Readings in the Psychology of Women

Readings in the Psychology of Women: Dimensions of the Female Experience

Carie Forden
Clarion University of Pennsylvania

Anne E. Hunter
Emory and Henry College

Beverly Birns
State University of New York at Stony Brook

Allyn and Bacon
Boston • London • Toronto • Sydney • Tokyo • Singapore

Vice President, Editor in Chief, Social Sciences: Sean W. Wakely
Series Editor: Carolyn Merrill
Editorial Assistant: Amy Goldmacher
Marketing Manager: Joyce Nilsen
Editorial Production Service: Marbern House
Manufacturing Buyer: Megan Cochran
Cover Administrator: Jennifer Hart

Library of Congress Cataloging-in-Publication Data

Readings in the psychology of women : dimensions of the female
    experience / Carie Forden, Anne E. Hunter, Beverly
    Birns.
        p.   cm.
    Includes bibliographical references.
    ISBN 0-205-26510-3
    1. Women—Psychology.   2. Women—Social conditions.   I. Forden,
Carie.   II. Hunter, Anne E.   III. Birns, Beverly.
HQ1206.R42   1998
305.42—dc21   98-21669
                                                                CIP

Printed in the United States of America

10   9   8   7   6   5   4   3   2   1   03   02   01   00   99   98

Contents

Preface

A student in a Psychology of Women course wrote in her journal, "the information you give is like a stone thrown into my pool of experience. The stone causes endless ripples of awareness, connections and realizations." Each of us had similar experiences when we began studying the psychology of women. It is a subject that alters dramatically our view of the world and our place in it, and one that empowers us to take action for change. This is accomplished when we place our individual experiences into the broader social context, and we learn that women's roles and subordinate status are not a biological given. We have compiled this reader in the hope that it will act as a "stone" in your "pool of experience," transforming your understanding of women's (and men's) lives.

PERSPECTIVE AND ORGANIZATION

To promote understanding of the complexity of the female experience, we have included a variety of approaches to the psychology of women. The readings include scientific research reports, theoretical discussions, and phenomenological descriptions of women's lives. To put this understanding in context, we have included an analysis of social, cultural, and historical influences on individual psychology, and we have brought to the foreground women whose lives are underrepresented in psychological research and theory.

Although this reader includes the work of a variety of authors with varying perspectives, it has also been shaped by the vision of its editors. Two of us are social psychologists (Forden and Hunter) and one of us is a developmental psychologist (Birns). All three of us are feminists. This means that we focus on the impact of social and cultural processes on the mind and behavior of females throughout the life cycle. It also means that we view these processes as keys to unlocking the human potential to transcend gender roles and inequalities. This focus does not deny the importance of biology; rather, we view gender and social inequality as arising from a complicated interplay among biology, society, and culture. Our complex and continually evolving brain allows us to construct gender in a variety of ways rather than being limited by genetic predispositions.

We have organized the readings in this book developmentally, with an emphasis on the multiple roles women experience in their adult lives: caregiving roles, work roles, and relationship roles.

Although a textbook allows instructors to present a large amount of information in a short amount of time, a book of readings provides students with the opportunity to study an issue in depth. Primary source material enables students to see how research is conducted and to evaluate the quality of the work for themselves. Rather than many short excerpts, we have chosen a smaller number of full-length articles and book chapters. Topic introductions provide an overview of the important issues and summarize the readings. "Questions to Consider" presented at the beginning of each reading give students the opportunity to think critically about the material.

ACKNOWLEDGMENTS

We would like to thank the writers whose work appears in this book for their contributions to our understanding of women's lives. We have also learned about women's lives from our students, and we thank in particular Sharon Russell, Alicia McEvoy-Replogle, Shannon Turner, April Cox, Ginger Hudson, Olivia Frasier, Amanda Broyden, Jamie McMinn, Amanda Warren, Greg Ward, Rhonda Barnett, Beth Rhodes, Roberta Davis, Donna Musser, Karen Fisher, Sharon Mast, Stephan West, Jim Winger, Nancy Edmondson, Diane Rhodes, Linda Wilbur, and Christopher Cramer. Their courage to go against the cultural grain in pursuit of their authentic selves continues to inspire us.

Our families have consistently championed our ideas and activities. We thank Bill and Toby Forden and Patricia Hunter for their endless practical and emotional support. Thanks to Charlene DiCalogero (cheerleader and proofreader extraordinaire), Matthew Donato for showing Alex the connection between masculinity and nurturing, Alexander Hunter Donato for many joyous moments, Harold Atkins for providing uncomplaining technical assistance, Susan Birns (colleague and daughter), Peter and Ann Kindfield, Matthew Atkins, and Michael Atkins.

We also are grateful to the friends who not only listened lovingly but also opened their homes to us and provided child care so we could work: Jean-Marie Luce, Ann Elliot, David Perry, and Sukie Zeeve. Thanks to Grey Hamm for her deep love and respect for children. Thanks also to Louisa Striver who assisted with photocopying and permissions.

We appreciate the support of the staff at Allyn & Bacon. We thank former senior editor Susan Badger, who provided the initial enthusiasm for this project, and Carolyn Merrill, our current editor, who took on the task of seeing it through and did it well. Thanks to editorial assistant Amy Goldmacher, who always had the answers to our questions; to John Beasley, who did an admirable copyedit; and to Marjorie Payne, former Senior Production Administrator at Allyn and Bacon, who guided the manuscript through the production process. Finally, thank you to the reviewers for their many helpful suggestions: Michelle Hunter, University of Connecticut–Waterbury; Veanne N. Anderson, Indiana State University–Terre Haute; Irene Frieze, University of Pittsburgh; Claire Etaugh, Bradley University; Carla Golden, Ithaca College; Judith Bridges, University of Connecticut–Hartford; Susan A. Lyman, University of Southwestern Louisiana; Joan S. Rabin, Towson University; and Michael Stevenson, Ball State University.

Introduction

ANNE E. HUNTER AND CARIE FORDEN

As you read this book you will learn the multiple truths of women's lives: that being female is not only a biological category, it is also a psychological, social, and cultural one; that women have been limited and that they have challenged those limits; and that the experience of being a woman differs between individuals and cultures, but that there are also commonalities that women share.

We have chosen readings that reflect a feminist perspective on gender, which means that we view gender as a *social construction*. From this perspective, societal processes play a central role in creating gender differences in thinking and feeling. Our feminist perspective on gender also includes the following interrelated themes:

1. Men have more power in society relative to women, and this is especially true for men who are white, economically privileged, and heterosexual.
2. Male dominance means that the experiences of males become the standard against which women are measured, which often results in gender differences being interpreted as female deficiencies.
3. Females often internalize their low status and behave in powerless ways, but they also resist their oppression.
4. Many of the ways in which females differ from males are strengths rather than deficiencies.
5. Women are a culturally diverse group. This means that although they have many experiences in common as women, they also have many different experiences.

GENDER AS A SOCIAL CONSTRUCTION

Simone de Beauvoir (1952) argued that "one is not born, but rather becomes, a woman" (p. 301). In making this statement, de Beauvoir was recognizing the social and cultural roots of women's lives. Our genetic heritage makes us anatomically and physiologically male or female, but the significance of these differences for the rest of our lives is influenced strongly by our social and cultural heritage.

Sex and Gender

Typically, feminist psychologists use the phrase *sex differences* to refer to biological factors—hormonal patterns, reproductive organs, and chromosomes—that differentiate females and males. Each society can then take these biological differences and create its own set of expectations for femininity and masculinity. Feminist psychologists typically use the phrase *gender differences* to refer to these socially constructed expectations. However, some feminist psychologists view this distinction as useful but oversimplified (Hyde, 1994; Lips, 1997). They view it as useful because it calls attention to the social and cultural influences on female–male behavioral differences.

They view it as oversimplified because sex and gender are overlapping concepts, which means that the effects of biology and environment on behavior are virtually impossible to separate. Hubbard (1990) describes how biological and social processes act on one another to produce an outcome. For example, gender-specific toys and games (such as dolls for girls and trucks for boys) not only teach children gender role behaviors, but they also influence the structure and chemistry of the developing brain. When sex and gender are viewed as overlapping rather than as distinct concepts, they are defined as follows: *Sex* refers to female–male differences that are related to anatomy and physiology; *gender* refers to female–male differences that are related to the interactions between biological and social processes (Lips, 1997).

Because gender is socially constructed, the meaning of femininity and masculinity can vary across time and place. We see this when we look at female and male roles. A society's definitions of femininity and masculinity arise from its history, economy, geography, and natural resources. These material conditions present challenges that demand solutions, and gender roles may be constructed as solutions. For example, during World War II, men in the United States were drafted into the armed services in such great numbers that women had to be recruited to work at the skilled jobs in manufacturing previously filled by men (e.g., welding, shipbuilding, and weapons manufacturing). The roles changed dramatically as they were asked by government and industry to move out of the home, leave traditionally "female" jobs, and enter the factory. Their physical strength and technical abilities were emphasized by those in power, while their caretaking roles were downplayed. In fact, women were encouraged to leave children in day care for five days a week.

After the war was over, a different construction of gender emerged to fit the new economic reality: Returning soldiers needed jobs, and there were not enough well-paid jobs for both men and women. The new gender ideology once again proclaimed that women were biologically inclined toward domesticity and child rearing, while men were inclined toward the competitive workplace. Consequently, the women who had filled the jobs that had been vacated by men were now expected to leave the factory and to find complete fulfillment in the home or back in their traditionally female jobs. Changing material conditions (the war versus the end of the war) brought about new economic challenges (unfilled jobs in manufacturing versus a shortage of jobs in manufacturing), and gender roles were constructed as part of the solution (women are physically and technically adept and belong in manufacturing versus women are naturally domestic and belong in the home). Similarly, changing economic conditions that began in the seventies have made it difficult for most two-parent families to exist on one income. This economic reality along with the women's movement, which began about the same time, have led the majority of women to expand their roles back into the workplace. Although most of these women are concentrated into low-power service jobs where they provide the same support and nurturance functions that they provide in the home, enough are making it into positions of power to initiate a new view of women.

The Flexible Human Brain

The idea that gender roles are socially constructed and, therefore, vary with changing material conditions challenges the widespread assumption that gender roles are a result of biological differences between women and men. Unlike most other animals, we are not constrained by our biology to engage in specific behaviors. Instead, our flexible and evolving brain allows us to continuously adapt our behavior patterns to meet the ever-changing demands of our environment. Therefore, characteristics such as female deference and male dominance are not inherent traits of women and men, but are assigned to them to meet the needs of the material conditions at a particular point in history. Thus, it is our biology, in the form of a flexible brain, that shapes our gender roles and allows us to adapt them in a variety of ways to a changing world.

Power and Social Structure

In the United States, as in most societies, the construction of gender happens within a social structure organized by power. We live in a hierarchical society where power is distributed unevenly, so that some groups of people have limited access to resources and to opportunities. Our gender (as well as our race, ethnicity, economic class, sexual orientation, and other social categories) plays an important role in determining our access to political, social, and economic power. Men have more power than do women in this society. We can see this when we look at our political system, economy, and social interactions. For example, in the United States Senate, only six of the one hundred senators are women; in the workplace, the majority of women are concentrated in low-paid, dead-end service jobs; and in romantic and sexual relationships, men are expected to act while women are to be acted upon.

Because men have more power relative to women, they have been able to construct a world that supports and maintains their power. Gender differences are not just interesting variations in human behavior; they are integral to a system of inequality. This system of inequality tied to sex and gender differences is called *sexism*. Sexism takes many forms, from individual sexism—prejudiced behavior of individual men toward individual women—to institutional sexism—the institutional rules and customs that restrict—intentionally or unintentional—opportunities for women. An example of an institutional rule is when height requirements are imposed for police officers that have the effect of excluding most women. An example of a custom is the "old boys network" that operates to assist men to obtain the most preferred jobs.

The Defined Norm

One aspect of this unequal power is that the ideas, experiences, and activities of white and economically privileged males have become the socially dominant ones, or the defined norm (Pharr, 1988). This means that the way in which this group of people view and experience the world is considered "normal," and that the mind and behavior of women is often interpreted against this male standard. In comparison to the defined norm, women are often seen as lacking or defective: less psychologically healthy, less intelligent, less independent, and less capable. Women of lower social status, such as poor women or women of color, are seen as even more inadequate because they are judged by both male standards and middle-class and/or white standards.

Much of the research and theory on the psychology of females incorporates this male bias, and consequently, the devaluation of the female experience. It is not the sex or gender difference itself that causes social inequality; rather, it is the interpretation of difference as deficiency that justifies and supports unequal power relations between women and men. It is important to remember, however, that the gender difference in power does not have to be permanent; it can be changed. As we discussed previously, gender ideology reflects material conditions. When conditions change, so does the ideology for gender roles. For example, physical strength is no longer needed in most contemporary jobs. Therefore, the stereotypes of the strong male and weak female no longer justify limited opportunities for women in the workplace.

Psychological Implications of Unequal Power

If gender ideology and gender roles can be changed, why don't we change them? The experience of low social and economic power is often incorporated in individual psychology as internalized oppression, or low self-worth. Members of low status groups often believe that they are unworthy and inferior because they do not measure up to the standards of the defined norm. They typically see themselves as unattractive, incapable, and powerless to affect change. Low-status people also tend to blame themselves for their low position in the social structure. Internalized oppression leads them to give up being in charge of their lives. This takes the forms of self-destructive behaviors, difficulty with being assertive, deference to members of dominant groups, and the tendency to settle for less in life on the assumption that one does not deserve any better. On the other hand, members of the dominant group (in this case, white economically privileged males) typically incorporate a sense of personal entitlement into their world view, thus taking for granted their inherent worthiness and their access to a wide range of opportunities.

When these socialization patterns are successful, male dominance is reinforced, along with the gender roles that reflect it. Women themselves reinforce male dominance when they view their own subordinate status as deserved, and behave accordingly; men in positions of power maintain it by using the powerless behaviors of many women (e.g., lack of assertiveness) to support the claim that gender differences in behavior are a reflection of biological differences and, consequently, are unchangeable.

Differences as Strengths

The defined norm assumes that differences are a source of inferiority. Feminist psychologists have argued that it is important to see that differences can also be strengths. For example, Caplan and Caplan (1994) point out that in a male-biased value system, females are viewed as more dependent than males—a characteristic that is undesirable in this value system and one that reflects low status. Evidence for the assumed greater dependency of women comes from studies showing that females look and smile more at other people,

sit and stand closer to others, and show more concern about and responsiveness toward others. The Caplans, who interpret this behavioral pattern within a feminist value system, argue that the behaviors actually reflect "interdependence" or "relational abilities," rather than dependency. From this value system, this typical female pattern is viewed as a strength rather than as a deficit, and is considered an essential behavioral pattern for males to develop also.

Not only can differences be reinterpreted as strengths in women and in other low-power groups—thereby contradicting the internalized oppression—but people who are victims of oppression often develop resistance to the oppression. For example, in recent history in the United States, we have seen resistance in the form of organized movements for change such as the civil rights movement, the women's movement, and the labor movement, to name a few. Furthermore, consciousness-raising groups, women's centers, women's shelters, birthing centers, and grassroots women's empowerment organizations continue to challenge both institutional and internalized oppression.

Similarity and Diversity among Women

As discussed previously, one of the contributions of the psychology of women has been to study women from their own perspective rather than through male eyes. A more recent contribution has been the recognition that women are not a homogeneous group in terms of their experiences, but that they have a variety of experiences related to their place in the social structure and to their cultural background. In many ways, the daily lives of women differ by social class, race, ethnicity, religion, age, sexual orientation, and so on. Therefore, a truly representative psychology of women must study the differences among groups of women as well as their similarities, and must also take into account any power relations that are built on these differences. For example, a poor

Native American woman may experience internalized oppression related to her low social status along three dimensions of her identity: sex, social class, and race. This means that she—like all women—suffers from sexism, but unlike middle-class women, and white women, she also suffers from classism and racism. Thus, she experiences and struggles against triple oppression in her daily life.

Optimistic View of Human Nature

The social constructionist perspective on gender offers an extremely optimistic view of human nature. If gender roles such as male competitiveness and female nurturance are deeply etched in our minds—rather than dictated by our genes—they are not inevitable. Because of the malleable human brain, our minds can be changed. This is true even if future research reveals that sex hormones predispose males and females toward different roles. From this perspective, gender equality becomes a real possibility. Widespread awareness of this possibility is of great significance, because if we cannot envision a society built on shared power, we will never take the steps to achieve it.

REFERENCES

Caplan, P. J. & Caplan, J. B. (1994). *Thinking Critically about Research on Sex and Gender.* New York: HarperCollins.

De Beauvoir, S. (1952). *The Second Sex.* New York: Vintage Books.

Hubbard, R. (1990). *The Politics of Women's Biology.* Rutgers, NJ: Rutgers University Press.

Hyde, J. S. (1994). "Should Psychologists Study Gender Differences? Yes, with Some Guidelines." *Feminism and Psychology,* 4(4), 507–512.

Lips, H. M. (1997). *Sex and Gender: An Introduction.* Mountain View, CA: Mayfield Publishing Company.

Pharr, S. (1988). *Homophobia: A Weapon of Sexism.* Little Rock, AK: Chardon Press.

Topic 1

Power and Ideology

Response to Patriarchy

Silent
so you cannot hear me.
Ignorant
so I will not know the truth.
Dependent
so you can protect me.
Beautiful
so you can show me off.
Nurturing
so I can take care of you.
Inexperienced
so I will think you are right.

Loud
so I will be heard.
Educated
so I will have the knowledge.
Strong
so I can support myself.
Experienced
so I will be able to choose.
Independent
so I can make my own decisions.
Beautiful
because I am a woman.

Courtesy of Kelly Mazaris

The four readings in this chapter were selected because they expand on the ideas and themes that were presented in the introduction to this book. They will deepen your understanding of how power structures and material conditions shape the social construction of gender, which in turn shapes individual experience and psychology.

As was discussed in the introduction, the defined norm has often biased our understanding of women and girls' lives. Janet Shibley Hyde, in the opening reading, "Should Psychologists Study Gender Differences?", questions whether psychologists should study gender differences because the research is so frequently faulty and often used against women. She points out that there is more interest in finding differences than similarities between males and females, and that this has led to publication bias, a lack of recognition of contradictory evidence, and the overemphasis on small differences. In addition, these differences are often interpreted as the result of biology, even when there is no evidence to support this explanation. When differences are found, the male experience often becomes the standard against which women are measured and found to be lacking. Further, gender difference findings have sometimes been reported and applied in ways that are harmful to women. While Hyde concludes that psychology should continue to study gender differences, she offers a set of guidelines designed to combat some of the problems she has found with this research.

Hyde critiques researchers who rush to attribute gender differences to biological causes. In the second reading, "Biological Essentialism," Sandra Bem examines two biological theories of gender roles and gender inequality that have dominated the scientific literature and the media for over two decades—sociobiology and prenatal hormone theory. She points out the ways these theories limit our understanding of the complex interaction between biology and culture in creating gender differences.

According to the first theory Bem describes, sociobiologists argue that males are genetically predisposed to be aggressive, competitive, dominant, and promiscuous, while females are predisposed to be nurturant, passive, sexually selective, and monogamous. Sociobiologists then claim that these particular genetic differences have evolved because these behaviors maximize the likelihood that a male's or female's genes will survive into the next generation. Therefore, males, because they can produce millions of sperm with minimal investment of energy, have evolved with an innate strategy to fertilize as many females as possible. On the other hand, females are limited in the number of offspring they can produce due to the time and energy that must be invested in pregnancy. Because of this, they tend to be more selective when choosing a sexual partner.

In the second theory examined by Bem, prenatal hormone theorists also overemphasize the impact of biological factors on gender differences in behavior while virtually ignoring the interaction between biology and social context. Hormonal theory proposes that there is differential brain organization in males and females due to the presence or absence of testosterone during a critical period in prenatal development. In turn, these differently organized brains lead to different male and female behavior patterns. Considerable animal evidence supports this theory, but there is little evidence to support a link between prenatal hormones and gender differences in human behavior.

Bem discusses the lack of evidence for the main assumptions of sociobiology and prenatal hormone theory. She also claims that sociobiologists and prenatal hormone theorists misunderstand the interaction between biology and culture. That is, they downplay the role of history and culture by minimizing the capacity of the flexible human brain to create technological advancements that transform our environments and, in turn, transform us. For example, advances in birth control have made it possible for women to avoid or to postpone pregnancy in pursuit of other goals. Bem claims, therefore, that the impact of any biological feature (e.g., reproductive systems) on behavior always depends on how it interacts with the environments that humans have created (e.g. the technological advancement of birth control). This means that even if universal gender roles do exist (and this is undetermined), such universals would be a product of a complex interaction between biology and culture, rather than primarily a product of biology, as sociobiologists and prenatal hormone theorists would have us believe.

In the third reading, "The Longest War: Gender and Culture," Carole Wade and Carol Tavris further challenge the idea that there is a biological explanation for gender differences in behavior. Using anthropological data, they provide many examples of historical and cultural variations in gender roles to demonstrate that what is considered natural in one society may be the exact opposite of what another culture considers natural. This is evidence that gender roles arise in specific material conditions (e.g., scarcity of resources in one New Guinea culture leading to the disparagement of women in order to discourage sexual intercourse and overpopulation). Further, as the material conditions change, so do the gender roles. The material conditions, in turn, give rise to ideology and social practices that support the new gender roles and which become deeply embedded in our thinking and in our social institutions. Wade and Tavris's analysis provides us with an explanation of the persistence of gender roles and gender inequality in our own culture, along with the expectation that they will change as our material conditions change.

We see a more detailed description of how cultural constructions of gender roles can shape individual psychology in the final reading by Teresa Keller, "Lessons in Inequality: What Television Teaches Us About Women." Keller argues that stereotyped portrayals of males and females on television perpetuate traditional gender roles and sexism. She demonstrates that the majority of the most popular television programs of the last 50 years portray white males as being in charge, and white females as physically attractive, as sex objects, and as family-focused. Women of color are consistently portrayed in even more limited and negative ways. Furthermore, in programs where women demonstrate power, they are often depicted as unhappy and as unappealing. Although some contemporary programs are challenging these limited and often harmful ideas about white women, nonstereotypic portrayals of minority women are still rare. Keller makes the point that such narrow images of women's lives reinforce the defined norm of male dominance and contribute to internalized oppression in women.

Reading 1   Should Psychologists Study Gender Differences? Yes, with Some Guidelines

JANET SHIBLEY HYDE

Questions to Consider:

1. Why are we all so intrigued by gender differences? Why do studies that demonstrate gender differences receive so much attention?

2. Do you agree with Hyde that psychologists should study gender differences? Why or why not?

3. What do you think of Hyde's guidelines? Do you think researchers will be interested in following them? Why or why not?

In 1887 Romanes argued that women were less intelligent than men and that this was a result of women's brains being smaller than men's. One hundred years later, in 1987, Kimura argued that there are gender differences[1] in the brain and that these brain factors create gender differences in abilities (see also Kimura, 1992). Psychologists and other scientists have a history of studying gender differences and attributing them to biological causes. In this article I contend that, like it or not, psychologists will continue to study gender differences and the media will continue to publicize the findings; the best course of action, then, is to institute guidelines so that the study of gender differences will be carried out in a manner that meets the highest standards of science and at

Reprinted by permission of Sage Publications Ltd and Janet Shibley Hyde from Janet Shibley Hyde, "Should Psychologists Study Sex Differences? Yes, With Some Guidelines," *Feminism and Psychology,* 4(4), pp. 507–512, Copyright Sage Publications Ltd, 1994.

the same time is not detrimental to women (for other discussions of this issue, see Baumeister, 1988; Rothblum, 1988).

THE NEVER-ENDING SEARCH FOR GENDER DIFFERENCES

The media and the lay public alike are greatly intrigued with gender differences. For example, within the last five years, *Time* (20 January 1992), *Newsweek* (28 May 1990), and *US News and World Report* (8 August 1988) have all carried cover stories on the question of psychological gender differences.

As noted at the beginning of this article, psychologists have studied gender differences from the very beginning of psychology in the late 1800s (Shields, 1975). Research and theorizing on gender differences, some of it by feminists and some by others, continued throughout the first six decades of the 20th century, including Helen Thompson Woolley's excellent early feminist review of the literature (1910), the famous psychologist Lewis Terman's study *Sex and Personality* (1936) and Eleanor Maccoby's edited volume of theory and empirical research (1966).

Beginning around 1970, stimulated in part by the feminist movement's emphasis on gender, there was a virtual explosion of theory and research on gender differences. This research has been reviewed in volumes such as those by Maccoby and Jacklin (1974), Hyde and Linn (1986), Halpern (1992), Eagly (1987a) and Hall (1984).

In short, the study of gender differences in psychology has been nothing but a growth industry. It shows no sign of declining. It's here to stay. The question then becomes one of how can we regulate this somewhat unruly growth industry so that it (1) becomes better science and (2) is used on behalf of women rather than against women.

PROBLEMS WITH EXISTING RESEARCH ON GENDER DIFFERENCES

A number of pernicious problems in the study of gender differences must be addressed if this research literature is to meet the twin goals of becoming better science and becoming beneficial to women.

The first problem is *publication bias,* a general bias in psychology toward publishing significant findings and not publishing null findings. This bias applies to the study of gender differences. It implies that there is a bias toward publishing findings of significant gender differences. A study finding nonsignificant gender differences may not be published. If the study is on another topic and the researchers conduct a routine test for gender differences, they are likely to report the finding if the difference is significant and make no mention of it if it is nonsignificant. The result of this bias is a general impression that there is a multitude of psychological gender differences and few gender similarities, because the latter tend not to be reported.

The second problem, related to the first, is the proliferation of *unreplicated findings of gender differences.* As a result of the tendency to report significant findings of gender differences, and the fascination of psychologists and the media with differences, a single report of a finding of a gender difference may receive widespread media coverage. Ten independent investigators may try to replicate the finding and all fail, i.e. all obtain a nonsignificant gender difference. These studies may not find their way into print or, if they do, they will attract no media attention. As a result, the original study reporting the difference stands as authoritative, with no recognition of the contradictory evidence.

The third problem is *failure to report effect sizes, so that tiny gender differences are given more attention than they merit.* An example comes from the extensive research on gender differences in mathematics performance. This gender difference has, for decades, been thought to be reliable and important—and, by implication, large. Yet meta-analysis shows the magnitude of the difference to be at most 0.15 standard deviation (Hyde et al., 1990). Had researchers all along reported the effect size d (Hyde et al., 1990) for their gender differences, we might have known long ago that the difference was small.

The fourth problem is that *findings of gender differences are often interpreted as indicating female deficits.* For example, there is a fairly consistent gender difference in self-confidence; on tasks such as estimating how many points they think they earned on an exam before the actual grades are known, females estimate fewer points, on the average, than males do (Hyde, 1991; Lenney, 1977). This finding has often been interpreted as indicating that females lack self-confidence—that is, that they have a deficit. An alternative interpretation might be that males are unrealistically over-confident. In fact, when estimated scores are compared with actual scores, it turns out that males overestimate their performance about as much as females underestimate theirs, although some studies find girls' estimates to be accurate and boys' to be inflated (Berg and Hyde, 1976; Crandall, 1969; Hyde, 1991). Therefore, there is little basis for saying that females have a deficit in self-confidence.

A fifth problem is that *findings of gender differences, when not reported and applied carefully, may be used in a manner that is harmful to females.* As an example, in a 1980 *Science* article, Benbow and Stanley made much of a very lopsided gender ratio (far more males than females) in their sample of highly mathematically precocious seventh graders. The media picked up this report and it appeared in national and international newspapers. Jacobs and Eccles (1985) were in the midst of a longitudinal study in which they had just asked parents for their estimates of their child's mathematical ability. They re-interviewed the parents following the publicity over the Benbow and Stanley report. They found that the media coverage had adversely affected the mothers of daughters. Mothers who had heard the media coverage had significantly lower estimates of their daughters' abilities than mothers who had not heard the media coverage. And, the mothers exposed to the media coverage, gave estimates that were lower than they had been before the media coverage. Mothers' confidence in their daughters' abilities, of course, is very important to girls' developing confidence in their own mathematical ability. In essence, then, the reporting of the Benbow and Stanley results, partly because of a lack of appropriate scientific caveats by the researchers, created outcomes that could be demonstrated to be harmful to females.

Finally, a sixth problem is that *gender differences are often interpreted as being due to biological factors in the absence of appropriate biological data.* An example is the Benbow and Stanley (1980) study reporting far more males than females among the mathematically gifted. Benbow and Stanley speculated that the difference was due to biological factors, when they actually had collected no biological measures.

GUIDELINES FOR NON-SEXIST RESEARCH ON GENDER DIFFERENCES

In order to address the problems previously listed, I propose the following guidelines for non-sexist research on gender differences (for related guidelines, see Denmark et al., 1988; McHugh et al., 1986):

1. Researchers should routinely conduct the appropriate significance tests for gender differences on all major measures in their study (Eagly, 1987b). Furthermore, researchers should take responsibility for reporting and publishing findings of nonsignificant gender differences, so they are reported on an equal basis with findings of significant gender differences.

2. Journal editors should take care to publish findings of nonsignificant gender differences, provided the study meets appropriate scientific standards.

3. Researchers should be required to report an effect size (such as d: cf. Hyde et al., 1990) for all findings of gender differences, whether significant or not, so that the reader is informed of the magnitude of the difference.

4. Researchers should be alert to the manner in which they interpret findings of gender differences. Interpretations implying a female deficit should always be questioned to see whether there is an equally tenable interpretation that does not imply a female deficit.

5. Biological explanations for gender differences should be made with great caution. Biological explanations should not be invoked when no biological measures were collected.

6. Researchers should apply appropriate scientific standards of conduct in ensuring that their data are appropriately interpreted so that the risk of the data being used inappropriately, in a manner detrimental to women, is minimized as much as possible.

CONCLUSION

I contend that psychologists will surely continue to do research on gender differences, the media will continue to publicize and glamorize the findings and the lay public will continue to be fascinated and influenced by these reports. It would be unwise in the extreme for feminist psychologists to abandon this area, thereby losing their power to influence it. It is of utmost importance to institute guidelines for non-sexist gender differences research. The six guidelines listed here should be very useful in remedying current problems in gender differences research.

NOTE

1. It seems safe to say that there is controversy and no consensus among feminist psychologists about the best system of nomenclature in using the terms 'sex' and 'gender'. One fairly common system is to use 'sex differences' to refer to innate or biologically produced differences between females and males (e.g. there are sex differences in the genitals) and to use 'gender differences' to refer to male-female differences that result from learning and the social roles of females and males (e.g. Unger, 1979). The problem with this terminology is that in many cases we do not know whether a particular male-female difference is biologically caused or culturally caused, and we should hold out the possibility of biology-environment interactions, with both contributing. In the latter case, the terminology becomes impossible.

I have adopted an alternative terminology that has worked well in my writing and conceptualizing. I use 'sex' to refer to sexual behaviors and anatomy, and 'gender' to the state of being male or female (e.g. Hyde, 1979). One advantage of this terminology is that it overcomes the ambiguous use of the term 'sex' in English, since it sometimes refers to sexuality and sometimes to maleness and femaleness. For example, does the book *Sex and Temperament in Three Primitive Societies* address the question of whether sexual expression influences one's temperament or does it address the question of gender roles and temperament? I therefore use 'gender differences' consistently to refer to male-female differences, leaving aside the issue of whether the differences are biologically or environmentally caused, or both, since we typically do not know the answer to this question.

REFERENCES

Baumeister, R. F. (1988) 'Should We Stop Studying Sex Differences Altogether?', *American Psychologist* 43: 1092–5.

Benbow, C. P. and Stanley, J. C. (1980) 'Sex Differences in Mathematical Ability: Fact or Artifact?', *Science* 210: 1262–4.

Berg, P. and Hyde, J. S. (1976) 'Gender and Race Differences in Causal Attributions', Paper presented at the September meeting of the American Psychological Association, Washington, DC.

Crandall, V. C. (1969) 'Sex Differences in Expectancy of Intellectual and Academic Reinforcement', in C. P. Smith (ed.) *Achievement-Related Motives in Children*. New York: Russell Sage Foundation.

Denmark, F., Russo, N. F., Frieze, I. H. and Sechzer, J. A. (1988) 'Guidelines for Avoiding Sexism in Psychological Research', *American Psychologist* 43: 582–5.

Eagly. A. H. (1987a) *Sex Differences in Social Behavior: A Social-Role Interpretation.* Hillsdale, NJ: Erlbaum.

Eagly, A. H. (1987b) 'Reporting Sex Differences', *American Psychologist* 42: 756–7.

Hall, J. A. (1984) *Nonverbal Sex Differences.* Baltimore: Johns Hopkins University Press.

Halpern, D. G. (1992) *Sex Differences in Cognitive Abilities,* 2nd edn. Hillsdale, NJ: Erlbaum.

Hyde, J. S. (1979) *Understanding Human Sexuality.* New York: McGraw-Hill.

Hyde, J. S. (1991) *Half the Human Experience: The Psychology of Women,* 4th edn. Lexington, MA: D.C. Heath.

Hyde, J. S., Fennema, E. and Lamon, S. J. (1990) 'Gender Differences in Mathematics Performance: A Meta-Analysis', *Psychological Bulletin* 107: 139–55.

Hyde, J. S. and Linn, M. C., eds (1986) *The Psychology of Gender: Advances Through Meta-Analysis.* Baltimore: Johns Hopkins University Press.

Jacobs, J. and Eccles, J. S. (1985) 'Science and the Media: Benbow and Stanley Revisited', *Educational Researcher* 14: 20–5.

Kimura, D. (1987) 'Are Men's and Women's Brains Really Different?', *Canadian Journal of Psychology* 37: 19–35.

Kimura, D. (1992) 'Sex Differences in the Brain', *Scientific American* 267(3): 118–25.

Lenney, E. (1977) 'Women's Self-Confidence in Achievement Settings', *Psychological Bulletin* 84: 1–13.

Maccoby, E. E., ed. (1966) *The Development of Sex Differences.* Stanford, CA: Stanford University Press.

Maccoby, E. E. and Jacklin, C. N. (1974) *The Psychology of Sex Differences.* Stanford, CA: Stanford University Press.

McHugh, M. C., Koeske, R. D. and Frieze, I. H. (1986) 'Issues to Consider in Conducting Nonsexist Psychological Research: A Guide for Researchers', *American Psychologist* 41: 879–90.

Romanes, G. J. (1887) 'Mental Differences Between Men and Women', *Nineteenth Century* 21(123): 654–72.

Rothblum, E. D. (1988) 'More on Reporting Sex Differences'. *American Psychologist* 43: 1095.

Shields, S. A. (1975) 'Functionalism, Darwinism, and the Psychology of Women: A Study in Social Myth', *American Psychologist* 30: 739–54.

Terman, L. M. (1936) *Sex and Personality.* New York: McGraw-Hill.

Unger, R. (1979) 'Toward a Redefinition of Sex and Gender', *American Psychologist* 34: 1085–94.

Woolley, H. T. (1910) 'A Review of the Recent Literature on the Psychology of Sex', *Psychological Bulletin* 7: 335–42.

Reading 2   Biological Essentialism

SANDRA LIPSITZ BEM

Questions to Consider

1. According to Bem, why can't biology alone account for differences between males and females? Give some examples to support your answer.

2. How has sociobiology been used to "rationalize and legitimize the sexual status quo"?

3. How could the interaction of biology and culture explain the results of the Money and Ehrhardt study?

4. Recently, biological explanations of gender differences have received a great deal of media attention. Why do you think these explanations are so popular?

Whether science has ever been—or can ever be—fully objective is the subject of lively debate among feminist scholars. Although challenging the objectivity of all scientific inquiry is not my intent here, I do argue that the biological accounts of male-female difference and male dominance that have emerged since the mid-nineteenth century have merely used the language of science, rather than the language of religion, to rationalize and legitimize the sexual status quo....

JUST-SO STORIES OF SOCIOBIOLOGY

Sexual Difference and Sexual Inequality

The sociobiological analysis of both sexual difference and sexual inequality is based on the sim-

ple fact that the number of offspring a male can produce is biologically limited only by the number of fertile females that he can manage to inseminate, whereas a female can produce only a limited number of offspring in her lifetime—a maximum of about twenty in the case of humans. In the days when evolution was still thought to operate on traits that benefited the species as a whole, the different reproductive capacity of the sexes was seen as far less important than their shared interest in the survival of the species. But now that evolution was thought to operate only at the level of the genes, that very same sex difference in reproductive capacity suddenly seemed all important. As Wilson put it in 1978,

> *During the full period of time it takes to bring a fetus to term, ... one male can fertilize many females but a female can be fertilized by only one male. Thus if males are able to court one female after another, some will be big winners and others will be absolute*

Sandra Lipsitz Bem, *The Lenses of Gender,* New Haven, Connecticut: Yale University Press, pp. 13–29. Copyright © 1993 by Yale University. Reprinted by permission.

losers, while virtually all healthy females will succeed in being fertilized. It pays males to be aggressive, hasty, fickle, and undiscriminating. In theory it is more profitable for females to be coy, to hold back until they can identify males with the best genes. In species that rear young, it is also important for the females to select males who are more likely to stay with them after insemination. Human beings obey this biological principle faithfully. (Pp. 124–125)

Wilson's "conflict of interest between the sexes" (p. 124) is described even more baldly by David Barash in *The Whisperings Within:*

Sperm are cheap. Eggs are expensive. . . . For males, reproduction is easy, a small amount of time, a small amount of semen, and the potential evolutionary return is very great if offspring are produced. On the other hand, a female who makes a "bad" choice may be in real evolutionary trouble. If fertilization occurs, a baby is begun, and the ensuing process is not only inexorable but immensely demanding. . . . The evolutionary mechanism should be clear. Genes that allow females to accept the sorts of mates who make lesser contributions to their reproductive success will leave fewer copies of themselves than will genes that influence the females to be more selective. Accordingly, genes inducing selectivity will increase at the expense of those that are less discriminating. For males, a very different strategy applies. The maximum advantage goes to individuals with fewer inhibitions. A genetically influenced tendency to "play fast and loose"— "love 'em and leave 'em"—may well reflect more biological reality than most of us care to admit. (P. 48)

In fairness to Wilson, it should be noted that his discussion of human evolution included the speculation that humans and a few other primates like the marmosets and the gibbons may have evolved under conditions that actually made it reproductively more advantageous for males to pair-bond with females and to cooperate in the rearing of young than to seek additional mates.

But other sociobiologists must have found the hypothesized conflict between the sexes to be much more compelling than the factors tempering that conflict because the consequences they extrapolated from it were truly extraordinary. On the male side, for example, sociobiologists offered up sexual promiscuity, rape, the abandonment of mates and children, intermale aggression, an intolerance for female infidelity, the sequestering of females, the killing of stepchildren, and universal male dominance. On the female side, they offered up the coy holding back of sex, the careful selection of sexual partners, the investment of time and energy in parental care, the preference for at least serial monogamy, and the deceiving of males with respect to paternity.

The sociobiological reasoning in all these cases was straightforward. Males are sexually promiscuous, they rape, and they abandon mates and offspring because these behaviors enable them to maximize the number of females they can inseminate and thus to maximize the reproduction of their own genes. They are aggressive toward other males (especially during the breeding season if they are not human) because they are in competition with those males for the scarce reproductive resources of females. They are intolerant of female infidelity, and they sequester females whenever possible to ensure that those scarce female resources are used to reproduce their own genes and not someone else's. They kill stepchildren to ensure that any investment they do make in parental care will benefit their genes and their genes alone. And finally, they are universally dominant over females because their reproductive strategies so highly select them for that particular trait.

Females, in contrast, withhold their sexual favors until they have found the best sexual partner because that strategy enables them to invest their scarce reproductive resources in both the best males and the best offspring. They invest far more time and energy in parental care than males do because they cannot so easily replace the offspring in whom they have already invested nine months of pregnancy. They prefer at least serial monogamy to promiscuity because that is the social organization that gets males to invest the most time and energy in the survival of female genes. And finally, they sometimes lie about paternity because that behavior, too, gets some male—even if not the father—to help them in the reproduction of their genes.

Not surprisingly, this sociobiological analysis of sexual difference and sexual inequality has generated enormous controversy, with feminists like Ruth Bleier (1984), Anne Fausto-Sterling (1985), and Janet Sayers (1982) seeing it as nothing more than the twentieth-century version of science stepping in to naturalize the status quo and with sociobiologists defending it as neither politically conservative nor biologically essentialist. David Barash, the sociobiologist who may be more criticized by feminist scholars than any other for his discussion of rape, explains that his "intent has been only to explore the evolutionary biology of male-female differences, not to espouse any particular social, political or ethical philosophy. Evolution simply *is*—or, better yet, evolution *does*. It says nothing whatever about what ought to be.... Furthermore, the inclinations predicted by sociobiology are just that: inclinations. They are not certainties" (1979, p. 70).

Critiques of Sociobiology

Sociobiologists begin their analysis of human behavior with what they construe to be the universal aspects of human social life and human social organization. In developing a theory of those universals, they focus on evolutionary and genetic factors, rather than cultural or historical factors, because they rightly see any purely environmental explanation as inadequate. One such explanation of sexual difference and dominance that is "common in social science," according to David Barash, and which sociobiology rejects outright, is that "boys act as they do because such behavior is taught to them, and the same for girls." Barash concedes that

> *we do do a great deal to inculcate gender identity among our children. Girls are more likely to be given dolls to play with, and boys ... airplanes.... But as an all-encompassing explanation for male-female differences, early social experience is simply insufficient. If we are to believe that there are no real male-female differences in behavior, and that such differences as we see are simply a result of the differential experiences that society provides little boys and little girls, we must also explain why such differences are promulgated independently by every society on earth. (1979, pp. 71–72)*

From the sociobiological point of view, the reason for this cross-cultural universality is clear. During our evolutionary prehistory, the males with more aggressive, dominant, and sexually promiscuous genes were able to leave many more copies of themselves, as were the females with more sexually selective and maternal genes. As a result of this evolutionary selection, genetic differences between the sexes that are directly related to behavior now exist in every culture, and these universal genetic differences ultimately explain why boys and girls are everywhere treated differently.

It is not only the universality of sexual difference and dominance that sociobiologists seek to explain with this model. They also seek to explain every other aspect of human behavior construed to be universal—including aggression, altruism, territoriality, xenophobia, and war. In every case, however, the reasoning is the same. Evolutionary selection enables certain behaviorally specific genes to leave many more copies of themselves than other behaviorally specific genes; as a result, the human species now has a genetic makeup that predisposes it to behave in more or less the same way in all cultures.

Critics of sociobiology have attacked at least three major aspects of this explanatory model. First, they have attacked the empirical claim of universality, arguing that in almost every instance, sociobiologists have distorted the human and the animal evidence, and in some cases, even the plant evidence, in order to create the appearance of many more human universals than may actually exist. Second, they have attacked the empirical base for the genetic claims of sociobiology, arguing that no evidence as yet exists for any link between human genes and the kinds of human behaviors that sociobiologists are trying to explain. And finally, they have attacked the nature of sociobiological reasoning itself, arguing that in the absence of any empirical evidence for the kinds of behaviorally specific genes that sociobiologists have postulated, the whole sociobiological enterprise becomes an exercise in tautological reasoning. To paraphrase Ruth Bleier:

> *Having selected a certain animal or human behavior, sociobiology makes it a* premise *that that behavior has a genetic basis; it then constructs a speculative story to explain how that behavior could have served to maximize the reproductive success of the individual, and could thereby have also been selected during the course of evolution,* if *it were genetically based; this* conjecture *then becomes evidence for the* premise *that the behavior is genetically based. (1984, p. 17)*

Precisely this circularity has led at least one set of critics to liken the evolutionary reasoning of

sociobiology to the just-so stories of Rudyard Kipling that were so popular during the nineteenth century (Lewontin, Rose & Kamin, 1984, p. 258).

Although I agree with all three of these earlier critiques, my own critique of sociobiology focuses less on the empirical question of whether behaviorally specific genes and human universals exist than on the more conceptual question of how sociobiology theorizes the interaction between biology and culture—and what role that theorizing gives to cultural invention. Sociobiologists have constructed what they consider to be a theory of biology and culture working together to create human universals. That theory, however, is so unimaginative about how biology and culture interact that it ends up treating culture and history almost as epiphenomena.

The sociobiological model of the interaction between biology and culture is easy to explain. Behaviorally specific genes provide genetically programmed predispositions for humans in all cultures to behave in particular ways. Those universal predispositions are differentially shaped by the social practices of different cultures, however. Put somewhat differently, culture adds a surface, or phenotypic, variability on top of what is a deeper, or genotypic, universality. In discussing how very little room biology allegedly allows for social change, E. O. Wilson argues that, like it or not, human cultures have but "three choices" (1978, p. 132). They can exaggerate genetic predispositions, they can fight against them, or they can leave them alone.

In fact, however, cultural invention can so radically transform the situational context of human life that the human organism can be liberated from what had earlier seemed to be its intrinsic biological limitations. Consider but three examples.

1. As a biological species, human beings require food and water on a daily basis, which once meant that it was part of univer-

sal human nature to live as survivalists. But now human beings have invented agricultural techniques for producing food, and storage and refrigeration techniques for preserving food, which means that it is no longer part of universal human nature to live as survivalists.

2. As a biological species, human beings are susceptible to infection from many bacteria, which once meant that it was part of universal human nature to die routinely from infection. But now human beings have invented antibiotics to fight infection, which means that it is no longer part of universal human nature to die routinely from infection.

3. As a biological species, human beings do not have wings, which once meant that it was part of universal human nature to be unable to fly. But now human beings have invented airplanes, which means that it is no longer part of universal human nature to be unable to fly.

As dramatically liberating as these three examples of technological innovation clearly are, the general principle that they illustrate is so mundane and noncontroversial that even sociobiologists would unhesitatingly endorse it. Simply put, the impact of any biological feature depends in every instance on how that biological feature interacts with the environment in which it is situated. That is why there is a technical distinction between a genotype and a phenotype in the first place. That is also why biologists never specify a one-to-one correspondence between biology and behavior but always specify a norm, or range, of reaction. More specifically, they say that in Environment 1, a given biological feature will produce Behavior A, but in Environment 2, that same biological feature will produce Behavior B.

Ironically, sociobiologists massively underestimate the contributions of culture and history to this interaction, not only because they pay too little attention to culture and history but because they also pay too little attention to what is arguably the most distinctively human feature of human biology: the ability of human beings to transform their environments through cultural invention and thereby to transform themselves. Just like the human capacity for language, this human capacity for cultural invention is a product of the evolution of the human brain.

Minimizing how the human brain has itself evolved leads sociobiologists to misconstrue the human organism as a being whose way of relating to the world is heavily constrained by genetic predispositions for specific behaviors, rather than as a being whose way of relating to the world is much more loosely constrained by a less specific set of genetic programs. It also leads sociobiologists to grossly underestimate how radically different the situational context of human life could be in different historical eras.

As noted earlier, sociobiologists are especially concerned with the universals of human social life and human social organization because they see these universals as the product of biology alone. If there is any single moral to my critique of sociobiology, however, it is that even universals are the product of an interaction between biology and culture. Accordingly, when trying to explain the emergence of a true human universal across time and place, scientists had better look for a constant in history and culture, as well as a constant in biology, because it is the interaction between those two constants that has produced that universal, not the constant in biology alone.

PRENATAL HORMONE THEORY

Long before sociobiologists came up with their own particular just-so story about the differential evolution of male and female genes, less fanciful biopsychologists offered a hormonal theory about the differential development in utero of male and female brains.* This prenatal hormone theory was an extrapolation of what was already known in the late 1940s about the differential development in utero of male and female bodies (Jost, 1953).

By the late 1940s, biopsychologists had established that regardless of their genetic sex, all mammalian embryos initially have the rudimentary tissue required for both male and female genitalia, as well as for both male and female reproductive organs. They had also established that what fashions this hermaphroditic embryo into either a male or a female body is the presence or absence of testosterone during a critical prenatal period. An embryo will thus develop into a male body if testosterone is present during this critical period; it will develop into a female body if testosterone is absent; and it will develop into a partly male and partly female—or pseudohermaphroditic—body if testosterone is present but either in the wrong amount or for the wrong period of time.

A decade later, this observation about male and female bodies becoming physically differentiated during a critical prenatal period was expanded into the theory of hormonally induced brain organization (Phoenix et al., 1959). According to this theory, prenatal hormones not only shape mammalian bodies into a male or female pattern during the critical period of sexual differentiation; they also irreversibly organize mammalian brains into a male or female pattern, and these hormonally organized brains, in turn, organize mammalian hormone function and mammalian behavior into a male or female pattern.

The evidence for this prenatal hormone theory is now extensive. In every mammalian species that has been comprehensively examined to date—including guinea pigs, rats, mice,

hamsters, dogs, sheep, ferrets, voles, rabbits, and rhesus monkeys but excluding humans—prenatal hormones have been shown to have some kind of permanent organizing effect on sexually dimorphic behaviors directly related to copulation, such as mounting and positioning one's body for penile penetration (Baum, 1979). In some of these mammalian species, prenatal hormones have also been shown to have a permanent organizing effect on sexually dimorphic behaviors not directly related to copulation, such as aggression and activity level (Beatty, 1979; Meaney, 1988), as well as on the cyclicity of hormone production—which is directly controlled by the hypothalamic portion of the brain in many species. Finally, in an even smaller number of species, prenatal hormones have been shown to have a permanent organizing effect on the structures of certain neurons within the brain itself (Arnold & Gorski, 1984; Feder, 1984).

In spite of the abundance of animal evidence supporting the prenatal hormone theory, there are at least two empirical reasons for thinking that this theory would not pertain to human beings as much as it does to other species.

1. Although prenatal hormones do shape the human body into a male or female pattern, they do not have any permanent effect on the cyclicity of hormone production in either humans or other primates (Karsch, Dierschke & Knobil, 1973; Kuhlin & Reiter, 1976; Goy & Resko, 1972; Valdés et al., 1979; Knobil et al., 1980). Breaking the link between the shaping of the body and the organizing of hormone function calls into question whether the functioning of the primate brain is even affected by prenatal hormones.

2. Even among rats, some of the effects of prenatal hormones on adult behavior are now known to be partially mediated not by a hormonally organized brain but by a social interaction pattern evoked by the male or female body of the young. To give but one

---

*This discussion of the history of, and the evidence for, the prenatal hormone theory relies heavily on Seiwert (1988).

example, male rat pups give off an odor different from that of female rat pups, and the additional anogenital licking that this odor evokes from their mothers is at least partially responsible for the higher rates of mounting behavior among male adults than among female adults (C. L. Moore, 1984). If sex differences are sometimes mediated by social interaction even among rats, they are even more likely to be mediated by social interaction among humans, whose social life is much more complex.

But however much reason there was to doubt the human applicability of the prenatal hormone theory, the animal evidence was so provocative—and the habit of looking at human sex differences biologically was so ingrained—that many studies were undertaken to test the prenatal model in humans. In addition, the results of those studies were widely seen as providing support for the prenatal model, even though they really didn't.

Two human studies are especially famous, and both are subject to many alternative interpretations: the Money and Ehrhardt study, which purports to show that prenatal testosterone in genetic females masculinizes the brain and thereby produces "tomboyism," and the Imperato-McGinley study, which purports to show that the prenatal masculinization of the fetal brain by testosterone is so directly related to the development of a male gender identity that for certain individuals, it can overcome even the experience of being reared as a female.

In contrast to all the animal studies on the prenatal hormone theory, which directly manipulate the level of a fetus's prenatal hormones and then measure the effect of that manipulation on later behavior, the human studies merely examine the effects on later behavior of unusual hormone conditions that a fetus happens to have experienced. In all cases, these unusual hormone conditions have either occurred naturally or are the side effect of some medical procedure that the mother underwent while pregnant, usually to save her pregnancy.

The Money and Ehrhardt Study

John Money and Anke Ehrhardt (1972) studied twenty-five genetic females who were exposed to abnormally high levels of testosterone in utero. Fifteen of these girls had a genetic disorder that caused their adrenal glands to malfunction, producing too few adrenocorticoids and too much adrenal testosterone. Ten of these girls had mothers who received progestins during pregnancy, a treatment now known to masculinize the external genitalia of girls. The fifteen girls with the adrenogenital syndrome (AGS) required cortisone treatment throughout their lives for their adrenal glands to function properly. All twenty-five girls had such male-looking genitalia that each required at least one surgery in order to look more like a girl. In many cases, several surgeries were required—including the cutting back of the clitoris, the conversion of the scrotum to labia, and the fashioning of a vagina—which sometimes brought the date of the last surgery well into adolescence.

At the time of the study, these twenty-five girls were between the ages of five and sixteen. For purposes of comparison, a control group of twenty-five medically normal girls was also studied. The girls in the control group were of the same age and socioeconomic background as the fetally masculinized girls.

On the basis of interviews with both the girls and their mothers, Money and Ehrhardt found that the fetally masculinized girls were more "tomboyish" than the normal girls. That is, they had a pattern of more intense energy expenditure in play; they had a higher preference for boys as playmates, for boys' toys, for boys' clothes, and for outdoor play and athletics; they had a lesser interest in dolls, in infant care, and in marriage; and they had a greater interest in a career. In their much-cited book, *Man and Woman, Boy and Girl,* Money and Ehrhardt concluded that the most likely explanation for this higher level of tomboyism was "a masculinizing effect on the fetal brain" (1972, p. 103).

In fact, at least three alternative explanations are even more likely.

1. Cortisone is a potent drug known to raise both activity level in general and the level of rough outdoor play in particular. The fifteen AGS girls may thus have become more "tomboyish" not because testosterone masculinized their fetal brains but because their lifelong cortisone therapy raised their activity level.

2. Because of either their continuing need for surgery or their continuing cortisone therapy or both, all twenty-five of the fetally masculinized girls were, in a sense, chronically ill during some portion of their childhood. This is especially true of the AGS girls who experienced the "salt-loss" form of the condition, which is associated with frequent hospitalization during the early years of life. Because all chronically ill children have to deal with a sense of inadequacy and a sense of uncertainty about the future and because some chronically ill children compensate for these feelings by developing a kind of bustling self-assurance, the possibility exists that the so-called tomboyism of the fetally masculinized girls resulted not from any masculinization of their brains but from their psychological reaction to the experience of being chronically ill.

   Support for this alternative hypothesis is available in a recent study in which a group of normal healthy girls between the ages of seven and seventeen was compared with three groups of chronically ill girls: AGS girls with salt loss, AGS girls without salt loss, and diabetic girls—who were chronically ill during childhood but had normal

hormones in utero (Slijper, 1984). Not only were all three groups of chronically ill girls more "boyish" than healthy girls on a test of their interests and values; in addition, the sicker AGS girls (those with salt loss) were significantly more boyish than the less sick AGS girls.

3. Finally, and perhaps most important, the girls' tomboyism may have resulted from the psychological impact on the girls and their parents of the girls' having masculinized genitalia. Among other things, for example, both the girls and their parents may have doubted what sex the girls actually were; they may also have wondered whether the girls' personalities had been altered along with their genitalia, whether the girls would ever be able to have children, and whether the girls would ever be able to find anyone to marry them. With all of this gender-related uncertainty, it would not be the least bit surprising if the parents of the fetally masculinized girls and the parents of the normal girls treated their daughters differently. Nor would it be surprising if the fetally masculinized girls themselves developed a somewhat different self-concept from that of the normal girls—and hence selected a somewhat different pattern of activities and friends.

Although several recent studies have tried to control for even these psychological effects of a girl's having masculinized genitalia, the "tomboy" experiments to date provide very little support for the theory that prenatal hormones differentially organize male and female brains.

The Imperato-McGinley Study

In contrast to Money and Ehrhardt, who studied girls with prenatally masculinized bodies, Julianne Imperato-McGinley and her colleagues (1979a, 1979b) studied boys with prenatally feminized bodies. More specifically, they studied eighteen genetic males living in the Dominican Republic who were suffering from a rare enzyme deficiency that prevented their prenatal testosterone from masculinizing their genitalia during the critical period in utero but did not later prevent their adolescent testosterone from masculinizing either their genitalia or their secondary sex characteristics at puberty. As a result of this enzyme deficiency, these boys not only looked like girls but were raised as girls from birth to puberty, when they finally began to look more like the boys they were genetically.

In spite of being reared as girls, sixteen of these eighteen genetic males allegedly changed their self-definition from female to male sometime after their physical masculinization at puberty. On the basis of this psychological change, Imperato-McGinley and her colleagues concluded that biology rather than environment is critical to the evolution of a male gender identity. "Just as the development of the male ... [body] is [normally] induced by androgens at a critical period in utero, the formation of a male gender identity is also an induced state with androgens acting on the brain at critical periods (in utero, neonatally, and puberty)" (1979b, p. 644).

Imperato-McGinley and her colleagues clearly believe that the feminized boys in their study switched at puberty from a female gender identity to a male gender identity because their high level of prenatal testosterone had already masculinized their brains, and their high level of pubertal testosterone was allowing that dormant masculinity to finally express itself psychologically. Their pubertal testosterone was accomplishing this by masculinizing their brains still further and by masculinizing their bodies as well.

This purely biological hypothesis has, however, an obvious interactionist alternative. Perhaps the brains of these individuals were never masculinized at all; perhaps when their bodies

began to be masculinized at puberty, both they and the others in their community began to believe that some kind of male identity would be much more appropriate than any kind of female identity. If so, the switch from female to male did not necessarily happen overnight or without conflict; nor was it necessarily a switch from one unambiguous gender identity to another unambiguous gender identity. Rather, the implication is that whatever the precise nature of the switch, (1) it was initiated by the masculinization of the body rather than by the masculinization of the brain, and (2) it was mediated by the reactions of both the self and others to that physical masculinization.

Imperato-McGinley and her colleagues did not gather the kind of detailed cultural or psychological information that would allow us to evaluate the importance of this biocultural interaction in the context of their sample of boys. Consistent with this interactionist interpretation, however, is the very detailed description by an anthropologist and a biologist of the process by which a group of Sambian boys in Papua, New Guinea, with the same enzyme deficiency made their switch from female to male. In the words of these two authors, "Sambian subjects who switched from the female to male role did so only under the greatest external public pressure. Once exposed, they had 'no place to hide,' and no public in which to continue to pose as 'female.'... *Only the failure of their own bodies to fulfill their social destiny as sex-assigned females seemed to have caused these individuals to change*" (Herdt & Davidson, 1988, p. 53).

As even this brief discussion of the literature makes clear, the fundamental conceptual problem with the prenatal hormone theory is strikingly similar to the fundamental conceptual problem discussed earlier with respect to sociobiology. In both cases, the importance of the individual's situational context is massively underestimated, and the importance of the individual's biology is massively overestimated. To put it somewhat differently, the interaction between situation and biology is insufficiently theorized; hence, the theorists jump too quickly to the conclusion that either sexual difference or sexual inequality is the product of biology alone.

REFERENCES

Arnold, A. P., & Gorski, R. A. (1984). Gonadal steroid induction of structural sex differences in the central nervous system. *Annual Review of Neuroscience, 7,* 413–442.

Barash, D. (1979). *The whispering within.* New York: Harper & Row.

Baum, M. J. (1979). Differentiation of coital behavior in mammals: A comparative analysis. *Neuroscience and Biobehavior Review, 3,* 265–284.

Beatty, W. W. (1979) Gonadal hormones and sex differences in nonreproductive behaviors in rodents: Organizational and activational influences. *Hormones and Behavior, 12,* 112–163.

Bleier, R. (1984). *Science and gender: A critique of biology and its theories on women.* New York: Pergamon.

Fausto-Sterling, A. (1985). *Myths of gender: Biological theories about women and men.* New York: Basic Books.

Feder, H. (1984). Hormones and sexual behavior. *Annual Review of Psychology, 35,* 165–200.

Goy, R., & Resko, J. A. (1972). Gonadal hormones and behavior of normal and pseudohermaphroditic nonhuman female primates. In E. B. Astwood (Ed.), *Recent progress in hormone research* (Vol. 28, pp. 707–754). New York: Academic Press.

Herdt, G. H., & Davidson, J. (1988). The Sambia "turnim-man": Sociocultural and clinical aspects of gender formation in male pseudohermaphrodites with 5-alpha-reductase deficiency in Papua New Guinea. *Archives of Sexual Behavior, 17,* 33–56.

Huxley, J. (1943). *Evolution: The modern synthesis.* New York: Harper.

Imperato-McGinley, J., Peterson, R. E., Gautier, T., & Sturla, E. (1979a). Androgens and the evolution of male gender identity among male pseudohermaphrodites with a 5-alpha-reductase deficiency. *New England Journal of Medicine, 300,* 1236–1237.

———. (1979b). Male pseudohermaphoditism secondary to 5-alpha-reductase deficiency: A model for the role of androgens in both the development of the male phenotype and the evolution of a male gender identity. *Journal of Steroid Biochemistry, 11,* 637–645.

Jost, A. (1953). Problems of fetal endocrinology: The gonadal and hypophyseal hormones. *Recent Progress in Hormone Research, 8,* 379–418.

Karsch, F. J., Dierschke, D. J., & Knobil, E. (1973). Sexual differences of pituitary function: Apparent difference between primates and rodents. *Science, 179,* 484–486.

Knobil, E., Plant, T. M., Wildt, L., Belchetz, P. E., & Marshall, G. (1980). Control of the rhesus monkey menstrual cycle: Permissive role of hypothalamic gonadotropin-releasing hormone. *Science, 207,* 1371–1373.

Kuhlin, H., & Reiter, E. O. (1976). Gonadotropin and testosterone measurements after estrogen administration to adult men, prepubertal and pubertal boys, and men with hypogonadotropism: Evidence for positive feedback in the male. *Pediatric Research, 10,* 46–51.

Lewontin, R. C., Rose, S., & Kamin, L. J. (1984). *Not in our genes: Biology, ideology, and human nature.* New York: Pantheon.

Meaney, M. J. (1988). The sexual differentiation of social play. *Trends in Neurosciences, 11,* 54–58.

Money, J., & Ehrhardt, A. (1972). *Man and woman, boy and girl.* Baltimore, Md.: Johns Hopkins University Press.

Moore, C. L. (1984). Maternal contributions to the development of masculine sexual behavior in laboratory rats. *Developmental Psychology, 17,* 347–356.

Phoenix, C. H., Goy, R. W., Gerall, A. A., & Young, W. C. (1959). Organizing action of prenatally administered testosterone propionate on the tissues mediating mating behavior in the female guinea pig. *Endocrinology, 65,* 369–382.

Sayers, J. (1982). *Biological politics: Feminist and anti-feminist perspectives.* New York: Tavistock.

Seiwert, C. (1988). The brain as a reproductive organ: An analysis of the organizational theory of hormone action. Unpublished manuscript, Cornell University.

Slijper, F. M. E. (1984). Androgens and gender role behaviour in girls with congenital adrenal hyperplasia (CAH). *Progress in Brain Research, 61,* 417–422.

Valdes, E., del Castillo, C., Gutiérrez, R., Larrea, F., Medina, M., & Pérez-Palacios, G. (1979). Endocrine studies and successful treatment in a patient with true hermaphroditism. *Acta Endocrinologica, 91,* 184–192.

Wynne-Edwards, V. C. (1962). *Animal dispersion in relation to social behavior.* New York: Hafner.

Reading 3   The Longest War: Gender and Culture

CAROLE WADE AND CAROL TAVRIS

Questions to Consider:

1. Why does our own cultural experience with gender make it difficult to conduct accurate observations of gender in other cultures?

2. Why do we need to know the history, environment, economy, and survival needs of a culture in order to understand its gender roles?

3. According to Wade and Tavris, why is it significant that gender roles vary across cultures and historical periods?

4. How do you think your culture will construct gender roles a century from now?

A young boy notices, at an early age, that he seems different from other boys. He prefers playing with girls. He is attracted to the work adult women do, such as cooking and sewing. He often dreams at night of being a girl, and he even likes to put on the clothes of girls. As the boy enters adolescence, people begin to whisper that he's "different," that he seems feminine in his movements, posture, and language. One day the boy can hide his secret feelings no longer, and reveals them to his parents.

The question: How do they respond?
The answer: It depends on their culture.

In twentieth-century North America and Europe, most parents would react with tears,

anger, or guilt ("Where did we go wrong?"). After the initial shock, they might haul their son off to a psychiatrist, who would diagnose him as having a "gender identity disorder" and begin intensive treatment. In contrast, if their daughter wanted to be "more like a man," the parents' response would probably be far milder. They might view a girl's desire to play hockey or become a construction worker as a bit unusual, but they probably wouldn't think she had a mental disorder.

These reactions are not universal. Until the late 1800s, in a number of Plains Indians and western Indian tribes, parents and other elders reacted with sympathy and understanding when a young person wanted to live the life of the other sex. The young man or woman was often given an honored status as a shaman, a person with the power to cure illness and act as an intermediary between the natural and spiritual worlds. A boy was permitted to dress as and perform the duties of a woman, and a girl might become a warrior.

Carole Wade and Carol Tavris, "The Longest War: Gender and Culture." In *Psychology and Culture,* W. J. Lonner & R. S. Malpars, eds. Copyright © 1994 by Allyn & Bacon. Reprinted by permission.

In some Native American cultures, the young man would be allowed to marry another man, the young woman to marry another woman.

In the Sambian society of Papua New Guinea, parents would react still differently. In Sambia, reports anthropologist Gilbert Herdt (1984), all adolescent boys are *required* to engage in oral sex with older men as part of their initiation into manhood. Sambians believe that a boy cannot mature physically or emotionally unless he ingests another man's semen over a period of several years. However, Sambian parents would react with shock and disbelief if a son said he wanted to live as a woman. Every man and woman in Sambian society marries someone of the other sex and performs the work assigned to his or her own sex; no exceptions.

What these diverse reactions tell us is that although anatomical *sex* is universal and unchangeable (unless extraordinary surgical procedures are used), *gender,* which encompasses all the duties, rights, and behaviors a culture considers appropriate for males and females, is a social invention. It is gender, not anatomical sex, that gives us a sense of personal identity as male or female. Cultures have different notions about what gender roles should entail, how flexible these roles ought to be, and how much leeway males and females have to cross the gender divide.

Perhaps, however, there is something essential about the sexes, something lying *beneath* the veneer of culture, immutable and eternal. That assumption is certainly widespread, and it has guided the research of social scientists as well as the beliefs of laypersons. Let us examine this assumption more closely. Are there some aspects of masculinity and femininity that occur at all times and in all places? If certain characteristics are common, why is that so? What determines how men and women should act toward each other, what their rights and obligations should be, and what it means, in psychological terms, to be female or male?

SEARCHING FOR THE ESSENTIAL MAN AND WOMAN

By comparing and contrasting different cultures around the world, social scientists have tried to identify those aspects of gender that are universally male or female. Their efforts may sound pretty straightforward. However, because researchers, like everyone else, are influenced by their own deeply felt perceptions and convictions about gender, the topic has been one of the most complex to study cross-culturally.

For many years American and European researchers looked for and found evidence that primate males (human and ape) were "by nature" competitive, dominant, and promiscuous, whereas primate females were "by nature" cooperative, submissive, and monogamous (Tavris, 1992). Because of their own preconceptions about male and female roles, based on their own cultural experiences, these observers often overlooked the evidence that contradicted their assumptions, even when the evidence was in front of their noses.

For example, many years ago the famous anthropologist Bronislaw Malinowski wrote a book on the Trobriand Islanders, in which he concluded that males controlled the economic and political life of the community. (Another of his biases is glaringly apparent in the title he gave his book: *The Sexual Life of Savages.*) But when Annette Weiner went to live among the Trobrianders many years later, she learned, by talking to the women, what Malinowski had not: that there was an important economic underground controlled by the labor and exchanges of women.

Similarly, in 1951, another famous anthropologist, E. E. Evans-Pritchard, reported that among the Nuer, a tribe living in the Sudan, husbands had unchallenged authority over their wives. Yet he himself described incidents in Nuer family life that contradicted his conclusion:

[Should a Nuer wife] in a quarrel with her husband disfigure him—knock a tooth out,

for example—her father must pay him compensation. I have myself on two occasions seen a father pay a heifer to his son-in-law to atone for insults hurled at the husband's head by his wife when irritated by accusations of adultery.

We don't approve of domestic violence, nor do we think the wife's actions cancel out men's political power over women in Nuer culture. However, as anthropologist Micaela di Leonardo observes, a husband's authority in the home is not absolute if his wife can insult him and knock his teeth out, and all he can do is demand that his father-in-law fork over a cow!

Many early researchers not only assumed that male dominance and aggression were universally the province of men; they also assumed that female nurturance was universally the province of women. Because of this assumption, Western researchers often overlooked the nurturing activities of men, or even *defined* nurturance in a way that excluded the altruistic, caring actions of men. When anthropologist David Gilmore (1991) examined how cultures around the world define manhood, he expected to find masculinity equated with selfishness and hardness. Instead he found that it often entails selfless generosity and sacrifice. "Women nurture others directly," notes Gilmore. "They do this with their bodies, with their milk and their love. This is very sacrificial and generous. But surprisingly, 'real' men nurture, too, although they would perhaps not be pleased to hear it put this way." Men nurture their families and society, he observes, by "bringing home food for both child and mother ... and by dying if necessary in faraway places to provide a safe haven for their people." (pp. 229–230)

Our own cultural stereotypes, then, affect what we see in other cultures and how we interpret what we see. Still, a few common themes— not universal, mind you, but common—do emerge from the cross-cultural study of gender.

Generally speaking, men have had, and continue to have, more status and more power than women, especially in public affairs. Generally speaking, men have fought the wars and brought home the meat. If a society's economy includes hunting large game, traveling a long way from home, or making weapons, men typically handle these activities. Women have had the primary responsibility for cooking, cleaning, and taking care of small children.

Corresponding with this division of jobs, in many cultures around the world people regard masculinity as something that boys must achieve through strenuous effort. Males must pass physical tests, must endure pain, must confront danger, and must separate psychologically and even physically from their mothers and the world of women. Sometimes they have to prove their self-reliance and courage in bloodcurdling initiation rites. Femininity, in contrast, tends to be associated with responsibility, obedience, and childcare, and it is seen as something that develops naturally, without any special intervention from others.

THE INVENTION OF GENDER

From these commonalities, some theorists have concluded that certain fundamental aspects of gender must be built into our genes. Biological factors—the fact that women are (so far) the only sex that gets pregnant and that men, on the average, have greater upper body strength—undoubtedly play some role in the sexual division of labor in many societies. But biology takes us only so far, because, when we remove our own cultural blinders and look at the full cross-cultural picture, the range of variation among men and women, in what they do and in how they regard one another, is simply astonishing.

For instance, in some places women are and have been completely under the rule of men, an experience reflected in the haunting words of the Chinese poet Fu Hsuan: "How sad it is to be a woman! Nothing on earth is held so cheap."

Women in Saudi Arabia today are not allowed to drive a car; many girls in India submit to arranged marriages as early as age nine; girls and women in the Sudan and other parts of Africa are subjected to infibulation (the practice of cutting off the clitoris and much of the labia, and stitching together the vaginal opening), allegedly to assure their virginity at marriage. Yet elsewhere women have achieved considerable power, influence, and sexual independence. Among the Iroquois, some of the older wives played an important role in village politics. Although they could not become members of the Council of Elders, the ruling body, they had a major say in its decisions. In this century, women have been heads of state in England, Israel, India, Sri Lanka, Iceland, and elsewhere.

Thus it is an oversimplification to say that men are the dominant sex, women the subordinate one. The status of women has been assessed by measures of economic security, educational opportunities, access to birth control and medical care, degree of self-determination, participation in public and political life, power to make decisions in the family, and physical safety. According to these indexes, the status of women worldwide is highest in Scandinavian countries and lowest in Bangladesh, with tremendous variation in between.

Similarly, cultures vary in many other aspects of male-female relations:

- The *content* of what is considered "men's work" and "women's work" differs from culture to culture. In some cultures, men weave and women do not; in others, it's the opposite. In many cultures women do the shopping and marketing, but in others marketing is men's work.
- In many cultures, women are considered the "emotional" sex and are permitted to express their emotions more freely than men. But in cultures throughout the Middle East and South America, men are permitted (and expected) to be as emotionally expressive as women, or even more so, whereas many Asian cultures expect *both* sexes to control their emotions. Moreover, the rules about which sex gets to display which emotion are quite variable. In one major international study, Israeli and Italian men were more likely than women to control feelings of sadness, but British, Spanish, Swiss, and German men were *less* likely than women to inhibit this emotion.
- Cultures differ in the degree of daily contact that is permitted between the sexes. In many farm communities and in most modern occupations in North America and Europe, men and women work together in close proximity. At the other end of the continuum, some Middle Eastern societies have a tradition of *purdah,* the veiling of women and the seclusion of wives from all male eyes except those of their relatives.
- In some cultures, as in Iran or the Sudan, women are expected to suppress all sexual feeling (and certainly behavior) until marriage, and premarital or extramarital sex is cause for the woman's ostracism from the community or even death. In others, such as Polynesia, women are expected to have sex before marriage. In still others, such as the Toda of India, women were allowed to have extramarital affairs (as long as they told their husbands and didn't sneak around).

Perhaps no society challenges our usual assumptions about the universal nature of psychological maleness and femaleness as profoundly as Tahiti. For over two centuries, Western visitors to Tahiti have marveled at the lack of sexual differentiation among its peaceful inhabitants. Early European sailors who arrived on the island reported that Tahitian women were free to do just about everything the men did. Women could be chiefs, they could take part in all sports, including wrestling, and they enjoyed casual sex with many different partners.

In the 1960s, anthropologist Robert Levy lived among the Tahitians and confirmed that they didn't share Westerners' ideas about gender. Men in Tahiti were no more aggressive than women, nor were women gentler or more maternal than men. Men felt no obligation to appear "manly" or defend "male honor," and women felt no pressure to be demure and "womanly." The Tahitians seemed to lack what psychologist Sandra Bem has called a "gender schema," a network of assumptions about the personalities and moral qualities of the two sexes. To Tahitians, Levy found, gender was just no big deal. Even the Tahitian language ignores gender: Pronouns are not different for males and females, and most traditional Tahitian names are used for both sexes.

The existence of cultures such as Tahiti, together with the wide variations in gender roles that exist around the world, suggest that the qualities that cultures link with masculinity and femininity are not innately male or female. Instead, they are, in the language of social science, *socially constructed.* As David Gilmore puts it, "gender ideologies are social facts, collective representations that pressure people into acting in certain ways."

WHERE DO THE RULES OF GENDER COME FROM?

When most people read about the customs of other cultures, they are inclined to say, "Oh, boy, I like the sexual attitudes of the Gorks but I hate the nasty habits of the Dorks." The point to keep in mind is that a culture's practices cannot easily be exported elsewhere, like cheese, or surgically removed, like a tumor. *A culture's attitudes and practices regarding gender are deeply embedded in its history, environment, economy, and survival needs.*

To understand how a society invents its notions of gender, we need to understand its political system and its economy, and how that economy is affected by geography, natural resources, and even the weather. We need to know who controls and distributes the resources, and how safe a society is from interlopers. We need to know the kind of work that people do, and how they structure that work. And we need to know whether there is environmental pressure on a group to produce more children, or to have fewer of them. In short, we need to know about *production* and *reproduction.*

For example, David Gilmore found that rigid concepts of manhood tend to exist wherever there is a great deal of competition for resources— which is to say, in most places. For the human species, life has usually been harsh. Consider a tribe trying to survive in the wilds of a South American forest; or in the dry and unforgiving landscape of the desert; or in an icy Arctic terrain that imposes limits on the number of people who can survive by fishing. When conditions like these exist, men are the sex that is taught to hunt for large game, compete with each other for work, and fight off enemies. (As we've noted, this division of labor may originally have occurred because of men's relatively greater upper-body muscular strength and the fact that they do not become pregnant or nurse children.) Men will be socialized to resist the impulse to avoid confrontation and retreat from danger. They will be "toughened up" and pushed to take risks, even with their lives.

How do you get men to do all this? To persuade men to wage war and risk death, argues anthropologist Marvin Harris (1974), societies have to give them something—and the something is prestige, power, and women. That in turn means you have to raise obedient women; if the King is going to offer his daughter in marriage to the bravest warrior, she has to go when given. In contrast, David Gilmore finds, in cultures such as Tahiti, where resources are abundant and there are no serious hazards or enemies to worry about, men don't feel they have to prove themselves or set themselves apart from women.

The economic realities of life also affect how men and women regard each other. Ernestine Friedl has described the remarkable differences between two tribes in New Guinea. One tribe, living in the highlands, believes that intercourse weakens men, that women are dangerous and unclean, and that menstrual blood can do all sorts of terrifying things. Sex is considered powerful and mysterious; if it is performed in a garden, the act will blight the crops. Antagonism between the sexes runs high; men often delay marriage and many remain single. Not far away, another tribe has an opposite view of women and sex. People in this tribe think sexual intercourse is fun and that it revitalizes men. Sex, they say, *should* take place in gardens, as it will foster the growth of plants. Men and women do not live in segregated quarters, as they do in the highlands, and they get along pretty well.

One possible explanation for these differences is that the highland people have been settled a long time and have little new land or resources. If the population increased, food would become scarce. Sexual antagonism and a fear of sexual intercourse help keep the birth rate low. The sexy tribe, however, lives in uncultivated areas and needs more members to work the land and help defend the group. Encouraging positive attitudes toward sex and early marriage is one way to increase the birth rate.

Cross-cultural studies find that when the sexes are mutually dependent and work cooperatively, as in husband-wife teams, sexual antagonism is much lower than when work is organized along sex-segregated lines. Among the Machiguenga Indians of Peru, where the sexes cooperate in growing vegetables, fishing, and recreation, husbands and wives feel more solidarity with each other than with their same-sex friends. Among the Mundurucu, however, women and men work in same-sex groups, and friendships rarely cross sexual lines; women therefore feel a sense of solidarity with other women, men with men.

In our own culture, changing conditions have profoundly influenced our ideas about gender as well as our family relationships. According to Francesca Cancian (1987), before the nineteenth century, the typical household was a cooperative rural community in which both spouses shared responsibility for the material and emotional well-being of the family. Men didn't "go to work"; work was right there, and so was the family. Women raised both chickens and children. This is not to say that the two sexes had equal rights in the public domain, but in psychological terms they were not seen as opposites.

But with the onset of the industrial revolution, shops and factories began to replace farming, and many men began to work apart from their families. This major economic change, argues Cancian, created a rift between "women's sphere," at home, and "men's sphere," at work. The masculine ideal adjusted to fit the new economic realities, which now required male competitiveness and the suppression of any signs of emotional "weakness." The feminine ideal became its opposite: Women were now seen as being "naturally" nurturant, emotional, and fragile.

WHAT'S AHEAD?

In the twentieth century, two profound changes in production and reproduction are occurring that have never before happened in human history. Most jobs in industrial nations, including military jobs, now involve service skills and brainwork rather than physical strength. Reproduction, too, has been revolutionized; although women in many countries still lack access to safe and affordable contraceptives, it is now possible for women to limit reliably the number of children they will have and to plan when to have them. The "separate spheres" doctrine spawned by the industrial revolution is breaking down in this post-industrial age, which requires the labor of both sexes.

As these changes unfold, ideas about the "natural" qualities of men and women are also being transformed. It is no longer news that a woman can run a country, be a Supreme Court justice or a miner, or walk in space. It is no longer news that many men, whose own fathers would no more have diapered a baby than jumped into a vat of boiling oil, now want to be involved fathers.

What a cross-cultural, historical perspective teaches us, then, is that gender arrangements, and the qualities associated with being male and female, are not arbitrary. Our ideas about gender are affected by the practical conditions of our lives. These conditions are far more influential than our hormones in determining whether men are expected to be fierce or gentle, and whether women are expected to be financially helpless or Wall Street whizzes.

The cross-cultural perspective reminds us too that no matter how entrenched our own notions of masculinity and femininity are, they can be expected to change—as the kind of work we do changes, as technology changes, and as our customs change. Yet many intriguing questions remain. Do men and women need to feel that they are psychologically different from one another in some way? Will masculinity always rest on male achievements and actions, and femininity on merely being female? Since most of us cannot move to Tahiti, but must live in a world in which wars and violence persist, is it wise or necessary to make sure that at least one sex—or only one sex—is willing to do the dangerous work?

Marvin Harris has argued that male supremacy was "just a phase in the evolution of culture," a phase that depended on the ancient division of labor that put men in charge of war and women in charge of babies. Harris predicts that by the 21st century, male supremacy will fade and gender equality will become, for the first time in history, a real possibility.

Is he right? How will gender be constructed by our own culture in the next century? What do you think?

REFERENCES

Cancian, Francesca (1987). *Love in America: Gender and self-development.* Cambridge, England: Cambridge University Press.

Gilmore, David (1991). *Manhood in the making.* New Haven, CT: Yale University Press.

Harris, Marvin (1974). *Cows, pigs, wars, and witches: The riddles of culture.* New York: Random House.

Herdt, Gilbert H. (1984). *Ritualized homosexuality in Melanesia.* Berkeley: University of California Press.

Kimmel, Michael S. (1987). *Changing men: New directions in research on men and masculinity.* Beverly Hills, CA: Sage.

Tavris, Carol (1992). *The mismeasure of woman.* New York: Simon & Schuster.

Reading 4 Lessons in Inequality: What Television Teaches Us about Women

TERESA KELLER

Questions to Consider:

1. Keller claims that television teaches us that men are in charge in society and that the roles of women (particularly white women) are to be beautiful and sexy for men's pleasure, and to take care of men, children, and the home. What historical and contemporary support does she provide for this claim? Is there other supporting evidence that she does not include in her article?

2. What, according to Keller, does television teach us about black women? How are these messages similar to and different from the messages about white women's roles? In what ways are they harmful to the self-image of black girls and women?

3. What lessons does television give us about women who act in powerful ways?

4. What are some examples of contemporary programs that challenge the "lessons in inequality"? Are there other examples? What alternative message do they give us about women and women's place in society? Is there an alternative message for black women too? Explain.

As you begin this article, take a moment to ponder the following questions. What picture forms in your mind when you think of a "welfare mother"? What do you see in your mind when you think of a "doctor"? What does the "ideal woman" look like?

You will likely discover that you have very strong ideas about people and behaviors, but you might have difficulty sorting out exactly where your ideas came from. In fact, we learn from everything we see and hear from the moment we are born: from the behaviors and words of mothers and fathers; from people in the communities where we grow up; from people in the streets, in stores, in churches, at parties, in school, at meetings; from our friends; on the little league field and soccer field; from the decorations in living rooms, basements, and garages in homes we visit; and yes, of course, from radio and television, newspapers, movies, music, magazines, and books.

In contemporary American discourse, radio, television, newspapers, and magazines tend to be clumped into a category referred to as "the media," implying a single, monolithic entity that many believe exerts strong influence on our thinking and behavior. As we look at how media affect

Courtesy of Teresa Keller.

our ideas and actions related to gender, the reader is encouraged to keep a couple of things in mind. First, the media are only among the many influences on a person; and, secondly, "the media" is a general term that includes all radio, television, film, and print that reaches a mass audience. With this understanding, we will begin an examination of the consistent messages the media present that influence our thinking and behavior related to gender, with a primary focus on television because of its dominant presence in American homes.

SHORT-TERM VERSUS LONG-TERM MEDIA IMPACT

Communication researchers have reached apparently contradictory conclusions about how strong media influence is. Studies show that media influence is both limited and very powerful. Scholars now differentiate between the very limited impact on individual behavior and the very powerful long-term impact on society (Dennis & DeFleur, 1996).

A single exposure to a media message is unlikely to have more than a minimal effect on attitudes and behaviors. For example, although you might watch a movie about a prostitute that ends happily for the prostitute, your likelihood of becoming a prostitute would not be directly related to watching the movie. You might, in fact, imitate, by your dress or mannerisms or speech, the behavior that you see in a pretty celluloid prostitute. The movie might inspire you to seriously consider what life as a prostitute would be like. But your career choice will be determined by many interacting factors, including your feelings about yourself, the attitudes you have learned toward careers from those around you, and your ability to persistently pursue long-term goals. In short, media impact on individuals can be very limited.

However, media impact can be very powerful also. Researchers now believe that the strongest influence of media comes with consistent, persistent, corroborated messages. As the introduction to this book discusses, women get messages early in life about their suitability for nurturing and domesticity. They quickly get the message that men hold the most powerful positions in politics and business. Young girls observe the importance of romantic relationships, appearance, and peacemaking to the women around them. They may watch their mothers, grandmothers, and aunts prepare and clean up after holiday meals while the men watch sporting events on television, indicating a subservient role for the females. They may see their sisters and mothers spend hours applying makeup and styling their hair in front of a mirror while their brothers and fathers jump in the shower and prepare for an evening out in a very few minutes. One first-year college student expressed her feelings of dissatisfaction with her body after looking through a well-known national catalog of underwear and sleepwear. "It made me feel like I didn't ever want to eat again," she said after studying the many slim, beautiful models. These messages that have a powerful effect on women, such as the importance of appearance and thinness, are almost always the same, continue over time, and are prevalent in personal lives as well as in the media. The accumulated effect is that women learn that expectations of them are different and sometimes lower than those of their brothers, boyfriends, and husbands.

CONSISTENT MEDIA MESSAGES TO WOMEN

Background

In the 1970s, leaders in the women's movement began questioning the most basic use of language across all media. Feminists complained that the masculine pronoun gave the unintended message that women didn't really count. Specifically, books and magazines referred to the condition of "man" or "mankind"; jobs were advertised for "policemen" and "firemen"; and writers referred to "congressmen" or "salesmen." Textbooks talked about a student as "he." Language usage in all media came under question, and supporters of traditional language usage accused feminists of absurd whining about trivialities. Despite those who preferred the status quo, however, language changed. Feminists insisted on using the title "Ms." as an address indicating sex, but nothing more, just as "Mr." gives no information about whether a man is married. Eventually, newspaper style guides were revised so that courtesy titles were omitted. Women began keeping their own names after marriage in protest of being labeled as "the wife of" Mr. So-and-So and in affirmation of their autonomy and equality. It seemed that the world had changed regarding media references to women.

Messages about the Importance of Women

A close examination of media today, however, shows that women remain surprisingly invisible in many ways. Even when they do appear, they are often in stereotyped roles. A large majority of prime-time television characters continue to be men, with women much more likely to appear in underwear, sleepwear, and skimpy bathing suits. Women do the housework. It is rare to see a man doing domestic chores in prime-time television, although men are much more likely to show up in kitchens and laundry rooms than they used to be ("Depiction of...," 1993). Men on television also appear in more capable roles than do women (Seggar, 1975), and they are almost always the voices of authority in television commercials.

Some analysts claim that reporting that "gets the widest coverage always seems to validate women's frailties" (Rivers, 1993). Stories about women's depression, PMS, and the risk of heart attack have all exploded in the media. Rivers contends that "PMS" is a common expression because of so much media attention. The media

has called repeated attention to the fact that women seek psychological help more than men, without acknowledging that recognizing problems and seeking help can be signs of strength.

Susan Faludi (1991) details extensive media coverage of the supposed horrors facing women who stray from the typical role of housewife and mother in her book *Backlash*. Single women face a "man shortage" if they aren't married by age 30. If a woman pursues a career instead of motherhood, her "biological clock" might run out before she can have a child, and a woman with both a child and a career will surely be doomed if she follows the "mommy track" instead of the "fast track." Faludi shows a consistent media portrayal of miserable working women despite research indicating that working women with children are more emotionally healthy compared to homemakers.

Another type of media message suggests that when women aren't alluring, they may be deadly, a pattern that has been dubbed "the psycho bitch phenomenon" and is exemplified by Glenn Close in *Fatal Attraction* and Sharon Stone in *Basic Instinct* (Rivers, 1993). This view of women might also explain *Newsweek*'s cover about wealthy tax-evader Leona Helmsley: "Rhymes With Rich," the cover blared.

Toy commercials support the narrow notion that girls are "sugar and spice and everything nice," but boys are "snakes and snails and puppy dog tails." Commercials aimed at boys are loud, with lots of running, climbing, and action, while the girls generally play quietly, designing hair styles and picking out clothing, or rocking and cuddling their dolls. The consistent, persistent, corroborated message indicates that boys act, whereas girls concentrate on looking good and nurturing others. What effect do these portrayals have on the girl who enjoys baseball or the boy who enjoys playing house? Do they get the message that they are abnormal and need to conceal their true interests? Do we wait for the little girl to outgrow her "tomboy" stage, and feel uncomfortable when little boys hug, kiss, carry, and cradle a baby doll?

The media often use the white male as the norm by which everyone else is judged (Gersh, 1992). News stories may lack descriptions of sex and race in stories about white men, but we may read about a "black leader" or a "female candidate," implying that they are different from the norm. When reporters include comments from experts, they usually choose men, reinforcing the message that men are more knowledgeable than women. When the focus is on women, the stories are more likely to be about poverty, family values, and welfare (Gersh, 1992). TV news will show pictures of welfare mothers while outlining educational and economic problems in single-parent homes.

Messages about Appearance

Despite the many messages of women's achievement and competence interspersed in all forms of media, columnist Linda Valdez (1997) says the message young girls get is that looking good is the most important achievement. Media messages can be very subtle. For example, women are often shown being looked at by men, an implication that men are making judgments about female appearance (Warlaumont, 1993). Women are more likely than men to be photographed with their mouths open, a presumably provocative pose (Dodd et al., 1989). More than twice as many TV women are blonde than are found in the general population ("Depiction of...," 1993). If there's any doubt about the consistent message to women regarding the importance of beauty and seductiveness, a visit to the magazine section of the corner store will reinforce the message that appearance and sexual relationships are THE priority.

There are many more corroborations for this message in addition to network prime time. MTV presents a fantasy world for men with nonstop images of writhing women as seducers or attractive backdrops for men. Violence against women can even be found as an MTV theme. Even though there are many more female rock stars now than ever before, they seem to be competing with each other to produce the most seductive music videos.

TV game shows are most always hosted by men and often feature glamour girls to model and adorn a display of prizes. Soap operas form a sea of upper-middle-class, exceptionally gorgeous people. In television, movies, magazines, and books, one plot continues to turn up over and over: a beautiful woman attracts a rich man; they have sex; they live happily ever after. Friendship and conversation never seem to enter the equation: The beauty of the woman is the primary requirement for "catching" the man.

IMPACT OF MEDIA MESSAGES

Stereotypical messages continue to have a strong influence on behavior in our culture. Because we still see many more images of seductive, sweet, scantily clad women than images of powerful women, we may be consciously or unconsciously displeased by behaviors that contradict the stereotype. When women take management positions in industry, others may resent their assertiveness or see expression of emotion as a weakness. A man may lose his temper, yet retain respect and authority, whereas a woman who loses hers is more likely to be labeled as "too emotional." Even in the workplace, women may be expected to plan menus and arrange social events in the belief that they are better suited for the tasks compared to men (Hamilton, 1993). Eventually, women stop getting promotions. They rise through the professional ranks, but somehow don't quite make it through to top positions in politics or business. Because the reasons are not apparent, the phenomenon is labeled the "glass ceiling." The same invisible reason that keeps women from assuming society's most powerful positions probably explains the fact that women with equal education and experience continue to make less money than do men. As Faludi (1991) points out, a woman with a college degree can expect earnings equivalent to a man with a high school diploma.

Women in politics are viewed as more honest, but have more trouble raising money. Voters expect them to be softer on crime and more concerned with domestic issues than are men ("Women in...," 1992). Strong women who do not fit the mold of sweetness and subservience to men may be judged harshly, as in the case of First Lady Hillary Clinton. Although she is a successful attorney and powerful political figure, media coverage consistently returns to her hair styles, clothing selection, and domestic activity, or to accusations of improper influence in the White House.

The consistent social message that women must look good undoubtedly contributes to the epidemic of eating disorders and to the fact that American women dislike their bodies more than women in any other culture (Faludi, 1991). Poor self-esteem, cigarette smoking, and mental health problems have all been linked to messages women receive about physical appearance (Lindsey, 1997). Little girls report that they don't expect boys to be handsome, but that boys expect girls to be perfect (Kilbourne, 1995). Is it any wonder that young girls place more emphasis on being sexy than on being active and engaged in personal pursuits?

AFRICAN AMERICAN WOMEN AND THE MEDIA

The general stereotypes about women in our society incorporate women of all races and ethnicity, but the media portrayal of minority women is especially horrific. For example, since the earliest television, white audiences have preferred portrayals of African American women as mammies or tarts. Bill Cosby introduced the first ongoing positive images of African American women in the 1980s in his major network hit *The Cosby Show* ("Black Women in Television," 1989). Otherwise, because black women have not fit the blonde, blue-eyed stereotype, they have often gotten the message that they are not considered attractive by society's standards. American television has also negated the sexuality of black women, partially through the dominance of the fat, jolly mammy figure. On American television, women in African tribes are regularly shown in full frontal nudity, but white women's breasts are considered indecent because of their strong sexuality.

TELEVISION PORTRAYALS OF WOMEN IN HISTORICAL PERSPECTIVE

Because television is the most pervasive medium and plays a major role in the socialization process, a brief and historical examination of televised portrayals of diverse groups of women is warranted. The top-rated situation comedies provide a focus as the most enduring, popular form of prime-time programming, although the successful dramatic programs in television history would presumably show similar trends. Consider the pictures that children receive of marriage, career, and relationships from viewing the following programs.

1950s

The happy, intact prime-time families of early television were generally guided by the wisdom of the father while the mother presided over the kitchen and the domestic chores. The families were white and middle class, featuring children that were college bound and destined for success. Examples of this type of programming include *The Adventures of Ozzie and Harriet* (1952–1956), *Father Knows Best* (1954–1963), *Leave It to Beaver* (1957–1963), and *I Love Lucy* (1951–1961).

At a time when blacks did not go to school with whites and were barred from most hotels and restaurants, their portrayals were stereotypical and unflattering. *Amos 'n Andy* (1951–1953) and *Beulah* (1950–1953) featured African American stars and cast members, but they were mammies and buffoons. As Brooks and Marsh (1995) say about *Amos 'n Andy,* "The humor certainly derived from the fact that these were shiftless, conniving, not-too-bright blacks. The very stereotypes that had so long been unfairly applied to an entire race were used throughout" (p. 47). In *Beulah,* actress Ethel Waters portrayed an efficient black maid in a white household, divorced from any family of her own, content to serve her white employers, and disconnected from the black community. As the civil rights era gained momentum and nine African American students attempted to enroll in a white Little Rock, Arkansas, high school, blacks virtually disappeared from prominent roles on television.

1960s

The 1960s programming relied heavily on westerns, detective shows, and medical dramas, all featuring white male central figures with minority portrayals at a minimum and women restricted to supporting roles. The situation comedy remained extremely popular and in those forms family life was white and middle class. If women were present, they often served as stay-at-home support systems for hardworking and beleaguered husbands. Divorce was practically nonexistent on television. Consequently, single-parent families resulted from the death of a spouse, usually the wife. Examples of 1960s story lines include *Andy Griffith* (1960–1968), *My Three Sons* (1960–1972), *Green Acres* (1965–1971), *Dick Van Dyke* (1961–66), *Bewitched* (1964–1972), *I Dream of Jeannie* (1965–70), and *The Brady Bunch* (1969–1974).

In a decade marked by civil rights marches and the assassinations of President John Kennedy and Martin Luther King, *Julia* (1968–71) brought African Americans back to the screen in a starring, but nonsubservient role. However, like

Beulah, Julia interacted primarily with whites, and critics claimed the husbandless character presented the stereotype of a black matriarch—so strong and antimale that she had emasculated her husband and destroyed the family (MacDonald, 1983, p. 117).

The 1970s

The 1970s ushered in a new television era, now widely hailed as more "relevant" to a world that seemed to be in upheaval. Divorce rates and the incidence of remarriage rose sharply in the 1970s, as did single-parent families, dual-career families, and singles living alone (Taylor, 1989). War was raging in Vietnam and students screamed in protest in streets and on campuses all across America. Young people challenged their parents; citizens challenged their government. All political and economic institutions seemed suspect, and the United States President resigned in disgrace. Television reflected the changes, including the first appearance of working-class family sitcoms and programs about unmarried single women struggling in careers, or divorcees raising children alone. The 1970s television family was troubled and faced "puzzling and painful new conditions" in society, especially in Norman Lear comedies, which dominated the Nielsen top 10 throughout the first half of the 1970s and confronted head-on the issues of racism and sexism (Taylor, 1989).

Norman Lear productions included *All In the Family* (1971–1979), *Sanford and Son* (1972–1977), *Maude* (1972–1978), *Good Times* (1974–1979), and *The Jeffersons* (1975–1985). The Evans family in *Good Times* was black, lower middle class, and originated with mother Florida who had been a maid on the series *Maude.* Husband James, unlike the white middle-class television fathers, was unable to hold a steady job. Son J.J. was a trade school student who was always on the lookout for a quick way to make money, sometimes less than honestly. Star Esther Rolle left the series objecting to the portrayal of J.J. as a "'jive-talking,' woman-chasing, less-than-honest character" (Brooks and Marsh, 1995, p. 411). In *Sanford and Son,* African American star Redd Foxx portrayed a proprietor of questionable character operating a junk yard.

In the story of a black family moving up the ladder of financial success, *The Jeffersons* introduced the first interracial couple on the small screen. In contrast to expectations in earlier family sitcoms, son Lionel was seen as exceptional for graduating from college.

Analysts point to *The Mary Tyler Moore Show* (1970–1977) as the beginning of a new feminist consciousness on television. The character of Mary Richards had rejected marriage, was pursuing a career, and made allusions to a sex life outside marriage, establishing a landmark change in television. While Mary was a revolutionary with an agreeable nature, Norman Lear's *Maude* challenged the notions of sweetness as an outspoken, thrice-divorced feminist with a deep, booming voice who no doubt fed social fears that any feminist must be unpleasant and difficult. Additionally, the character had an abortion during the series, which stirred viewer anger and protest.

In *One Day at a Time* (1975–1984), the divorced character of Ann Romano made it clear that she was searching for independence from controlling men, be it father or husband, and wanted to raise her daughters in a less protective, less stifling environment than she had experienced.

The 1980s

Successful television shows in the 1980s presented much more varied roles for women, with more career choices and more independence, but network prime time remained predominantly white and middle class, with the exception of *The Cosby Show* (1984–1992). *The Cosby Show* presented an African American version of the nearly perfect middle-class family model of the 1950s,

but was criticized on a variety of fronts. Some claimed the show was misrepresentative of the struggles of many black families, supported by the fact that issues of race were rarely explored. Others appreciated a portrayal of educated African Americans where both mother and father held professional positions. *Cosby* spun off another hit, *A Different World* (1987–1993), set on a predominantly black college campus.

Other hit shows featured some African Americans and all varieties of women stars presiding over their own fates, including older women enjoying their mature years in the series *Golden Girls* (1985–1992).

Murphy Brown (1988–1997) represents the opposite extreme of the 1950s television woman—ambitious regardless of the impact on anyone around her and generally sarcastic and manipulative. During the 1992 season, the single, career-oriented Murphy decided to have a baby, sparking a national controversy when the vice president of the United States, Dan Quayle, criticized the show for contributing to a decline in family values.

The 1990s

Although many popular TV sitcoms of the 1990s continued to present portrayals of women as jiggly, brainless sexpots, new kinds of women began to appear.

In *Roseanne* (1988–1997), Roseanne Barr broke new ground and created one of the all-time most popular family comedies, with a program centered around the mother's perspective in a nonperfect, non–middle-class, nongorgeous family. Roseanne herself became a media event as she openly insulted and challenged network authority and flouted most social conventions.

The sitcom, *Ellen* (1994–1998), also became a landmark program when the central character revealed her homosexuality during the 1997 season. ABC sanctioned the controversial event after much revision and supervision of script, but the show became the first sitcom in history to star an openly homosexual character. Waves of protest arose, along with calls for a boycott of the Disney Company, owner of ABC.

Designing Women (1986–1993) centered around four strong women operating a decorating business in Atlanta. The show dealt directly and forcefully with issues of sexism and showed women finding strength and support in each other. After viewer protest, the network changed plans to cancel the program.

In *Home Improvement* (1991–present), Tim and Jill Taylor are raising three boys in another upper-middle-class family sitcom. The show attempts to present the struggles of an equal partnership in marriage, and Jill points up feminist issues from time to time. However, comic actor Tim Allen is the show's superstar, his television show helper is a very stereotypical buxom blonde, and wife Jill appears to stay home most of the time.

These programs present a broad overview of many of television's most popular situation comedies. Although there is no stated message that men are more important than women or that women must be both gorgeous and sexy—plus proficient in domestic matters—the implied message is everywhere. Most actors, most stars, most voices have been male, and white. Minorities have most often been seen in unflattering roles. White television males have long been seen as successful and powerful; women who have achieved power have often been portrayed as difficult and alone. Since the beginning, television audiences have been most comfortable with soft-spoken, seductive white women, or with wives and mothers busy caring for children, husbands, and households.

CONCLUSION

Television and other media comprise a strong component in the socialization of diverse women. The media have their most powerful effect when a single message is presented consistently over time and is corroborated by other media, in addition to real-life experiences.

The prevailing media message to women has shown that men are the authorities and that women must be attractive, seductive, and focused on family. The consistent portrayal of African American and other minority women has been in subservient or secondary roles, when they were portrayed at all. Women have seen that concentrating on careers and social achievement leads to an unhappy fate of remaining unmarried and childless. If women gain power, they may lose their appeal. The most popular television programs of the last half century have supported these social constraints. Only recently have a few programs presented positive portrayals of a variety of women: working class, middle class, homosexual and heterosexual, married and single, thin and heavy. Positive portrayals of minority women remain woefully lacking. The challenge for women today is to recognize the consistent media messages that limit their possibilities, to demand liberation from social constraints, and to insist on improved public gender portrayals.

REFERENCES

Bridges, J. (1993). "Pink or blue: Gender-stereotypic perceptions of infants as conveyed by birth congratulations cards." *Psychology of Women Quarterly,* 17: 193–205.

Brooks, T., & Marsh, E. (1995). *The Complete Directory to Prime Time Network and Cable TV Shows.* New York: Ballantine Books.

Dennis, E., & DeFleur, M. (1996). *Understanding Mass Communication.* Boston: Houghton Mifflin.

"Depiction of women in mainstream TV shows still stereotypical, sexual." (1993). *Media Report To Women,* 21 (Winter): 4.

"Discrimination in employment." (1990). *Boston Globe,* March 12, Newsbank EMP 18:C13.

Dodd, D., Harcar, V., Foerch, B., & Anderson, H. T. (1989). "Face-ism and facial expressions of women in magazine photos." *The Psychological Record,* 39(3): 325.

Faludi, S. (1991). *Backlash: The Undeclared War Against American Women.* New York: Crown Publishers.

Gersh, D. (1992). "Promulgating polarization." *Editor & Publisher.* Oct. 10, pp. 30, 31, 48.

Hamilton, P. (1993). "Running in place." *D&B Reports.* March/April, pp. 24–26.

Hawkins, J., & Aber, C. (1993). "Women in advertisements in medical journals." *Sex Roles,* 28(3/4): 223–242.

Hernandez, D. G. (1994). "Religious stereotyping by the media." *Editor & Publisher,* Sept. 3, 127(36): 16.

Hernandez, D. G. (1994). "Stereotypes refuse to die." *Editor & Publisher,* August 27, 127(35): 21.

Hill, G., Raglin, L., & Johnson, C. (1990). *Black Women in Television.* New York: Garland Publishing, Inc.

Kilbourne, J. (1995). "Beauty and the beast of advertising." In Paula S. Rothenberg (Ed.), *Race, Class, and Gender in the United States: An Integrated Study.* New York: St. Martin's.

Lindsey, L. (1997). *Gender Roles: A Sociological Perspective,* 3rd ed. Upper Saddle River, NJ: Prentice Hall.

"Long-awaited global media monitoring study released at NGO Forum." (1995). *Media Report to Women.* Fall, 23(4): 2.

MacDonald, J. F. (1983). *Blacks and White TV: Afro-Americans in Television since 1948.* Chicago: Nelson-Hall Publishers.

Marc, D., & Thompson, R. (1995). *Prime Time Prime Movers.* Syracuse, NY: Syracuse University Press.

Rivers, C. (1993). "Bandwagons, women and cultural mythology." *Media Studies Journal,* Winter, 7: 1–17.

Seggar, J. F. (1975). "Imagery of women in television drama: 1974." *Journal of Broadcasting,* 19: 273–181.

Stein, M. L. (1994). "Racial stereotyping and the media." *Editor & Publisher.* Aug. 6, 127(32): 12.

Taylor, E. (1989). *Prime Time Families: Television Culture in Postwar America.* University of California Press. Berkeley, Los Angeles, London.

Valdez, L. (1997). "Baby boomer moms send mixed message to daughters." *Liberal Opinion,* May 26, p. 18.

Warlaumont, H. G. (1993). "Visual grammars of gender." *Journal of Communication Inquiry.* Winter, 17(1): 25.

"Women in politics" (1992). *Dallas Morning News.* July 29, Newsbank 1992 POL 71:C2.

Topic 2

Theories of Development

Growth

Seeds, smothered
by soil, rock, blacktop
dwell in the seamless dark.

Like a toddler's first steps,
one seedling creeps up,
denting the strata's collusion.

The single blade of grass
overthrows the pavement
seizing our attention.

Courtesy of Beth Rhodes

How do young people learn about and adopt their gender roles? What forces shape their identity as a male or a female? This section presents three different perspectives on these questions—based in socialization theory, cognitive theory, and psychoanalytic theory. Each approach provides us with an important piece of the puzzle of how children learn about gender.

In the first reading, "Gender-Role Socialization: Lessons in Femininity," Hilary Lips summarizes socialization research in the learning of gender roles. Socialization theorists examine how children are taught the behaviors that are expected of males and females. Lips describes the ways that parents, peers, and teachers communicate these expectations to boys and girls. Children internalize these messages and act out their appropriate gender roles. While socialization is a process that occurs in all cultures, there are cultural differences in the socialization of gender, both in what behaviors are expected of boys and girls and how these expectations are communicated.

Sandra Lipsitz Bem introduces gender schema theory in the second reading, "Gender Schema Theory and its Implications for Child Development." In contrast to socialization theory, where children are seen as passive recipients of social messages, gender schema theory sees children as active participants in developing their gender roles. In this perspective, children construct mental models of what males and females are like (for example, that females wear dresses and males wear pants). These models, or schemas, help children make sense of the world as they use them to organize their experiences. Gender schemas become very powerful in maintaining gender roles because children will approach situations expecting males and females to behave in ways that are consistent with their models, and will ignore behaviors that violate the models. For example, they will continue to believe that all doctors are male even when they encounter a female doctor. As Bem points out however, there is nothing inherent about gender as a basic organizing schema of a child's world. This schema arises because a culture sees it as important and brings it to a child's attention through distinctions between boys' and girls' toys, clothing, activities, and so on. Like socialization theory, gender schema theory assumes that while children in all cultures will make use of schemas, the content of these schemas will vary according to cultural values.

The third reading, "The Development of Women's Sense of Self," by Jean Baker Miller, takes a critical look at theories of personality development that she sees as neglecting the experience of girls. Personality development has been explained by theorists such as Erik Erikson and Daniel Levinson as a process of separating from others in order to become a unique individual. Miller argues that this model is based on male experience, and for females, personality development involves constructing a sense of self through connections with others. This process begins in infancy as babies learn to notice and respond to their caregivers' emotions and to see themselves as being in a relationship with another person. A sense of self arises as infant and caregiver attend to each other's mental states and emotions. For Miller, this developmental process occurs for both males and females, but gender differences in personality emerge because from birth, female children are encouraged to develop skills of "being-in-relationship," while males are pushed toward achievement and competition with others. She sees this as detrimental to both women and men because women's sense of self in relationships is devalued, and men develop deficiencies in connecting with other people.

In all of these developmental theories, children learn to act out gender roles only when their culture has constructed differences between male and female behavior. There is the possibility then, that gender roles can be changed if we change our cultural values and the child-rearing practices that teach those values to new generations.

Reading 1   Gender-Role Socialization: Lessons in Femininity

HILARY M. LIPS

Questions to Consider:

1. As you read this article, look for similarities in your own gender socialization. Did your parents, peers, and teachers socialize you in the ways described?

2. What cultural differences does Lips describe in the socialization of gender? Do you see any examples of cultural similarities?

3. What gender role socialization messages are present in both childhood and adolescence? What messages are different?

4. If you wanted to end gender roles, what changes would you make in childhood and adolescent socialization?

When two researchers examined the creative writing of elementary-school children attending a "young authors conference" in Michigan, their findings with respect to gender roles were striking: Male characters outnumbered female ones in stories written by both girls and boys, and male characters were credited with more attributes—both positive ones, such as courageous and determined, and negative ones, such as mean and nasty—than were female characters (Trepanier & Romatowski, 1985). Most striking of all was the difference in the occupational roles assigned to female and male characters: Of 127 occupa-

tions assigned by the young authors to their protagonists, 111 (87 percent) were assigned to males and only 16 (13 percent) to females. The occupational assignments clearly reflected the assumption that females' capabilities limited them to gender-stereotypic jobs: The few roles allotted female characters included those of princess, cook, hula dancer, babysitter, nurse, and housekeeper.

It is early indeed that children show an awareness of the message that males are active while females watch from the sidelines, and that females are generally less interesting and less important than males are and have narrower horizons and less impact on the world than males do. The (often inadvertent) bearers of this message include parents, peers, and teachers, with reinforcement from a variety of media sources and cultural institutions.

CHILDHOOD SOCIALIZATION

Parents

Perhaps because it is one of the earliest distinguishing pieces of information available about a child, gender appears to be an important dimension of socialization for parents in virtually every cultural, ethnic, and class group. Among white, middle-class North American parents, female infants are viewed, as early as twenty-four hours after birth, as softer and more delicate than are their male counterparts (Rubin, Provenzano, & Luria, 1974). Mothers playing with another woman's six-month-old infant have been found to offer gender-stereotypic toys and to smile at and hold the baby more closely when told it is a girl than when told it is a boy (Will, Self, & Datan, 1976). Furthermore parents provide their daughters and sons with different kinds of toys, games, and environmental surroundings (Bradbard, 1985; Lytton & Romney, 1991; Miller, 1987; Peretti & Sydney, 1985; Rheingold & Cook, 1975).

Though parents do not treat their young daughters and sons as differently as gender norms might suggest (Lytton & Romney, 1991), some apparently "minor" differences in childhood can lay the groundwork for larger differences later on. In this sense, parental gender-role socialization has a more global impact than merely the communication of a particular set of "gender-appropriate" behaviors. Girls and boys are taught by their parents to take different approaches to problem solving, to challenge, and to life in general. Specifically, parents are more likely to encourage dependency in daughters than in sons (Lytton & Romney, 1991). Noting the research showing that parents give male infants more stimulation and varied responses than they give to females, give more contingent responses to boys than to girls, and allow boys more freedom to explore than they do girls, Jeanne Block (1984) argued that boys are socialized to "develop a premise system that presumes or anticipates mastery, efficacy, and instrumental competence" (p. 131). The socialization

practices directed at girls tend toward "fostering proximity, discouraging independent problem solving by premature or excessive intervention, restricting exploration, and discouraging active play" (p. 111). Speaking in even stronger terms, Block suggested that the end result of the differing patterns of socialization for females and males is that boys develop "'wings'—which permit leaving the nest, exploring far reaches, and flying alone" (p. 137), while girls develop "'roots'— roots that anchor, stabilize and support growth" (p. 138), but allow fewer chances to master the environment.

Block's conclusions are supported by a wealth of research besides her own. For example, one study showed that parents used different strategies when working on jigsaw-puzzle and memory tasks with their six-year-old sons and daughters. They were more likely to try to teach general problem-solving strategies to their sons and to make specific solution suggestions to their daughters. With a daughter, parents were more likely to work with the child cooperatively and to provide her with information about whether her performance was correct. With a son, parents were more likely to be physically uninvolved in the task but to direct and order the child's activities and to give him praise (such as "You did well") or negative reactions (such as "Stop acting silly") (Frankel & Rollins, 1983). What these parents seemed to be communicating to their children is that it is more important for the sons than for the daughters that they not only solve this problem, but also learn how to solve others like it—and that they do it, as far as possible, on their own.

Other research also shows that parental behavior toward children may lay the groundwork for gender differences in patterns of thinking and problem solving. North American mothers' speech to their female and male toddlers differs significantly on dimensions thought to stimulate cognitive development. In one study, mothers used more questions, more numbers, more verbal teaching, and more action verbs when talking to their sons than they did when talking to their daughters (Weitzman, Birns, & Friend, 1985). Moreover, parents tend to expect more of their children in gender-stereotypic areas of performance and to communicate these differential expectations to children at a young age. For example, after tracking 1,100 children semester by semester over the first three grades of school, one research team found that boys developed higher expectations for their performance in mathematics than girls did, despite the fact that arithmetic marks and general aptitude were similar for girls and boys in the first grade. Boys' higher expectations for their own performance seemed to be related not to past performance or to teachers' evaluations but rather to mothers' expectations for their children's performance (Baker & Entwisle, 1987; Entwisle & Baker, 1983).

Even the different toys and play activities parents encourage for girls and boys influence not only children's conceptions of what activities are appropriate for females and males but also what thinking, problem-solving, and social skills these children develop. For example, when mechanical toys such as models and tools are defined as "boys' toys" and are not given to girls, the outcome is a chance for boys to develop both their spatial ability and the attitude that this ability is a peculiarly masculine one. A study by Cynthia Miller (1987) used adults' ratings to classify children's toys on twelve functional dimensions, illustrating that the toys selected as appropriate for boys and girls do differ in the kinds of skills they promote. Toys rated as "boys' toys" were also rated as high in the promotion of symbolic or fantasy play, competition, constructiveness (adding pieces or combining with another toy to create something new), handling, sociability, and aggressiveness; "girls' toys" were rated higher on manipulability (ease of removing and replacing parts), creativity, nurturance, and attractiveness.

Although parents in various cultural groups differ in the rules they attach to gender, it is not unusual to find that parents (particularly fathers, according to some research) pay more attention to boys than to girls, emphasize cooperation and nurturance more for girls and achievement and autonomy more for boys. For example, a study of Mexican families by Phyllis Bronstein (1984) showed that, when interacting with their school-aged children, fathers but not mothers listened more to boys than to girls and were more likely to show boys than to show girls how to do things. In contrast, they treated girls especially gently, but with a lack of full attention and a readiness to impose opinions on them. Overall, these fathers were communicating to their children that what boys have to say is more important than what girls have to say and that boys are more capable than girls are of learning new skills.

Within North American society, there are variations among groups in gender-role socialization. A number of studies have shown that gender stereotyping tends to be stronger and restrictions on girls greater in working-class than in middle-class families (McBroom, 1981; Rubin, 1976). Perhaps as a result, middle-class children's ideas about gender roles reflect more sharing of characteristics between the sexes than do those of working-class children (Romer & Cherry, 1980). Ethnicity is also linked to variations in parental gender-role socialization. Romer and Cherry (1980) found that black children viewed men and women as being equally emotionally expressive, whereas children from Jewish and Italian families thought it more characteristic of women than of men. Studies of both Mexican-American and Puerto Rican families indicate greater emphasis on feminine subservice and the wife–mother role for women than in non-Hispanic families (Garcia, 1991; Mirande, 1977; Fitzpatrick, 1971). The opposite is true of black families. While black parents are more concerned than white parents that girls be feminine and boys masculine (Dugger, 1991; Price-Bonham & Skeen, 1983), research suggests that they are less likely than are white families to polarize *behavioral* expectations. The female role in particular differs from that of white middle-class Americans. In black families female strength, independence, and resourcefulness are admired; weakness is not.

Peers

As soon as they are old enough to have peers outside the home, children begin to rely heavily on these peers as a source of information and approval about social behavior. Peer interactions promote gender-role socialization first of all by a tendency to segregate the sexes. School-aged children tend to play in same-sex groups (Katz & Boswell, 1984; Maccoby, 1990), thus minimizing contact between girls and boys and promoting an "us–them" rhetoric that contributes to the exaggeration of female–male differences, self-serving gender prejudice on the part of both groups, and a tendency to react negatively to children who "break the rules" by behaving in non–gender-stereotypic ways. There is some evidence that peers even help to shape girls' and boys' different orientations toward mastery and power.

Researchers have found consistently that children evaluate their own gender group more positively than they do the other (Etaugh, Levine, & Mennella, 1984; Olsen & Willemsen, 1978). There is also strong evidence that preschoolers, kindergartners, and elementary-school children are active and effective at maintaining gender-stereotypic behavior in their peers. Very young children make harsh judgments about and punish other children, especially boys, who violate gender stereotypes (Fagot, 1977, 1984, 1985; Langlois & Downs, 1980). The girl who tries to join a boys' game is likely to be told "You can't play—you're a girl"; the boy who picks up a girls' toy is likely to be taunted "now you're a girl." Young children are also active in reinforcing peers who engage in gender-appropriate behavior, and the peers do adjust their behavior to conform to the gender roles thus enforced (Lamb, Easterbrooks, & Holden, 1980; Lamb & Roopnarine, 1979). When researchers interviewed children in kinder-

garten and in the second, fourth, and sixth grades about their attitudes toward hypothetical peers who violated gender-role norms, the vast majority of the children, while indicating that cross-gender behavior was not wrong, said that they would prefer not to associate with children who violated these norms (Carter & McCloskey, 1983/84). Reactions to cross-gender behavior were more negative among older than among younger children, suggesting that children become more sure of their gender stereotypes as they progress through elementary school. These children also reported that they would react more negatively toward males than toward females who exhibited cross-gender behavior. The negative reactions listed by children in the interviews indicate just how strong the gender stereotypes can be at a young age: "I would push him and call him a weirdo"; "I'd probably hit him and take away the doll"; "I'd call him a sissy and make fun of him"; "I wouldn't go anywhere near him." Other research indicates that same-sex peers are the most effective socializers: Girls respond more to the pressures of female peers, boys to those of male peers (Fagot, 1985). It is not clear whether children are aware of their power to keep their peers "in line" with gender-role expectations or even exactly what motivates them to exert these pressures. It is evident, however, that peers do act as strict enforcers of gender-role norms in the areas of activities, toy preference, friendship choices, and traits.

Not only do peers enforce gender roles in specific content areas, but they also play an important part in the creation and maintenance of gender-differentiated approaches to power, mastery, and influence. Among toddlers, the beginnings of gender differences in power and effectiveness can be noted in the finding that girls paired with male playmates behave more passively than do girls paired with other girls or than boys paired with either girls or boys, and that vocal prohibitions (such as "Stop! Don't do that!") are most likely to be ignored when addressed to a boy by a girl (Jacklin & Maccoby,

1978). Power is still problematic for females, even in elementary school. A study of first- and second-graders in same-sex groups showed that, although both the female and male groups were structured by power hierarchies that were maintained in essentially similar ways, reactions to power holders differed in female and male groups. Boys who held top positions in the hierarchy were liked and accepted by their peers; powerful girls, in contrast, were rejected (Jones, 1983).

Among preschoolers, boys make a greater number of influence attempts on their male and female peers than girls do—a difference that is almost entirely due to boys' greater use of "direct" requests and that becomes more pronounced with age (Serbin, Sprafkin, Elman, & Doyle, 1982). Between the ages of three and five years, boys become more likely to use influence attempts, such as ordering a peer to "give me the truck," announcing "you have to give me the truck," or specifying roles, as in "pretend you're the doctor." Across the same ages, girls become more likely to use "indirect" requests, in which either the request is implied rather than clearly spelled out (e.g., "I need the truck"), or it is bracketed in polite phrases (e.g., "May I please have the truck?"). Furthermore, boys become less and less responsive with age, from three to five, to peer influence attempts, particularly indirect requests, whereas the responsiveness of girls to influence attempts seems to be relatively stable across the same ages. Another interesting finding is that girls in this age range are more effective in their direct requests of other girls than in those of boys. The researchers suggest that the social effectiveness that girls experience with other girls, relative to boys, helps to perpetuate the high levels of same-sex play found in preschool classrooms, and that this sex segregation, in turn, fosters the development of increasingly differentiated verbal social influence styles and perhaps differences in cognitive and social problem-solving skills.

Even the way that children talk to one another underlines and reinforces differences in gender roles with respect to power. Research by Austin, Salehi, and Leffler (1987), who studied the discourse of samples of mainly white children from working- and middle-class homes, uncovered gender differences in the degree to which children "took charge' of conversations as opposed to simply facilitating continuing interaction. Boys of all ages studied (preschool, third, and sixth grades) were more likely than were girls to initiate conversations and to use verbal (e.g., "Hey look at me") and nonverbal (e.g., tapping another child on the arm) attention-getting devices. Girls were more likely than were boys to say things that facilitated an ongoing conversational theme and to use reinforcers, especially positive ones, that acknowledged their partner's speech or behavior. These gender differences are similar to those that have been found for adults and suggest that peers play a role in the early development of patterns of conversational dominance by males. There may also be long-term consequences of these different interaction styles. Girls become accustomed through childhood patterns of female–female interaction to a cooperative style of communication that encourages listening and turn-taking in speaking. As young women, they may later feel uncomfortable and ineffective when they are working or socializing with males who take a more competitive approach to social interaction, in which speakers restrict one another's access to the conversation (Maccoby, 1990).

Peers may play a more important role in socialization for some groups than for others. For example, Ladner (1971), studying girls in a lower-class black American inner-city community, noted that the peer group had a broader function for these children than for their middle-class counterparts. The girls tended to have a lot of unsupervised contact with peers and began at an early age to rely heavily on them for company, emotional support, advice, comfort, and other intangible resources that might, in other groups, be expected to come from parents. Thus, according to Ladner, in poor inner-city communities, peers are an extremely important force in shaping black American girls' images of womanhood.

Teachers

Teachers' behavior adds to gender-role-socialization pressure as soon as children enter the educational system. Part of teacher influence occurs through the teachers' choice of textbooks and other curriculum materials that depict gender in traditional ways and present females as invisible or incompetent (e.g., Hahn & Blankenship, 1983; Marten & Matlin, 1976; Pursell & Stewart, 1990; United States Commission on Civil Rights, 1980; Weitzman & Rizzo, 1974). Moreover, teachers reinforce sex-differentiated activity patterns by introducing toys and play activities in gender-stereotypic ways (Serbin, Connor, & Citron, 1981; Serbin, Connor, & Iler, 1979). In one study, researchers asked teachers of preschoolers to introduce one of three toys to their classes each day: a magnetic fishing set, a set of sewing cards, and a number puzzle. To introduce the toy, they were to show it to the class and then call on four to six children to assist in demonstrating the toy and to try it out. When the toy in question was a fishing set (a stereotypically masculine toy), these teachers were far more likely to call on boys than on girls to demonstrate it, thus effectively restricting the play experience of the girls. For the other two toys, rated by observers as feminine and neutral respectively, the teachers showed no overall preference for either girls or boys as demonstrators (Serbin, Conner, & Iler, 1979). In a second study, the same researchers showed that gender-stereotyped introductions of toys to preschoolers lead the children to make gender-stereotypic toy choices. For example, when a teacher introduced a set of trucks and cars by saying "Daddies can go to work and drive a trailer truck" and then called on only boys to demonstrate the trucks, girls were much less likely to play with the trucks than they were when the teacher introduced the toys by saying "We can pretend to be policemen and policewomen driving the police car" and called on children of both sexes to demonstrate.

Perhaps the most important influence of teachers on the development of gender roles, however, is that teachers respond differently to girls and boys. Even in preschool, teachers, apparently unaware of the differential treatment they are handing out, pay more attention to boys and respond more to boys who act aggressive and to girls who act dependent (Serbin & O'Leary, 1975). Moreover, these researchers found that teachers actually teach boys more than they teach girls, with boys twice as likely as girls to receive individual instruction in how to do things. For example, in one classroom where the children were making paper baskets, it was necessary to staple the paper handles onto each basket. The teacher circulated through the room, helping each child individually to do this task. With boys, she held the handle in place and allowed the child to staple it; for girls, unless the child spontaneously stapled the handle herself, the teacher simply took the basket and stapled it for her rather than showing her how to do it.

Even teachers' evaluations of the intellectual competence of children is biased by gender-role considerations. For example, a preschool child's compliance to teachers does not significantly predict teachers' evaluations of that child's competence, providing the child is a boy. However, for girls, compliance to teachers is a significant factor in teacher evaluation of intellectual competence, with the less compliant girls being viewed as less competent (Gold, Crombie, & Noble, 1987). Even gender stereotypes with respect to physical appearance affect teachers' reactions to their young students. For example, the stereotype that females should be dainty and petite disadvantages girls who do not fit this mold. In one study, teachers of children in kindergarten through fourth grade rated each child's academic, athletic, and social skills. Girls who were larger and heavier than their peers were rated by teachers as lower in all three areas of skill. Moreover, teachers gave lower grades to these large girls. The same pattern was not found for teachers' ratings of boys (Villimez, Eisenberg, & Carroll, 1986).

In elementary-school classrooms, girls and boys are treated in ways that tend to produce relatively more feelings of control among boys and relatively more feelings of helplessness among girls. From preschool onward, teachers focus more on boys, spend more time interacting with boys than with girls, allow boys to talk and to interrupt them more in class, and even have more out-of-class conversations with boys (e.g., BenTsvi-Mayer, Hertz-Lazarowitz, & Safir, 1989; Brophy, 1985; Ebbeck, 1984). In addition, teachers punish girls and boys for different kinds of behaviors: girls for academic mistakes and boys for being disruptive. In contrast, when teachers praise students, they are more likely to be responding to good appearance or conduct for girls and good academic performance for boys (Dweck, 1975; Dweck, Goetz, & Strauss, 1980; Dweck & Leggett, 1988; Elliott & Dweck, 1988). Teachers also encourage girls and boys to react differently to the children's own mistakes. Boys are given more precise feedback and are encouraged to keep trying until they get the right answer; girls are more often told not to worry about a mistake, and teachers spend less time with them suggesting new approaches and encouraging them to keep trying. In fact, girls are often simply left in the dark about whether their answers are right or wrong (Sadker & Sadker, 1985).

Studies of teacher–student interactions that have included race as a variable suggest strongly that the classroom is a place where white middle-class conceptions of gender roles are enforced. Among elementary-school students, Irvine (1985) found that white females received significantly less total communication from teachers than did white males or black females or males. More-

over, when teacher–student interactions are examined across grade levels, it becomes clear that black females are being socialized by teachers to join their white sisters in invisibility. In early elementary school (grades K through 2), black girls do not receive less teacher feedback than do their male counterparts; by later grades (3 through 5), however, they fit the pattern of inconspicuousness and low salience to the teacher that holds for white girls from the beginning (Irvine, 1986). Irvine suggests that it is because black girls are not socialized to the passive and submissive behaviors encouraged in white girls that they receive more teacher attention than do white girls in the early grades. As noted by Lightfoot (1976), black female students in the classroom may be more likely to be seen as "assertive and bossy" than as fitting the white-female-student image of "submissive and cuddly" (p. 259). However, as found by Irvine (1986), as black girls move from lower to upper elementary-school grades, there is a significant decline in the total amount of teacher feedback they receive, in the amount of positive teacher feedback they receive, and in the number of opportunities to respond in class they are given. As Irvine notes, "Black female students present an active, interacting and initiating profile in the early grades but join their white female counterparts in the later grades in what appears to be traditional female sex role behaviors" (p. 20). The teachers in Irvine's study were predominantly white and female; this research leaves unanswered questions as to the importance of teacher race and sex, and of the race and gender composition of the classroom, in producing the patterns Irvine found.

Other research supports the notion that children's approach to school achievement is influenced by gender-role socialization and that these gender roles vary among ethnic groups. Studies of white middle-class children show that, as early as the third grade, boys begin to predict more successful performance for themselves than do females (Erkut, 1983; Vollmer, 1984). However, when samples include a high proportion of black and low-socioeconomic-status children, gender differences in expectations for success on specific tasks are not found (Fulkerson, Furr, & Brown, 1983). One reason for this may be that teachers tend to hold lower academic expectations for black males than for black females (Ross & Jackson, 1991). Even when it comes to actual achievement, the mediation of gender roles by cultural and ethnic factors is evident. In mathematics achievement, where studies of white middle-class children have generally shown an advantage for boys, some studies of black American children show no gender differences (Fulkerson, Furr, & Brown, 1983), and research on children of a number of different racial backgrounds in Hawaii shows a consistent advantage for females (Brandon, Newton, & Hammond, 1987).

Specific Consequences of Childhood Socialization

Aggression.   Researchers generally agree that boys are more likely than are girls to behave in aggressive ways. The difference was noted by Maccoby and Jacklin (1974), after an extensive review of the literature, as one of the few female–male behavioral differences that is found consistently. Since then, the greater tendency of male than of female children toward such physical aggression as hitting and pushing has been demonstrated repeatedly in free-play situations (e.g., Archer & Westeman, 1981; Di Pietro, 1981), and boys have also been found to surpass girls in the use of verbal aggression such as insults (Barrett, 1979). Although well established, however, gender differences in aggression are neither large nor completely consistent. They are largest in situations in which expectations for female and male behavior differ most strongly (Eagly & Steffen, 1986). Janet Hyde's (1984) analysis of 143 studies indicated that the amount of variation in the aggressive behavior measured in these studies that can be attributed to gender is about 5 percent.

Some researchers have noted that the apparent overall gender difference can sometimes be traced to extremely aggressive behavior by a few boys (Archer & Westeman, 1981).

It is clear that socialization plays an important part in the formation of whatever gender differences in aggression exist. For example, while cross-cultural research shows that, within any given society, boys tend to be at least slightly more aggressive than girls, the variation *among* societies in children's aggressive behavior is far more dramatic than is the gender difference. In some societies, children of both sexes have violent temper tantrums and learn to scream insults as soon as they learn to speak; in others, children tend not to quarrel at all. In fact, in any particular society, the level of aggression displayed by children of one sex is strongly and positively related to the level of aggression displayed by the other (Rohner, 1976, pp. 61–62). Clearly, social reactions to and tolerance of aggression affect the likelihood that children of either sex will engage in it.

Researchers have shown that, when girls and boys are similarly rewarded for aggressive behaviors, girls are as aggressive as boys (Bandura, 1973). It has been established, however, that boys are more rewarded by their peers than females are for aggressive behavior and that aggression in females meets with disapproval, even among children. One study showed that aggression by girls in the classroom was far more likely to be ignored, by both peers and teachers, than was aggression by boys. For the girls in this study, more than 50 percent of their aggressive actions received no response whatsoever (Fagot & Hagan, 1985). Since any response, either positive or negative, is better than none at all for maintaining a behavior, it is easy to see the large part that the social environment plays in making boys more aggressive than girl

Performance on Cognitive Tests: Language and Mathematics.   For years it was consistently reported in the psychological literature that females outperformed males on verbal tasks, while males outperformed females on quantitative and spatial tasks (Anastasi, 1937/1958; Hyde, 1981; Maccoby & Jacklin, 1974; Tyler, 1947/1965). Research comparing test performances of samples of children between 1947 and 1983 shows that gender differences in verbal performance, as well as in other cognitive skill areas, have declined drastically over the years (Feingold, 1988). A recent review of 165 studies found no gender differences in verbal performance, either across all types of verbal tests or within such specific tests as vocabulary, reading comprehension, and essay writing (Hyde & Linn, 1988). However, some researchers continue to report gender differences in verbal performance. For instance, a study of high school students in Japan and the United States indicated that in both countries girls averaged significantly higher scores than boys on a word fluency test (Mann, Sasanuma, Sakuma, & Masaki, 1990).

The gender gap in mathematics performance is also decreasing (Friedman, 1989; Hyde, Fennema, & Lamon, 1990) and is often negligible. The latter review showed that gender differences in mathematics performance were greater for white Americans than for black, Hispanic, or Asian Americans or for Canadian or Australian samples. A similar pattern of larger gender differences in samples of white American students than in studies based on minority samples is reported by Friedman (1989).

Until early adolescence, most studies show no gender differences in performance on general mathematics achievement tests—a finding that holds across a variety of cultures (Lummis & Stevenson, 1990). Girls show a slight advantage in computation in elementary and middle school. Some studies find that boys do better than girls on one type of quantitative performance, mathematical problem solving, as early as the first grade (Lummis & Stevenson, 1990). However, gender differences favoring males in mathematical problem solving appear most reliably in high

school and are maintained or increased in college. About 43 percent of high school females and 57 percent of high school males would score above the average score for the whole high school sample (Hyde et al., 1990).

On the whole, gender differences seem to be smallest, and may favor females, when the samples studied are from the general population. The differences are larger with more selective samples and appear largest for samples of highly precocious persons (Hyde et al., 1990). There are some indications that gender and social class interact with respect to mathematics achievement test results. Smaller gender differences in performance are found in samples from lower than from higher socioeconomic groups (Fischbein, 1990).

Despite the finding that by high school males tend to outperform females on standardized tests of mathematical problem solving, girls often obtain higher grades in mathematics than boys do (Kimball, 1989). This fact, along with the wide individual variation within each gender group, is frequently ignored when people use cognitive gender differences as a basis for arguing that girls and boys are naturally suited for different kinds of tasks and should prepare for different kinds of work.

Because the differences are so small, they cannot explain the large differences in occupation. For example, Hyde (1981), making the initial assumption that a person would have to be in the top 5 percent of the range of spatial abilities to be qualified for a profession such as engineering, calculated that, if spatial ability were the only determining factor, the ratio of males to females in such professions would be 2 to 1. Since the ratio of men to women in engineering is currently 25 to 1, gender differences in spatial ability could conceivably explain only a small part of the male dominance of the engineering professions.

The gender difference in mathematics achievement is linked more strongly to gender-role socialization than to ability differences. Parents and teachers have differing expectations for girls and boys, and these expectations are communicated early. One study of the parents of mathematically gifted children in the Johns Hopkins Talent Search found that the boys' parents were considerably more likely than were the girls' parents even to be aware that their child was mathematically talented (Tobias, 1982), and parents of boys were more likely than were parents of girls to have given their children science-related gifts, such as science kits, telescopes, and microscopes (Astin, 1974). Parents tend to credit their sons' success in mathematics more to talent and their daughters' success more to effort (Yee & Eccles, 1988). Furthermore, even within the same class, girls and boys tend not to get the same education. When one team of researchers observed thirty-three second-grade teachers in the classroom, they found that these teachers spent more time teaching reading than mathematics to individual girls and more time teaching mathematics than reading to individual boys (Leinhardt, Seewald, & Engel, 1979).

A large-scale study of Baltimore first-graders indicates that, even as children enter school, girls and boys have already begun to learn that different things are important (Entwisle, Alexander, Pallas, & Cardigan, 1987). At this stage, academic competence and the student role formed a more important and distinct aspect of self-concept for boys than for girls. Boys were more concerned with learning quickly; girls were more concerned with obeying rules and being honest. Being able to do arithmetic was an important aspect of the academic self-concept for boys; for girls, it was irrelevant. The girls did not view their ability in mathematics as relevant to their academic self-image, even though they did as well in mathematics as the boys did and were exposed to the same mathematics instruction classes as the boys. Where do these differences come from? The study suggests that, for girls at least, they originate partly in parental expectations—and parental expectations of girls focus strongly on "being good" rather than on academic achievement. However when data for black children and white children in this study are examined separately, it appears that black parents give a less gender-stereotypic message about mathematics to their daughters than white parents do. For black girls but not for white girls, parents' mathematics-achievement expectations were significant predictors of their daughters' academic self-image.

REFERENCES

Anastasi, Anne (1937/1958). *Differential psychology: Individual and group differences in behavior.* New York: Macmillan.

Archer, John, & Westeman, Karin (1981). Sex differences in the aggressive behaviour of schoolchildren. *British Journal of Social Psychology, 20,* 31–36.

Astin, Helen (1974). Sex differences in mathematical and scientific precocity. In Julian C. Stanley, D. P. Keating, & Lynn Fox (Eds.), *Mathematical talent: Discovery, description and development.* Baltimore: Johns Hopkins University Press.

Austin, Ann M. B. A., Salehi, Mahshid, & Leffler, Ann (1987). Gender and developmental differences in children's conversations. *Sex Roles, 16* (9/10), 497–510.

Baker, David P., & Entwisle, Doris R. (1987). The influence of mothers on the academic expectations of young children: A longitudinal study of how gender differences arise. *Social Forces, 65* (3), 670–94.

Barrett, David E. (1979). A naturalistic study of sex differences in children's aggression. *Merrill Palmer Quarterly, 25* (3), 193–203.

BenTsvi-Mayer, S., Hertz-Lazarowitz, R., & Safir, M. P. (1989). Teachers' selections of boys and girls as prominent pupils. *Sex Roles, 21,* 231–45.

Block, Jeanne H. (1984). Psychological development of female children and adolescents. In Jeanne H. Block, *Sex role identity and ego development* (pp. 126–42). San Francisco: Jossey-Bass.

Bradbard, Marilyn R. (1985). Sex differences in adults' gifts and children's toy requests at Christmas. *Psychological Reports, 56,* 969–70.

Brandon, Paul R., Newton, Barbara J., & Hammond, Ormond W. (1987). Children's mathematics achievement in Hawaii: Sex differences favoring girls. *American Educational Research Journal, 24* (3), 437–61.

Bronstein, Phyllis (1984). Differences in mothers' and fathers' behavior toward children: A cross-cultural comparison. *Developmental Psychology, 20* (6), 995–1003.

Brophy, J. (1985). Interactions of male and female students with male and female teachers. In L. C. Wilkinson & C. B. Marrett (Eds.), *Gender influences in classroom interaction* (pp. 115–42). Orlando, FL: Academic Press.

Carter, D. Bruce, & McCloskey, Laura A. (1983/84). Peers and the maintenance of sex-typed behavior: The development of children's conceptions of cross-gender behavior in their peers. *Social Cognition, 2* (4), 294–314.

Di Pietro, Janet A. (1981). Rough and tumble play: A function of gender. *Developmental Psychology, 17* (1), 5O–58.

Dugger, K. (1991). Social location and gender-role attitudes: A comparison of black and white women. In J. Lorber & S. A. Farrell (Eds.), *The social construction of gender* (pp. 38–59). Newbury Park, CA: Sage.

Dweck, Carol S. (1975). The role of expectations and attributions in the alleviation of learned helplessness. *Journal of Personality and Social Psychology, 31,* 674–85.

Dweck, Carol S., Goetz, Therese E., & Strauss, Nan L. (1980). Sex differences in learned helplessness: IV: An experimental and naturalistic study of failure generalization and its mediators. *Journal of Personality and Social Psychology, 38,* 441–52.

Dweck, Carol S., & Leggett, Ellen L. (1988). A social-cognitive approach to motivation and personality. *Psychological Review, 95,* 256–73.

Eagly, Alice H., & Steffen, Valerie J. (1986). Gender and aggressive behavior: A meta-analytic review of the social psychological literature. *Psychological Bulletin, 100,* 309–30.

Ebbeck, M. (1984). Equity issues for boys and girls: Some important issues. *Early Child Development and Care, 18* (1/2), 119–31.

Elliott, E. S., & Dweck, Carol S. (1988). Goals: An approach to motivation and achievement. *Journal of Personality and Social Psychology, 54,* 5–12.

Entwisle, Doris R., Alexander, Karl L., Pallas, Aaron M., & Cardigan, Doris (1987). The emergent academic self-image of first graders: Its response to social structure. *Child Development, 58,* 1190–1206.

Entwisle, Doris R., & Baker, D. P. (1983). Gender and young children's expectations for performance in arithmetic. *Developmental Psychology, 19* (2), 200–209.

Erkut, Sumru (1983). Exploring sex differences in expectancy, attribution, and academic achievement. *Sex Roles, 9,* 217–31.

Etaugh, Claire, Levine, Diane, & Mennella, Angela (1984). Development of sex biases in children: 40 years later. *Sex Roles, 10,* 911–22.

Fagot, Beverly I. (1977). Consequences of moderate cross-gender behavior in preschool children. *Child Development, 48,* 902–7.

Fagot, Beverly I. (1984). Teacher and peer reactions to boys' and girls' play styles. *Sex Roles, 11,* 691–702.

Fagot, Beverly I. (1985). Beyond the reinforcement principle: Another step toward understanding sex role development. *Developmental Psychology, 21* (6), 1097–1104.

Fagot, Beverly I., & Hagan, Richard (1985). Aggression in toddlers: Responses to the assertive acts of boys and girls. *Sex Roles, 12* (3/4), 341–51.

Feingold, A. (1988). Cognitive gender differences are disappearing. *American Psychologist, 43* (2), 95–103.

Fischbein, S. (1990). Biosocial influences on sex differences for ability and achievement test results as well as marks at school. *Intelligence, 14* (1), 127–39.

Fitzpatrick, J. (1971). *Puerto Rican Americans: The meaning of migration.* Englewood Cliffs, NJ: Prentice-Hall.

Frankel, Marc T., & Rollins, Howard A., Jr. (1983). Does mother know best? Mothers and fathers interacting with preschool sons and daughters. *Developmental Psychology, 19* (5), 694–702.

Friedman, L. (1989). Mathematics and the gender gap: A meta-analysis of recent studies on sex differences in mathematical tasks. *Review of Educational Research, 59* (2), 185–213.

Fulkerson, Katherine Fee, Furr, Susan, & Brown, Duane (1983). Expectations and achievement among third-, sixth-, and ninth-grade black and white males and females. *Developmental Psychology, 19* (2), 231–36.

Garcia, A. M. (1991). The development of Chicana feminist discourse. In J. Lorber & S. A. Farrell

(Eds.), *The social construction of gender* (pp. 269–87). Newbury Park, CA: Sage.

Gold, Dolores, Crombie, Gail, & Noble, Sally (1987). Relations between teachers' judgments of girls' and boys' compliance and intellectual competence. *Sex Roles, 16* (7/8), 351–58.

Hahn, C., & Blankenship, G. (1983). Women and economics textbooks. *Theory and Research in Social Education, 11* (3), 67–75.

Hyde, Janet S. (1981). How large are cognitive gender differences? A meta-analysis using ω and δ. *American Psychologist, 36,* 892–901.

Hyde, Janet S. (1984). How large are gender differences in aggression? A developmental meta-analysis. *Developmental Psychology, 20* (4), 722–36.

Hyde, Janet S., Fennema, Elizabeth, & Lamon, S. J. (1990). Gender differences in mathematics performance: A meta-analysis. *Psychological Bulletin, 107* (2), 139–55.

Hyde, Janet S., & Linn, Marcia C. (1988). Gender differences in verbal ability: A meta-analysis. *Psychological Bulletin, 104* (1), 53–69.

Irvine, Jacqueline Jordan (1985). Teacher communication patterns as related to the race and sex of the student. *Journal of Educational Research, 78* (6), 338–45.

Irvine, Jacqueline Jordan (1986). Teacher–student interactions: Effects of student race, sex, and grade level. *Journal of Educational Psychology, 78* (1), 14–21.

Jacklin, Carol Nagy, & Maccoby, Eleanor Emmons (1978). Social behavior at thirty-three months in same-sex and mixed-sex dyads. *Child Development, 49,* 557–69.

Jones, Diane C. (1983). Power structures and perceptions of power holders in same-sex groups of young children. *Women and Politics, 3,* 147–64.

Katz, Phyllis A., & Boswell, S. L. (1984). Sex-role development and the one-child family. In T. Falbo (Ed.), *The single-child family.* New York: Guilford Press.

Kimball, Meredith (1989). A new perspective on women's math achievement. *Psychological Bulletin, 105,* 198–214.

Ladner, Joyce A. (1971). *Tomorrow's tomorrow: The black woman.* Garden City, NY: Doubleday.

Lamb, Michael E., Easterbrooks, M. Ann, & Holden, George W. (1980). Reinforcement and punishment among preschoolers: Characteristics, effects, and correlates. *Child Development, 51,* 1230–36.

Lamb, Michael E., & Roopnarine, Jaipaul L. (1979). Peer influences on sex-role development in preschoolers. *Child Development, 50,* 1219–22.

Langlois, Judith H., & Downs, A. Chris (1980). Mothers, fathers, and peers as socialization agents of sex-typed play behaviors in young children. *Child Development, 51,* 1237–47.

Leinhardt, G., Seewald, A. M., & Engel, M. (1979). Learning what's taught: Sex differences in instruction. *Journal of Educational Psychology, 71,* 432–39.

Lummis, M., & Stevenson, H. W. (1990). Gender differences in beliefs and achievement: A cross-cultural study. *Developmental Psychology, 26* (2), 254–63.

Lytton, H., & Romney, D. M. (1991). Parents' differential socialization of boys and girls: A meta-analysis. *Psychological Bulletin, 109* (2), 267–96.

Maccoby, Eleanor E. (1990). Gender and relationships: A developmental account. *American Psychologist, 45* (4), 513–20.

Maccoby, Eleanor E., & Jacklin, Carol N. (1974). *The psychology of sex differences.* Stanford, CA: Stanford University Press.

Mann, V. A., Sasanuma, S., Sakuma, N., & Masaki, S. (1989). Sex differences in cognitive abilities: A cross-cultural perspective. *Neuropsychologia, 28* (10), 1063–77.

Marten, Laurel A., & Matlin, Margaret W. (1976). Does sexism in elementary school readers still exist? *The Reading Teacher, 29,* 767–76.

McBroom, William H. (1981). Parental relationships, socioeconomic status, and sex role expectations. *Sex Roles, 7,* 1027–33.

Miller, Cynthia L. (1987). Qualitative differences among gender-stereotyped toys: Implications for cognitive and social development in girls and boys. *Sex Roles, 16* (9/10), 473–87.

Mirande, Alfredo (1977). The Chicano family: A reanalysis of conflicting views. *Journal of Marriage and the Family, 39,* 747–56.

Olsen, Nancy J., & Willemsen, Eleanor W. (1978). Studying sex prejudice in children. *The Journal of Genetic Psychology, 133,* 203–16.

Peretti, Peter O., & Sydney, Tiffany M. (1984). Parental toy choice stereotyping and its effect on child toy preference and sex-role typing. *Social Behavior and Personality, 12* (2), 213–16.

Price-Bonham, Sharon, & Skeen, Patsy (1982). Black and white fathers' attitudes toward children's sex roles. *Psychological Reports, 50,* 1187–90.

Pursell, P., & Stewart, L. (1990). Dick and Jane in 1989. *Sex Roles, 22* (3/4), 177–85.

Rheingold, Harriet L., & Cook, Kaye V. (1975). The contents of boys' and girls' rooms as an index of parents' behaviors. *Child Development, 46,* 459–63.

Rohner, Ronald P. (1976). Sex differences in aggression: Phylogenetic and enculturation perspectives. *Ethos, 4* (1), 57–72.

Romer, Nancy, & Cherry, Debra (1980). Ethnic and social class differences in children's sex-role concepts. *Sex Roles, 6,* 245–63.

Ross, Sandra I., & Jackson, Jeffrey M. (1991). Teachers' expectations for black males' and black females' academic achievement. *Personality and Social Psychology Bulletin, 17* (1), 78–82.

Rubin, Jeffrey Z., Provenzano, Frank J., & Luria, Zella (1974). The eye of the beholder: Parents' views on sex of newborns. *American Journal of Orthopsychiatry, 44,* 512–19.

Rubin, Lillian (1976). *Worlds of pain: Life in the working class family.* New York: Basic Books.

Sadker, Myra, & Sadker, David (1985, March). Sexism in the schoolroom of the '80s. *Psychology Today, 19,* 54–57.

Serbin, Lisa A., Connor, Jane M., & Citron, Cheryl C. (1981). Sex-differentiated free play behavior: Effects of teacher modeling, location and gender. *Developmental Psychology, 17,* 640–46.

Serbin, Lisa A., Connor, Jane M., & Iler, Iris (1979). Sex-stereotyped and non-stereotyped introductions of new toys in the preschool classroom: An observational study of teacher behavior and its effects. *Psychology of Women Quarterly, 4,* 261–65.

Serbin, Lisa A., & O'Leary K. Daniel (1975, December). How nursery schools teach girls to shut up. *Psychology Today, 9* (7), 56–58, 102–3.

Serbin, Lisa A., Sprafkin, Carol, Elman, Meryl, & Doyle, Anna-Beth (1982). The early development of sex-differentiated patterns of social influence. *Canadian Journal of Behavioural Science, 14* (4), 350–63.

Tobias, Sheila (1982, January). Sexist equations. *Psychology Today,* 14–17.

Trepanier, Mary L., & Romatowski, Jane A. (1985). Attributes and roles assigned to characters in children's writing: Sex differences and sex-role perceptions. *Sex Roles, 13* (5/6), 263–72.

Tyler, Leona (1947/1965). *The psychology of human differences.* New York: Appleton-Century-Crofts.

U.S. Commission on Civil Rights (1980). *Characters in textbooks.* Washington, D.C.: U.S. Government Printing Office.

Villimez, Carolyn, Eisenberg, Nancy, & Carroll, James L. (1986). Sex differences in the relation of children's height and weight to academic performance and to others' attributions of competence. *Sex Roles, 15* (11/12), 667–81.

Vollmer, Fred (1984). Sex differences in personality and expectancy. *Sex Roles, 11,* 1121–39.

Weitzman, Lenore J., & Rizzo, Diane (1974). *Image of males and females in elementary school textbooks.* New York: National Organization for Women's Legal Defense and Education Fund.

Weitzman, Nancy, Birns, Beverly, & Friend, Ronald (1985). Traditional and nontraditional mothers' communication with their daughters and sons. *Child Development, 56,* 894–98.

Will, Jerrie, Self, Patricia, & Datan, Nancy (1976). Maternal behavior and perceived sex of infant. *American Journal of Orthopsychiatry, 46,* 135–39.

Yee, Doris K., & Eccles, Jacquelynne S. (1988). Parent perceptions and attributions for children's math achievement. *Sex Roles, 19,* 317–33.

Reading 2   Gender Schema Theory and Its Implications for Child Development: Raising Gender-Aschematic Children in a Gender-Schematic Society

SANDRA LIPSITZ BEM

Questions to Consider:

1. What attributes and behaviors made up your childhood gender schema? Do you still organize gender in the same ways you did as a child?

2. What parts of cognitive-developmental theory and social learning theory are incorporated in gender schema theory?

3. How do children learn to organize information according to gender?

4. What do you think of Bem's suggestions for raising gender-aschematic children?

As every parent, teacher, and developmental psychologist knows, male and female children become "masculine" and "feminine," respectively, at a very early age. By the time they are four or five, for example, girls and boys have typically come to prefer activities defined by the culture as appropriate for their sex and also to prefer same-sex peers. The acquisition of sex-appropriate preferences, skills, personality attributes, behaviors, and self-concepts is typically referred to in psychology as the process of sex typing.

The universality and importance of this process is reflected in the prominence it has received

Sandra Lipsitz Bem, "Gender Schema Theory and its Implications for Child Development: Raising Gender-Aschematic Children in a Gender-Schematic Society," *Signs: Journal of Women in Culture and Society, 8,* (4). Copyright © 1983 by The University of Chicago. Reprinted with the permission of Sandra Lipsitz Bem and The University of Chicago Press.

in psychological theories of development, which seek to elucidate how the developing child comes to match the template defined as sex appropriate by his or her culture. Three theories of sex typing have been especially influential: psychoanalytic theory, social learning theory, and cognitive-developmental theory. More recently, a fourth theory of sex typing has been introduced into the psychological literature—gender schema theory.

This article is designed to introduce gender schema theory to feminist scholars outside the discipline of psychology. In order to provide a background for the conceptual issues that have given rise to gender schema theory, I will begin with a discussion of the three theories of sex typing that have been dominant within psychology to date.

PSYCHOANALYTIC THEORY

The first psychologist to ask how male and female are transmuted into masculine and feminine was Freud. Accordingly, in the past, virtually every major source book in developmental psychology began its discussion of sex typing with a review of psychoanalytic theory.[1]

Psychoanalytic theory emphasizes the child's identification with the same-sex parent as the primary mechanism whereby children become sex typed, an identification that results from the child's discovery of genital sex differences, from the penis envy and castration anxiety that this discovery produces in females and males, respectively, and from the successful resolution of the Oedipus conflict.[2] Although a number of feminist scholars have found it fruitful in recent years to work within a psychoanalytic framework,[3] the theory's "anatomy is destiny" view has been associated historically with quite conservative conclusions regarding the inevitability of sex typing.

Of the three dominant theories of sex typing, psychoanalytic theory is almost certainly the best known outside the discipline of psychology, although it is no longer especially popular among research psychologists. In part, this is because the theory is difficult to test empirically. An even more important reason, however, is that the empirical evidence simply does not justify emphasizing either the child's discovery of genital sex differences in particular[4] or the child's identification with his or her same-sex parent[5] as a crucial determinant of sex typing.

SOCIAL LEARNING THEORY

In contrast to psychoanalytic theory, social learning theory emphasizes the rewards and punishments that children receive for sex-appropriate and sex-inappropriate behaviors, as well as the vicarious learning that observation and modeling can provide.[6] Social learning theory thus locates the source of sex typing in the sex-differentiated practices of the socializing community.

Perhaps the major virtue of social learning theory for psychologists is that it applies to the development of psychological femaleness and maleness the very same general principles of learning that are already known to account for the development of a multitude of other behaviors. Thus, as far as the formal theory is concerned, gender does not demand special consideration; that is, no special psychological mechanisms or

1. See, e.g., Paul H. Mussen, "Early Sex-Role Development," in *Handbook of Socialization Theory and Research,* ed. David A. Goslin (Chicago: Rand McNally & Co., 1969), pp. 707–31. For a more recent review that does not even mention psychoanalytic theory, see Aletha C. Huston, "Sex-Typing," to appear in *Carmichael's Manual of Child Psychology.* ed. Paul H. Mussen, 4th ed. (New York: John Wiley & Sons, in press).

2. Urie Bronfenbrenner, "Freudian Theories of Identification with Their Derivatives," *Child Development* 31, no. 1 (March 1960): 15–40: Sigmund Freud, "Some Psychological Consequences of the Anatomical Distinction between the Sexes (1925)," in *Collected Papers of Sigmund Freud,* ed. Ernest Jones, 5 vols. (New York: Basic Books, 1959), 5: 186–97; Sigmund Freud, "The Passing of the Oedipus Complex (1924)," ibid., 2: 269–76.

3. E.g., Nancy Chodorow, *The Reproduction of Mothering: Psychoanalysis and the Sociology of Gender* (Berkeley: University of California Press, 1978); Gayle Rubin, "The Traffic in Women: Notes on the 'Political Economy' of Sex," in *Toward an Anthropology of Women,* ed. Rayna Reiter (New York: Monthly Review Press, 1975), pp. 157–210.

4. Lawrence Kohlberg, "A Cognitive-Developmental Analysis of Children's Sex-Role Concepts and Attitudes," in *The Development of Sex Differences,* ed. Eleanor E. Maccoby (Stanford, Calif.: Stanford University Press, 1966), pp. 82–173; Maureen J. McConaghy, "Gender Permanence and the Genital Basis of Gender: Stages in the Development of Constancy of Gender Identity," *Child Development* 50, no. 4 (December 1979): 1223–26.

5. Eleanor E. Maccoby and Carol N. Jacklin, *The Psychology of Sex Differences* (Stanford, Calif.: Stanford University Press, 1974).

6. Walter Mischel, "Sex-Typing and Socialization," in *Carmichael's Manual of Child Psychology,* ed. Paul H. Mussen, 2 vols. (New York: John Wiley & Sons, 1970), 2:3–72.

processes must be postulated in order to explain how children become sex typed beyond those already used to explain how children learn other socialized behaviors.

Interestingly, the theory's generality also constitutes the basis of its appeal to feminist psychologists in particular. If there is nothing special about gender, then the phenomenon of sex typing itself is neither inevitable nor unmodifiable. Children become sex typed because sex happens to be the basis of differential socialization in their culture. In principle, however, any category could be made the basis for differential socialization.

Although social learning theory can account for the young child's acquiring a number of particular behaviors that are stereotyped by the culture as sex appropriate, it treats the child as the relatively passive recipient of environmental forces rather than as an active agent striving to organize and thereby to comprehend the social world. This view of the passive child is inconsistent with the common observation that children themselves frequently construct and enforce their own version of society's gender rules. It is also inconsistent with the fact that the flexibility with which children interpret society's gender rules varies predictably with age. In one study, for example, 73 percent of the four-year-olds and 80 percent of the nine-year-olds believed—quite flexibly—that there should be no sexual restrictions on one's choice of occupation. Between those ages, however, children held more rigid opinions, with the middle children being the least flexible of all. Thus, only 33 percent of the five-year-olds, 10 percent of the six-year-olds, 11 percent of the seven-year-olds, and 44 percent of the eight-year-olds believed there should be no sexul restrictions on one's choice of occupation.[7]

This particular developmental pattern is not unique to the child's interpretation of gender rules. Even in a domain as far removed from gender as syntax, children first learn certain cor-

rect grammatical forms through reinforcement and modeling. As they get a bit older, however, they begin to construct their own grammatical rules on the basis of what they hear spoken around them, and they are able only later still to allow for exceptions to those rules. Thus, only the youngest and the oldest children say "ran"; children in between say "runned."[8] What all of this implies, of course, is that the child is passive in neither domain. Rather, she or he is actively constructing rules to organize—and thereby to comprehend—the vast array of information in his or her world.

COGNITIVE-DEVELOPMENTAL THEORY

Unlike social learning theory, cognitive-developmental theory focuses almost exclusively on the child as the primary agent of his or her own sex-role socialization, a focus reflecting the theory's basic assumption that sex typing follows naturally and inevitably from universal principles of cognitive development. As children work actively to comprehend their social world, they inevitably "label themselves—call it alpha—and determine that there are alphas and betas in the environment. Given the cognitive-motivational properties of the self,...the child moves toward other alphas and away from betas. That is, it is the child who realizes what gender he or she is, and in what behaviors he or she should engage."[9] In essence, then, cognitive-developmental theory postulates that, because of the child's need for cognitive consistency, self-categorization as female or male motivates her or him to value that which is seen as similar to the self in terms of gender. This gender-

7. William Damon, *The Social World of the Child* (San Francisco: Jossey-Bass, 1977).

8. Courtney B. Cazden, "The Acquisition of Noun and Verb Inflections," *Child Development* 39, no. 2 (June 1968): 433–48; Herbert H. Clark and Eve V. Clark, *Psychology and Language: An Introduction to Psycholinguistics* (New York: Harcourt Brace Jovanovich, 1977).

9. Michael Lewis and Jeanne Brooks-Gunn, *Social Cognition and the Acquisition of Self* (New York: Plenum Publishing Corp., 1979), p. 270.

based value system, in turn, motivates the child to engage in gender-congruent activities, to strive for gender-congruent attributes, and to prefer gender-congruent peers. "Basic self-categorizations determine basic valuings. Once the boy has stably identified himself as male, he then values positively those objects and acts consistent with his gender identity."[10]

The cognitive-developmental account of sex typing has been so influential since its introduction into the literature in 1996 that many psychologists now seem to accept almost as a given that the young child will spontaneously develop both a gender-based self-concept and a gender-based value system even in the absence of external pressure to behave in a sex-stereotyped manner. Despite its popularity, however, the theory fails to explicate why sex will have primacy over other potential categories of the self such as race, religion, or even eye color. Interestingly, the formal theory itself does not dictate that any particular category should have such primacy. Moreover, most cognitive-developmental theorists do not explicitly ponder the "why sex" question nor do they even raise the possibility that other categories could fit the general theory just as well. To the extent that cognitive-developmental psychologists address this question at all, they seem to emphasize the perceptual salience to the child of the observable differences between the sexes, particularly biologically produced differences such as size and strength.[11]

The implicit assumption here that sex differences are naturally and inevitably more perceptually salient to children than other differences may not have cross-cultural validity. Although it may be true that our culture does not construct any distinctions between people that we perceive to be as compelling as sex, other cultures do construct such distinctions, for example, distinctions between those who are high caste and those who are low caste, between those who are inhabited by spirits and those who are not, between those who are divine and those who are mortal, between those who are wet and those who are dry, or between those who are open and those who are closed.[12] Given such cross-cultural diversity, it is ironic that a theory emphasizing the child's active striving to comprehend the social world should not be more open to the possibility that a distinction other than sex might be more perceptually salient in another cultural context. What appears to have happened is that the universality and inevitability that the theory claims for the child's cognitive processes have been implicitly and gratuitously transferred to one of the many substantive domains upon which those processes operate: the domain of gender.

This is not to say, of course, that cognitive-developmental theory is necessarily wrong in its implicit assumption that all children have a built-in readiness to organize their perceptions of the social world on the basis of sex. Perhaps evolution has given sex a biologically based priority over many other categories. The important point, however, is that the question of whether and why sex has cognitive primacy is not included within the bounds of cognitive-developmental theory. To understand why children become *sex* typed rather than, say, race or caste typed, we still need a theory that explicitly addresses the question of how and why children come to utilize sex in particular as a cognitive organizing principle.

10. Kohlberg, p. 89.

11. Kohlberg; Lewis and Brooks-Gunn; Dorothy Z. Ullian, "The Child's Construction of Gender: Anatomy as Destiny," in *Cognitive and Affective Growth: Developmental Interaction,* ed. Edna K. Shapiro and Evelyn Weber (Hillsdale, N.J.: Lawrence Erlbaum Associates, 1981), pp. 171–85.

12. For a discussion of the wet-dry distinction, see Anna S. Meigs, "Male Pregnancy and the Reduction of Sexual Opposition in a New Guinea Highlands Society," *Ethology* 15, no. 4 (1976): 393–407; for a discussion of the open-closed distinction, see Sally Falk Moore, "The Secret of the Men: A Fiction of Chagga Initiation and Its Relation to the Logic of Chagga Symbolism," *Africa* 46, no. 4 (1976): 357–70.

GENDER SCHEMA THEORY

Gender schema theory[13] contains features of both the cognitive-developmental and the social learning accounts of sex typing. In particular, gender schema theory proposes that sex typing derives in large measure from gender-schematic processing, from a generalized readiness on the part of the child to encode and to organize information—including information about the self—according to the culture's definitions of maleness and femaleness. Like cognitive-developmental theory, then, gender schema theory proposes that sex typing is mediated by the child's own cognitive processing. However, gender schema theory further proposes that gender-schematic processing is itself derived from the sex-differentiated practices of the social community. Thus, like social learning theory, gender schema theory assumes that sex typing is a learned phenomenon and, hence, that it is neither inevitable nor unmodifiable. In this discussion, I shall first consider in some detail what gender-schematic processing is and how it mediates sex typing; I shall then explore the conditions that produce gender-schematic processing, thereby providing an explicit account of why sex comes to have cognitive primacy over other social categories.

GENDER-SCHEMATIC PROCESSING

Gender schema theory begins with the observation that the developing child invariably learns his or her society's cultural definitions of femaleness and maleness. In most societies, these definitions comprise a diverse and sprawling network of sex-linked associations encompassing not only those features directly related to female and male persons—such as anatomy, reproductive function, division of labor, and personality attributes—but also features more remotely or metaphorically related to sex, such as the angularity or roundness of an abstract shape and the periodicity of the moon. Indeed, no other dichotomy in human experience appears to have as many entities linked to it as does the distinction between male and female.

But there is more. Gender schema theory proposes that, in addition to learning such content-specific information about gender, the child also learns to invoke this heterogeneous network of sex-related associations in order to evaluate and assimilate new information. The child, in short, learns to encode and to organize information in terms of an evolving gender schema.

A schema is a cognitive structure, a network of associations that organizes and guides an individual's perception. A schema functions as an anticipatory structure, a readiness to search for and to assimilate incoming information in schema-relevant terms. Schematic information processing is thus highly selective and enables the individual to impose structure and meaning onto a vast array of incoming stimuli. More specifically, schematic information processing entails a readiness to sort information into categories on the basis of some particular dimension, despite the existence of other dimensions that could serve equally well in this regard. Gender-schematic processing in particular thus involves spontaneously sorting attributes and behaviors into masculine and feminine categories or "equivalence classes," regardless of their differences on a variety of dimensions unrelated to gender, for example, spontaneously placing items like "tender" and "nightingale" into a feminine category and items like "assertive" and "eagle" into a masculine category. Like schema theories generally,[14] gender schema theory thus construes perception as a constructive process in which the interaction between incoming informa-

13. Sandra L. Bem, "Gender Schema Theory: A Cognitive Account of Sex Typing," *Psychological Review* 88, no. 4 (July 1981): 354–64; and "Gender Schema Theory and Self-Schema Theory Compared: A Comment on Markus, Crane, Bernstein, and Siladi's 'Self-Schemas and Gender,'" *Journal of Personality and Social Psychology* 43, no. 6 (December 1982): 1192–94.

tion and an individual's preexisting schema determines what is perceived.

What gender schema theory proposes, then, is that the phenomenon of sex typing derives, in part, from gender-schematic processing, from an individual's generalized readiness to process information on the basis of the sex-linked associations that constitute the gender schema. Specifically, the theory proposes that sex typing results, in part, from the assimilation of the self-concept itself to the gender schema. As children learn the contents of their society's gender schema, they learn which attributes are to be linked with their own sex and, hence, with themselves. This does not simply entail learning the defined relationship between each sex and each dimension or attribute—that boys are to be strong and girls weak, for example—but involves the deeper lesson that the dimensions themselves are differentially applicable to the two sexes. Thus, the strong-weak dimension itself is absent from the schema to be applied to girls just as the dimension of nurturance is implicitly omitted from the schema applied to boys. Adults in the child's world rarely notice or remark upon how strong a little girl is becoming or how nurturant a little boy is becoming, despite their readiness to note precisely these attributes in the "appropriate" sex. The child learns to apply this same schematic selectivity to the self, to choose from among the many possible dimensions of human personality only that subset defined as applicable to his or her own sex and thereby eligible for organizing the diverse contents of the self-concept. Thus do children's self-concepts become sex typed, and thus

do the two sexes become, in their own eyes, not only different in degree, but different in kind.

Simultaneously, the child also learns to evaluate his or her adequacy as a person according to the gender schema, to match his or her preferences, attitudes, behaviors, and personal attributes against the prototypes stored within it. The gender schema becomes a prescriptive standard or guide,[15] and self-esteem becomes its hostage. Here, then, enters an internalized motivational factor that prompts an individual to regulate his or her behavior so that it conforms to cultural definitions of femaleness and maleness. Thus do cultural myths become self-fulfilling prophecies, and thus, according to gender schema theory, do we arrive at the phenomenon known as sex typing.

It is important to note that gender schema theory is a theory of process, not content. Because sex typed individuals are seen as processing information and regulating their behavior according to whatever definitions of femininity and masculinity their culture happens to provide, the process of dividing the world into feminine and masculine categories—and not the contents of the categories—is central to the theory. Accordingly, sex-typed individuals are seen to differ from other individuals not primarily in the degree of femininity or masculinity they possess, but in the extent to which their self-concepts and behaviors are organized on the basis of gender rather than on the basis of some other dimension. Many non-sex-typed individuals may describe themselves as, say, nurturant or dominant without implicating the concepts of femininity or masculinity. When sex-typed individuals so describe themselves, however, it is precisely the gender connotations of the

---

14. Ulric Neisser, *Cognition and Reality* (San Francisco: W. H. Freeman & Co., 1976); Shelley E. Taylor and Jennifer Crocker, "Schematic Bases of Social Information Processing," in *Social Cognition, the Ontario Symposium,* ed. E. Tory Higgins, C. Peter Herman, and Mark P. Zanna (Hillsdale, N.J.: Lawrence Erlbaum Associates, 1981), 1:89–135.

15. Jerome Kagan, "Acquisition and Significance of Sex Typing and Sex Role Identity," in *Review of Child Development Research,* ed. Martin L. Hoffmann and Lois W. Hoffman (New York: Russell Sage Foundation, 1964), 1:137–67.

attributes or behaviors that are presumed to be salient for them.

EMPIRICAL RESEARCH ON GENDER-SCHEMATIC PROCESSING

Recent empirical research supports gender schema theory's basic contention that sex typing is derived from gender-schematic processing. In a variety of studies using different subject populations and different paradigms, female and male sex-typed individuals have been found to be significantly more likely than non-sex-typed individuals to process information—including information about the self—in terms of gender.[16]

One study, for example, used a memory task to determine whether gender connotations are, in fact, more "cognitively available" to sex-typed individuals than to non-sex-typed individuals, as gender schema theory claims.[17] The subjects in this study were forty-eight male and forty-eight female undergraduates who had described themselves as either sex typed or non-sex typed on the Bem Sex Role Inventory (BSRI).[18]

During the experimental session, subjects were presented with a randomly ordered sequence of sixty-one words that included proper names, animal names, verbs, and articles of clothing. Half of the proper names were female, half were male; one-third of the items within each of the other semantic categories had been consistently rated by undergraduate judges as feminine (e.g., butterfly, blushing, bikini), one-third as masculine (e.g., gorilla, hurling, trousers), and one-third as neutral (e.g., ant, stepping, sweater). The words were presented on slides at

16. Susan M. Anderson and Sandra L. Bem, "Sex Typing and Androgyny in Dyadic Interaction: Individual Differences in Responsiveness to Physical Attractiveness," *Journal of Personality and Social Psychology* 41, no. 1 (July 1981): 74–86; Bem, "Gender Schema Theory"; Kay Deaux and Brenda Major, "Sex-related Patterns in the Unit of Perception," *Personality and Social Psychology Bulletin* 3, no. 2 (Spring 1977): 297–300; Brenda Girvin, "The Nature of Being Schematic: Sex Role Schemas and Differential Processing of Masculine and Feminine Information" (Ph.D. diss., Stanford University, 1978); Robert V. Kail and Laura E. Levine, "Encoding Processed and Sex-Role Preferences," *Journal of Experimental Child Psychology* 21, no. 2 (April 1976): 256–63; Lynn S. Liben and Margaret L. Signorella, "Gender-related Schemata and Constructive Memory in Children," *Child Development* 51, no. 1 (March 1980): 11–18; Richard Lippa, "Androgyny, Sex Typing, and the Perception of Masculinity-Femininity in Handwriting," *Journal of Research in Personality* 11, no. 1 (March 1977): 21–37; Hazel Markus et al., "Self-Schemas and Gender," *Journal of Personality and Social Psychology* 42, no. 1 (January 1982): 38–50; Shelley E. Taylor and Hsiao-Ti Falcone, "Cognitive Bases of Stereotyping: The Relationship between Categorization and Prejudice," *Personality and Social Psychology Bulletin* 8, no. 3 (September 1982): 426–32.

17. Bem, "Gender Schema Theory," pp. 356–58.

18. The Bem Sex Role Inventory, or BSRI, is an instrument that identifies sex-typed individuals on the basis of their self-concepts or self-ratings of their personal attributes. The BSRI asks the respondent to indicate on a seven-point scale how well each of sixty attributes describes himself or herself. Although it is not apparent to the respondent, twenty of the attributes reflect the culture's definition of masculinity (e.g., assertive), and twenty reflect its definition of femininity (e.g., tender), with the remaining attributes serving as filler. Each respondent receives both a masculinity and a femininity score, and those who score above the median on the sex-congruent scale and below the median on the sex-incongruent scale are defined as sex typed. That is, men who score high in masculinity and low in femininity are defined as sex typed, as are women who score high in femininity and low in masculinity. The BSRI is described in detail in the following articles: Sandra L. Bem, "The Measurement of Psychological Androgyny," *Journal of Consulting and Clinical Psychology* 42, no. 2 (April 1974): 155–62; "On the Utility of Alternative Procedures for Assessing Psychological Androgyny," *Journal of Clinical and Consulting Psychology* 45, no. 2 (April 1977): 196–205; "The Theory and Measurement of Androgyny: A Reply to the Pedhazur-Tetenbaum and Locksley-Colten Critiques," *Journal of Personality and Social Psychology* 37, no. 6 (June 1979): 1047–54; and *A Manual for the Bem Sex Role Inventory* (Palo Alto, Calif.: Consulting Psychologists Press, 1981).

three-second intervals, and subjects were told that their recall would later be tested. Three seconds after the presentation of the last word, they were given a period of eight minutes to write down as many words as they could, in whatever order they happened to come to mind.

As expected, the results indicated that although sex-typed and non-sex-typed individuals recalled equal numbers of items overall, the order in which they recalled the items was different. Once having recalled a feminine item, sex-typed individuals were more likely than non-sex-typed individuals to recall another feminine item next rather than a masculine or a neutral item. The same was true for masculine items. In other words, the sequence of recall for sex-typed individuals revealed significantly more runs or clusters of feminine items and of masculine items than the sequence of recall for non-sex-typed individuals. Thinking of one feminine (or masculine) item could enhance the probability of thinking of another feminine (or masculine) item in this way only if the individual spontaneously encodes both items as feminine (or masculine), and the gender schema thereby links the two items in memory. These results thus confirm gender schema theory's claim that sex-typed individuals have a greater readiness than do non-sex-typed individuals to encode information in terms of the sex-linked associations that constitute the gender schema.

A second study tested the hypothesis that sex-typed individuals have a readiness to decide on the basis of gender which personal attributes are to be associated with their self-concepts and which are to be dissociated from their self-concepts.[19] The subjects in this second study were another set of forty-eight male and forty-eight female undergraduates who had also described themselves as sex typed or non-sex typed on the Bem Sex Role Inventory. During each of the individual experi-

mental sessions, the sixty attributes from the BSRI were projected on a screen one at a time, and the subject was requested to push one of two buttons, "Me" or "Not Me," to indicate whether the attribute was or was not self-descriptive. Of interest in this study was the subject's response latency, that is, how long it took the subject to make a decision about each attribute.

Gender schema theory predicts and the results of this study confirm that sex-typed subjects are significantly faster than non-sex-typed subjects when endorsing sex-appropriate attributes and when rejecting sex-inappropriate attributes. These results suggest that when deciding whether a particular attribute is or is not self-descriptive, sex-typed individuals do not bother to go through a time-consuming process of recruiting behavioral evidence from memory and judging whether the evidence warrants an affirmative answer—which is presumably what non-sex-typed individuals do. Rather, sex-typed individuals "look up" the attribute in the gender schema. If the attribute is sex appropriate, they quickly say yes; if the attribute is sex inappropriate, they quickly say no. Occasionally, of course, even sex-typed individuals must admit to possessing an attribute that is sex inappropriate or to lacking an attribute that is sex appropriate. On these occasions, they are significantly slower than non-sex-typed individuals. This pattern of rapid delivery of gender-consistent self-descriptions and slow delivery of gender-inconsistent self-descriptions confirms gender schema theory's contention that sex-typed individuals spontaneously sort information into categories on the basis of gender, despite the existence of other dimensions that could serve equally well as a basis for categorization.

ANTECEDENTS OF GENDER-SCHEMATIC PROCESSING

But how and why do sex-typed individuals develop a readiness to organize information in general, and their self-concepts in particular, in

---

19. Bem, "Gender Schema Theory," pp. 358–61.

terms of gender? Because gender-schematic processing is considered a special case of schematic processing, this specific question is superseded by the more general question of how and why individuals come to organize information in terms of any social category, that is, how and why a social category becomes transformed into a cognitive schema.

Gender schema theory proposes that the transformation of a given social category into the nucleus of a highly available cognitive schema depends on the nature of the social context within which the category is embedded, not on the intrinsic nature of the category itself. Given the proper social context, then, even a category like eye color could become a cognitive schema. More specifically, gender schema theory proposes that a category will become a schema if: (*a*) the social context makes it the nucleus of a large associative network, that is, if the ideology and/or the practices of the culture construct an association between that category and a wide range of other attributes, behaviors, concepts, and categories; and (*b*) the social context assigns the category broad functional significance, that is, if a broad array of social institutions, norms, and taboos distinguishes between persons, behaviors, and attributes on the basis of this category.

This latter condition is most critical, for gender schema theory presumes that the culture's insistence on the functional importance of the social category is what transforms a passive network of associations into an active and readily available schema for interpreting reality. We all learn many associative networks of concepts throughout life, many potential cognitive schemata, but the centrality or functional importance assigned by society to particular categories and distinctions animates their associated networks and gives these schemata priority and availability over others.

From the perspective of gender schema theory, then, gender has come to have cognitive primacy over many other social categories because the culture has made it so. Nearly all societies teach the developing child two crucial things about gender: first, as noted earlier, they teach the substantive network of sex-related associations that can come to serve as a cognitive schema; second, they teach that the dichotomy between male and female has intensive and extensive relevance to virtually every domain of human experience. The typical American child cannot help observing, for example, that what parents, teachers, and peers consider to be appropriate behavior varies as a function of sex; that toys, clothing, occupations, hobbies, the domestic division of labor—even pronouns—all vary as a function of sex.

Gender schema theory thus implies that children would be far less likely to become gender schematic and hence sex typed if the society were to limit the associative network linked to sex and to temper its insistence on the functional importance of the gender dichotomy. Ironically, even though our society has become sensitive to negative sex stereotypes and has begun to expunge them from the media and from children's literature, it remains blind to its gratuitous emphasis on the gender dichotomy itself. In elementary schools, for example, boys and girls line up separately or alternately; they learn songs in which the fingers are "ladies" and the thumbs are "men"; they see boy and girl paper-doll silhouettes alternately placed on the days of the month in order to learn about the calendar. Children, it will be noted, are not lined up separately or alternately as blacks and whites; fingers are not "whites" and thumbs "blacks"; black and white dolls do not alternately mark the days of the calendar. Our society seeks to deemphasize racial distinctions but continues to exaggerate sexual distinctions.

Because of the role that sex plays in reproduction, perhaps no society could ever be as indifferent to sex in its cultural arrangements as it could be to, say, eye color, thereby giving the gender schema a sociologically based priority over many other categories. For the same reason, it may even be, as noted earlier, that sex has evolved to be a basic category of perception for our species, thereby giving the gender schema a biologically based priority as well. Be that as it may, however, gender schema theory claims that society's ubiquitous insistence on the functional importance of the gender dichotomy must necessarily render it even more cognitively available— and available in more remotely relevant contexts—than it would be otherwise.

It should be noted that gender schema theory's claims about the antecedents or gender-schematic processing have not yet been tested empirically. Hence, it is not possible at this point to state whether individual differences in gender-schematic processing do, in fact, derive from differences in the emphasis placed on gender dichotomy in individual's socialization histories, or to describe concretely the particular kinds of socialization histories that enhance or diminish gender-schematic processing. Nevertheless, I should like to set forth a number of plausible strategies that are consistent with gender schema theory for raising a gender-aschematic child in the midst of a gender-schematic society.

This discussion will, by necessity, be highly speculative. Even so, it will serve to clarify gender schema theory's view of exactly how gender-schematic processing is learned and how something else might be learned in its place. As we shall see, many of the particular strategies recommended for raising gender-aschematic children are strategies that have already been adopted by feminist parents trying to create what is typically called a nonsexist or a gender-liberated form of child rearing. In these cases, what gender schema theory provides is a new theoretical framework for thinking about the psychological impact of various child-rearing practices. Sprinkled throughout the discussion will be examples taken from my own home. These are meant to be illustrations and not systematic evidence that such strategies actually decrease gender-schematic processing.

RAISING GENDER-ASCHEMATIC CHILDREN

Feminist parents who wish to raise gender-aschematic children in a gender-schematic world are like any parents who wish to inculcate their children with beliefs and values that deviate from those of the dominant culture. Their major option is to try to undermine the dominant ideology before it can undermine theirs. Feminist parents are thus in a difficult situation. They cannot simply ignore gender in their child rearing as they might prefer to do, because the society will then have free rein to teach their children the lessons about gender that it teaches all other children. Rather, they must manage somehow to inoculate their children against gender-schematic processing.

Two strategies are suggested here. First, parents can enable their children to learn about sex differences initially without their also learning the culture's sex-linked associative network by simultaneously retarding their children's knowledge of sex's cultural correlates and advancing their children's knowledge of sex's biological correlates. Second, parents can provide alternative or "subversive" schemata that their children can use to interpret the culture's sex-linked associative network when they do learn it. This step is essential if children are not simply to learn gender-schematic processing somewhat later than their counterparts from more traditional homes. Whether one is a child or an adult, such alternative schemata "build up one's resistance" to the lessons of the dominant culture and thereby enable one to remain gender-aschematic even while living in a gender-schematic society.

TEACHING CHILDREN ABOUT SEX DIFFERENCES

Cultural Correlates of Sex

Children typically learn that gender is a sprawling associative network with ubiquitous functional importance through their observation of the many cultural correlates of sex existing in their society.

Accordingly, the first step parents can take to retard the development of gender-schematic processing is to retard the child's knowledge of these cultural messages about gender. Less crudely put, parents can attempt to attenuate sex-linked correlations within the child's social environment, thereby altering the basic data upon which the child will construct his or her own concepts of maleness and femaleness.

In part, parents can do this by eliminating sex stereotyping from their own behavior and from the alternatives that they provide for their children, just as many feminist parents are already doing. Among other things, for example, they can take turns making dinner, bathing the children and driving the car; they can ensure that all their children—regardless of sex—have both trucks and dolls, both pink and blue clothing, and both male and female playmates; and they can arrange for their children to see women and men in nontraditional occupations.

When children are quite young, parents can further inhibit cultural messages about gender by actually censoring books and television programs whose explicit or implicit message is that the sexes differ on nonbiological dimensions. At present, this tactic will eliminate many children's books and most television programming. Ironically, it will also temporarily eliminate a number of feminist books designed to overcome sex stereotypes; even a book which insists that it is wrong for William not to be allowed to have a doll by implication teaches a child who has not yet learned the associative network that boys and dolls do not normally go together.

To compensate for this censorship, parents will need to seek out—and to create—materials that do not teach sex stereotypes. With our own children, my husband and I got into the habit of doctoring books whenever possible so as to remove all sex-linked correlations. We did this, among other ways, by changing the sex of the main character; by drawing longer hair and the outline of breasts onto illustrations of previously male truck drivers, physicians, pilots, and the like; and by deleting or altering sections of the text that described females or males in a sex-stereotyped manner. When reading children's picture books aloud, we also chose pronouns that avoided the ubiquitous implication that all characters without dresses or pink bows must necessarily be male: "And what is this little piggy doing? Why, he or she seems to be building a bridge."

All of these practices are designed to permit very young children to dwell temporarily in a social environment where, if the parents are lucky, the cultural correlations with sex will be attenuated from, say, .96 to .43. According to gender schema theory, this attenuation should retard the formation of the sex-linked associative network that will itself form the basis of the gender schema. By themselves, however, these practices teach children only what sex is not. But children must also be taught what sex is.

Biological Correlates of Sex

What remains when all of the cultural correlates of sex are attenuated or eliminated, of course, are two of the undisputed biological correlates of sex: anatomy and reproduction. Accordingly, parents can make these the definitional attributes of femaleness and maleness. By teaching their children that the genitalia constitute the definitive attributes of females and males, parents help them to apprehend the merely probabilistic nature of sex's cultural correlates and thereby restrict sex's associative sprawl. By teaching their children that whether one is female or male makes a difference only in the context of reproduction, parents limit sex's functional significance and thereby retard gender-schematic processing. Because children taught these lessons have been provided with an explicit and clear-cut rule about what sex is and when sex matters, they should be predisposed to construct their own concepts of femaleness and maleness based on biology, rather than on the cultural correlates to which they have been exposed. And to the extent that young children tend to interpret rules and categories rigidly rather than flexibly, this tendency will serve to enhance their belief that sex is to be narrowly defined in terms of anatomy and reproduction rather than to enhance a traditional belief that every arbitrary gender rule must be strictly obeyed and enforced. Thus there may be an irony, but there is no inconsistency, in the fact that an emphasis on the biological differences between the sexes should here be advocated as the basis for feminist child rearing.

The liberation that comes from having an unambiguous genital definition of sex and the imprisonment that comes from not having such a definition are nicely illustrated by the story of what happened to our son Jeremy, then age four, the day he decided to wear barrettes to nursery school. Several times that day, another little boy told Jeremy that he, Jeremy, must be a girl because "only girls wear barrettes." After trying to explain to this child that "wearing barrettes doesn't matter" and that "being a boy means having a penis and testicles," Jeremy finally pulled down his pants as a way of making his point more convincingly. The other child was not impressed. He simply said, "Everybody has a penis; only girls wear barrettes."

In the American context, children do not typically learn to define sex in terms of anatomy and reproduction until quite late, and, as a result, they—like the child in the example above—mistakenly treat many of the cultural correlates of sex as definitional. This confusion is facilitated, of course, by the fact that the genitalia themselves are not usually visible and hence cannot be relied on as a way of identifying someone's sex.

Accordingly, when our children asked whether someone was male or female, we frequently denied certain knowledge of the person's sex, emphasizing that without being able to see whether there was a penis or a vagina under the person's clothes, we had no definitive information. Moreover, when our children themselves began to utilize nonbiological markers as a way of identifying sex, we gently teased them about that strategy to remind them that the genitalia—and only the genitalia—constitute the definition of sex: "What do you mean that you can tell that Chris is a girl because Chris has long hair? Does Chris's hair have a vagina?"

We found Stephanie Waxman's picture book *What Is a Girl? What Is a Boy?* to be a superb teaching aid in this context.[20] Each page displays a vivid and attractive photograph of a boy or a girl engaged in some behavior stereotyped as more typical of or more appropriate for the other sex. The accompanying text says such things as, "Some people say a girl is someone with jewelry, but Barry is wearing a necklace and he's a boy." The book ends with nude photographs of both children and adults, and it explicitly defines sex in terms of anatomy.

These particular lessons about what sex is, what sex is not, and when sex matters are designed to make young children far more naive than their peers about the cultural aspects of gender and far more sophisticated than their peers about the biological aspects of sex. Eventually, of course, their naiveté will begin to fade, and they too will begin to learn the culture's sprawling network of sex-linked associations. At that point, parents must take steps to prevent that associative network from itself becoming a cognitive schema.

PROVIDING ALTERNATIVE SCHEMATA

Let us presume that the feminist parent has successfully produced a child who defines sex in terms of anatomy and reproduction. How is such a child to understand the many sex-linked correlations that will inevitably begin to intrude upon his or her awareness? What alternative schemata can substitute for the gender schema in helping

20. Stephanie Waxman, *What Is a Girl? What Is a Boy?* (Culver City, Calif.: Peace Press, 1976).

the child to organize and to assimilate gender-related information?

Individual Differences Schema

The first alternative schema is simply a child's version of the time-honored liberal truism used to counter stereotypic thinking in general, namely, that there is remarkable variability of individuals within groups as compared with the small mean differences between groups. To the child who says that girls do not like to play baseball, the feminist parent can thus point out that although it is true that some girls do not like to play baseball, it is also true that some girls do (e.g., your Aunt Beverly and Alissa who lives across the street) and that some boys do not (e.g., your dad and Alissa's brother Jimmy). It is, of course, useful for parents to supply themselves with a long list of counterexamples well in advance of such occasions.

This individual differences schema is designed to prevent children from interpreting individual differences as sex differences, from assimilating perceived differences among people to a gender schema. Simultaneously, it should also encourage children to treat as a given that the sexes are basically similar to one another and, hence, to view all glib assertions about sex differences as inherently suspect. And it is with this skepticism that feminist consciousness begins.

Cultural Relativism Schema

As the child's knowledge and awareness grow, he or she will gradually begin to realize that his or her family's beliefs and attitudes about gender are at variance with those of the dominant culture. Accordingly, the child needs some rationale for not simply accepting the majority view as the more valid. One possible rationale is cultural relativism, that notion that "different people believe different things" and that the coexistence of even contradictory beliefs is the rule in society rather than the exception.

Children can (and should) be introduced to the schema of cultural relativism long before it is pertinent to the domain of gender. For example, our children needed the rationale that "different people believe different things" in order to understand why they, but not the children next door, had to wear seat belts; why our family, but not the family next door, was casual about nudity in the home. The general principle that contradictory beliefs frequently coexist seems now to have become a readily available schema for our children, a schema that permits them to accept with relative equanimity that they have different beliefs from many of their peers with respect to gender.

Finally, the cultural relativism schema can solve one of the primary dilemmas of the liberal feminist parent: how to give one's children access to the riches of classical literature—as well as to lesser riches of the mass media—without abandoning them to the forces that promote gender-schematic processing. Happily, the censorship of sex-stereotyped materials that is necessary to retard the initial growth of the sex-linked associative network when children are young can end once children have learned the critical lesson that cultural messages reflect the beliefs and attitudes of the person or persons who created those messages.

Accordingly, before we read our daughter her first volume of fairy tales, we discussed with her the cultural beliefs and attitudes about men and women that the tales would reflect, and while reading the tales, we frequently made such comments as, "Isn't it interesting that the person who wrote this story seems to think that girls always need to be rescued?" If such discussions are not too heavy-handed, they can provide a background of understanding against which the child can thoroughly enjoy the stories themselves, while still learning to discount the sex stereotypes within them as irrelevant both to their own beliefs and to truth. The cultural relativism schema thus brings children an awareness that fairy tales are fairy tales in more than one sense.

Sexism Schema

Cultural relativism is fine in its place, but feminist parents will not and should not be satisfied to pretend that they think all ideas—particularly those about gender—are equally valid. At some point, they will feel compelled to declare that the view of women and men conveyed by fairy tales, by the mass media—and by the next-door neighbors—is not only different, but wrong. It is time to teach one's children about sexism.

Moreover, it is only by giving children a sexism schema, a coherent and organized understanding of the historical roots and the contemporaneous consequences of sex discrimination, that they will truly be able to comprehend why the sexes appear to be so different in our society: why, for example, there has never been a female president of the United States; why fathers do not stay home with their children; and why so many people believe these sex differences to be the natural consequence of biology. The child who has developed a readiness to encode and to organize information in terms of an evolving sexism schema is a child who is prepared to oppose actively the gender-related constraints that those with a gender schema will inevitably seek to impose.

The development of a sexism schema is nicely illustrated by our daughter Emily's response to Norma Klein's book *Girls Can Be Anything*.[21] One of the characters is Adam Sobel, who insists that "girls are always nurses and boys are always doctors" and that "girls can't be pilots,...they have to be stewardesses." After reading this book, our daughter, then age four, spontaneously began to label with contempt anyone who voiced stereotyped beliefs about gender an "Adam Sobel." Adam Sobel thus became for her the nucleus of an evolving sexism schema, a schema that enables her now to perceive—and also to become morally outraged by and to oppose—whatever sex discrimination she meets in daily life.

As feminist parents, we wish it could have been possible to raise our children with neither a gender schema nor a sexism schema. At this historical moment, however, that is not an option. Rather we must choose either to have our children become gender schematic and hence sex typed, or to have our children become sexism schematic and hence feminists. We have chosen the latter.

A COMMENT ON PSYCHOLOGICAL ANDROGYNY

The central figure in gender schema theory is the sex-typed individual, a shift in focus from my earlier work in which the non-sex-typed individual—the androgynous individual in particular—commanded center stage.[22] In the early 1970s, androgyny seemed to me and to many others a liberated and more humane alternative to the traditional, sex-biased standards of mental health. And it is true that this concept can be applied equally to both women and men, and that it encourages individuals to embrace both the feminine and the masculine within themselves. But advocating the concept of androgyny can also be seen as replacing a prescription to be masculine or feminine with the doubly incarcerating prescription to be masculine and feminine. The individual now has not

21. Norma Klein, *Girls Can Be Anything* (New York: E. P. Dutton, 1973).

22. Sandra L. Bem, "Sex-Role Adaptability: One Consequence of Psychological Androgyny," *Journal of Personality and Social Psychology* 31, no. 4 (April 1975): 634–43; Sandra L. Bem, Wendy Martyna, and Carol Watson, "Sex-Typing and Androgyny: Further Explorations of the Expressive Domain," *Journal of Personality and Social Psychology* 34, no. 5 (November 1976): 1016–23; Sandra L. Bem, "Beyond Androgyny: Some Presumptuous Prescriptions for a Liberated Sexual Identity," in *The Future of Women: Issues in Psychology,* ed. Julia Sherman and Florence Denmark (New York: Psychological Dimensions, Inc., 1978), pp. 1–23; Sandra L. Bem and Ellen Lenney, "Sex-Typing and the Avoidance of Cross-Sex Behavior," *Journal of Personality and Social Psychology* 33, no. 1 (January 1976): 48–54.

one but two potential sources of inadequacy with which to contend. Even more important, however, the concept of androgyny is problematic from the perspective of gender schema theory because it is based on the presupposition that there is a feminine and a masculine within us all, that is, that "femininity" and "masculinity" have an independent and palpable reality and are not cognitive constructs derived from gender-schematic processing. Focusing on androgyny thus fails to prompt serious examination of the extent to which gender organizes both our perceptions and our social world.

In contrast, the concept of gender-schematic processing directs our attention to the promiscu- ous availability of the gender schema in contexts where other schemata ought to have priority. Thus, if gender schema theory has a political message, it is not that the individual should be androgynous. Rather, it is that the network of associations constituting the gender schema ought to become more limited in scope and that society ought to temper its insistence on the ubiquitous functional importance of the gender dichotomy. In short, human behaviors and personality attributes should no longer be linked with gender, and society should stop projecting gender into situations irrelevant to genitalia.

Reading 3   The Development of Women's Sense of Self

JEAN BAKER MILLER

Questions to Consider:

1. Does Miller's description of the "self-in-relation" describe your sense of self? Explain.

2. Why does Miller feel it is important to recognize that women develop a sense of self through relationships?

3. How does Miller's description of development differ from Erikson's during infancy, childhood, and adolescence?

4. If gender roles were ended, how would the sense of self develop?

The concept of the self has been prominent in psychological theory, perhaps because it has been one of the central ideas in Western thought. While various writers use different definitions, the essential idea of a "self" seems to underlie the historical development of many Western notions about such vast issues as the "good life," justice, and freedom. Indeed, it seems entwined in the roots of several delineations of fundamental human motives or the highest form of existence, as in Maslow's self-actualizing character.

As we have inherited it, the notion of a "self" does not appear to fit women's experience. Several recent writers have spoken to this point, for

Jean Baker Miller, "The Development of Women's Sense of Self," in Judith V. Jordan, Alexandra G. Kaplan, Jean Baker Miller, Irene P. Striver, and Janet L. Surrey (Eds.), *Women's Growth in Connection.* New York: Guilford Press. Reprinted by permission.

example, literary critic Carolyn Heilbrun (1979) and psychologist Carol Gilligan (1982). A question then arises: Do only men, and not women, have a self? In working with women the question is quite puzzling, but an examination of the very puzzle itself may cast new light on certain long-standing assumptions. Modern American theorists of early psychological development and, indeed, of the entire life span, from Erik Erikson (1950) to Daniel Levinson (1978), tend to see all of development as a process of separating oneself out from the matrix of others—"becoming one's own man," in Levinson's words. Development of the self presumably is attained via a series of painful crises by which the individual accomplishes a sequence of allegedly essential separations from others, thereby achieving an inner sense of separated individuation. Few men ever attain such self-sufficiency, as every woman knows. They are usually supported by wives, mistresses, mothers, daughters, secretaries, nurses, and other women (as well as other men who are lower than they in the socioeconomic hierarchy). Thus, there is reason to question whether this model accurately reflects men's lives. Its goals, however, are held out for all, and are seen as the preconditions for mental health.

Almost every modern theorist who has tried to fit women into the prevalent models has had much more obvious difficulty, beginning with Freud and extending through Erikson and others. Some have not even tried. In Erikson's scheme, for example, after the first stage, in which the aim is the development of basic trust, the aim of every other stage, until young adulthood, is some form of increased separation or self-development. I am not referring at this point to the process by which each aim is attained (although that is an intimately related point that will be discussed below), but to the aim itself, the goal. It is important to note that the aim is not something like development of greater capacity for emotional connection to others; or for contributing to an interchange between people; or for playing a part in the growth of others as well as one's self. When the individual arrives at the stage called "intimacy," he is supposed to be able to be intimate with another person—having spent all of his prior development striving for something very different.

Much recent writing deploring men's inability to engage in intimacy has come from the women's movement. But men, too, have been making the same point. Almost all of modern literature, philosophy, and commentary in other forms portrays men's lack of a sense of community—indeed, it denies even the possibility of communicating with others.

Thus, the prevailing models may not describe well what occurs in men; in addition, there is a question about the value of these models even if it were possible to fulfill their requirements. These two questions are related, as I will try to suggest. It is very important to note, however, that the prevalent models are powerful because they have become prescriptions about what *should* happen. They affect men; they determine the actions of mental health professionals. They have affected women adversely in one way in the past. They are affecting women in another way now, if women seek "equal access" to them. Therefore, we need to examine them carefully. It is important not to embrace them because they are the only models available.

THE BEGINNINGS

What are some of the questions that arise when we try to bring women's experience into the picture? We can take Erikson's theories as a starting point, not to attempt a thorough examination of them, but to use them as a framework for consideration of a few of the many features in women's development.

In the first stage of life, according to Erikson, the central goal is the infant's development of a sense of basic trust. Another important dimension, however, is also involved. Even at that early stage in all infants, but encouraged much more in girls, the young child begins to be like and act like the main caretaker, who, up until now, has usually been a woman—not to "identify" with that person as some static figure described only by gender, but with what that person *actually* is doing. I think that the infant begins to develop an internal representation of itself as a kind of being that, for the moment, I will call by a hyphenated term—a "being-in-relationship." This is the beginning of a sense of "self" that reflects what is happening *between* people. The infant picks up the feelings of the other person, that is, it has an early sense that "I feel what is going on in the other as well as what is going on in myself." It is more complex because it involves "knowing"—feeling—what is going on in that emotional field between us. The child experiences a sense of comfort only as the other is also comfortable, or, more precisely, only as they are both engaged in an emotional relationship that is moving toward greater well-being, rather than toward the opposite—that is, only as the interactions in the emotional field between the infant and the adult are moving toward a "better" progression of events.* In this sense, the infant, actively exerting an effect on the relationship, begins to develop an internal sense of itself as one who changes the emotional interplay for both participants—for good or ill.

The beginnings of a mental construction of self are much more complicated than those suggested by such commonly used terms as *fusion* or *merger* for the mental constructions of the first stages of infancy, as drawn from Mahler (1975), object relations theorists, and others. New research on infant-caretaker interactions also indicates the inappropriateness of those terms (see, for example, Stern, 1980, Stechler and Kaplan, 1980; Klein, 1976). This research suggests that these constructs are not likely to describe adequately the complex internal representations of the self and the "other," or, rather, the internal self—other relational patterns that the infant is likely to create even from the earliest age.

When we talk about a sense of self in this field, we have been referring to a "man-made" construct meant to describe an internal mental representation. The suggestion here is that from the moment of birth this internal representation is of a self that is in active interchange with other selves. Moreover, this interaction has one central characteristic, and that is that people are attending to the infant—most importantly, attending to the infant's core of being, which means the infant's emotions—and the infant is responding in the same way, that is, to the other person's emotions. The earliest mental representation of the self, then, is of a self whose core—which is emotional—is attended to by the other(s) and in turn, begins to attend to the emotions of the

other(s). Part of this internal image of oneself includes feeling the other's emotions and *acting on* them as they are in interplay with one's own emotions. This means that the beginnings of the concept of self are not those of a static and lone self being ministered to by another (incidentally, this construct has a strong male flavor), but rather of a self inseparable from dynamic interaction. And the central character of that interaction involves attending to each other's mental states and emotions.

This early "interacting sense of self" is present for infants of both sexes, but the culturally induced beliefs of the caretakers about girls and boys play a role from the moment of birth. These beliefs are, of course, internalized even in the woman caretaker, although more so in fathers, according to suggestions from some studies (e.g., Rubin et al., 1974; Block, 1978). Girls are encouraged to augment their abilities to "feel as the other feels" and to practice "learning about" the other(s). Boys are systematically diverted from it—to their deprivation and detriment, in my opinion. (In my opinion, this redounds, too, to the detriment of the whole construction of our societal structure and of our models of thinking.)

Out of this interplay of experience one certainly develops a sense of one's self, that is, an internal or mental representation of one's self. Moreover, one develops a sense of one's self as a person who attends to and responds to what is going on in the relationships between two or more people.

Much of the literature tends to suggest that because she is the same sex as the caretaker, the girl cannot develop an internal sense of self; that is, that boys develop a sense of self because they separate themselves from the female caretaker. This is truly an incredible notion. First, it ignores all of the complexity of the interaction between caretaker and infant. It is as if there were no interaction because mother and child are both of the same sex—an amazing negation of the very idea of girls and women.

---

*This point has been made in various ways by many theorists, such as M. Klein, H. S. Sullivan, and several others. The features that they emphasize, however, are different.

Second, the literature has generally ignored the extraordinarily important character of the interaction—that of attending to and responding to the other. This is the essential feature of what comes to be called "caretaking." It is also the basis of all continuing psychological growth; that is, all growth occurs within emotional connections, not separate from them. Current theories ignore, too, the likelihood that the early self is built on the model of this very process—as opposed to the very different kinds of interaction that exist in the current world. The very notion of true caretaking precludes anything that would lead the infant to feel submerged, fused, or merged with the other. These words may describe some of the phenomena observed after *distortions* in caretaking have occurred, but they are unlikely to characterize the infant's prototypic sense of self.

Third, current notions tend to ignore the likelihood that the only possibility of having any sense of self at all is built on the core process I have described. As suggested above, it begins to be discouraged early on in boys. For girls, it is encouraged, but complications are added at this and at each succeeding phase of development.

Surrey has suggested that this early mental representation of the self in girls can be described as a more *encompassing* sense of self, in contrast with the more boundaried, or limited, self that is encouraged in boys from a very young age. She suggests, too, the term "oscillating" sense of self as compared to the current, more linear model, with the "oscillation" following from the ongoing growth of empathy in the child as well as in the mother (see Surrey, 1991; Jordan, Surrey, & Kaplan, 1991). Many implications follow. To begin with, certain events in later life that other models see as detracting from the self are instead seen as satisfying, motivating and empowering. For example, to feel "more related to another person" means to feel one's self enhanced, not threatened. It does not feel like a loss of part of one's self; instead it becomes a step toward more pleasure and effectiveness—because it is the way the girl and woman feel

"things should be," the way she wants them to be. Being in relationship, picking up the feelings of the other and attending to the "interaction between" becomes an accepted, "natural-seeming" way of being and acting. It is learned and assumed; not alien or threatening. Most important, it is desired; it is a *goal*, not a detraction or a means to some other end, such as one's own self-development. Thus, it forms a *motivation*.

We have come to think of this whole experience as so "foreign," I believe, because our cultural tradition has emphasized such a different direction. In the dominant and official culture, attending to the experience of others and to the relationships between people is not seen as a *requirement* of all of life. It has been relegated to the alien and mysterious world of mothers and infancy—and misunderstood. Sometimes, when I have tried to talk about this, psychiatrists have said, "Oh, I see what you mean. All right, I agree that women are more altruistic." That is not what I mean. That is attempting to slot this description into the old categories. It suggests a "sacrifice" of parts of a kind of self that has developed in a different fashion. To engage in the kind of interaction I am discussing is not a sacrifice; it is, in fact, a source of feeling better and more gratified, as well as more knowledgeable—about what is really happening. I believe it is closer to the elementary human necessities from which our dominant culture has become unnecessarily removed.

Another implication relates to self-esteem, or the sense of self-worth. The girl's sense of self-esteem is based in feeling that she is a part of relationships and is taking care of those relationships. This is very different from the components of self-esteem as usually described and, incidentally, as measured by most available scales. Another ramification involves the issue of competence or effectiveness. The girl and woman often feel a sense of effectiveness as arising out of emotional connections and as bound up with and feeding back into them. This is very different from a sense of effectiveness (or power) based in lone action and in acting against or over others. This sense of effectiveness can develop further in the next and all subsequent ages, but it grows upon this base.

AGENCY WITHIN COMMUNITY

To move quickly through the next ages of life, I will sketch a few suggestions about each of them, leading only as far as adolescence. Erikson speaks about the second stage of childhood as one in which the goal is autonomy; others have spoken about separation and individuation. I would suggest, instead, that we could think of this as a period when the child has more abilities, more possibilities "to do," and more physical and mental resources to use. The child also has an enlarged "point of view" on all events, as it were, that is, a more developed sense of how she or he sees things. There is not, however, nor need there be, any increased separation. Instead, there are new configurations and new "understandings" *in the relationship*. Maintaining the relationship(s) with the main people in her or his life is still *the* most important thing.

We might think of this as something like a phase called "agency-in-community." These words are borrowed from Bakan (1966) but not used with his definitions. Instead, by "agency" I am searching for a word again, a word that means being active, using all of one's resources, but without the connotations of aggression—another large topic, but one that cannot be developed here (see Miller, 1991). Here, again, the "doing" is different from what has been described in the past. Often for little girls, it means doing *for* following the model of what the mother is doing (see Jordan, Surrey, & Kaplan, 1991; Surrey, 1991). What the mother is still doing with little children is attending to their feelings and "*doing for*" them, although not totally. So the action, again, has a different character—it is doing for other(s) within a relationship, with the little girl using increased powers, an increased number of "opinions" about

how and what she wants "to do," and an increased assertion of what she can do.

In her internal representation of herself, I suggest, the girl is developing not a sense of separation, but a more developed sense of her own capacities and her greater ability to put her "views" into effect. That is, she has a sense of a larger scope of action—but still with an inner representation of a self that is doing this in relation to other selves. A larger scope of action is not equivalent to separation; it requires a *change* in her internal configuration of her sense of self and other, but not a separation.

The child can move on to a larger, but a more articulated sense of herself *only because* of her actions and feelings *in* the relationship. These actions and feelings are inevitably different from the other person's. They are obviously not identical. The point is that she is attuned to the feelings of the other person; and just as her feelings are influenced by other's feelings, so too, do they influence the other's feelings. She has a wide range of feelings and actions, and they vary at different times, with one or another in ascendancy, but they occur within the relational context.

Of course, the character of the relationship differs from that of infancy; new qualities come in. But this does not lead to a "separate" sense of self. It leads to a more complex sense of self in more complex relationships to other selves.

The whole notion of describing human interaction in geographic or spatial terms, along a scale of close or distant (i.e., separated), seems questionable. Surely it is the *quality* of the interaction that is the question—the interplay of "conceptualized feelings" (i.e., feelings *cum* concepts), the doing of good or bad to the other—in relation to the nature of each's needs. A growing child has the potential to do more than he or she could do before. The caretaker who recognizes and supports this enlarged ability does not become more distant. The caretaker becomes *more caring* in one more way—that is, *more related*—and the child does, too.

CHILDHOOD

When we move to the next stage, which is based on the oedipal stage, we may ask whether one reason that people, beginning with Freud, have had such trouble delineating this stage in girls is that it may not exist. There is no major crisis of "cutting off" anything, and especially relationships. And there is no need to fulfill the goal of "identifying with an aggressor," that is, the threatening and dominant male figure. (Several theorists believe that all of society, culture, and thought is built on this oedipal moment of identification with the aggressive father. It is interesting to think about the possibility that society need not be built on this base.) However, there is a message that may come in to play more forcefully at this time (though it begins earlier and it continues later)—that the girl should now focus all her energies on the well-being, growth, and development of men. Nonetheless, the relationship to the mother and to other women continues. A pronounced turning away from the mother and toward the father may occur because of particular conditions in particular families, especially when the mother herself encourages and models this way of being. Western culture has dictated that mothers should uphold the superior importance and power of the man. These forces begin to affect deeply the girl's sense of herself and her relationship to her mother and to complicate the relationship in many ways. However, the relationship to the mother and to other women continues, although it may be less obvious and it may be made to seem less important. There are ethnic, class, and historical variations in the degree of influence of the mother or father within the family, but, in general, the greater importance, value, and power of the father—and the devaluation of the mother— seems to come through psychologically.

In latency, or the period that, according to Erikson, has "industry" as its goal, there is increasing evidence that girls are not very latent. What girls may do is learn to hide more, if we are talking about sexuality, as Freud was when he initiated the use of the term. But if we are talking about relationships, this is certainly the time when the girls are very intensely involved in all of their relationships, especially with other girls. Many girls are very interested in men and boys, too, but the boys are often either not interested or actively deprecating and destructive to girls. The boys are out learning "industry," which others have talked about as "learning the rules of the game and how to play it" (Gilligan, 1982). Most of these rules, incidentally, seem directly traceable to war games. In a study of this period, Luria (1981) describes the events in a grade school playground. She talks about the boys' learning not only how to be "warlike" and to win out over others, but how to cheat and get away with it. When she asked the girls what they were doing, they often said, "Nothing." The girls are hanging around the edges of the playground "just talking." What are they talking about? They are talking about the issues in their families and how to solve them. In discussing their families, the girls are, of course, very involved in an emotional interaction with one another. Surrey (1991) has pointed out that the vast amount of psychological development that occurs within the relationships between girls at this time has been one of the major neglected areas in psychological study.

ADOLESCENCE

Adolescence has been seen as a time when the individual has greatly increased capacities. Traditionally, psychologists have *divided* them in several ways: for example, sexual capacities; aggressive capacities—which I will call, for the moment, agentic (the ability to act); and cognitive capacities, with the development of formal thought that greatly expands the universe. However, many studies still indicate that this is a time when girls begin to "contract" rather than expand. Clara Thompson (1942) noted this long ago. She said that for boys, adolescence is seen as a period of opening up, but for girls it is a time for shutting down. In different terms, Freud said this, too. Freud believed that girls now had to learn that they were not actively to use all of themselves and all of their life forces from a base centered in their own bodies and in their own psychological constructions. For Freud, this meant, of course, the derivatives of their sexual drive. Instead, these forces are now to be turned to the use of others—men, in the first instance, and to the service of the next generation, via childbearing. That is, girls had to resolve their psychological issues by becoming passive and masochistic—to accomplish the necessary submission to the man and to "sacrifice" themselves for children.

Freud's observations may have reflected much of what happened—and still happens. That is, in regard to sexuality, most girls still learn that their own sexual perceptions, sensations, and impulses are not supposed to arise from themselves, but are to be brought forth by and for men. Thus girls still tend to experience their physical and sexual stirrings as wrong, bad, evil, dirty, and the like. This is to say that part of what has been going on in the girl's earlier internal representations of herself has included several problematic parts. One of these involves bodily and sexual experience. This situation can lead to an attempt to deal with this experience by turning to passivity and submission. The girl picks up the strong message that her own perceptions about her bodily and sexual feelings are not acceptable. They acquire connotations of badness and evil. They become parts of her self that are shameful and wrong. She has sought to bring these parts of herself into relationships with others all along, but has had difficulty in doing so. She still seeks to act on these desires within relationships with others. But she meets opposition. In the face of this, the solution of "doing it for others" can seem to offer a ready answer. The problem is that this solution is one that attempts to leave her—and her sense of herself, with all of her own psychological constructions—out of the relationship.

In heterosexual relationships, if the girl or young woman tries to have her own perceptions, to follow her own desires, and to bring them into sexual experience with boys, she still is destined for conflict. Despite all of the recent talk, the girl's attempt to act on the basis of her own sexuality still leads to conflict with her potential male partners. It will also lead to internal conflict with certain components of her sense of self. One is the part that says she should—and that she wants to—be attuned to others, which leads to a conflict if the other is behaving in ways that are excluding her perceptions and desires from the relationship. Another is the part that has made sexuality an unacceptable aspect of her internal sense of self and therefore prevents her from bringing a large part of herself into the relationship.

A similar dynamic exists in regard to "agency," that is, the girl's capacity to perceive and to use her powers in all ways. Women are not supposed to do this, and they have incorporated the idea that to do so is wrong and shameful. The girl has learned and done many things, until now, within a relationship. However, because of societal influences, she has also incorporated a sense—again, to varying degrees—that she is not fully and freely to use all of her powers. During adolescence, however, she receives this as a much stronger message.

Thus her sense of self as an active agent—in the context of acting within a relationship and for the relationship—has been altered to some degree all along by a sense of a self who must defer to others' needs or desires. However, at adolescence she experiences a much more intense pressure to do so. Her sense of self as developed so far now faces a more serious conflict with the external forces she confronts.

The question is how she will deal with this conflict. As with sexuality, I believe that the major tendency is for the girl to opt for the relationship both in her overt actions and in an alteration of her internal sense of self. She will tend to want most to retain the self that wants to be a "being-in-relationship" but she will begin to lose touch with the definition of herself as a more active "being-within-relationship." If one part has to go, and until now it did, most girls lose more of the sense that they can bring their agency and sexuality, as they experience it, into the relationship.

To restate some of these points, at adolescence the girl is seeking fulfillment of two very important needs: to use all of her capacities, including her sexual capacity, but seeking to do so within a context that will fulfill her great desire to be a "being-in-relationship." This wish to do so has developed all through earlier ages. She wishes that the other person will be able to enter into a relationship in this fashion. I believe that the boy really has the same needs, at bottom. However, he has been much more preoccupied with trying to develop "himself" and a sense of his independent identity. The culture has made the very heavy demand that he be so preoccupied. It has been doing so all along, but it does so at adolescence in an even more forceful way. He has also picked up the idea that the girl should adapt to him, and he has not been encouraged to continue the development of the sense that he is primarily a boy-in-relationship with a primary responsibility for others and a desire to concentrate on the relationship between himself and others.

Thus girls are not seeking the *kind* of identity that has been prescribed for boys, but a different kind, one in which one is a "being-in-relation," which means developing all of one's self in increasingly complex ways, in increasingly complex relationships.

The model of a "being-in-relationship" that women are seeking is not easy to attain in present conditions. As I have tried to suggest, it is a very valuable model and, I believe, a model more related to reality—the reality of the human condition. In the current situation, however, it still tends to mean for women the old kind of relationship, with the suppression of the full participation of the woman's way of seeing and acting. This has been the historical pattern, certainly. For most women it is still the case. Even so, the woman's struggle continues into later life; but many more factors now complicate it.

PRACTICAL IMPLICATIONS

The practical implications are many. To suggest just a few, women probably do talk about relationships more often, and this is often misinterpreted as dependency. It is very important to listen carefully to what women are saying. Often it is not about wanting or needing to be dependent *or* independent, but about wanting to be in relationship with others and, again, to really comprehend the other; wanting to understand the other's feelings; wanting to contribute to the other; wanting the *nature* of the relationship to be one in which the other person(s) is engaged in this way (see Stiver, 1991; Surrey, 1991; Jordan, Surrey, & Kaplan, 1991). Thus, very often I have heard described as dependent women who are taking care of (and still developing psychologically from taking care of) about six other people. Sometimes they were doing so within a framework that contained many factors of realistic dependency, such as economic dependency or social dependency. Sometimes they had to adopt the psychological framework of the other because that is what their partners expected or demanded. But that is better described as the condition of a subordinate (Miller, 1976), which is still the social condition. This distinction is important.

It is not because of relationships per se that women are suppressed or oppressed. The issue is the *nature* of the relationships. In fact, without the recognition of the importance of relationships to women, we do not help women to find a path that leads them to growth and development. Some psychologists fall into a tendency to encourage "independence" or "separation," which is not what many women want. In the past, mental health professionals encouraged dependency with submission. The point is that the construction of concepts on that axis is inappropriate and misleading.

Perhaps I can illustrate these points by referring briefly to parts of the therapeutic work with one young woman, Ms. D. Ms. D., a 23-year-old woman, had been depressed and had felt worthless in an extreme way since about the age of 13. She was clearly very intelligent and also had a profound quality of thought. She was exceptionally physically attractive.

She did not know where all of the troubles were coming from and could not connect their onset with any specific events. She saw her father as a sort of nice guy; he was light, humorous, and the parent she liked. By contrast, she perceived her mother as a difficult, agitated, "screaming" person, someone no one would want to be like or even to be around. This is one description of parents that therapists hear frequently.

There was one thing that seemed related to the trouble beginning at age 13, although Ms. D. did not make this connection initially. The main part of her relationship with her father appeared to center around her tagging along with him in what seemed his major interest, football. From the time she was about 12 or 13, he did not let her tag along anymore, nor did he let her play with him, her brothers, and the other neighborhood boys. This also is one fairly common occurrence.

She had two brothers, 2 and 4 years younger, to whom she felt very devoted. From young childhood, she had always been very sympathetic to them, felt she understood them, and did a great many things for them.

Something else began around age 13: Many boys began to pursue her. Some were clearly making a straightforward dash for sex; others seemed to seek her ability to hear their needs, to understand them, to be responsive, to be sympathetic, to help them—all of which she did. In neither case, however, were the boys interested in her feelings and concerns if she tried to bring these into the relationship. By the time of therapy, she had lost much of her ability to do so.

I will highlight in abbreviated fashion some of the features that emerged in therapy. Ms. D.

came to see that she had developed in many ways, even with all that was bad and lacking in her life. She had related to others in a way that fostered their development. She did this and did it with pleasure and willingness, but she herself was not given much sense of self-worth and self-validation for doing so. No one recognized it fully, or gave her much affirmation for it. Thus, for one thing, she lacked a huge portion of the basis for self-esteem that she could and should have had. Second, almost no one reciprocated, that is, wanted to know and to respond to her needs and desires as she perceived and felt them.

Only after some time in therapy did she see that she had worked at bolstering her father (which she felt was her task) and her brothers; most important, she connected some of this to the "life's work" that had preoccupied her mother all along. She could see, for instance, that a great part of her mother's "ranting and raving," as she called it, resulted from the attempt to "shore up" her father and help her more valued brothers. Her father always had been shaky in his work, and there was a lot to do in the effort to help him "succeed." Her mother had been trying to do that. A large part of her mother's behavior was, however, both a cry for help at her felt obligation to accomplish an impossibility and a "protest" against having to accomplish that impossibility. Late in therapy, Ms. D. could begin to feel a sense of connection to her mother in the recognition that they both had been engaged in that task. Both had gained little sense of value from it. Simultaneously, her mother had not been able to value her daughter, as she had not been able to value herself.

After this recognition, Ms. D. was able to alter some of her resentment toward her mother, although acknowledging the ways that her mother had failed her. Later, too, she came to see her father as someone who had never been prepared or able to hear her concerns or to be responsive to her. She was able to perceive this only after she had finally become able even to *think* of seeking this kind of interaction with him. When she tried to bring her own needs into discussions with him, she perceived his inability to relate to her in this way. It was not like football.

Ms. D. had to confront her anger. She had a large amount of anger at both her father and her mother, for different reasons. It took a long time, but she became more able to allow herself her anger, as she also became able to see how much she had really contributed to others' development. That is, she had first to feel some sense of value before she could tolerate a view of herself as a person with anger (see Miller, 1991). Then, the understanding and redirection of her anger further relieved her sense of worthlessness. Very importantly, she came to see that she would not have had a large amount of anger if she had not had her own set of perceptions, expectations, wishes, desires, and judgments, that is, the sense of self that she had thought she never had. She was angry because of the violation of the self she really had. She, like many people, particularly women, had said originally that she had no sense of self at all; she was able to discover one and then to go on to build on it.

Her biggest problem in a way remains: how to be the kind of self she wants to be, a being-in-relationship, now able to value the very valuable parts of herself, along with her own perceptions and desires—and to find others who will be with her in that way. She still encounters situations, particularly but not only with men, in which she feels annihilated as a person. I think she is experiencing situations that are common to all of us.

RICHER MODELS

To generalize from this example, then, the model of self-development as it has been defined so far does not help us to understand or to help women well. Many women perceive the prospects held out by this model as threatening, for good reason. I think their perception reflects at bottom a fear of forfeiting relationships. By contrast, men's fears occur in different forms. Indeed, most men see the prospect of self-development not only as desirable but also as a basic definition of what they must do in life. Moreover, seeking to understand women opens paths to enlargement of a model of a "self" to one that encompasses more fully the range of human necessities and possibilities.

For Ms. D. there had been problems in relationships, especially in having directed a large portion of her life to relationships that primarily benefited others. However, to have overlooked their value, and her value in them, would have robbed Ms. D. of the major source of her strength and her potential for greater strengths.

The features I have suggested are present even in many highly accomplished women and women who do not care for families in the concrete sense. There is a small group of women today who seek a sense of self similar to that which has been advocated for men. But even many of these women express many of the same themes. They are often the relatively advantaged women who feel very pressured to advance in careers. They often find that their desire to live and work in a context of mutually enhancing relationships conflicts with male norms. There is pressure to believe that the latter are better and to devalue the relational desires in themselves.

Important evidence is emerging from other parts of the psychological field. Notably, Gilligan's (1982) work in developmental psychology suggests that women's sense of self and of morality revolves around issues of responsibility for, care of, and inclusion of other people. It is embedded in a compelling appreciation of context and an insistent unwillingness to construct abstractions that violate their grasp of the complexities of the connections between people. Women were previously seen as deficient or at a low level of development as a consequence of their encompassing these realms of context and of psychological connection. These features are found even in as accomplished a group as current women Harvard students. In other studies, McClelland (1979) finds that women tend to define power as having the strength to care for and give to others, which is very different from the way men have defined power.

As always, the artists have said it long ago. It is interesting to note that in much of literature the man has been in search of his self, as in *David Copperfield, Portrait of the Artist as a Young Man,* and many other novels. Women express desires, but they have tended to cast them in the overarching terms of wanting to make deep connection with another (others) and usually to enhance another, as in George Eliot's *Middlemarch* or Charlotte Bronte's *Villette.*

Overall, then, the concept of a "self" as it has come down to us has encouraged a complex series of processes leading to a sense of psychological separation from others. From this there would follow a quest for power over others and power over natural forces, including one's own body. This would seem to be inevitable if one cannot be grounded in *faith* in the kind of interconnections I have tried to suggest. Have such definitions of a separated self become conceivable *only* because half of the species has been assigned to the realms of life that involve such necessities as attending to the complex particularities of building the day-to-day emotional connections with others? This means, in effect, giving primary attention to participating in and fostering the development of other people—and even direct concentration on sustaining of the sheer physical life of others. Simultaneously, these realms delegated to women have been granted inferior value. They have not been incorporated into our perceptions as sources of growth, satisfaction, and empowerment. It then becomes difficult to conceive of them as the wellsprings of true inner motivation and development. But they are.

Another way to put this is to say that women's actual practice in the real world and the complex processes that those practices entail have not been drawn upon, nor elaborated on, as a basis of culture, knowledge, theory, or public policy. They then come to sound almost unreal or idealistic, but they are real; they are going on every day. If they were not, none of us would have lived and developed at all. But they have been split off from official definitions of reality.

An underlying question may be: Has our tradition made it difficult to conceive of the possibility that freedom and maximum use of our resources—our initiative, our intellect, our powers—can occur within a context that requires simultaneous responsibility for the care and growth of others and of the natural world? We cannot hope that such a sense of responsibility will develop *after* the person develops first as a separated "self," as currently defined. I believe that the search for the more appropriate study of women in women's own terms can not only lead to understanding women, certainly a valid goal in itself, but can also provide clues to a deeper grasp of the *necessities* for all human development and, simultaneously, to a greater realization of the realities of the vast, untapped human capacities. This is not an easy thing to do, because our whole system of thought, our categories, the eyes with which we see and the ears with which we hear have been trained in a system removed from this activity.

We have all been laboring under only one implicit model of the nature of human nature and of human development. Much richer models are possible. Glimpses of them have always been struggling to emerge, through the artists and the poets, and in some of the hopes and dreams of all of us. Now, perhaps, we can work at learning about them in this field.

An earlier version of this paper was presented at The Stone Center Dedication Conference in October 1981.

REFERENCES

Belenky, M. F., Clinchy, B. M., Goldberger, N. R., & Tarule, J. M. (1986). *Women's Ways of Knowing: The Development of Self, Voice and Mind.* New York: Basic Books.

Block, J. H. (1978). "Another look at sex differentiation in the socialization behaviors of mothers and fathers." In J. A. Sherman & F. L. Denmark (Eds.), *Psychology of Women: Future Directions of Research.* New York: Psychological Dimensions.

Erikson, E. (1950/1963). *Childhood and Society.* New York: W. W. Norton.

Gilligan, C. (1982). *In a Different Voice: Psychological Theory and Women's Development.* Cambridge: Harvard University Press.

Heilbrun, C. (1979). *Reinventing Womanhood.* New York: W. W. Norton.

Jordan, J. V., Surrey, J. L., & Kaplan, A. G. (1991). "Women and empathy: Implications for psychological development and psychotherapy." In J. V. Jordan, A. G. Kaplan, J. B. Miller, I. P. Stiver, & J. L. Surrey (Eds.), *Women's Growth in Connection.* New York: Guilford Press.

Klein, G. (1976). *Psychoanalytic Theory: An Explanation of Essentials.* New York: International Universities Press.

Levinson, D. (1978). *The Seasons of a Man's Life.* New York: Alfred A. Knopf.

Luria, Z. (1981, October). Presentation at the Dedication Conference, Stone Center, Wellesley College, Wellesley, MA.

Mahler, M. (1972). "On the first three subphases of the separation-individuation process." *International Journal of Psychoanalysis,* 53, 333–338.

Mahler, M. S., & Goslinger, B. J. (1955). "On symbiotic child psychosis: Genetic, Dynamic, and Restitutive aspects." *The Psychoanalytic Study of the Child,* 10, 195–212.

Mahler, M., Pine F., & Berman, A. (1975). *The Psychological Birth of the Human Infant: Symbiosis and Individuation.* New York: Basic Books.

McClelland, D. (1979). *Power. The Inner Experience.* New York: Irvington.

Miller, J. B. (1976). *Toward a New Psychology of Women.* Boston: Beacon Press.

Miller, J. B. (1991). "The construction of anger in women and men." In J. V. Jordan, A. G. Kaplan, J. B. Miller, I. P. Stiver, & J. L. Surrey (Eds.), *Women's Growth in Connection.* New York: Guilford Press.

Rubin, J., Provenzano, F., & Luria, Z. (1974). "The eye of the beholder: Views on sex of newborns." *American Journal of Orthopsychiatry,* 44, 512–519.

Stechler, G., & Kaplan, S. (1980). "The development of the self: A psychoanalytic perspective." *Psychoanalytic Study of the Child,* 35, 85–106.

Stern, D. (1980, October). "The early differentiation of self and other." In *Reflections on Self Psychology.* Symposium at the Boston Psychoanalytic Society, Boston, MA.

Stiver, I. P. (1991). "Beyond the oedipus complex: Mothers and daughters." In J. V. Jordan, A. G. Kaplan, J. B. Miller, I. P. Stiver, & J. L. Surrey (Eds.), *Women's Growth in Connection.* New York: Guilford Press.

Surrey, J. L. (1991). "The 'self-in relation': A theory of women's development." In J. V. Jordan, A. G. Kaplan, J. B. Miller, I. P. Stiver, & J. L. Surrey (Eds.), *Women's Growth in Connection.* New York: Guilford Press.

Thompson, C. (1942). "Cultural pressures in the psychology of women." *Psychiatry,* 5, 331–339. Reprinted in J. B. Miller (Ed.), *Psychoanalysis and Women.* New York: Brunner-Mazel and Penguin Books, 1973.

Topic 3

Adolescence

Sister

I get scared
watching your stretch marks
spread into elaborate spiderwebs
as your mouth clamps shut
against mirror images
of womanly curves

I tell you how once upon a time
I also suffered motion sickness
from curvy one-lane backroads
and longed for stick straight freeway

In the dark of night
I hear you cradling your sharp ribs
like a loving mother caressing
each milk white bone

With warning glances
against fashion models
whose runway legs stretch
taller than your body's length
I try to hold the mirror in a new light
capturing the strength of your body
the beauty of your mind

One day I will awaken
to your repetitions:
Mirror, mirror on the wall
I am woman, I am strong

Courtesy of April Cox

Feminist research on adolescent girls demonstrates the importance of this time of life for understanding the psychology of women. Much of this work challenges traditional developmental theory, which views the creation of an autonomous identity as the critical task of adolescence. A major problem with this theory is that it is based on studies of males, but the findings have been generalized to females. Subsequent research based on the identity development of girls reveals a different pattern—one in which close relationships are of central importance (see Jean Baker Miller, this volume). Before this research, the pattern of identity development typical of males was considered the norm, while the different path typical of girls was viewed as deficient. That is, the female emphasis on intimacy was interpreted as dependency, which was viewed as a weakness. The feminist perspective points out the male bias in this model, as well as the importance of connections to others in the formation of a healthy identity. The central research focus of this perspective becomes the pinpointing of personal and social factors that aid the creation of a connected but unique self, and which discourage a loss of self.

The first reading in this section is a chapter from the book titled, *Reviving Ophelia: Saving the Selves of Adolescent Girls,* by Mary Pipher. In it, Pipher describes the cultural pressures on girls beginning at around age 12 to disown their true selves and to replace it with false, more socially acceptable selves. Through her interviews and case studies, Pipher discovered that to avoid social rejection, many girls learn to be nice rather than honest (because girls who speak the truth are labeled as bitches), and to focus their creative energy and dreams on the pursuit of physical perfection. As self-worth comes to depend more and more on external approval, the internal (authentic) self withers from lack of use. Pipher believes that this cultural training in femininity deprives adolescent girls of their humanity. To prevent this tragic loss, she helps girls to develop "intelligent resistance" to the social pressures to disown the authentic self.

Unfortunately, most of the research to date on girls' identity development is based on the experiences of white, middle-class teens. Just as it is a mistake to generalize to females based on the experiences of males, it is inappropriate to assume that the identity development of adolescent girls from diverse backgrounds is identical to that of white, middle-class girls. For example, several of the black adolescent girls that Pipher interviewed were trained to view femininity in terms of assertiveness and strength. Similarly, research reported in the reading titled "Body Image and Weight Concerns Among African American and White Adolescent Females: Differences That Make a Difference," by Sheila Parker and her colleagues, reveals that girls from African American communities are often encouraged to develop and nurture their authentic selves.

Another important aspect of life during adolescence are the physical changes that accompany puberty. On the positive side, these changes give rise to exciting opportunities for new and gratifying sexual and emotional experiences. However, in certain contexts, these changes may also contribute to common problems of adolescence such as depression, teen pregnancy, and eating disorders. Two of the readings in this section address these changes.

In the reading, "Putting a Big Thing into a Little Hole: Teenage Girls' Accounts of Sexual Initiation," Sharon Thompson reveals two different stories of first sexual encounters (one passive and one active), and relates the stories to the social and family contexts surrounding them. Her interviews with 100 sexually active teens from diverse backgrounds reveal that the majority come from environments that inhibit early sexual self-pleasuring and sexual knowledge and tend to experience their first intercourse completely unprepared and passive. They commonly describe the encounter as "something that just happened," and as "disappointing, boring and painful." Several of these girls also reported sexual initiation without consent. Because of their lack of preparation and passive involvement, these girls are at high risk of teen pregnancy, sexually transmitted diseases, and sexual exploitation.

A totally different story was told to Thompson by a smaller group of about 25 percent of the teens she interviewed. Labeled as "pleasure narrators" by Thompson, these teens recount childhood sexual curiosity and self-pleasuring, and considerable sexual initiative and pleasure in later years. These teens are sexually initiated in a context of family and friends who think childhood masturbation is healthy rather than sinful, who reject the double standard of sexuality for males and females, and who encourage the pursuit of bodily pleasure. These teens were at much lower risk of pregnancy, diseases, and exploitation than those who recounted the first story because they were much more likely to take charge of their sexual behavior and feelings.

The final reading in this section, "Body Image and Weight Concerns among African American and White Adolescent Females: Differences That Make a Difference," outlines differences in body image and dieting behaviors between white and African American adolescent females following puberty. It also pinpoints the cultural factors that underlie these differences. Research shows that the majority of white adolescent females are involved in some form of dieting. It also reveals that cases of anorexia (self-starvation) and bulimia (binging and purging) are comparatively rare among African American females. The authors attribute these findings to differences in cultural standards for acceptable body weights, and different conceptions of beauty. Their own data, drawn from a three-year longitudinal study on dieting, smoking, and body image, suggest that white adolescent females are often taught to equate thinness with social acceptability and happiness, and to compete with other women for social approval based on appearance. Compared to white females, African American females are more likely to grow up in environments where a girl's character is valued over her physical attributes (although physical appearance is certainly valued too), and where competition and envy among women are considerably less common.

Reading 1   Reviving Ophelia:
Saving the Selves of Adolescent Girls

MARY PIPHER

Questions to Consider:

1. What does Pipher mean by the concept "false self," and how does she account for its development and maintenance in adolescent girls?

2. Which description do you (or a female close to you, if you are male) fit best, the "false self" or the "true (authentic) self"? Explain your choice.

3. In your experience, do people respond to the "false self" differently than they respond to the "true self," as Pipher claims? If so, what effect have you observed on behavior—either your own or that of someone close to you?

4. What does Pipher mean by the concept, "intelligent resistance"? Describe ways in which you resist intelligently, or can support a female to resist intelligently.

CAYENNE (15)

In a home video made when she was ten, Cayenne was wiry and scrappy, all sixty-eight pounds of her focused on the ball as she ran down the soccer field. Her red ponytail bobbed, her face shone with sweat as she ducked in and around the other players, always hustling. When she scored a goal, she held her arms over her head in a moment of self-congratulation. She tossed her parents a proud smile and moved into position for another play.

Her parents loved her willingness to take on the universe. One day she dressed up like a belly dancer, the next like an astronaut. She liked adults and babies, boys and girls, dogs and sparrows. An absolute democrat, Cayenne treated everyone with respect, and she expected the same.

When outraged, she took on the world. She got a black eye from fighting with a boy who said that girls couldn't play soccer. Once she dunked a much older boy who was throwing rocks at a little turtle. She threatened to hit kids who were racist. Because she was good at standing up for herself and concerned with justice, her teachers predicted she'd go to law school.

In elementary school Cayenne didn't fret much about her appearance. She weighed in once a year at the doctor's office and was pleased with gains in her height and weight chart. She wore jeans and T-shirts unless forced to dress up. Her mother had to beg her to go shopping and remind her to brush her hair.

She walked to school every day with her best friend, Chelsea. She and Chelsea biked together, watched television, played on the same ball teams and helped each other with chores. They talked about everything—parents, school, sports and interests. They shared their dreams. Chelsea wanted to be a pilot, and Cayenne wanted to be a doctor. They made up elaborate fantasies in which Chelsea would fly Cayenne into a remote Alaskan village to deliver a baby or amputate the leg of a fisherman.

Cayenne liked school. Her grades were good and she loved projects, especially science projects. Twice she was on the Olympics of the Mind team. She'd known most of the kids in her class since kindergarten. She played ball with them and went to their houses for birthday parties.

Cayenne got along well with her parents. Marla, her older sister, had been the moodier and more disobedient child. As an adolescent, Marla sneaked out of the house to drink with her friends. Cayenne felt sorry for her parents when Marla yelled or made them worry, and she promised she would never act that way.

Of course, Cayenne wasn't perfect. She'd never liked to clean her room and was fidgety in church. She preferred junk food to fruits and vegetables. About twice a year Cayenne would be cranky and sullen for a day, but mostly she was easy-going. Bad days were so rare that they were events, like Groundhog Day. Her parents came to depend on Cayenne as their emotional centerboard, and they jokingly called her "Old Faithful."

At twelve, Cayenne had her first period. As her body grew rapidly, it became awkward and unpredictable. She gained weight, especially in her hips, and she got acne. Cayenne moved from her neighborhood school to a junior high with 2,000 students. She was nervous the first day because she'd heard rumors that seventh-graders' heads were stuffed in the toilets and that boys pulled down the girls' blouses. Fortunately these things didn't happen, but she came home upset that some boys teased her and that the girls wore makeup and expensive clothes. She was criticized for her JCPenney jeans, and even Chelsea begged her to give up soccer practice and spend Saturday at the mall.

Cayenne grew quieter and less energetic. For the first time she needed to be coaxed into doing things with the family. She stopped wanting hugs from her parents and brushed them away when they approached her. She didn't laugh or talk to them.

Her parents expected some of this. When Cayenne became self-conscious about her appearance, it saddened them, but they knew this was "normal." They were more upset when she quit playing soccer and when her grades dropped, even in science, which Cayenne now considered hard and boring.

Meanwhile Chelsea's parents divorced and Chelsea fell in with a wild crowd. She invited Cayenne to join and called her a "Muffy" when she hesitated. Eventually Cayenne became part of the group. Her parents suspected that this crowd might be using alcohol or drugs. They encouraged Cayenne to do more with other girls, but she complained about cliques. They tried to steer her toward sports and school activities, but she felt these things were for nerds.

I met Cayenne the winter of her ninth-grade year. Her family physician had referred her to me after she was diagnosed with herpes. He believed that the family and Cayenne needed help dealing with this infectious disease.

She scrunched between her parents wearing a T-shirt that said "If you don't like loud music, you're too fucking old." Her body posture signaled "My parents can force me to be here but nobody can make me talk." When I offered her a soda, she rolled her eyes and said, "Color me excited."

Her mother said, "Cayenne acts like she's allergic to us. Everything we do is wrong."

Her dad talked about her grades, her friends, her herpes and depression, but most of all he mourned their lost relationship. Cayenne had been so close to them and so much fun. She was no longer "Old Faithful"—her bad days outnumbered her good. He thought that even Marla had been easier. At least she hadn't contracted a sexually transmitted disease. After he shared his concerns, he asked, "Does Cayenne need to be hospitalized, or is she just acting like a fifteen-year-old?"

Good question, I thought to myself. Later I met with Cayenne alone. Her blue eyes were icy under her frizzy red hair. She glared at me, almost daring me to make her talk. I sensed that while her surface behavior was angry and withdrawn, underneath she was hurting. I searched for a way to begin.

Finally Cayenne asked, "Do shrinks analyze dreams?"

"Do you have one?"

Cayenne told me of a recurring dream in which she was asleep in her upstairs bedroom. She heard footsteps on the stairs and knew who was coming. She listened, terrified, as the steps grew louder. An old man leading a goat walked into her room. He had a long, sharp knife. Cayenne lay in her bed unable to move while he began slicing at her toes. He sliced off pieces of her and fed her to the goat. She usually awoke when he reached her knees. She'd be covered with sweat and her heart would be racing wildly. Afterward she was afraid to go back to sleep for fear the man would return.

When she finished I asked her what she thought the dream meant. She said, "It means I'm afraid of being cut up and eaten alive."

Over the next few months Cayenne talked in fragments, almost in code. Sometimes she talked so softly that I couldn't hear her. She wasn't happy in junior high and missed her old school. She missed her sister, Marla, who was away at college. Although she was sure it was they, not she, who had changed, Cayenne missed the closeness she had had with her parents.

Cayenne's demeanor was cautious and her speech elliptical, but she kept coming. She hated her looks. She thought her hair was too bright,

her hips and thighs too flabby. She tried to lose weight but couldn't. She dyed her hair, but it turned a weird purple color and dried out. She felt almost every girl was prettier. She said, "Let's face it, I'm a dog."

She didn't feel comfortable around her old friends. We talked about the girls in her class who teased her about her clothes and about the boys who gave her a hard time. Cayenne had problems with most of her friends. Everything was unpredictable. One week she felt reasonably comfortable and accepted, the next she felt like a pariah. She told her friends secrets only to have them spread all over the school. She was included one day in a clique and left out the next. Some days guys called her a slut, other days these same boys would flirt with her.

She felt pressure to use drugs and alcohol. She said, "I was the perfect angel in grade school. I never planned to smoke or drink, but all of a sudden, alcohol was everywhere. Even the president of the Just Say No Club got loaded all the time."

School, which had once been fun, was now a torment. She felt stupid in her math and science classes and bored in everything else. She said to me, "School's just the way the government babysits kids my age."

We talked about her parents' rules, which had grown much stricter after the herpes. Her protests were surprisingly weak. She felt ambivalent about her parents—part of her felt guilty about all the fights with them, while another part blamed them for not understanding the pressure she was under and keeping her safe.

I recommended she write down three things every day that she felt proud of. I asked her to write me a letter telling me her good qualities. She wrote that she was proud of mowing the lawn, doing dishes and going to church with her grandmother. As for good qualities, she liked her navel and her feet. When I pressed her for personality characteristics, she liked her courage and directness. At least, she could remember being that way.

One session, dressed in sweats and red-nosed from a bad cold, Cayenne told me that Chelsea was afraid she was pregnant. She had missed a period and showed positive on a home testing kit. We had a general discussion of girls getting pregnant, teenage mothers, abortion and birth control pills. Cayenne was happy to discuss her friend's sexual behavior, but volunteered nothing about her own.

The next session she said that Chelsea was not pregnant and had renounced sex until she was sixteen. She and Chelsea had gone to the movies to celebrate. We talked about *Mermaids,* the movie they had seen, in which a teenage girl has graphic sex with a guy she barely knows. I asked Cayenne what she thought of that. She said, "It tells it like it is."

I'd just seen *Medicine Man,* the story of a male scientist who is in the rain forest searching for a cure for cancer. Sean Connery is visited by a female scientist forty years younger than he, wearing short shorts and a tight, low-cut top. He's shocked to find that a scientist is female and refuses to work with her. She's snooty and terrified of snakes. Then she has an accident, Sean saves her, and she falls weeping into his arms. Reduced to a helpless blob of jelly, the female scientist becomes more feminine and likable. She follows Sean around and he rewards her with smiles and caresses. In the end she gives up her career to help him find the cure for cancer.

I thought it was sexist and told her why. "This movie says it's okay for women to be scientists if they are beautiful, young and seductive. But they must allow themselves to be rescued by a man and give up their careers to serve his needs."

As I wondered aloud if a movie like this could influence a girl's grades in science, I told Cayenne about the MTV I had watched in a hotel room in Chicago. I was shocked by the sexual lyrics and scenes. In the first video, openmouthed and moaning women writhed around the male singer. In the second video, four women with vacant eyes gyrated in low-cut dresses and high

black boots. Their breasts and bottoms were photographed more frequently than their faces. When I expressed dismay, she said, "That's nothing; you should see the Guns 'N' Roses videos."

We talked about *Silence of the Lambs.* Much to my dismay, she insisted on describing to me the pictures of skinned women and oozing body parts. I realized as she talked how different we were. Violence and casual sex that upset me didn't bother her. In fact, Cayenne was proud of being able to watch scary and graphic scenes—it proved she wasn't a wimp. Despite our different reactions to media, the talk raised important issues—lookism, sexism, cultural stereotypes of men and women, and the importance of sex and violence in movies.

Finally Cayenne was ready to talk about her own sexual experiences, at first in a tentative way, and later in a more relaxed manner. She made fun of the school films with their embryos and cartoon sperm that looked like tadpoles. She said her parents told her to wait for sex until she was out of high school and involved with someone whom she loved.

I asked, "How does your experience fit with what your parents told you?"

Cayenne looked at me wide-eyed. "My parents don't know anything about sex."

She pushed back her frizzy bangs. "In seventh grade everyone was sex-crazy. Kids kept asking me if I did it, if I wanted to get laid, stuff like that. Guys would grab at me in the halls. I was shocked, but I didn't show it. Later I got used to it."

By the middle of her eighth-grade year, Cayenne wanted to have sex. Her friends said it was fun and they teased her about being a virgin. But she was scared—she wondered if it would hurt, if she would get AIDS or become pregnant or if the boy would lose respect for her. She knew that "boys who have sex are studs, but girls who do it are sluts."

The summer before ninth grade she and Chelsea went to an unsupervised party. A guy she knew from the Olympics of the Mind team was there. Tim had been innocent and clean-cut in sixth grade. Now he was a sophomore with long hair pulled back in a headband and a sarcastic sense of humor.

Tim's friend had invited ten girls and nine guys. He opened his parents' liquor cabinet and poured créme de menthe for the girls and scotch for the guys. Cayenne hated the cough-syrupy taste of liqueur, but because she was nervous, she drank it. Tim came over and sat by Cayenne. He complimented her shirt and joked about all the geeks at the party. He poured refills. Tim's friend put on a Madonna tape and turned off all the lights.

Cayenne was nervous and excited. Tim put his arm around her and kissed her on the forehead. They whispered for a while, then began to make out. All the other kids were doing the same thing or more. Some moved off into other rooms.

Cayenne told me, "I knew this would be the night. I was scared, but ready. I was surprised by how fast things happened. We had sex in the first hour of the party."

After that night she and Tim called each other for the next month. They talked about school, music and movies—never sex. They lived in different parts of town and couldn't figure out how to meet each other. Twice they made elaborate plans that fell through. After a while both became interested in kids at their own schools and they drifted apart.

I asked her how she felt about Tim now. Cayenne rubbed her forehead. "I wish it had been more romantic."

Cayenne was a typical therapy client. She had had a reasonably happy childhood. With puberty, the changes and challenges in her life overwhelmed her, at least temporarily. Her grades fell, she dropped out of sports and relinquished her dream of being a doctor. As she moved from the relatively protected space of an elementary school into the more complex world of junior high, all her relationships grew turbulent. She had decisions to make about adult issues such as alcohol and sex. While she was figuring things out, she contracted herpes.

When I first worked with girls like Cayenne, I was lost myself. I had been educated by male psychologists in the 1970s. With the exception of Carol Gilligan's work, almost all theory about teenagers had been authored by men such as Lawrence Kohlberg and E. H. Erikson, who had mainly studied boys.

I found girls to be obsessed with complicated and intense relationships. They felt obligated and resentful, loving and angry, close and distant, all at the same time with the same people. Sexuality, romance and intimacy were all jumbled together and needed sorting. Their symptoms seemed connected to their age and their common experiences. Certain themes, such as concern with weight, fear of rejection and the need for perfection, seemed rooted in cultural expectations for women rather than in the "pathology" of each individual girl. Girls struggled with mixed messages: Be beautiful, but beauty is only skin deep. Be sexy, but not sexual. Be honest, but don't hurt anyone's feelings. Be independent, but be nice. Be smart, but not so smart that you threaten boys.

Adolescent girls presented me with all kinds of problems that my education and experience didn't help me solve. When I stubbornly tried traditional methods of psychotherapy, they didn't work. Girls dropped out of therapy, or even worse, they came in obediently, chatted obligingly and accomplished nothing. Because they were my most difficult cases, I thought a great deal about my adolescent clients. I wanted to conceptualize their problems in a way that actually led to positive action, and I tried to connect their surface behaviors with their deeper struggles. I found help from the writings of Alice Miller.

Alice Miller was an expert on the sacrifice of wholeness. In *The Drama of the Gifted Child,* she describes how some of her patients lost their true selves in early childhood. She believed that as young children her patients faced a difficult choice: They could be authentic and honest, or they could be loved. If they chose wholeness, they were abandoned by their parents. If they chose love, they abandoned their true selves.

Her patients' parents, because of their own childhood experiences, regarded parts of their children's personalities as unacceptable. They taught their children that only a small range of thoughts, emotions and behaviors would be tolerated. The children disowned that which wasn't tolerated. If anger was not tolerated, they acted as if they felt no anger. If sexual feelings were not permitted, they acted as if they had no sexual urges.

As children, her patients chose parental approval and experienced a loss of their true selves. They stopped expressing unacceptable feelings and engaging in the unacceptable behaviors, at least in front of adults. They stopped sharing the unsanctioned thoughts. The part of them that was unacceptable went underground and eventually withered from lack of attention. Or that part of them that was unacceptable was projected onto others.

Miller believed that as the true self was disowned, the false self was elevated. If others approved, the false self felt validated and the person was temporarily happy. With the false self in charge, all validation came from outside the person. If the false self failed to gain approval, the person was devastated.

This loss of the true self was so traumatic that her patients repressed it. They had only a vague recollection of what was lost, a sense of emptiness and betrayal. They felt vulnerable and directionless—happy when praised and devastated when ignored or criticized. They were like sailboats without centerboards. Their self-worth changed with whatever way the wind blew.

Miller contrasted adults with false selves to authentic adults who experienced all feelings, including pain, in an honest way. Authentic adults accepted themselves rather than waiting for others to accept them. This state of psychological health she called vibrancy.

Her weapon against mental illness was "the discovery and emotional acceptance of the truth of each individual." She encouraged her patients to accept what happened to them as young children. Only then could they become authentic people.

Miller wrote about this process as if it were an either-or phenomenon. But in fact this process of creating false selves in children follows a continuum that ranges from basic socialization to abuse. It is present in all families: All parents accept and reject some of their children's behaviors and teach children to sacrifice some wholeness to social acceptability. However, even the most authoritarian parents usually don't succeed in totally destroying the true selves of their children.

Miller wrote in a different time and place about a different kind of family from the average family in America in the 1990s. What is timeless and important about Miller's work is her description of the process by which the self splits. With great clarity she describes the splitting into political versus personal selves. She documents the damage that this splitting can do and describes the process by which healing can occur.

I think that a process analogous to Miller's occurs for girls in early adolescence. Whereas Miller sees the parents as responsible for the splitting in early childhood, I see the culture as splitting adolescent girls into true and false selves. The culture is what causes girls to abandon their true selves and take up false selves.

Often parents are fighting hard to save their daughters' true selves. Parents encourage their daughters to stay with their childhood interests and argue with them over issues such as early sexual activity, makeup, diets and dating. They encourage athletics and math and science classes. They dislike the media values and resist cultural definitions of their daughters as consumers or sex objects. They do not want their daughters to sell their souls for popularity. They are fighting to preserve wholeness and authenticity.

But because of girls' developmental stage, parents have limited influence. Cayenne, for example, would barely speak to her parents. As daughters move into the broader culture, they care what their friends, not their parents, think. They model themselves after media stars, not parental ideals.

With puberty, girls face enormous cultural pressure to split into false selves. The pressure comes from schools, magazines, music, television, advertisements and movies. It comes from peers. Girls can be true to themselves and risk abandonment by their peers, or they can reject their true selves and be socially acceptable. Most girls choose to be socially accepted and split into two selves, one that is authentic and one that is culturally scripted. In public they become who they are supposed to be.

Authenticity is an "owning" of all experience, including emotions and thoughts that are not socially acceptable. Because self-esteem is based on the acceptance of all thoughts and feelings as one's own, girls lose confidence as they "disown" themselves. They suffer enormous losses when they stop expressing certain thoughts and feelings.

Cayenne exemplifies the process of disowning the true self. With puberty she went from being a whole, authentic person to a diminished, unhappy version of herself. Her dream of being cut into pieces and fed to a goat reflects quite exactly her loss of wholeness. Many girls report dreams like Cayenne's. They dream of drowning, of being paralyzed and of being stuck in quicksand. A common dream is of being attacked and unable to scream or fight back in any way. The attackers can vary—men, schoolmates, insects or snakes. The important elements of the dream are the attack, the paralysis and the imminent destruction of the self.

With adolescence, Cayenne begins to operate from a false self. When she says "Let's face it, I'm a dog," she is accepting society's right to define her solely on the basis of her appearance. She is even defining herself that way. Earlier, she fought to save a turtle or defend an ideal, now she

is used to being "grabbed," and no longer protests when her bodily integrity is threatened.

As she adopts a false self, Cayenne loses her confidence and calmness. She loses her clear, direct speech. She distances from her parents, who encourage her to remain true to her self. Her surface behavior and her deeper feelings are not congruent. She no longer behaves in a way that meets her true needs.

Her decisions are not thoughtful, conscious choices, but rather reactions to peer pressure. She's pressured to use chemicals and to have sex. Cayenne is off course and unfocused. Her long-term goal to be a doctor is abandoned.

Cayenne experienced what all girls experience in early adolescence—rigorous training for the female role. At this time girls are expected to sacrifice the parts of themselves that our culture considers masculine on the altar of social acceptability and to shrink their souls down to a petite size. Claudia Bepko and Jo-Ann Krestan call it "indoctrination into the code of goodness," which they argue is essentially unchanged since the fifties. The rules remain the same: be attractive, be a lady, be unselfish and of service, make relationships work and be competent without complaint.

This is when girls learn to be nice rather than honest. Cayenne told me, "The worst punishment is to be called a bitch. That will shut anyone up." She continued, "Girls are supposed to smile. If I'm having a bad day, teachers and kids tell me to smile. I've never heard them say that to a guy."

Adolescent girls discover that it is impossible to be both feminine and adult. Psychologist I. K. Broverman's now classic study documents this impossibility. Male and female participants in the study checked off adjectives describing the characteristics of healthy men, healthy women and healthy adults. The results showed that while people describe healthy men and healthy adults as having the same qualities, they describe healthy women as having quite different qualities than healthy adults. For example, healthy women were described as passive, dependent and illogical, while healthy adults were active, independent and logical. In fact, it was impossible to score as both a healthy adult and a healthy woman.

The rules for girls are confusing and the deck is stacked against them, but they soon learn that this is the only game in town. One friend remembered that when she was in seventh grade, she wished someone would tell her what the rules were. She said, "It was so hard to play the games correctly without knowing the rules."

While the rules for proper female behavior aren't clearly stated, the punishment for breaking them is harsh. Girls who speak frankly are labeled as bitches. Girls who are not attractive are scorned. The rules are reinforced by the visual images in soft- and hard-core pornography, by song lyrics, by casual remarks, by criticisms, by teasing and by jokes. The rules are enforced by the labeling of a woman like Hillary Rodham Clinton as a "bitch" simply because she's a competent, healthy adult.

Many of the girls I teach at the university can remember some of their choices—the choice to be quiet in class rather than risk being called a brain, the choice to diet rather than eat when they were hungry, the choice to go out with the right crowd rather than the crowd they liked, the choice to be polite rather than honest, or to be pretty rather than have fun. One girl put it this way: "You have to suffer to be beautiful." But generally, girls are inarticulate about the trauma at the time it happens. The issues that adolescent girls struggle with are barely discussed in the culture. Language doesn't fit their experiences. Protest is called delinquency, frustration is called bitchiness, withdrawal is called depression and despair is labeled hormonal. Many battles for the self are won and lost without reports from the front lines.

There are many different experiences that cause girls to relinquish their true selves. In early adolescence girls learn how important appearance is in defining social acceptability. Attrac-

tiveness is both a necessary and a sufficient condition for girls' success. This is an old, old problem. Helen of Troy didn't launch a thousand ships because she was a hard worker. Juliet wasn't loved for her math ability.

The *Ladies' Guide to Health,* written in 1888, pointed out that while boys were dressed for winter in wool pants, jackets and sweaters, girls were dressed in silks and laces that fell gracefully from their shoulders and left their arms exposed. The author bemoaned the deaths of girls from diphtheria and pneumonia.

Teen magazines are a good example of the training in lookism that girls receive. Once when my daughter was sick I wanted to buy her some light reading. When I picked up her antibiotics at the drugstore, I leafed through the magazines. The models all looked six feet tall and anorexic. The emphasis was on makeup, fashion and weight. Girls were encouraged to spend money and to diet and work out in order to develop the looks that would attract boys. Apparently attracting boys was the sole purpose of life, because the magazines had no articles on careers, hobbies, politics or academic pursuits. I couldn't find one that wasn't preaching the message "Don't worry about feeling good or being good, worry about looking good."

Girls come of age in a misogynistic culture in which men have most political and economic power. Girls read a history of Western civilization that is essentially a record of men's lives. As Dale Spender says, "Women's accomplishments are relegated to the lost and found." As girls study Western civilization, they become increasingly aware that history is the history of men. History is His Story, the story of *Man*kind.

I discovered this when I read H. G. Wells' *Outline of History* and Winston Churchill's *History of the Western World.* Both are primarily histories of war and the distribution of property. Women's lives were ignored except as they influenced the course of men's lives. I remember wondering, Where were the women during all these events? My daughter made the same observation about her history text: "It's so boring, just a bunch of kings and generals fighting each other. What were the women doing anyway?"

Girls move into a culture with a Constitution that gave white men, not all Americans, the right to vote, and that has yet to pass an equal rights amendment. They join a culture in which historical documents proclaim the rights of man. As Tillie Olson observed, women's voices have been silenced through the ages, and the silencing continues in the present.

By junior high girls sense their lack of power, but usually they cannot say what they sense. They see that mostly men are congressmen, principals, bankers and corporate executives. They notice that famous writers, musicians and artists are mostly men. But they don't focus on the political—their complaints are personal.

What girls say about gender and power issues depends on how they are asked. When I ask adolescent girls if they are feminists, most say no. To them, feminism is a dirty word, like communism or fascism. But if I ask if they believe men and women should have equal rights, they say yes. When I ask if their schools are sexist, they are likely to say no. But if I ask if they are ever harassed sexually at their school, they say yes and tell me stories. If I ask who writes most of the material they study at school, they know it's men. If I ask who is more likely to be a principal, they say a man. If I ask who has more power, they say men.

I encourage girls to think about these issues and bring me examples of discrimination. One girl noticed that the mountains in Colorado that were named for men had their last names. She brought in a map to point out Mount Adams, Mount Audubon, Babcock Peak, Mount Edwards, Mount Garfield, Hilliard Peak, Mount Sneffels and Mount Richthofen. The few natural features that are named for women are named with only the woman's first name, such as Mount Alice, Mount Emma, Mount Eva, Lake Emma-

line, Lake Agnes, Maggie Gulch and Mount Flora.

Girls complain that they do more chores than their brothers. Or that they make less money baby-sitting than their brothers do mowing lawns. Or that parents praise brothers' accomplishments more than theirs. An athlete complained that her track coach spent more time with the boys. Another noted that only the female gymnasts had to weigh in at practices. A softball player complained that sports coverage was better for men's events than for her own. A musician noticed that most rock stars were male.

I was a reader and I remember the trouble I had with misogynistic writers. I loved Tolstoy, but it broke my heart to realize when I read *The Kreutzer Sonata* that he detested women. Later I had the same experience with Schopenhauer, Henry Miller and Norman Mailer. My daughter, Sara, read Aristotle in her philosophy class. One night she read a section aloud to me and said, "This guy doesn't respect women." I wondered what it means to her that one of the wisest men of the ages is misogynistic.

It's important for girls to be exposed to more women writers, but it's equally important to change the way women are portrayed in the media. Not many girls read Tolstoy today, but almost all watch television. On the screen they see women mainly depicted as half-clad and half-witted, often awaiting rescue by quick-thinking, fully clothed men. I ask girls to watch the ways women are portrayed on television. We'll talk about their observations and I'll ask, "What does this teach you about the role of women?"

Cayenne noticed that television almost never features old, heavy or unattractive women. She also noticed that on TV even if a woman is a doctor or a scholar, she looks like a *Playboy* bunny. Another noticed that women are often victims of violence. Lots of plots have to do with women being raped, beaten, chased or terrorized by men. She also noticed that some sex scenes have scary music and some violent scenes have sexy music so that sex and violence are all mixed up.

She noticed that male voices carry more authority in commercials. Men are the doctors and scientists who give product endorsements. She observed that women's bodies sell products that have nothing directly to do with women—tires, tractors, liquor and guns.

Another client hated the Old Milwaukee beer ads that feature the Swedish Bikini Team in which a group of bikini-clad women parachute onto a beach to fulfill the sexual fantasies of a beer-drinking man. She said, "Women are portrayed as expensive toys, as the ultimate recreation." She brought in cologne ads. A Royal Copenhagen ad shows a semi-naked woman kissing a man. The tag line is: "Some of the wildest things happen below deck." A Santa Fe ad has a couple in bed with the woman's body in the foreground and it reads: "It's pretty hot in Santa Fe." She showed me a Courvoisier ad showing a woman in a short tight skirt sitting on a man's lap locked in a passionate embrace. She said, "It looks like he'll get sex if he buys this alcohol."

To my embarrassment, one client brought in a magazine from my own waiting room. It was an alumni magazine that features arts and sciences. In the glossy thirty-five-page magazine, there were forty-five photographs, forty-four of which pictured males. The one female pictured was on the last page in an article on ballet classes. A male teacher posed with a young girl in a tutu.

My psychology students are aware that the field is male-dominated. While 90 percent of the students are women, almost all the theorists and the famous therapists are men. It's hard to find books about psychotherapy written by women or films of women psychotherapists.

Ironically, bright and sensitive girls are most at risk for problems. They are likely to understand the implications of the media around them and be alarmed. They have the mental equipment to pick up our cultural ambivalence about women, and yet they don't have the cognitive,

emotional and social skills to handle this information. They are paralyzed by complicated and contradictory data that they cannot interpret. They struggle to resolve the unresolvable and to make sense of the absurd. It's this attempt to make sense of the whole of adolescent experience that overwhelms bright girls.

Less perceptive girls may miss the meaning of sexist ads, music and shows entirely. They tend to deny and oversimplify problems. They don't attempt to integrate aspects of their experience or to "connect the dots" between cultural events and their own lives. Rather than process their experience, they seal in confusion.

Often bright girls look more vulnerable than their peers who have picked up less or who have chosen to deal with all the complexity by blocking it out. Later, bright girls may be more interesting, adaptive and authentic, but in early adolescence they just look shelled.

Girls have four general ways in which they can react to the cultural pressures to abandon the self. They can conform, withdraw, be depressed or get angry. Whether girls feel depression or anger is a matter of attribution—those who blame themselves feel depressed, while those who blame others feel angry. Generally they blame their parents. Of course, most girls react with some combination of the four general ways.

To totally accept the cultural definitions of femininity and conform to the pressures is to kill the self. Girls who do this are the "Muffys" and "Barbie dolls" with hair and smiles in place and a terrible deadness underneath. They are the ones who make me want to shout, "Don't give up, fight back." Often girls who try to conform overshoot the mark. For example, girls with anorexia have tried too hard to be slender, feminine and perfect. They have become thin, shiny packages, outwardly carefully wrapped and inwardly a total muddle.

Girls have long been trained to be feminine at considerable cost to their humanity. They have long been evaluated on the basis of appearance and caught in myriad double binds: achieve, but not too much; be polite, but be yourself; be feminine and adult; be aware of our cultural heritage, but don't comment on the sexism. Another way to describe this femininity training is to call it false self-training. Girls are trained to be less than who they really are. They are trained to be what the culture wants of its young women, not what they themselves want to become.

America today is a girl-destroying place. Everywhere girls are encouraged to sacrifice their true selves. Their parents may fight to protect them, but their parents have limited power. Many girls lose contact with their true selves, and when they do, they become extraordinarily vulnerable to a culture that is all too happy to use them for its purposes.

Alice Miller said, "It is what we cannot see that makes us sick." It's important for girls to explore the impact the culture has on their growth and development. They all benefit from, to use an old-fashioned term, consciousness-raising. Once girls understand the effects of the culture on their lives, they can fight back. They learn that they have conscious choices to make and ultimate responsibility for those choices. Intelligent resistance keeps the true self alive.

Reading 2   Putting a Big Thing into a Little Hole: Teenage Girls' Accounts of Sexual Initiation

SHARON THOMPSON

Questions to Consider:

1. In what key ways do the two stories about sexual initiation differ, and how does Thompson account for these differences?

2. How well do each of these stories fit with your own experiences and/or observations? Is there a third story? Explain.

3. How does each story make you feel about your own sexual self?

4. Why, according to Thompson, do most girls need an erotic education, and what would it consist of? What is your reaction to her recommendations?

The rise in adolescent coitus in the late 1970s and early 1980s provoked many studies of teenage contraceptive practice. Drawing on 400 in-depth interviews with teenage girls, this article considers the quality of teenage girls' sexual initiations, comparing the family and sexual histories of girls who describe sexual initiation as painful, boring, or disappointing with those of girls who emphasize sexual curiosity, desire, and pleasure. In conclusion, the article draws several recommendations for sexual education.

Reprinted with permission of the Society for the Scientific Study of Sexuality. *The Journal of Sex Research (JSR)*. Vol. 27, No. 3, 85–106.

Thanks to Carole S. Vance for several heartening and clarifying discussions and to the teenage girls who understood so well that talk is the first step toward change. The comments of Edna Haber, Ann Snitow, and Carol Pollis made the process of revision a great deal easier than it would otherwise have been.

In the expansive economic growth and social upheavals of the 1960s and 70s, competing interests—family planning, juvenile justice, and feminism—rewrote the rules of adolescence, changing the relationship between "gender and generation" (McRobbie & Nava, 1984). By the late 1970s, when the largest generation of teenagers in U.S. history came of age, teenage girls had new rights to due process, privacy, and autonomy, and they could obtain contraception and abortion without parental consent (Moore & Burt, 1982; Paul et al., 1976). These developments were by no means unilateral or stable. The Supreme Court affirmed age of consent laws in the early 1980s, and adolescent reproductive autonomy and contemporary juvenile justice arrangements remain hotly contested political issues. But school, the body, and the zeitgeist are the authorities that girls know best. To try teenage sex out made more sense to most girls—even born-again Christian girls—than it had in a hundred years. By the beginning of the 80s, almost 7 in 10 girls under age 20 in metropolitan areas said they had intercourse (Ministry, 1987; Pratt & Hendershot, 1984).

In the past decade and a half, mainstream research has focused on why the majority of teenage girls do not use reliable contraception for first intercourse and why only one in three sexually-active young women always contracept (Trussell, 1988). Major studies have investigated the variables of race, age, sex education, mother-daughter communication, relationship with first partner, and sexual planning, but not sexual arousal. All teenage girls are assumed by these researchers to be perpetually "at risk" of being "swept away" "on the spur" of any moment by "unanticipated, unintentional passion." They don't specify whose desire, and rape did not even arise as a research consideration until the mid-1980s (Cassell, 1984; Moore, Winquist, & Peterson, 1989; Zelnik & Kantner, 1980; Zelnik & Shah, 1983).

Feminists and family-planning counselors, in contrast, have long remarked that girls and women are all too rarely "swept away" by their own sexual desires, which are, as Vance has observed, "suspect from the first tingle, questionable until proven safe, and frequently too expensive when evaluated within the larger cultural framework which poses the question: Is it really worth it?" (Vance, p. 4, 1984). Most ascribe the scarcity of female desire to developmental and social conditions that constrict rather than develop a sense of sexual entitlement and an understanding of how to have pleasure, a view that sexology has, by and large supported (Benjamin, 1988; Chilman, 1983; Clower, 1980; Dodson, 1974; Fine, 1988; Gagnon & Simon, 1973; Kelley, 1983).

This paper explores teenage girls' assessments of early sexual experience and first intercourse. The material is drawn from a 1978–1986 narrative study of 400 teenage girls' sexual, romantic, and reproductive histories. About 75 percent narrated either heterosexual intercourse or extensive lesbian sex-

ual experience. I am working here with a representative subsample of a hundred narratives gathered from the three hundred sexually-initiated girls. The narrators in the subsample all went well beyond answering direct questions to elaborate life stories about sex, romance, or pregnancy. About 15 percent are African-American, another 15 percent are Hispanic–Puerto Rican, Cuban, and Chicana. About a quarter are teenage mothers. Ten percent identified themselves as lesbian; a few more had had sexual experiences with girls but did not identify as lesbian. The interviews took place in the northeast, mid- and southwest. I interviewed all the narrators, some several times, in open-ended sessions. Girls went to great lengths to introduce me to their friends, but they rarely referred across class, race, reproductive status, or even sexual attitude. To obtain multiple perspectives, I began several snowball samples, through various groups as well as personal contacts. The names below are changed for confidentiality.

"Now That I Think about It, Everybody Used the Same Story"

"Everybody talked about it. You know, that was the big thing in school to talk about sex."—16-year-old girl, 1985.

Teenage girls have a wealth of experience in talking about friendship and romance, but sex has traditionally been a ruinous secret for them, and they have mainly kept their lips sealed. Not until the 70s did young college women and men reportedly tell their experiences with similar frequency (Kallen & Stephenson, 1982). In the 1940s sociologist August Hollingshead observed that a "conspiracy of silence" surrounded teenage sex; Kinsey noted the "covert culture" of the 50s. As recently as the 1960s, one researcher observed that young college women only told their friends about having sex when they could construe it as a sign of progress in love. Even then they told far fewer friends than boys did—

an average of two to boys' five (Hollingshead, 1949; Kinsey, 1963; Carns, 1973).

By the early 80s, the talk of initiates was valuable as a source of knowledge, a guidebook to the body. "My first time" had become a staple in girls' oral tradition, but girls still had few conventions to draw on to open or develop the subject. In this study, most girls said that all their experienced friends told the "same story" about first intercourse. However, the "same story" some girls said they heard reversed the "same story" that other girls said they heard.

SAME STORY #1

Asked to describe the circumstances of first coitus, many girls blink and freeze, dropping predicates and leaving passive sentences dangling as if under a posthypnotic suggestion to suppress. "It was something that just happened," they say finally (Rogel et al., 1980). They don't know how it happened.

I tell you, I don't know why or how I did it. Maybe I just did it unconsciously.

And:

I don't know what came over me that night. I really don't. I mean, I can't really answer it. But it happened.

Girls have many reasons to deny sexual volition. Many still believe that they should not be sexual, or have parents and teachers who believe this, and the language of denial is traditional. Nevertheless, the claim these girls make that they don't know what happened is credible under the circumstances they describe. Girls who have received no sexual education at all, say, for example:

I had no idea. I had no idea at all. I knew I would be taking off my clothes, and I knew he'd be taking off his clothes. But as far as

what would happen, I didn't know. I didn't know, you know, that a guy would put his penis in me like that, you know. I didn't know that.

Most girls report some instruction in the biology of intercourse and say they knew but they didn't really know. The facts hadn't really sunk in; there was a cognitive gap.

I didn't really know what I was doing. I knew what I was doing but I didn't actually know *what I was doing.*

While girls who tell stories of sexual anticipation and pleasure describe childhood and preadolescent sexual fantasies and experimentation, the narrators who tell Story #1 speak as if they had no sexual consciousness at all before first penetration—no memories, no experiences. Asked about childhood, they talk about pets, homes, family arguments, best friendships, and crushes, but not about masturbation, sex play, or the development of sexual curiosity or understanding. Some describe themselves as nonsexual, others as presexual (virginal). Even well beyond puberty, the girls who identify as either asexual or virginal cannot believe they chose to have sex:

I'm telling you I did it unconsciously because I wouldn't do a thing like that.

Some passages suggest that part of the problem is that coitus itself comes and goes too fast. In Kinsey's era, petting was the most common adolescent sexual experience for girls (Kinsey, 1953). To the extent that petting represented the outer limits of permissible sexual expression in adolescence, it was notoriously frustrating, as the narrators of the movie "Heavy Petting" hilariously recalled, but petting is also a sexual learning experience, a way to discover and open the trick locks of pleasure.

Petting continued to be a common adolescent sexual practice through the 1960s and into the 1970s (Sorenson, 1973; DeLamater & Mac-Corquodale, 1979), but in the late 1970s and early 80s, many teenagers came to think of petting, including foreplay, as kid stuff. Believing that intercourse was the real thing, they began to rush into bed with almost no sexual preliminaries (Thompson, 1984; Haffner, 1988). Between the instant ejaculation characteristic of teenage boys' sex and the absence of sexual preparation, many girls say they barely realize what is happening before it is over.

It was just like—psssst, one minute here, the next minute it was there. It happened. That was it.

Others report the rude awakening of painful penetration.

The pain was like I couldn't stand it.

And:

It hurt. It hurt a lot. It hurt a lot.

And:

It felt like there was a knife going through me.

Pain has become so much a part of the Grand Guignol lore of teenage sexuality that girls' own stories increase their fear of sex.

Everybody said, "Oh, it's going to really hurt and there's going to be a pool of blood..."

They almost seem to be scaring each other off; or playing dare doubledare.

While girls hold their lovers responsible for virtually all the emotional pain they experience in relationships, they rarely blame them for sexual pain during first coitus. Instead, they blame their own bodies:

It was very, very painful. I don't know. My mother had a very—had a hard time giving birth to us so I think perhaps—to my sister and I both. It took her maybe 48, 36 hours. I think we have small pelvises if that has anything to do with it.

In an uninformed and undesirous state, girls find it hard to distinguish choice and coercion, and they aren't at all certain of how to make such a distinction. They may talk about voluntary first intercourse as involuntary not because they were forced to have sex, but because the sexual experience they choose to have conflicts with their sense of identity. Abby, for example, had first sex with a girlfriend's boyfriend at a keg party. She was seduced, not coerced, after she had "peck kissed" him all night. But even though she did it with him voluntarily, she blamed him on the grounds that what happened was contrary to her belief system but not his. "I really didn't want to because it's her boyfriend." In a supreme act of displacement, she saved her greatest outrage for his girlfriend who comforted her later: His girlfriend should have been angry, she reasoned. "How could she not care?"

Conversely, girls may fail to recognize or name coercion when sex takes place with someone they really care about or have a steady relationship with. Linda's first intercourse took place within a relationship. When she began to talk about the experience, she couched it as "special," adding it put "a special bond" between her boyfriend and her. "We'll always be close." As she continued to tell what happened, it became clear that her steady boyfriend took her totally by surprise.

I was just really stunned.

Thinking it over:

Uhm, probably if I would have had my eyes opened, I would have realized it was going to happen, it was gonna...

The reason "it was gonna happen, it was gonna," was not because, say, petting had become so frustratingly exciting for them both that coitus was inevitable—but because:

> He was over here once and my parents weren't—home—and I didn't realize basically what I got myself into.

She had wanted to "experience" sex but not then:

> I don't think I was emotionally capable of handling it at the time. And I don't know. I GOT REAL MAD AT HIM BUT . . .

She continued to see him for several months, and they continued to have sex. Her assertion, "He'll always be special to me," is an ironic reminder of how important it is to many girls to cherish their first lovers.

Coercion and pain are not the only characteristics of first sex in this group. Boredom is also a feature. Sex is supposed to be great—a major deal, some of the girls in this narrative group say accusingly. By report, it "makes" love and pleasure but for them, it made boredom and disappointment.

> It wasn't that I didn't like it. It was just kind of a letdown.

> It wasn't really that good. There was nothing I really liked about it.

> Oh, why would they even bother to leave that out of the movies?

Some start to say it felt "nice" and then lower the ante or add irony. Cheri had listened in as I conducted an interview with a friend of hers and knew the line of my questions ahead of time. Before I could ask how it was, she filled in:

> Cheri: So. We did it. It was nice—before you ask me that question.

> Q: Yeah? It was really nice?

> Cheri: It was all right. It wasn't nothing to brag to my mother about, but it was nice.

A number of narratives combine pain and boredom:

> It didn't really hurt. It hurt a little bit. It was uncomfortable. I was pretty bored actually. I didn't see anything very nice about it at all.

Others include the pain of first intercourse and their own ignorance as two aspects of "nothing":

> The first time I had sex I was in junior high school. . . . This is the way we used to do it. It would be two girls or three girls and there'd be two or three guys that were, you know, their type. So you'd all play hooky from school and you went over to his house. . . . And I had sex—I didn't even realize what I was doing. He did. It occurred to me that he had done this before but not me. He was like, "Come on, let's go in the bedroom," or whatever. "Take off your clothes and everything." And I had sex just—you know, it was like—I can't say it was rape. . . . To me it, it hurted. And I even bled and everything and I thought my period was coming on or something. But it wasn't that. It was just having sex for the first time. And I got sick after it too. And I said, "Just for this?" It wasn't nothing to me.

The letdown so many girls describe is not wholly physical. It is romantic as well. Girls often expect that having sex will transform an uneven relationship into a blissful fusion or transform their lover into a devotee. When, instead, he cools abruptly, their disappointment pervades the memory of first coitus (Thompson, 1984).

OK, This Is The Way It's Supposed to Be: Lesbian Narratives

Until they began to talk about their first, typically orgasmic, experiences with other girls, teenagers who defined themselves as lesbian frequently sounded more "heterosexual" than "heterosexual" narrators describing heterosexual experience. Perhaps because they have more sexual preparation—more petting and kissing—or perhaps because concerns about sexual identity force them to think consciously about sex, lesbian narrators report more comfort with penetration than girls who take heterosexuality for granted. Barbara thought not caring may have been what made heterosexual coitus easy.

> I guess because it was a sexual energy but there wasn't much real love or affection there.... I thought nothing of just taking off all my clothes and just going into bed. I mean, it didn't—I wasn't shy.

When a male lover does something he has said he would not, lesbian narrators are quick to point an incriminating finger:

> He wasn't supposed to penetrate, and, uhm, he did by mistake. Of course, that was what he said, but I don't think it was a mistake.

But they, too, blame shortfalls in pleasure on themselves, often deducing that pain and boredom prove they are lesbian. Several related determined efforts to change—to learn how to get pleasure out of heterosexual coitus. Two of Yolanda's former female lovers turned to male lovers in senior high school:

> They said it was good. It was fun and it was exciting and they looked forward to doing it again and I said, "OK." They said, "Well, you should try it." And I said, "OK." So—I did.

> Q: Did you report back to your friends?

> A: But I didn't tell them it was boring. I said, "Yeah, it was just as good as you said it was going to be." I'm saying, "Well, no." But you know—I kept trying, because I said, OK, this is the way it's supposed to be. I guess, with time, I'll grow to like it. But it didn't happen.

Out of a Sow's Ear

Many of the same girls who describe pain, boredom, and disappointment nevertheless conclude that first intercourse is "worth it." Love mitigates pain, some girls declare. Pat "just liked being with him." Regina recalled:

> I felt really good in his arms, and it was like a fantasy.

More pragmatically, as if coitus opens a door they couldn't find for themselves, several exulted in their new ability to put in a tampon. (None of the narrators in this group recalled masturbating.) Other girls understand first intercourse as a rite of passage. Even if intercourse seems like "nothing," "a letdown," "a big pain," doing it transforms them into initiates. Enduring pain proves courage and maturity.

> It hurted but I did it.

Others turn their endurance into a proof of superiority over other girls who don't have what it takes to be women. To me it was nothing, they brag.

> I really didn't feel nothing special. Most girls say, "Oh, god, it really hurt, and like that." It was nothing to me. And I had never done it before.

Other girls celebrate resisting or truncating penetration, using vaginal muscles and pelvic thrust to expel the penis. These passages begin to explain why many girls say they aren't "sure" they had sex.

I almost was 15 and that was, that was at a party and, uhm, it wasn't—I didn't even really sleep with him. I really didn't. It was just like for two seconds. And it was just really strange, you know. And I was like Nope.

Expulsion of the penis is frequently a long, graphic, comic story—often told with gales of laughter. Its triumphal quality is virtually unparalleled in the other stories. Hilary's account, for example, combines comedy and victory. When Hilary said she couldn't remember her first date with her boyfriend, I laughed and indicated I was sure she was joking. She said, No, she had been hit on the head when she was very young, and had trouble remembering ever since. As she grew sadder with each "I don't remember," I cut directly to first intercourse. She brightened and launched into a resistance story.

I don't know how it started. It just happened one night. All of a sudden one night.

She was wholly unprepared:

I had never thought about it like that. At all.

They were in the backseat of his car. Although she repeatedly said she was frightened, she rendered the experience itself as a cartoon, treating her panicked pre-initiated self as hilarious.

And it was real funny. I was getting real scared. I was just like backing off and stuff. . . . Everything was like going wrong.

Partly what made the whole thing cartoonlike was that "nothing would just work." The experience had a Boing!—springs popping, skin sticking, knocks, bumps, Laurel & Hardy quality. Her giggles and shrieks conveyed that she wasn't ready for sex without provoking her sometimes violent boyfriend. How could he be angry? She

was too scared, giggly, tight, a cartoon of a child-like virgin. In retrospect, she glowed with pride. She had held her own against a strong and possibly abusive opponent, and she treasured the memory as fiercely as she fought him off.

Some reports of expulsion suggest that proving virginity is one point of resisting penetration. Victoria said she tried to cooperate but it didn't work.

So he starts opening my legs. He's—I was tight, just like you were—boy! talk about clamps!

So he starts opening and opening. It started hurting because it's like—I don't know. It's like trying to put a big thing into a little hole. So he pushed and pushed.

I go, "I'm sorry. I'm scared. Forget about it. I changed my mind."

So he goes, "Okay. So forget about it." So we put our clothes back on. We waited in the room. He—he proposed to me that day as a matter of fact. He said, "Will you marry me?"

I go, "Yeah."

So at about 3 years later, we did get married. That was in August.

Post-Coital Reform

In the wake of a painful or dull first intercourse and romantic disappointment, many girls tell themselves and each other that they'll never have sex again, or they might "but it won't be soon." Rather than the secondary virginity that Right-to-Life literature extols as a second chance at chastity, what follows is a waiting period not for marriage but for desire or for a better boyfriend. After a time, they test the waters; then wait; then test. (When girls are asked the ideal age for first intercourse, they usually state a higher age than that of their own first intercourse, perhaps the age at which intercourse began to pleasure them or they commenced a "committed" relationship [Zabin, 1981; Thompson, 1984]). Each reform is accompanied by the same pattern of denial that precedes first intercourse, and many girls are stunned by sex several times before they realize that they are very likely to have sex again, and prepare for that eventuality by obtaining contraception. Even girls who have been pregnant, or had children, may believe that they will not have sex again until the time is, at last, right. But pregnancy is not the only unhappy ending to this collective story (nor is it necessarily an unhappy ending). The pain, fear, and disappointment that most girls reported especially in the early years of this study were hurtful in and of themselves. They not only decreased the probability of effective contraceptive practice. They undercut girls' sense of well-being and hope and generated depression and amnesia (Thompson, 1984).

In isolation, these grim reports seem to support the various arguments against teenage coitus. But as girls' talk reveals again and again, the most common experience does not tell the whole story, and stories change as culture changes, with experience, with time, with knowledge, with context. Who you are, when you live, who loves you, who is your friend, who taught you, who listens to you, what comes as a surprise: These variables make the differences in sexual experience that they make in life as a whole. Not all girls are as alienated from the sexual body as the narrators above seem to be, nor is first intercourse always painful or boring (Sorenson, 1983; Weiss, 1983, 1985). An increasing minority of teenage girls, about a quarter of my total sample, tell a totally different story of sexual curiosity, exploration, and pleasure. What do these girls say? And who are they? How do they come to construct such a different report?

SAME STORY #2

Those who tell Same Story #2, the pleasure narrators, imagine listeners—friends, parents, a community—who believe in pleasure: who think masturbation and childhood sexuality are good omens, not sins, and that the double standard is a dead issue; who encourage the search for the body's wellsprings and for supportive and exciting lovers. Expecting a compassionate and humorous response, these narrators recall their first sexual experiences well and relate them in lavish, realistic, and often comic detail. Their stories of sexual pleasure have a rich variousness that stands in eloquent contrast to the constrained, repetitive narratives above of pain and boredom. Early sexual experience is a voyage of discovery. The body is a treasure chest that they take with them.

The narrators who told the first story didn't look ahead to sex. They didn't prepare. They didn't explore. Often they didn't even agree to sex. They gave in, they gave up, they gave out. At most they waited. At least, that's how they told it. The pleasure narrators describe taking sexual initiative; satisfying their own sexual curiosity; instigating petting and coital relations. If it's "yes," they say so. If it's not, they say that too. From earliest childhood, they seem to take sexual subjectivity for granted.

The pleasure narrators describe several sources and forms of precoital sexual knowledge and experience. Most tell stories about trying to use tampons. All recount some precoital familiarity with the vagina. Several recall becoming sexually stimulated by things they have read and experiencing orgasm either involuntarily or through masturbation or petting. Caron opened with a childhood dream: "It was all these wedding cakes and I was jumping up and down on a bed with a boy that I liked." Elodia remembered "sex play" in nursery school—running "around naked," playing doctor, and "experimenting with kids my age." Phyllis recalled the mimicry of childhood sex play—its ventriloquism and athletic variation:

I call that having intercourse, because he did put it in, you know, and he was doing all the movements.... I tried to, you know, do what I hear and I seen, and I started making noises...not knowing why I'm making them.

Ivorine doubled over with laughter remembering the time she and two little boys were playing sex on the bathroom floor. When Ivorine's little boy tried to go "in the wrong hole," it hurt. Lili also recalled playing sex at a very young age:

It wasn't very sexual actually.... It's like when you're little you're playing these games and you're going through the motions...but it's not the deep impulse. It's very unpassionate.

The pleasure narrators not only acknowledge the masturbation experience but make it a part of the story of their sexual and romantic experience. Jenny's masturbation account is lengthy:

Don't know how I started—it was a combination of curiosity, as in "what does this feel like?" because I have all—I have several books about the teenage body and Our Body Our Selves, *and all these things about sex. And I read about masturbation. And I was wondering what an orgasm felt like. So I decided, I have to try this.*

And I felt really strange and really stupid and I could imagine someone walking in any moment. So I thought the only time when no one's going to walk in is when I'm in the shower. So...I used to lie on the bottom of the bathtub and angle the shower water to hit my clitoris. And I had a lot of orgasms that way but my showers would last too long. So I decided this—no—I'm wasting New York's water and I can't do this.

And, you know, people would start knocking on the door, "Come on, Jen, you've been in there for 25 minutes." I'm lying on the bot-

tom of the bath like "Ooo, don't walk in now." That had some scary moments. So I decided to forget the shower. And I thought, How am I going to masturbate, you know, without the water? I didn't know if I'd be able to do it—without water, because the water was a lot harder. A lot more stimulating. And then I discovered that I could rub my clitoris and it did feel good. And so I have—I'd m-masturbate in bed at night. Which meant I didn't get to sleep for ages.

Q: And which meant you didn't have any trouble, in fact, figuring out how to have an orgasm.

J: No, actually I didn't. No. Has my life been too simple?

Elodia's first memory of masturbation was at age five:

Q: Do you remember how you figured it out?

A: Yeah, it kind of like, uhm, it just all of a sudden dawned on me that I had all these amazing nerves down there and that was a sense of all these weird feelings.... I kind of felt like Wow! you know. I can actually manipulate these nerves and feel wonderful.

Elodia remembered all the details of that moment, as if it had been a first kiss.

Vestigial Petting, Contemporary Pleasure

A few rare narrators recounted referring to their own bodies and feelings as primary justifications in sexual decision making, and described lovers willing to be governed by their findings who may even make similar inquiries of themselves. Cindy's boyfriend complained in the beginning of their relationship that it "was too much based on sex." At the same time "he really wanted to have sex," and she knew that they would, as she had known she and her previous boyfriend never would.

And it wasn't because I wasn't attracted to him. It was only because I just knew that he wasn't the person I wanted to have sex with. So when I met Timothy I knew that I wanted to have sex with him, and maybe not at the immediate time, but I knew that some time I wanted to.

These narrators relate a slow steady progression through petting in early adolescence to mid-adolescent intercourse. Their histories are not marred by the fearful stop-start quality common to accounts of adolescent sexual experience in the 1950s but characterized, rather, by a gradual, intentional ascension toward erotic understanding.

A larger group of narrators, mainly those enrolled in accelerated academic programs or active in sports or some other extracurricular activity, related long, often increasingly anxious, waits to become sexually—or at least heterosocially—active. They made do with a sluggish period of romantic daydreaming, which was followed by a sudden bout of heavy petting. The petting was sensuous and sexually illuminating.

It was pretty far into the party but I was just standing in the middle of the living room… staring into space. There was a little group of people sitting on the floor, which included Clark…and Clark said, "Elise, come here!" …and so I sat down and joined them and started talking and it was just magic. I mean, Clark sort of started massaging my foot and then after that we smoked some pot…and we just lay on the floor and listened to music. And it was so incredible. It was so great and you know, Clark and I were lying there sort of under a blanket making out in a very stoned way. And I was very pleased.

Perhaps because less rides on petting, or perhaps because they have waited for so long, these narrators feel they have a right to improve their chances of experiencing pleasure by telling their lovers what pleases them. Beth, for instance, told Jason:

I—I would—I liked it when he would, you know, stroke my body and kiss my neck and things like that. And uhm, so he just started doing that and it was really nice.

The most charged noncoital sexual experiences were related by teenage girls who identified themselves as lesbian.

And then we kissed, and it was the most incredible—I knew I was gay at that minute for the first time, because I had made out before and it never felt like that. And it was just so incredible.

And:

This was the first time we ever did anything besides kiss. And I just put her down and then I touched her through her little yellow panties. She was soaked!

If they have not already, lesbian and heterosexual girls alike begin to think of themselves as sexual beings in the course of petting experiences. Girls who define themselves as lesbian talk about beginning to realize, or wholeheartedly embrace, a lesbian sexual identity. Girls who define themselves as heterosexual describe having a premonition of what intercourse will entail:

I had never really thought about it. And I remember thinking, Wow.

Like Mother, Like Daughter

Pleasure narrators frequently related that their mothers have always been "open." These narrators relish this openness, and return it in kind. The comfort they report in talking with their mothers sets them apart from most girls who, several studies have shown, are uncomfortable talking with their mothers about sex and would rather talk about it less than their mothers would (Fox & Inazu, 1980; Furstenberg, Herceg-Baron, et al., 1984). The quality and content of the talk creates this difference. Most mothers who believe they "should" talk with their daughters about sex, the life histories indicate, either restrict their sexual communications to the facts of life or become entangled in judgmental no-win, no-holds-barred arguments. Such discussions may retard the transition to coitus, but this says nothing about their effect on the quality of that transition. The mothers of the pleasure narrators are forthcoming not just as the biological facts of life, but about adult life itself. They are active women with full lives, and they have a great deal to impart about the adventure of sex; the juggle of love and work, passion and maternity. With enormous gusto, their daughters regaled me with their mothers stories of sexual pleasure and adventure as well as their own. Jen:

Mom had always talked very casually about sex. I mean, I have sat at the dinner table and discussed with mom what contraceptive she used when she was, uh, uh, you know, having an affair with my dad for the year before she married him. And, uhm, actually we have discussed what sex was like with my father and what she did in—in the way of fooling around before she got married. She told me all these wonderful incidents about the back seat of the car, which I thought was hysterical. I can't imagine anybody bothering to use the back seat of a car. Yeah, and we once over dinner talked about pregnancy and giving birth. Sitting in a restaurant. While we ate.

And Elodia:

We were just around listening to older women talking about sex, you know, sometimes in very intricate details, sometimes,

you know, just jokes about it. Also, you know, problems with men—like, you know, "Oh god, stood up again. Those jazz musicians always stand us up.... Next time I'm going to get a man with a car and a job."

Through these conversations, these daughters gain invaluable insights into the body and intimate relations, and they learn that talking about their pleasures, sorrows, and furies will strengthen, inform, and enrich their lives. They also learn a lesson that feminist psychoanalyst Jessica Benjamin has suggested is crucial: that women can be subjects of their own desire (Benjamin, 1988).

With one or more of the advantages above—childhood sexual experience, masturbation, a gregarious, empowered mother, petting—these girls say they approach sexual initiation prepared by a knowledge of the pleasure their bodies hold in store and a sense of knowing their own minds. They are desirous:

Like I was totally ready to have sex, uhm, all day—like for a week before.

They understand that they have a right to consult their own desire in deciding whether or not to have sex, as Victoria, for example, narrated:

Then he told me how he really feel about me.... Then he said, "Can I make love to you?" I said, "What?" He said, "Can I make love to you?" I said, "Why do you ask me that now?" He said, "Because I think now you're ready to handle it." I said, "I might be." [Her voice took on a very considered, sensuous tone.] Then he said, "I think you are." So then, he said, "You're sure?" I said, "Wait a minute. Let me think." Then I say, "Yeah, I'm sure."

Because these teenage girls are looking forward to first sex, rather than grimly holding their breath until it's over, they usually prepare for it, even carrying sponges and diaphragms and creams in their bags, even obtaining the pill, considerably before their boyfriends have imagined that sex might be imminent. They hold out for kisses, foreplay, oral sex, passion. Lesbian girls make sure there will be a private time and place for something to happen. All wait for the right time (the moment when they feel desire). When that time has come and gone, they report a far better time than most girls. First sex isn't ecstasy, they say, but it is a promising beginning:

Annie said:

I wasn't really that shy because I had grown up around it [sex] and it seemed sort of natural to me.

Anja summed her assessment of first sex with characteristic precision:

I felt good because I liked [him] and good also because I was very attracted to him and good because…it was another thing I could get out of the way but also because it felt like the right time…. I'd always said to myself, "I'm not going to do it if it's the wrong time." You know, "I'm not going to do it when I don't want to. I'll just wait until I really want to." And I did want to. I was glad I wanted to, and, you know, the moment was right. So that was fun…. It wasn't very different from what I thought but…I hadn't thought of it really that far…. So it was kind of not surprise, but, you know, something new. I wasn't thinking of. But it—I liked it.

Jen thought her lover's penis "felt big, like owwwww!" But, she added, "It also felt good."

Instead of mourning the lost chance virginity represents, they work to recall every detail. Instead of swearing off sex, they begin making plans for a more sensuous and satisfying future.

Tracy:

Oh, well, it didn't live up to everything that the romances say it will, but it's worth it. It was fun. I was definitely going to try it again.

They assume they have a right to orgasm, and they know it's possible. They have a point of comparison:

You know, I had been masturbating and it felt wonderful and now this was such a far cry from that.

Orgasm is reported as a representative sexual experience by lesbian teenagers even before sexual initiation. "You just kissed me," one remarked to her lover, "and I had one." They also report orgasmic sexual experiences with other girls involving clitoral stimulation, digital penetration, or oral sex. Heterosexual girls traditionally report greater difficulty in achieving orgasm in first intercourse (Kinsey, 1953; Masters & Johnson, 1966), and even pleasure narrators rarely report orgasm.

I didn't even know what it was. I didn't think—I thought it was something that somebody made up. To sound good, you know.

Those with more faith aren't sure that sex "counts" if they haven't had an orgasm, and several inquired how to go about coming. Elodia found first sex "pleasing in a way that wasn't sexual." She worried: "Am I frigid? Is he not a good lover? You know, what's the problem?" Elodia's lover said all his other lovers came. "Through intercourse." She found that "hard to believe." She went back to her mother.

And she said that she didn't and that a lot of people she knew didn't. And then I went back to the books and the books said that what? Fifty percent of the women, according to reports, don't. And so I figured they must have faked it on you or something, you know, to make you feel good. But I—I need to feel good so I can't do that.

Not surprisingly, her boyfriend didn't want to accept her analysis.

He didn't seem to believe that they were faking it or he didn't want to believe it.

Nevertheless, her complaint had an effect.

Basically, he overcompensated.... He pleased me other ways so that I could... Okay, he would masturbate me and it took a while but eventually we started to have oral sex.... He said, "Let's do each other at the same time." So. You know, that was nice.

Others tell their boyfriends to go more slowly, take time with pleasure. They look for lovers with slower hands, more exploratory tongues, wiser cocks. They work on their own minds:

I was so nervous...was very—nervous about my performance all the time.... I remember this experience of him going down on me and saying—in my mind going, OK, is this going to work? Is this going to work? And then I remember saying to myself, Shut up. And then being able to come. That was the first time. And then the second time was figuring out how to make myself come when I was on top of him. And we were having intercourse. And that was really—that was the only way I could come with him from fucking. I think maybe once I came when I was—underneath him.

The first group of narrators described having sex without the preparation of masturbation, petting, foreplay, desire, or contraception. They did not recall or acknowledge ever touching their clitorises or vaginas. They saw the penis as "a big thing" that had to go into "a small hole" that they were not familiar with. They didn't think they had any sexual choice. They felt rushed into and through coitus, but they didn't see a way out or a way to make it easier. They even feared pleasure might make them pregnant. When they turned out to be too tight and dry for penetration to proceed, they exulted in a sexual victory that brought intercourse to a speedy conclusion. When coitus was over, they put it out of their minds so thoroughly that they could barely recall the details.

The second group of narrators relished sexuality, its stories and its pleasures. They approached first intercourse with a foretaste of desire from earlier experiences—masturbation, childhood sex play, and heavy petting—and from their mothers' accounts. Frequently, they obtained contraception before first intercourse. Desire and foreknowledge did not eliminate pain entirely, or ensure orgasm, but they did provide points of comparison. In the wake of first intercourse, these narrators were able to recall their first sexual experience in detail. They made plans for better and safer sex to come—going quickly to a doctor or a clinic, asking friends and mothers about the question of pleasure.

JUST SAY, NOT UNTIL I KNOW I WANT YOU...NOTES TOWARD AN EROTIC EDUCATION

Adolescent sexual exploration, adventure, and pleasure constitute, on the whole, a newer story in girls' tradition than that of pain and boredom, which appears, although not so emphatically or in such detail, in earlier accounts (Schofield, 1965; Chilman, 1983). This new story represents a fine outcome of the sexual reforms and hopes of 1960s and 70s but one that remains, unfortunately, a minority experience—a serendipitous outcome of social and personal history.

To take possession of sexuality in the wake of the anti-erotic sexist socialization that remains the majority experience, most teenage girls need an erotic education. Like the conversations above between gregarious mothers and avid daughters, an erotic education would be narrative as well as expository and provide a psychological context for understanding sexual experience. It would include lessons in how to explore the body: how to masturbate; how to come; how to respect another's desire; how to bring another—of either gender—to orgasm; how to fuck; and it would include narrative exchange. It would teach boys to continue making love beyond premature ejaculation until their partners were ready for them to stop or to slow their sexual response time and girls to make conscious moment-by-moment decisions as choice proceeds to experience. This is far from the direction of "just say no" or "not now" education. If curricula strongly advised teenagers to begin sexual life with masturbation, which, we know, promotes girls' sexual pleasure and knowledge more successfully than any other sexual experience, or to defer coitus until they have experienced genital desire or orgasm, they might make some sense as a sex-positive response to reasonable medical and developmental concerns (Abramson, 1973; Arafat & Cotton, 1974; Clower, 1980; Chilman, 1983; Gagnon & Simon, 1973; Kelley, 1983). But they do not. Instead, they reinforce girls' tendency to deny that they *are* sexual.

To adjure teenagers "just say no" or "just say not now" is to join conservatives in sabotaging the sense of sexual confidence upon which the pleasure narratives—and effective contraception—depend. This is not fair to girls and it does not make educational sense. Sexual education and counseling must, rather, counter the triple-whammy that love, ignorance, and guilt already exercise over girls' ability to accept themselves as sexual beings by lightening rather than increasing the load of cultural weight that love must bear; dealing with sex fully and straightforwardly; giving girls the clues they need to recognize desire (Fine, 1988; Petchesky, 1984). Granted, in the current political context, it is difficult, to say the least, to imagine instituting a

sexual education curriculum that teaches desire. But informal materials and discussion groups can add cognition and desire—lubrication, vaginal premonition, clitoral demand, lust, excitement—to the issues teenagers are advised to think about.

Sol Gordon's classic comic *Ten Heavy Facts About Sex* (1971, revised 1983) follows up the advice "no sex unless you are ready for it" with this checklist clarifying the meaning of readiness:

Are you mature?
Are you in love?
Are both of you ready for a baby, or if you aren't
Are you using birth control?
What about marriage?

A brochure that addressed girls' sexual perspective might inquire rather:

Do you get wet when you have a romantic or sexual daydream? When you think about kissing or petting?
Do your genitals become warm or feel pleasure?
Do you know where your clitoris (joy button, little man in a boat) is? Have you touched it? Excited it?
Are you sexually excited when you and your prospective lover are together or making out? That is:
   Does your heart beat differently than usual?
   Is your clitoris warm? pulsing? swollen?
   Is your mouth watering?
   Is your vagina (hole) moist? warm? Does it seem to be opening and
     contracting, fluttering, reaching out?
   Are your toes curling or spreading?
   Are your nipples stiff? Sensitive? Quick to pleasure?
Do you have an idea of what an orgasm is?
Have you visualized or imagined what it will be like to be naked with someone? To

kiss or pet without clothes on? Have you tried it?

Have you touched your breasts and genitals? Have you touched yourself inside?

If you are considering having intercourse, have you imagined what penetration may feel like?

Have you looked into the various forms of birth control? Obtained one? Tried using it? Talked with your friends about their experiences?

Does the idea of having sex with the person you are considering it with excite you?

Does the touch of that person excite or pleasure you?

Do you think your prospective lover will take the time to pleasure, or learn how to pleasure, you? Stop whatever he or she is doing if you insist? Continue until you want to stop?

No amount of sexual education—and certainly no brochure—will eliminate the feeling of surprise at first being nude together; touching genitals; trying penetration. Sexual initiation is, by definition, a new experience, and surprise is an aspect of sexual pleasure. But when the "big thing" goes into the "little hole," it does not have to be a knockout punch.

REFERENCES

Abramson, P. (1973). The relationship of the frequency of masturbation to several aspects of personality and behavior. *The Journal of Sex Research, 9,* 132–142.

Arafat, I., & Cotton, W. (1974). Masturbation practices of males and females. *The Journal of Sex Research, 10,* 293–307.

Benjamin, J. (1988). *The Bonds of Love: Psychoanalysis, feminism and the problem of domination.* New York: Pantheon Books, Random House, Inc.

Carns, D. E. (1973). Talking about sex: Notes on first coitus and the double sexual standard. *Journal of Marriage and the Family, 35,* 677–688.

Chilman, C. S. (1983). *Adolescent sexuality in a changing society: Social and psychological perspectives for the human services professions.* New York: John Wiley & Sons, 2nd ed.

Clower, V. L. (1980). Masturbation in women. In M. Kirkpatrick (Ed.), *Women's sexual development* (pp. 147–166). New York: Plenum Press.

Dinnerstein, D. (1977). *The mermaid and the minotaur: Sexual arrangements and human malaise.* New York: Harper and Row.

Dodson, B. (1974). *Liberating masturbation: A meditation on self love.* New York: Bodysex Designs.

Fine, M. (1988). Schooling, sexuality, and adolescent females: The missing discourse of desire. *Harvard Educational Review, 58,* 29–53.

Fox, G. L., & Inazu, J. K. (1979). Talking about sex: Patterns of mother-daughter communication. Conference paper, Society for the Study of Social Problems. Detroit: The Merrill-Palmer Institute.

Fox, G. L., & Inazu, J. K. (1980). Mother-daughter communication about sex. *Family Relations, 29,* 347–352.

Fox, G. L., & Inazu, J. K. (1980). Patterns and outcomes of mother-daughter communication about sexuality. *Journal of Social Issues, 36*(1), 7–29.

Furstenberg, F. F., Jr., Herceg-Baron, R., Shea, J., & Webb, D. (1984). Family communication and teenagers' contraceptive use. *Family Planning Perspectives, 16,* 163–170.

Gagnon, J. H., & Simon, W. (1973). *Sexual conduct: The social sources of human sexuality.* Chicago: Aldine Publishing Company.

Gordon, S. (1980, revised 1983). *How can I tell if I'm really in love?* Fayetteville, NY: Ed-U Press, Inc.

Gordon, S. (1971, revised 1983). *Ten heavy facts about sex.* Fayetteville, NY: Ed-U Press, Inc.

Haffner, D. W. (1988). Safe sex and teens. *SIECUS Report, 17,* 9.

Hollingshead, A. (1949). *Elmtown's youth: The impact of social classes on adolescents.* New York: John Wiley & Sons, Inc.

Kallen, D. J., & Stephenson, J. J. (1982). Talking about sex revisited. *Journal of Youth and Adolescence, II,* 11–23.

Kelley, K. (1983). Adolescent sexuality: The first lessons. In D. Byrne and W. A. Fisher (Eds.), *Adolescents, sex, and contraception* (pp. 125–142), Hillsdale, NJ: Lawrence Erlbaum Associates.

Kinsey, A. C., Pomeroy, W. B., Martin, C. E., & Geb-
hard, P. H. (1953). *Sexual behavior in the human
female.* Philadelphia & London: W. B. Saunders
Company.

Masters, W., & Johnson, V. (1966). *Human sexual
response.* Boston: Little, Brown.

McRobbie, A., & Nava, M. (1984). *Gender and generation.* London: Macmillan.

Ministry, J. M. (1987). *Teen sex survey in the evangel-
ical church.* Dallas, TX.

Moore, K., & Burt, M. R. (1982). *Private crisis, public
cost.* Washington, DC: The Urban Institute Press.

Moore, K. A., Winquist, C., & Peterson, J. L. (1989).
Nonvoluntary sexual activity among adolescents.
Family Planning Perspectives, 21, 110–114.

Paul, E., Pilpel, H. F., & Wechsler, N. F. (1976). Pregnancy, teenagers and the law, 1976. *Family Planning Perspectives, 8,* 16–21.

Petchesky, R. (1984). *Abortion and woman's choice.*
New York: Longman.

Pratt, W. F., & Hendershot, G. E. (1984). The use of
family planning services by sexually active teenage women. Paper presented at the annual meeting of the Population Association of America,
Minneapolis, MN.

Rogel, M., Zuehlke, M. E., Petersen, A. C., Tobin-
Richards, M., & Shelton, M. (1980). Contraceptive behavior in adolescence: A decision-making
perspective. *Journal of Youth and Adolescence, 9,*
491–506.

Schofield, M. (1965). *The sexual behaviour of young
people.* Boston: Little, Brown and Company.

Sorenson, R. C. (1973). *Adolescent sexuality in contemporary America: Personal values and sexual
behavior, ages 13–19.* New York: The World Publishing Company.

Thompson, S. (1984). Search for tomorrow: On feminism and the reconstruction of teen romance. In
C. S. Vance (Ed.), *Pleasure and danger: Exploring female sexuality* (pp. 350–384). Boston: Routledge & Kegan Paul.

Trussell, J. (1988). Teenage pregnancy in the United
States. *Family Planning Perspectives, 20,* (6),
262–272.

Vance, C. S. (1984). Pleasure and danger: Toward a
politics of sexuality. In C. S. Vance (Ed.), *Pleasure and danger* (pp. 1–27). Boston: Routledge &
Kegan Paul.

Weiss, D. L. (1985). The experience of pain during
women's first sexual intercourse: Cultural
mythology about female sexual initiation.
Archives of Sexual Behavior, 14, 421–438.

Winter, L. (1988). The role of sexual self-concept in
the use of contraceptives. *Family Planning Perspectives, 20,* 123–127.

Zabin, L. S., & Clark, S. D. (1981). Why they delay.
Family Planning Perspectives. 13, 211–217.

Zabin, L. S., et al. (1984). Adolescent sexual attitudes
and behavior: Are they consistent? *Family Planning Perspectives, 16,* 181–185.

Zelnik, M., & Kantner, J. D. (1980). Sexual activity,
contraceptive use and pregnancy among metro-
politan-area teenagers: 1971–1979. *Family Planning Perspectives, 12,* 230–238.

Zelnik, M., & Shah, F. (1983). First intercourse among
young Americans. *Family Planning Perspectives,
15,* 64–72.

Reading 3 Body Image and Weight Concerns among African American and White Adolescent Females: Differences that Make a Difference

SHEILA PARKER, MIMI NICHTER, MARK NICHTER, NANCY VUCKOVIC, COLETTE SIMS, AND CHERYL RITENBAUGH

Questions to Consider:

1. What is your view of the ideal female? If you are female, how does this view make you feel about yourself? If you are male, how does this view affect your attitudes about women?

2. What are the two different cultural conceptions of beauty that are identified by the authors? What cultural factors do they use to explain the origins of each conception? What cultural factors have shaped your own view of the ideal female?

3. In the title of their article, the authors refer to "Differences that make a difference." What do they mean by this phrase? Do you agree? Explain your answer.

4. The authors identify some limitations of survey research for investigating cultural differences. What are these limitations, and what suggestions do you have for research methods that would more accurately assess the African-American experience?

Dissatisfaction with weight and inappropriate dieting behaviors are reported to be pervasive among adolescent Caucasian females. Survey research has suggested that there is an "epidemic" of dieting among White adolescent females (Rosen and Gross 1987) with estimates that as many as 60–80% of girls are dieting at any given time (Berg 1992). By contrast, research on African American adolescents suggests that

Reprinted from *Human Organization, 54*, (2), 1995, pp. 103–114, by permission of The Society for Applied Anthropology.

these girls are less dissatisfied with their body weight and are far less likely to engage in weight reducing efforts than their White peers (Casper and Offer 1990; MMWR 1991). Explanations of such ethnic differences typically revolve around the statement that "cultural factors" are somehow implicated (Rosen and Gross 1987).

Utilizing data collected from a multi-ethnic study of adolescent females, this paper explores cultural factors which have an impact on weight perception, body image, beauty, and style. African American perceptions of beauty, characterized by informants as flexible and fluid, will be contrasted with White images which tend to be more rigid and fixed.[1] Ramifications of this difference will be broadly considered.

ETHNIC DIFFERENCES IN PERCEPTIONS OF WEIGHT AND DIETING

Weight has been identified as an important health concern, source of psychological stress, and measure of self-esteem among White females (Attie and Brooks-Gunn 1987; Moses *et al.* 1989). Numerous surveys have documented the pervasiveness of dieting and body dissatisfaction among White adolescent females (Desmond *et al.* 1986; Greenfield *et al.* 1987; Koff and Rierdan 1991). In one study among White high school students, 80% of girls surveyed felt they were above the weight at which they would be happiest and 43% said they would like to weigh at least 10 pounds less (Fisher *et al.* 1991). Storz and Greene (1983) found that 83% of White adolescent girls they surveyed wanted to lose weight, though 62% were in the normal weight range for their height and gender.

Results of recent nationwide surveys have revealed that White and Hispanic girls perceived themselves to be overweight even when their weight for height fell within "normal" parameters as established by the National Center for Health Statistics. By comparison, African American adolescent females were found to be less likely to perceive themselves as overweight (MMWR 1991). Desmond, Price, Hallinan, and Smith (1989) contend that both African American and White adolescents maintain distorted perceptions of their body weight, but in opposite directions. Their study suggests that African American adolescents of normal and heavy weight tend to perceive themselves as thinner than they actually are, while White adolescents of thin and normal weight perceive themselves as heavier than they actually are. Such studies call attention to differences in standards of acceptable weight and their variability across cultures.

A study conducted by Casper and Offer (1990) found that African American female adolescents were less preoccupied with weight and dieting concerns than White adolescent females. In an item by item comparison, African American adolescents had fewer thoughts about dieting, were less fearful of weight gain, and had a less negative valuation of overeating. Rosen and Gross (1987) concluded that African American girls were more likely to be engaged in weight gaining than weight loss efforts when compared to their White and Hispanic counterparts.

Differences in cultural standards for acceptable weights have been reported both among adult women as well as among adolescent females. Using a structured interview technique, Rand and Kuldau (1990) assessed the prevalence of obesity and self-defined weight problems in a large sample (n = 2,115) of African American and White women. Almost half (46%) of African American women in their study (n = 306) were overweight by an average of 25 pounds, an amount which exceeded the average of all other groups. Significant differences emerged when acceptable weights by race and age were considered. Younger White women (aged 18–34) who considered themselves to have "no weight problem" were thin and were an average of 6–14 pounds under the lower limit of the "ideal weight range." African American women of the same age category who reported "no weight problem" had an average (rather than thin) body weight. Acceptable weights for this group fell within the recommended weight range, but acceptance of "overweight" became more pronounced as women became older. At older ages (55–74), African American women who reported "no weight problem" were on average 17–20 pounds overweight. Kumanyika (1987) has noted that "controlling for socioeconomic status does not eliminate the obesity prevalence differences between Black women and White women" (1987:34).

Allen (1989), in a study of weight management activities among African American women, reported that although most of her informants had been overweight for years by biomedical standards, they did not perceive themselves to be overweight. Awareness of being overweight came from outside the immediate family—a social or health encounter. As Allen notes, these women had not evaluated their body size "in relation to the White ideal in the media but in comparison to other African American women who on the average are heavier than white women" (1989:17). Most informants did not define overweight as unhealthy. These findings are corroborated in a National Health Interview Survey (NHIS) which found that fewer African American women than White women considered themselves overweight, even when they were by actual weight.

Kumanyika, Wilson, and Guilford-Davenport (1993), drawing from a sample of 25- to 64-year-old African American women (n = 500), found that about 40% of the women in the overweight categories (based on BMI) considered their figures attractive or very attractive.[2] Almost all of these women recognized that they were overweight by biomedical standards. Furthermore, only half of the women who were moderately or severely overweight reported that their husband or boyfriend was supportive of their dieting efforts. Almost unanimously, overweight women reported that their body size had not been the source of difficulties in their personal or family relationships.

Anorexia and bulimia are estimated to affect 2–3% of the White population. To date, few cases of anorexia and bulimia among African American females have been reported in the literature. A comparative study of bulimia among African American and White college women found that fewer African American women experienced a sense of fear and discouragement concerning food and weight control than did their White counterparts (Gray *et al.* 1987). Researchers have suggested that the cultural milieu of African Americans offers "protective factors" against the development of eating disorders. Such factors include family and community appreciation of a fuller and physiologically healthier body size and less emphasis on physical appearance as measured solely by one's weight (Root 1989). There

has been some concern, however, that increased affluence and acculturation of African Americans into White culture may result in higher incidence of eating disorders as African Americans seek to emulate White middle class ideals (Hsu 1987).[3] Silber (1986) has suggested that professionals misdiagnose eating disorders among African Americans due to stereotypical ideas that such problems are restricted to White women.

Beyond considerations of weight, several researchers have noted that women of color are compelled, at various points in their lives, to compare their appearance to the dominant White ideal. Such comparisons extend beyond body shape to hair and skin color (Gillespie 1993; Lakoff and Scherr 1984; Okazawa-Rey *et al.* 1987). Okazawa-Rey, Robinson and Ward (1987) have argued that the African American women are twice victimized and in "double jeopardy" because they must respond to the desires and expectations of African American men and to White cultural values and norms.

Research conducted up until the last decade tended to highlight the self-contempt some African Americans feel about their appearance as a result of the hegemony of the White beauty ideal.[4] Researchers have recently pointed to the manner in which African American women are supportive and appreciative of one another's efforts to fashion a positive identity in a proactive and aggressive manner (Cross 1991; Okazawa-Rey *et al.* 1987[5]). Little research has focused on the lived experience of African American adolescent females and the extent to which conflict about appearance affects their lives in various social interactional settings.

Survey research suggests that there is greater satisfaction with body weight and less dieting among African American than among White adolescent populations. This does not mean that African American adolescent females are less concerned about their appearance than are their White counterparts. At issue here is: *what type of self presentation is culturally valued by African American females, in what context, and for what reasons.*

To date, little research has focused on African American females although issues relating to self presentation of males has been discussed. Research on African American males suggests that one coping strategy adopted to deal with oppression and marginality has been "cool pose" (Majors and Billson 1992). Animation marks African American style expressed verbally, non-verbally, at the site of the body, and through a wide range of performance (Fordham 1993). Cool pose is a "ritualized form of masculinity that entails behaviors, scripts, physical posturing that deliver a single, critical message: pride, strength and control" (Majors and Billson 1992:4). According to these authors, cool pose empowers black males in their daily lives by helping them stay in control of their psychological and social space. "Styling" provides an individual voice for males who might otherwise go silent and unnoticed.[6]

While Majors and Billson (1992) do not specifically discuss African American women, other researchers (Fordham 1993) have noted the importance of styling and *ad hoc* construction of a gendered self in an environment where style is both valued and commented upon. The existing literature does not address how African American adolescent girls negotiate their identities and relate to their bodies in a variety of settings. Toward this end, the present study examines African American perceptions of weight and beauty in a Southwestern city marked by ethnic diversity and a geographically diffuse as distinct from centralized African American population. African American and White adolescent females' attitudes about appropriate body size and dieting are contrasted to highlight important differences between these groups.

METHODOLOGY

Data for our analysis are drawn from a three-year longitudinal study (the Teen Lifestyle Project) on dieting, smoking, and body image among adolescent girls. Two hundred fifty girls were recruited into the study while they were in the 8th grade (junior high) and 9th grade (senior high school). Informants were 75% White, 16% Mexican American, and 9% Asian Americans. In the final year of the project, a second sample of 46 African American adolescent girls, drawn from grades 9–12 and other community groups in the same city was added to the study. Both the White and African American participants in the study were from a range of lower middle to middle class families. Similarity in socioeconomic status between girls in the two ethnic groups precluded analysis of body image and dieting behaviors by social class.

Data collection during the study took place primarily in four schools and community organizations. Each girl in the study participated in one in-depth semi-structured interview each year. Each interview took about 45 minutes and was conducted in the school. In addition to individual interviews, focus groups were also conducted with groups of four to five girls on issues regarding perceptions of beauty, ideal body shape, and dieting practices. Ethnographic techniques enabled the researchers to gather data on the natural language of teens and the meaning of beauty, body, and dieting references in context. Interviews were tape recorded and later transcribed and entered into Notebook II software to permit retrieval of quotations on particular topics. Individual interview and focus group data were analyzed through thematic analysis.

Each participant in the study completed a survey questionnaire each year on a range of issues including body image, eating, and dieting behaviors. Questions on the survey were derived from the literature and from issues which emerged as salient to this adolescent population during interviews. Culturally appropriate response categories were also drawn from ethnographic interview data (Nichter *et al.* 1994). Height and weight were measured at the time of each survey.

Our study of African American adolescent girls utilized both ethnographic interview and survey methods. Ten focus group discussions with 4–5 girls per group were conducted by African American researchers in order to identify the

TABLE 1   How satisfied are you with your present weight? Responses of African American girls, aged 14–18 (n = 44)[+]

BMI	Very Dissatisfied	Dissatisfied	Satisfied	Very Satisfied	Total
Low*	25%	25%	25%	25%	10%
Mid**	4%	11%	71%	14%	72%
High***	14%	57%	29%	—	18%

[+]Forty six girls responded to the survey, but two girls did not supply information on their height and weight. Thus, the n of the table is 44.

*Low BMI indicates girls below the 15th percentile of BMI.

**Mid BMI indicates girls who were above the 15th and below the 85th percentile.

***High BMI indicates girls above the 85th percentile.

These are drawn from NHANES I data for African American girls (Must *et al.* 1991).

perceptions and concerns that African American girls held about their weight, body image, dieting, and other broader health and lifestyle factors. Focus group discussions averaged about one hour in duration. These discussions were followed by individual interviews with several key informants. Two surveys were administered to the African American participants. The first survey was the same as that given to the larger multiethnic sample. The second survey was designed specifically for African American girls based on issues generated in interviews.

The research team consisted of both White and African American researchers. Focus group and individual interviews were transcribed, read, and discussed by members of the research team. Cultural differences and similarities which emerged from the data were analyzed in weekly meetings among the authors. Later, a panel of community members were asked to comment on findings.

RESULTS

Teen Lifestyle Project Survey Results

In this section a comparison will be drawn between responses to the Teen Lifestyle Project survey (year 3) collected from the sample of White, Hispanic, and Asian-American girls (n = 211) and African American girls (n = 46). Responses show distinct differences with regard to the issue of satisfaction with weight.[7] In response to the question, "How satisfied are you with your weight?" 70% of the African American informants responded that they were satisfied or very satisfied with their current weight. While 82% of these girls were at or below the normal weight for height range for African American girls of their age, 18% were significantly overweight (above the 85th percentile).[8] Only 12% of girls who were normal weight expressed dissatisfaction with their present weight (see Table 1).

Among Whites, results of a survey question about satisfaction with body shape revealed that almost 90% of these informants expressed some degree of negative concern about their body shape. Dissatisfaction with body weight and shape among White girls, even when their weight/height ratio is normal, has been continually confirmed in the literature (Fisher *et al.* 1991; Storz and Greene 1983).

Despite the differences in body satisfaction expressed by African American and White girls, responses to survey questions on weight control behaviors reveal few significant differences between the two groups. This was initially puzzling for the researchers. In response to the question "How often have you tried to lose weight during the past year?" 48% of African American girls stated that they had not tried to lose weight, as compared to 39% of White girls. Approximately 30% of girls in both ethnic groups had tried to lose weight one or two times in the past year. In both groups, 11% said that they always dieted. No significant differences between White and African American girls emerged (see Table 2).

In response to the question "Are you trying to change your weight now?" 54% of African American girls said they were trying to lose weight as compared to 44% of White girls. No significant differences emerged between ethnic group responses (see Table 3).

Data derived from this survey seemed contradictory. While African American informants seemed similar to White informants with regard to dieting practices, they expressed much greater satisfaction with their weight than White girls. Why did these African American girls report trying to lose weight if they were satisfied with how much they weighed? During discussions among project staff and a panel of African American youth, several issues emerged:

Did answering questions on a survey primarily designed for a White population mask differences in attitudes and behaviors of African American girls?

To what extent were their answers shaped by the questions asked and the context in which they were asked?

Was it plausible that the language of the survey indexed dominant cultural values?

Would language which engaged African American girls yield different responses?

Did this African American sample have characteristics which would lead them to adopt forms of behavior similar to White girls?

Were their friends mainly White girls and did this influence their practices and attitudes?[9]

Members of the research team expressed concern that the survey results from the African American girls did not reflect differences in body image and perceptions of self expressed during focus groups and individual interviews. In the next section, data are presented which highlight cultural differences identified during ethnographic interviews and focus groups. Data will also be presented from a second survey designed specifically for African American girls. This survey employed language and addressed themes which emerged from key informant interviews and focus group discussions. A series of juxtapositions between White and African American adolescents with regard to beauty and thinness ideals are presented.

Being Perfect: Beauty Ideals among White Adolescents

Females, particularly those who are White and middle class, are socialized through a host of influences from the media to fantasy play with Barbie dolls to believe that slenderness is essen-

TABLE 2   How often have you tried to lose weight during the past year?

	haven't tried	1–2 times	4–6 times	once a month or more	always trying
White (n = 211)	39%	28%	14%	9%	11%
Black (n = 46)	48%	30%	6%	4%	11%

TABLE 3   Are you trying to change your weight now?

	No	Yes, I'm trying to gain	Yes, I'm trying to lose
White (n = 211)	51%	5%	44%
Black (n = 46)	39%	7%	54%

tial for attractiveness and is a key component for interpersonal success (Freedman 1984; Hawkins and Clement, 1980). Many adolescent females strive for the bodily perfection depicted in the media, believing that they are somehow inadequate in comparison to the American ideal. As Freedman (1989) has noted, the adolescent search for a personal identity has been distorted into a search for a packaged image.

The ideal, "perfect" girl was often described by our White informants as being 5′7″ tall and between 100 and 110 pounds. She was usually a blonde and her hair was long and flowing, "the kind you could throw over your shoulder." Descriptions mirrored those of fashion models: "I think of her as tall—5′7″, 5′8″, long legs, naturally pretty, like a model's face with high cheekbones." To many informants, the ideal girl was a living manifestation of the Barbie doll. The researchers were continually struck by the uniformity of descriptions of the ideal girl, regardless of what the speaker herself looked like. This led us to conclude that there was a prototypic, ascribed standard of beauty that girls struggle to achieve. The attributes of the ideal girl were encapsulated by the word "perfect." This sense of beauty was fixed: fixed on the pages of magazines, fixed on the airbrushed faces of models, and fixed in the minds of our adolescent informants.

For the vast majority of girls, "being perfect" was an unattainable dream which led to a devaluing of their own looks and a sense of personal dissatisfaction and frustration. This was particularly striking when informants were in junior high school and their bodies were undergoing rapid change. Some girls described their practices of bodily concealment in an effort to hide their bodies. As one girl explained:

I just want to look like one of those models in the swimming suits when they walk on the beach—like a flat stomach, little hips, little waist, and skinny thighs, so you don't, like me, have to put on the shorts and the shirt and the sunglasses.

In focus group interviews, girls were asked to describe what kind of attributes made another girl's life seem perfect. One girl answered, "I don't know. Their friends and their attitude, their looks and their weight." Another girl in the group elaborated on the weight issue:

Well, they're not like malnutritioned or anything, I mean they look healthy. I mean, you don't look at them and say, 'Oh my God, they're too skinny' or 'Oh my God they're too fat.' They're just perfect.

Interviews revealed that the right weight was often perceived as a ticket to the perfect life. The girl with the perfect body who can "eat and eat and eat and not gain anything" was described as being "perfect in every way." By extension, the girl with the perfect body has a perfect life: She gets the boy of every girl's dreams.

Most girls buy Seventeen magazine and see all the models and they're really, really skinny and they see all these girls in real life that look like that. They have the cutest guy in the school and they seem to have life so perfect...

Girls, particularly in junior high school, described how being thin was a prerequisite for popularity. Girls equated being thin with being "totally happy" and noted "how being skinny makes you fit in more." Many girls thought that boys wanted them to be thin. As one girl said "Guys always say they don't want big chunky girls, they want skinny, slim girls."

Dieting among White Adolescent Females: An Attempt to Achieve Perfection

To many White adolescents, achieving the thin body ideal was viewed as the key which opens the door to success, popularity, and romance. In group discussions, girls talked about wanting to lose weight. They spoke of dieting not just as a way to become thinner, but as a way to gain control of other aspects of their lives. This logic was explained succinctly by one high school girl:

> ...*if I went on a diet, I'd feel like it was a way of getting control...like a way to make myself thinner, and make my appearance, and my social life better. So it would be like getting control over lots of different things I guess.*

Dieting, a mode of producing a more perfect thin body, held the promise of control over one's present and future. A thin body constituted symbolic capital having exchange value for popularity. As one girl noted:

> *I think the reason that I would diet would be to gain self-confidence...but also that self-confidence I would want to use to like get a boyfriend. Do you know what I mean? It seems like that's the only way that I would be able to...to be accepted.*

For many White girls, talking about body dissatisfaction and the need to lose weight is a strategy for establishing group affiliation. It reproduces a model of, as well as a plan for, achieving a more perfect life. Drawing on focus group and individual interview data from the Teen Lifestyle Project, Nichter and Vuckovic (1994)

explored the commonality of the expression "I'm so fat" among adolescent girls. This discourse, which they term "fat talk," was commonly used among White informants to express dissatisfaction with themselves as well as a broad range of other negative feelings. "Fat talk" was also used to maintain group affiliation and served as a leveling device: in order to be part of a group, a girl had to express some degree of dissatisfaction with herself. Calling attention to one's physical imperfections afforded girls a sense of belonging with those who shared similar concerns.

Analysis of interview and survey data revealed that although talk about body dissatisfaction and the need to diet is pervasive, this does not always result in actual sustained dieting behavior among White adolescent females. Quantitative data analysis confined that more girls engaged in "watching what they ate" as a strategy to maintain their weight and to be healthy than were actually dieting (Nichter *et al.* 1994). "Watching what you eat" was usually defined as "eating right, like eating a lot of fruits and vegetables and avoiding junk foods." A thin, toned body was clearly identified as a symbol of being healthy by White adolescent informants.

Competition among White Girls

Ironically, White girls who were closest to the image of the ideal girl were admired, but at the same time were the object of envy and dislike. The perfect girl provokes frustration for other girls, sometimes to the point where these girls feel their own efforts are futile:

> *You just see all these older girls, like when you go to the mall, and there's like, it's like, "why was I born?" because they're so perfect.*

Despite the desire to be perfect, a White female who is extremely attractive may find herself shunned by her female peers, as she represents all that her peers are not and aspire to be. Adolescent girls as well as boys scrutinize and evaluate her "reified parts" and envy is gained at the cost of self-alienation (Goldman 1992). Some informants noted that when they saw a beautiful girl at school, in the mall, or even on television, they would label her a "bitch." Since the perfect girl's flaw is not visible, it is assumed to exist in her personality. As one girl noted:

> *Girls, they completely stare at another girl. If a new girl would walk in I would like notice every single flaw and then I'd wait for her to make me happy—I mean show me that she is really okay and then I kind of blow off her flaw, but until then I'm like "god do you see that big thing between her teeth...do you see how much makeup she's wearing?" I like have to know everything...If she is really pretty, then I want to see her flaw... all of it. All of it. I want to know every single part of her flaw.*

Not uncommonly, girls would state that they hated this girl, despite the fact that they didn't know her. Some girls remarked "I want to hurt her" or "I feel like killing her."

Comparing themselves to other girls and failing to measure up to self-imposed standards of beauty made some girls feel bad about themselves. As one girl noted, "A lot of times I envy other people and then I start to feel bad...that I'm ugly or something." Rather than accentuate the positive aspects of their looks, many White girls expressed a desire to alter their perceived imperfections in order to achieve the ideal.

Using What You've Got: Body Image and Beauty among African American Adolescents

African American perceptions of beauty are markedly different than White perceptions despite frequent media images of African American models and dancers who depict White beauty ideals. In focus groups, African American girls were asked to describe their sense of an ideal girl. Commonly, girls responded with a request for clarification: Were we asking about an African American ideal girl or a White one? This response signaled to the researchers that the girls were keenly aware of differences in ideals of beauty between the African American and the dominant White culture.

This was confirmed in the second survey administered to African American girls in which they were asked whether there was a difference between their ideal of beauty and that of White girls. Sixty three percent of the girls agreed that there was, while the rest reported that there was little difference. In response to the open-ended question "If yes, what is the difference?" girls wrote comments such as: "White girls have to look like Barbie dolls and Cindy Crawford to be beautiful", and "White girls want to be perfect." African American girls noted that "their attitudes and the way they wear their clothes is different" and that White girls "want to be tall, be thin and have long hair."

When the researchers asked African American girls for their description of an ideal African American girl, their response often began with a list of personality traits rather than physical attributes. The ideal African American girl was smart, friendly, not conceited, easy to talk to, fun to be with, and had a good sense of humor. Many girls noted that their ideal girl did not have to be "pretty," just "well-kept" (i.e., well-groomed). In terms of physical attributes, girls tended to respond by calling attention to an ideal girl having it "going on." This indexed making what they had work for them: long nails, pretty eyes, big lips, nice thighs, a big butt—whatever. The skin color of the "ideal girl" was described as dark, medium, or light depending on the skin color of the respondent.

What was particularly striking in African American girls' descriptions, when compared to those of white adolescents, was the deemphasis on external beauty as a prerequisite for popularity. As one girl noted:

There's a difference between being just fine or being just pretty. . .because I know a lot of girls who aren't just drop-dead fine but they are pretty, and they're funny, all those things come in and that makes the person beautiful. There are a lot of bad-looking (physically beautiful) girls out there, but you can't stand being around them.

Girls were aware that African American boys had more specific physical criteria for an "ideal girl" than they had themselves. They commented that boys liked girls who were shapely, "thick" and who had "nice thighs". One girl noted that "guys would be talkin' about the butt. . .it be big." Another girl explained:

I think pretty matters more to guys than to me. I don't care. Just real easy to talk to, that would be the ideal girl for me, but the ideal girl from the guy's perspective would be entirely different. They want them to be fine, you know what guys like, shapely. Black guys like black girls who are thick—full figured (laughs).

African American girls were notably less concerned with standards for an "ideal girl" depicted in the media. What emerged from interviews was a sense of self esteem which led several girls to describe the ideal girl in terms of themselves—not somebody "out there" to be emulated. As one girl noted:

. . .the ideal girl? That's me. I don't know. I'm happy with the way I am. My friends like me the way that I am and they don't think that I should change and neither do I.

Beauty was not described in relation to a particular size or set of body statistics. Girls noted that beauty was not merely a question of shape. It was important to be beautiful on the inside as well as on the outside, and to be beautiful a girl had to "know her culture." One girl explained that "African American girls have inner beauty in themselves that they carry with them—their sense of pride." This sense of pride was commonly described as a legacy they received from their mothers.

We asked girls to describe what kinds of qualities they admired in a Black woman. Girls noted that they admired a woman who "keeps herself up and acts like herself" and "is strong on the inside, knows what she wants, and looks good on the outside and inside." One girl explained that a beautiful Black woman is "a woman who accepts who she is but yet can stand up for herself, and a woman who truly believes in herself, works hard and doesn't accept negative things in her life that will bring her down." Having a positive attitude and "not worrying about your looks too much" were important components of a beautiful woman. Attitude eclipsed body parts as a measure of value.

In focus group interviews we asked girls if they heard or engaged in much talk about being fat with their friends.

I don't hear that a lot. I hang out with black people and they don't care—we don't worry if we're fat because we'd all be drawn away from that. We want to talk about what's going on, you know, about where we're going for lunch. We're not concerned with that.

We asked girls what they would do if a friend did complain about being fat. One girl responded in the following manner: "I'd tell her 'Don't think negative. People who think negative aren't gonna get nowhere'."

Standards for body image and beauty among these African American adolescents can be summed up in what these girls term "looking good." "Looking good" or "got it goin' on" entails making what you've got work for you, by creating and presenting a sense of style. In a recent article on body size values among White and African American women, Allan *et al.* (1993) similarly report that "looking good" among African American women is related to public image and overall attractiveness rather than to weight. Adolescent informants explained that regardless of a girl's body size or shape, height, weight, skin color, hairstyle, etc., if you can clothe and groom yourself and have the personality to carry off your personal style, you are "looking good." "Looking good" had to do with projecting one's self image and confidence—having "tude" (i.e., attitude), and "flavor." "Throwing your attitude" entails establishing one's presence, creating a "certain air about yourself," being in control of your image and "things around you," being able to improvise effectively, and maintaining poise under pressure. "Flavor" refers to the sensual dimension of one's presence beyond gross physical appearance.

African American perceptions of beauty are flexible; they include, and go beyond, physical characteristics. In the second survey administered to African American girls, they were asked to select one of several possible answers to complete the statement "In my opinion, beauty is. . . ." Almost two thirds (63%) of these girls responded that beauty is "having the right kind of attitude and personality when you deal with others." Thirty five percent of girls responded that beauty is "making what you got work for you in your own way." Only 2% of our sample noted that beauty is "making yourself look as close as possible to an ideal body shape and face."

Another theme which emerged in discussions with African American informants was that beauty is fluid rather than static. Beauty is judged on the basis of "how one moves" rather than on what one weighs. Participant observation with African American girls and women trying on clothes and looking in the mirror revealed a greater tendency for these women to move with the clothes being tried on than to strike a series of static poses, a behavior more typical of White women. The importance of movement and body language has likewise been noted with reference to Black English. Speicher and McMahon (1992:391) discuss how their informants described style in conversation as a means of projecting self. As one woman noted, "When you're trying to get your point across, there's style, there's movement, there's a lot of moving". Another informant described Black English as a "very interactive form of language" noting that "it has to do with eliciting an audience's response, not just an audience's listening and understanding, but very much a visceral response, a physical response." The emphasis was as much on how you moved and the sense of style that was projected, as what was actually said.

Style among African American Girls: Using What You've Got

Style is appreciated and commented upon by peer group members. "Putting it together" entails creating style that not only fits one's person, but projects an attitude. African American girls in the study were far less likely to purchase ready made "looks" off a rack or to derive identity from wearing the label of a particular brand. The wearing of brand name clothes and recognizable styles was a major identity issue among adolescent White girls, especially in junior high school.[10] Economics, as well as the cut of clothing (most ready made clothes are fit for a Caucasian body), affected African American girls' efforts to create a style. While brand names continued to be recognized as a sign of status, brands did not dominate African American girls' fashion statement. Style demanded that resources once marshaled be tailored, adapted, and appropriated. Brands did not create distinction in and of themselves.

Creation of a style "which works" involves making a personal statement and projecting a unique presence. This presence reflects not only on one's person, but on the African American community at large. As Taylor (1982:61) notes, style is a domain of life strongly linked to ethnic pride:

Black style is our culture. It's our collective response to the world. Our style is rooted in our history and in knowledge of our inner power—our power as a people. Black style is the opposite of conformity. It's what others conform to. In fact, quiet as it's kept, our style is envied and emulated throughout the world.

Beginning in early adolescence, an African American girl is encouraged to develop a look which "works" given her own physical endowments and her social and economic environment. In a context in which the beauty standards of the larger society are often the antithesis of African American physical attributes (facial features, body shape, body size, and hair), positive feedback from other members of the African American community is important. This feedback is essential given the constant barrage of ideal standards from the dominant White culture and negative stereotypes generated about African Americans (Gillespie 1993:75):

For who among us has not at some point in time succumbed to the propaganda, looked in a mirror felt ourselves to be wanting? Wanting, because our skin is too dark, or our noses too wide or our hips too large, or because our hair wouldn't grow and never blew in the wind, or just because we never seemed to measure up.

How an African American female is valued within her family and community will determine whether she does or does not succumb to this constant assault on her person.

African American girls in the study reported routinely receiving compliments from other African Americans of both genders for "looking good" and "having it going on." Compliments were received from people of close as well as casual acquaintance, in public as well as in private, as a matter of course without any offense taken. Interview data strongly suggested that African American girls received far more positive feedback about how they look from their families and friends than negative feedback. At the same time, however, they are taught to maintain their composure in verbal battles (such as playing the dozens) in which one's opponents attempt to exploit areas of potential sensibility and vulnerability. All in all, however, African American girls reported receiving far more positive feedback for creating their own style around their given attributes than did White girls who received support for altering their looks to fit established beauty ideals. Support for dieting was commonly articulated by White girls but rarely mentioned by African American girls. Allan *et al.* (1993) confirm these findings and note that African American adult women in their sample were influenced by friends and family to maintain a larger body size.

Positive Feedback among African American Girls

Juxtaposed to the envy and competitiveness which mark White girls' comments of others whom they perceive to be attractive, African American girls described themselves as being supportive of each other. In focus groups, girls talked about receiving positive feedback from family members, friends, and community members about "looking good."[11] This is consistent with Collins (1989:762) who noted that in traditional African American communities, Black women "share knowledge of what it takes to be self-defined Black women with their younger, less experienced sisters." Collins further contends that there is a sisterhood among Black women in their extended families, in the church, and in the community-at-large.

On the survey designed for African Americans, we asked girls what their response was when they saw a girl "who's got it going on"—a girl who has put her personal resources and attributes together. Almost 60% of our informants noted that they would "tell her she's looking good," while another 20% of girls noted that they "would admire her but wouldn't say anything." Only 11% of girls noted that they "would be jealous of her." These findings stand in stark contrast to the earlier discussion about competition among White girls.

A girl's peer group serves an important function in her socialization among African Americans. Being the same age as other group members is not as necessary a prerequisite for group membership as it is among White girls. Broader based group membership and support contributes to flexibility in the way beauty and style is perceived and accepted. Groups do engage in surveillance, however, and hold members accountable for how they look, how they carry themselves, and whether or not they are "taking care of business." As one girl noted:

> Other people, our peers like when they don't like what you have on they will tell you and if they like it they will say so ('that's fresh') ...the white girls, oh whatever, they say 'that's nice' even if it's not, they will say it anyway.

Beauty and Aging

Another difference between White and African American perceptions of beauty involves the manner in which age is represented. Age is represented as physical deterioration in the dominant White culture. Age is an enemy to be fought with vigilance through the use of wrinkle creams, dieting, and exercise programs, and when all else fails cosmetic surgery. Wolf (1991), citing interviews with editors of women's magazines, notes that the airbrushing of age from women's faces is routine. Wolf contends that to airbrush age off a woman's face is to erase her identity, individuality, power, and history. With regard to adolescence, the lack of portrayal of adult White women as beautiful adds an increasing tension to achieve the beauty ideal during the teenage years.

Among African Americans less emphasis is placed on being young as a criteria for being beautiful. This theme emerged during focus groups and was queried on the African American survey. In response to the question "As women get older, what will happen to them in terms of how they look?" 65% of girls said that they would get more beautiful and 22% said they would stay the same. Only 13% of girls thought women would lose their looks as they became older.

For African American girls, beauty is not associated with a short window of opportunity as it is in dominant White culture. It may be achieved, maintained, and enhanced as one grows older and more sure of herself. The number of African American girls who spoke of their mothers as "beautiful" far exceeded White girls who tended to speak of their mothers either in terms of their youth ("when she was young..."), or as "alright for a mother," implying that as one became older, the possibilities of being beautiful were reduced.

Attitudes toward Dieting among African American Adolescents

Beauty work is closely tied to dieting in dominant White culture. Among African Americans, dieting carried less significance. On the African American survey we asked girls to complete the statement "For your health, is it better to be...." Responses included "a little overweight" or "a little underweight." Sixty four percent of the girls thought it was better to be "a little overweight," while the remaining 36% chose being "a little underweight" as a response. In the same survey, girls were asked to respond to the question "For people who are normal weight or underweight, I think dieting is...." Responses indicate that 40% of girls thought it was "okay if you want to do it" while 42% thought dieting was "harmful to your body." Only twelve percent of girls thought it was "good because it puts you in control of your life."

During interviews with African American girls, most agreed that dieting was appropriate for someone who was "very overweight." "Very overweight" was defined in focus group interviews as "someone who takes up two seats on the bus." Some girls noted that harming the body through dieting was a sin in as much as one's body was God given. Notably, informants who reported dieting behavior on surveys, articulated a different set of cultural values related to dieting and body image in focus groups and individual interviews.

Self-Esteem

In addition to one's peer group, the African American family and community are sources of positive feedback that serve to enhance self-esteem and supplant negative comments directed against individuals from outside (Bames 1980). African American children, especially those in lower socioeconomic groups, are taught by their parents to function in and deal with an oppressive and hostile society in which they are expected to survive and excel (Ladner 1971). Children are raised with the knowledge of "how it is." Parents teach their children that resources may not be available to them, but they can succeed if they learn to "make what they got work for them."

During focus groups, African American girls expressed a greater acceptance of their physical bodies than did White girls as well as a sense of self and style based on making what they had work. Rather than reaching for an abstract ideal, these girls talked about achieving their own personal ideal. As one girl noted:

> *I think that Black people, Black kids, we're all brought up and taught to be realistic about life and we don't look at things the way you want them to be, or how you wish them to be. You look at them the way they are.*

Acceptance of self is also a message girls take home from the church. African American parents must prepare their children to understand and live in two cultures. W.E.B. Dubois wrote in the early 1900s about the idea of a double consciousness: "Blacks have to guard their sense of blackness while accepting the rules of the game and cultural consciousness of the dominant white culture" (1903). To achieve the former, children are raised to be part of an African American community as well as a member of an African American family. For many African American women, this entails developing a spiritual self which becomes "the greenhouse in which a woman can nurse her self-image and build her self-esteem" (Lewis 1988:64). In Christian spiritual belief, one's body is conceptualized as the temple of the holy spirit. In many communities, the church is one of the places where one's sense of style is displayed and appreciated.

CONCLUSION

Existing studies have identified cultural differences in body image and weight control behavior among adolescents of different ethnic groups. They have not, however, explored reasons underlying such differences. In this article, the authors point out differences in the conceptualization of beauty and style which influence how White and African American adolescent girls perceive themselves and relate to others around them. Two distinct ideologies have been contrasted that are articulated at the site of the body. While these ideologies coexist, they have an impact on White and African American women in different ways.

The ideology of advanced capitalist society is reproduced at the site of the body through the mode of working toward bodily perfection. This task engages the imagination if not the lives of a majority of young White women in America. This ideology has promoted critical assessment leading to dissatisfaction with one's physical attributes, fostered competition and envy among women, and encouraged the pursuit of goals impossible to obtain/maintain (Nichter and Nichter 1991; Goldman 1992). In a multicultural nation, the idealized beauty of White culture has been valorized and a multitude of products made available to women of color promising "melting pot" success in the form of products which help one pass/blend in mainstream America.

A second ideology, propagated within African American culture, is built around egalitarian ideals, the principle of reciprocity, and the recognition of strength and balance in diversity (Fordham 1993). Fostered is an approach to life where improvisation is valued and identity is constructed through creativity and style. Writing about the ways in which knowledge is transmitted between mothers and daughters in an African American community, Carothers (1990:239) notes:

Daughters learn competency through a sense of aesthetics, an appreciation for work done beautifully…This aesthetic quality becomes one of the measures of competently done work as judged by the women themselves and by other members of their community.

African American girls learn from their mothers and through interactions with their peer group and community that they can project an image and attitude of power through the way they dress and carry themselves. Competency is required in knowing how to present oneself in bicultural contexts ranging from the school and street to the church and job market.[12] In focus groups, girls continually noted the importance of style not only to project an image of themselves as individuals, but in their role as representatives of the family and African American community.[13]

One way in which lessons about freedom, competency, and community are learned is through aesthetic appreciation in African American culture. Beauty is defined less in relation to static images and more in terms of performative competence in a multicultural world marked by conflict as well as egalitarian ideals. In contrast to a more static image of beauty as bodily perfection, a more fluid, flexible image of beauty prevails. Instead of competition which fosters envy and alienation, an egalitarian ethos is promoted, marked by mutual appreciation, cooperation, and approval of someone "who's got it going on."

Several researchers (e.g., Collins 1990; Stack 1974; Valentine 1978) have noted that American racial-ethnic communities have developed collective social strategies that contrast with the individuation of the dominant culture. Among African Americans, creating one's own style as an individual statement is important, but equally important is a positive presentation of one's community. An egalitarian ethos does not imply the absence of hierarchy nor the absence of historical tensions and interpersonal power struggles that form part of daily existence (Fordham 1993)[14]. What it does imply is that individuality, while respected in the form of personal style, attitude, and improvisation, is also encompassed by sociocentric values.[15]

A review of the Teen Lifestyle Project focus group and individual interview data identified striking differences with regard to body satisfaction and notions of ideal body shape between African American and White adolescent females. African American females were far less rigid in their concepts of beauty than their White counterparts and spoke more positively of "making what you've got work for you". While both White and African American girls articulated the importance of developing one's own style, White images of style were built around a more restricted set of beauty ideals. This led most White girls interviewed to express dissatisfaction with their bodies, especially in terms of their desire to lose weight as a way to "be perfect" and popular.

While talk about feeling fat was pervasive among White girls, reported dieting attempts rarely resulted in sustained weight loss behavior.

Dissatisfaction with weight (and consequently with one's self) and talk about feeling fat was discovered to be a culturally appropriate way for girls to show that they were concerned with their bodies and that they were working toward an ideal of perfection (Nichter and Vuckovic 1994). This contrasts with the African American ideal of "making what you got work for you" which pays greater credence to individual difference. The first ideal is reflected in how women measure up on the scale and strike a series of static poses in front of the mirror. The second ideal is reflected in women who move in front of the mirror in order to see if they "have it going on" and who pay less attention to scales and decontextualized measures of perfection.

Okazawa-Rey, Robinson, and Ward (1990: 100) contend that African American women are becoming increasingly proactive in their negotiation of identity:

Rising above externally sanctioned characterizations of womanhood, some black women are fashioning their identities based upon an analysis and understanding of their own struggles and successes. Further, Black women have united to support one another's efforts in the creation of newly defined roles and identities. Within this dynamic of self-determination, the black woman is proactive rather than reactive, aggressive rather than passive, and assertive rather than receptive.

Many of the African American girls interviewed during the Teen Lifestyle Project expressed positive feelings about their bodies and their sense of style. Their responses may well reflect egalitarian ideals and play down internal conflicts which may emerge in contexts where positive feedback is not forthcoming. It remains to be seen whether they will be able to maintain these self perceptions as they become older and obtain jobs in mainstream American society. As Root (1989) has noted, increased opportunities

are available to women of color, particularly those who can operate in ways that conform to the norms of the dominant White culture. Middle class African American women may be more likely to deemphasize their black identities in order to get ahead, and may be particularly vulnerable to the message of dominant White society that "thin is everything" (Villarosa 1994). For example, Bordo (1993) claims that African American women are as likely to have disturbed relationships with food as all other women. For evidence of this, she points to African American magazines which have an increased number of articles on weight, dieting, and exercise issues. The extent to which hegemonic values articulated in popular magazines are ignored and/or resisted by individuals or groups of women bears consideration. Entering the mainstream job market may increase pressure for women of color to be "perfect" in order to counteract negative racial stereotypes. Will this translate into body discipline in the form of dieting to obtain a thin body by girls who aspire to make it, or will preexisting and/or postmortem sensibilities alter the way in which beauty and success are perceived in this community?[16]

A final note on project methodology is in order. The initial Teen Lifestyle Project survey administered to a multi-ethnic, but largely White, population of adolescents did not reveal pronounced differences in perceptions of beauty, body image, or weight management between White and African American girls. These differences only emerged when a culturally sensitive survey was constructed following ethnographic research and administered by African American researchers. Two lessons were learned. First, survey instruments on body image and weight control designed largely for White populations mask important differences that exist between African American and White girls. Second, performance on such surveys by African American youth attending predominantly White schools reveals more about their bicultural competency than the way in which they think about beauty and body image. Because questions asked in the initial Teen Lifestyle Project survey did not address issues relevant to African American girls and because the survey was administered in a space associated with dominant White cultural ideals, responses tended to conform to those expected of the dominant population.

Follow-up research in the African American community of a sprawling Southwestern city revealed that adolescents expend considerable time and energy negotiating a sense of style in contexts where they are on display to their peers. The dominant White beauty ideal was clearly recognized, but did not play an influential role in negotiating identity. Similar studies need to be carried out in other regions and "school cultures" within America to ascertain the degree to which the findings of the present study are generalizable.

NOTES

1. Our use of the terms African American and White is an heuristic. We do not mean to infer that either a monolithic African American or White culture exists. The depiction of cultural ideals related to weight and body image presented in this article is drawn in broad strokes so that differences in orientation may be discussed. We are aware that these differences are cross-cut by class considerations and that cultural heterogeneity exists.

2. An issue that has been raised is whether Black-White differences in bone-size, body proportions, and frame can affect measurement of African American women. Kumanyika (1987) suggests that these errors are not significant, and in any case, would affect African American women after adolescence.

3. A concern about affluence and anorexia deflects attention away from eating problems as women's struggle against a "simultaneity of oppression" (Clarke 1982; Naylor 1985; White 1990). These researchers suggest that eating problems in the African American community constitute responses to oppression, being undervalued and overburdened at home as well as in the workplace. Thompson (1992) notes that eating problems begin as coping strategies against traumas ranging from sexual abuse to racism.

4. See Cross (1991) for a critique of early studies of group identity preferences and self-esteem that were based largely upon pre-school studies.

5. The extent to which African American consciousness has affected self-esteem associated with physical appearance has been the subject of little research (Smith, Burlew, and Lundgren 1991).

6. To our knowledge, a comparable literature among White males does not exist.

7. For this analysis, a comparison is drawn between the longitudinal sample (largely White) and the African American sample. Although it would be useful to separately consider ethnic differences among Hispanic, Asian American and White adolescents, it is beyond the scope of the present article.

8. Classification of girls into these categories was done by computing BMI from height and weight measurements. BMI was compared to normal values for African American girls based on NHANES I data (Must *et al.* 1991).

9. Limitations of the present study should be noted. First, the region in which the study was conducted has a small African American population. It would be important to explore the same issues in a community which was largely African American. Second, informants in the present study were drawn from a range of lower- to upper-middle class families. Social differences in weight related attitudes and behaviors need to be examined within samples drawn for this paper. Third, the study was conducted in the Southwest where housing among African Americans is scattered as distinct from being centralized. Future studies should be conducted in areas with a higher population density in the African American community.

10. White girls in junior high school were more label conscious than their counterparts in high school. It is important to note that White youth are also involved in the creation of style (McRobbie 1989) which may take the form of symbolic repression of commodities as a mean of actualizing opposition and resistance (Hebdige 1979, 1988). Irrespective of differences in the ways in which White adolescent girls dress based upon the clique to which they belong, a thin body ideal is maintained (Nichter and Nichter 1991; Nichter and Vuckovic 1994). Hegemony carried out at the site of the body coexists with acts of resis-

tance and attempts to express individual identity. The body is an immediate, proximate terrain where social truths and contradictions are played out and agency expressed (Scheper-Hughes and Locke 1987). It is a site of sensuality and creativity as well as domination and struggle, a medium of expression affected by a confluence of meanings flowing from a variety of life spaces.

11. It has been observed (Abrahams 1975) that African American society involves a highly flexible and personalistic approach to interaction. The expressive or personalistic, rather than the instrumental or institutional, dimension of role validation is stressed. Respect must continually be earned and negotiated. In this context, smart talk and body language are important and a competitive spirit is encouraged within the home as a survival skill (Ward 1971). Given this pattern of interaction, positive feedback about one's looks is perceived far to exceed negative feedback by adolescent girls.

12. Collins (1989) has described how knowledge of how to behave is essential to the survival of the subordinate.

13. A crucial part of African American aesthetics involves doing their own thing while contributing to the overall sense of the whole (Abrahams 1975).

14. The egalitarian ethos found in contemporary African American "communities" is, in part, the result of an externally imposed lack of differentiation between "Black peoples" associated with enslavement.

15. African American scholars writing on management styles and organizational environment have repeatedly drawn a distinction between Eurocentric and Africentric perspectives of social organization (Ak'bar 1984, Asanti 1988, Baldwin 1986, Nobles 1980, Schiele 1990). The Eurocentric model places emphasis on group and system survival which views the individual as part of a collective wherein horizontal communication and affective ties within the group are high. The virtue of the Africentric approach is its flexibility in responding to turbulent changes in the environment (Daly 1994). As distinct from a Eurocentric model of organization, where emphasis is placed on the "the correct way of doing the job," an Africentric approach places greater emphasis on raising group consciousness of where problems lie and a consideration of alternatives that may work given a set of contingencies. This parallels our discussion of the value of

"making a look work for you" and "community feedback" about one's sense of style and aesthetic as a reflection on self as well as community. Researchers of African American child socialization have also laid emphasis on the way children are taught to bear individual burdens (self-suffering) as well as to adapt for the good of kin as a sign of strength and character (Higgenbotham and Weber 1992).

16. While it is important to recognize the ways in which the bodies and voices of women of different ethnic and class backgrounds are influenced by material forces in society (Martin 1990), it is also necessary to challenge the extent to which such influence is totalizing given pre-existing dispositions (physical as well as cultural), situated knowledge, and fractured identities (Haraway 1991). Following Jameson (1981), it seems prudent to examine cultural aesthetics as a sedimentary genre. Every new appropriation of a genre to express contemporary realities passes through the sedimentary layers of its previous appropriations.

REFERENCES CITED

Abrahams, Roger
    1975   Negotiating Respect: Patterns of Presentation Among Black Women. Journal of American Folklore 88:58–80.
Ak'bar, Na'im
    1984   Africentric Social Sciences for Human Liberation. Journal of Black Studies 14(4):395–414.
Allan, Janet D.
    1989   Weight Management Activities Among Black Women. Presented at the Annual Meeting of the American Anthropological Association, Washington, D.C. November 15–19, 1989.
Allan, Janet D., Kelly Mayo, and Yvonne Michel
    1993   Body Size Values of White and Black Women. Research in Nursing and Health 16:323–333.
Asanti, Molefi K.
    1988   Afrocentricity. Trenton, NJ.: Africa World Press, Inc.
Attie, Ilana and Jeanne Brooks-Gunn
    1987   Weight Concerns as Chronic Stressors in Women. In Gender and Stress. Rosalind Barnett, Lois Biener and Grace Baruch, eds. New York: Free Press.

Baldwin, Joseph
  1986   African (Black) Psychology: Issues and Synthesis. Journal of Black Studies 16(3):235–249.
Barnes, Edward J.
  1980   The Black Community as the Source of Positive Self Concept for Black Children: A Theoretical Perspective. *In* Black Psychology. Reginald Jones, ed. Pp. 106–130. New York: Harper and Row.
Berg, Frances
  1992   Harmful Weight Loss Practices are Widespread among Adolescents. Obesity and Health July/Aug:69–72.
Bordo, Susan
  1993   Unbearable Weight: Feminism, Western Culture and the Body. Berkeley: University of California Press.
Carothers, Suzanne C.
  1990   Catching Sense: Learning from Our Mothers to be Black and Female. *In* Uncertain Terms: Negotiating Gender in American Culture. Faye Ginsberg and Anna Lowenhaupt Tsung, eds. Boston: Beacon Press.
Casper, Regina C. and Daniel Offer
  1990   Weight and Dieting Concerns in Adolescents: Fashion or Symptom? Pediatrics 86(3):384–390.
Clarke, Cheryl
  1982   Narratives. New Brunswick, NJ: Sister Books.
Collins, Patricia Hill
  1989   The Social Construction of Black Feminist Thought. Journal of Women in Culture and Society 14(4):745–761.
  1990   Black Feminist Thought: Knowledge, Consciousness and the Politics of Empowerment. Boston: Routledge.
Cross, William E., Jr.
  1991   Shades of Black: Diversity in African-American Identity. Philadelphia: Temple University Press.
Daly, A.
  1994   African American and White Managers: A Comparison in One Agency. *In* Diversity and Development in Community Practice. A. Faulkner, M. Roberts-DeGennaro, and M. Weil, eds. New York: Haworth Press.

Desmond, Sharon, James Price, Christopher Hallinan, and Daisy Smith
  1989   Black and White Adolescents' Perceptions of Their Weight. Journal of School Health 59:353–358.
Desmond, Sharon, James Price, Nancy Gray and Janelle K. O'Connel
  1986   The Etiology of Adolescents' Perception of Their Weight. Journal of Youth and Adolescence 15:461–474.
Dubois, William Edward Burghardt
  1903[1961] The Souls of Black Folk. Greenwich, Conn: Fawcett Publications.
Fisher, Martin, Marcie Schneider, Cynthia Pegler, and Barbara Napolitano
  1991   Eating Attitudes, Health-risk Behaviors, Self-esteem, and Anxiety Among Adolescent Females in a Suburban High School. Journal of Adolescent Health 12:377–384.
Fordham, Signithia
  1993   "Those Loud Black Girls": (Black) Women, Silence, and Gender "Passing" in the Academy. Anthropology and Education Quarterly 24(1):3–32.
Freedman, Rita
  1984   Reflections on Beauty as it Relates to Health in Adolescent Females. Women's Health 9:29–45.
  1989   Bodylove: Learning to Like Our Looks—and Ourselves. New York: Harper and Row.
Gillespie, Marcia Ann
  1993   Mirror Mirror. Essence, January 1993, pp. 73–79.
Goldman, Robert
  1992   Reading Ads Socially. London: Routledge.
Gray, James, Kathryn Ford, and Lily M. Kelly
  1987   The Prevalence of Bulimia in a Black College Population. International Journal of Eating Disorders 6:733–740.
Greenfield, David, Donald M. Quinlan, Pamela Harding, Elaine Glass and Anne Bliss
  1987   Eating Behavior in an Adolescent Population. International Journal of Eating Disorders 6(1):99–111.
Haraway, Donna
  1991   Simians, Cyborgs and Women: The Reinvention of Nature. New York: Routledge.

Hawkins, Raymond C. and P. F. Clement
1980 Development and Construct Validation of a Self-report Measure of Binge Eating Tendencies. Addictive Behaviors 5:219–226.

Hebdige, Dick
1979 Subculture: The Meaning of Style. London: Methuen.
1988 Hiding in the Light. London: Routledge.

Higginbotham, Elizabeth, and Lynn Weber
1992 Moving Up with Kin and Community: Upward Social Mobility for Black and White Women. Gender and Society 6:416–440.

Hsu, George
1987 Are Eating Disorders Becoming More Common among Blacks? International Journal of Eating Disorders 6:113–124.

Jameson, Frederic
1981 The Political Unconscious: Narrative as a Socially Symbolic Act. Ithaca: Cornell University Press.

Koff, Elissa, and Jill Rierdan
1991 Perceptions of Weight and Attitudes toward Eating in Early Adolescent Girls. Journal of Adolescent Health 12:307–312.

Kumanyika, Shiriki
1987 Obesity in Black Women. Epidemiologic Reviews 9:31–50.

Kumanyika, Shifiki, Judy Wilson, and Marsha Guilford-Davenport
1993 Weight-related Attitudes and Behaviors of Black Women. Journal of the American Dietetic Association 93 (4):416–422.

Ladner, Joyce
1971 Tomorrow's Tomorrow. New York: Doubleday.

Lakoff, Robin and Raquel Scherr
1984 Face Value: The Politics of Beauty. Boston: Routledge Kegan Paul.

Lewis, Mary C.
1988 Herstory: Black Female Rites of Passage. Chicago: African American Images.

McRobbie, Angela
1989 Second-hand Dresses and the Role of the Ragmarket. In A. McRobbie ed., Zoot Suits and Second-hand Dresses. London: MacMillan.

Martin, Emily
1990 Science and Women's Bodies: Forms of Anthropological Knowledge. In Body/Politics.

Mary Jacobus, Evelyn Fox Keller, and Sally Shuttleworth eds. New York: Routledge, 69–82.

Majors, Richard and Janet Mancini Billson
1992 Cool Pose: The Dilemmas of Black Manhood in America. New York: Lexington Books.

Moses, Nancy, Mansour-Max Banilivy, and Fima Lifshitz
1989 Fear of Obesity among Adolescent Girls. Pediatrics 83(3):393–398.

Must, Aviva, Gerald E. Dallal, and William H. Dietz
1991 Reference Data for Obesity. American Journal of Clinical Nutrition 53:839–846.

Morbidity and Mortality Weekly Report
1991 Body Weight Perceptions and Selected Weight Management Goals and Practices of High School Students—United States, 1990. Morbidity and Mortality Weekly Review 40:741–750.

Naylor, Gloria
1985 Linden Hills. New York: Ticknor and Fields.

Nichter, Mark and Mimi Nichter
1991 Hype and Weight. Medical Anthropology 13:249–284.

Nichter, Mimi and Nancy Vuckovic
1994 Fat Talk: Body Image among Adolescent Females. In Mirror, Mirror: Body Image and Social Relations. N. Sault, ed. New Brunswick, NJ: Rutgers University Press.

Nichter, Mimi, Cheryl Ritenbaugh, Mark Nichter, Nancy Vuckovic, and Mikel Aickin
1995 Dieting and "Watching" Behaviors among Adolescent Females: Report of a Multi-method Study. Journal of Adolescent Health. in press.

Nobles, Wade
1980 African Philosophy: Foundations for Black Psychology. In Black Pyschology. Reginald Jones, ed. New York: Harper & Row.

Okazawa-Rey, Margo, Tracy Robinson, and Jamie Victoria Ward
1987 Black Women and the Politics of Skin Color and Hair. Women and Therapy 6(1/2):89–102.

Rand, Colleen and John Kuldau
1990 The Epidemiology of Obesity and Self-defined Weight Problem in the General Population: Gender, Race, Age and Social Class. International Journal of Eating Disorders 9:329–343.

Root, Maria
1989 Treating the Victimized Bulimic: The Functions of Binge-purge Behavior. Journal of Interpersonal Violence 4:90–100.

Rosen, James C. and Janet Gross

1987   Prevalence of Weight Reducing and Weight Gaining in Adolescent Girls and Boys. Health Psychology 6:131–147.

Rosenberg, Morris and Roberta Simmons

1972   Black and White Self-esteem: The Urban Schoolchild. Arnold and Caroline Rose Monograph Series. Washington, DC: American Sociological Association.

Scheper-Hughes, Nancy and Margaret Lock

1987   The Mindful Body: A Prolegomenon to Future Work in Medical Anthropology. Medical Anthropology Quarterly 1(1) 6–41.

Schiele, Jerome H.

1990   Organizational Theory from an Africentric Perspective. Journal of Black Studies 21(2):145–161.

Silber, Tomas

1986   Anorexia Nervosa in Blacks and Hispanics. International Journal of Eating Disorders 5:121–128.

Simmons, Roberta, and Florence Rosenberg

1975   Sex, Sex-roles and Self Image. Journal of Youth and Adolescence 4:229–258.

Smith, Lori, Anne Kathleen Burlew, and David C. Lundgren

1991   Black Consciousness, Self-esteem, and Satisfaction with Physical Appearance among African-American Female College Students. Journal of Black Studies 22(2):269–283.

Speicher, Barbara, and Seane McMahon

1992   Some African-American Perspectives on Black English Vernacular. Language in Society 21:383–407.

Stack, Carol

1974   All Our Kin. New York: Harper and Row.

Storz, Nancy and Walter H. Greene

1983   Body Weight, Body Image, and Perceptions of Fad Diets in Adolescent Girls. Journal of Nutrition Education. 15:15–19.

Taylor, Susan L.

1982   In the Spirit: Cherishing Black Style. Essence, October 1982, p. 61.

Valentine, Bettylou

1978   Hustling and Other Hard Work. New York: Macmillan.

Villarosa, Linda

1994   Dangerous Eating. Essence, January 1994, p. 19.

Ward, Martha Coonfield

1971   Them Children: A Study in Language Learning. New York: Holt, Reinhart and Winston.

White, Evelyn C.

1990   The Black Woman's Health Book: Speaking for Ourselves. Seattle, WA: Seal Press.

Wolf, Naomi

1991   The Beauty Myth: How Images of Beauty are Used against Women. New York: William Morrow and Company.

Topic 4

Academic and Career Achievement

The Famous Jewish-Russian Woman Poet Termanowsky

If you found out your great grandmother was a poet,
if there was one obscure book that you discovered
one off-day at the bottom of a dusty cardboard box,

in the corner basement room, covered up by pickle jars,
slid behind your father's moth-eaten war uniforms,
a volume slim as a small hand, the cover a fainted blue,

layered and sealed with mold, the pages tearing with each touch,
the letters in Yiddish, and there's her name: *Termanowsky,*
your name, you realize, like a body suddenly twitching

for the missing limb, before it was shortened by the authorities
the way they would slice off anything unpronounceable.
Termanowsky, the famous Jewish-Russian woman poet,

her daguerreotype on the title's facing page, her face,
the one you recognize from other portraits, but younger, a beauty,
no babushka but a frilled scarf wrapped about the neck,

her dark thick hair flowing from beneath a tilted-
to-one-side beret, a few strands loose across her cheeks,
translucent as porcelain, dangling from her lips a cigarette.

You turn the pages as if they were faded rose petals,
study the words, the lines and stanzas, wonder
about the pressure of her fingers pressing the pen

to the page, the blood in the hand, the composure
that would call her to sneak down a thought or a mood,
between the pogrom and the poverty, the praying

for a relative in America to sponsor her over,
the baking of the bread she had to peddle in the marketplace,
having to worry over who would print and publish poems

by a woman named Termanowsky about being a girl
in the *shtetl,* the smell of challah rising,
horses and wagons in the dawn air, the mud streets,

the learned huddled toward the eastern wall, old men
in black coats, how it shamed her to have to sit
on her side of the synagogue—even if she had the space,

even if she had the time to save her moments
in words, the way she kept buttons in a box,
and was assured of the support to write them all down.

Courtesy of Philip Terman

Currently, women are the majority of students on most college campuses, and they make up almost half of the total workforce. Women have been moving into male-dominated fields, and there are now laws that protect equality of educational and work opportunity. However, women still confront many barriers to success in both school and in the workplace. In this section, we explore these challenges that women face in achieving their educational and career goals.

Recent research on the educational system from elementary school to college makes it clear that males and females are not receiving equal education. Women experience biased treatment from their teachers (including sexual harassment), study sexist textbooks, and become silent as they internalize the messages they are given about their abilities (Sadker and Sadker, 1994).

In the workplace, women continue to earn less than men earn, about 70 cents compared to every dollar paid to men. The pay gap is even wider for women of color, who as a group are in the lowest-paid jobs of all workers. The workforce is also segregated by sex, and the jobs typically held by females are lower in status. For example, over 90 percent of secretaries, nurses, and early childhood educators are women while fewer than 30 percent of engineers, police officers, and physicians are female (U.S. Department of Labor, 1995).

Women have been limited by lowered expectations for their educational and career achievement. This is particularly evident in the fields of math and science, where widespread assumptions about women's lack of ability exist—in spite of evidence to the contrary. Many women have been steered away from pursuing these fields. Further, because they often internalize these messages, women may limit their own aspirations. The first reading of this section, "Are Boys Better Than Girls at Math?" by Paula and Jeremy Caplan, explores this issue. Their critique of gender difference research debunks the idea that boys are innately better than girls at math. When the Caplans examine the research, they find that, contrary to popular belief, gender differences in math ability are nonexistent or small, and don't show up until adolescence. In addition, much of the research on gender and math is flawed by the invalid measurement of math ability, an overgeneralization of data, and inappropriate speculation regarding the cause of gender differences. The Caplans contend that even if there are sex differences in math, they are likely not the result of biology, but rather follow from (1) an educational system that does not encourage girls' math abilities and (2) social expectations that say boys are better than girls at math.

Another limit to women's achievement may be bias in performance standards. For example, Caplan and Caplan point out that one factor that might contribute to a gender difference in math performance is that math teachers may teach in a quantitative, abstract style that emphasizes power and control, a style that might appeal more to males than females. In the workplace, the quality of women's performance is often evaluated in relation to the male standard (the defined norm set by the group in power). From this perspective, any new approaches that women may bring to the profession (such as consensus building in decision making) are viewed as deficiencies, rather than as potential strengths.

The second reading, "The Development of Thoughtfulness in College Women," examines the issue of biased performance standards. Blythe McVicker Clinchy describes two ways that students approach learning, separate and connected knowing. In separate knowing, the knower tries to be objective and impersonal, employing procedures such as scientific methodology to analyze ideas and data. This method of knowing is central to most college classrooms, where students are encouraged to doubt and to argue in order to learn. In connected knowing, the knower learns by entering into another's perspective in order to understand it. Such knowing is deeply personal, and it involves empathy and connection to the material under investigation. Learning here is seen as a collaborative process in which students and teacher create knowledge together. Clinchy feels that many women prefer connected knowing and therefore are silenced in college classrooms where students are asked to argue and debate rather than to listen and collaborate. Separate knowing has become the defined norm, and the skills of connected knowing are not valued. The result is that women who do not learn the skills of separate knowing may leave college feeling convinced that they are stupid, while those who do learn the skills may become alienated and disenchanted with learning. Clinchy argues that all students would benefit if both ways of knowing were valued and integrated into college education.

Sexual harassment is another barrier to educational and career success for women. The U.S. Equal Employment Opportunity Commission defines sexual harassment as "unwelcome sexual advances, requests for sexual favors, and other verbal or physical conduct of a sexual nature." Studies have demonstrated that this abuse is widespread and that women of all ages and in all job categories are vulnerable. The courageous women who are making inroads into male-dominated jobs may be at the greatest risk of harassment. They face hostility from both coworkers and supervisors who are attempting to preserve their position of social power over women.

The third reading in this section, "Gendered Relations in the Mines and the Division of Labor Underground," by Suzanne Tallichet, provides a disturbing case study of sexual harassment in the male-dominated occupation of mining. Tallichet connects the oppressive treatment of women miners underground to the attempts by men in the broader society to maintain their privileged status. She also documents ways in which some women miners effectively resisted the oppression and asserted their rights to the same opportunities as male miners.

The combination of work and family roles creates additional opportunities for fulfillment for women. However, it can also create competing demands between the workplace and home, as well as work overload. Two-thirds of all mothers are currently in the labor force, and most married couples work two jobs. As stated earlier, most employed mothers do not have the option of staying home because either their families depend on two incomes or they are the sole breadwinners. Unfortunately, while husbands now share the burden and role of economic provider with their wives, most of them do not share the workload at home. This situation has caused many women to experience a double burden between the home and the workplace.

The last reading in this section is a study of the double burden of employed women. It is titled "A Speed-Up in the Family," and it is taken from a book by Arlie Hochschild with Anne Machung, *The Second Shift: Working Parents and the Revolution at Home.* In this reading, Hochschild summarizes interviews she conducted with 50 two-job couples from a variety of cultural and social-class backgrounds. Her research documents a "second shift" for employed mothers, but not for fathers. One shift takes place at the office or factory, and the other shift is at home. Hochschild's study also explores how the women experienced their double shifts, and its effects on their marriage and on their health. Widespread awareness of this phenomenon is extremely important so that couples can address these issues and can negotiate a more equitable distribution of labor early in the relationship. Furthermore, with increased awareness of the hardships of dual-career families, couples are more likely to pressure the government and the workplace to design policies that ease the burden of working families.

The readings in this section demonstrate the ways that gendered power differences are an integral part of education and work. If we are to have equity, not only must we eliminate discriminatory practices and bias, we also need to incorporate the strengths women and girls bring to the classroom and the workplace.

REFERENCES

Sadker, D., and Sadker, M. (1994). *Failing at Fairness: How America's Schools Cheat Girls.* New York: Simon & Schuster.

U.S. Department of Labor, Women's Bureau. (1995). *Facts on Working Women,* #95-1, May.

Reading 1   Are Boys Better Than Girls at Math?

PAULA J. CAPLAN AND JEREMY B. CAPLAN

Questions to Consider:

1. What experiences did you have with math growing up? Do you feel that those experiences may have been related to your gender?

2. Why were Benbow and Stanley's findings so popular?

3. What can we do to encourage girls to be more involved with math?

Mathematics is a science, not an art. In math, you are either *right* or *wrong*. In subjects such as English and even in chemistry or physics, an answer can be partly right, but in beginning math and much of high school math, an answer is either right or wrong; you can check your answer in math to see whether it is correct. This makes math a unique arena in which to study sex differences. For instance, girls are more likely than boys to be taught to seek adults' approval (see Caplan, 1973, for a review), and one way to win approval is to give a teacher the right answer to a question. Girls may be more upset than boys by being asked questions that have single, correct answers, rather than, say, being asked to describe a character from a novel, since for the latter you can be partly right, and it is hard to be totally wrong. If a group of students take a math test, and the boys score higher than the girls, you might conclude that the boys were simply better at math. However, it is possible that the girls were worried about giving the wrong answer, and so they were less likely to try some items. This would mean that the boys were not necessarily better at that particular math skill even if their score were higher.

Much of what we found with regard to spatial abilities also applies to the study of mathematical abilities: Most of the research yields either small sex differences or no sex differences, and the differences that do appear don't tend to emerge until around adolescence, after girls and boys have been exposed to many years of socialization about which sex is supposed to be good or bad at which school subjects. Furthermore, the results of some studies (e.g., Decore, 1984) show that females' grades in mathematics courses are actually *higher* than those of males. Decore, for instance, found that, between 1970 and 1982 at the University of Alberta, females' grades in both elementary and intermediate calculus were nearly always higher than those of males. And Hanna (1988) reports, based on her study of math ability in 18 different countries, that "gender-related differences in achievement vary considerably both within and among countries" (p. 14).

Since it is so generally believed that not only are boys and men superior at math but also that this alleged difference is *innate,* it is important to look at a number of socialization factors—at least within North America—that would tend to enhance male students' math performance and interfere with that of female students. Eccles and Jacobs (1987) found that their research indicated that junior and senior high school students' grades and the likelihood that they would even enroll in math courses are more influenced by social and attitudinal factors than by their actual ability to do mathematics. One of the best-known of these factors is math anxiety, which has been shown to be higher in girls than in boys (Eccles & Jacobs, 1987). It is interesting that students' math anxiety does not seem to be based very much on how well they have done in math in the past. In other words, girls have greater anxieties about their math ability, but this is not because their ability is inferior. Math anxiety *is* related to the grades students get in math courses and their plans to take more math courses in the future. Other social and attitudinal factors include parents' belief that math is harder for girls than for boys (Eccles & Jacobs, 1987); the tendency for fathers to help their children with math homework more than mothers do (Meece, Parsons, Kaczala, Goff, & Futterman, 1982); the greater preponderance of men than women as teachers of advanced math courses (Meece et al., 1982); the stereotyping of math textbook materials and math games as more appropriate for boys than for girls; teachers' higher expectations for boys than for girls in terms of math performance (Meece et al., 1982); and teachers' tendency to spend more time instructing and interacting with boys than with girls in math courses (Meece et al., 1982). The production in 1992 of talking Barbie dolls that complained about math being difficult was a recent, glaring example of the persistence of such stereotyping.

Probably the most influential work on sex differences in math has been done by Benbow and Stanley (1980, 1983), and it illustrates some of the most common kinds of methodological problems in research on sex differences in math, so we shall examine one of their most important studies in some detail. One major reason for its importance is that it was widely publicized in the media. Some of the typical headlines (cited by Eccles & Jacobs, 1987) were:

Are Boys Better at Math?
(*New York Times,* December 7, 1980)

Do Males Have a Math Gene?
(*Newsweek,* December 15, 1980)

The Gender Factor in Math. A New Study Says Males May Be Naturally Abler Than Females
(*Time,* December 15, 1980)

Clearly, the media took the Benbow and Stanley research very seriously. Those headlines strongly suggest that boys are actually better at math than girls. Furthermore, people have believed for a long time that males are superior to females in mathematical ability, so the interpretation of Benbow and Stanley's results agreed with the accepted outlook. If we look deeper, however, we find that the reality of their work doesn't match the headlines. Moreover, the flaws in Benbow and Stanley's research are typical of the majority of sex-difference studies of math.

Benbow and Stanley (1980, 1983) studied the scores that Grade 7 and Grade 8 gifted students achieved on the mathematics portion of the Scholastic Aptitude Test (SAT-M), a test widely used to help determine who is admitted to college. Students scoring in at least the top 2–5 percent of any standardized math achievement test were invited to take the SAT. They came mainly from the Middle Atlantic area, although later on, some students from elsewhere in the United States were included. Nearly 50,000 students accepted the invitation. Benbow and Stanley found that, overall, the boys achieved higher scores than the girls.

They therefore concluded that boys have greater "math reasoning ability."

There are several major errors in that research. Some of these are embedded in the design of the study, while others are just wrong interpretations of the results. Each will be discussed in detail, but briefly, they are:

1. **Measuring Math Reasoning Ability.** The researchers used the SAT-M as an indicator of "math reasoning ability," even though this test is not an accurate indicator of math aptitude.
2. **Obtaining a Uniform Sample.** We can only reasonably conclude that a difference exists between the sexes if the groups are identical in all other ways. The researchers stated that the boys and girls in the study had equal amounts of formal education. This may be true, but even when the subjects spend the same number of hours in the classroom, many factors are involved in learning other than simply the quantity of time spent in the classroom. For instance, having heard that "girls aren't very good at math" or "girls who are good at math aren't very feminine" could have important effects on students of both sexes. Futhermore, in keeping with traditional female socialization, more intelligent girls than boys may have had too little self-confidence to accept the invitation to take the SAT and participate in the research.
3. **The Power of Suggestion.** The researchers did not consider the fact that the students' expectations about their own performance, as well as other people's expectations of them, might have affected their performance on the SAT-M.
4. **From Specific to General.** The researchers wrote as though the results from their study would apply to all females and males, everywhere. This is not a valid assumption.
5. **The Unjustified Claim That Males' Superiority Is Innate.** Nowhere do they cite conclusive evidence of this.

MEASURING "MATH REASONING ABILITY"

Benbow and Stanley wanted to compare the "mathematical reasoning ability" of boys and girls. They neglected, however, to define the phrase, so we don't know what they intended to study. How can we know whether or not the SAT-M accurately measures what they call "mathematical reasoning ability"? Since the acronym, SAT, stands for Scholastic Aptitude Test, perhaps we were meant to assume that Benbow and Stanley felt they were measuring aptitude. However, scores on the SAT-M are influenced by many factors other than pure aptitude. If you ask a person to solve a problem, but the problem requires the person to know the quadratic formula, it is impossible to solve the question without that knowledge. Then, does the question measure aptitude or achievement? It means nothing about the person's ability to solve the problem if they don't know the formula.

One possible use of a test of mathematical ability might be to predict how well a student would do in college math courses; however, the test Benbow and Stanley studied is not very useful in making such predictions. Slack and Porter (1980) found in their research that high school math grades, and even math achievement test scores, were more reliable than SAT-M scores for predicting a student's math achievement in college. Furthermore, Fox and Cohn studied students in junior high school and found that the girls' SAT-M scores were unreliable predictors of their achievement later in school.

Fox, Tobin, and Brody (see Kolata, 1980) interviewed many of the girls in the Benbow and Stanley study and found that a great many of them did not want to participate in accelerated math classes. They were afraid that their peers would think of them as "different," and they thought that the accelerated classes were dull and that the boys in the classes were "little creeps." Although the researchers did not interview the boys in the same way, their results suggest that girls believe it is not socially acceptable or desirable for them to do well in math; this belief could certainly hinder their math performance, especially since girls are more likely than boys to seek social acceptance (Caplan, 1973).

THE PROBLEM OF OBTAINING A UNIFORM SAMPLE

Benbow and Stanley called what they found a "sex difference" in math. If the girls and boys they tested were identical in every way except for their sex, it would be fairly safe to assume that something about maleness and femaleness led to the difference in math scores. But it is *not* legitimate to make that assumption if the girls and boys differ in some way besides their sex. One of Benbow and Stanley's major assumptions was that all of their students had the same amount of formal education. Their reason for believing this was that every student was in Grade 7 in a U.S. school. However, the issue of the quantity of educational experience is much more complex. Grade 7 girls and boys don't necessarily receive the same amount of formal education, even when they are in the same classes (Eccles & Jacobs, 1987). Leinhardt, Seewald, and Engel (1979) found that by Grade 7, math teachers have spent up to 36 more hours instructing boys than girls. With less exposure to math, it is easy to see how girls might have less desire to study math.

Aside from simply the number of hours spent with each student, there is also the factor of how the teacher treats the child. Stanley himself (reported by Holden, 1987) noticed that females are more oriented toward social interaction and aesthetics, while males tend to be more oriented toward the quantitative, abstract, "power and control" (p. 661). If he is right about this, then maybe math teachers tend to teach in a style that appeals more to males than to females. This could easily explain the discrepancy in females' and males' scores. In fact, Patricia Casserly

(reported by Kolata, 1980) studied 20 schools in which the members of both sexes scored equally on the math achievement tests and found they had several common features; for instance, the math teachers of these students communicated a love of and enthusiasm for math. This may have enhanced their interpersonal connections with students—a factor that the girls might have found particularly encouraging (Gilligan, 1982).

People don't learn from formal education alone; therefore girls' and boys' SAT-M scores might have been affected differentially by experiences outside the classroom. Someone who plays math-related games will be expected to learn a lot more about math than someone who doesn't. It has been shown that boys are more likely to be involved in mathematical games and math-related activities, and to read more math-related books than are girls (Astin 1974; Fox & Cohn, 1980; Leinhardt, Seewald, & Engel, 1979).

In several ways other than biological sex, then, the girls and boys in the Benbow and Stanley study may well have differed from each other, and those other ways could certainly have led to a sex difference in the sexes' average math scores. This raises the possibility that boys may not be innately better than girls at math—as the headlines have implied—but simply have more experience with math.

THE POWER OF SUGGESTION

In our society, boys are expected to be better at math than girls. This expectation could heavily influence the results of the SAT-M. If you lead a person to expect something, they tend to interpret whatever happens as bearing out what they were led to expect. For instance, teachers who are told that a child is not very bright tend to notice things that confirm that expectation (Rosenthal & Jacobson, 1968).

In the same way, children who are told "you cannot do math" tend to come to believe that. (Of course, usually these messages are more subtle, but just as powerful.) Then, whenever they are confronted with a mathematical problem, they are likely to conclude automatically that they cannot solve the problem and, therefore, they are less motivated to try or persist. After studying the various influences on students' math grades, Eccles and Jacobs (1987) concluded that the strongest influence on a student's math ability was how their mother thought they would do.

Miele (1958) found that as children get older, the difference in scores for boys and girls on the Wechsler Intelligence Scale for Children (WISC) becomes greater and greater (with boys doing better). Also, in her review of the literature on sex-difference research using the WISC, Attard (1986) concluded, "It appears that, on the whole, no gender differences are evident on the arithmetic sub-test [of the WISC and WAIS] up to approximately age 16" (p. 14). These results seem to reinforce the hypothesis that sex differences in math result at least partly from other people's influence; as children approach age 16, they accumulate more and more years of exposure to the idea that boys are better than girls at math. Since people in our society tend to *believe* that boys are better than girls at math, it ends up appearing to be true on test results.

FROM SPECIFIC TO GENERAL

Finally, Benbow and Stanley did not take into account what are called *sampling errors*. Since they studied a sample of about 50,000 Grade 7 students in the United States, even if their results were valid, they should only be assumed to apply to Grade 7 students in the United States. It is quite possible that even the results that Benbow and Stanley produced would be different for Grade 1 students or college students or 40-year-olds or 80-year-olds. It is also quite possible that the results would be different in another country, since Hanna (1988) and Schildkamp-Küngider (1982) tested tens of thousands of students from all over the world and found that in some areas,

girls got the higher scores, while in other places, boys did.

Even if Benbow and Stanley's results had been otherwise accurate, they would still only apply to the specific people they tested. And it must be remembered that the people they studied were a *highly* selected group: They represent not students in general but only students who had scored in the top 2–5 percent on one of several math tests *and* who accepted the invitation to participate in the study. If, for instance, there is no sex difference in math ability for 95–98 percent of students, then Benbow and Stanley's claim to have found sex differences in math is a serious distortion.

If there *were* compelling evidence that most or all boys have better math abilities than most or all girls, then it might have been reasonable to consider adjusting our education system and our way of thinking accordingly (for example, having teachers spend more time teaching girls). However, if there *is* no sex difference, or only a small, unreliable, and late-developing one or a difference for only a small fraction of people, then it is dangerous to talk about "a sex difference"; to talk in that way leads people to believe that girls just can't do math. Indeed, that claim *has* been made, and many females who might have done quite well in a math career—in teaching of math; in accounting; in statistics, surveys, and poll-taking; in computer-related fields have therefore not pursued one.

As a result, for sex-difference studies about math, as for all sex-difference research, it is essential to be aware of possible sources of error, since these distort our view of the truth about females and males.

THE UNJUSTIFIED CLAIM THAT MALES' SUPERIORITY IS INNATE

When Benbow and Stanley's work was reported at the 1986 American Association for the Advancement of Science meeting, Benbow claimed that hormonal differences lead to males' greater proficiency in math. Naturally, the media eagerly reported this story. What they did *not* mention was that hormonal levels of the students in their study were never measured, thus making Benbow's claim entirely unjustified (Caplan, 1987). This is a particularly important issue, since when there is, or seems to be, a biologically based and innate difference such as a hormonal one, people are likely to assume that little or nothing can be done to reduce the supposed inferiority of one sex.

A careful exploration of the nature of Benbow's claim about a hormonal basis for males' alleged superiority in math is useful because it reflects so many of the errors that can occur when theory and research are not thought about carefully. Although the following discussion is very detailed and complicated, it is worth going through, because it illustrates how an unfounded theory can be used as a basis for assumptions, predictions, and hypotheses. Then, data are gathered on the basis of those assumptions and hypotheses, and authors tend to try to interpret them in a way that supports the shaky theory. It is very important to remember that, *once data have been gathered to test a theory, the theory often comes to seem to be true, even if the data do not support the theory particularly well.*

In a paper titled "Extreme mathematical talent: A hormonally induced ability?" (1987), Camilla Benbow and Robert Benbow presented their "yes" answer to the question in the title of their paper. As you will see, their argument is very roundabout and complicated, and there are problems every step of the way. It is based on the unsupported theory of two other researchers.

Benbow and Benbow (1987) noted that Geschwind and Behan (1982) had reported that left-handed people are more likely than right-handers to suffer from immune disorders, learning disabilities, and migraines, and that Geschwind and Behan "hypothesized" that this was due to high levels of the "male" hormone, testosterone. Benbow and Benbow (1987) failed to mention that

this claim by Geschwind and Behan has been vigorously criticized and has not actually been proven true by solid research. The Benbows suggested that testosterone slows down the development of the left hemisphere of the brain, so that the right hemisphere compensates by growing stronger, and that this improves mathematical abilities. Therefore, they concluded, excellent math students should have more immune problems and be more likely to be left-handed than would the general population. They decided to test those speculations on a group of students, but for no apparent reason they left out migraines. So, they were investigating the *implications* of only *part* of a theory, and the theory itself was not well supported in the first place. Furthermore, as we shall see, the students they studied were a highly unusual group.

The Geschwind and Behan theory was based partly on the idea that the immune disorders result from the effects of testosterone on the immune system's thymus gland. However, Benbow and Benbow (1987) cite no evidence for this idea. The theory was also based partly on the idea that testosterone slows down the development of the brain's left hemisphere, so that the right hemisphere compensates by growing stronger. However, Benbow and Benbow (1987) cite no evidence for this idea either.

What about the Benbows' speculation that mathematical tasks are better carried out by the right than the left hemisphere of the brain? They cite no evidence for this claim but simply assert that this is "considered to be" the case. In fact, however, many aspects of math involve the ability to think analytically, which in most people is located in the left hemisphere, and other aspects of math involve the ability to deal with spatial relationships of the kind that in most people are housed in the right hemisphere. Thus, it is just too simplistic to say that math tasks should be better performed when the right hemisphere is doing them.

Even *if* all of the claims and speculations by both pairs of authors had been proven to be true, then one would expect *most* males to be far better at math and much more likely to develop immune disorders and migraines and to be left-handed than most females. But that is certainly not the case.

Based on all of these unproven propositions, the Benbows *speculated* that, since males tend to have more testosterone than females, *some* males would be both left-handed and skilled at math, due to the hormone's effect on the right hemisphere, and that same testosterone would affect their thymus gland, so that they would have immune disorders. Next, they predicted that, in their very special, unusual group—the most extremely skilled math students (they had scored 700 or more on the college entrance SAT-M *before age 13* and were 1 in 10,000 students!)—left-handedness and high mathematical *reasoning* ability would be correlated with each other. They did not explain why they chose to look at math reasoning rather than at any other math abilities, and nowhere in their paper did they present any evidence that math reasoning is more likely to be affected by testosterone or by hand preference or by the brain hemispheres than any other math ability.

The Benbows claimed that they had supported their hypothesis when they found that, in their highly unusual group, there were about twice as many left-handers and twice the frequency of allergies (an immune disorder) as in the general population. However, as every introductory psychology student learns, left-handers are more common in a wide range of unusual populations, including prisoners and students at Harvard University. Therefore, it is extremely difficult to know how to interpret yet another example of a high incidence of left-handers in an extreme population. And as for the unusually high frequency of allergies in the top math students, so little is understood about allergies themselves and about possible effects of hormones on allergies that it is premature to make too much of that finding. Furthermore, a carefully done study would include investigation of the whole spec-

trum of immune disorders, when we have been given no reason to believe that only one specific type would be affected by testosterone levels.

Then we might wonder how the Benbows might explain why only *some* members of their highly selected group fit the pattern that their questionable theory predicted. In fact, they again plunge into speculation, suggesting that *those* students *might have been* exposed before birth to higher than normal testosterone levels. Do they present any data to support this claim? Their argument here becomes quite strange and again convoluted. They had no proof that these students had had such prenatal exposure, but they hauled out the finding that they were more likely than most students to have been born during months that have more than 12 hours of daylight per day. Then, they stated, "Daylight affects pineal gland secretion, altering the level of melatonin, which in turn has an inhibitory effect on reproductive hormones" (pp. 150–151). In other words, daylight affects Factor A, which affects Factor B, and *that* can reduce the hormone level. Aside from the sheer length of this unproven explanation about how top math students *might* have been exposed to high levels of testosterone, their reasoning is simply wrong. If more daylight is supposed to *reduce* the reproductive hormones, then these students should have had *less* testosterone, not more, than most students. And according to the Benbows' own (unsupported) chain of reasoning, lower testosterone levels should lead to *poorer* mathematical abilities.

If you look back at the headlines cited earlier in this chapter, it may seem surprising that the public could be presented such claims when they are based on highly speculative theories, research on extreme groups of people, and just plain poor reasoning. However, such presentations are not uncommon. When some journalists hear what seems to be a "hot" story, they do not stop to learn whether or not there is any scientific basis for it.

We hope that, through the scrutiny of the range and variety of problems in the Benbow and

Stanley study, you have some sense of the complexity and difficulty of the field of sex differences in mathematics. This sense should be helpful to you as you read other research or plan your own.

REFERENCES

Astin, H. (1974). Sex differences in mathematical and scientific precocity. In J. Stanley, D. Keating, & L. Fox (Eds.), *Mathematical talent: Discovery, descriptions, and development* (pp. 70–86). Baltimore, MD: Johns Hopkins University Press.

Attard, M. (1986). *Gender differences on the Arithmetic and Coding subtests of the Wechsler Intelligence Scale for Children.* Unpublished master's thesis, University of Toronto.

Benbow, C. P., & Benbow, R. M. (1987). Extreme mathematical talent: A hormonally induced ability? In David Ottoson (Ed.), *Duality and unity of the brain* (pp. 147–157). London: Macmillan.

Benbow, C., & Stanley, J. (1980, December 12). Sex differences in mathematical ability: Fact or artifact? *Science, 210,* 1262–1264.

Benbow, C., & Stanley, J. (1983, December 2). Sex differences in mathematical reasoning: More facts. *Science, 222,* 1029–1031.

Caplan, P. J. (1987, February). *Do sex differences in spatial abilities exist?* Presented at the Symposium on Bias in Sex-Differences Research, American Association for the Advancement of Science, Annual Meeting, Chicago.

Caplan, P. J. (1973). *Sex differences in determinants of antisocial behavior.* Unpublished doctoral dissertation, Duke University.

Decore, A. M. (1984). Vive la différence: A comparison of male-female academic performance. *Canadian Journal of Higher Education, 14*(3), 34–58.

Eccles, J. S., & Jacobs, J. E. (1987). Social forces shape math attitudes and performance. In M. R.Walsh (Ed.), *The psychology of women: Ongoing debates* (pp. 341–354). New Haven: Yale University Press.

Fox, L., & Cohn, S. (1980). Sex differences in the development of precocious mathematical talent. In L. Fox, L. A. Brody, & D. Tobin (Eds.), *Women and the mathematical mystique* (pp. 94–112). Baltimore: Johns Hopkins University Press.

Geschwind, N., & Behan, P. (1992). Left-handedness: Association with immune disease, migraine, and developmental learning disorder. *Proceedings of the National Academy of the Sciences, 79,* 5097–5100.

Gilligan, C. (1982). *In a different voice: Psychological theory and women's development.* Cambridge, MA: Harvard University Press.

Hanna, G. (1988). Mathematics achievement of boys and girls: An international perspective. In D. Ellis (Ed.), *Math 4 girls* (pp. 14–21). Ontario Educational Research Council.

Holden, C. (1987, May 8). Female math anxiety on the wane. *Science, 236,* 660–661.

Kolata, G. B. (1980, December 12). Math and sex: Are girls born with less ability? *Science, 210,* 1234–1235.

Leinhardt, G., Seewald, A., & Engel, M. (1979). Learning what's taught: Sex differences in instruction. *Journal of Educational Psychology, 71*(3),432–439.

Meece, J. L.; Parsons, J. E.; Kaczala, C. M.; Goff, S. B.; & Futterman, R. (1982). Sex differences in math achievement: Toward a model of academic choice. *Psychological Bulletin, 91,* 324–48.

Miele, J. A. (1958). Sex differences in intelligence: The relationship of sex to intelligence as measured by the Wechsler Adult Intelligence Scale and the Wechsler Intelligence Scale for Children. *Dissertation Abstracts International, 18,* 2213.

Rosenthal, R., & Jacobson, L. (1968). *Pygmalion in the classroom: Teacher expectation and pupils' intellectual development.* New York: Holt, Rinehart & Winston.

Schildkamp-Küngider, E. (Ed.) (1982). *International review on gender and mathematics.* ERIC Clearinghouse for Science, Mathematics, and Environmental Education, Columbus, OH.

Slack, W., & Porter, D. (1980). Training, validity, and the issue of aptitude: A reply to Jackson. *Harvard Educational Review, 50*(3), 392–401.

Reading 2   The Development of Thoughtfulness in College Women

BLYTHE MCVICKER CLINCHY

Questions to Consider:

1. Do you agree that women are often silent in college classrooms? Is this silence most frequent in classrooms where argument is encouraged?

2. Give an example of a time you have used separate knowing to understand something. Give an example of a time you have used connected knowing. What are the benefits and drawbacks of each approach to knowing?

3. What might learning look like in a classroom based on connected knowing? Would you prefer this type of classroom? Why or why not?

Last year there appeared in the *New York Times* an article by Michael Gorra (1988), and assistant professor of English at Smith College. The title of Gorra's piece was "Learning to Hear the Small, Soft Voices," and it began this way:

> *"You at a women's college?" a friend said just after I'd been hired to teach English at Smith. "That's a scandal waiting to happen." He never made it clear if I was to be the debaucher or the debauchee. Another friend, a Smith alumna, told me its students saw the young male faculty, married or not, as "fair game." My mother told me to get a heavy doorstop for my office and to keep my wife's picture on the desk [p. 32].*

Blythe McVicker Clinchy, "The Development of Thoughtfulness in College Women," *American Behavioral Scientist, 32*(6), pp. 647–657, copyright © 1989 by Sage Publications, Inc. Reprinted by permission of Sage Publications, Inc.

THE SILENCE OF WOMEN STUDENTS

Gorra does not tell us whether he took his mother's advice or not. If he did, it seems to have worked. He has been at Smith for several years now, and the lurid fantasies of his friends and relations so far have not been fulfilled. The difficulties that Gorra has encountered in teaching women students have to do not with their sexuality but with their silence. Gorra has trouble getting a class discussion off the ground, because the students refuse to argue. They will not argue with him, even when he tries to lure them into it by taking a devil's advocate position. They will not even argue with each other. Gorra tells about a recent incident in which two students, one speaking right after the other, offered diametrically opposed readings of a W. H. Auden poem. The second student, Gorra says,

> *didn't define her interpretation against her predecessor's, as I think a man would have. She didn't begin by saying, "I don't agree*

with that." She betrayed no awareness that she [had] disagreed with her classmate, and seemed surprised when I pointed it out [1988: 32].

Gorra has found the feminist poet Adrienne Rich's (1979) essay, "Taking Women Students Seriously," helpful in trying to understand this phenomenon. Rich says that women have been taught since early childhood to speak in "small, soft voices" (p. 243). And Gorra says,

Our students still suffer, even at a woman's college, from the lessons Rich says women are taught about unfemininity of assertiveness. They are uneasy with the prospect of having to defend their opinions, not only against my own devil's advocacy, but against each other. They would rather not speak if speaking means breaking with their classmates' consensus. Yet that consensus is usually more emotional, a matter of tone, than it is intellectual [1988: 32].

I have been teaching at a woman's college much longer than Gorra has and have had experiences similar to his. A few years ago, I might have described and analyzed the experiences in the same way he does, but in the course of research over the last 10 years I have interviewed a great many women students, both at my own college and at a broad range of other institutions, and as a result of that research, I have come to interpret the phenomenon of silence among women students differently. As my colleagues (Mary Belenky, Nancy Goldberger, and Jill Tarule) and I poured over the interviews with 135 women, which we had collected in preparation for writing our book, *Women's Ways of Knowing* (Belenky et al., 1986), we were astonished to see how often the women referred to matters of voice: "speaking out," "speaking up," "being silenced," "not being heard," "really listening," "really talking," "words as weapons," "feeling deaf and dumb,"

"saying what you mean," and so on. We subtitled the book *The Development of Self, Voice and Mind* because issues of voice seemed so intricately intertwined with the development of women's minds and selves.

Our interviews confirm Gorra's sense that many young women are reluctant to engage in argument, and I agree—and so would many of the women we interviewed—and this is a limitation. But argument is not the only form of dialogue, and if asked to engage in other types of conversation—"in a different voice," to borrow Carol Gilligan's (1982) phrase—we found that women could speak with eloquence and strength. Gorra may not know about this different voice, as I did not, because, like most of us professionals, he does not invite it to speak in his classroom. In Gorra's classroom, as in most classrooms run by teachers who pride themselves on encouraging discussion, discussion means disagreement, and the student has two choices: to disagree or to remain silent.

To get a somewhat different slant on the problem, Gorra might take a look at another of Adrienne Rich's essays (1979). It is called "Toward a Woman-Centered University," and in it she says that our educational practice is founded upon a "masculine, adversarial form of discourse" (p. 138). Here, Rich defines the problem of silence not as a deficiency in women, but as a limitation in our educational institutions. Argument is not the only style of discourse that exists, but it is the only kind that has found much favor in the groves of academe.

Now, I do not mean to imply that women are incapable of argument. We interviewed a good many students, especially from the more traditional elite colleges, who, Gorra would be pleased to know, had become skilled in argument and valued their skill. For some, adversarial thinking had become automatic. For example, one young woman told us, "As soon as someone tells me his point of view, I immediately start arguing in my head the opposite point of view.

When someone is saying something, I can't help turning it upside down." And another said,

> I never take anything someone says for granted. I just tend to see the contrary. I like playing devil's advocate, arguing the opposite of what somebody's saying, thinking of exceptions to what the person has said or thinking of a different train of logic.

SEPARATE KNOWING

These young women are playing what the writer Peter Elbow (1973) calls the "doubting game." They look for what is wrong with whatever it is that they are examining. They think up opposing positions. The doubting, argumentative, adversarial mode of discourse is the voice that is appropriate to a way of knowing we call separate knowing. I will not dwell upon separate knowing here, because we all know what it is. It is the way we are supposed to think, according to most of our professors. Separate knowing includes activities like critical thinking, scientific method, and textual analysis. The heart of separate knowing is detachment. The separate knower keeps her distance from the object she is trying to analyze. She takes an impersonal stance. She follows certain rules or procedures that will ensure that her judgments are unbiased. All our various disciplines and vocations have these impersonal procedures for analyzing things. All of the various fields have impersonal standards for evaluating things, criteria that allow one to decide whether a novel is well constructed or an experiment has been properly conducted or a person should be diagnosed as schizophrenic.

Separate knowing is obviously of great importance. It allows us to criticize our own and other people's thinking. Without it, we could not write second drafts of our papers; the first draft would look just fine. Without it, we would be at the mercy of all of the authorities who try to tell us what to believe. Separate knowing is a powerful way of knowing.

But it is not the only way of knowing.

CONNECTED KNOWING

In the research that my colleague, Claire Zimmerman, and I did at Wellesley, we interviewed undergraduate women each year and asked them to respond to comments made by other undergraduates, including the one that I quoted earlier to illustrate separate knowing made by the woman who says she automatically starts "arguing the opposite point of view." Most of the students said that they did not like the quotation much; they said that they were not into that kind of thing.

They could recognize disagreement all right, but they did not deal with disagreement by arguing. For instance, a woman we call Grace[1] said that when she disagreed with someone she did not start arguing in her head. She started trying to imagine herself in the person's situation. She said, "I sort of fit myself into it in my mind and then say, 'I see what you mean.'" She said, "There's this initial point where I kind of go into the story, you know? And become like Alice in Wonderland falling down the well."

It took Claire and me a long time to hear what Grace was saying. We thought at the time that she was just revealing her inability to engage in critical thinking. To us, her comment indicated not the presence of a different way of thinking but the absence of any kind of thinking—not a difference but a deficiency. Now we see it as an instance of what we call connected knowing, and, as we go back over the interviews we have done with women over the years, we see it everywhere. It is clear to us that many women have a proclivity for connected knowing.

Here is an especially clear illustration of connected knowing from a student we call Priscilla:

> When I have an idea about something, and it differs from the way another person's thinking about it, I'll usually try to look at it from that person's point of view, see how they could say that, why they think they're right, why it makes sense.

Now, contrast this quotation with the ones illustrating separate knowing. When you play devil's advocate, you take a position contrary to the other person's, even when you agree with it, even when it seems intuitively right. Priscilla turns this upside down. She allies herself with the other person's position even when she disagrees with it. Another student, Leonora, said she seldom played devil's advocate. She said, "I'm usually a little bit of a chameleon. I really try to look for pieces of truth in what the person says, instead of going contrary to them. Sort of collaborate with them." These women are playing what Elbow (1973) calls the "believing game." Instead of looking for what is wrong with the other person's idea, they look for why it makes sense, how it might be right.

Connected knowers are not dispassionate, unbiased observers. They deliberately bias themselves in favor of the thing they are examining. They try to get right inside it, to form an intimate attachment to it. The heart of connected knowing is imaginative attachment. Priscilla tries to get behind the other person's eyes, to "look at it from that person's point of view." This is what Elbow means by "believe." You must suspend your disbelief, put your own views aside, and try to see the logic in the idea. Ultimately, you need not agree with it, but while you are entertaining it you must, as Elbow says, "Say yes to it"; you must empathize with it, feel with and think with the person who created it.

The connected knower believes that in order to understand what a person is saying, one must adopt the person's own terms. One must refrain from judgment. In this sense, connected knowing is uncritical, but it is not unthinking. It is a personal way of thinking, and it involves feeling. The connected knower takes a personal approach even to an impersonal thing like a philosophical treatise; she treats the text, as one Wellesley student put it, "as if it were a friend." In Martin Buber's (1970) terms, the text is a "thou," a subject, rather than an "it," an object, of analysis.

So, while the separate knower takes nothing at face value, the connected knower, in a sense, takes everything at face value. She does not try to evaluate the perspective she is examining. She tries to understand it. She does not ask, "Is it right?"; she asks, "What does it mean?" When she says, "Why do you think that?" she does not mean, "What evidence do you have to support that belief, how can you back it up?" She means, "What in your experience led you to that position?" She is looking for the story behind the idea. The voice of separate knowing is argument; the voice of connected knowing is a narrative voice.

Women spend a lot of time sharing stories of their experience. It sometimes seemed to us that first-year students spent most of their time this way. This may help to account for the fact that most studies of intellectual development among college students show the major growth occurring during the first year. The students worry that they waste time chatting with their friends when they should be in the library reading books. But we came to believe that, at least for women, the sharing of stories is a major avenue of growth. When a student who has known many Jews but has never before laid eyes on an Arab listens to her Arab roommate tell her life story, she can stretch beyond the boundaries of her own limited experience. As a separate knower might say, she expands her data base or, to paraphrase the philosopher Ned Noddings (1984), the other person's reality becomes a possibility for her. Connected knowing, then, is not only a way of knowing but a way of growing. It opens up new ways of being.

We call these conversations "connected conversations." In connected conversations each participant tries to draw the other one out. These conversations may begin rather like clinical interviews. In interviewing, a still soft voice is an asset. The skilled interviewer says little; mainly, she listens. But the listening is active, although it may appear passive: The skilled interviewer offers support and invites elaboration at the appropriate moments. She is thoughtful: She thinks along with her informant and offers her careful consideration.

This kind of dialogue can be one-sided. One risks being always the interviewer and never the interviewee, always the listener and never the primary speaker. There is the risk of losing one's self in the other person's story, rather than using the story to expand the self. The psychologist Robert Hogan (1973) identified a group of people who scored relatively high on a measure of empathy and relatively low on a measure of autonomy. The behavior of these "overempathizers" suggests, Hogan says, that "unleavened role taking can produce an equivocating jellyfish as well as a compassionate person with a broad moral perspective" (p. 224). Connected knowers sometimes look like equivocating jellyfish, "clones" or "chameleons," even to themselves. For example, Adrienne, in her first year at college, laments,

> It's easy for me to take other people's points of view. It's hard for me to argue, sometimes, because I feel like I can understand the other person's argument. It's easy for me to see a whole lot of different points of view on things and to understand why people think those things. The hard thing is sitting down and saying, "Okay, what do I think, and why do I think it?"

This may be what is going on behind the apparent "consensus" in Gorra's classroom. His silent students may find it easy to think *with* their classmates and their teacher, hard to think against them, and hard to think for themselves; but connected knowing need not end in static consensus. If we cultivate our students' skills in connected knowing and nourish their development, connected knowing can attain a higher form. In this form, connected conversations involve a *community* of students and teachers engaged in the collaborative construction of knowledge. When we asked women to describe a "good class" they had had, many told of classes that had taken this form, with students and teachers drawing out each other's ideas, elaborating upon them, and building together a truth none could have constructed alone. In *Women's Ways of Knowing,* we quoted one such student:

> We were all raising our hands and talking about I forget what book, and some of the students brought up things that [the teacher] hadn't thought about that made him see it in a whole different way, and he was really excited, and we all came to a conclusion that none of us had started out with. We came up with an answer to a question we thought was unanswerable in the beginning, and it just made you all feel really good when you walked out of class. You felt you had accomplished something and that you understood the book [Belenky et al., 1986: 220].

This sort of discussion moves well beyond bland agreement. In fact, many women see this sort of discussion as dynamic, while they see arguments as static. Arguments, they say, leave the participants in the same place they began, while collaborative conversations can lead the speakers into territory none has ventured into before.

THE QUESTION OF GENDER

Recently, my students and colleagues and I have been interviewing both men and women, asking them to respond to the sorts of comments I have quoted here, illustrating argument and connected conversation. This is highly exploratory research, and I do not want to make too much of it, but so far, typically, the men we have interviewed describe arguments as useful in clarifying their own thinking and helping others to think more clearly. Unlike many women, who see argument as a zero-sum game in which only one side could win, men see arguments as useful for both participants. Men reported that arguments had stimulated their intellectual growth, whereas women—not always, but often—described them as crippling. They told about men in their lives—teachers, lovers, husbands, and, most often, fathers—who had used devil's advocacy against them, reducing them to silence and frequently to tears.

However, many of these women were ambivalent. Although arguments made them uncomfortable, they were ashamed of their discomfort and of their ineptitude. They wished that they could argue better.

Typically, the men's responses to our questions about connected knowing reflected an ambivalence similar to the women's attitudes toward argument. These men said that they knew they ought to try harder to enter the other person's perspective, but it made them uncomfortable, and they found it difficult to do, as they did not do it much.

It is possible that men like this might feel as constricted in the kind of connected class discussion I envisage as the women seem to feel in Gorra's classroom. In a connected class, men might sit in silence, and the teacher would worry about what it was in their upbringing that had retarded their intellectual development.

Ideally, we would encourage our men and women students to speak in both voices, and we would help them to integrate the voices. But that is not the way it is. In classrooms that sanction only separate knowing, men can speak up more easily than women, but they may never learn to speak in a connected voice

Given the present situation, what about the women? Here, we need not imagine the outcomes, because women have told us about them. Some women, unable to acquire the skills of separate knowing, will graduate from college convinced that they are stupid. Others will learn the skills, but often at the cost of alienation and repression. The kind of connected thinking for which they have a predilection is disallowed, and the utterly objective, impersonal, detached reasoning that they think they are asked to use in academic life comes to seem increasingly empty and pointless. In playing the doubting game, Elbow (1973) says, you try to "extricate your-self," "weed out the self," "make your thinking more like using a computer.... The less involvement of the self the better" (p. 171).

Some students use mechanical metaphors like this to describe their production of essays. They speak of "cranking out" papers. Others, like Simone, use biological metaphors: They call their papers "bullshit." Simone says she can write "good papers" when she tries. By "good papers," she means papers that teachers like. Simone, herself, does not like them very much. She says,

> I can write a good paper, and someday I may learn to write one that I like, that is not just bullshit, but I still feel that it's somewhat pointless. I do it, and I get my grade, but it hasn't proved anything to me.

Simone calls her papers bullshit because she does not care about what she is writing about, and reason, in the absence of feeling, is bullshit. The problem, she says,

> is that I don't feel terribly strongly about one point of view, but that point of view seems to make more sense. It's easier to write the paper, supporting that point of view than the other one, because there's more to support it. And it's not one of my deep-founded beliefs, but it writes the paper.

Simone does not write the paper. "It" writes the paper.

This, to me, is the really insidious effect of an education that emphasizes separate knowing to the virtual exclusion of connected knowing: The student removes her self from her work and dissociates thinking and feeling. She learns to think only about things she does not care about and she cares only about things she does not think about. The contemporary philosopher Sara Ruddick (1977) tells us that in college she became, in our terms, an ultraseparate knower. She writes, "In college I learned to avoid work done out of love.

My intellectual life became increasingly critical, detached, and dispensable" (p. 135). Think of that word: *dispensable.*

Simone seemed to have dispensed with intellectual life. Nominated by the science faculty at her college as the most outstanding student of her year, Simone in her senior year aborted her thesis, withdrew her applications to the most prestigious graduate schools in the country, and, after graduating without honors, returned to her hometown, married her high school boyfriend, and settled into an undemanding job. Simone's professors were horrified, of course, and I, interviewing her, was worried. Simone seemed to feel that she had to choose between her mind and her heart. Her work had become heartless. I worried that the decision to marry was mindless. Will Simone ever achieve some sort of integration between heart and mind?

Sara Ruddick did, but not until years after she had graduated from college and earned a Ph.D. in philosophy. In rearing her two children Ruddick developed what we call connected knowing. She watched her children closely, attentively, in detail, her attention sharpened rather than clouded by her feeling for them. As a sort of hobby, she began to study Virginia Woolf, and she found that the way of thinking she developed in reading Woolf was closer to the way of thinking she used in rearing children than to the way she had been taught in college and graduate school. She writes,

I seemed to learn new ways of attending.... This kind of attending was intimately connected with caring; because I cared I reread slowly, then found myself watching more carefully, listening with patience.... The more I attended, the more deeply I cared. The domination of feeling by thought, which I had worked so hard to achieve, was breaking down. Instead of developing arguments that could bring my feelings to heel, I allowed feeling to inform my most abstract thinking.... I now care about my thinking

and think about what I care about [Ruddick, 1984: 151].

Surely we can find ways to help our students achieve this sort of integration while they are still in college. As the philosopher Janice Raymond (1986) reminds us, the word *thoughtfulness* contains two meanings: the use of reason and the practice of consideration and care. We are awash these days in rhetoric setting forth the proper aims of higher education. I will settle for thoughtfulness.

NOTE

1. All students' names are pseudonyms.

REFERENCES

Belenky, M. B., B. M. Clinchy, N. R. Goldberger, and J. M. Tarule (1986) Woman's Ways of Knowing. New York: Basic Books.

Buber, M. (1970) I and Thou. New York: Scribner's.

Elbow, P. (1973) Writing Without Teachers. London: Oxford Univ. Press.

Gilligan, C. (1982) In a Different Voice: Psychological Theory and Women's Development. Cambridge, MA: Harvard Univ. Press.

Gorra, M. (1988) "Learning to hear the small, soft voices." New York Times Sunday Magazine (May 1): 32, 34.

Hogan, R. (1973) "Moral conduct and moral character: a psychological perspective." Psych. Bull. 70: 217–232.

Noddings, N. (1984) Caring. Berkeley: Univ. of California Press.

Raymond, J. B. (1986) A Passion for Friends. Boston: Beacon.

Rich, A. (1979) On Lies, Secrets, and Silence: Selected Prose 1966–1978. New York: Norton.

Ruddick, S. (1977) "A work of one's own," pp. 128–143 in S. Ruddick and P. Daniels (eds.) Working it Out. New York: Pantheon.

Ruddick, S. (1984) "New combinations: learning from Virginia Woolf," pp. 137–159 in C. Asher, L. DeSalvo, and S. Ruddick (eds.) Between Women. Boston: Beacon.

Reading 3   Gendered Relations in the Mines and the Division of Labor Underground

SUZANNE E. TALLICHET

Questions to Consider:

1. In what ways do the gender relations documented in this study reflect the patriarchal ideology of the larger society?

2. What does Tallichet mean by the "sexualization of work relations and the workplace," and what are some examples documented by her study? What is your reaction to her findings?

3. In what ways did the women miners resist their oppressive treatment? How would you resist (or have you resisted) in a similar situation?

4. Are there ways in which the findings from this study can be generalized to other male-dominated jobs? (Consider this issue in terms of both blue- and white-collar jobs.) What implications do these findings have for the experience of women of color in white, male-dominated jobs?

This article focuses on how men's sexualization of work relations and the workplace contributes to job-level gender segregation among coal miners. The findings suggest that sexualization represents men's power to stigmatize women in order to sustain stereotypes about them as inferior workers. In particular, supervisors use ste-

Suzanne E. Tallichet, "Gendered Relations in the Mines and the Division of Labor Underground," *Gender and Society,* 9(6), pp. 697–711, copyright © 1995 by Sage Publications, Inc. Reprinted by Permission of Sage Publications, Inc.

Author's Note: I appreciate the encouragement and assistance of Comelia B. Flora, Constance L. Hardesty, David R. Rudy, and Carolyn E. Sachs during various stages of the article. I would also like to thank the anonymous reviewers and those women miners who so kindly consented to be a part of this research.

reotypes to justify women's assignments to jobs in support of and in service to men. Once in these jobs, men's positive evaluations of women workers become contingent upon their fulfillment of men's gendered expectations. These processes foster the gender typing of jobs and lead to the gendered division of labor underground.

Among those women who entered nontraditional blue-collar occupations almost two decades ago, many have remained in entry-level jobs (Reskin 1993). Despite federal antidiscrimination regulations and the threat of litigation, men still dominate the channels of upward mobility and retain the better-paying positions of authority. Numerous studies have examined how men's reactions to women workers have contributed to job-level gender segregation in different blue-collar occupations (Walshok 1981), among auto workers (Gruber and Bjorn 1982), and corrections officers (Jurik 1985), in manufacturing (Harlan and O'Farrell 1982), policing (Martin 1980), steel making (Deaux 1984), and forestry (Enarson 1984). Even so, there are still relatively few studies investigating women's on-the-job experiences in other masculine-identified blue-collar occupations, such as coal mining. The present investigation examines how supervisors' and coworkers' resistance to women coal miners' integration has inhibited their job advancement at a single mining establishment.

THEORY AND PAST RESEARCH

The most recent theoretical formulations appropriate to this investigation are social closure theory and the concept of patriarchy. Social closure theory states that "a status group creates and preserves its identity and advantages by reserving certain opportunities for members of the group" using exclusionary and discriminatory practices (Tomaskovic-Devey 1993, 61). Patriarchy is the system of beliefs and corresponding behaviors by which men preserve their advantages (Cockburn 1991; Hartmann 1976; Reskin 1988). In workplaces dominated by men, their privilege is manifested primarily through the functional differentiation of workers by gender (Reskin 1988; Reskin and Roos 1987).

According to Reskin and Roos, the gendered division of labor is "grounded in stereotypes of innate sex differences in traits and abilities" and operates through "various social control mechanisms" (1987, 9). Because women pose a threat to men's masculine-based privileges, men will tend to emphasize women's presumed incapability for doing male-identified work. Their behavior toward women workers underscores the terms by which they are willing to accept them. As women become integrated into the job hierarchy, they are expected to occupy subordinate positions requiring their deference to men; thus, men are able to "tolerate women in predominantly

male work settings if they work in 'women's' jobs...but resist women doing traditionally male jobs in male work settings" (Reskin 1988, 67).

The gendered status hierarchy is preserved through certain "social practices that create or exaggerate the social distance between status groups" (Reskin and Roos 1987, 7). These practices dictate subordinates' behavior in the presence of dominant group members and shape the casual interaction between them. When gendered status hierarchies are maintained this way, they are usually seen by both men and women as natural and, thus, appropriate, because they recreate gendered social relations occurring in the larger culture. Because women who do "men's jobs" are challenging the routinization of the presumably natural order of gendered relations, they are "at risk of gender assessment" (West and Zimmerman 1987, 136). They are held accountable for engaging in gender-inappropriate behavior through other women's and men's evaluations of their behavior based on "normative conceptions of appropriate attitudes and activities" for their gender category (West and Zimmerman 1987, 139); thus, these women are under pressure to prove their femininity.

Kanter (1977a, 1977b) was among the first to document that women's conspicuous token presence leads to men's exaggeration of the differences between them. This is accomplished via men's "sexualization of the workplace," during which work relations between men and women are "sexualized" (Enarson 1984; Swerdlow 1989). Sexualizing the workplace and work relations consists of behaviors that express "the salience of sexual meanings in the presumably asexual domain of work" (Enarson 1984, 88). As the literature on women in nontraditional blue-collar occupations has documented, many men engage in at least one of several forms of workplace sexualization using sexual harassment, sexual bribery, gender-based jokes and comments, and profanity in order to make gender differences a salient aspect of work relations (Enarson 1984;

Gruber and Bjorn 1982; Swerdlow 1989). These behaviors, according to Enarson, constitute a continuum of abuse and reflect "a cultural tradition which sexualizes, objectifies, and diminishes women" (1984, 109).

Men's sexualization of work relations directly expresses the expectation that women should "act like women" by making their integration into a sexualized workplace contingent upon their production of gender as they interact with men. Because men's sexualization of work relations identifies women primarily by their gender category and not by their work roles, it objectifies them. As Schur (1984) has pointed out, this objectification of women workers leads to their stigmatization about their work-related inferiority. Objectification and work-related trivialization are mutually reinforcing processes (Schur 1984, 142), which is how women workers are matched with gender-typed jobs requiring few skills, if any. Under these circumstances, jobs to which women are assigned mirror their relations with men, since these jobs require women's support of and service to men occupying more skilled jobs. Because there are simply too few women present in a workplace dominated by men, women are usually unable to directly counter men's expressions of the negative stereotypes upon which this gender-typed matching process is based (Kanter 1977b).[1]

Studies have shown that men's gender-role expectations of women workers negatively affect women's success in nontraditional employment because these expectations color the men's perception of women's potential for or actual job performance (for a review, see Roos and Reskin 1984). Accordingly, "male workers may inhibit integration both by their ability to shape employer's decisions and by affecting the preferences of female workers" (Reskin 1993, 248). Reskin and Padavic (1988) found that supervisors' stereotypes about women's capabilities for doing sex-atypical work prevented them from objectively evaluating the women's performance. They tend to selectively perceive only that behav-ior that confirms their beliefs about women's lesser suitability for doing men's jobs.[2] In examining women miners' day-to-day social relations with men coworkers and supervisors in several western states, Yount found that "women are assigned to positions that are conducive to perceptions of sex-stereotypical traits. In turn, these perceptions (based on the work they perform) provide legitimation for the assignments" (1986, 29).

The present study investigated how men's sexualization of work relations and the workplace have contributed to coal mining women's concentration in entry-level jobs at a large underground coal mine. As the women pointed out, men's sexualization has reinforced men's, particularly supervisors', stereotypical beliefs about women's incapability for doing more masculine-identified work. Stereotypes, they said, have influenced supervisors' job assignments and have contributed to the gender typing of jobs. The women's perceptions of opportunities and, for some women, the availability of necessary training and experience also constituted barriers to their advancement; moreover, certain organizational constraints, such as realignments of the workforce and shift work, have negatively influenced their advancement decisions. Women's resistance was reflected in their awareness of the consequences of men's negative stereotypes and of the process by which the gender typing of jobs occurred. Their continual individual efforts to prove their competence as coal miners represented their solution to a collective dilemma.

METHODOLOGY

Primary data were collected from in-depth interviews, on-site observation, and document study done at a large coal mine in southern West Virginia during the fall of 1990. After getting permission from the company's home office, local mine officials gave me tours of the compound and the mine. Interviews with women and men were solicited between shifts in the women's bath house and lamp house, respectively. Being a woman in my early thirties and dressed in a faded army jacket, flannel shirt, jeans, and boots facilitated my initial contact with the women miners. Ten of the women contacted were interviewed later in either their homes, my motel room, or other places where they felt at ease. Seven other women were willing to talk only in the bath house because they feared reprisals from the company, saying, "Sorry, but I need this job." Four women flatly refused to be interviewed. Two were unavailable because of illness and injury. Relatively speaking, men miners were considerably more difficult to interview than women. As revealed later, they believed I was only interested in "women's problems," not their experiences. This was not surprising since managerial personnel often referred to me as "the lady here to talk to our lady miners."

In sum, in-depth interviews were conducted with 10 women and the mine superintendent. On several occasions, 20-minute discussions were held with seven more women. Conversations were also held with the local union president and several other men miners. All these individuals were contacted repeatedly. Sampling among men was based on convenience. Sampling among women miners was a combination of snowball and purposive techniques. The first few women interviewed provided the names of other women who were selected because of their tenure, job rank, and other job-related experiences, such as sexual harassment or discrimination. With two exceptions, interviews were taped.

The women in the sample were diverse in terms of their age, education, marital status, and child bearing. The youngest woman in the sample was 29; the oldest was 50. One woman finished the tenth grade, seven had high school diplomas, and two had attended college. When they were hired, three women were married with at least one child. Four were divorced with one or more children to support. The remaining three were single without children. All of the women said they needed a coal mining job to support themselves or their families. By the time of the study, one of the married women divorced and three of the divorced women had married or were cohabiting, so half of the women in the sample were coupled with children. Two of the women were divorced with one or two children to support. Two had remained single and childless. The youngest woman, a single mother, was Black. The rest of the sample was White.

Coal mining jobs are arranged according to five ranks, each containing job families. Six of the 10 women in the case study sample were classified in laboring jobs, three of whom were certified for higher grade jobs. Grade 1 jobs are laboring jobs usually involving mine maintenance. These jobs require few skills and more physical strength and endurance.[3] The four other women held jobs in each one of the higher grades. These jobs are more closely involved with coal production and require operative skills or certification, or both. The women's experience in mining ranged between 9 and 15 years. Two of the women in the sample had been working together. The rest were working as token members of their crews, as were most women at the mine.

Similar to other large coal companies involved in the hiring discrimination litigation of 1978, the case study company did not begin employing women in appreciable numbers until it was forced to do so. In 1975, only three women were working there. By the early 1980s the company employed approximately 800 miners. Between 80 and 90 were women; however, several years later the industry's economic slump forced the company to lay off almost half of its miners, including more than two-thirds of the women. At the time of the study, the company employed 466 miners, including 23 women. All the miners were members of the United Mine Workers of America (UMWA). The company also employed a dozen men as assistant foremen or "bosses." Their duties underground were strictly supervisory, so they were not members of the UMWA.

During their first few months on the job, new miners are considered trainees and are assigned to Grade 1 jobs, usually as general inside laborers ("GIs") or beltmen. At the end of this period, they receive their miner's certificate, meaning they can bid on any newly posted job in the mine. By UMWA contract, jobs are awarded by seniority defined as length of service and a miner's ability to perform the job (United Mine Workers of America 1988). Since the mid-1980s, new job postings at the case study mine had been infrequent and realignments of the working force were occurring regularly. At the time of the study, the concentration of women in Grade 1 jobs at the mine was substantial. Eighteen of the 23 women miners (78 percent) were so classified, compared with 148 (33 percent) of the men. The following analyses identify the social processes that contributed to job-level gender segregation at the case study site.

ANALYSES AND FINDINGS

Although most of the men treated them with some measure of respect, all the women in the sample reported that during their first few years underground, they encountered men's sexualization of work relations in the form of either sexual harassment, propositioning, or sexual bribery. More often than men coworkers, foremen tended to sexually bribe women through the misuse of their authority. In response to the women's complaints about the men's behavior, the company issued a formal set of rules forbidding obscene or abusive language. According to the women, the more direct forms of sexualization became less prevalent, in part, because of the men's fear of sanctions; however, other forms of workplace sexualization, such as gender-based jokes, comments, and profanity have persisted. These conditions, they said, have contributed to the endurance of the negative stereotypes that justify women's assignments to lesser-skilled jobs.

Sexualization of Work Relations

Half of the women in the sample said they had been sexually harassed by either men coworkers or foremen, who used verbal innuendo and body language to convey a sexual message (Gruber and Bjorn 1982). Two women reported that occasionally some of the men coworkers grabbed their own genitals and then pretended to have gotten "caught" urinating. Another woman reported an incident of homosexual buffoonery with a particularly potent message accentuating men's sexuality and solidarity:

> They was pretending they was queers in front of me. One was humping the other one, but they had their clothes on. And the boss said, "You scared of us, ain't you?" I said, "No, I'm not scared of you all." And he said, "Well, this is our little world down here and you don't belong."

Some men coworkers and foremen either directly solicited sexual favors from the women or repeatedly asked them for dates. When women first started working at the mine, one woman said that they were treated "like a piece of pussy." Another recalled that "a boss [said] all the women made beds out of rock dust for the men. You know, like that's all we did was go in there to sleep with them?"

Because of the power differential, sexual propositioning by foremen posed a much greater threat to a woman's work status than propositioning by men coworkers. It was well known by women in the sample that when a woman failed to capitulate to a foreman's sexual demands, she usually faced the prospect of getting a more difficult work assignment. One woman who had been reassigned for such an offense was told by a man coworker, "If you let these bosses pinch your titties, you'll get along. If you don't, you'll get the awfullest job that ever was." She allowed that she preferred the "awful" job every time.

Another form of punishment used by a foreman was social derogation designed to humiliate the woman who refused his sexual requests:

One time [the foreman] told the guys behind my back that I had "sucked his dick," is the way he put it. It came back to me about a week or so later. I went through pure misery for about a year because the boss lied to the crew that I worked with, telling them stuff. I didn't even know why everybody all of a sudden quit speaking to me, giving me the cold shoulder.

In front of her men coworkers, she retaliated:

I walked up to him and I said. "When did I suck your goddamned dick down the jackline?" He goes, "I don't know what you're talking about." I said, "You're a goddamned liar. You told everyone of them and you didn't think that they'd find out I'm not doing the shit you said I was doing and come back and tell me things, did you?" Right there it proved to the guys [he was lying].

In the above case, the foreman's rumors lead to her coworkers' lack of on-the-job cooperation, but even in the absence of rumors, the women's potential for becoming socially isolated was especially great because of their token status. This seriously hindered their ability to do their jobs and made them vulnerable to the perception that they were incapable of doing the work. A miner's reputation is important not only for being respected and appreciated by coworkers but also for gaining the opportunities necessary for advancement. Men's sexualization of work relations underscored the women's sexuality at the expense of their work-role performances and substantiated the cultural contradiction of a woman doing a man's job.

Although the women in the sample recognized that the men's sexual harassment was usually unprovoked, some tended to place the responsibility for the men's actions almost entirely on women themselves. This was especially true among those women who had received little or no sexual harassment. According to one woman:

The majority of the men up there are good to you if you let them. But they'll treat you how they see you act. See, men, they tend to watch women more, I believe it's just the male in them.

When the women were treated as sex objects, each woman was regarded by the men as a representative of her gender category; hence, each woman was made to feel that she had a moral responsibility to herself and to all her women coworkers for avoiding "loose" behavior.[4] Conversely, the sexual indulgences of other women were also a reflection upon each of them. As one woman explained:

[The foreman] wanted to sleep with me. I wouldn't have anything to do with him. He thought if a woman worked for him, she had to sleep with him because there was one woman working on the section [who was] sleeping with him. Everybody knew it. When it came my turn, I wouldn't sleep with him.

In order to thwart the men's sexual advances and uphold the image of fidelity, several of the women reported doing the following:

When I first came here, I set myself up right away. I've made it known: Don't bother me, I'm here to work. I'm not here for romance [but for] finance. Once you establish yourself, they know your boundaries.

Because of her behavior, this single and childless woman had challenged men's heterosexist beliefs. As a result, a man coworker once asked her if she was a lesbian, to which she responded, "What difference does it make what I tell you?

You already have your mind made up." No one ever asked her that again. She explained that not only were the men intimidated when women could handle coal mining jobs, but they were also intimidated by the possibility of a woman's homosexuality. In this case, a woman could remain not only financially independent but also sexually independent of men and their control.

When the company issued its mandate against harassment, the superintendent told me it was necessary to "teach the men what harassment was." His subsequent negative remarks implied that the men were so accustomed to regarding women in terms of their sexuality that they would find it difficult, if not unnatural, to develop egalitarian work relationships with them. Although the rule has effectively eroded these incidents of sexual harassment, the women added that its enforcement put the onus of responsibility on them. Using the rule had a double binding or "damned if you do, damned if you don't" quality, because it was the women, not other men (such as foremen), who were solely responsible for reporting harassment. Some women indicated that they were often reluctant to do so because it created tension among crew members. It also violated a UMWA oath of solidarity, defeating the women's attempts to become socially integrated as unionized members of their crews; moreover, those women who reported infractions said that it was they, not their harassers, who ended up being transferred to other work locations.

At the time of the study, most of the women insisted that any kind of sexual harassment was largely a thing of the past. A few also said that its saliency was the result of media hype and was not indicative of their current experiences. As one women said:

I think things have changed so much since the first woman come into the mines. She was harassed a lot [said with emphasis], but things have changed because they've accepted us.

Another woman agreed that sexual harassment was declining, but for a vastly different reason:

Oh, they've just about quit now because after all this time they see they're not going to get in my pants. At first they get mad at you and don't speak. Eventually they'll start talking to you, but they don't harass you no more for sex.

Another added, "I think it's still going on, it's just more subtle now." Her comment indicated that although the men's sexualization of work relations had changed form, it certainly had not disappeared.

Sexualization of the Workplace

Typically, men will continue to relate to women in sexual terms as long as the division of labor provides the potential for women to be equal to men (Reskin and Roos 1987). Over time it had become clear to the women that their successful integration had done little to seriously disrupt men's sexualization of the workplace. As one woman put it:

It's a man's world. And when I started I knew I was going into a man's world and men have their ways. When the first women went into the mines, it was hard for a man to change his ways.

Two types of men's behavior that contributed to workplace sexualization were sexual jokes and stories and profanity.

Gutek (1985) concluded that sex in the forms of graffiti, jokes, comments, and metaphors for work is a part of workplaces dominated by men regardless of women's presence. As women enter the work setting, they are obligated to set limits on some of the men's activities in order to avoid being degraded. Sometimes the men miners were careful about telling jokes in the women's presence. At other times, the women found themselves in the position of having to "draw the line" on the men's unacceptable behavior. On her crew, one woman said that, although she generally "laughs stuff off," she was careful not to "get rowdy with them," because invariably the action would escalate. She commented that if they got carried away, she would "make them stop." Another woman attempted to curb the men's "sex talk":

> They would start making sexual remarks about their girlfriends and women: So I'd say, "Hey, you shouldn't talk like that! What's the matter with you guys? You ought to be ashamed of yourself!" to get them to watch what they say.

Although she stated "you're not going to change people," she concluded, "all you can do is have them have respect for you."

Similar to other workers employed in dangerous occupations, coal miners are notorious for using profanity. The women said that men would apologize if they thought a woman had overheard them using foul language. Their apologies strongly imply that there is a difference between men's and women's language. Language maintains role boundaries. If profanity is not fit language for a woman to hear, then certainly she should avoid using it. The women varied considerably in their use of foul language and in their willingness to tolerate it from others. A few women did not swear and had no tolerance for it; however, most of the women miners admitted to using what constituted "men's language," but they said they were careful to conceal or curtail their use of it. For example:

> There's a lot of stuff I will say. I used to not cuss too bad, but I'll cuss now. I'll say it under my breath. I don't think they've ever heard it. They'd die if they heard me say what I say to myself.

Another said, "I cuss some when I get mad, but I always try to watch what I say because I'll lose

that edge." That "edge," she explained, was the men's respect.

The emphasis some men place on sexuality and gender differences in the workplace reasserts the subordinate status of women by focusing on their gender-role behavior at the expense of their work-role performances. As one woman put it, "The men look at our bodies and not at what we can do." The sexualization of work relationships and the workplace had the effect of stigmatizing women as a group, allowing the imputation of stereotypes about women's inferiority relative to men when it came to doing "men's work."

Men's Stereotypes and the Gender Typing of Jobs

In a masculine-identified workplace, men's sexualization maintains the gendered relations between women and men, but it also defines women's appropriate positions in the work hierarchy based on the stereotypical differences in women's and men's respective abilities. All of the women in the sample identified men's stereotypes as a means for justifying women's work assignments. These stereotypes were expressed verbally by some men coworkers but were also demonstrated by foremen's behavior toward the women.

During their first few years at the mine, all of the women complained that at least some men coworkers had made derisive remarks questioning the appropriateness of their presence or their work-related competence. One woman's account captures the nature of these remarks:

> Even some of our union brothers [said] I don't think women ought to be in here. They ought to get out of here and let a good man have this job. They said we should be home cleaning house, raising kids.

Another woman was asked why she had taken a coal job if she could not do the work. She said "they didn't want you to [work]. They don't even want you to try because you're crowding in on their turf."

Several of the women said that when they first started working, some of the men told them that mining jobs were too physically difficult for them. On the job, their men coworkers made the women's jobs unnecessarily difficult by ignoring them or reducing their own efforts. Other men responded in a chivalrous fashion by offering women unnecessary assistance. The women recognized the implication this had for their presumed inadequacy and refused their help. As one man miner said with a sneer, "They wouldn't let nobody help them do nothing. They'd chew you right out. And they've stayed here and become real independent."

Even at the time of the study, however, men miners were still expressing the same views. The women felt that these men had exaggerated their claims and asserted that these ideas constituted men's mythology designed to keep them from becoming miners. They likened the men's views to the superstition that women were bad luck in a coal mine. Under these circumstances, most of the women agreed that establishing a good work reputation was harder for women than it was for men. In order to avoid fulfilling the men's prophecies about their presumed incapability, the women felt they had to constantly prove themselves.

Foremen also communicated to the women that they were not suited for running machinery. Half the women in the sample said that they had been passed over for a man when skilled work was being assigned. As one woman commented:

We've had a couple of bosses up there that thought that women couldn't do nothing but shovel. I had one foreman [who] had me on a section as an extra person to hang rag. I roof bolted before that and roof bolters would be off. He would send the other [men] GIs to roof bolt. Well, I went to the union to file a grievance on it. After that night I roof bolted until they sent me to [another shift].

And from another woman:

This one boss just bypassed me on a job he knew I could do for another guy who never even run a motor. He just looked at me and went on. I've been on a motor. Taking it in and out wasn't a problem. The boy that I work with just looked at me after we got around to the other side and started laughing. He understood. Most of the men [coworkers] did.

Not only did foremen "have it in their minds that we are the weaker sex," another woman miner said, but the superintendent insisted that "men had a more mechanical approach" to their work, and the women had the more menial mining jobs because of "the natural settling of their skills and their application."

As documented elsewhere in the literature on women in nontraditional occupations (Deaux 1984; Harlan and O'Farrell 1982), the women miners perceived themselves as having less opportunity for advancement than men. Before the company implemented its training policy, getting on-the-job training on mining machinery was almost impossible, according to one of the earliest women miners. Although she heard that some women had been shown how to run equipment, she had not been shown.

I was put on the belt line shoveling and then on the belt head running the coal into the cars. As far as running equipment, I didn't get that [because] we were kept out of the face. They didn't offer us any chance to run any equipment. I don't know how to today and I don't care. I like my job. Stay where you're at and you really know what you're doing.

Even after management instructed senior miners to honor new miners' requests for on-the-job training, the women said that getting the training or the temporary assignment to get the experience was rare. Men coworkers and foremen "think women are harder to train," one woman said, "like we're dumb or something."

Three Grade 1 women in the sample said they had the skills to run machinery, but were not really interested in bidding on higher-grade jobs requiring operative skills. Those few higher-grade operative jobs that were posted were on night shifts and conflicted with their family responsibilities. Others indicated that they did not want the added pressures and responsibility that those jobs entailed. As one woman explained:

> Sometimes a general inside labor job, it's not easy, but there's no pressure. There's no major head-busting decisions to make. Somebody else tells you what to do and takes the blame if it does not get done right. Sometimes it's easy to fall into a situation where I don't have to make any decisions, [so] if you don't advance, you don't take a chance on being wrong or messing up.

She added that when a woman did operate machinery and made "a mistake, [the men] really don't let you live it down." She concluded by saying that the women were less likely to take such a chance "probably because we are women and we're feeling inferior." Likewise, those women who had jobs operating machinery said they were more closely scrutinized than the men working in similar jobs.

Some women who had once held operative jobs had been reassigned to Grade 1 jobs as the result of workforce realignments.[5] They contended that women were disproportionately downgraded relative to men. Like these women, another woman miner who had once bid unsuccessfully on a higher-grade job had become discouraged at the prospect of trying again. Another said that one time she had bid on a job knowing that she had the necessary seniority and skills, but was turned down. When she complained to the foreman who had assigned a man in her place, "he went over [to the posted assignment sheet] and

rubbed his name off there and put mine on it." As another woman who had advanced concluded, "The women have to stand up for their rights. If you want to advance, you got to make waves." Most of the women, she contended, were not willing to risk the men's hostility by doing so. Even when these jobs came up for bid, they did not bid on them. As one woman miner said about most of the women in Grade 1 jobs, "I think they just accept theirself in that position. They like it [or] they don't like it, but they're there, and they're afraid to advance theirself." About herself she said:

> For the past 10 years I felt like I was the underdog, that I shouldn't be stepping on their toes. I haven't felt like I was a person. They tell me to go shovel and I used to stand back and let things [jobs] go by. If there was a top-paying job, if I thought I could do it, most of the time I'd say let him do it.

Some of the Grade 1 women also said they could not compete with the men's greater seniority; however, one women who had advanced said that "a lot of them women got the seniority to bid over half them guys out." Data from company documents substantiated her claim. As previous studies on women in occupations dominated by men has shown, "the perceptions of opportunities are in part dependent on evidence that members of one's own group occupy particular positions within the organization" (Deaux 1984, 292). Indeed, the women in Grade 1 jobs were unable to name any or only one or two more advanced women at the mine, even though there were five women so classified at the time of the study.

The sex bias occurring at the mine also substantiated the suitability of assigning women to certain jobs requiring those characteristics that women are presumed to possess in relation to men. During one of my conversations with several men miners, one exclaimed that "there are some jobs women can do in the mines!" According to women in the sample, they were often expected to perform duties that mirrored the work they traditionally performed in their homes in service to or in support of men.[6]

> *Sunday I carried cinder block and rock dust behind them, I cleaned up the garbage, I carried their junk to them if they wanted it. It's just like you're a gofer or something. When they set up, they throw down everything. It's up to us to go clean up their mess. I know all the women experience the work discrimination because most of us are gofers, hard manual labor.*

And from another woman:

> *I've had bosses that treat you worse than the men. They make you go pick up things. When I was general inside labor, it didn't matter what section I went to they'd expect me to clean the dinner hole.*

When I asked one woman if there were "women's jobs" in the mine, she exclaimed, "Oh yeah! You got yourself on the belt, that's a woman's job. You go shovel the belt, you help the mason build stoppings." Conversely, these jobs, such as general inside labor and beltman, carry a certain stigma. The same woman told me, "[As a GI] you're the flunky. I mean you're the gofer. It's real hard." And another said, "It's just like you don't have no sense to do nothing else."

Over time, the men's, particularly the foremen's, gendered stereotyping about women's work capabilities have remained prevalent, making token women's negotiations with men over how they evaluate themselves and other women as miners highly problematic. The men's expectations that women should perform support activities requiring few, if any, technical skills has resulted in the gender typing of jobs at the mine. At least some of the men have acted to restrict the women's advancement by redefining the women's

and men's respective places in the underground work hierarchy.

CONCLUSIONS

Sexualization of work relations and the workplace reinforces the assumption that men and women are inherently different in terms of their physical and mechanical abilities. Accepting these differences as natural implies that their consequences, such as job-level gender segregation, are beyond organizational control. As the findings of this research have shown, sexualization and the resulting stigmatization of women as inferior to men maintains the potency of sex stereotypes that negatively affect their employment outcomes through the application of organizational procedures. The strength of job-level gender segregation rests upon the endurance of men's stereotypical beliefs about women's capabilities for doing men's work. These beliefs, behaviors, and corresponding organizational consequences constitute the preservation of men's privilege. As long as these beliefs are supported by management in the form of reactive as opposed to proactive antidiscriminatory policies and their enforcement, advancement for women miners will be unnecessarily difficult.

Over the years, despite their pessimistic advancement attitudes, women have been tireless in resisting men's attempts to stereotype their abilities through their own hard work. Their resistance can be furthered in at least two ways. First, despite some personal differences, the women share a common sense of being subordinates in a "man's world." They could gain an even greater collective consciousness by forming a support group at the mine. Then, as one woman told me, "we'd be a force to be reckoned with."

Second, there is strong evidence that nonsexual, egalitarian relationships have developed between at least some of the men miners and their women coworkers. Despite the women's disillusionment with weak local leadership, their allegiance to the union and their union brothers has remained strong; hence, the bonds between women and men miners could be strengthened through union solidarity. Women miners could remind their less-accepting union brothers that their entry represents the inevitable changes in the larger culture; that their presence should be regarded as a source of strength and not weakness; and that while some men are busy looking at women's bodies, management is busy using all miners' bodies to their own advantage. Specifically, management's use of making selective job assignments has been a powerful tool for dividing and controlling miners. The belief that an injury to one is an injury to all needs to be reasserted because the informal exclusion of women as union members diminishes the potential effects of union solidarity. Together, miners could pressure the company to more vigorously enforce its own policies for all miners, thereby recognizing that women deserve to be accepted as competent and not merely tolerated as "here to stay."

Coal mining is only one of many male-identified blue-collar occupations into which women have made important inroads. More research needs to be done delineating their experiences with men coworkers and supervisors in these nontraditional settings. Other studies could focus on the women's relationships with each other and the collective strategies they have devised to resist how men have attempted to discredit and exclude them.

NOTES

1. When women's resistance to men's stereotypical work-role expectations is minimal or nonexistent, they fall victim to what Nieva and Gutek (1981) have labeled "sex-role spillover." This occurs when workers in men's jobs are expected to "'act like men' to be perceived as good workers" (Gutek 1985, 133). For women in nontraditional jobs, being perceived as competent is problematic.

2. Women who disconfirmed these stereotypes by successful advancement were regarded as "exceptional" (Reskin and Padavic 1988).

3. Typically, the entry-level jobs of beginning miners consist of rock dusting, hanging ventilation curtain, setting timbers for roof support, shoveling coal along a belt line, moving heavy belt line structures and power cables, and laying track.

4. Not only did the women miners place the burden of sexual responsibility upon themselves, but miner's wives' opposition to women miners reinforced it and, according to women in the sample, partially accounted for the men's negative behavior toward them.

5. Realignments were done to accommodate major changes in the extraction of coal. Before realignments occurred, miners indicated in writing their job and shift preferences to management. Miners were then reassigned on the basis of their preferences and seniority in years and qualifications.

6. A few women in the sample likened their crew membership to being in a family, a social unit in which patriarchal control and women's subordinate status have already been defined (See Crull 1987, 233–4).

REFERENCES

Cockburn, Cynthia. 1991. *In the way of women: Men's resistance to sex equality in organizations.* Ithaca, NY: ILR Press.

Crull, Peggy. 1987. Searching for the causes of sexual harassment: An examination of two prototypes. In *Hidden aspects of women's work,* edited by Christine E. Bose, Rosyln Feldberg, and Natalie J. Sokoloff. New York: Greenwood.

Deaux, K. 1984. Blue-collar barriers. *American Behavioral Scientist* 27:287–300.

Enarson, Elaine Pitt. 1984. *Woods-working woman: Sexual integration in the U.S. forest service.* Birmingham: University of Alabama Press.

Gruber, James S., and Lars Bjorn. 1982. Blue-collar blues: The sexual harassment of women autoworkers. *Work and Occupations* 9:271–98.

Gutek, Barbara A. 1985. *Sex and the workplace: The impact of sexual behavior and harassment on women, men and organizations.* San Francisco: Jossey Bass.

Harlan, Sharon L., and Brigid O'Farrell. 1982. After the pioneers: Prospects for women in nontraditional blue-collar jobs. *Work and Occupations* 9:363–86.

Hartmann, Heidi. 1976. Capitalism, patriarchy, and job segregation by sex. In *Women and the work-*

place: The implications of occupational segregation, edited by Martha Blaxall and Barbara Reagan. Chicago: University of Chicago Press.

Jurik, Nancy C. 1985. An officer and a lady: Organizational barriers to women working as correctional officers in men's prisons. *Social Problems* 32:375–88.

Kanter, Rosabeth Moss. 1977a. *Men and women of the corporation.* New York: Harper and Row.

———. 1977b. Some effects of proportions on group life: Skewed sex ratios and responses to token women. *American Journal of Sociology* 82:965–90.

Martin, Susan. 1980. *Breaking and entering: Policewomen on patrol.* Berkeley: University of California Press.

Nieva, V. F., and B. A. Gutek. 1981. *Women and work: A psychological perspective.* New York: Praeger.

Reskin, Barbara F. 1988. Bringing the men back in: Sex differentiation and the devaluation of women's work. *Gender & Society* 2:58–81.

———. 1993. Sex segregation in the workplace. In *American Sociological Review.* Vol. 19, edited by Judith Blake and John Hagen. Palo Alto: Annual Reviews.

Reskin, Barbara, and Irene Padavic. 1988. Supervisors as gate-keepers: Male supervisors' response to women's integration in plant jobs. *Social Problems* 35:536–50.

Reskin, Barbara E, and Patricia A. Roos. 1987. Sex segregation and status hierarchies. In *Ingredients for women's employment policy,* edited by Christine Bose and Glenna Spitze. Albany: State University of New York Press.

Roos, Patricia A., and Barbara F. Reskin. 1984. Institutional factors affecting job access and mobility for women: A review of institutional explanations for occupational sex segregation. In *Sex segregation in the workplace: Trends, explanations, and remedies,* edited by Barbara F. Reskin. Washington, DC: National Academy Press.

Schur, Edwin M. 1984. *Labeling women deviant: Gender, stigma and control.* Philadelphia: Temple University Press.

Swerdlow, Marian. 1989. Entering a nontraditional occupation: A case of rapid transit operatives. *Gender & Society* 3:373–87.

Tomaskovic-Devey, Donald. 1993. *Gender and racial inequality at work.* Ithaca, NY: ILR Press.

United Mine Workers of America. 1988. *National bituminous coal wage agreement.* Indianapolis, IN: Allied Printing.

Walshok, Mary L. 1981. *Blue collar women: Pioneers on the male frontier.* New York: Anchor Books.

West, Candace, and Don H. Zimmerman. 1987. Doing gender. *Gender & Society* 1:125–51.

Yount, Kristen. 1986. Women and men coal miners: Coping with gender integration underground. Ph.D. diss., University of Colorado, Boulder.

Reading 4   The Second Shift: Working Parents and the Revolution at Home

ARLIE HOCHSCHILD WITH ANNE MACHUNG

Questions to Consider:

1. What does Hochschild mean by the "leisure gap" between employed mothers and fathers? Does this finding fit with your own experiences and/or observations?

2. Hochschild claims that the second shift of employed mothers is responsible for the leisure gap documented by her research. Why do you think this second shift exists for women?

3. How, according to Hochschild, does the second shift affect the health and well-being of employed mothers?

4. What changes need to be made in marriage and society to eliminate the leisure gap? Do you see any hopeful signs of these changes? Explain.

She is not the same woman in each magazine advertisement, but she is the same idea. She has that working-mother look as she strides forward, briefcase in one hand, smiling child in the other. Literally and figuratively, she is moving ahead. Her hair, if long, tosses behind her; if it is short, it sweeps back at the sides, suggesting mobility and progress. There is nothing shy or passive about her. She is confident, active, "liberated." She wears a dark tailored suit, but with a silk bow or colorful frill that says, "I'm really feminine underneath." She has made it in a man's world without sacrificing her femininity. And she has done this on her own. By

"A Speed-up in the Family," from *The Second Shift* by Arlie Hochschild with Anne Machung. Copyright © 1989 by Arlie Hochschild. Used by permission of Viking Penguin, a division of Penguin Books USA Inc.

some personal miracle, this image suggests, she has managed to combine what 150 years of industrialization have split wide apart—child and job, frill and suit, female culture and male.

When I showed a photograph of a supermom like this to the working mothers I talked to in the course of researching this book, many responded with an outright laugh. One daycare worker and mother of two, ages three and five, threw back her head: "Ha! They've got to be *kidding* about her. Look at me, hair a mess, nails jagged, twenty pounds overweight. Mornings, I'm getting my kids dressed, the dog fed, the lunches made, the shopping list done. That lady's got a maid." Even working mothers who did have maids couldn't imagine combining work and family in such a carefree way. "Do you know what a baby *does* to your life, the two o'clock feedings, the four o'clock feedings?" Another mother of two said:

"They don't show it, but she's whistling"—she imitated a whistling woman, eyes to the sky—"so she can't hear the din." They envied the apparent ease of the woman with the flying hair, but she didn't remind them of anyone they knew.

The women I interviewed—lawyers, corporate executives, word processors, garment pattern cutters, daycare workers—and most of their husbands, too—felt differently about some issues: how right it is for a mother of young children to work a full-time job, or how much a husband should be responsible for the home. But they all agreed that it was hard to work two full-time jobs and raise young children.

How well do couples do it? The more women work outside the home, the more central this question. The number of women in paid work has risen steadily since before the turn of the century, but since 1950 the rise has been staggering. In 1950, 30 percent of American women were in the labor force; in 1986, it was 55 percent. In 1950, 28 percent of married women with children between six and seventeen worked outside the home; in 1986, it had risen to 68 percent. In 1950, 23 percent of married women with children under six worked. By 1986, it had grown to 54 percent. We don't know how many women with children under the age of one worked outside the home in 1950; it was so rare that the Bureau of Labor kept no statistics on it. Today half of such women do. Two-thirds of all mothers are now in the labor force; in fact, more mothers have paid jobs (or are actively looking for one) than nonmothers. Because of this change in women, two-job families now make up 58 percent of all married couples with children.[1]

Since an increasing number of working women have small children, we might expect an increase in part-time work. But actually, 67 percent of the mothers who work have full-time jobs—that is, thirty-five hours or more weekly. That proportion is what it was in 1959.

If more mothers of young children are stepping into full-time jobs outside the home, and if most couples can't afford household help, how much more are fathers doing at home? As I began exploring this question I found many studies on the hours working men and women devote to housework and childcare. One national random sample of 1,243 working parents in forty-four American cities, conducted in 1965–66 by Alexander Szalai and his coworkers, for example, found that working women averaged three hours a day on housework while men averaged 17 minutes; women spent fifty minutes a day of time exclusively with their children; men spent twelve minutes. On the other side of the coin, working fathers watched television an hour longer than their working wives, and slept a half hour longer each night. A comparison of this American sample with eleven other industrial countries in Eastern and Western Europe revealed the same difference between working women and working men in those countries as well.[2] In a 1983 study of white middle-class families in greater Boston, Grace Baruch and R. C. Barnett found that working men married to working women spent only three-quarters of an hour longer each week with their kindergarten-aged children than did men married to housewives.[3]

Szalai's landmark study documented the now familiar but still alarming story of the working woman's "double day," but it left me wondering how men and women actually felt about all this. He and his coworkers studied how people used time, but not, say, how a father felt about his twelve minutes with his child, or how his wife felt about it. Szalai's study revealed the visible surface of what I discovered to be a set of deeply emotional issues: What should a man and woman contribute to the family? How appreciated does each feel? How does each respond to subtle changes in the balance of marital power? How does each develop an unconscious "gender strategy" for coping with the work at home, with marriage, and, indeed, with life itself? These were the underlying issues.

But I began with the measurable issue of time. Adding together the time it takes to do a paid job and to do housework and childcare, I averaged estimates from the major studies on time use done in the 1960s and 1970s, and discovered that women worked roughly fifteen hours longer each week than men. Over a year, they worked an *extra month of twenty-four-hour days a year.* Over a dozen years, it was an extra year of twenty-four-hour days. Most women without children spend much more time than men on housework; with children, they devote more time to both housework and childcare. Just as there is a wage gap between men and women in the workplace, there is a "leisure gap" between them at home. Most women work one shift at the office or factory and a "second shift" at home.

Studies show that working mothers have higher self-esteem and get less depressed than housewives, but compared to their husbands, they're more tired and get sick more often. In Peggy Thoits's 1985 analysis of two large-scale surveys, each of about a thousand men and women, people were asked how often in the preceding week they'd experienced each of twenty-three symptoms of anxiety (such as dizziness or hallucinations). According to the researchers' criteria, working mothers were more likely than any other group to be "anxious."

In light of these studies, the image of the woman with the flying hair seems like an upbeat "cover" for a grim reality, like those pictures of Soviet tractor drivers smilingly radiantly into the distance as they think about the ten-year plan. The Szalai study was conducted in 1965–66. I wanted to know whether the leisure gap he found in 1965 persists, or whether it has disappeared. Since most married couples work two jobs, since more will in the future, since most wives in these couples work the extra month a year, I wanted to understand what the wife's extra month a year meant for each person, and what it does for love and marriage in an age of high divorce.

MY RESEARCH

With my research associates Anne Machung and Elaine Kaplan, I interviewed fifty couples very intensively, and I observed in a dozen homes. We first began interviewing artisans, students, and professionals in Berkeley, California, in the late 1970s. This was at the height of the women's movement, and many of these couples were earnestly and self-consciously struggling to modernize the ground rules of their marriages. Enjoying flexible job schedules and intense cultural support to do so, many succeeded. Since their circumstances were unusual they became our "comparison group" as we sought other couples more typical of mainstream America. In 1980 we located more typical couples by sending a questionnaire on work and family life to every thirteenth name—from top to bottom—of the personnel roster of a large, urban manufacturing company. At the end of the questionnaire, we asked members of working couples raising children under six and working full time jobs if they would be willing to talk to us in greater depth. Interviewed from 1980 through 1988, these couples, their neighbors and friends, their children's teachers, daycare workers and baby-sitters, form the heart of this book.

When we called them, a number of baby-sitters replied as one woman did "You're interviewing us? Good. We're human too." Or another, "I'm glad you consider what we do work. A lot of people don't." As it turned out, many daycare workers were themselves juggling two jobs and small children, and so we talked to them about that, too.

We also talked with other men and women who were not part of two-job couples; divorced parents who were war-weary veterans of two-job marriages, and traditional couples, to see how much of the strain we were seeing was unique to two-job couples.

I also watched daily life in a dozen homes during a weekday evening, during the week-end, and during the months that followed, when I was invited on outings, to dinner, or just to talk. I found myself waiting on the front doorstep as weary parents and hungry children tumbled out of the family car. I shopped with them, visited friends, watched television, ate with them, walked through parks, and came along when they dropped their children at daycare, often staying on at the baby-sitter's house after parents waved good-bye. In their homes, I sat on the living-room floor and drew pictures and played house with the children. I watched as parents gave them baths, read bedtime stories, and said good night. Most couples tried to bring me into the family scene, inviting me to eat with them and talk. I responded if they spoke to me, from time to time asked questions, but I rarely initiated conversations. I tried to become as unobtrusive as a family dog. Often I would base myself in the living room, quietly taking notes. Sometimes I would follow a wife upstairs or down, accompany a child on her way out to "help Dad" fix the car, or watch television with the other watchers. Sometimes I would break out of my peculiar role to join in the jokes they often made about acting like the "model" two-job couple. Or perhaps the joking was a subtle part of my role, to put them at ease so they could act more naturally. For a period of two to five years, I phoned or visited these couples to keep in touch even as I moved on to study the daily lives of other working couples—black, Chicano, white, from every social class and walk of life.

I asked who did how much of a wide variety of household tasks. I asked who cooks? Vacuums? Makes the beds? Sews? Cares for plants? Sends Christmas or Hanukkah cards? I also asked: Who washes the car? Repairs household appliances? Does the taxes? Tends the yard? I asked who did most household planning, who noticed such things as when a child's fingernails need clipping, cared more how the house looked or about the change in a child's mood.

INSIDE THE EXTRA MONTH A YEAR

The women I interviewed seemed to be far more deeply torn between the demands of work and family than were their husbands. They talked with more animation and at greater length than their husbands about the abiding conflict between them. Busy as they were, women more often brightened at the idea of yet another interviewing session. They felt the second shift was *their* issue and most of their husbands agreed. When I telephoned one husband to arrange an interview with him, explaining that I wanted to ask him about how he managed work and family life, he replied genially, "Oh, this will *really* interest my *wife*."

It was a woman who first proposed to me the metaphor, borrowed from industrial life, of the "second shift." She strongly resisted the *idea* that homemaking was a "shift." Her family was her life and she didn't want it reduced to a job. But as she put it, "You're on duty at work. You come home, and you're on duty. Then you go back to work and you're on duty." After eight hours of adjusting insurance claims, she came home to put on the rice for dinner, care for her children, and wash laundry. Despite herself her home life *felt* like a second shift. That was the real story and that was the real problem.

Men who shared the load at home seemed just as pressed for time as their wives, and as torn between the demands of career and small children.... But the majority of men did not share the load at home. Some refused outright. Others refused more passively, often offering a loving shoulder to lean on, an understanding ear as their working wife faced the conflict they both saw as hers. At first it seemed to me that the problem of the second shift was hers. But I came to realize that those husbands who helped very little at home were often indirectly just as deeply affected as their wives by the need to do that work, through the resentment their wives feel toward them, and through their need to steel themselves against that resentment. Evan Holt, a warehouse furniture salesman…did very little housework and played with his four-year-old son, Joey, at his convenience. Juggling the demands of work with family at first seemed a problem for his wife. But Evan himself suffered enormously from the side effects of "her" problem. His wife did the second shift, but she resented it keenly, and half-consciously expressed her frustration and rage by losing interest in sex and becoming overly absorbed with Joey. One way or another, most men I talked with do suffer the severe repercussions of what I think is a transitional phase in American family life.

One reason women take a deeper interest than men in the problems of juggling work with family life is that even when husbands happily shared the hours of work, their wives felt more *responsible* for home and children. More women kept track of doctors' appointments and arranged for playmates to come over. More mothers than fathers worried about the tail on a child's Halloween costume or a birthday present for a school friend. They were more likely to think about their children while at work and to check in by phone with the baby-sitter.

Partly because of this, more women felt torn between one sense of urgency and another, between the need to soothe a child's fear of being left at daycare, and the need to show the boss she's "serious" at work. More women than men questioned how good they were as parents, or if they did not, they questioned why they weren't questioning it. More often than men, women alternated between living in their ambition and standing apart from it.

As masses of women have moved into the economy, families have been hit by a "speed-up" in work and family life. There is no more time in the day than there was when wives stayed home, but there is twice as much to get done. It is mainly women who absorb this "speed-up." Twenty percent of the men in my study shared housework equally. Seventy percent of men did a

substantial amount (less than half but more than a third), and 10 percent did less than a third. Even when couples share more equitably in the work at home, women do two-thirds of the *daily* jobs at home, like cooking and cleaning up—jobs that fix them into a rigid routine. Most women cook dinner and most men change the oil in the family car. But, as one mother pointed out, dinner needs to be prepared every evening around six o'clock, whereas the car oil needs to be changed every six months, any day around that time, any time that day. Women do more childcare than men, and men repair more household appliances. A child needs to be tended daily while the repair of household appliances can often wait "until I have time." Men thus have more control over *when* they make their contributions than women do. They may be very busy with family chores but, like the executive who tells his secretary to "hold my calls," the man has more control over his time. The job of the working mother, like that of the secretary, is usually to "take the calls."

Another reason women may feel more strained than men is that women more often do two things at once—for example, write checks and return phone calls, vacuum and keep an eye on a three-year-old, fold laundry and think out the shopping list. Men more often cook dinner *or* take a child to the park. Indeed, women more often juggle three spheres—job, children, and housework—while most men juggle two—job and children. For women, two activities compete with their time with children, not just one.

Beyond doing more at home, women also devote *proportionately more* of their time at home to housework and proportionately less of it to childcare. Of all the time men spend working at home, more of it goes to childcare. That is, working wives spend relatively more time "mothering the house"; husbands spend more time "mothering" the children. Since most parents prefer to tend to their children than clean house, men do more of what they'd rather do. More men than women take their children on "fun" outings to the park, the zoo, the movies. Women spend more time on maintenance, feeding and bathing children, enjoyable activities to be sure, but often less leisurely or "special" than going to the zoo. Men also do fewer of the "undesirable" household chores: fewer men than women wash toilets and scrub the bathroom.

As a result, women tend to talk more intently about being overtired, sick, and "emotionally drained." Many women I could not tear away from the topic of sleep. They talked about how much they could "get by on"…six and a half, seven, seven and a half, less, more. They talked about who they knew who needed more or less. Some apologized for how much sleep they needed—"I'm afraid I need eight hours of sleep"—as if eight was "too much." They talked about the effect of a change in baby-sitter, the birth of a second child, or a business trip on their child's pattern of sleep. They talked about how to avoid fully waking up when a child called them at night, and how to get back to sleep. These women talked about sleep the way a hungry person talks about food.

All in all, if in this period of American history, the two-job family is suffering from a speed up of work and family life, working mothers are its primary victims. It is ironic, then, that often it falls to women to be the "time and motion expert" of family life. Watching inside homes, I noticed it was often the mother who rushed children, saying, "Hurry up! It's time to go," "Finish your cereal now," "You can do that later," "Let's go!" When a bath is crammed into a slot between 7:45 and 8:00 it was often the mother who called out, "Let's see who can take their bath the quickest!" Often a younger child will rush out, scurrying to be first in bed, while the older and wiser one stalls, resistant, sometimes resentful: "Mother is always rushing us." Sadly enough, women are more often the lightning rods for family aggressions aroused by the speed-up of work and family life. They are the "villains" in a process of which they are also the primary victims. More than the

longer hours, the sleeplessness, and feeling torn, this is the saddest cost to women of the extra month a year.

NOTES

1. U.S. Bureau of Labor Statistics, *Employment and Earnings, Characteristics of Families: First Quarter* (Washington, D.C.: U.S. Department of Labor, 1988).

2. Alexander Szalai, ed., *The Use of Time: Daily Activities of Urban and Suburban Populations in Twelve Countries* (The Hague: Mouton, 1972), p. 668, Table B. Another study found that men spent a longer time than women eating meals (Shelley Coverman, "Gender, Domestic Labor Time and Wage Inequality," *American Sociological Review* 48 [1983]: 626). With regard to sleep, the pattern differs for men and women. The higher the social class of a man, the more sleep he's likely to get. The higher the class of a woman, the less sleep she's likely to get. (Upper-white-collar men average 7.6 hours sleep a night. Lower-white-collar, skilled and unskilled men all averaged 7.3 hours. Upper-white-collar women average 7.1 hours of sleep; lower-white-collar workers average 7.4; skilled workers 7.0 and unskilled workers 8.1.) Working wives seem to meet the demands of high-pressure careers by reducing sleep, whereas working husbands don't. For more details on the hours working men and women devote to housework and childcare, see the Appendix of this book.

3. Grace K. Baruch and Rosalind Barnett, "Correlates of Fathers' Participation in Family Work: A Technical Report," Working Paper no. 106 (Wellesley, Mass.: Wellesley College Center for Research on Women, 1983), pp. 80–81. Also see Kathryn E. Walker and Margaret E. Woods, *Time Use: A Measure of Household Production of Goods and Services* (Washington, D.C.: American Home Economics Association, 1976).

Topic 5

Intimate Relationships

Lilly's Porch on the Last Night of July

Sylvia is moving to Boulder
and the table is draped

in white linen. White napkins. White candles.
A table for three.

This tiny sideporch has become a French
cafe in Lilly's white

and Sylvia is leaving
for Boulder.

Chicken on wheat bread. Lettuce. Tomato.
Plums. Blueberries. Green grapes.

Rice pudding with raisins and cinnamon.
A dust of nutmeg. Wine.

The candles melt, drip.
Light flickers

on Lilly's face, blooms on Sylvia's. Dark,
light, dark, multi-shaded like a bed

of pansies. Beloved flowers. The moth
loves us, wants to be us so much

that it flits too close, too close.
Sylvia, caught mid-sentence,

brushes it away, flicks her fingers
to warn it, but it circles

and hurls
itself into the fire. Goblets are lifted,

lowered. We pass the jug. Over-
flow in the dark, but it's just

cheap chablis, and we are rich
in talk and poems that spill

over the wrought-iron bannister
into the hedge where we threw the ends

of cigarettes,
the charred moth.

Courtesy of Nancy Edmondson

Gender role expectations play an important part in shaping our experiences with intimacy. For example, as we saw in earlier discussions of developmental psychology, women are taught to be responsible for intimate relationships, and so invest much time and energy in thinking about and doing for others. This investment in relationships can be important for a woman's identity development and can provide her with a sense of fulfillment, but it can also be a burden. As we will see in the sections on caregiving and work, relationships can become a burden when the expectation is that women hold primary responsibility for providing emotional and physical support to husbands, lovers, children, parents, and friends.

In this section, we look at how socially constructed expectations for gender roles and intimacy affect our understanding of and experience with friendship, marriage, and sexuality. We will see that these expectations have limited women (and men), but we will also see that as gender roles have become less rigid, our choices in intimate relationships have widened. For example, as Beverly Birns and Rhoda Selvin point out in the first reading of this section, "Marriage: Something Old, Something New," it is no longer taken for granted that women will marry. More women are remaining single, and women are also more likely to initiate divorce if they are unhappily married.

Birns and Selvin demonstrate that change in the intimate relationship of marriage is connected to larger social changes. They describe how our vision of the ideal marriage and the ideal wife has been influenced by women's role in the workplace. As this role has fluctuated, so has our view of women's role in marriage. After World War II, women were pushed out of the workforce because of the slowdown in weapons production and the view that the better-paid jobs should be offered to returning soldiers. The popular image of women's role was to be at their homes in the suburbs, devoting themselves full-time to promoting the happiness of their husbands and children. More recently, as rising numbers of women have entered the workforce for the purposes of self-fulfillment and/or economic necessity, women have gained greater independence, but also have the pressure of being expected to "do it all."

According to Birns and Selvin, another social change that has impacted our view of marriage is the development of effective birth control. Once women could control reproduction, sexual activity outside of marriage became more acceptable. As sexual permissiveness has grown, and there has been more openness about sexual behavior, women have gained a greater understanding and therefore greater control over their sexual and reproductive lives. They are more likely to have sex outside of marriage, more likely to postpone childbearing, and more likely to see themselves as equal partners in sex.

These social changes have given women more power and greater choice in the intimate relationship of marriage, but as Birns and Selvin point out, women do not yet have full equality in that relationship. The institution of marriage has been integral to the maintenance of sexism, and challenges to it have been met with resistance and backlash. While more and more women and men are viewing an egalitarian marriage as the ideal, legal, economic, and cultural change in women's roles will be essential to that idea's becoming a reality.

Carla Golden, in her reading, "Diversity and Variability in Women's Sexual Identities," further develops the theme of choice for women in intimate relationships. Golden points out that social definitions of sexuality divide people into one of four sexual groups: heterosexual, homosexual, bisexual, or asexual. It is assumed that there is a match between people's sexual behavior and their identification with one of these groups. What Golden discovered, however, in her work with young college women who were exploring their sexuality, was that women's personally constructed sexual identities did not always match with these socially constructed categories. She found that, in every sexual group, there was a great deal of variability and diversity. To illustrate this, she describes how women who defined themselves as lesbians understood that identity. One major distinction she discovered was that some women saw themselves as "born" lesbians, who had always felt different because they were attracted to women, while others saw themselves as "elective" lesbians because they did not have a history of thinking of themselves as sexually "different," and because they felt they had consciously chosen to become lesbians. Another major difference was that some of these women saw their attraction to women as an unchanging and essential aspect of their identity, while others saw this attraction as more fluid and open to change.

Women have often been reluctant to reveal aspects of their identity or behavior that do not fit into socially constructed roles for fear of reprisal. Golden makes the argument that just as it has been important for feminists to challenge traditional gender roles in order to open up new possibilities for women's lives, it is also important to challenge rigid and inflexible sexual categories so that women can define for themselves what it means to be sexual.

Gender role expectations have also contributed to the devaluation and misunderstanding of female friendships. As Fern Johnson and Elizabeth Aries discuss in the third reading, "The Talk of Women Friends," women's relationships to men and to the family have been seen as primary, so friendship between women has rarely been seen as a subject worthy of study. Women's friendships have also been misunderstood because gender stereotypes assume that women rival each other for men and so cannot be good friends. Finally, as Johnson and Aries discover, talk is a central feature of women's friendships, and since women's talk is stereotyped as trivial, women's friendships may also be regarded that way.

Johnson and Aries interviewed an economically diverse group of white women in order to begin an exploration of women's friendships. In these interviews, they found certain common elements to women's friendships. Women usually visited with one friend, rather than in groups, most conversations took place in the women's homes, and often, the friendships included favors. Talk was a central feature of their time together. This talk included noncritical listening and enabled women to share feelings, provided support in times of need, enhanced self-worth, and promoted personal growth and self-discovery.

As women move out of traditional gender roles and into the workplace, overwhelming demands may make it difficult for them to have the time and energy for women friends. Despite this, Johnson and Aries find that women make these relationships a high priority and struggle to find ways to be together.

The readings in this section help us understand how the social construction of gender and sexuality, marriage and friendship can shape the dynamics of our individual intimate relationships. It is exciting to recognize that as the social expectations that structure these relationships become less rigid, we are more able to define for ourselves the kinds of relationships we want in our lives.

Reading 1   Marriage: Something Old, Something New

BEVERLY BIRNS AND RHODA SELVIN

Questions to Consider:

1. According to Birns and Selvin, how does economic class affect the experience of marriage? What factors make Black marriages differ from White marriages?

2. According to Birns and Selvin, are women equal partners in marriage today? Why or why not?

3. What is your vision of the ideal marriage? What factors (if any) make it difficult for you to achieve that ideal relationship?

4. Birns and Selvin document the ways that social changes such as the move to the suburbs, women's entry into the workforce, and development of birth control, have changed women's role in marriage. What future social changes do you believe are likely to occur? How will these changes affect marriage?

Most women, now as in the past, marry, and bring to marriage a whole set of expectations, dreams, hopes, and fears. Although some weddings look similar to those of yesteryear, and some marriages continue the old traditions, most marriages today are different from those of old. Today, women are older when they first marry. They enter marriage with more knowledge about sexuality, they have more control over childbearing, they are more likely to be in the paid labor force, and they are more likely to divorce. To understand these changes in marriage, we must look at the social context of marriage. In the last fifty years we have seen families move from the cities to the suburbs, seen women become more educated and increase their wage earning status, and seen changes in sexual mores and the technology of birth control.

All of these changes have played a role in making marriage "something new."

THE END OF WORLD WAR II AND THE MOVE TO THE SUBURBS

Fifty years ago America was recovering from the greatest economic depression in its history, as well as from the Second World War. The changes during the postwar period must be understood to appreciate both the current status of women as wives and the alternate life styles that are now more acceptable. Many more women choose to remain single, and some form long-term lesbian relationships. "Serial monogamy" and "open marriage" are terms describing forms of relationships not spoken of 50 years ago. All of these changes mean that young women contemplating marriage, as well as women who are already married, know of the diverse possibilities of sharing one's life with a partner, but also some of the advantages of remaining single. While 50 years ago single women of 25 or 30 were called "old maids" or "spinsters," today many women happily choose not to marry.

Statistics reveal major changes in the marital scene over the last 50 years (Wetzel, 1990). The age at which most men and women marry is later than it was 50 years ago. In 1950, the average age of women when they married was 20; by the late 80s it was 23.6; and in 1994 it was 24.5 (Saluter, 1997). The number of women who choose not to marry has also increased. The divorce rate hit an all-time high of almost 50 percent in the mid 70s but has now stabilized. Many who divorce remarry, and third and fourth marriages are not uncommon.

A new image of wives and mothers was fostered during the Second World War as women were encouraged to enter industry. The men were at war and women were needed to manufacture supplies for the war effort. For the first time in American history even mothers with young children were encouraged to work; day care centers were federally funded. "Rosie the Riveter," the woman of the year, was portrayed at work in pants and a shirt, looking pretty and feminine. Even during the war, however, it was clearly stated that married working women were a "war measure" and not intended as a permanent fixture (Rothman, 1978). When the men returned, child care center funding was cut and women were given the message, loud and clear, that their place was in the home.

Society fostered a new image of marriage to facilitate women's return to the home. Children's school books, as well as newly evolving television and movies, portrayed women as white, middle-class, happily married mothers of two or more children. The happy, albeit infantile, wife and mother maintained her pretty suburban home. She was available all day every day to provide physical and emotional care to her children and husband.

During the 50s, mental health professionals proclaimed that the normal female was infantile, selfish, and neurotic while they berated women for being inadequate at fulfilling their normal functions as wives and mothers. A woman's responsibilities included not only the physical health and welfare of their husbands and children, but also their mental health. As often occurs today, women were portrayed as being responsible for all the social ills of their time. Single women who chose not to marry were considered pathological and unfeminine. Popular and professional books on child rearing listed "working mothers" under the heading of PROBLEMS. Single, poor women worked for low wages and were portrayed by the press and the authorities as lacking in skills and even in the ability to care for their families.

A major social change of the postwar years was the suburbanization of America. White veterans could buy homes with a deposit of less than $100 and low interest rates. The first Levittown was built on Long Island, a development of 17,000 homes. Such huge housing developments in the suburbs meant the exodus of working-class and middle-class whites from inner cities. The inner cities became home to new immigrants, most often poor, and to the many blacks who had migrated north in the hope of finding jobs, less discrimination, and a better standard of living than was possible in the South.

With the suburbs came the malls, television, and the extraordinary expansion of the consumer society. The role of women expanded to their becoming educated, avid consumers. The many labor-saving devices on the market were advertised as time-savers too. Not known then, however, but well documented now was the fact that electrical machines created more work and not less for the housewives. Although not as physically tiring, more washes were done, more floors were cleaned more often, and the time invested in housework increased (Cowan, 1983).

The mandate to women was clear: Father earns the bread, mother bakes and serves it, and has dinner ready at the end of the day. The young children would be fed, bathed by six, and ready for bed when father came home. Evenings for older children would be consumed with Little League, Boy Scouts, and supervised homework. At the end of the day of cleaning, shopping, and cooking the women were expected to be beautiful and ready for exciting sex.

Most women actively looked forward to this life, and many happily followed the script. For others, however, the proverb, "Be careful what you wish for; you may get your wish," was all too true. The dream did not become the reality for many postwar wives. Although women were told that their role was wife and mother, descriptions of the family were clearly prescriptions about what women should do rather than reflections of reality. The stereotype of the 50s woman never reflected all women's lives.

For black Americans, the dream was not even a possibility. When black men who served in the army returned home, their families could not move to the "for whites only" suburbs (New York Times, 1997). Discrimination followed the mass migration of blacks from the South to the North. Jobs, housing, and education in inner cities declined, and for many blacks life in the segregated, discriminatory North became as painful as life had been in the South.

Even for white families, many difficulties existed. The domesticity that was touted as most desirable created its own problems. As sociologist Herbert Gans described (cited in Rothman, 1978) the suburban paradise was seriously marred, and many participants in the new way of life found not happiness, but loneliness. One result of the postwar life, which became the "American dream," was the turning inward and alienation of the family. Americans, historically committed to family privacy as a right, believed that they would find only happiness in this new lifestyle. For many wives, however, all this privacy was too much. Suburban lifestyle separated young couples from their families who had traditionally provided physical and social support in times of need, but who were too far away when the need came. Although the cities were congested, one benefit was having another family member in the same building or "down the block" and neighbors to pitch in when families needed help. Suburban wives, by definition, would expect more social support of their marriages than could be provided. Without this support, many suffered from depression.

In 1963, after interviewing a group of Smith College graduates, Betty Friedan wrote *The Feminine Mystique*. She gave a name to the problem of educated women who were not finding wifehood and motherhood as fulfilling as expected. Rather, many complained of feeling empty and devoid of self-respect. Friedan's book had a major impact on the formation of the women's movement for sexual equality.

Friedan also helped stimulate a new element in women's conversation in the 70s. As women gathered together and discussed their lives, they articulated their dissatisfaction with their current roles and relationships. With the realization that dissatisfaction was not just an individual problem, they began to advocate change. Some became active in the women's movement for equality, but even those who rejected "feminism" were profoundly affected by the women writers who articulated women's concerns. Feminists at this time advocated women's paid labor force participation as the way for women to find their own identities. This advocacy, however, was only one factor contributing to growing numbers of women going to work outside the home. Another factor was the steady increase in the cost of raising families. Although suburban living made holding a job difficult for women, each decade led to greater participation of women in the paid labor force.

EDUCATION AND WORK

The social change that has had the most pervasive effect on women's lives and marriages is women's participation in the paid labor force. As long as men were the primary breadwinners, women were economically dependent on husbands for food, housing, and clothing and for the support of children. As one analyst pointed out, unemployed women were and remain one man away from welfare. For women who can support themselves, economic independence changes not only their financial but their psychological sense of independence. Greater education and higher earnings increase women's sense of self and in many cases reduce the degree of inequality between spouses (Hochschild, 1997). In general, as women's pay approaches parity with men, increased employment status increases their involvement in family decision making.

In contrast to 50 years ago, currently most American women are in the paid labor force. Women's employment status varies according to their marital status. The most dramatic difference is between married and divorced women. Sixty percent of married women work, but among divorced women the rate is 74 percent (U.S. Department of Labor, 1995). At the present time more than half of the women with babies under one year of age are working. Women continue to work in many of the lowest-paid fields, and even for full-time working women holding the same jobs as men, there is a 30 percent gap in salaries. Not only are most American women working, but women have been entering professions where their representation was unknown or from which they were excluded in the 50s and 60s. For example, women physicians were rare in the 50s, but one-quarter of all physicians today are women, as are one-half of medical school classes (U.S. Department of Labor, 1995).

Not only did more women continue to enter the labor force, they increasingly went to college and became eligible for better jobs. For instance, in 1950, 7 percent of women aged 18 to 24 were in college, in 1970 the figure was 20 percent, and by 1993 there were more women enrolled in colleges than men (U.S. Census, 1997). In general, the more education people attain, the greater the potential to work and to earn a living wage. Although this applies to women when they are compared to other women, it has not led to pay equity between men and women, as there remains a gap between their salaries.

The financial contribution to the family income by working women is essential for most American families. It is used for providing food, shelter, clothes, and education, not for "extras." In addition to salaries, women clearly gain social contacts, a network of friends and colleagues, and improved self-esteem when they go to work. However, married women often experience a conflict between their work and home lives. We see this conflict in the "mommy track," where women work less than full time and take longer to reach higher status because they have children. Women also face a "second shift" when they return home from their paid jobs and must do most of the housework. Many women and their families are caught in a "time bind" (Hochschild, 1997), as home life is more scheduled and pressured.

Black families in America are in the worst economic position. Marriage rates among them are low. Plagued by discrimination that leads to restricted job opportunities, inferior and inadequate housing, and segregated and inadequately supported schools, black children are the most impoverished (Edelman, 1987). Many of the children live in single-parent families. Like all groups subjected to discrimination, black mothers are frequently blamed for their own poverty. They are pilloried for the high rates of out-of-wedlock births to teenage mothers.

A careful analysis conducted by the Children's Defense Fund (Edelman, 1987) demonstrates the many reasons that black pregnant teens do not marry the fathers of their children. The major reason is the high unemployment rate among black men; only a minority earn a sufficient living to support a family. According to Zinn (1989) 50 percent of black men lost jobs in industry between 1979 and 1984. Another important factor is the shortage of black men; black males are disproportionately murdered during childhood and adolescence and are also disproportionately in jail or in the army. What Edelman (1987) documents is that black marriage rates fluctuate in direct relationship to employment rates for black men. Among middle-class blacks, marital rates are similar to those of whites.

SEXUALITY AND BIRTH CONTROL

The ability to decide whether, when, and how many children to have is a major factor that determines women's attitudes and behavior within marriage. In addition to the relative effectiveness of birth control today, women have more knowledge about their bodies. Although some women throughout history have found means to limit their childbearing, birth control as it is practiced today is a twentieth-century phenomenon.

Although many speak of the "sexual revolution" as liberating female sexuality, the most profound influence in changing sexual behavior has been the ability to control childbearing by the use of relatively safe means of birth control and the legalization of abortion. One need only read the pleading letters written by poor women to Margaret Sanger, the pioneer of modern means of contraception, to realize the complete despair of married women who were told by their physicians that if they wanted to stop becoming pregnant every year, to have their husbands sleep up on the roof of their tenements. Being able to control reproduction has been a powerful factor in the sexual behavior of women and men, and also in women's attitudes toward marriage and childbearing.

In the first half of this century and until *Roe v. Wade* (1972), the unmarried woman who became pregnant was pressured to either marry the father of her child, have an illegal abortion (painful, dangerous, and at times leading to death), or give the child up for adoption. Wealthy women had the additional choice of a trip to Europe, where abortions were legal and safe.

When the culture as well as practicing physicians told women that childbearing later in life was dangerous, many women were motivated to marry early in order to have children safely in their 20s. Now, in the late twentieth century, not only is birth control more effective than earlier, but also many changes in knowledge and practice have led women to give birth for the first time in their late 30s or 40s. Although women today speak about the biological clock winding down, the possibility of having children late has altered women's attitudes toward marriage. The acceptance of women's sexuality apart from marriage and childbearing allows them to choose the lives they want.

Once women could control their fertility, and sexuality no longer automatically led to pregnancy or the fear of pregnancy, the sexual mores changed. An important feature of the 60s and the hippie culture was greater permissiveness concerning sexuality. Sex was no longer considered as a "right" only acceptable in marriage. Recreational sex began to be talked and written about in the popular press.

It is difficult for the youth of today to recognize that 40 years ago women students could be expelled from college if a man entered their room. The men, of course, did not endure similar sanctions. Women students in the 50s were asked to leave college should they get married, single pregnant women were expelled, and married pregnant women were also forced to leave. Pregnant women were forbidden to teach in the public schools. Coed dorms were as unimaginable as computers in schools. In the 50s, unmarried couples who wanted to be sexually active had a choice among the back seats of cars, haylofts, or at home if their parents were out. Today the desire to have sex no longer automatically propels women or men into marriage. Unmarried couples may now vacation together and buy houses together. Years ago this behavior was scandalous; unmarried cohabitation was almost impossible.

In the second half of the century, knowledge about the anatomy and physiology of sex came under scrutiny, initially through the use of questionnaires by Kinsey and his collaborators. The Kinsey Reports in 1948 and 1953 sampled over 11,000 people and provided information on the average frequency of intercourse, peak ages for sexual desire, and the wide range of sexual experiences. Following the Kinsey research, the next major breakthrough came from Masters and Johnson (cited in Sussman, 1976). They were specifically interested in the anatomy and physiology of sexual arousal and orgasms and used complex technology to find their answers. When Masters and Johnson realized that almost all women were capable of orgasm but frequently did not experience them, they turned to the study of sexual dysfuntion and its treatment.

More recently, Sheri Hite turned attention to an understanding of how women perceive their own sexuality. She sent out 100,000 questionnaires and received 3,000 responses. Her book is criticized by some for her sampling techniques, which entailed recruiting through women's organizations, churches, and magazines. Indeed, her sample, similar to other studies in human sexuality, can reflect only the opinions on bodily functioning in people who are willing to participate in sexuality research. Keeping in mind this limitation, her major finding was that many women are dissatisfied with their partners' interest in providing them with sexual fulfillment.

Now, as in the past, factors other than love determine sexual behavior. Today fear of AIDS may be having the greatest effect on nonmarital sex, and indirectly on a greater interest in marriage, rather than casual sex. In the 50s, young girls were told "nice girls don't before marriage." In the 60s and 70s women were told "you can and

not become pregnant," and also that "the sexual revolution means that women can and may." Now women are told to "be careful, since AIDS is becoming more common in women, and casual sex may be life threatening."

As women consider marriage in the late twentieth century, they do so with much knowledge about sexuality. If we believe that knowledge is always advantageous, we need also to consider in what direction the knowledge leads us. What it points to in the realm of sexuality and marriage is the certainty that each woman should be free to express her sexuality and to find sex pleasurable. To achieve this goal, however, the social context must change so that, in the realm of sex and other aspects of marriage, men acknowledge women as equal partners.

CONCLUSIONS

Educated women who marry today have much greater information available to them than did their mothers. Since one aspect of mental health is the ability to see options and to make wise choices, they have a healthy advantage. The freedom for women to choose is paramount today— to choose whether to marry, whether to become highly educated, whether to have traditional marriages or no marriage at all, whether and when to have children. Late twentieth-century feminists have helped to change some of the old ideas and replace them with new ones. We know now that women are intellectually equal to men. We know that satisfaction in work can be very important in a woman's life. We know that living with men who believe in the equality of women is a possibility.

We also know that social change comes slowly and not without struggle. We know that changes in the law are imperative, and many women have won many legal battles. We also know that changing attitudes may be our hardest job. It is only when men and women are equally valued, when obstetricians no longer give men a knowing wink as they congratulate them on being father to a son, when television portrays men as nurturant and nonviolent and women as being heroines of their own lives that marriages will be more egalitarian and therefore happier.

REFERENCES

Brecher, E. M. (1976). "History of human sexual research and study." In B. J. Saddock, H. I. Kaplan, & A. M. Freedman (Eds.), *The Sexual Experience.* Baltimore: Williams and Wilkins.

Cowan, R. S. (1984). *More Work for Mother.* NY: Basic Books.

Edelman, M. B. (1987). "The black family in America." In L. Tepperman & S. Wilson (Eds.), *Next of kin* (pp. 241–245). Englewood Cliffs, NJ: Prentice Hall.

Hite, S. (1976). *The Hite Report: A Nationwide Study of Female Sexuality.* New York: Macmillan.

Hochschild, A. (1989). *The Second Shift: Working Parents and the Revolution at Home.* New York: Penguin.

Hochschild, A. (1997). *The Time Bind: When Work Becomes Home and Home Becomes Work.* New York: Holt.

Lambert, B. (1997). At 50, Levittown Contends With Its Legacy of Bias. *New York Times,* 12/28/97, 1, 23:2.

Rothman, S. M. (1978). *Women's Proper Place: A History of Changing Ideals and Practices, 1870 to the Present.* New York: Prentice Hall.

Saluter, A. F. (1997). *Marital Status and Living Arrangements.* Bethesda, MD: U.S. Census Bureau.

Skolnick, A. (1997). "The triple revolution: Social sources of family change." In S. Dreman (Ed), *The Family on the Threshold of the 21st Century: Trends and Implications.* Mahwah, NJ: Erlbaum.

Sussman, N. (1976). "Sex and sexuality in history." In B. J. Saddock, H. I. Kaplan, & A. M. Freedman (Eds) *The Sexual Experience.* Baltimore: Williams and Wilkins.

Anon. (1970). *We the American Women,* U.S. Department of Commerce, Social and Economic Statistics Administration, Bureau of the Census.

Anon. (May 1995). *Facts on Working Women.* U.S. Department of Labor, Women's Bureau. No. 95-1.

Anon. *Nontraditional Occupations for Women in 1995.* (March 1995). U.S. Department of Labor, Women's Bureau.

Wetzel, J. R. (1990). "American families: 75 years of change." *Monthly Labor Review, 4,* 4–13.

Zinn, M. B. (1989). Family, race and poverty. *Signs: Journal of Women in Culture and Society, vol. 14,* no. 4. Reprinted in: Skolnick, A. S. and J. H. Skolnick. *Family in Transition,* 9th edition (pp. 316–329), 1997. Addison-Wesley Educational Publishers, Inc., New York.

Reading 2   Diversity and Variability in Women's Sexual Identities

CARLA GOLDEN

Questions to Consider:

1. What do you see as your sexual identity? What factors are important to you in choosing that description for yourself?

2. Golden notes that many women privately considered themselves bisexual but that they seemed to be reluctant to publicly claim that identity. How does she explain this finding? Do you agree with her explanation?

3. Do you agree with Golden that it would be beneficial to be more flexible in the ways we think about sexual identity? Why or why not?

Psychologists and feminists alike tend to assume that most persons can be neatly categorized according to membership in one of four groups: heterosexual, homosexual, bisexual, or asexual (celibate). Furthermore, they tend to accept uncritically the notion that when a person's behavior fits into one of those four sexual preference categories, that person adopts a corresponding sexual identity to match the behavior. If such beliefs are not questioned, it seems logical to assume that a person whose sexual behavior is exclusively heterosexual would also assume a heterosexual identity, and conversely, that a person with a heterosexual identity would only engage in heterosexual behavior. The same con-

nection between sexual behavior and sexual identity would be assumed of homosexuality as well.

The relation between sexual behavior and sexual identity may not be so clear-cut, however. For women, sexuality may be an aspect of identity that is fluid and dynamic as opposed to fixed and invariant. I came to think of women's sexuality in this way as a function of interviews and more general discussions with young college women who were exploring their sexuality. Many of these women were defining themselves as lesbians despite the fact that their current or previous sexual experience was heterosexual. I was confused by this, because I had tended to think of sex between women as rather central to the definition of lesbianism. However, as I read more feminist literature on sexuality and spoke with women who were feminists and/or lesbians, I came to see that the definition of a lesbian is both problematic and far from unambiguous. As a psychologist, I am primarily interested in how

From *Lesbian Psychologies: Explorations and Challenges*. Copyright 1987 by the Board of Trustees of the University of Illinois. Used with permission of the University of Illinois Press.

women subjectively experience their identities, and how they react when their personally constructed identities are not concordant with social definitions. Exploring these issues led me to a new view of women's sexuality.

I will review here some of the controversial definitional issues that have been identified in the feminist sexuality literature, and then will present the findings from interviews with college women. These interviews suggest that there is enormous diversity and variability in women's self-defined sexual identities, and that these identities are often at odds with social definitions. Finally, I will discuss how the exploration of sexuality from the perspective of a "deviant" group (i.e., lesbians) sheds some important light on the nature of women's sexuality in general.

How do feminist theorists interested in women's sexuality define lesbianism? Adrienne Rich's conception of the lesbian continuum provides an interesting introduction to the problematic nature of the term.[1] Instead of using the word *lesbianism,* which for her has connotations both clinical and pejorative, Rich suggests thinking in terms of a lesbian continuum. She notes that across history and cultures, women have in a variety of ways been primarily committed to other women, and she uses the term *lesbian continuum* to refer to the range of such women-identified experiences. That a woman has actually had, or has consciously desired, genital sexual experience with another woman is but one point on the lesbian continuum. By conceiving of lesbianism in these terms, Rich suggests that many more forms of primary intensity between and among women (including emotional bonding) can be included than would be possible with a narrower definition based solely on sexual behavior. Furthermore, according to Rich's definition, a woman need not identify herself as a lesbian in order to be considered one. By defining lesbianism in terms of primary intensity between women, she allows for women from previous historical periods to be considered as lesbians, even

though at the time when they lived there may have been no cultural conception of lesbianism.

Rich's formulation holds that neither sexual relations nor sexual attraction between women is necessary for inclusion in the category *lesbian*. It should be noted that such a contention is not new. In 1973, the Radicalesbians, in their "Woman-Identified Women" article, focused on the political, as opposed to specifically sexual, nature of lesbianism when they defined it as "the rage of all women condensed to the point of explosion."[2] Blanche Wiesen Cook, in her *Chrysalis* article on "Female Support Networks and Political Activism," defined a lesbian as "a woman who loves women, who chooses women to nurture and support and to create a living environment in which to work creatively and independently, whether or not her relations with these women are sexual."[3] Such definitions, which have de-emphasized sexual feelings and behavior, have not been uncontroversial. Not only do they suggest that with whom one has sexual relations is not critical, but they also imply that a woman who never consciously considers herself to be a lesbian may in fact be thought of as one.

Ann Ferguson has argued that defining lesbianism in such a manner incorrectly downplays the importance of sexual feelings and behavior.[4] Such a definition in effect unsexes lesbianism and makes it more agreeable to some people by diminishing what is undeniably a significant difference. Furthermore, Ferguson argues that it isn't meaningful to talk about a woman as a lesbian if she doesn't acknowledge herself to be one. She suggests that, because before the twentieth century there was no cultural conception of lesbianism, one cannot and should not attempt to consider women lesbians who did not consider themselves to be such. As an alternative, Ferguson offers the following definition: "A lesbian is a woman who has sexual and erotic-emotional ties primarily with women or who sees herself as centrally involved with a community of self-identified lesbians whose sexual and erotic-emotional ties are primarily with women *and* who is herself a self-identified lesbian."[5] Without de-emphasizing the role of sexual behavior, this definition includes both celibate and bisexual women as lesbians, as long as they identify themselves as such.

The issue of self-conscious acknowledgment of lesbian identity is important, especially if we are talking about contemporary women for whom a definite cultural category of lesbian exists. The issue of sexual behavior is a bit more complicated, and Ferguson's definition reflects this in her use of the word "primarily," which allows for inclusion in the category *lesbian* women whose sexual relations are not exclusively with women. It is my observation that within certain lesbian communities there has tended to be more ready acceptance of celibate and of sexually inexperienced women who choose to call themselves lesbians than there has been of bisexual women who choose to identify themselves as lesbians. Thus, it seems that for some members of the lesbian community the critical issue in determining the "legitimacy" of a woman's claim to a lesbian identity is not whether or not she is sleeping with women, but whether she is sleeping with men. This kind of thinking is problematic because women's relations to men are given greater weight than are women's own self-conscious voices.

Some have argued that attempts to define who is and who is not a lesbian will only be divisive, and it seems undeniable that to a certain extent it has been. Jacquelyn Zita has aptly referred to this judging and weighing of who does and does not qualify for membership as the "Lesbian Olympics."[6] However, it does seem both intellectually important and socially useful for groups to define themselves. It is critical for any minority or oppressed group to break free from the confining definitions of the dominant culture and to create their own. In collectively resisting oppression, minority groups need to foster not only a positive group identity, but also a sense of the cohesiveness of the group based at least partially on shared characteristics and self-definitions.

While acknowledging that it is important for minority groups to define themselves (as opposed to being defined by the dominant group), it must be recognized that it is a sociopolitical task to do so, and that there are certain limitations inherent in such an enterprise. That is, to construct a definition is to identify a set of criteria according to which individual women can be considered to fit or not. Describing a social group is quite different from the psychological task of understanding what it means to any particular woman to identify as a member of that group. In fact, the construction of a categorical definition of lesbian is bound to obscure the personal and variable meanings of lesbian identity as it is experienced by real women. I say this because sexual feelings, attractions, and behavior are not necessarily fixed and invariant with regard to the sex of the person toward whom they are directed. When definitions of lesbian are conceptualized with primary reference to sexual feelings and activities, it may be difficult (if one wishes to allow for the complexity of lived experience) to construct unambiguous criteria that would specify who does and does not belong in the category *lesbian*.

A precise definition of lesbian that establishes unchanging sexual criteria according to which individual women can be judged as legitimate members of the category may not have the flexibility to account for the diversity and variability in subjectively experienced lesbian identities. One serious problem that results is that individual women may find their experience of themselves at odds with the socially constructed category, even when it emanates from the lesbian community. At this point in history when so many women are self-consciously asking who they are and how they can understand their place in society, it is possible to explore these issues with them directly.

Between 1977 and 1983, I taught at a northeastern women's college, where I served, albeit unofficially, as a counselor to young women exploring their sexual and personal identities. For many of the women I spoke with over the years, these were times of change and transition, and among the most prominent changes were those in their sexual feelings, activities, and identities, and in their sense of possibilities for the future. Although many of these young women had been sexual (in varying degrees and with different sexual object choices) before coming to college, several features of their new environment converged to make the issue of sexuality in general, and their own sexuality in particular, more salient than it had been in their high school years.

One important aspect of their new environment was that they were away from their parents and had the option of engaging in sexual relations without having to be overly concerned about their parents' discovery of their behavior. Second, they were in an all-women's environment where close connections between women were valued, and where they were free to develop in ways not often matched in coeducational environments. In women's colleges, relationships between women can and do flourish; women have the opportunity to live, love, learn, work, and grow together. Although such environments are special in any historic time period, there was something unique about their atmosphere in the last ten years. As a result of the women's movement, the visibility of a small but dedicated number of feminist faculty, and the presence in the curriculum of women's studies courses, a certain self-consciousness about being women existed among a majority of the students. This consciousness gave rise to both self-exploration and a broader consideration of women's lives and possibilities, including the variety of vocational choices and sexual life-styles available to women. Added to this was a highly visible and active Lesbian Alliance on campus. At a time when many students were having to deal with themselves as sexual beings, they were also being exposed to "out" lesbians, many of whom

were in more than a few respects indistinguishable from themselves. Workshops conducted by the Lesbian Alliance did a tremendous job in raising consciousness, and they also served, for some students, to heighten questions and thinking about their own sexuality.

Let me digress to address the issue of lesbianism at women's colleges, specifically whether it is more prevalent at such institutions than at coeducational colleges. Although the president and public relations officials at the college where I taught have steadfastly maintained that the proportion of lesbians at the college is not higher than in the population at large, it is still the case that alumnae, parents of prospective students, and some of the prospective students themselves, express strong concern about both the prevalence and the visibility of lesbianism on campus. Although I did not make a systematic survey, it is my impression that the incidence of lesbianism at this women's college was higher than in the population at large, even significantly so. Young women who had previously thought of themselves as heterosexual, as well as those who had suspected that they were lesbians but had tried to deny it, found in their four years at this college that there was something positive and good in lesbian relationships, and some of them began to identify proudly as lesbians. I believe that the environment at a women's college is both structurally and psychologically conducive to lesbianism. But I do not think that the concern expressed by alumnae, parents, and students is entirely attributable to the existence and visibility of lesbianism on campus. At least some of their concern is actually unrelated to the level of lesbianism on campus. For one thing, it is still considered unusual for a woman to choose to spend four years in an all-women environment, especially now that there are equivalently excellent coeducational liberal arts colleges. As is typically the case with women who make different choices, who choose to take themselves and other women so seriously that they decide not to organize four years or more of their lives around men, they get labeled deviant. And we all know what that means. Expressed concern about lesbianism at women's colleges is at least partially based on a failure to understand why women would choose to be together and on a fear of what that kind of choice suggests.

Second, I think fear or concern about lesbianism is at least partially a displaced fear among parents about their daughters' sexuality. Parents know that their daughters are going to engage in sexual explorations while away at college, and for a great many of those daughters, the explorations will involve heterosexual sex. I think it may be difficult for both mothers and fathers to conceive of this consciously; even if they do, it may be difficult to express to themselves, each other, and their daughters, some of their real concerns (e.g., that their daughters may be coerced or taken advantage of). Psychologically, parental concerns about their daughter's sexuality (in the broadest sense) may get displaced and expressed in relation to something about which, in a homophobic culture, concern can more readily be articulated and discussed, that is, lesbianism. I have often had the sense that parental preoccupation with lesbianism serves to assuage more deeply hidden or more difficult to acknowledge fears about the (hetero)sexual behavior of daughters.

Whether or not lesbianism is more prevalent at women's colleges is difficult to establish, and the expressed concern about it may in fact mask other issues and fears concerning women's choices. What is abundantly clear, however, is that at the women's college where I taught, there was a significant minority of young women who were actively engaged in the process of sexual self-definition. Let me return to some of the definitional concerns that emerged as particularly salient in my discussions with these women. I had extensive contact with students who were active members of the Lesbian Alliance (and who were thus viewed as "the lesbian community" on campus), as well as with students who were not publicly affiliated with

the Alliance. I will articulate as well as I can from their perspective some of the ways in which these young women were defining themselves, and how they made sense of their pasts, their present, and their futures.

One major distinction that emerged from interviews with women who defined themselves as lesbian was between those who felt their lesbianism was essentially beyond their control and those who felt it was self-consciously chosen. Some of these women had from an earlier age (usually between six and twelve) considered themselves to be different from other girls. Whether or not they had a label for it, they experienced themselves as different in that they felt sexually attracted to and oriented toward other girls or women. Their feelings could be independent of actual sexual experiences. In other words, they may or may not have had lesbian relationships, and they may even have had heterosexual ones, but regardless, they felt themselves to be different in that they were attracted to females. Furthermore, this was experienced either at the time, or in retrospect, as something beyond their control; these women had not chosen to be attracted to women, they just were. Some of these women offered comments to the effect that they were "born" lesbians and would spontaneously contrast themselves with women who described their lesbianism as resulting from a conscious decision. Following a distinction made by Barbara Ponse in her study of a southern lesbian community, I have characterized these women as primary lesbians; that is, women who from an early age have a conscious sense of difference based on sexual attraction toward members of the same sex, and who do not perceive this difference to be based on any kind of conscious choice.[7]

In contrast to primary lesbians were women who could be characterized, again following the distinction made by Ponse, as elective lesbians. For these women, their lesbian identity is perceived as consciously chosen. This is not to imply that it is strictly a political choice; for the majority it is experienced as an erotic choice as well. Unlike primary lesbians, these women did not have a conscious sense of being different from other girls at a younger age. But in similarity with primary lesbians, their sense of identity was independent of their actual sexual history. As girls, some of these elective lesbians had crushes on other girls; they may even have engaged in sexual play and exchanges with other girls. Despite such lesbian-like experiences, they did not think of themselves as different. No one had ever labeled their behavior as deviant, and it had not occurred to them that others might consider it to be.

These women usually had some heterosexual experience as they got older, and even when they had not, they had heterosexual identities. However, regardless of their actual sexual experience, they never thought of themselves as different from the "average" female in terms of their sexual orientation. Although they may never have explicitly called themselves heterosexuals, neither did they consider the possibility that they were anything else (much in the manner of white people who never give much explicit thought to their race). I have characterized as elective lesbians women who perceive of their lesbianism as a conscious choice, and who do not have a history of thinking of themselves as different from other females in the realm of sexual inclinations.

Among elective lesbians, I found two distinctive sub-patterns that suggested another salient dimension of lesbian identity. Some of these women viewed their sexual attraction to women as a central, basic, and unchanging aspect of who they were, and it seemed to me that this was not merely a political stance but a strongly experienced subjective feeling about their essential natures. In light of this sense of themselves, their past heterosexual behavior and identity presented an inconsistency. Unwilling to accept this apparent discontinuity and given their belief in the stability and enduring quality of their sexual orientation, they repeatedly expressed the view that there was something "unreal" about their previous heterosexuality. This was reflected in their tendency to reinterpret their past history to suggest a continuity between past and present senses of self. As one woman put it, "In high school when I had a steady boyfriend, the real me, the lesbian, was suppressed. I just wasn't my real self back then." For other women, their less-than-satisfactory heterosexual experiences confirmed that they had really been lesbians all along. Still others pointed to their intense friendships with girlfriends as suggestive of their true lesbian identities. Sexual feelings and behaviors were central to the lesbian identities of these women, and they believed in the essentiality of their lesbianism.

Other elective lesbians did not view their lesbianism as an essential and enduring aspect of who they were. They did not show any tendency to reinterpret their past history, and did not experience dissonance or contradiction in describing themselves as lesbians with heterosexual pasts. As one woman put it quite simply, "Then I was heterosexual, and now I'm a lesbian." These women expressed the view that there was nothing inconsistent or in need of explanation about their present identity and the one they had assumed in the past. Some of these women revealed, upon questioning, that they had engaged in childhood sexual play with other girls or had had strong attachments to camp counselors and teachers, but had never thought of these as lesbian feelings. Although they currently identified themselves as lesbians, they saw no reason to reconstruct their pasts as implicitly lesbian. Unlike the elective lesbians previously described, they did not view sexual attraction to women as an essential and unchanging aspect of who they were, although they strongly believed they would continue to have their primary (if not all) relationships with women. Some women said they considered themselves to be lesbians whose sexual feelings could be most accurately characterized as bisexual, or just sexual; however, these comments tended to be private as opposed to publicly stated. Other lesbians in this subgroup defined themselves as lesbian and let its essentiality be assumed, while privately they experienced their sexuality as fluid, or potentially so.

To summarize, in the sample of college women with whom I worked, one major difference that emerged was in whether their lesbianism was experienced as determined (i.e., primary) or self-consciously chosen (i.e., elective). Another major difference had to do with whether their lesbianism was experienced as a central and enduring aspect of who they were, or whether it was experienced as more fluid and dynamic in nature. These two dimensions of difference were not entirely independent of one another. Among those lesbians whose identity was a chosen one, some experienced their sexuality as essential, others as fluid; among those lesbians whose identity felt determined, sexuality was experienced as essential by definition.

With respect to these dimensions of sexuality, there appear to be some interesting age differences. I have spoken with elective lesbians in their late twenties, thirties, and forties who described shifts in their thinking about the nature of their lesbianism. Some had at an earlier age experienced their sexuality as essential and fixed, that is, invariantly focused on women, but later in the development of their lesbian identity had come to feel that their sexuality was in fact more fluid. For a few, this shift resulted from bisexual experiences later in life. Others who felt this way had continued to have relationships only with women. They attributed their earlier position to their more adamant lesbian feminist politics or to what they thought was a developmental phase many lesbians go through.

Alternatively, some elective lesbians felt that in their younger years, when they were engaged in sexual exploration and discovery, their sexuality was more fluid, but that in the context of lesbian culture and relationships they had developed a very explicit preference for women. These women thought of their sexuality as having become more fixed as they got older. Whereas the

college women with whom I worked characterized their sexuality as either fixed or fluid, some older women had experienced shifts over the life-cycle in this aspect of their sexuality

It seems that as lesbians engage in the continuing process of self-definition, their sense of the essentiality or fluidity of their sexuality may change. In contrast, the distinction between primary and elective lesbianism seems to remain more dichotomous over the course of development. Women of all ages with whom I have spoken made reference to such a distinction; they tended to identify as one or the other, and experienced this identification as one that was stable.

Let me return to my discussion of these differing dimensions of lesbian identity as they were experienced by the students with whom I spoke. Because among themselves some of these students discussed lesbianism and their differing experiences of it, they were often aware that not all lesbians described themselves similarly. Sometimes they had distinct opinions about themselves in relation to other lesbians who described themselves differently. For example, some women whom I have characterized as primary lesbians referred to themselves as "born" or "real" lesbians with the implicit designation of elective lesbians as "fake."

It was not uncommon for an elective lesbian to express to me privately her speculations about whether she was "really" a lesbian. At times she wondered whether she wasn't "really" bisexual, or even heterosexual. While some primary lesbians interpret such uncertainty as difficulty in coming out, unwillingness to give up heterosexual privilege, or internalized homophobia, it seems to me that at least some of the elective lesbian's uncertainty can be traced back to the belief within the campus lesbian community that women who choose to be lesbians are somehow less real, or legitimate, than those who felt they had no choice about it.

Despite this belief, there did seem to me to be a tolerance within the community for differences based on primary, compared with elective, lesbianism. In contrast, the issue of whether sexuality was thought of as essential or fluid was a much more sensitive one. For example, there was a noteworthy asymmetry in the application of the concept of the fluidity of sexual attractions when discussed in relation to lesbian and heterosexual women. I spoke with more than a few lesbians who were quite intolerant of (some) heterosexual women's insistence that they simply were not sexually attracted to women and that they couldn't imagine ever feeling differently. Implied in their intolerance was the belief that, despite heavy socialization pressures, sexual attraction is never so fixed and unmalleable as to be irrevocably focused just on persons of one sex. Yet some of these same women were equally intolerant of the opposite stance, that sexual feelings could exist toward persons of either sex, when expressed by a lesbian.

The assumption was often made about lesbians who were unwilling to state that they were (forever) uninterested sexually in men, that they must be having difficulty coming out, or were unwilling to accept a stigmatized identity. Sometimes they were assumed to be going through a bisexual phase, or worse yet, to be male-identified and operating under a false consciousness. The assumption that bisexuality is simply a phase in the coming-out process of lesbians, and that those who call themselves bisexuals are really lesbians unwilling to call themselves that, has been countered by the contention from self-proclaimed bisexuals that their lesbianism was a phase in their coming out as bisexuals.[8]

The problem with all of these assumptions is that one person or set of persons presumes an attitude of knowing and understanding the meaning of another person's experience better than the person who is herself experiencing it. In this climate, individual women may have a difficult time finding their own voices and defining their own experiences. To the extent that lesbianism is very narrowly defined, the categories will restrict, rather than give full expression to, the diversity among women who subjectively define themselves as lesbian.

The question of sexual identity and how it is formed is not well understood, but some of our psychological conceptions do not do justice to the complexity of the process. We have often simplistically assumed that people have sexual attractions to persons of one or the other sex (but not both), that they act on those exclusive attractions, and that they eventually come to adopt the identity appropriate to their sexual activities, although there may be resistance when that identity is a stigmatized one. It appears to be the case, however, that sexual feelings and activities change; they can be fluid and dynamic. And furthermore, the reality is that feelings, activities, and self-conscious identities may not at all times be congruent. It has been suggested by social psychologists that people strive for congruence between their thoughts and feelings,[9] and that with respect to sexual identity in particular, we are motivated to achieve congruence between our feelings, activities, and self-proclaimed identities.[10] This suggestion, however, does not accord with what I observed during my six-and-a-half years at a women's college in the late seventies and early eighties.

What particularly struck me, among this select sample of college women, was the diversity in self-definitions and the degree of incongruence between their sexual activities and their sexual identities (as expressed both publicly and privately). Every possible permutation of feelings and activities existed within each sexual identification category. Further, I was impressed by the way in which these young women were able to tolerate the ambiguity without significant internal distress.

Let me elaborate on the observation that every possible permutation existed. Among women who identified themselves to me as lesbians, there were some whose sexual behavior was explicitly and exclusively lesbian, and some whose behavior was exclusively heterosexual or bisexual (these latter also described themselves as "political lesbians"). In addition, I spoke with sexually inexperienced women who considered themselves to be lesbians. Although no student ever self-consciously identified herself as a celibate lesbian, this is a distinct possibility and has been described by Susan Yarborough.[11] Thus, among women who call themselves lesbians, a wide range of sexual behavior is evident.

Far fewer women described themselves to me as having a bisexual identity, and those who did made it quite clear that this was a confidential disclosure. The small number of self-identified bisexuals was particularly interesting in light of the findings from a survey of sexual behavior and attitudes taken in a psychology of women class I taught. The survey was constructed by students in the class and administered in such a way as to insure complete anonymity. In response to the question of how they would label their sexuality to themselves, regardless of their actual sexual experiences, 65 percent (of 95 students) identified as heterosexual, 26 percent identified as bisexual, and 9 percent identified as lesbian. When asked what their actual sexual experiences were, the responses were as follows: 72 percent heterosexual, 20 percent bisexual, 4 percent lesbian, and 4 percent lacking sexual experience. Two things are interesting about these figures. First, they reveal that the way in which women sexually identify themselves does not always coincide with their actual sexual experience. Second, although three times as many women privately considered themselves to be bisexual as contrasted with lesbian, their concerns were never publicly raised, nor were their bisexual identities ever acknowledged in class. In comparison, lesbian concerns and identities were much more visible in the classroom. It began to occur to me that acknowledging one's bisexuality, or raising such issues publicly, was as stigmatized as discussing lesbianism, if not more so.

To return to the question of the various permutations of sexual activity and identity: Among those interviewed women who identified themselves to me as bisexual, some were engaged in exclusively lesbian activity, some were engaged in exclusively heterosexual activity, while others actually had bisexual experience. Some women who were sexually inexperienced considered themselves on the basis of their potential sexual behavior to be bisexual.

Finally, to complete consideration of the various permutations, consider women who identified themselves to me as heterosexual. Here too, I found women whose current sexual behavior was exclusively lesbian (of the "I just love Mindy; I'm not a lesbian" variety) as well as those whose sexual behavior was exclusively heterosexual. A few women considered themselves to be basically heterosexual even though they had had bisexual experience. And again, some women who were sexually inexperienced nevertheless asserted that they knew they were heterosexual.

The point I wish to make by describing these combinations is not simply that one's sexual identity is not always predictable on the basis of one's sexual behavior, but rather that the assumption that we inherently strive for congruence between our sexual feelings, activities, and identities may not be warranted, and that given the fluidity of sexual feelings, permanent congruence may not be an achievable state. The women with whom I spoke were not personally distressed by the fact of discrepancies between sexual behavior and sexual identity. For example, women who identified as lesbians but found themselves to be occasionally sexually attracted to men were made more uncomfortable by the thought of what other lesbians might think than by their own fluid and changing attractions. These were women who wanted to be considered legitimate members of the lesbian community, but who often felt that they were not welcome, or that if they were, they were not trusted. Although very often they felt compelled to identify themselves publicly and unequivocally as lesbians whose sexuality was stable and enduring and exclusively focused on women, they privately experienced their sexuality in a more fluid and dynamic manner. The pressure to be congruent and to proclaim an identity that was in line with their sexual activities was often more externally than internally motivated.

These women are real, not hypothetical. Although the kind of lesbian they represent did not constitute a majority of the self-defined lesbians with whom I spoke, I think that the way they experienced their identities and their relation to the community has implications for how psychologists talk about sexuality and sexual identity.

Identity is constructed both societally and psychologically; it is both a social and a personal process. The process of psychological self-definition takes place within the context of existing dominant culture definitions as well as those that emanate from within the minority community itself. Not only are lesbians a stigmatized and oppressed group, with the result that many have internalized negative images of self, but they are also a group whose central characteristic is debatable and not altogether invariant. Hence its boundaries are more permeable than those of other minority groups. Unlike one's sex or race, which is typically both highly visible and unchanging, one's sexuality (like one's class) is less visible and not so static over the course of a lifetime. Thus, the process of lesbian identity formation is complicated not only because of homophobia, but also because of the nature of sexuality itself.

When counselling women who are engaged in the act of sexual self-definition, therapists need to be aware of the variations in the process of identity formation. On the basis of the findings presented here, it is suggested that psychologists need to take a more serious look at the assumptions inherent in the phrase "coming out." It is not uncommon to hear clinicians talk about women who are in the process of coming out, or who have difficulty with coming out, as if they know what the "right" result looks like. We should begin to question not only whether there is a "right" way to come out, but also whether there is some static end point at all. Liberal teachers and clinicians often think their appropriate role with lesbians is to help them deal with coming out, but I would urge us to think seriously about the relationship between coming out and self-definition. It seems to me that the aim ought to be to encourage each woman as she struggles to define herself. This may mean facilitating her search for authenticity rather than assuming a fixed sexuality that the therapist will help her discover. If being authentic entails accepting the fluidity of one's sexual feelings and activities and identifying as a lesbian, therapists should support this rather than convey the impression that the woman is confused or unwilling to accept a stigmatized identity.

These interviews suggest that sexuality is experienced by some women (both heterosexual and lesbian) as an aspect of identity that may change over the course of their lives. Although there has not been research on this issue with male homosexuals, from reading gay male literature, speaking with a small sample of gay men, and exchanging views with therapists who work with them, my sense is that gay men do not experience their sexuality in the fluid manner that some lesbian and heterosexual women do. I have no strong data on this, but I suspect that very few gay men could be characterized as elective homosexuals. Although this observation might at first seem puzzling and lead one to wonder why the nature of sexuality would be different for women and for men, I think it becomes more understandable with reference to psychoanalytic theories of mothering that place emphasis on the primary human need for social relationship and then examine the expression of that need in terms of the infant's first love object: its mother. Specifically, object relations theory can provide the framework for understanding how the conditions of early infancy might lead women to have greater bisexual potential than men. Dorothy Dinnerstein has discussed how the first relationship with a woman establishes a homoerotic potential in women,[12] and Nancy Chodorow has elaborated on the early psychic foundations of women's homoemotional needs and capacities.[13] The writings of both of these authors can provide the basis for formulation of a new question: Why do so many women become exclusively heterosexual as opposed to bisexual or lesbian?

One of the most important insights of both feminist psychology and the women's movement is that our being born female does not mean that we automatically and naturally prefer certain roles and activities. We have recognized that the category *woman* has been socially constructed, and that societal definitions notwithstanding, women are a diverse group with interests, attitudes, and identities that do not always conform to what is traditionally considered feminine. We have long been told that we are not "real" women unless we are wives and mothers, and to counter this, feminists have been forceful and articulate in asserting that one's sex is not related in any inevitable or natural way to one's sexual preference or societal role. In a similar vein I suggest, on the basis of my discussions with a select sample of college women, that sexual feelings and activities are not always accurately described in either/or terms, nor do they exist in a simple one-to-one relation to our sexual identities. Just as we have protested the constricting social definition of what a real woman is, precisely because it has served to oppress women and to limit the expression of our diverse potentials, so too must we be careful in our social construction of sexuality not to construct categories that are so rigid and inflexible that women's self-definitions put them at odds with the social definitions. To do so only limits the expression of the diversities and variabilities in women's sexual identities.

NOTES

1. Adrienne Rich, "Compulsory Heterosexuality and Lesbian Existence," *Signs* 5 (Summer 1980): 631–60.

2. "Radicalesbians, Woman-Identified Women," in *Radical Feminism,* ed. Ann Koedt, Ellen Levine, and Anita Rapone (New York: Quadrangle Books, 1973).

3. Blanche Wiesen Cook, "Female Support Networks and Political Activism," *Chrysalis* 3 (1977): 43–61.

4. Ann Ferguson, "Compulsory Heterosexuality and Lesbian Existence: Defining the Issues," *Signs* 7 (Autumn 1981): 158–72.

5. Ferguson, "Compulsory Heterosexuality," 166.

6. Jacquelyn Zita, "Compulsory Heterosexuality and Lesbian Existence: Defining the Issues," *Signs* 7 (Autumn 1981): 172–87.

7. Barbara Ponse, *Identities in the Lesbian World* (Westport, Conn.: Greenwood Press, 1978).

8. Lisa Orlando, "Loving Whom We Choose: Bisexuality and the Lesbian/Gay Community," *Gay Community News,* Feb. 25, 1984.

9. Leon Festinger, *A Theory of Cognitive Dissonance* (Evanston, Ill.: Row, Peterson, 1957).

10. Vivienne Cass, "Homosexual Identity Formation: A Theoretical Model," *Journal of Homosexuality* 4 (Fall 1979): 219–35.

11. Susan Yarborough, "Lesbian Celibacy," *Sinister Wisdom* 11 (Fall 1979): 24–29.

12. Dorothy Dinnerstein, *The Mermaid and the Minotaur: Sexual Arrangements and Human Malaise* (New York: Harper & Row, 1976).

13. Nancy Chodorow, *The Reproduction of Mothering: Psychoanalysis and the Sociology of Gender* (Berkeley: University of California Press, 1978).

Reading 3   The Talk of Women Friends

FERN L. JOHNSON AND ELIZABETH J. ARIES

Questions to Consider:

1. According to Johnson and Aries, why hasn't friendship between women been studied? Do you feel it is important to study women's friendships? Why or why not?

2. Has talk been a central part of your friendships? Have you found that the role of talk is different in your relationships with men than it is with women?

3. This study described the friendships of a small sample of white women. Do you think you would see differences between women of color? Would there be differences between the friendships of lesbians and the friendships of heterosexual women?

Synopsis—The talk of women friends has, for a variety of reasons, received little serious attention. We review (1) the sources of prejudice against this topic, (2) the dimensions of social context that shape women's friendships, and (3) the major differences between male friendships and female friendships. On the basis of prior research and an interview study, we propose that talk is central to close friendships between women. Our interview data reveal a broad range of conversational topics among women friends. The women we interviewed report that talk with their close friends creates a mosaic of noncritical listening, mutual support, enhancement of self-worth, relationship exclusiveness, and personal growth and self-discovery. We conclude by addressing issues pertaining to research methodology, to cross-cultural and sub-cultural differences, and to the politics of female friendship.

Writing about the talk of women friends is an act infused with contemporary import. From at least three vantage points, the topic emerges from an historical context of both inattention and selected attention.

First, there is the issue of friendship itself. Friendship is certainly not a contemporary invention, yet friendship as a significant and important part of the continuing fabric of personal existence has received nowhere near the attention given to other relationships, notably kinship, marriage, work, and neighborhood relationships. Bott (1971) concludes that investigators in the past may have been too 'bedazzled by kinship to take proper note of friendship' (p. 234). Anthropologists are cited for their inattention to friendship (Paine, 1969). And the author of a recent book on friendship (Bell, 1981) comments that 'over the

Reprinted with permission from *Women's Studies International Forum, 6,* Fern L. Johnson and Elizabeth Aries, "The Talk of Women Friends," 1983, Elsevier Science Ltd, Oxford, England.

years sociologists have shown little interest in the study of friendship' (p. 7).

The inattention to friendship probably rests more on omission that it does on some conscious rejection of the topic. The easy 'bedazzlement' with relationships other than friendships most likely occurs because these other relationships bear clear ties to the institutional and structural foundations of a society. Friendships, of all human relationships, exhibit the weakest structural ties because they imply neither permanence, as does the kinship link, nor face-to-face constancy, as does the work or neighborhood link (Litwak and Szelenyi, 1969). The bonds of friendship rest on voluntary association and affective ties (Wright, 1978). Friendships bond individuals in intensely personal and private ways: 'persons may break their friendship, revise it, or simply drift away from one another without notifying anyone else,' observes Suttles (1970, p. 97). Even when friendships are embedded in more structurally obvious relationships, the dynamic remains distinct. The dynamic of friendship evolves through the *internal* character of the relationship rather than being defined by criteria *external* to the relationship (Allan, 1979: 4–5). We suspect, in short, that friendship has not received due attention because it appears elusive and fragile, sometimes co-exists with other relationships, or is considered to be subordinate or ancillary to more publicly visible and structurally stable relationships.

Second, there is the issue of *female* friendship. Just as friendship has taken a back seat to other relationships, female friendship has historically taken a back seat to male friendship. Looking back on the literature, Bell (1981) finds that history records the great friendships of men. This is no surprise since men are valued above women in most societies and since men have done most of the historiography. It is also the case that males in most societies enjoy greater mobility and social contact outside of the kinship system, and therefore have greater opportunities for forming friendships independent of kinship ties (DuBois,

1974). Seiden and Bart (1975) aptly describe the attention paid to female friendship as follows: 'Significant female friendships are either not portrayed at all, are interpreted as lesbian, or considerably depreciated in importance' (p. 194). The slighting of female friendship is part, then, of the more general slighting and devaluation of those activities of women that go beyond their traditional connections to men and family.

Much of what we are about when we address any issue pertaining to female friendship is rectifying the pervasive stereotypes and preconceptions about the differential capabilities of men and women for friendships. Marking the polarities, we have on the male side, the glorification of male bonding so clearly conceptualized by Tiger (1969) who sees biological evolution and 'biograms' as the unique logical force behind the supremacy of male relationships. On the female side, we have the rampant conception (our female students still speak of it) that females are opposed rather than joined to one another. de Beauvoir (1952), along with her construction of feminine friendships as precious and strength-giving, sees women as against each other, seeing 'in every other an enemy' (p. 607). Seiden and Bart (1975) distill this viewpoint:

> 'There has been a popular cultural stereotype that women do not really like each other very much. It has been said that women do not really trust women friends, do not have grounds for trusting them, do not work well for women supervisors, and are inherently in competition for the available men. This competition is said to override the possibility of genuine friendships' (p. 192).

Treating female friendships seriously and treating them as they exist, rather than as they are presumed to exist, is an important part of the contemporary movement to reclaim and recount women's lives. The friendships that women have with one another serve important functions for their participants, and the value of these relationships deserves careful attention.

Finally, the issue of studying the *talk* of female friends shapes the focus of this paper and defines what we believe may be the most significant component of female friendship. Featuring talk takes on importance both within the context of studying friendship and within the content of studying women.

The bulk of empirical research on friendship has been directed to the psychological and social conditions that draw individuals together in friendship. At the personal/psychological level, major topics have included personality similarity of friends, e.g. Duck (1973); commonality of attitudes, beliefs, and values, e.g. Black (1974); and similarity of activity preference, e.g. Werner and Parmelee (1979). At the sociological level, research includes explorations of the role of proximity in friendship choice, e.g. Athanasiou and Yoshioka (1973); the effects of social status and social class on friendship ties, e.g. Simon *et al.* (1970); Verbrugge (1977); and the manner in which one's position in the life cycle implies different patterns of friendship relationships, e.g. Candy *et al.* (1981); Lowenthal *et al.* (1976); Shulman (1975).

The only major perspective to emphasize any aspect of talk among friends comes from the literature on self-disclosure. Among many other variables, this literature explores the types and amount of self-disclosure that occur between friends; and sex differences in patterns of self-disclosure between friends, e.g. Cozby (1973); Hacker (1981); Morgan (1976).

We believe that talk has been neglected in the research literature because it is viewed as mundane, is difficult to study, and is not the basis of friendships among men. Within the context of studying women's friendships, talk may also have been neglected because of the more general devaluation of *women's talk*. Certainly scholars of both speech communication and sociolinguistics take talk (or speech) as central to their studies, but the substance of women's talk rarely, until

recently, appears as a legitimate focus for investigation, e.g. Kramarae (1981); Lakoff (1975); Spender (1980). Folk wisdom has long denigrated women's talk as 'idle chatter,' 'yackedy yack,' 'hen cackling,' 'gabbing,' and 'gossip.' Such folk wisdom pejoratively places women in the position of having nothing better to do with their time than talk and of having nothing important to talk about. Kramer's (1977) study of perceptions of male and female speech among high school and college students confirmed this folk wisdom: her respondents thought that 'gossip,' 'talk a lot,' 'talk about trivial topics,' and 'gibberish' were much more characteristic of female than male speakers.

We are focusing on the talk of women friends not simply because talk is a variable that has received little attention but because our research demonstrates that talk is the substance of women's friendship. By highlighting and featuring talk as the *central feature* of women's friendship, we are attempting to contribute to the more general trend of feminist scholars to reconceptualize women's experience in terms that grow from and validly capture their experience. A large part of this task requires exposing the double standard that operates to defame an activity when performed by women while inflating a similar activity when performed by men. In her discussion of woman talk, Spender (1980) views the double standard as serving patriarchal order: *'No matter what women may say* it fosters the conviction that you cannot trust the words of a woman and that it is permissible to *dismiss* anything she might say' (p. 107, first emphasis added).

The focus of this paper is on providing a clearer understanding of the nature of female friendship and, in particular, the function of talk in this relationship. We will begin from the perspective of the socio-cultural forces that shape the friendship relationship, looking at the conditions in which close friendships flourish between females. We will then take a closer look at female friendship through qualitative interview data that we have collected.

PERSPECTIVES ON WOMEN'S FRIENDSHIP

The character of women's friendship emerges from a number of social factors that influence the manner in which women interact with one another. We briefly review here (1) the relationships between social context and the ties that females have to one another and (2) the differences in friendship patterns that are attributable to sex and gender roles.

Social Context

Social factors serve as powerful preconditions for the types of friendships that women experience. Female friendships may vary in form, intensity, or function, depending on the nature of sex-role differentiation and of male-female relations within the family and in society generally.

Several compelling historical accounts of female friendship now exist that together depict how female friendships take on special importance in the context of rigid gender-role differentiation. Faderman (1981) traces romantic friendships between women from the sixteenth century through the present, arguing that the twentieth century rupture of an historical tolerance of these relationships came in part because woman's role changed:

> 'Passionate romantic friendship was a widely recognized, tolerated social institution before our century. Women were, in fact, expected to seek out kindred spirits and form strong bonds.... It was not unusual for a woman to seek in her romantic friendship the center of her life, quite apart from the demands of marriage and family.... When women's role in society began to change, however—when what women did needed to be taken more seriously because they were achieving some of the powers that could make them adult persons—society's view of romantic friendship changed' (p. 411).

Prior to Faderman's book, both Cott (1977) and Smith-Rosenberg (1975) described female friendships during the first half of the nineteenth century, noting that the separate spheres of men and women established sharp gender boundaries. The male sphere was associated with discernment, judgment, knowledge, reason, and superiority. The female sphere was associated with the heart, with sensibility, grace, tenderness, and compliance (Cott, 1977).

Within this historic social context, women formed very close, passionate, long-lasting, and devoted friendships with other women. The biological realities associated with reproductive functions helped to create a physical and emotional intimacy that bound women together. In a world where relations with men were formal and where men were not socialized to share the same sensitivities and sensibilities, women turned to each other to provide the emotional richness and complexity to their lives that men could not. Women shared with one another their joys and sorrows, births and marriages, stressful events, sicknesses, deaths, and offered aid with domestic chores. It was only with members of their own sex that women could have truly reciprocal relationships. While women remained subordinate to men, they could possess status and power among women. Here their intellectual capacities were respected, not disparaged. Here they could develop a sense of inner security and self-esteem.

A similar picture of female friendships emerges from more contemporary research on working class families in England, Australia, and the United States. Working-class couples live in a world with marked sexual segregation both inside and outside the family. Husbands and wives have their own separate social networks (Bott, 1971; Fallding, 1961; Young and Willmott, 1957). Working-class women form close bonds with women kin and friends, existing in a female world in which they share together the daily realities of child care and managing the home. Women turn to each other to fill their needs for emotional expression and understanding, as well as to pro-vide mutual aid in times of trouble (Rubin, 1976). In this context, female friendships help women maintain an emotional balance in their marriages where communication with husbands is difficult and meager (Komarovsky, 1967).

Role differentiation is not as extreme within contemporary middle and upper classes. Male and female spheres are less sharply defined, with greater overlap in the interests and activities of both sexes. Here communication between spouses is greater (Komarovsky, 1967), and friendships between married couples often replace sex-segregated relations (Lopata, 1973). What is inter-esting, however, is that even when couples get together, wives share confidences with wives, hus-bands with husbands (Babchuck, 1965). Thus, even when sexual segregation is greatly reduced, females continue to seek close friendships with members of their own sex.

Sex Differences

Female friendships are frequently described in contrast to male friendships. 'There is no social factor,' writes Bell (1981), 'more important than that of sex in leading to friendship variations' (p. 55). Females engage in more intimate, one-to-one relationships involving mutual explora-tion, understanding and security, while males form friendships in groups, showing less concern for the relational aspects of friendship and putting more stress on activities (Douvan and Adelson, 1966; Lowenthal *et al.*, 1976; Wright and Crawford, 1971).

One of the most salient dimensions of this difference is in what men and women talk about with their same-sex friends. Females are more self-disclosing to same-sex friends (Jourard, 1971; Mulcahy, 1973), and in particular about intimate topics (Morgan, 1976). In adulthood, close female friends converse more frequently than close male friends about personal and fam-ily problems, intimate relationships, doubts and fears, daily activities, and hobbies and shared activities; male friends, on the other hand, dis-cuss sports more frequently than female friends (Aries and Johnson, in press). Adult women also report greater depth of discussion with their female friends about personal problems, family activities, and reminiscences about the past; men report greater depth in conversations with same-sex close friends about the topics of work and sports (Aries and Johnson, in press).

The major contrast, then, between male friendships and female friendships appears to grow from different orientations toward close relationships. Male friendships involve more communication about matters peripheral to the self; they engage more in sociability than in intimacy (Pleck, 1975). Female friendships encompass personal identities, intimacy, and the immediacy of daily life.

THE INTERVIEW STUDY

As part of a larger research program on same-sex close friendships (Aries and Johnson, in press; Johnson and Aries, in press), we conducted a depth interview study with a small sample of men and women from a New England city. This was an exploratory study employing the richness of idio-graphic response to provide a general description of the close friendship relationship. We report here on the interviews with women.

Procedures and Sample

We arrived at a sample of 20 adult females through a procedure that would ensure socio-economic heterogeneity among participants. We began by randomly selecting 40 female names from the street list of the city we had targeted, stratifying the sample by areas within the city. Each woman in the sample was sent a letter describing the study and was phoned several days later to determine her willingness to participate. Half accepted our invitation, and half declined.

While the sample is not random, it is representative of a diverse group of women.

The final sample of 20 included white women only. They ranged in age from 27 to 58 yr, with a mean age of 39 yr. All but one completed high school; five had finished college; and three had done graduate work. Seventy-five per cent of the women had engaged at some time in full- or part-time work outside the home as nurses, teachers, secretaries, dressmakers, home economists, telephone operators, etc. In terms of marital status, fifteen were currently married, two were widowed, one was divorced, and two were single. All but three had children. For those who were or had been married, the husband's occupational category ranged from blue-collar to professional, e.g. factory worker, firefighter, lawyer. Because the sample was small, it was not possible to examine the effects of demographic variables on the nature of close friendship relationships.

We interviewed all participants in their homes at their convenience. The interviews were audio recorded and ranged in length from 45 to 90 min. During the interview, each woman first was asked some general questions about the role of friendship in her life, and then was asked a number of questions about one relationship with a woman she defined as a close friend. Questions covered the history of the friendship, types of interaction between the two friends, functions of the friendship, and feelings about the friendship.

Qualitative Analysis of the Interviews

We found considerable diversity in the nature of the close friendships that the women described. For some women, the close friend was a person known for only a year or two; for others, the relationship had been ongoing for 20 or 30 yr. Half reported that their closest friend had always lived nearby, but four reported their closest friend to be a person currently living hundreds or thousands of miles away. Seventy-five per cent said they carried out their relationships through daily or weekly visits and phone conversations, while a few, e.g. a 41-yr old teacher and mother of five, said that phone calls were very frequent, with visits occurring only monthly or less often. For those friends living far apart, lengthy letters and/or phone conversations provided the connection.

We also found some common characteristics to the friendships. First, all but one of the women reported substantial dyadic contact with the close friend, although six women said that they also spent time with their friends in a group setting. Second, when asked 'Where do you usually see each other?' the women over and over gave the same answer: at each other's homes. Even those women whose best friend was a co-worker spent time together with her outside of work in each other's homes.

Here they often enjoyed a cup of coffee or tea and some conversation: viz. 'We never did anything together. We just sat around and talked. We sit and eat and talk and drink tea.' Third, half engaged in activities together such as sewing, knitting, baking, canning, crafts, and in one case, research. When the friends saw each other outside of their homes, they shopped, went out to eat or have a drink, and sometimes took their children to a park or for a walk. Finally, we found that for more than half of the women, there was an ongoing exchange of favors and services between friends. A few women depended upon their friends for transportation, for weekly trips to the grocery store, or simply for time away from home. Others exchanged household items, cooking utensils, dishes, tools, recipes, sewing patterns, and clothes. Friends were there for each other to help out with babysitting and household chores, especially in times of sickness or trouble.

What emerges from these reports is the centrality of talk in all their contacts. Situations in which women meet are occasions for conversation:

—*It doesn't matter if the kids are running through the house or the phone is ringing. We sit down and pick up with our conversation.*

The women we interviewed isolate talk as the most important aspect of the relationship. When asked 'What is the most important thing you feel you get out of the relationship?' almost identical words were spoken:

—*Someone to talk to.*
—*Just knowing I've got somebody I can talk to about anything.*
—*Just the fact that we can talk.*
—*You need somebody you can talk to.*

When one women described her visits to her closest friend who had moved away, she reported:

—*We would get up in the morning and talk for several hours.*
Then P. would go off. We'd stay up half of the night talking more.

Women also gave the same answers again and again to the question. 'What do you talk about?':

—*We talk about anything and everything.*
—*We talk about everything from A to Z. We talk about the kids a lot, cooking, furniture, or if she has a problem or I have a problem.*
—*We talk about a lot of personal things that you wouldn't discuss with just anybody.*

Women talk about the significant relationships in their lives: their children, their husbands, their families of origin, and their inlaws. They talk of their relationships with co-workers, with other friends, and with each other. They discuss their work and daily lives and activities. They engage in 'very personal talk', sharing their deepest feelings, problems, concerns, things they often can discuss with no one else. While some women report that they discuss politics, civic affairs, religion, or books and articles they've been reading, these topics are discussed with less frequency

and are usually spoken of as less important to the fabric of the friendship.

Several themes emerge from these descriptions of talk between female friends. First, friends listen to one another and do so in a noncritical fashion:

—*If I had a problem or I was upset, she would listen to me and talk and not try to tell me, 'Well, you should ought to do this, or you should ought to do that.' She's willing to accept me the way I am. . . . She's willing to listen when I need someone to listen. Day or night, it doesn't make any difference.*
—*We don't cut each other down. We just accept what's going on, and I feel this is different from relatives who always want you to be a certain way.*

The willingness of a close friend to listen noncritically appears to be the key to a second theme in the descriptions of talk. Almost all of the women spoke of the support they got from their close friends:

—*There have been some family problems, and I've needed a lot of encouragement, and she gives me that encouragement. She makes me feel really good about being myself.*
—*I've gone through a time in the past few years when I've found that I needed a lot of support that I haven't gotten from the marriage situation, and my friends have been able to provide the support that I needed as a person.*
—*She's somebody you can depend on, someone you can turn to when you need any help at all in any way.*
—*I just always know that she's there.*
—*If I've got a problem and I want someone to talk to, I'd go to her. . . . If I've got any problems, she's going to feel sorry for me or make me feel better.*

As a result of the kind of talk these women report, the close friends enhance each other's feelings of self-worth. Although expressed in many different ways, this theme characterized almost every interview.

These comments are typical:

—*If I had to capture the friendship overall, she makes me feel good about myself. I mean, she's the kind of person who I think values friendship and does lots of little things to tell you that. Whenever she knows that I'm not feeling well, she calls. She calls if something important is going on in my life, you know, she wants to wish me well or check up on me, so that she's very careful about those kinds of things.*

—*I get a sense of self worth because there's somebody out there who I like and who I respect in a number of ways who feels the same way about me.*

—*She lets me like myself. She lets me value myself.*

As one woman put it, a close friend 'makes you feel like a worthwhile human being—that you are capable of loving and sharing.'

These conversations give life and validity to aspects of the self that cannot be shared with other people. In this way, the conversations between close friends establish what we see as a theme of exclusiveness:

—*I can discuss things with her—whatever—that I don't with other people...things that involve something personal.*

—*She makes me get in touch with myself again.*

—*You can't survive without friends. Everything is inside, so you have to let it out. If S. weren't there, I'd be lost.*

—*I feel when I'm with her, I'm totally honest. I can say whatever I want to. Sometimes*

I feel there are very few times in my life when I really can do that.

As a particular part of this theme of exclusiveness, half of the married women noted that the type of communication they engage in with their close friend is not something they can experience with their husbands. Husbands have a difficult time listening to or understanding what is being said, or responding appropriately. As one woman put it:

—*You can't talk to your husband. My husband keeps things inside. He doesn't tell me what's on his mind or what bothers him. You have to really get after him. When I get close to someone, I'm there body, soul, and mind, all the way, and him...he isn't like this. You can't talk to your husband the way you can to your best girlfriend. I wish I could.*

Husbands, too, often make if difficult for women friends to talk with one another. One woman commented that husbands are 'always telling you to stop gossiping.' This simply provides further conformation that what appears senseless or mindless to men is of considerable importance to women. Chesler (1972) writes that female dialogue 'on its most ordinary level...affords women a measure of emotional reality and a kind of comfort that they cannot find with men' (p. 268).

A final theme (and one that certainly grows from the others) captures the importance of the close friend in the process of self-discovery and personal growth. The specifics are far-ranging, but the theme was uniform:

—*She's made me realize that if I had to be independent, I could hack it. She's told me that and made me really aware of what I am.... E. really taught me a lot—to really have more self-confidence.*

—*My relationship with P. has helped me get over being overly sensitive and to develop my own sense of humor about myself.*

    —B. helped bring me out of my shell to a certain degree. She gave me much more confidence in myself than I had ever had before she and I met.

    —She encouraged me to go and study and do what you want to do. You've got to better yourself.

Another woman whose friend had recently moved to another part of the country discussed her letter writing in these terms:

    —Right now I'm involved in school business, and, you see, I went through a whole thing and decided I really do have more potential in my life than to be just a secretary, so I'm trying to find some direction, where I'm going. She really helps me with that, so I write a lot about what I'm thinking and how things are going.

    In sum, we find consistent evidence in our interview data that talk—either as the *raison d'être* for being together or as an outcome of other activities—creates for female friends an elaborate and on-going mosaic of noncritical listening, mutual support, enhancement of self-worth, relationship exclusiveness, and personal growth and self-discovery. Through extensive talk about the most routine of daily activities to the most private of personal problems and crises, women friends establish connections with one another that function significantly in their lives.

    Our description of women's close friendships is, of course, a portrayal of what is typical. Not everyone follows the pattern: one of our interviewees who expressed affection for her close friend also admitted that she did not care to share intimacies with anyone but her husband; another women was skeptical of the likelihood that she and her friend would remain close because they shared little of what was important in their lives. The first case probably shows an individual departure from what is typical, while the second case may be more related to the constraints of a specific situation or time of life.

CONCLUSIONS

We see the continued study of all aspects of women's friendships as important to building a conscious awareness for women about women's experiences. Close friendships among women persist despite their social diminution. Women's talk, which cements friendships, also persists despite its social diminution. This persistence certainly tells us something about the value that women derive from the closeness they build with other women. We are reminded here of Jones's (1980) serious treatment of 'gossip' as an important component of the oral culture of women. She turns the tables on the social construal of gossip as mere trifling, idle, and groundless rumor by viewing it as well structured, highly functional, and an important vehicle for transmitting female values and concerns. The same turning of the tables is now well under way regarding women's friendship. Rather than viewing these relationships as vacuous fillers of time that are rife with idle chatter, we are now redefining this closeness as a primary social relationship holding unique values for women that are elsewhere unattainable.

    Like any research, ours raises more issues than it settles. We mention some of the major ones here.

    First, there are limitations to the conclusions that can be drawn from an interview study with a small sample of women. Self-selection may have played a part in the sample characteristics such that those women most predisposed to the importance of female friendship agreed to participate. In addition, the study relies on accounts by women about the centrality of talk in their friendships rather than on direct behavioral observation. Ideally, the character of women's friendships is best captured through a variety of research approaches. Expanding the interview format used in the present research to include both members of the friendship pair would provide insights about both co-perceptions and relationship types. Field studies too would be helpful in providing valid data about female friendships, but it is unlikely that field studies could penetrate the intimate, dyadic quality of interaction shared between friends. The point, simply, is that any method imposes constraints on the type of data gathered. Diverse methods will ultimately enrich our understanding of the properties of female friendship.

Second, there is the issue of cross-cultural comparisons. To what extent do the women we interviewed and the women studied by other researchers speak to the experience of female friends in other cultures? Obviously we have no adequate answer. There is, however, one important structural dimension to suggest at least some cross-cultural similarity. Since most societies substantially differentiate male and female roles, subordinating the latter to the former, women across a broad range of societies may bond together for similar functional reasons. As so cogently stated by Bernikow (1980):

> —'Women friends help each other to remain perpendicular in the face of cultures that attempt to knock them over with the hurricane forces of ideology about what a woman should be or pull the ground out from under them by denying the validity of their experience, denigrating their frame of reference, reinforcing female masochism, self-doubt, passivity, and suicide.' (p. 144).

So although the specific ways in which women friends in different cultures interact will probably vary depending on world view and values, e.g. differences in the value of talk, we suspect that there may be a strong resemblance in the functions and outcomes of close female bonds from culture to culture. We hope that future

anthropological work will address this issue and that friendship will receive attention even in societies where it is largely embedded in kinship.

The related issue of sub-cultural comparison also needs further study. With the exception of social class, the empirical research on women's friendship bypasses systematic investigations of sub-cultural patterns. Race, affectional preference, and ethnicity, for example, may shape female relationships in important ways, and we need to pay much closer attention to these factors.

Finally, there are political issues and questions that arise about the bonds established among women through friendship. On one level, the themes we found in our respondents' descriptions of their talk with female friends (noncritical listening, supportiveness, enhancement of self-worth, exclusiveness, and self-discovery and growth) reflect a humaneness that is admirable. But on another level, these themes reveal a response against global deficiencies in the larger social world that women confront on a daily basis. Women accomplish in the privacy of friendship what is publicly denied to them. Their friendships may well provide a strength-giving buffer between themselves and the persistent social denial of female integrity. If female friendship functions this way, whether consciously or unconsciously, it has tremendous subversive value; it subverts the devaluation of women by allowing them to develop a self-defined identity. Gerda Lerner (1979), for example, has asserted that women's close and essential ties have historically been to men rather than women, making women collaborators in their own subordination. Female ties are a powerful force in opposition to this pattern. We suspect that many men may understand this—at least on some level—and that this understanding accounts in part for male attempts to trivialize women's friendships and to trivialize or scorn the female proclivity for talk with other females. The threat that female friendship poses for men is the possibility that it can disrupt the asymmetry between male and female and ultimately lead females to reject male-female pairing as the pinnacle of human relationships.

These speculations lead logically to questions about the impact of female liberation on female friendship. The character of close female friendship obviously owes much to women's historic social position. The quintessence of these friendships is deeply rooted in sex-segregation and its division of male and female spheres. Where sex-segregation occurs, women come together as friends quite naturally. Women who devote most of their time to family nurturance and homemaking usually find it both convenient and desirable to seek relationships with women in similar positions; they find in these relationships many bases for sharing and many opportunities for mutual support and comfort. Similarly, women in the work force who hold positions that are sex-typical will find their most natural alliances with women in like positions—secretaries with secretaries, nurses with nurses, etc.

As women move out of sex-typical roles, particularly in the work place, there are several potential obstacles to their relationships with other women. Some women find themselves almost exclusively in the company of men; their jobs afford few opportunities to meet and form friendships with women, and in some cases may set them against women either by forcing them to compete with one another or by structurally placing them in superior-subordinate relationships. Professional women, especially those with families, often find themselves consumed by the overwhelming demands of both work and domestic life; they have little time left over for either keeping up with old friends or developing new ones.

Do these obstacles militate against the bonds of female friendship? Or do women continue despite these obstacles to establish close bonds with other women? Answers to these questions depend in large part on whether women continue to embrace female values or whether they abandon them. Our informal evidence (and we hope that it is not idiosyncratic) suggests that even in situations where women have little time and opportunity for friendship with other women, they still place high priority on these relationships. For married women, the contacts may occur in the couples context—much like the pattern observed by Babchuck (1965). Or they might grow quite independently through other relationship networks. For single women and for women who are single parents, the contacts can be diverse, ranging from strong similarity of position to great difference in personal situation. For lesbian women, the search is for others with whom to build a community that fosters the values they cherish.

Whatever the pattern, there are many women who are struggling to maintain and to build new ties with women friends. That struggle often entails transcending the pressures of the work situation itself, the simultaneous pressures of work and domestic demands, and the all too frequent pressures on women to relinquish their women-centered activities as a way of achieving professional accomplishment. One very positive force in helping women in their continuing struggle to be with one another is the growing recognition of the value of sisterhood. No matter how intensely or mildly political the sentiment, sensing the commonalities and attachments of women helps focus more specific values about female friendship.

REFERENCES

Allan, Graham A. 1979. *A Sociology of Friendship and Kinship.* George Allen & Unwin, London.

Aries, Elizabeth J. and Fern L. Johnson. In press. Close friendship in adulthood: conversational conduct between same-sex friends. *Sex Roles.*

Athanasiou, Robert and Gary A. Yoshioka. 1973. The spatial character of friendship formation. *Environment and Behavior* **5:** 43–65.

Babchuck, Nicholas. 1965. Primary friends and kin: a study of the associations of middle class couples. *Social Forces* **43:** 483–493.

Beauvoir, Simone, de. 1952. *The Second Sex.* Vintage, New York.

Bell, Robert R. 1981. *Worlds of Friendship*. Sage, Beverly Hills.

Bernikow, Louise. 1980. *Among Women*. Crown, New York.

Black, Harvey K. 1974. Physical attractiveness and similarity of attitude in interpersonal attraction. *Psychological Rep.* **35**: 403–406.

Bott, Elizabeth. 1971. *Family and Social Networks: Roles, Norms and External Relationships in Ordinary Urban Families.* 2nd edn. Tavistock, London.

Candy, Sandra Gibbs, Lillian E. Troll and Sheldon G. Levy. 1981. A developmental exploration of friendship functions in women. *Psychology Women Q.* **5**: 456–472.

Chesler, Phyllis. 1972. *Women and Madness*. Avon, New York.

Cott, Nancy. 1977. *The Bonds of Womanhood: 'Woman's Sphere' in New England, 1780–1835.* Yale University Press, New Haven.

Cozby, Paul C. 1973. Self-disclosure: a literature review. *Psychological Bull.* **79**: 73–91.

Douvan, Elizabeth A. M. and Joseph Adelson. 1966. *The Adolescent Experience.* John Wiley, New York.

DuBois, Cora. 1974. The gratuitous act: an introduction to the comparative study of friendship patterns. In Elliott Leyton, ed. *The Compact: Selected Dimensions of Friendship,* pp. 15–32. University of Toronto Press, Toronto.

Duck, Steven. 1973. *Personal Relationships and Personal Constructs.* Wiley, London.

Faderman, Lillian. 1981. *Surpassing the Love of Men.* William Morrow, New York.

Fallding, Harold. 1961. The family and the ideal of a cardinal role. *Human Relations* **14**: 329–350.

Hacker, Helen Mayer. 1981. Blabbermouths and clams: sex differences in self-disclosure in same-sex and cross-sex friendships dyads. *Psychology Women Q.* **5**: 385–401.

Johnson, Fern L., and Elizabeth J. Aries. 1983. Conversational patterns among same-sex pairs of late adolescent close friends. *J. Genet. Psychology* **142**: 225–238.

Jones, Deborah. 1980. Gossip: Notes on women's oral culture. *Women's Studies Int. Q.* **3**: 193–198.

Jourard, Sydney, 1971. *Disclosure: An Experimental Analysis of the Transparent Self.* John Wiley, New York.

Komarovsky, Mirra. 1967. *Blue Collar Marriage.* Random House, New York.

Kramarae, Cheris. 1981. *Women and Men Speaking.* Newbury House, Rowley, Mass.

Kramer, Cheris. 1977. Perceptions of female and male speech. *Language and Speech* **20**: 151–161.

Lakoff, Robin. 1975. *Language and Woman's Place.* Harper & Row, New York.

Lerner, Gerda. 1979. *The Majority Finds Its Past: Placing Women in History.* Oxford University Press, Oxford.

Litwak, Eugene and Ivan Szelenyi. 1969. Primary group structures and their functions: kin, neighbors, and friends. *Am. sociol Rev.* **34**: 465–481.

Lopata, Helena Z. 1973. The effect of schooling on social contacts of urban women. *Am. J. Sociol* **79**: 604–619.

Lowenthal, Marjorie F., Majda Thurnher, David Chiriboga, and associates. 1976. *Four Stages of Life.* Jossey-Bass, San Francisco.

Morgan, Brian S. 1976. Intimacy of self-disclosure topics and sex differences in self-disclosure. *Sex Roles* **2**: 161–166.

Mulcahy, Gloria A. 1973. Sex differences in patterns of self-disclosure among adolescents: A developmental perspective. *J. Youth Adolescence* **2**: 343–356.

Paine, Robert. 1969. In search of friendship: An exploratory analysis in 'middle-class' culture. *Man* **4**: 506–524.

Pleck, Joseph H. 1975. Man to man: is brotherhood possible? In Nona Glazer-Malbin, ed., *Old Family/New Family,* pp. 229–244. Van Nostrand, New York.

Rubin, Lillian. 1976. *Worlds of Pain: Life in the Working Class Family.* Basic Books, New York.

Seiden, Anne M. and Pauline B. Bart. 1975. Woman to woman: is sisterhood powerful? In Nona Glazer-Malbin, ed., *Old Family/New Family,* pp. 189–228. Van Nostrand, New York.

Shulman, Norman. 1975. Life-cycle variations in patterns in close relationships. *J. Marriage Family* **37**: 813–821.

Simon, Rita James, Gail Crotts, and Linda Mahan. 1970. An empirical note about married women and their friends. *Social Forces* **48**: 520–525.

Smith-Rosenberg, Carroll. 1975. The female world of love and ritual: Relations between women in nineteenth-century America. *Signs: J. Women Culture.* **1:** 1–29.

Spender, Dale. 1980. *Man Made Language.* Routledge & Kegan Paul, London.

Suttles, Gerald D. 1970. Friendship as a social institution. In George J. McCall, ed., *Social Relationships,* pp. 95–135. Aldine, Chicago.

Tiger, Lionel. 1969. *Men in Groups.* Thomas Nelson & Sons, London.

Verbrugge, Lois M. 1977. The structure of adult friendship choices. *Social Forces* **56:** 576–597.

Werner, Carol and Pat Parmelee. 1979. Similarity of activity preferences among friends: Those who play together stay together. *Social Psychol. Q.* **42:** 62–66.

Wright, Paul H. 1978. Toward a theory of friendship based on a conception of self. *Human Commun. Res.* **4:** 196–207.

Wright, Paul H. and Andrea C. Crawford. 1971. Argument and friendship: a close look and some second thoughts. *Representative Res. social Psychol.* **2:** 52–69.

Young, Michael and Willmott, Peter, 1957. *Family and Kinship in East London.* Penguin, Baltimore.

Topic 6

Caregiving

Azande Wood Figure: Mother and Child

Her vulva hangs between her legs like a trophy
while she holds up a child for all to see
what dropped through it.

They are joined at the hip, these two,
carved from the same trunk of wood,
as seamless as night and day.
Their mouths, their noses, their eyes connect them
to the lineage that their nakedness shares.

The child's feet straddle the mother's waist,
but her feet are rooted to the ground
that allows her to bear the child's whole weight
without losing the balance she needs
Her feet are stronger than an elephant's.

Courtesy of Felicia Mitchell

Until recently, authorities on the family and mental health viewed women as being the most happy and fulfilled when in their caregiving roles. Child-care manuals listed working mothers under the heading of "problems" (Birns and Selvin, this volume). In the 50s, middle-class women had to choose between a career and motherhood. For example, many colleges, including nursing and teaching colleges, forced women to withdraw when they became pregnant. Of course, very poor women had no choice but to work and have children. Being a wife and mother was a privilege (although not without drawbacks) for the middle class and a burden for the poor.

Today, most women and most mothers are in the paid workforce. However, their responsibility for the care of spouses, children, and aging parents has scarcely diminished. In addition, women remain the majority of the "caregiving workers." Most nurses, secretaries, teachers, and domestic workers for example, are women. For many women, days are spent out of the home taking care of the needs of others (for which they are usually poorly paid) and nights and weekends are filled by caring for their own families—the very young and the very old.

Caregiving can be a very rewarding activity when caregivers are not overburdened and unsupported. When women mother however, they are asked to do an impossible job. We expect mothers to possess infinite patience, love unconditionally, and meet all of a child's needs. When women fail at this task, as they inevitably will, they are blamed. If a woman chooses not to become a mother, she is frequently seen as unwomanly and selfish. The expectations that surround motherhood have important consequences for the well-being of both mothers and children.

The readings in this section examine these historical, social, and cultural contexts of women's experiences with caregiving. The first reading, "History and Current Applications of Attachment Theory," by Susan Franzblau, describes the history of attachment theory and its influence on the practice of mothering. According to attachment theory, a secure bond between a mother and her child is the key to healthy psychological development in the child. Although the research that supports this idea has been heavily criticized, attachment theory has played a central role in shaping thinking about child custody, childbirth, and day care. Franzblau argues that attachment theory has been used to restrict women's reproductive and parenting choices, and proposes alternative ways of thinking about the needs of mothers and their children.

In the second reading, "Overcoming Stereotypes of Mothers in the African American Context," Elizabeth Sparks discusses stereotypes of African American mothers and their effect on African American women. She explores the history of these stereotypes, and shows how images of motherhood are used to justify oppression. Sparks is a psychotherapist who has seen how the internalization of these images has hindered her clients' recovery. She offers suggestions for counteracting stereotypes in therapy, and argues that in addition to such individual solutions, it is necessary to challenge stereotypes with a new definition of African American motherhood.

The final reading of this section, "The Sandwich Generation: Women's Roles as Multi-Generational Caregivers," broadens the discussion of caregiving to include the work women do in elder care. Joan Kuchner looks at the "sandwich generation," the group of women who postponed parenthood into middle age, and now find themselves struggling with the competing demands of aging parents and young children. As with motherhood, the ideology of caregiving places most of the burden for the care of elderly parents on women's shoulders. Kuchner discusses the problems the women face in meeting the demands of caregiving, and offers directions for change.

As these readings demonstrate, social change is essential if caregiving is to be an activity that women and men can freely choose and enjoy. Caregiving can no longer be seen as primarily a woman's job, and the work of caregivers must be valued and supported.

Reading 1   History and Current Applications of Attachment Theory

SUSAN FRANZBLAU

Questions to Consider:

1. According to Franzblau, how has attachment research shaped the policies and practices that affect mothers?

2. If fathers had been considered as important to child development as mothers, would attachment research have been conducted differently? Explain.

3. Should mothers stay at home full-time with their children? Why or why not?

INTRODUCTION

In this reading, I will discuss the role that Darwin's theory of evolution, social Darwinism, and eugenics played in the development of attachment theory, followed by a discussion of the implications of attachment theory for girls and women who are presently thinking about or making decisions about issues related to reproduction.

Both popular and scientific discourse about mother-child relationships in the United States and England have influenced us in a variety of ways. Our ideas about whether, when, and how to have children; natural versus surgical births; bottle versus breast feeding; whether women should stay at home or work and for how long; the meaning of childhood; and the meaning of motherhood—all have an ideological history. Our own thinking on motherhood reflects not simply the advice of our own mothers, or some genetic predisposition, but the influences of more powerful authority figures, most of whom have been men

(Eyer, 1992). Their theories, the research they conducted, and the social policies emanating from these theories and research are imbedded in a historical and political context as well.

There is a pervasive and commonsensical notion that the social relationship between a woman and her newborn has a strong biological/evolutionary basis. Many developmental psychologists argue that if this bond is broken by the mother, either consciously or unconsciously, the child will suffer psychological harm. This idea has been formalized as "attachment theory." The following is the history of attachment theory and the influence it has had on the lives of girls and women.

DARWIN'S THEORY OF EVOLUTION

Charles Darwin, at first a gentleman-naturalist and later a scientist (Himmelfarb, 1959), observed the dramatic changes in England brought on by the Industrial Revolution, as well as changes over time and place in the morphology of rocks, animals, birds, and insects. Darwin, in his determination to find a universal explanation for all change and adaptation, rejected divine causality, and centered his theory of evolution on material changes resulting from natural selection. He argued that over evolutionary time, competition for scarce resources determines which races would survive (reproduce) and which races would die out. "[I]t suddenly flashed upon me that this self-action process would necessarily *improve the race,* because in every generation the inferior would inevitably be killed off and the superior would remain—that is, *the fittest would survive*" (Darwin, 1858, quoted in Himmelfarb, 1959, p. 246; italics his).

Darwin suggested that evolution determined the development of morphological and functional differences in males and females of all species, for the purpose of sexual selection of a mate. Any differences between men and women, therefore, had evolutionary significance. In humans, he noted, "Man is more courageous, pugnacious and energetic than woman, and has a more inventive genius" (Darwin, 1871, p. 867). Citing the writings of his cousin, Francis Galton, who founded the eugenics movement, Darwin proposed that because men have a greater capability than women in a variety of areas, "the average of mental power in man must be above that of woman" (Darwin, 1871, p. 873). Both social Darwinian and psychoanalytic thinking about infant-mother relationships emerged from Darwin's belief that differences in survival reflected evolutionary fitness.

Social Darwinism

The principle behind *social* Darwinism is that the social and economic status quo, including the existence of vast class and gender inequalities, derives naturally from biologically predetermined human variability (Lewontin, Rose, & Kamin, 1984). Both Darwin's theory of evolution and social Darwinism took shape within the framework of the social and economic inequalities created by the Industrial Revolution of the early 1800s, that brought with it the need for a cheap and reserve labor force. In the United States, this labor force was made up of black migrants from the south and immigrants from Eastern Europe, the Mediterranean, Ireland, and Scandinavia. A major concern of the new entrepreneurial classes in both England and the United States was that they would lose control over this vast, politically sophisticated labor force who made up the majority of the population. These ruling class concerns led to a number of trends, including (1) a movement to increase the marriage and fertility rates of middle- and upper-class white women; (2) a movement to establish early parental bonding between these same women and their infants to ensure the perpetuation of "race culture" (white middle and upper classes); and (3) a trend to decrease the marriage and fertility rates of working class/poor women, immigrant women, and women of color. The attempt to selectively increase reproduction of "fit" classes/races was termed "eugenics"; the attempt to selectively decrease reproduction of "unfit" classes/races was termed "dysgenics." With the support of Darwin's theory, social Darwinian thought and the eugenics movement, an ideological base was created for theories and research supporting the glorification of heterosexual love, early marriage, motherhood, and early mother-infant bonding/attachment.

The period from 1850 through the late 1800s marked the zenith of industrialization in England. It was during this period that the philosopher Herbert Spencer argued that the compelling inequalities among peoples of differing social classes, races, and genders, were an inevitable consequence of evolution. Society, he argued, must not artificially preserve those least able to survive. "[T]he quality of a society is physically lowered by the artificial preservation of its feeblest members...the quality of a society is lowered morally and intellectually, by the artificial preservation of those who are least able to take care of themselves" (Spencer, 1880/1961, p. 313).

Spencer believed that women's role in securing the evolutionary superiority of the "white race" [quotes mine] was primarily reproductive, which was why, he argued, that a woman's intellectual activity was in direct conflict with and must be sacrificed for reproduction, so that "species life" may be maintained (Spencer, 1897, p. 564). When a woman becomes a wife and mother, he suggested, all the vanities of individualized life should disappear (Spencer, 1897).

The Eugenics Proposal

[Eugenics'] first object is to check the birthrate of the Unfit, instead of allowing them to come into being, though doomed in large numbers to perish prematurely. The second object is the improvement of the race by furthering the productivity of the Fit by early marriages, and healthful rearing of their children. Natural Selection rests upon excessive production and wholesale destruction; Eugenics on bringing no more individuals into the world than can be properly cared for, and those only of the best stock.

–Galton, 1908, quoted in
Journal of Heredity, 1914, p. 560

The eugenics movement in England, the United States, and Germany was organized to ensure racial purity, prevent racial suicide, and preserve the inheritance of so-called superior stock (Haraway, 1989). Its founder, Francis Galton, thought it was more appropriate to conceive of human nature as *rising* from a low state to a higher one (an evolutionary idea) rather than the reverse tendency, advocated by religion, that man (sic!) *falls* from grace (Kevles, 1985). Galton believed that eugenics would "accelerate the process...[by breeding] out the vestigial barbarism of the human race and manipulate evolution to bring the biological reality of man into consonance with his advanced moral ideals" (Kevles, 1985, p. 12). Four proposals of importance to

women emerged from social Darwinian thought and infused the eugenics movement in the United States, England, and Germany with a fervor that kept it going until after the Second World War, when the Nazis use of eugenics ideology as the excuse for its genocidal activities could no longer be defended on moral grounds (Kevles, 1985). These proposals were: (1) to increase the marriage and fertility rates of middle- and upper-class white women (cf. Leslie, 1911); (2) to restructure education for women, including the postponement of women's intellectual studies until after the active reproductive period (cf. Robie, 1984); (3) to selectively sterilize "unfit" women (cf. Robie, 1984); and (4) to promote the primacy of reproductive sex and glorify sexual intercourse (cf. Popenoe, 1984; Yerkes, cited in Haraway, 1989, p. 71). A fifth proposal, to promote the early maternal-child relationship, by framing it in evolutionary terms, appeared earlier in skeletal form (Bell, 1914; Popenoe, 1984), but finally emerged as a theoretical paradigm in the form of attachment theory after the Second World War (cf. Bowlby, 1951).

Setting the Stage for Attachment Theory

Despite propagandist efforts to persuade women to marry and have families in the service of eugenics ideals, the general marriage rate had plummeted to an all-time low by the 1930s, aided by the depression that began in 1929 (May, 1988). Between 1940 and 1945, however, women began marrying at a younger age, and the birthrate increased from 19.4 to 24.5 per one thousand. A desire to keep men out of the war, and fear of losing men to the war, precipitated these changes. The war also drew women into the public sphere, where they were encouraged to do work previously done by men who were now soldiers. Although the number of employed women leaped from 30 percent to 60 percent (May, 1988), there was widespread uneasiness and suspicion of the implications of women's role in the workforce, including the "destruction of the family" and the "looseness" of female sexuality, including non-marital sex and homosexuality (May, 1988).

Despite these concerns, women continued to work, as well as marry and reproduce, until the end of the war when they were expected to give up their jobs and return to the home full-time. During the period from 1944 until 1950, federally funded day care centers, that provided some working women with day care during the war, closed down; and the range of jobs available to women narrowed. Mature sexuality was portrayed in various media as reproductive heterosexuality, beginning and ending in marriage (May, 1988).

It was within this context that, in 1950, English psychiatrist John Bowlby was asked by the World Health Organization (WHO) to report on the effects of familial absence on children who had been evacuated from London during World War II (Ainsworth & Bowlby, 1991). Familial absence was operationally defined as separation from the mother (Ainsworth & Bowlby, 1991). Before this assignment, however, Bowlby had already been convinced that there was a relationship between the orphaning of children, which he termed "maternal deprivation," and children's feelings of anxiety, isolation, as well as later delinquent behavior (Ainsworth & Bowlby, 1991). Although Bowlby's training was psychoanalytic and he continued to ally himself with Freud's thinking that the mother was ultimately responsible for the "normal" social/emotional/sexual development of the child (Birns & Ben-Ner, 1988; Silverstein, 1991), evolution provided him with the principal justification for the necessity of infant-mother bonding. He argued that there was an evolutionary basis for the infant-mother relationship, which relationship was critical for the normal emotional and behavioral development of the child.

"Attachment" is a reference to discrete patterns of behaviors (e.g., proximity seeking, crying), based in the evolutionary need to develop a social relationship with the mother. This selective attachment provides emotional security and creates the basis for later social relationships. Bowlby argued, for example, that fear of being placed with strangers is an evolutionary adapted atypical behavior pattern assuring attachment (Bowlby, 1973). The attachment figure activates an attachment behavior in the child via her or his feelings of separation anxiety in a number of ways; (1) when she is separated from the child; (2) by giving attention to someone else; or (3) through outright rejection (Ainsworth & Bowlby, 1991). Not only is the response of mother to the child consequential for the development of attachment, but *all* mother-child separations lead to immediate infant distress and possible long-term detrimental effects (Rutter, 1991; Silverstein, 1991).

In 1952 Bowlby wrote:

> *the provision of* constant attention day and night, seven days a week and 365 days in the year, *is possible only for a woman who derives profound satisfaction from seeing her child grow from babyhood through the many phases of childhood.... One of the principle social functions of an adult is that of parenthood.*
> —Bowlby, 1952, pp. 67–68 [emphasis mine]

Bowlby argued for various social policies that ensured that this constant attention take place, including: (1) marriage guidance about sexual techniques necessary for happy marriages; (2) the redistribution of monies from day care services to housekeeping services for mothers, so that they stay home with their children; and (3) the creation of rest homes where both mothers and their children could go during times of marital stress, in order to prevent marital breakdown. A rest [sic!] home for both mother and child, he contended, would lessen the need for out-of-family child care (Bowlby, 1952). The father's role was to help the mother maintain an harmonious contented mood (Bowlby, 1952).

Bowlby's work drew strong support from eugenics publications (cf. Notes of the Quarter, 1951).

Bowlby's WHO report on consequences of the institutionalization of children (Bowlby, 1951) and the later research of Ainsworth and Bowlby (Bowlby, Ainsworth, Boston, & Rosenbluth, 1956; Bowlby & Ainsworth, 1965) significantly influenced the thinking of specialists (cf. Belsky, 1988) and lay people (cf. Keogh, 1993) concerned with the effects of early parent-child relationships on later emotions, morality, and behavior. During the early 1950s and 1960s however, the basic and immediate question for working and middle-class women centered on whether they should put their young children in the care of others, or stay home during the first few years of their children's lives. Of course, the answer to this question had different implications depending upon whether or not the family's income depended on her work.

In this light, it is important to note that the first study of attachment relied upon a small sample of middle-class, home-reared infants. "The subjects of Ainsworth's [original] study are fifty-six infants, aged one year, of white American middle-class families, reared within their family in ways typical of the 1960s" (Bowlby, 1973, p. 40). This small sample comprised the standard upon which later comparisons were made. The Strange Situation Procedure (Ainsworth & Wittig, 1969) involved placing the child in an unfamiliar physical environment, and in series of eight 3-minute episodes, alternately separating the child from the mother and providing contact with a strange woman. Three types of attachment were classified: avoidant, securely attached, and resistant. Generally, studies using this sample report approximately 66 percent securely attached; 22 percent insecure-avoidant, and 12 percent insecure-resistant infants.

Critique of Attachment Research

Because the samples were small, variations from the norm would appear to have greater effects on

group differences than they would in larger, more random samples (Thompson, 1991). Further, because attachment labels are defined as types and do not fall on a continuum, between-group differences are accentuated and within-group variation is diminished (Thompson, 1991). Despite these problems and contrary to the assumption that avoidant infants reject mothers, it has been found that securely attached infants also behave avoidantly (Thompson, 1991), along with a variety of other within-culture variations (van Ijzendoorn & Kroonenberg, 1987, reported in Thompson, 1991). These findings may be accounted for by individual differences in response, including differences in temperament and differences in reactions to stress (Kagan, 1984).

Outside of the laboratory, not all separations can be explained by attachment theory. For example, distress reactions at the time of admittance to a hospital or residential nursery can result from the acuteness of the separation, the lack of opportunity to build relationships with caregivers because caregivers keep changing, and the strange, unpleasant, and often frightening nature of these kinds of environment (Rutter, 1991).

Another factor affecting to whom the infant gravitates may be the father's *lack* of caregiving (Silverstein, 1991). Because Bowlby initially assumed that the mother was primarily responsible for early caregiving, effects on the child of a father's emotional distance/disengagement were never considered. Father absence may be as powerful an influence on the child's proximity seeking as the mother's presence.

Social class differences in childrearing, and two-parent or extended family attitudes toward child rearing, which may be considered a cultural as well as a social class variable, may also affect proximity behaviors of the infant (Silverstein, 1991). Cultural factors could include attitudes toward frequency of contact with strangers, regularity of separations from caretaker, and cultural child-rearing norms, including the variety of people who interact with the child in a village-rearing or community-rearing culture.

Finally, the unnatural brief separation in the Strange Situation paradigm, including only the unusual leaving of the mother, and the unusual encounter with the stranger, may act as a confound. This unusual environment, along with the brief separations and encounters may interact to produce stress. Thus the *meaning* of the behavior in the Strange Situation paradigm may differ from the behavior of a child in an actual day care situation.

Despite the massive critiques of attachment theory and the Strange Situation Procedure, attachment research goes on unabated and researchers continue their quest for negative effects of mother-child separation (cf. Belsky, 1988). Attachment theory is being used by clinicians as a tool to explore the reasons for adult behavioral, emotional, and social problems (Ainsworth & Bowlby, 1991); organizations have been formed for adult "sufferers" of early separation anxiety (Keogh, 1993) and insecure attachment as a result of "bad" mothering has been linked with adolescent violence (Keogh, 1993). In fact, defense counsel can now rely on current "findings" about lack of attachment for legal arguments that clients are not mentally competent to take responsibility for their actions (Keogh, 1993; E. P. Trevino, Personal Communication, 1994).

I would like to concentrate on three implications of attachment theory: Its use in legal arguments in custody cases; its function in the natural childbirth movement; and how it figures in the argument for or against day care.

Legal Implications of Attachment Theory

The question of who is fit to mother continues to influence social policies in England and the United States. Bad/unfit mothers have often been characterized as women who work full time or part time, those who choose education over child rearing, and others (e.g. lesbians, single mothers) who do not fall within the confines of the "traditional family." Many debates over fitness to mother find their way into the legal system. In a number of recent cases, the courts have awarded custody rights based on attachment/bonding arguments. In one case involving the right of a mother to put a child in day care while she attended the University of Michigan, the lower court of the state of Michigan argued that day care was not suitable because "in no way…can a single parent, attending an academic program at an institution …do justice to her studies and the raising of an infant child" (In re: *Custody of Maranda Kate Ireland-Smith; Jennifer Ireland v. Steven J. Smith, 1994,* p. 349). Yet this same court was willing to give the child to the father, even though he worked, because he lived at home with his mother who was "a blood relative and not a stranger" (p. 349). Ironically, the grandmother was more of a stranger than the day care providers, given that she had not been in the child's life other than as a giver of gifts. In a 1988 case dealing with the termination of parental rights (In re: *C.M.T., A Child,* 1988), the court denied the mother visitation rights to her child based on lack of "bonding between the child and mother" (p. 57). The court made the assumption that bonding should *preexist* any relationship developing out of consistent visitation with her child. In a West Virginia 1995 custody case (*Campbell v. Campbell,* 1995) the court argued that, because the mother "returned to work…only two months after the second child was born" (p. 472), custody should be awarded to the father. The court found that two months of primary caregiving by the mother after the birth of the child was too short a period of time. It is interesting to note that even though the father was temporarily at home with an injury and would go back to work as soon as his injury healed, the appeals court awarded him custody. In a number of contested custody hearings, the issue of immediate and early bonding between the caregiver and the child determines custody (Halon, 1994; Johnson & Torres, 1994). In many child custody cases, two attachment scales—the ATC Scale and Social Competence scale—are used to measure whether a child is strongly attached to the parent(s) (Marcus & Mirle, 1990).

The "Nurturing Is Natural" Movement

Recently, researchers isolated a gene that they argue affects nurturing tendencies of mice (Brown, Ye, Dikkes, & Greenberg, 1996). In a giant hypothetical leap, Brown and his colleagues postulated that this mouse research may lead to early determination of innate nurturing tendencies in humans. This research is only the latest justification of attachment theory's evolutionary base. Religion has also been used to justify early infant-mother attachment. In the late 1800s, pain was believed to lead to motherly love, and doctors who tried to relieve women's childbirth pain were attacked for "daring to circumvent the biblical condemnation of women to childbed agony" (Eyer, 1992, p. 170). In the 1950s, the natural childbirth movement was established by a fundamentalist Christian group who argued that the attachment of the child to his or her caregiver and the bonding of the caregiver to the child was rooted in the Bible, and that the suffering of women during childbirth was biblically mandated as well (Eyer, 1992). In fact, both Christians and psychoanalysts stated that "a woman's destiny was to bear and rear children...[and] the experience of pain would heighten her awareness of this sublime beginning" (Eyer, 1992, p. 170). The advocates of natural childbirth and early bonding stated that by placing the baby skin-to-skin on the mother right after birth, bonding would promote family stability, leading to a reduction in the rates of divorce (Eyer, 1988, in Eyer, 1992). Of course, there was and is absolutely no empirical support for any of these assertions.

There have been many famous advocates of attachment/bonding theories, including Drs. T. Berry Brazelton, Benjamin Spock, anthropologist Margaret Mead, leaders of the La Leche breast-feeding movement and the Boston Women's Health Collective (Eyer, 1992). Via scientific and popular tracts, they popularized the still unsubstantiated idea that infants and mothers are biologically predisposed to develop strong attachments to one another. Some of these advocates have gone so far as to claim that low scores on intelligence and language tests as well as violent crimes, including terrorism, could result from lack of close early contact between babies and their mothers (Eyer, 1992).

Given the increase in the medicalization of birth and the profit to doctors and hospitals of surgical births, doctors were reluctant to buy into the natural childbirth movement; however, in the 1970s "some doctors viewed natural childbirth (and bonding) as a means to make women more tractable patients, giving them a sense of control while retaining the power to define and manage birth for themselves" (Eyer, 1992, p. 184).

Despite the fact that most claims of the attachment/bonding research have been discredited (cf. Birns & Hay, 1988; Eyer, 1988), the view that early attachment (of the infant to the mother) and bonding (of the mother to infant) is necessary for normal development to occur remains popular. Obstetrical nurses are trained to encourage it and use a checklist to determine if proper bonding/attachment has not occurred (Eyer, 1988).

Working Women and Day Care

Perhaps the most serious question that attachment theory poses to working women is whether or not leaving children in the care of "strangers" negatively affects later emotional, psychological, and behavioral development. We live during a time when most women need to work so that their families may survive economically. These women may be single mothers, members of two-parent families, or members of extended or alternative family arrangements. Because we live during a time when families are often separated by great distances, and when most adults in a family work, in-home child care by family members is not always possible. Therefore, day care often presents itself as the only solution and is, in fact, the "fastest growing type of supplemental care in [the United States]" (Gamble & Zigler, 1986, p. 26).

The issue presented by attachment theorists is whether infants and toddlers who are separated from their primary caregivers for eight or so hours a day/five days a week, can form the necessary attachment to their primary caregivers (mothers). Of course, this argument assumes that this "gluelike" attachment to one individual is both necessary and sufficient for successful development to occur. We know, however, from our own experiences that infants and toddlers form strong social and emotional relationships with many other people in their lives, including brothers and sisters, grandparents, fathers, day care providers, and other loving adults (Birns & Ben-Ner, 1988). It is also the case that early separation from a primary caregiver is not sufficient to explain problems children may have later in life. After an extensive review of the literature on effects of early separations, including severe deprivation, Birns and Ben-Ner (1988) conclude that "postinfancy experience alters the results of early deprivation" (p. 64). Thus, early experience is insufficient to explain later behavior. Children are active participants in their lives. The relationship between children and their caretakers is dialectic or interactive rather than monotropic. Further, the home is not the only context within which children learn and form relationships. Finally, children are malleable, influencing and influenced by many factors during the course of their development.

Most important to the argument about day care is who needs it. Although some women work because they want to, 90 percent of women work because they have to (Silverstein, 1991). The social Darwinian argument underlying attachment theory inevitably punishes working women, who can least afford to stay home with their infants/toddlers. The problems children and their mothers experience often result from the stress a woman experiences when she takes on multiple jobs, only one of which is child care. Research shows quite clearly that the reduction in women's stress is directly related to the willingness of the men in their lives to take on equal responsibility for child care and house care (Kamerman, 1980b, in Silverstein, 1991). Family stress also results

from "a society that is unresponsive to the needs of families" (Kamerman, 1980b, in Silverstein, 1991, p. 1029). For the 90 percent of women who have to work, their need is for quality and inexpensive day care. Two decades of studies have failed to show that children suffer from being placed in alternative care situations while their mothers work (Silverstein, 1991).

We need stronger regulation of quality day care centers so that all children, not only the children of wealthy parents, have the opportunity for the most enriching experiences possible; we need to pay day care workers a livable wage with adequate health care and retirement benefits so that day care workers can play a stable role in the daily lives of infants and toddlers; we need to make day care more affordable so that working women, in their desperation, do not leave their children at home alone, or in temporary babysitter situations.

Women have the right to determine for themselves whether or not to have children; and once they give birth, the right to the social/economic resources to adequately care for them. That these issues are still debated today; that women are targets of social, economic, and political violence; that poor women and women of color suffer disproportionately from this legal, social, and economic violence suggest that eugenics ideology is not dead. We need to take notice, however, that the struggle against eugenics ideologies, whatever their form, has also heightened. The international pressure from women to change the focus of the International Population Conference in Cairo (1994) from overpopulation to women's reproductive and sexual rights shows quite clearly that women are collectively demanding sexual and reproductive freedom, as well as the economic, political, social, and educational resources to make freedom a reality.

REFERENCES

Ainsworth, M. D., & Bowlby, J. (1991). "An ethological approach to personality development." *American Psychologist,* 46 (4), 333–341.

Ainsworth, M. D., & Wittig, B. A. (1969). "Attachment and exploratory behaviour of one-year-olds in a strange situation." In B. M. Foss (Ed.), *Determinants of Infant Behavior* (vol. 4, pp. 111–136). London: Metheun.

Bell, A. G. (1914). "How to improve the race." *Journal of Heredity,* 5(1), 1–7.

Belsky, J. (1988). "The effects of infant day care reconsidered." *Early Childhood Research Quarterly,* 3, 235–272.

Birns, B., & Ben-Ner, N. "Psychoanalysis constructs motherhood." In B. Birns & D. Hay (Eds.). (1988). *The Different Faces of Motherhood* (pp. 47–72). New York: Plenum Press.

Bowlby, J. (1951). *Maternal Care and Mental Health: A Report Proposed on Behalf of the World Health Organization as a Contribution to the United Nations.* Geneva, Switzerland: World Health Organization.

Bowlby, J. (1952). *Maternal Care and Mental Health.* Geneva, Switzerland: World Health Organization.

Bowlby, J. (1973). *Attachment and Loss: Vol. 2. Separation: Anxiety and Anger.* New York: Basic Books.

Bowlby, J., & Ainsworth, M. D. S. (1965). *Child Care and The Growth of Love* (2nd ed.). Harmondsworth, England: Penguin Books.

Bowlby, J., Ainsworth, M. D., Boston, M., & Rosenbluth, D. (1956). "Effects of mother-child separation." *British Journal of Medical Psychology,* 29, 169–201.

Boyer, R. O., & Morais, H. M. (1955). *Labor's Untold Story.* New York: United Electrical, Radio & Machine Workers of America.

Brown, J., Ye, H., Dikkes, P., & Greenberg, M. (1996). "A defect in nurturing in mice lacking the immediate early gene FosB." *Cell,* 86, 297–309.

Campbell v. Campbell, 460 S.E.2d, 469 (W. Va. App. 1995).

Darwin, C. (1871). *The Descent of Man.* New York: The Modern Library.

Eyer, D. E. (1992). *Mother-Infant Bonding: A Scientific Fiction.* New Haven, CT: Yale University Press.

Flexner, E. (1959, 1975 rev. ed.). *Century of Struggle.* Cambridge, MA: Harvard University Press.

Franzblau, S. H. (Fall, 1996). "Social Darwinian influences on conceptions of marriage, sex, and motherhood." *The Journal of Primary Prevention,* 17(1), 47–73.

Freud, S. (1962). *Three Contributions to The Theory of Sex.* New York: Dutton. (Original work published in 1920)

Galton, F. (1914). "Conclusion to memories of my life." *Journal of Heredity,* 5 (12), 560.

Gamble, T. J., & Zigler, E. (1986). "Effects of infant day care: another look at the evidence." *American Journal of Orthopsychiatry,* 56, (1), 26–41.

Halon, R. (1994). Child custody "move away" cases: McGinnis and psychology. *American Journal of Forensic Psychology, 12,* 43–54.

Haraway, D. (1989). *Primate Visions: Gender, Race, and Nature in The World of Modern Science.* New York: Routledge.

Harlow, H., & Mears, C. (1979). *The Human Model: Primate Perspectives.* New York: Wiley.

Himmelfarb, G. (1959). *Darwin and The Darwinian Revolution.* New York: W. W. Norton & Company.

Hirsch, I. S. (1991). "Poverty comes home: women and children in the 90's." *Clearinghouse Review,* 24(4). Chicago, IL: National Clearinghouse for Legal Services, Inc.

In re: Custody of Maranda Kate Ireland-Smith; Jennifer Ireland v. Steven J. Smith, No. 177431 (Michigan Court of Appeals), 1994.

Johnson, R. H. (1914). "Marriage selection." *Journal of Heredity,* 5(3), 102–110.

Kagan, J. (1984). *The nature of the child.* New York: Basic Books.

Keogh, T. (1993, Jan/Feb). "Children without a conscience." *New Age Journal,* 53–57, 128–130.

Kevles, Daniel J. (1985). *In The Name of Eugenics.* Berkeley, CA: University of California Press.

Leslie, R. M. (1911). "Women's progress in relation to eugenics." *The Eugenics Review,* 2(4), 282–298.

Lewonton, R. C., Ross, S., & Kamin, L. J. (1984). *Not in Our Genes.* New York: Pantheon Books.

Marcus, R., & Mirle, J. (1990). Validity of a child interview measure of attachment as used in child custody evaluations. *Perceptual and Motor Skills, 70,* 1043–1054.

May, E. T. (1988). *Homeward Bound.* New York: Basic Books.

Notes of The Quarter: Obituary of Margaret Sanger. (1966). *The Eugenics Review,* 58(4), 179–181.

Popenoe, P. (1984). "Marriage counseling." In C. Rosenberg (Ed.), *The History of Hereditarian Thought: A Decade of Progress in Eugenics. Scientific Papers of the 3rd International Congress of Eugenics, New York, 1932* (pp. 210–211). New York: Garland Publishing, Inc.

Rifkin, J. (1983). *Algeny.* New York: The Viking Press.

Robie, T. J. (1984). "Selective sterilization for race culture." In C. Rosenberg (Ed.), *The History of Hereditarian Thought: A Decade of Progress in Eugenics. Scientific Papers of the 3rd International Congress of Eugenics, New York, 1932* (pp. 201–209). New York: Garland Publishing, Inc.

Robinson, W. J. (1916). *Birth Control or The Limitation of Offspring.* New York: The Critic and Guide Co.

Rosenberg, C. (Ed.). *The History of Hereditarian Thought: A Decade of Progress in Eugenics. Scientific Papers of the 3rd International Congress of Eugenics, New York, 1932* (pp. 201–209), New York: Garland Publishing, Inc.

Rothman, B. K. (1987). "Comment on Harrison: The commodification of motherhood." *Gender & Society,* 1(3), 312–316.

Rowbotham, S. (1973). *Hidden From History.* London: Pluto Press.

Rutter, M. A. (1991). "A fresh look at 'maternal deprivation.'" In P. Bateson, (Ed.), *The Development and Integration of Behavior: Essays in Honour of Robert Hinde* (pp. 331–374). Cambridge: Cambridge University Press.

Siegel, L. (1990). "The criminalizaton of pregnant and child-rearing drug users." *Drug Law Report,* 17(4), 6–10.

Silverstein, L. B. (1991). "Transforming the debate about child care and maternal employment." *American Psychologist,* 46 (10), 1025–1032.

Spencer, H. (1961). *The Study of Sociology.* Ann Arbor: The University of Michigan Press. (Original work published in 1880)

Spencer, H. (1978). *The Principles of Ethics* (Vol. 1). Indianapolis: Liberty Classics. (Original work published in 1897)

Spencer, H. (1978). *The Principles of Ethics* (Vol. 2). Indianapolis: Liberty Classics. (Original work published in 1897)

Thompson, R. A. (1991). "Infant day care: concerns, controversies, choices." In J. V. Lerner (Ed.), *Employed Mothers and Their Children.* New York: Garland Publishing, Inc.

Van-Ijzendoorn, M. H. (1990). "Developments in cross-cultural research on attachment: Some methodological notes." *Human Development,* 33 (1), 3–9.

Reading 2   Overcoming Stereotypes of Mothers in the African American Context

ELIZABETH E. SPARKS

Questions to Consider:

1. According to Sparks, how have stereotypes of African American mothers affected African American women? Have you or someone you know been affected by these stereotypes? Explain.

2. How do stereotypes of African American mothers blame the victim for the consequences of racism and discrimination?

3. How has your view of what a mother should be been affected by your racial and ethnic heritage? Your social class?

4. What do you think about the suggestions Sparks makes for a new definition of motherhood?

I am an African American, middle-aged professional woman who has spent the past twenty years thinking about and discussing with others what it means to be an African American woman in this society. Because of the clients with whom I have interacted over the years, I have been particularly interested in what it means to be an African American mother in contemporary America. My viewpoint has undergone changes during this time, and the perspective expressed in this chapter is the culmination of my personal experiences as an African American daughter (who is not a mother), experiences that I have shared with

Approximately twenty pages from *Women's Ethnicities: Journeys through Psychology* edited by Karen Fraser Wyche and Faye Crosby. Copyright © 1996 by West-viewPress. Reprinted by permission of WestviewPress.

female kin and friends (most of whom are mothers), and from my work as a psychotherapist with African American mothers. We have all struggled to understand what it means to be a woman and mother, both within our own cultural context and as we are perceived by the White-majority culture. Our experiences of motherhood range from feeling strong and empowered because of who we are to feeling overwhelmed, burdened, and unfulfilled.

In this chapter I explore some of the stereotypes of African American women that have been promulgated by the White establishment and which have been internalized by at least some of my clients. In the first part of the chapter, I look at the historical roots of these images of motherhood and outline current stereotypical conceptualizations of African American women. I next present a set of case examples. In them, we see women who are struggling with difficult situations in their lives and whose recovery has been hindered by the internalization of these stereotypical images. In the third section, I discuss the personal journey required to free myself from these controlling images and my work in helping clients overcome the negative impact of this internalization process. Finally, I argue for a new definition of African American motherhood and for rekindling the sense of collectivism that has been so highly valued within the African American community throughout its history.

STEREOTYPES

African Roots and Transformations During Slavery

The analysis of motherhood that is presented in this chapter incorporates the broader perspective of African American womanhood because of the intricate connection that exists between these two identities for African American women. In traditional African society, reproduction and mothering formed a valued and integral aspect of women's identity (Mbiti, 1969). The tradition involved not only nurturing one's biological offspring but also caring for other, often nonrelated children (Oppong, 1973). Child rearing was thought to be a shared responsibility of the community, and there was a common African practice of fostering children as a means of minimizing what was viewed as a dysfunctional emphasis on individualism within a communal setting (James, 1993; Sudarkasa, 1993). Although enslaved West Africans were unable to replicate traditional family and communal patterns and values in America, some traditions, including the emphasis on the interconnectedness and interdependence between families, appear to have been adapted as a means of coping with slavery's highly destructive system of exploitation and oppression (Gutman, 1976).

African American slave women played an integral role in the maintenance and survival of the family. However, the control of motherhood (reproduction) and mothering (caretaking) was ultimately held by the White slave master. African American female slaves were generally not seen as women at all, but as beasts whose reproductive capacities (as well as their physical labor) were used to produce commodities for someone else's benefit (Fox-Genovese, 1988; Greene, 1994). In some instances, women were able to establish solid relationships with male partners and to provide caretaking for their children. Slave narratives provide stories of women who stole food and clothing from their White masters in order to supplement the meager provisions allocated for their children and stories of women who made valiant attempts to keep their children with them (Shaw, 1994). However, there was a darker side to this struggle between African American slave women and their White masters for the control of motherhood, which sometimes resulted in drastic measures being used by the slave women to influence the fate of their offspring. Documents written by slave owners during this era indicate that there were high rates of infant mortality, including deaths by natural causes and those that were the result of infanticide (Shaw, 1994). Some documents also indicate the use of self-induced abortions as a means of controlling reproduction.

Despite the attempts made by women to provide consistent caretaking for their children, slave owners' disregard for the sanctity and unity of the family often led to instability (James, 1993; Greene, 1994). It was against the law for African American slaves to marry; however, documents in counties throughout the South indicate that many couples who had been informally married and living together during slavery had their marriages legalized and registered after emancipation (Billingsley, 1992). Both official documents and slave narratives suggest that slaves created patterns of family life that were functionally integrative and that did more than prevent the destruction of personality. Family life also created the conditions out of which came African American pride, identity, culture, and community (Billingsley, 1992).

The conditions of slavery made it necessary for mothers and fathers to be psychologically prepared, and their children socialized, for possible separation. This led to a conceptualization of "mother" that was collective. The term "mother" was used to refer to birthmothers and any other adult slave woman who provided basic caretaking for the child. Thus, the African tradition of fostering was adapted to meet the needs of the enslaved community in America, and the practice of "othermothering" played a critical role in child rearing (James, 1993). This tradition of women-centered units being primarily responsible for the nurturing and rearing of children has continued in the African American community since the times of slavery. It reflects both a continuation of West African cultural values and functional adaptations to race and gender oppression faced by African Americans in this society (Tanner, 1974; Stack, 1974; Sudarkasa, 1981).

What is most important about these years in slavery, and the period of time immediately following emancipation, is the way in which African Americans developed their own socially constructed definition of family. This definition included those adults (whether birth parents, relatives, or fictive kin) who accepted responsibility for the nurturance and socialization of children and who shared strong feelings of loyalty and trust. The work of contemporary scholars such as Carol Stack (1974) and Joyce Aschenbrenner (1975) show that these patterns of cooperation have been a very important factor in the survival of African American families in cities as well as in rural areas throughout America. During slavery, othermothers cared for children orphaned by sale or death of their parents and children conceived through rape whose mothers were unable to bond with them. In more contemporary times, othermothers support children born into extreme poverty or to alcoholic or drug-addicted mothers,

children of young mothers, as well as children who for other reasons cannot remain with their birthmothers (Young, 1970; Dougherty, 1978).

Although there is little discussion in the literature about the quality of the relationships between birthmothers and othermothers, the interactions are described as cooperative and seem to reflect the importance of women working together collectively to raise children successfully under oppressive conditions (Collins, 1990). Cross-residential or transresidential cooperation among African Americans was, and continues to be, an important factor in rearing children, providing financial support in times of need, caring for aged family members, and providing shelter for various kinfolk who need it from time to time. Thus, many contemporary mothers rely on women-centered communities as their basis for support in caring for their children (Sudarkasa, 1993).

Stereotypical Images from Slavery to the Civil Rights Era

In addition to supporting each other and caring for their partners and children under severe conditions of racism, sexism, and oppression, African American women have also had to struggle to counteract negative stereotypes promulgated by the White-majority culture since the time of slavery (hooks, 1981; Greene, 1994). A stereotype is defined as a belief about a group of people that gives insufficient attention to individual differences among members of that group (Brislin, 1993). In situations where these stereotypes are negative, pervasive, and have existed for many generations, they become part of the culture into which children are socialized and reflect prejudicial feelings about this group. Throughout the history of this country, the White-majority culture has created negative stereotypes about African American women as mothers, and these stereotypes have been used to legitimize their oppression (Collins, 1990).

In her sociopolitical analysis of race, class, and gender bias in America and its impact on African American women, Patricia Hill Collins identifies stereotypes that seem to have penetrated the consciousness of African American women today. Collins's thesis represents a bringing together of sociological research, ideas of Black feminist theorists, her own experiences as an African American woman, and experiences of other women she has encountered in many different arenas. She examines the complexity of ideas that exist in both scholarly and everyday life and formulates a perspective that helps us understand the experiences of African American women as they attempt to find an authentic "voice" in the current social, political, and economic climate (Collins, 1990). In identifying these stereotypical images, Collins utilizes observations taken from African American literature, historical documents, the media, and research. She highlights the controlling nature of these stereotypical images and describes how each has contributed to the oppression and subjugation of African American women. Two of these images, "Mammy" and "Jezebel," were developed during slavery. Three others evolved later.

The stereotypical Mammy was portrayed as the faithful, obedient domestic servant who loved, nurtured, and cared for White children without any thought or attention to her own needs or to those of her family (Collins, 1990). This image not only characterized African American women as having exceptional nurturing and care-taking skills, but it also promoted the belief that she preferred to care for White children, even if this meant neglecting her own. Thus, the Mammy image was one that provided support for White superiority while it characterized African American women as both understanding and accepting of their subordinate place in society. The Mammy image buttressed the ideology of the cult of true womanhood, in which sexuality and fertility are severed. "Good" White mothers were expected to deny their female sexuality and

to devote their attention to the moral development of their offspring. In contrast, Mammy was an asexual, surrogate African American mother who handled the more basic child care needs for White children (Collins, 1990). This image was used to justify the economic exploitation of African American women both as slaves and later as domestic workers (Gilkes, 1994).

In the Jezebel stereotype, African American women were portrayed as being sexually aggressive and responsible for their own sexual victimization. This image was created by Whites as a way of justifying the widespread sexual assaults on African American women by White males that occurred during slavery (Davis, 1981; hooks, 1981; White, 1985). By their acceptance of the Jezebel stereotype, the White establishment was able to rationalize using African American women as "breeders" for the financial gain of slaveholders. This stereotype has continued to be applied to African American women even in more modern times, as evidenced by the fact that White males who were accused of raping African American women received no legal sanctions in courts in many southern states from the time of emancipation through more than two-thirds of the twentieth century (White, 1985). In a similar way, the Jezebel stereotype was reflected in the treatment received by African American domestic workers in White homes during the early 1900s. According to narratives from women who were domestics during that time period, African American women often risked sexual harassment and victimization by White male employers. As one woman remarked in 1912: "I believe that nearly all White men take, and expect to take, undue liberties with their colored female servants—not only the fathers, but in many cases the sons also. Those servants who rebel against such familiarity must either leave or expect a mightily hard time, if they stay" (quoted in Mann, 1990, p. 148).

Although the Jezebel stereotype is not directly focused on mothers, as is the Mammy stereotype, it has affected the perception of African American mothers within the larger White-majority culture because of the complex, often contradictory, connection between sexuality and motherhood that exists in this society. Although children are conceived through sexual activity, the prevailing notion of motherhood is of one that is relatively asexual, with "good mothers" expected to have rigid control over their sexuality. As a result, women are often seen as being either a "Madonna," who is a devoted, asexual mother figure, or as a "Whore," whose maternal feelings and instincts are thought to be minimal at best. The Jezebel stereotypical image portrays African American women as having excessive sexual appetites; therefore, it follows that these women could not possibly be good mothers because of their preoccupation with sexuality. During slavery, this stereotype contributed to the rationalizations used by the White establishment to legitimize separating slave children from their mothers, as these women were believed to have little, if any, commitment to mothering the children who resulted from their sexual activity. Although the Jezebel stereotype may have freed African American women from the rigid, puritanical attitudes toward sexuality that affected the lives of most White women of that day, it ultimately made them vulnerable to sexual assault and held them responsible for their own sexual victimization and for the removal of their children.

The third stereotypical image, the "Matriarch," was constructed by the White establishment during the 1960s. She is an African American woman who has failed to fulfill her traditional "womanly" role by working outside the home and who is so negative and critical toward her male partner (or spouse) that he is unwilling to live with her (Collins, 1990). This stereotype presents African American women as bad mothers, since, according to this stereotype, their work outside of the home forces them to neglect their children, and their critical, negative interaction with the children's father causes him to abandon the family. Although the Matriarch image does present African American women as strong and powerful maternal figures, in opposition to the then prevailing cultural image of White women as being weak, passive, and submissive, it is nonetheless used as a means of controlling African American women.

The Matriarch stereotype allows the White establishment to blame African American women for the success or failure of their children and for the economic circumstances of African American families (Collins, 1990; Greene, 1994). White scholars, journalists, and policymakers have claimed that the African American family structure is the main cause of the high rates of crime, unemployment, school dropouts, teenage pregnancies, drug abuse, and disaffection among young people in the inner cities (Moynihan, 1967). This perspective, although challenged by many researchers of color (e.g., Billingsley, 1968; Hill, 1972; McAdoo, 1981), is an extremely difficult myth to overcome because many in this country, including some African Americans, believe the stereotype and accept it as truth (Sudarkasa, 1988).

Current Stereotypical Images

The fourth image is that of the "Welfare Mother," which labels the fertility of women who are not White and middle class as unnecessary and even dangerous to the values of this country (Collins, 1990). Unlike the Matriarch, who was seen as too aggressive, the Welfare Mother is not aggressive enough. She is seen as too lazy to work and as having repetitive pregnancies in order to collect more money from the state. She is portrayed as a mother who does not appropriately socialize her children to accept the societal values and normative behaviors surrounding the work ethic, thereby causing her family to remain in poverty. The Jezebel image can be seen underneath the Welfare Mother stereotype, since the latter is also seen as being sexually promiscuous and having little emotional connection to her offspring, who result from her heightened sexual activity. As with the other stereotypical images of African American women, the Welfare Mother image allows the White-majority culture to blame the victims for their own oppression and victimization and shifts the focus away from the institutional and structural factors that perpetuate poverty.

The final stereotypical image is that of the "Superwoman." Unlike the earlier stereotypes, which were constructed by the White establishment to justify its exploitative behavior toward African American women, the Superwoman image has been perpetuated by the African American community and is embraced by many as being an "idealized" image of motherhood. The Superwoman image requires that African American women sacrifice their own needs for those of their children and families, while being committed to maintaining the economic viability of their families by working and contributing to the advancement of the African American community as a whole through their participation in service work. Michele Wallace (1991) describes the Superwoman as follows:

[She is a woman] of inordinate strength, with an ability for tolerating an unusual amount of misery and heavy, distasteful work. This woman does not have the same fears, weaknesses, and insecurities as other women, but believes herself to be and is, in fact, stronger emotionally than most men. Less of a woman in that she is less "feminine" and helpless, she is really more of a woman in that she is the embodiment of Mother Earth, the quintessential mother with infinite sexual, life-giving, and nurturing reserves. In other words, she is a Superwoman. (p. 107)

The Superwoman image is deceptive because it builds on the efforts that African American women have made through the years to oppose negative stereotypes prevalent in the White-majority culture, particularly the Matriarch and Welfare Mother images. Because it appears to be positive and to represent the strengths of African American motherhood, it is one that many African American women have internalized (Boyd-Franklin, 1991; Greene, 1994). In the 1980s the Superwoman image was expanded to include another criterion—she must also be a highly educated, professional woman. This newer image has been labeled the "Super/Essence woman," after the popular magazine geared toward professional African American women (Edwards, 1992). The Super/Essence woman is expected to be a supportive, and at times submissive, partner to her spouse, a devoted mother who is actively involved in her children's lives, while also being aggressive, competent, and career-focused in her professional life. She must be able to create and maintain a viable marriage, while also being prepared to care for herself and her children alone if necessary.

This stereotype has a strong influence on mothering and on the mother-daughter relationship for African American women. Mothers strive to equip their daughters with the skills necessary to meet these expectations, making every effort to ensure that their daughters have the stability and emotional strength to overcome whatever obstacles are in their way (Collins, 1990).

With the Super/Essence woman image held up as an ideal, life for African American women can become a gauntlet race. Some succeed, but there are many casualties. The "wounded" are those women who make up the 42.8 percent (1988 figures) of Black female heads of households who live at or below the poverty level (Mullings, 1994). They are the mothers of the 70.1 percent of Black children who are living in families with incomes less than twice the poverty level (Edelman, 1985). These women head families that constitute what has been called the "underclass," which refers to those individuals who live in persistent poverty and who have "dropped out" of the struggle to attain economic stability and security. Many of these women living in poverty are young. Statistics indicate that the African American female head of household has become younger over the past forty years, which compounds the difficulties that these women and their children face. In 1980, figures indicated that 1 in 8 female-headed African American families were headed by women under twenty-five years of age (Smith, 1988). Among this number, three-fourths of these young women have never been married. They tend to be women from low-income families whose incomes are depressed even further as they form their own families out of wedlock (Smith, 1988). Clearly, teen mothers are quite disadvantaged in their capacity to attain the Super/Essence woman ideal. For those who have internalized the image, the result can be depression and guilt.

THE INTERNALIZATION OF STEREOTYPES

Case Examples

Claudine. Claudine is a 35-year-old African American woman who is the single parent for her two boys, ages 8 and 6. She was married to, and lived with, the boys' father for seven years, during which time he was physically and emotionally abusive to her. When Claudine left her husband, she had a high school education but no specific job-related skills. She applied for and received Aid to Families with Dependent Children (AFDC) and began living in an inner-city apartment near her mother and sisters. Once her children were in school all day, Claudine requested job training through the Welfare Department. She hoped to be able to find a job that would provide her with a livable income so that she would no longer need AFDC. Claudine was referred to a program that trained women to work as instrument technicians, preparing surgical kits for hospitals. She faithfully attended the training, and at graduation she received an award

for being the most consistent and conscientious trainee in the program.

For six months after completing the training, Claudine applied for jobs in local hospitals. Although she received a few interviews, she was not hired. From time to time, Claudine found temporary work (usually during the Christmas season) in a local department store. However, she could never seriously consider taking a full-time position and terminating her AFDC benefits because the minimum-wage salary that she could earn would not be sufficient to compensate for the benefits she would lose. In addition to the stipend, Claudine's AFDC benefits included subsidized housing, Medicaid coverage for herself and the children, and food stamps.

Claudine is in therapy because one of her sons developed severe behavior problems following the parental separation. She actively participates in his treatment and in supportive sessions for herself. In her individual sessions, Claudine expresses frustration with her life. She very much wants to establish a "better life" for her children, and she blames herself for not being able to figure out a way to work and take care of her family. Although she does not want to return to her abusive husband, she sometimes wonders whether she caused him to be abusive, often blaming herself for some "defect" that made her a "failure" as a wife and mother.

Claudine's life situation reflects at least two of the prevailing stereotypes of African American women—that of the Matriarch and that of the Welfare Mother. She is a single head of household and feels personally responsible for the plight of her family and for the failure of her marriage. In many ways, Claudine has internalized these stereotypical images, which contributes to her feelings of worthlessness, guilt, and depression.

Annette. Annette is a 22-year-old African American young woman who has been in treatment since she was 14 years old. She was raised by her mother in a single-parent household and has a history of physical and sexual abuse. At age 15, Annette ran away from her mother and went to live with a family friend (she was Annette's fictive aunt). While in her aunt's home, she was raped, which resulted in her being placed in a Department of Social Services (DSS) foster home. Annette became pregnant during her senior year in high school and decided to keep her child. This disrupted her foster placement, and, after the baby's birth, she (and her child) went to live with a biological aunt. Annette, with the help of an adult female cousin, was able to adequately parent the child for the first two years. She completed high school and was admitted to a small two-year college in the area. Annette's situation is complicated by the regulations of the social services system, which made her ineligible for AFDC benefits because she was still considered a foster child under the jurisdiction of DSS. The financial support Annette received from DSS was not sufficient to care for herself and her child, and the agency refused to provide support for the child since she was technically not in foster care. Although Annette's therapist attempted to advocate, she was unsuccessful. Eventually, Annette no longer had the financial resources or the emotional energy to continue both attending college and adequately parenting her child. After a great deal of deliberation, Annette released custody of the child to her cousin. She is currently attempting to complete her college education and is employed as a temporary worker.

In Annette's case, we see internalization of the Super/Essence woman image by a young, single mother who has had a problematic life history. Her decision to attend college was based on a firm belief that as an African American woman, she was expected to educate herself so that she could obtain a professional-level job in order to adequately care for herself and her child. Annette's early history and life experiences undoubtedly complicate her situation; however, she has continued to feel totally responsible for her plight. Annette faced tremendous stress, both emotionally and physically, when she tried to parent her daughter and attend college at the same time, but she frequently comments that other African American women have been able to do these things successfully. She blames herself (and feels that others also blame her) for this perceived failure. Annette gives little credence to the financial hardships she faced being unemployed and receiving a small stipend from the DSS and to the contradictions in the social services system that contributed to the problems she faced. The internalization of the Super/Essence woman stereotype is certainly not the only factor responsible for Annette's distress; however, it has contributed to her self-perception and expectations in a way that is detrimental.

Darlene.   Darlene is a 35-year-old African American mother of four children. The children have two different fathers, and she has little consistent contact with either man. Darlene lost custody of her children two years prior to her entering treatment because of her chronic alcoholism and neglect. The children are placed with Darlene's mother, who altered her retirement plans in order to care for them. Darlene's relationship with her mother is strained, although they try to cooperate in the caretaking of the children. Darlene hopes to have her children returned to her care and custody some day, but she has been unable to consistently follow through with treatment for her alcoholism. She seems to have also internalized the Matriarch and Super/Essence woman images and blames herself for her situation. She suffers from depression, low self-esteem, and a sense of failure about her inability to appropriately take care of her children. Darlene believes that she has had every opportunity to "make it" in life and feels that she is solely responsible for her failure to be a strong, resilient woman who could overcome all of the obstacles inherent in the society in order to adequately care for herself and her children.

PROBLEMS WITH THE IMAGE

The Super/Essence woman stereotype, like the other negative stereotypes of African American women, attributes total responsibility for the status of one's life situation to the individual, while ignoring the prevailing sociopolitical conditions that have a negative impact on women's lives. In a society where almost 30 percent of all African American families live under oppressive conditions that threaten their survival, such as pervasive poverty, joblessness, drugs, and violence, the Super/Essence woman image can be used by the White establishment to once again blame African American women for their own (and their family's) plight. Those African American women who have been able to embody the Super/Essence woman image have been written about in many different sources, and their self-sacrifice, struggle, and commitment to family and to the broader community should not be discredited (Gilkes, 1994; Collins, 1990; Greene, 1990). However, maintaining this strength in the face of oppression and poverty is quite costly, and many African American mothers have not been able to successfully overcome these barriers (Collins, 1990).

The often difficult nature of motherhood within the African American cultural context explains the range that is found in women's reactions to motherhood and the ambivalence that many feel about mothering (Collins, 1990). In a unique way, some contemporary African American mothers are like the voices heard in slave narratives and the slave mothers portrayed in Toni Morrison's book *Beloved*, whose losses are so deep and pervasive that they are driven to desperate acts. African American women living in poverty are often overwhelmed by the task of caring for children, and they may experience motherhood as a challenge that they have no hope of winning. Some women may simply give up and let go of the attempt to nurture and provide for their children. They are the victims of the structural conditions of racism and discrimination that limit their access to adequate resources to care for themselves and their children and victims of the depression and hopelessness experienced as a result of their internalization of the stereotypes. African American women like the ones described in the above case examples represent those who have been unable to reach the stereotypical, idealized image of the Super/Essence woman. Even within the African American cultural context, their voices have seldom been recorded or heard (Weems, 1993).

The silence that has surrounded these African American mothers who are "not so sturdy bridges" for their children is a reaction within this community against the negative stereotypes that are prevalent in the White-majority culture. Some, however, have begun to speak out about this issue and to call for a deeper understanding of the complex experience of African American motherhood (Bell-Scott, Guy-Sheftall, Jones-Royster, Sims-Wood, DeCosta-Willis, and Fultz, 1991; Wade-Gayles, 1984; Weems, 1993). They suggest that it is critical that we not romanticize the struggles of African American mothers by failing to acknowledge and understand fully the psychological and physical costs to their survival (Greene, 1990). The mothers in the case examples would be considered failures in their attempts to achieve the Super/Essence woman ideal, and their internalization of the stereotype has contributed to their feelings of depression, guilt, and self-blame. In the treatment process, it is essential to find a way to counteract these stereotypes, while helping the women construct a more comprehensive understanding of the experience of African American motherhood in order to facilitate positive growth and empowerment.

COUNTERACTING STEREOTYPICAL IMAGES

In clinical work with clients like Claudine, Annette, and Darlene, I try to find a way to effectively counteract their internalization of stereo-typical images. Most often this is done by providing information about the controlling nature of these stereotypes and explanations of how they have been used to blame African American women for their condition in life and for the plight of their families and the community. I have done most of my clinical work with low-income African American women who are struggling with economic and personal hardships and who are parenting alone. Therefore, I also inform them of the systemic and institutional forces that contribute to their continuing poverty and limited access to resources.

To be able to work with African American women in this way, I first had to struggle to counteract my own internalization of the Super/Essence woman stereotype. I was socialized to believe that this was an ideal image for an African American woman, and I began my professional career thinking that I would "have it all" by the time I was 35 years old—a husband, beautiful children, and a successful, exciting career. I knew that women sometimes were not able to achieve all of these things, but I felt that I had been taught how to effectively handle the stress involved and therefore would be one of the "successful" ones. I quickly learned that this was an almost impossible task. The amount of time involved in establishing and maintaining a successful professional career interfered with developing relationships, and I could never figure out when I would have the time to absent myself from work long enough to have a child. Gradually, I began to realize that all women (including African American women) must make choices about their lives and that often something had to be put "on hold." As I came to terms with this insight, I also realized that African American women (including myself) have been attempting to reach a mythical image, one that is not possible to achieve in reality. I began to understand that the sociopolitical forces that keep many of

my African American clients in poverty also drive me to work extra hard to develop a professional career. I realize that I have purchased my professional success at a high price.

After gaining this personal perspective on the stereotypical nature of the Super/Essence woman image, I was ready to utilize my experiences to help clients better understand their lives. I decided to use the psychotherapeutic relationship to help strengthen their "psychological armor." This term describes the behavioral and cognitive skills used by African Americans and other persons of color to decrease their psychological vulnerability in encounters where there is a potential for racism (Faulkner, 1983; Greene, 1993). African American mothers socialize their daughters in such a way that they can make psychological sense out of the racist and sexist messages that they receive on a routine basis in this society, thereby creating a psychological barrier that protects one's self-esteem and identity.

Many of my clients have grown up in dysfunctional families where they have been deprived of an effective racial socialization process. Since they have not received the type of training that would prepare them to confront institutional barriers and negative stereotypes in an adaptive manner, my clients are especially vulnerable to the effects of racism. I see my job as helping them overcome the inadequate training they received, while strengthening their adaptive strategies for coping with racism.

Within the context of the therapeutic relationship, I engage with the client in a form of racial socialization. The therapy sessions are an opportunity for us to discuss appropriate responses to situations reflecting institutional racism that occur within a woman's life and to develop strategies for self-advocacy. The racial socialization process also involves my understanding of, and empathy for, the experiences of racism and sexism that occur in my clients' lives, and I provide emotional support for the feelings of anger and impotence that result from their attempts to overcome these barriers.

To see psychotherapy as the building of this psychological armor represents a culture-specific approach to treatment. In the more traditional models of psychodynamic psychotherapy, an individual's difficulties in functioning are thought to be the result of intrapsychic conflicts and anxiety that is not effectively being controlled because the client has poor coping skills or is using inappropriate defenses. Effective psychotherapy with African American clients requires that the therapist identify *both* the internal and external sources of stress and not just assume that the problem has an internal locus of etiology. The internal sources of stress are treated in much the same way as they would be in nonminority clients. There is a recognition, however, that the external sources of stress can exacerbate any internal conflicts that may be present. In working with African American mothers, the therapist must find a way to challenge the internalization of stereotypical images that can contribute to the client's feelings of frustration, anger, and helplessness. The therapeutic focus can then move beyond self-blame and feelings of helplessness toward helping the client envision ways to effectively maneuver around these barriers. In addition to psychological armoring, another adaptive strategy that is often observed in African Americans is "cultural paranoia" (Grier and Cobbs, 1968). Therapists working with African American clients need to understand that these behaviors, and the complex attitudes that accompany them, are necessary for survival in this society and should not conclude that their presence in the clinical picture is evidence of psychopathology.

THE NEED FOR A NEW DEFINITION OF MOTHERHOOD

In many instances, the clinical interventions that I provide for my African American female cli-

ents are helpful in facilitating their ability to understand the internalization of negative stereotypes and the mythical nature of the Super/Essence woman image. More than this is needed, however, to overcome the impact that these controlling images have on the psychological well-being of African American women. The Super/Essence woman stereotype must be challenged as an idealized image of African American motherhood. It does not acknowledge the negative impact that racism and discrimination have on the lives of African Americans or how these factors can inhibit a woman's ability to effectively care for her children. What is called for is a redefinition of motherhood: one that not only takes into account the strengths and resilience of African American women but also incorporates the sociopolitical and economic issues that act as barriers to success.

Prior to the civil rights movement of the 1960s there was an understanding in the African American community that poverty was directly attributable to the racist, discriminatory practices of the larger society. The changes in discriminatory laws and social policies that resulted from this movement have been accompanied by the attribution of complete personal responsibility for one's success or failure in life. Some segments of the African American community, along with the White-majority culture, seem to believe that equal opportunity exists for all, and they cite intraindividual deficits as the only causal factor involved when someone is chronically unemployed and living in pervasive poverty. This attribution of individual responsibility for success and failure in life underlies the Super/Essence woman stereotype.

The belief in intraindividual causality is only one thesis that has been proposed to explain chronic poverty. A related theory, the cultural-deficiency model, assumes that the African American culture holds a value system that is characterized by low aspirations and accepts female-headed families as normative (Corcoran,

Duncan, Gurin, and Gurin, 1985). It attributes poverty to the disintegration of the traditional male-dominated family structure, embracing the notion that welfare creates disincentives to work and incentives to have children out of wedlock (Moynihan, 1967). From this perspective, the African American culture is seen as maladaptive and creating thought processes within individuals that cause the continuation of poverty in the Black community (Zinn, 1990). This cultural-deficiency model is reflected in the stereotypes of the Matriarch and the Welfare Mother.

The structural model challenges this perspective and provides an alternative explanation of the existence of chronic poverty. It focuses on the socioeconomic conditions and institutional forces that work to keep ethnic-minority groups in poverty (Zinn, 1990; Wilson, 1987). Within this model, attention is drawn away from psychological and cultural issues and is focused on the social structures that allocate economic and social rewards (Zinn, 1990). The structural model explains such conditions as the prevalence of female-headed households in the African American community as being the result of poverty, not the cause of it. Researchers cite such statistics as the decline in the male-female ratio that occurs by ages 25 to 44 and attribute causality to early mortality (1 in 10 African American males dies before age 20), high levels of incarceration (1 in 4 African American males are either in prison or on parole), and the number of African Americans who marry outside of their ethnic group (Jenkins, 1994). They also suggest that the chronic joblessness experienced by many African American men contributes to the problem of female-headed families, since men who are unable to obtain consistent employment are unlikely to marry their partners (Wilson, 1987).

Utilizing this model, we can now begin to see how an African American woman's difficulties in caring for herself and her children are not solely the result of intrapersonal deficits but have roots in the socioeconomic conditions that limit access to employment, the amount of income she can earn even if employed, and the likelihood that she will be able to establish and maintain a viable marital partnership with an African American male. With clients who are low-income mothers living on welfare, I often discuss the structural model and use examples from their own lives to illustrate the fact that the conditions under which many African American women (and men) live are extremely vulnerable to economic change. The client is then able to understand that as an African American mother living in poverty, she is being hampered in her efforts to rise out of this condition even when she follows all of the "rules" of the society. When she is able to work, she is the lowest paid among all employed individuals. If she is unable to find a job, which will most likely be the case if she resides in the inner city, the welfare benefits she receives will keep her at or below poverty level. And even if she longs for the traditionally female role of homemaker and nurturer of children, she is unlikely to have a male partner who is in a position to adequately provide for the family and with whom she can share the challenge of survival.

As a clinician, I am particularly concerned with African American women's internalization of the stereotypical images described above, since this can have a powerful negative effect on their psychological well-being (Greene, 1994; Jenkins, 1993). When women have internalized the Super/Essence woman stereotype, they often feel that they have somehow failed to attend appropriately to all of their burdens or to solve all of their family members' problems. These clients rarely wonder whether their responsibilities are too extensive or if their expectations of themselves are realistic. They express the fear that coming to therapy means that they are "weak" or "couldn't take it" and believe that it is "indulgent" to spend time talking about their own personal concerns (Childs, 1990; Jenkins, 1994; Greene, 1992). These women not only blame themselves for their inability to function, but they may also harbor attitudes and beliefs that interfere with their ability to seek and sustain important support and validation from other women (Greene, 1994). The conditions that exist today in the African American community highlight the need to return to women-centered communities that care for children—in much the same way that they were needed during slavery. Yet, the Super/Essence woman image hinders the development of this sense of community.

The current idealized image of African American motherhood (the Super/Essence woman), buttressed by the negative stereotypes of poor African American mothers in the White-majority culture (the Matriarch and Welfare Mother), creates a dilemma for most women and makes it difficult for many to succeed. Both low-income and professional women must struggle to deal with the controlling nature of each of these stereotypes, and their internalization contributes to feelings of guilt and shame, which complicate the treatment process. Further, the attribution of total individual responsibility for success or failure that underlies each of the stereotypes makes it difficult for African American women to join together across social class lines to form a collective sisterhood. Challenging the existing Super/Essence woman image and creating a new definition of African American motherhood should help to counteract the internalization of these stereotypes and to enhance cooperation and collective support for mothering. Although this new definition acknowledges the negative effects of institutional racism and other sociopolitical factors on the lives of African Americans, I am not suggesting that there should be no attribution of personal responsibility, since there is always a component of individual agency under even the most oppressive conditions. However, there is an interaction between these systemic forces and individual skills that must be taken into account if we are to truly understand the complexities of African American motherhood.

With the new definition that I am suggesting, it should be possible for African American mothers to overcome the arbitrary class divisions that have kept them apart and women would realize that we are all adversely affected by the sociopolitical and institutional conditions in society. This perspective should also help reduce the tendency to blame one segment of the community for its own victimization, thereby contributing to a more cooperative social climate. Communities of women (as birthmothers, othermothers, and community othermothers) could provide support and caring for each other while working together to nurture African American children in this hostile environment. This definition challenges us to remember, and to put into practice once again, the patterns of collectivism, mutual support, and interdependency that have been highly valued in the African American community throughout its history. These values helped African American families survive the most brutal years of our history in America. They can also effectively lead us through this modern-day maze of social ills.

REFERENCES

Aschenbrenner, J. (1975). *Black families in Chicago.* Prospect Heights, IL: Waveland Press.

Bell-Scott, P., Guy-Sheftall, B., Jones-Royster, J., Sims-Wood, J., DeCosta-Willis, M., and Fultz, L. P. (Eds.) (1991). *Double stitch.* New York, NY: HarperCollins.

Billingsley, A. (1968). *Black families in White America.* Englewood Cliffs, NJ: Prentice-Hall.

Billingsley, A. (1992). *Climbing Jacob's ladder.* New York, NY: Simon and Schuster.

Boyd-Franklin, N. (1991). Recurrent themes in the treatment of African American women in group therapy. *Women and Therapy, 11*(2), 25–40.

Brislin, R. (1993). *Understanding culture's influence on behavior.* New York, NY: Harcourt Brace Jovanovich.

Childs, E. K. (1990). Therapy, feminist ethic, and the community of color with particular emphasis on the treatment of Black women. In H. Lerman and

N. Porter (Eds.), *Feminist Ethics in Psychother-apy* (pp. 195–203). New York, NY: Springer.

Collins, P. H. (1990). *Black feminist thought.* Boston, MA: Unwin Hyman.

Corcoran, M., Duncan, G. J., Gurin, G., and Gurin, P. (1985). Myth and reality: The causes and persis-tence of poverty. *Journal of Policy Analysis and Management, 4*(4), 516–536.

Davis, A. (1981). *Women, race and class.* New York, NY: Vintage.

Dougherty, M. C. (1978). *Becoming a woman in rural Black culture.* New York, NY: Holt, Rinehart and Winston.

Edelman, M. W. (1985). The sea is so wide and my boat is so small: Problems facing Black children today. In H. McAdoo and J. McAdoo (Eds.), *Black children: Social, educational and parental environments.* Newbury Park, CA: Sage.

Edwards, A. (1992). *Children of the dream: The psychol-ogy of Black success.* New York, NY: Doubleday.

Faulkner, J. (1983). Women in interracial relation-ships. *Women and Therapy, 2,* 193–203.

Fox-Genovese, E. (1988). *Within the plantation house-hold: Black and White women of the old south.* Chapel Hill, NC: University of North Carolina Press.

Gilkes, C. T. (1994). "If it wasn't for the women…": African American women, community work, and social change. In M. B. Zinn and B. Thorton Dill (Eds.), *Women of color in U.S. society.* Philadel-phia, PA: Temple University Press.

Greene, B. (1990). What has gone before: The legacy of racism and sexism in the lives of Black moth-ers and daughters. *Women and Therapy, 9*(1–3), 207–230.

Greene, B. (1992). Black feminist psychotherapy. In E. Wright (Ed.), *Feminism and psychoanalysis.* Oxford, England: Blackwell.

Greene, B. (1993). Psychotherapy with African Amer-ican women: Integrating feminist and psychody-namic models. *Journal of Training and Practice in Professional Psychology, 7*(1), 49–66.

Greene, B. (1994). Diversity and difference: The issue of race in feminist therapy. In M. Mirkin (Ed.), *Women in context: Toward a feminist reconstruc-tion of psychotherapy.* New York, NY: Guilford.

Grier, W. H., and Cobbs, P. (1968). *Black rage.* New York, NY: Basic Books.

Gutman, H. G. (1976). *The Black family in slavery and freedom: 1750–1925.* New York, NY: Vintage Books.

Hill, R. B. (1972). *The strengths of Black families.* New York, NY: Emerson Hall.

hooks, b. (1981). *Black women and feminism.* Boston, MA: South End Press.

James, S. M. (1993). Mothering: A possible black fem-inist link to social transformation? In S. M. James and A. P. A. Busia (Eds.), *Theorizing Black femi-nisims: The visionary pragmatism of Black women* (pp. 44–54). New York, NY: Routledge.

Jenkins, L. (1994). African-American identity and its social context. In E. P. Salett and D. R. Koslow (Eds.), *Race, ethnicity and self: Identity in multi-cultural perspective* (pp. 63–88). Washington, DC: National Multicultural Institute.

Jenkins, Y. (1993). African American women: Ethnoc-ultural variables and dissonant expectations. In J. L. Chin, V. De La Cancela, and Y. Jenkins (Eds.), *Diversity in psychotherapy: The politics of race, ethnicity and gender* (pp. 117–136). West-port, CT: Praeger.

Mann, S. A. (1990). Slavery, sharecropping, and sex-ual inequality. In M. R. Malson, E. Mudimbe-Boyi, J. F. O'Barr, and M. Wyer (Eds.), *Black women in America* (pp. 133–157). Chicago, IL: University of Chicago Press.

Mbiti, J. (1969). *African religions and philosophies.* New York, NY: Anchor.

McAdoo, H. P. (1981). *Black Families.* Beverly Hills, CA: Sage.

Moynihan, D. P. (1967). The Negro family: The case for national action. In L. Rainwater and W. L. Yancy (Eds.), *The Moynihan report and the poli-tics of controversy* (pp. 39–132). Cambridge, MA: MIT Press.

Mullings, L. (1994). Images, ideology, and women of color. In M. B. Zinn and B. T. Dill (Eds.), *Women of color in U.S. society.* Philadelphia, PA: Temple University Press.

Oppong, C. (1973). *Growing up in Dagbon.* Tema, Ghana: Ghana Publishing Corporation.

Shaw, S. (1994). Mothering under slavery in the ante-bellum south. In E. N. Glenn, Chang, G., and Forcey, L. R. (Eds.), *Mothering: Ideology, expe-rience and agency* (pp. 237–258). New York, NY: Routledge.

Smith, J. P. (1988). Poverty and the family. In G. Sandefur and M. Tienda (Eds.), *Divided opportunities: Minorities, poverty and social policy* (pp. 141–172). New York, NY: Plenum.

Stack, C. B. (1974). *All our kin: Strategies for survival in a Black community.* New York, NY: Harper and Row.

Sudarkasa, N. (1981). Interpreting the African heritage in Afro-American family organization. In H. P. McAdoo (Ed.), *Black families* (pp. 37–53). Beverly Hills, CA: Sage.

Sudarkasa, N. (1988). Interpreting the African heritage in Afro-American family organization. In H. P. McAdoo (Ed.), *Black families* (2d ed., pp. 27–43). Newbury Park, CA: Sage.

Sudarkasa, N. (1993). Female-headed African American households: Some neglected dimensions. In H. P. McAdoo (Ed.), *Family ethnicity: Strength in diversity* (pp. 81–89). Newbury Park, CA: Sage.

Tanner, N. (1974). Matrifocality in Indonesia and Africa and among Black Americans. In M. Z. Rosaldo and L. Lamphere (Eds.), *Women, culture, and society* (pp. 129–156). Stanford, CA: Stanford University Press.

Wade-Gayles, G. (1984, Fall). The truth of our mother's lives: Mother-daughter relationships in Black women's fiction. *Sage: A Scholarly Journal on Black Women, 1,* 8.

Wallace, M. (1991). *Black macho and the myth of the superwoman.* New York, NY: Verso Press.

Weems, R. J. (1993). *I asked for intimacy: Stories of blessings, betrayals, and birthings.* San Diego, CA: Lura Media.

White, D. G. (1985). *Ar'n't I a woman? Female slaves in the plantation south.* New York, NY: W. W. Norton.

Wilson, J. (1987). *The truly disadvantaged: The inner city, the underclass and public policy.* Chicago, IL: University of Chicago Press.

Young, V. H. (1970). Family and childhood in a southern Negro community. *American Psychologist, 72,* 269–288.

Zinn, M. B. (1990). Family, race, and poverty in the eighties. In M. R. Malson, E. Mudimbe-Boyi, J. F. O'Barr, and M. Wyer (Eds.), *Black women in America.* Chicago, IL: University of Chicago Press.

Reading 3   The Sandwich Generation: Women's Roles as Multi-Generational Caregivers

JOAN F. KUCHNER

Questions to Consider:

1. According to Kuchner, how has women's caregiving role contributed to the creation of the sandwich generation?

2. How is the experience of caregiving for a parent different from the experience of caregiving for a child?

3. Who do you have caregiving responsibility for? What do you like about caregiving? What is hard about caregiving for you?

4. What would change in women's lives if caregiving were truly valued?

INTRODUCTION

Personal choice and improved quality of life have been watchwords for the closing decades of the twentieth century. In pursuit of these goals, women have continued their education longer and launched careers, married later and postponed parenthood, while their parents have benefited from medical advances that have reduced the mortality risks of progressive and degenerative disease. However, the social, scientific and economic forces that made these initial wishes come true have also wedged a generation of adults between the competing caregiving demands of children and frail elderly. This is the sandwich generation. A generation who anticipated that the middle years of life would be years of personal fulfillment now face the reality of weighing the needs of their own children against those of aging

parents: needs that are financial, such as paying for nursing home care versus saving for college; needs that involve the allocation of time, such as attending a school play or a teacher's conference versus driving elders to doctors' appointments; and the overarching needs to listen and to provide emotional support to both children and parents (Kuchner, 1993). The personal story of one woman who alternates shifts with her two sisters in providing bedside care to her paralyzed mother illustrates this predicament (Monson, 1993). After a 48-hour shift, she arrives home, ready to collapse, without any energy or time to take part in her son's activities. Even with sisters to share the burden, the guilt as well as the responsibility have made her "career, peace of mind and normal existence" (Monson, 1993, p. E1) a thing of the past.

As children, both boys and girls heard the messages that each individual should be all he or she could be and that the modern world held the egalitarian promise of options and opportunity for all. However, the caregiving role of women, shaped by centuries, has been resistant to change. Even when egalitarian parenting is the expressed ideal within a dual-career family, only 20 percent of couples equitably divide child care responsibilities (Basow, 1992). The reality is that family caregiving is overwhelmingly the responsibility of women throughout the life cycle. From the orchestration and supervision of the myriad details of personal hygiene to the basics of household chores, food purchases and preparation, room care and cleanliness, and appropriateness and availability of clothing all ultimately fall on the shoulders of women (Ahlberg & De Vita, 1992). When men participate in these tasks, they are viewed as assistants. The recent and dramatic increase in life expectancy has added a new dimension to family caregiving responsibilities, the need to provide supervision and daily assistance to familial frail elderly. The 1982 National Long-Term Care Survey clearly documents that the family caregivers for the elderly are overwhelmingly women in each and every category: wives providing more direct care than husbands, daughters providing more care than sons, daughters-in-law more care than either biological sons or sons-in-law, and sisters more assistance than brothers (Coward, Horne, & Dwyer, 1992). This article will explore the implications of these trends for today's women within the social and political climate that persists in overlooking the impact of the uneven distribution of care responsibilities within the family circle.

POSTPONED PARENTHOOD AND ELDER CARE

A sense of limitless flexibility made possible by advances in medical technology has encouraged more women to postpone motherhood until the third and even fourth decade of life. In 1978, approximately 76 percent of women aged 31–35 years old had given birth to their first child by age 21 (U.S.

Bureau of the Census, 1978). Ten years later, only 39 percent of ever-married women had become mothers prior to their 25th birthday (U.S. Bureau of the Census, 1987); and by 1992, the births to women 40–44 years old had nearly doubled the 1980 rate (U.S. Bureau of the Census, 1995).

However, the optimism associated with increased procreative choice has a hidden shadow. Many women who enter into motherhood in their mid to late 30s and earlier 40s have parents approaching or well into their 70s. The numbers of individuals aged 65 years old and older are rapidly growing, with the portion 85 years old and older expanding more rapidly than any other segment of the American population (Treas, 1995). Individuals with injuries or diseases that would have been fatal a generation ago can now expect to live a normal lifespan (Neal et al., 1993). The same burgeoning of medical advances that heralded increased flexibility in the timing of motherhood has enabled people with such degenerative diseases as heart disease, strokes, and cancer to live longer (Olshansky, Carnes, & Cassel, 1993). While the years between 65 and 85 are increasingly years of health, nearly half of those individuals 85 years old and older need assistance in carrying out some, if not all, of the activities of daily living (Soldo & Agree, 1988). Although frailty is not synonymous with old age, longer life spans have resulted in longer periods of incapacitation. "Frailty and disability (still remain) the dark side of aging (Olshansky, Carnes & Cassel, 1993, p. 52). The National Council on Aging predicts that by 2040, nineteen million elderly "baby boomers," who represent an overall population bulge, will become dependent on the care of others, leaving more dependent parents per employee than dependent children (Friedman, 1991).

These trends are occurring at a time when government financial support for institutional-based health care is being undermined and both the numbers of women working full time outside of the home and the shrinking total population point to a decreasing availability of potential caregivers. For example, a systematic reduction in the duration of inpatient hospital stays was initiated by the federally financed Medicare program without consideration for the complexity of illness or the complications associated with advanced age. The result is that all patients are sent home from the hospital with a long recuperative period still ahead of them and in need of continued care by family members. As policy makers increasingly emphasize the role of the family in providing assistance and care to the growing population of frail elderly, they are continuing to overlook the fact that there are fewer adult family members to care for the sick at home. Women are disproportionately expected to add this caregiving responsibility onto an already full schedule of child rearing and wage earning, without specialized training and without community supports.

WORKFORCE PARTICIPATION AND CAREGIVING

The continuous labor force participation by today's cohort of women in the childbearing years represents a third dynamic part of the equation. Eighty-five per cent of new mothers return to work shortly after the birth of their children (Friedman, 1991), and they remain in the workforce during their children's preschool, elementary, and secondary school years. Half of this group has one or more children aged 6 or younger (Bouvier & De Vita, 1991). In 1994, 57 percent of women with children younger than 3 were in the labor force, and the figure rises to 60 percent of women with children under 6 years of age (Children's Defense Fund, 1996). This group constitutes one of the fastest growing segments of the employed population. The majority of women 45–54 years of age, and 42 percent of women in the 55–64 age bracket, are also gainfully employed (Brody & Schoonover, 1986). Labor force participation for women throughout the life cycle has become the norm, with women making

up over half of the total labor force of the United States (U.S. Bureau of the Census, 1995). According to the National Association of Working Women, nearly 60 percent of women employed outside of the home are the main or primary wage earner (Basow, 1992). Their participation in the workforce is fueled by the economic realities of high taxes, low wages, and spiraling costs for the basics including housing, groceries, and education. While business experiments with downsizing and eliminating higher-paid positions through reorganization and nonvoluntary early retirement, many women attempt to keep the lives of their families together on salaries that are routinely lower than those of men at all skill and educational levels (Lott, 1994). During an informal interview, one woman whose husband just turned 50 spelled out her own set of pressures. Their two sons, one in third grade and the other in seventh grade will need college educations. There are two older children from her husband's first marriage who are still being supported. Government downsizing has placed the specter of her husband's forced early retirement on the horizon. Although the family has tried to put aside money from her work as a part-time teacher's aide, she has had to turn down employment offers to care for her widowed 84-year-old mother-in-law, who recently returned from the hospital in need of daily assistance. Fear of income loss combined with the increased expenses of caring for two generations haunt both single and married women.

Employment does not exempt women from carrying a second shift at home, that of homemaker. Married employed fathers report that, whether or not their wives are employed, the wives spend almost four times as many hours a week on home chores and child care than they do (Friedman, 1991). Care for elderly family members is added on to the care of children and the maintenance of the primary household. Forty-four percent of women who assume the care of elders in their family are employed, and 20 percent of these caregivers still have children in the home (Bouvier & DeVita, 1991). On average, elder supervision and care require over 6½ hours per day, extending over six or more years (Noller & Fitzpatrick, 1993). Estimates based on weekly responsibilities are more conservative, placing the figure at 16 hours a work-week for women, which is added onto the approximately 75–85 hours a week women normally spend at work and on child care (Friedman, 1991). While the Family and Medical Leave Act requires businesses with 50 or more employees to grant up to 12 weeks of unpaid leave to men or women who request it—in order to care for a new biological or adopted child or to provide care to another adult family member without losing their health insurance or their old job—many individuals who could access this option cannot afford this extended time without pay. Although it is available to 40 percent of the workforce (Lott, 1994), the option of unpaid leave does not cover care in extended chronic situations. These require women to rearrange their schedules, coming into work late or leaving early in order to accommodate elder care, a choice that over 35 percent of women elect, according to the National Long Term Care study (Friedman, 1991). Although there is increased absenteeism among employees due to elder care, the perception among managers is that the rate of absenteeism is higher than actually recorded (Friedman, 1991). This false perception is also damaging in its implication for women's career paths.

In general, when men participate in child or elder caregiving, they generally remain in the background on a reserve basis, completing delegated tasks rather than taking on the routine daily requirements. The pattern of divorce and remarriage, as well as the proliferation of single-parent households among the sandwich generation, means that, in some instances, women may be responsible for children, parents, step-parents, and parents-in-law, as well as elderly aunts and uncles.

While the media and the community are quick to glorify individual men who voluntarily take on routine caregiving activities for infants and young children or the frail elderly, they ignore women's responses to the culture's caregiving directive. Employers still view the mere possibility of compliance with this cultural mandate on the part of women as a significant threat to career advancement. "A man is typically seen as bringing more than one full time person to the job with the wife as an asset, while a women is seen as less than one full time worker, with the family a distraction" (Friedman, 1991, p. 20).

The assumption that caregiving is natural for women has many repercussions, including the misplaced belief that caregiving by women is both free and of little value. The general invisibility of women's caregiving efforts is highlighted by the reaction when it is a male family member who takes on this responsibility. Men who assume routine caregiving are more likely to receive supplemental assistance from formal services, that is, services that cost someone money (Dwyer & Coward, 1995). Furthermore, society does not include among the cost of women's caregiving the personal financial losses, either those to current personal or family income or those that have implications for future financial security, such as contributions to retirement plans and Social Security (Walker, 1992).

CAREGIVING CHOICES

During 1981 and 1982, Brody and Schoonover (1986) interviewed 150 families in order to understand the pattern of care provided to elders by working women and nonworking women. While daughters who were not employed outside of the home tended to spend somewhat more of their helping hours doing laundry, preparing meals, and assisting with personal care, the researchers found that shopping and emotional support were the most frequent types of assistance provided by both groups, followed by assistance with managing money and arranging for services. Members of the sandwich generation have many examples from their own families, friends, and acquaintances of women trying to provide emotional and practical support across generations, to parents, spouse and children. Just such an example is the 48-year-old elementary school teacher with a son in fourth grade who spends evenings during the week on the phone listening to her mother cry out her frustrations. Her 76-year-old mother is recuperating from heart surgery, one in a long list of medical crises. Checking on mother's care and condition has become one of the many required weekend activities.

Although combining multiple roles during midlife has become the norm for most adults, the reality of the experience has different implications for women than men (Brody, Johnson & Fulcomer, 1994). In the United States, older women outnumber older men, particularly in the years after 85 (Treas, 1995). Gender distribution in this older age group is 100 women for every 39 living men (Treas, 1995). The bulk of the care for older, frequently widowed women is carried out by daughters or daughters-in-law (Soldo & Agree, 1988). It has been argued that the reason that women are usually the primary caregivers of the elderly is because the majority of the frail elderly are also women. Direct personal care from sons may appear psychologically threatening. The intimate assistance required in washing and dressing can make both parties uncomfortable, as it may involve close physical contact. Avoiding such contact is a traditional means of supporting the incest taboo that governs relationships between mothers and sons (Lee et al., 1993). However, this does not explain why women generally assume the role of primary caregiver for both male and female elders, even when additional assistance is available from male family members and formal agencies (Brody, Hoffman, Kleban & Schoonover, 1989). Adult sons become caregivers of frail parents only in the absence of an available female sibling or spouse (Lee et al., 1993) or in families without daughters or daughters-in-law to pick up this role (Dwyer &

Coward, 1995). The aid proffered by sons is usually managerial in nature, involving arranging for others to be available to assist on a daily basis (Friedman, 1991; Noller & Fitzpatrick, 1993). Only 4 percent of sons provide any direct care to either fathers or mothers (Lee et al., 1993).

Although men recognize the financial responsibility for the care of their parents, they usually handle it at a geographical and psychological distance. While members of both generations express the idea that all adult children should help meet necessary expenses of elder care, a majority of women of all ages expect adult daughters but not sons to adjust their schedules as well as their finances to provide care as needed (Brody, Johnson, & Fulcomer, 1994). Women tend to live up to this expectation. The routine nature of the caregiving tasks undertaken by men and women is substantially different. Researchers have documented that adult daughters are three times more likely than sons to provide their parents with assistance in eating, getting in and out of bed, dressing, and bathing; they are twice as likely to be involved with housework, laundry, meal preparation, assistance, reminders to take medications, shopping, and getting around outside of the house—as well as money management (Lee et al., 1993).

The marital status of adult children appears to affect the choice of primary caregiver. Longitudinal data from 1984–1986 representing a national sample of over 20,000 households in the United States documented that older women were more likely to be living with their children than were older men, even when age is taken into account (Speare & Avery, 1993). Unmarried women are the most likely adult children to become the primary caregiver of frail parents (Speare & Avery, 1993) and the least likely to receive help from other informal sources (Brody et al., 1994); whereas, married and remarried women received assistance in their parental caregiving from their husbands (Brody et al., 1994) and children (Suitor & Pillemer, 1993).

Although the role of principal caregiver usually falls on the adult daughter with the fewest competing responsibilities, taking on the additional demands of caring for an elderly parent can also place limits on the daughter's access to other roles and social networks. There is a growing body of evidence that caregiving for elderly parents may deter participation in the workforce for many adult daughters (Brody & Schoonover, 1986). As one 28-year-old woman explained to a reporter from the *Wall Street Journal,* she left her administrative job on the eve of a promotion interview so that she could keep her 61-year-old father out of a nursing home (Shellenberg, 1996). However, other women who first consider quitting work do remain in the workforce. They are more likely to be better educated, in higher-status jobs, or from families whose incomes place them in a higher socioeconomic category (Brody & Schoonover, 1986).

CAREGIVING AND SUPPORT NETWORKS

Women predominantly face the multiple stress of caregiving alone (Skinner, 1986). Employment outside of the home often inhibits the development of neighborhood social structures, while opting for periods of time at home after the birth of a child may result in distancing from colleagues at work (Kuchner & Porcino, 1988) and other forms of subtle ostracism. Integrating the roles of wage earner and caregiver involves continuously tapping emotional reserves to attempt to satisfy the needs of others. At the same time, it systematically eliminates the availability of discretionary time that could be used to replenish these resources. Society does not require this psychological task of men.

Although caring for young children is stressful, adults who are caring for an aging relative experience even more stress than a parent with child-care responsibilities, and are more likely than the recipients of elder care to report symptoms of depression and anger (Friedman, 1991).

Caring for an infant or young child is frequently undertaken as a matter of choice; caring for the daily needs of a frail parent is a matter of duty, undertaken with a great deal of emotional ambivalence on both the giving and receiving end of the transaction. For both men and women, distress is higher when the adult child is caring for his or her own biological parent (Spitz et al., 1994). The older generation may attempt to shield their adult children from the reality of their needs while, at the same time, expecting them to be met and exhibiting anger when these issues are not understood and anticipated. Mothers frequently feel guilty for intruding into their adult daughters' lives, while simultaneously wanting their personal attention. This mixed bag of feelings may include anger, resentment, fear, sadness, and guilt as well as a close identification between the adult child and the aging parent. Caring for a frail parent invokes fears for one's own aging. During an informal conversation, a woman in her mid 50s who was waiting in a hospital lobby for her mother's surgery to be completed expressed it this way. "I don't want to grow old," she said. "These are not golden years, they are rusty years." Adult children begin to contemplate the inevitable death of the parent while attempting to cope with changes in their parent's abilities and memory. This slow destruction clouds the adult child's memory of the parent in younger years.

The way that adult children relate to their aging parent reflects the nature of their relationship throughout their lives. For some relationships, this means providing care for a parent who may have been viewed as unlovable in the past and whose current actions do nothing to erase these feelings. Writing in *Newsday* with the assurance of anonymity, one women explained "I believe that there are other families with children like myself who feel the obligation, have resentment and yet believe this is their parent and they must do what is right (Dialogue, 1997, B18).

In other instances, the adult child may mourn the loss of motherliness. Illness or decreased capacity may leave the adult daughter bereft of her lifelong advisor and confidant. Within this same close relationship, she may be faced with the role of being the one who listens, cajoles, comforts, and gives advice. The changing relationship between adult children and elderly parents involves both a renegotiation of issues of power and control and a letting go of the need to be parented. The ability of adult children to establish a peer relationship with their own parents during early adulthood has been found to be associated with lower levels of stress and emotional turmoil, even under close contact, as their relationship with their parents evolves over its closing years (Rabin, Bressler, & Prager, 1993).

A history of involvement and intimate sharing that is characteristic of the mother-daughter bond is a strong foundation for the caregiving role (Lee et al., 1993), but it may also be a source of additional emotional distress. Women feel an emotional closeness to their mothers, frequently identifying with the needs of their elderly mothers and occasionally denying the reality of their aging (Kuchner, 1993). An additional source of emotional stress for women revolves around their perceptions of their ability to assist their parents—the actions that they are taking and what they feel they should be doing. The central meaning of the caregiving role for women accentuates each of these issues.

Currently, married women appear to be able to weather the role of caregiver to parents better than women who were never married or those currently separated or divorced (Brody, Litvin, Albert, Hoffman, & Kleban, 1992). They show fewer overt signs of depression and express fewer worries about substitute caregivers for their parents in the event that they are unable to continue the care. Adult children with more education and higher income have also been found to experience lower levels of stress in their role as caregiver for parents (Spitz et al., 1994). Some women whose identities are closely linked to the lifelong caregiving role may even retrospectively evidence a sense of satisfaction from successfully rising to the challenge of elder care responsibilities (Spitz et al., 1994).

Family members can be a source of support or an additional source of stress for caregivers. Most caregivers receive criticism and complaints from their social networks as well as concrete assistance and emotional support (Suitor & Pillemer, 1993). While both friends and siblings provide instrumental help such as running errands, occasional respite caregiving, helping with housework, and providing information, friends are more likely to be a source of emotional support, particularly those who have lived through similar experiences. As caregiving demands increase, so does the squabbling and tension between siblings (Brody et al., 1989). Not only does the primary caregiver feel the brunt of the criticism, but also sibling assistance rarely lives up to expectations (Suitor & Pillemer, 1993). The one exception is when two adult sisters live near each other (Brody et al., 1989). Sisters are more likely to share both decision making and caregiving (Brody et al., 1989). However, even-handed turn taking and shared caregiving without regard for parental wishes may cause resentment in parents (Eisenhandler, 1992). Sisters who are not the primary caregiver often report feelings of guilt for not doing enough for their parent(s), even when their geographical distance from the parent would make direct caregiving unfeasible (Brody et al., 1989). Distance from parent does not appear to be as much of an impediment to providing care for daughters as it does for sons (Lee et al., 1993). Among nonprimary caregiving siblings, brothers rarely report the same level of emotional conflict around caregiving to parents (Brody et al., 1989). However, "when men take on family responsibilities that women now perform, they suffer the same conflicts and consequences, personally and professionally" (Friedman, 1991, p. 21).

Daughters frequently share households with their parents during the parents' elder care years (Brody et al., 1994). Sharing a household with a frail parent may require adjustments that are both physical and psychological in order to accommodate his or her safety, hygiene, and dietary needs. Compared to their own siblings, individuals in shared households experience more disruptions in their work, as well as their social and family lives (Brody et al., 1989). Both privacy and time alone with spouse or with children may be difficult to attain. With less time for family members, leisure and taking care of one's own health become chronic sources of caregiving stress (Friedman, 1991). Although time spent caring for elderly parents and loss of privacy may become a focus of arguments between husband and wife (Noller & Fitzpatrick, 1993), seeking assistance from outside the family is usually viewed as a last resort (Soldo & Agree, 1988).

When changes in living arrangements are precipitated by elder care needs, children may feel threatened or embarrassed by these changes and the intrusion in their lives. However, close relationships between grandchildren and grandparents do develop reciprocally over time. As grandparents age, grandchildren may provide instrumental assistance and even direct care. In discussing the reasons for close ties to grandparents, many college students acknowledge that caregiving for their elderly grandparents is one component of this relationship (Smith, 1995).

ANOTHER LOOK AT THE SANDWICH GENERATION: GRANDMOTHERS AS CAREGIVERS

In 1992, approximately 1.6 million children under 6 years old were living in their grandparents' home (Young Children, 1994). Some of this is associated with the increasingly high rate of teenage pregnancies (Children's Defense Fund, 1996). In the case of teenage mothers, living with parents is generally associated with a more successful outcome, including likelihood of completing high school and subsequent self-sufficiency (Brooks-Gunn & Chase-Lansdale, 1995).

Over 40 percent of contemporary young adults return to their parents' homes after initially leaving (Goldscheider & Goldscheider, 1994), yet the relationship of parents and coresident adult children is shadowed by the implication that living with parents at this age indicates some form of failure (Spitz et al., 1994). Using survey data from 1984–1986, Speare and Avery (1993) found that over 79 percent of unmarried 18- to 24-year-olds and over 38 percent of unmarried 25- to 29-year-olds lived with their parents. Women in these age groups were more likely to have been previously married and living away from their parents' homes than were unmarried males who were more likely never to have left. Among 30- to 35-year-olds, over 40 percent of those who live with their parents had one or more children living in the household (Speare & Avery, 1993). Adult children return with young children to their parents' homes for a range of reasons including divorce or failed relationships, battles with illness, or the need to adjust to financial setbacks. Fewer than 25 percent of them provided a share of the household income (Speare & Avery, 1993). While these adult children generally do not require assistance with the minutia of daily living, adult children do receive services from parents, including assistance with household tasks and child care (Speare & Avery, 1993).

Grandmothers provide child care to assist their children emotionally and financially, even when the mother is married (Jendreck, 1993) or not residing in her parents' home. Grandparents are the primary caregivers for 16 percent of children younger than 5 years old whose mothers are employed outside of the home (Young Children, 1994). Over 8 percent of these children are under one year old (U.S. Bureau of the Census, 1995). There is also a growing population of grandparents, middle aged and older, who are not merely caring for grandchildren during working hours but who are raising their grandchildren. The U.S. Census Bureau estimates that over 3.5 million children are cared for solely by a grandparent, a jump of nearly 36 percent since 1994 (Woodworth, 1996). The women who are providing this caregiving assistance are primarily members of the sandwich generation. These midlife grandmothers may also have the responsibility for aging parents and may face the challenge of juggling work, elder care, and child care.

CONCLUSION AND DIRECTIONS FOR CHANGE

As the twenty-first century approaches, changes in life expectancy, population shifts, scientific advances, and new social realities have combined to create a challenge to the inevitability of growth in personal flexibility. For women, the anticipation of extended years in the workforce and a need to acquire the education to support employment options have led to entry into motherhood later, at a time when additional family care responsibilities are being required. The major biomedical advances that have enabled individuals to stretch their years of productivity have left communities unprepared to deal with the overlapping needs of its youngest and oldest members for daily assistance and care. The first attempts have turned to traditional patterns of caregiving responsibility and rhetoric without taking into account current economic realities.

Providing for the expanding population of elderly without sacrificing the needs of the youngest members of the community will occur only when there is appropriate recognition for the role of caregiver. It is only then that society will begin to relieve the pressures of the sandwich generation. This necessitates acknowledging the true value of caregiving and recognizing its contribution to the family and to society in the coin of the realm that speaks the loudest—a worthy wage in the workforce and ensured access to family income and financial resources for men and women who take on these caregiving responsibilities. Providing assistance for women in their

roles as caregivers throughout the life cycle is a first step.

However, appropriate recognition needs to be incorporated into the legal and business ethos. Women who spend time in family caregiving need to have equal access to pensions in their own right without being penalized for time spent outside the workforce. This includes access to pension resources through divorce settlements. Today, this occurs only when such benefits are specifically spelled out in court orders (Frug, 1992). In addition, implementation of the Family Leave Act needs to be monitored to ensure that positions are held for women whose absence from the workplace is temporary. At the same time, creative ways of expanding this option to small businesses should be explored. America is the only industrialized nation that measures its caregiving allotment in unpaid weeks.

It is important to expand the availability of care options for both young children and the elderly and to create legislation that will ensure that the individuals who are providing care both inside and outside of the home have specialized education and training: (a) requiring the registration and certification of home care providers for both youngsters and oldsters; (b) increasing the availability of community and workplace child care centers to provide affordable education, care, and guidance for infants, toddlers, and preschoolers; (c) increasing the range of supervised care environments that provide appropriate activities and services for the frail or impaired elderly; (d) developing respite care for families caring for frail elderly; (e) establishing community networks to exchange skills and services; and (f) providing tax credits for home improvements that facilitate independent living for the elderly or that add safety measures for the care of young children. In addition, neighborhood supports should be created to counteract the frequent emotional and social isolation of caregiving. Home visits by community companions could bring both social and recreational enrichment into a home setting.

Lists of individuals trained to supervise or assist frail elderly on an hourly basis could be compiled through a community center or library. Recent advances in communication technology could support both telephone- and computer-assisted discussion groups and resources for both regular and emergency contact.

Both boys and girls need continued education about the value of caregiving. Establishing elementary, junior high school, and high school links with child and adult day care centers could teach responsible caregiving skills to both young men and women through observation, interaction, and discussion. The heightened generational interdependence that will be the hallmark of the next century is an opportunity for reevaluating the nation's priorities. It is an opportunity to recognize the true cost and value of caregiving throughout the life cycle.

REFERENCES

Ahlberg, D., & DeVita, C. (1992). "New realities of the American family." *Population Bulletin,* Vol. 47, No. 2.

Basow, S. (1992). *Gender Stereotypes and Roles* (3rd ed.). Pacific Grove, CA: Brooks/Cole Publishing.

Bouvier, L., & DeVita, C. (1991). "The baby boom entering midlife." *Population Bulletin,* Vol. 46, No. 3.

Brody, E., Hoffman, C., Kleban, M., & Schoonover, C. (1989). "Caregiving daughters and their local siblings: Perceptions, strains, and interactions." *The Gerontologist,* Vol. 29, No. 4, 529–538.

Brody, E., Johnsen, P., & Fulcomer, M. (1984). "What should adult children do for elderly parents? Opinions and preferences of three generations of women." *Journal of Gerontology,* Vol. 39, No. 6, 736–746.

Brody, E., Litvin, S., Albert, S., & Hoffman, C. (1994). "Marital Status of daughters and patterns of parent care." *Journal of Gerontology,* Vol. 9, No. 2, S95–S103.

Brody, E., Litvin, S., Albert, S., Hoffman, C., & Kleban, M. (1992). "Differential effects of daughters' marital status on their parent care experiences." *The Gerontologist,* Vol. 32, No. 1, 58–67.

Brody, E., & Schoonover, C. (1986). "Patterns of parent-care when adult daughters work and when they do not." *The Gerontologist,* Vol. 26, No. 4, 372–381.

Brooks-Gunn, J., & Chase-Lansdale, P. (1995). "Adolescent parenthood." In Marc Bornstein (Ed.), *Handbook of Parenting,* Vol. 3, 113–150.

Brooks-Gunn, J., & Kirsh, B. (1984). "Life events and the boundaries of midlife for women." In G. Baruch & J. Brooks-Gunn (Eds.), *Women in Midlife.* New York: Plenum Press.

Children's Defense Fund. (1996). *State of America's Children.* Washington, DC: Children's Defense Fund.

Coward, R., Horne, C., & Dwyer, J. (1992). "Demographic perspectives on gender and family caregiving." In J. Dwyer & R. Coward (Eds), *Gender, Families, and Elder Care.* Newbury Park, CA: Sage Publications.

Dialogue. (1997). "The burden of caregiving." *Newsday,* February 27, B18.

Dwyer, J., & Coward, R. (1992). "Gender, family, and long-term care of the elderly." In J. Dwyer & R. Coward (Eds.), *Gender, Families, and Elder Care.* Newbury Park, CA: Sage Publications.

Eisenhandler, S. (1992). "Lifelong roles and cameo appearances: Elderly parents and relationships with adult children." *Journal of Aging Studies,* Vol. 6, No. 3, 243–257.

Friedman, D. (1991). *Linking Work-Family Issues to the Bottom Line.* New York: The Conference Board.

Frug, M. (1992). *Women and the Law.* Westbury, NY: The Foundation Press, Inc.

Goldscheider, F., & Goldscheider, C. (1995). "Leaving and returning home in 20th century America." *Population Bulletin,* Vol. 48, No. 4.

Jendrek, M. (1993). "Grandparents who parent their grandchildren: Effects on lifestyle." *Journal of Marriage and the Family,* Vol. 55, 609–621.

Kuchner, J. (1993). "Motherhood postponed: The impact on family and society." *Resources in Education.* (ED 365 417), March.

Kuchner, J., & Porcino, J. (1988). "Delayed motherhood." In B. Birns & D. Hay (Eds.), *The Different Faces of Motherhood.* New York: Plenum Press.

Lee, G., Dwyer, J., & Coward, R. (1993). "Gender differences in parent care: Demographic factors and same-gender preferences." *Journal of Gerontology,* Vol. 48, No. 1, S9–S16.

Lott, B. (1994). *Women's Lives: Themes and Variations in Gender Learning.* Pacific Grove, CA: Brooks/Cole Publishing Co.

Monson, G. (1993). "Caught in the middle." *Los Angeles Times, May 12,* E1.

Neal, M., Chapman, N., Ingersoll-Dayton, B., & Emlen, A. (1993). *Balancing Work and Caregiving for Children, Adults, and Elders.* Newbury Park, CA: Sage Publications.

Noller, P., & Fitzpatrick, B. A. (1993). *Communication in Family Relationships.* Englewood Cliffs, NJ: Prentice Hall.

Olshansky, S., Carnes, B., & Cassel, C. (1993). "The aging of the human species." *Scientific American, 268* (4), 46–53.

Rabin, C., Bressler, Y., & Prager, E. (1993). "Caregiver burden and personal authority: Differentiation and connection in caring for an elderly parent." *The American Journal of Family Therapy,* Vol. 21, No. 1, 27–39.

Shellenberger, S. (1996). "Care-giver duties make generation Xers anything but slackers." *Wall Street Journal,* May 22, B1.

Skinner, D. (1986). "Dual-career family stress and coping." In R. Moos (Ed.), *Coping with Life Crisis: An Integrated Approach.* New York: Plenum Press.

Smith, P. (1995). "Grandparenthood." In Marc Bornstein (Ed.), *Handbook of Parenting,* Vol. 3, 89–112.

Soldo, B. J., & Agree, E. M. (1988). "America's elderly." *Population Bulletin.* Vol. 43, No. 3.

Speare, A., Jr., & Avery, R. (1993). "Who helps whom in older parent-child families." *Journal of Gerontology,* Vol. 48, No. 2, S64.

Spitz, F., Logan, J., Joseph, F., & Lee, E. (1994). "Middle generation roles and the well-being of men and women." *Journal of Gerontology,* Vol. 49, No. 3, S107–S116.

Stoller, E. (1992). "Gender differences in the experiences of caregiving spouses." In J. Dwyer & R. Coward (Eds), *Gender, Families, and Elder Care,* Newbury Park, CA: Sage Publications.

Suitor, J., & Pillemer, K. (1993). "Support and interpersonal stress in the social networks of married daughters caring for parents with dementia." *Journal of Gerontology,* Vol. 48, No. 1, S1–S8.

Treas, J. (1995). "Older Americans in the 1990s and beyond." *Population Bulletin,* Vol. 50, No. 2.

U.S. Bureau of the Census. (1978). "Perspectives on American fertility." *Current Population Reports.* Series P-23, No. 1, 338.

U.S. Bureau of the Census. (1987). *Statistical Abstract of the United States; 1987.* Washington, DC: U.S. Government Printing Office.

U.S. Bureau of the Census. (1995). *Statistical Abstract of the United States; 1995* (115th ed.). Washington, DC: United States Government Printing Office.

Walker, S. (1992). "Conceptual perspectives on gender and family caregiving." In J. Dwyer & R. Coward (Eds.), *Gender, Families, and Elder Care.* Newbury Park, CA: Sage Publications.

Woodworth, R. (1996). "It's not the same the second time around: Grandparents raising grandchildren." *Zero to Three,* Vol. 16, No. 4, 21–26.

Young Children. (1994). "Changing roles of grandparents." *Young Children,* Vol. 49, No. 6, 3.

Topic 7

Women's Bodies, Women's Health

Body Language
(for Betty McKisson)

Gentle touch
firm touch
putting me in touch
with the sacredness of this body

> this body that gathers
> in its hive
> the swarming bees
> of my senses

> this body that opens
> like a flower
> to the warmth
> of a touch

> this body that whispers
> ancient wisdom
> in the quiet
> of my mind

Courtesy of Mary C. Bragg

Women are given contradictory messages about their bodies. On the one hand, women are seen as being in need of specialized medical care because their bodies appear to be more complicated than the bodies of men. On the other hand, women's health concerns are given considerably less attention by physicians and medical researchers than those of men. The readings in this section document the effects that these contradictory messages have on women's physical health and make suggestions for improving women's health care.

In the first reading of this section, "How to Think about Women's Health," Martha Livingston describes the ways that women's health is shaped by the social construction of gender. Because of sexism, the male body is seen as the norm, and this makes female bodily functions such as menstruation, menopause, and childbirth seem "unhealthy." As a result, women may receive too much health care, or "overdoctoring," for normal female body functions.

A second way that the social construction of gender affects health is through the problem of "underdoctoring." As Livingston describes, when it comes to the parts of their bodies that are not uniquely female, women generally receive a lower quality of care. It has been shown for example, that women and men with identical complaints receive different treatment—different amounts of time from the physician, different amounts of tests, and different medications. Women are also neglected in medical research, both by a lack of funding for research into women's diseases such as breast cancer, and by a lack of representation in research on health issues such as heart disease.

As Livingston points out, overdoctoring has been a problem in pregnancy and childbirth. The second reading "Midwives and Women-Centered Care," by midwives Lisa Ross and Linda Cole, suggests an alternative to the illness model. Ross and Cole see labor and birth as usually normal processes requiring minimal medical intervention. Midwives offer care that sees the birthing woman not as a "patient," but rather as a powerful person in charge of her labor and delivery. Ross and Cole claim that the midwife's view of childbirth as a normal and empowering experience has many physical and psychological benefits for both mother and child.

In seeking better health care for women, women's health activists have challenged the medical profession to broaden its definition of what it is to be a human being. As we come to a clearer understanding of how women's bodies are different from men's and begin to see this difference as a normal variation rather than a disease, women's health care improves. Similarly, Deborah Lisi in the final reading "Found Voices: Women, Disability and Cultural Transformation," contends that a clearer understanding of the experiences of disabled women can broaden our view of what it is to be human, and help us embrace difference. For example, disabled women may not fit into stereotypic views of women, and so they have the opportunity to define what it is to be female outside of rigidly defined roles, thus opening up new possibilities for all women. People with disabilities challenge us to be more inclusive of physical and emotional difference.

The readings in this section demonstrate the negative impact that occurs when we set standards for health based solely on the experience of a dominant group (in this case, able-bodied males). If we want a system that provides effective health care for all of us, we must incorporate the experience of all humans into our understanding of health.

Reading 1   How to Think about Women's Health

MARTHA LIVINGSTON

Questions to Consider:

1. According to Livingston, "the conditions of our daily lives shape our health status." What are two conditions of your daily life that shape your health status? Explain.

2. Have you or someone you know had an experience of "overdoctoring"? Describe. Have you or someone you know had an experience of "underdoctoring"? Describe.

3. Should women's health become a new medical specialty? Why or why not?

4. Is the quality of your health care affected by your gender? What changes, if any, would you like to see happen in your health care?

INTRODUCTION

This article couldn't have been written before 1970, because before then, there *was* no field called women's health. There was, to be sure, a medical specialty called obstetrics and gynecology, but that's not the same thing at all. The women's health movement grew out of the women's movement, which itself grew out of the African American freedom (commonly called the "civil rights") movement and the anti–Vietnam War movement, when women activists began to notice that while our typing and coffee-making skills were very much in demand, those leading the charge were almost exclusively male. With the birth of the women's movement, women began to study how we had been systematically oppressed and marginalized, and developed an interest in our treatment and mistreatment by the medical establishment. We began to study our bodies, challenging the medical establishment's

Courtesy of Martha Livingston

view, criticizing patronizing, often inadequate care and risky treatments, demanding a full range of reproductive services including abortion, forming women's health centers throughout North America and developing a wealth of activist research (see, for example, Seaman, 1969; Kushner, 1984). A group of women in Boston worked to produce, in 1971, a newsprint volume called *Our Bodies, Our Selves,* which was run off and distributed by the New England Free Press and sold for 30 cents. This group, the Boston Women's Health Course Collective, later the Boston Women's Health Book Collective, went on to produce *Ourselves and Our Children* (1978), *Ourselves, Growing Older* (Doress-Waters and Siegal, 1987) and a volume for adolescents, *Changing Bodies, Changing Lives* (Bell, 1981). The original book and later editions were snapped up by women and used as texts in emerging women's studies courses. Now called *The New Our Bodies, Our Selves,* the book celebrated its 25th anniversary in 1996. Another group, the Washington-based National Women's Health

Network, began, in 1976, to monitor women's health research and treatment, perform independent research, publish a newsletter and other resource material, and testify about women's health issues. The National Black Women's Health Project grew out of the work of Byllye Avery of the Network, and came into being in 1983 (see, e.g., White, 1994).

The purpose of this article is to provide the reader with a set of tools with which to think about *any* issue in women's health; these concepts include medicalization, social control, the view of our bodies as complicated and problematic, over- and undertreatment, our invisibility in most medical research, and risk-benefit analysis. Also implicit in much of this discussion is the role of the for-profit health care system.

BACKGROUND: THE PUBLIC HEALTH PERSPECTIVE ON HEALTH AND ILLNESS

Before we can understand the major issues in *women's* health, we first need to understand the *public* health perspective. In public health, we say that the conditions of our daily lives shape our health status, and we call those conditions the social determinants of health. These social, economic, and political forces include social class and poverty in an economic system in which there are fewer secure jobs to go around, in which the disparity between rich and poor is larger than it's ever been and larger than it is in any other country on Earth.

Another major determinant is racism, which works in two ways. First, racism denies people of color the same opportunities as white people—to education, appropriate employment, advancement in employment, decent housing, equal access to an equal quality of health care. But even when people of color hold the same kinds of jobs, live in the same kinds of neighborhoods, and have similar educations and similar economic and social resources available to them, the stress related to daily racism results in poorer health for

Americans of color (e.g., Reed, Darity, & Roberson, 1993; Navarro, 1990).

Gender and sexism, of course, have an enormous impact on health; more about that later. Our physical and social environments, what kind of work we do, and what kinds of neighborhoods we live in are important contributors to our health. The American food system, which makes it hard for us to eat healthfully in the midst of an abundant (for some of us) but unhealthy food supply, has enormous health consequences. Our ability to get health care when we need it in a country in which health care is seen as just another commodity to be purchased, rather than as a human right, has a powerful impact on us when we need health care. Our social relationships and social support networks affect our health in numerous ways: We get material help, information, and education, and emotional support from family, friends, government, and organizations. Taken together, these contributors are called the social determinants of health, and define the public health perspective on health and illness.

WOMEN'S HEALTH AND THE SOCIAL CONSTRUCTION OF WOMEN'S ROLES

Of course, the most important determinant of women's health status is our role and position in society, just as it is for men, and this role varies from place to place and time to time. Most obviously, our access to the necessities of life—food, clothing, shelter, education, health care—is produced by our location in society. In some cultures, when food and other resources are scarce, men get them first because they are the breadwinners; little boys, as future breadwinners, come second, mothers are third, and little girls last. Depending on our access to resources, women's lives are either longer or shorter relative to men's (Waldron, 1997; Doyal, 1995). So this undoubtedly *biological* variable, sex, becomes one of the *social* determinants of health, gender. We think of "society" as variable and "biology" as fixed, but since biology doesn't exist in a vacuum, even seemingly unchangeable biological characteristics manifest themselves very differently depending upon the culture in which we live. For example, Hubbard (1990, pp. 125–127) illustrates this point by contrasting North American women's experience of menstruation with that of the !Kung women of the Kalahari Desert in Southern Africa. In North America, due in part to exposure to a diet heavily laden with animal protein and fat, girls begin to menstruate, on average, at 12 or 13. This biological event probably occurred years later in most of our grandmothers, especially those who came from other parts of the world, where menarche occurs at between 16 and 18 years. The typical American woman menstruates for 36 to 40 years, experiencing menopause at 48 to 52. Depending on her childbearing history, the American woman is likely to experience between four and five hundred menstrual cycles. By contrast, the !Kung woman of the Kalahari will experience her first menstruation at 16 to 18 years. She will marry early, and have about five or six children. Each of her children will be completely breastfed for about two years. ("Complete" breastfeeding means feeding on demand around the clock, and not supplementing the breastmilk with other food or drink. This form of breastfeeding inhibits ovulation and is a remarkably effective form of birth control.) The !Kung woman will experience menopause a few years earlier than her North American counterpart, and have had, in her reproductive life, a few dozen, rather than a few hundred, menstrual cycles. However, this is not a "biological difference"; should the !Kung woman move, say, to Johannesburg, and adopt a western-style life and diet, her menstrual cycles will look just like ours.

When we live also shapes our health status. For example, in the United States in the nineteenth-century, a kind of wasting disease affected mainly wealthy women of European descent. This condition was a common result of the use-

less lives these women were expected to lead and the unhealthy, tightly corseted, pale appearance they were expected to cultivate. They were not allowed to pursue careers or higher education, which would detract from the health of their uteri (the uterus was seen as the source of female intelligence at the time, and thus pursuing intellectual interests was seen as draining energy from women's primary function). Women were expected to marry well, bear children but not perform the arduous work of raising them, and run households but not do the actual housework. Many women of this class took to their beds soon after marriage, spending the rest of their lives as invalids, literally wasting away. One such sufferer, Alice James, sister of writer Henry James and psychologist William James, wrote in her diary, upon learning that she had breast cancer, that she was relieved, because her burdensome life would not last much longer (Ehrenreich & English, 1978, p. 94). Of course, women of color and working-class women were not viewed in the same way; although the ideology held that women were delicate creatures, the delicacy of slave women and women working in factories was hardly a concern. The current epidemic of eating disorders, especially among young, upper- and middle-class white women, is another expression of the shaping of our health status by the social roles expected of us.

MEDICALIZATION AND SOCIAL CONTROL

Because women's hormones cycle instead of being emitted at a steady rate (like men's), our bodies are seen as *complicated,* and our bodies' normal physiological functions are *pathologized,* described as conditions requiring expert medical intervention. Doctors then become the experts on normal female physiological functions. This is called *medicalization* and medicalization has transformed normal female life events such as menarche (the onset of menses), birth control, childbirth, and menopause into medical conditions or diseases requiring medical attention. We cede social control of womanly activities to (mostly male) doctors, who make pronouncements on many things about which they know little, such as our sexuality, control of our fertility, our interpersonal relationships, and child rearing.

Medical Education

If medical education were gender-neutral, women's bodies would be seen simply as a variation of the norm. Instead, as one woman doctor put it (Barbara Newman, 1994, personal communication), the human norm is conceptualized, in medical school, as the "70-kilogram white male."

Even our anatomy and physiology—our parts and how they work—are often controversial and poorly researched and understood by the medical profession. Human sexuality researchers claim to have located the Grafenberg ("G") Spot, which has yet to be anatomically identified, and which is said to be one location of female sexual response. The Federation of Feminist Women's Health Centers (1981), long active in women's anatomy and physiology research, contests the standard medical view of the clitoris and includes in its depiction the entire introitus to the vagina, basing its model on research into women's sexual response.

Just how contemptuously the medical system views women's bodies has been well described by two women physicians, Michelle Harrison (1982) and Adriane Fugh-Berman. Fugh-Berman (1992, pp. 1, 54) described viewing her first autopsy as a medical student:

The prevailing attitude toward women was demonstrated on the first day of classes by my anatomy instructor, who remarked that our elderly cadaver "must have been a Playboy bunny" before instructing us to cut off her large breasts and toss them into the thirty-gallon trash can marked "cadaver

waste." Barely hours into our training, we were already being taught that there was nothing to be learned from examining breasts. Given the fact that one out of nine American women will develop breast cancer in her lifetime, to treat breasts as extraneous tissue seemed an appalling waste of an educational opportunity, as well as a not-so-subtle message about the relative importance of body parts.

One doctor drastically expressed his opinion of our female parts: Having decided that Mother Nature had goofed when she placed the clitoris outside the vagina, he "rectified" this mistake when performing other gynecological surgery on his patients, without their knowledge. He called his procedure the "surgery of love," but his patients and the medical board disagreed, and he lost his license ("$5 Million," 1991).

Medical Treatment: (1) Overdoctoring. We find ourselves in a peculiar situation, in which women are simultaneously both overdoctored and underdoctored. Our "female" parts are overtreated, with frequent checkups and monitoring, making women anxious about these "problematic," "complicated" parts and functions, and accepting of medical treatments such as hormone "replacement therapy," hysterectomy, and cesarean section.

Birth is one example. The medicalization of birth can be understood as the mostly male medical profession's takeover of control of the quintessential womanly function (e.g., Rothman, 1982). The medical model of birth views the process as inherently dangerous and life-threatening, requiring medical and often surgical intervention to produce a safe outcome. The smooth physiological progress of birth is so tampered with in the medical model—isolating women from loved ones, starving us during a marathon-like activity, forcing us into bed when we need to be mobile, wiring us up to monitors and IV fluids, drugging us and cutting us—that few of us can produce our babies normally (e.g., Haire, 1972; Mitford, 1992; Wagner, 1994). One result has been, in the United States, a leap in the rate of cesarean section from 5.5 percent of all births in 1970 to 24 percent today (Centers for Disease Control and Prevention, 1993), with a three- to fourfold increase in maternal mortality, and no benefit to the newborn. This high-tech interference in birth is also enormously expensive. But it didn't stop a prominent gynecologist (Feldman and Freiman, 1985) from calling, in a major medical journal, for "prophylactic cesarean at term," for *all* babies to be delivered by cesarean, on the assumption that women's problematic bodies often fail us during labor in unanticipated ways. Out of this misunderstanding of the normal physiology of birth, and the consequent rampant mistreatment of birthing women, grew the modern childbirth reform movement, with its interest in promoting normal birth attended by midwives, a profession largely suppressed by the medical establishment in the United States during the early part of the twentieth century but now once again on the rise (e.g., Edwards & Waldorf, 1984; Livingston, 1987; Wertz & Wertz, 1989).

Our "problematic" parts are often removed for little reason, or when less drastic medical treatments are available. It has been estimated, for example, that from 35 percent to 90 percent of the more than half a million hysterectomies performed each year in the United States are unnecessary (Angier, 1997; Hufnagel & Golant, 1989; Strausz, 1993; West & Dranov, 1994). The dominant late-twentieth-century medical view of the uterus-as-baby-carriage suggests that we need our uteri only for childbearing; a common saying about hysterectomy is that doctors "take out the baby carriage but leave the playpen behind" [Hufnagel, 1989, p. 81]. The long-term health effects of *not* having a uterus have been poorly or not at all documented, and include loss of sexual response, depression, and chronic fatigue. Many women undergoing hysterectomy are counseled to have their ovaries, healthy though they may be,

removed at the same time, with the rationale that if you don't have ovaries, you can't get ovarian cancer. Removal of the uterus and both ovaries, with the consequent drastic plunge in hormone secretion, results in immediate surgical menopause, and the most dramatic menopausal symptoms. But since the hormone-regulating function of the ovaries can seemingly be supplied by hormone pills, no further thought is given to the problem, and long-term risks of hormone supplementation are downplayed. A commonly heard medical expression is, "No ovary is good enough to leave in; no testicle is bad enough to take out."

Menopause itself has become a major growth industry (Coney, 1994; National Women's Health Network, 1995), with artificial hormones among the best-selling pharmaceuticals. Rather than being celebrated as a major turning point in women's lives as it is in many cultures, the normal female aging process and end of the childbearing years are described in uniformly depressing terms as a "condition" that modern pharmacology can "treat." Robert A. Wilson (Coney, 1994, p. 69), the gynecologist who first developed hormone "replacement," described postmenopausal women as being in a state of "living decay." Although it is likely that fewer than 10 percent of menopausal women have symptoms serious enough to warrant medical and pharmaceutical intervention, the vast majority of us are offered artificial hormones as a treatment for our "condition." One difficulty is that of the clinical *versus* random sample, gynecologists' waiting rooms may be filled with menopausal women in distress seeking medical relief. So these doctors mistakenly project their daily work experience onto the majority of the menopausal population, assuming that all menopausal women are in distress. The clinical sample—women seeking medical help—does not, however, reflect the population as a whole. But these days, getting through menopause *without* taking hormones is now seen as the "alternative!" (see, e.g., Greenwood, 1989).

Medical Treatment: (2) Underdoctoring.
Paradoxically, the rest of our bodies is *under-treated*: Women have to be a lot sicker than men for similar conditions, such as heart problems, to be taken seriously (e.g., Iezzoni, Ash, Shwartz and Mackiernan, 1997; Altman, 1991; Saslow, 1992; Nechas and Foley, 1994). First, it is presumed that women rush to their caregivers with trivial complaints, while macho men who present for treatment must *really* be sick. Then, the symptoms that sick women present with when they seek medical attention are not as well known and catalogued as those of men, since little medical research has included women, and this results in slower or more often incorrect diagnosis. For example, since AIDS was first seen as a gay male disease, the conditions that women living with HIV and AIDS present with are less well known than they should be, and the Centers for Disease Control has still not listed many of these conditions as "AIDS-defining." As a result, many living women are never diagnosed with AIDS, but AIDS is discovered on autopsy (ACT UP/ New York Women and AIDS Book Group, 1990). Women presenting with symptoms of heart disease identical to men's are far less likely to be given the same diagnostic tests, and the tests themselves, not having been designed for women, are not as useful, and are sometimes misleading (e.g., Altman, 1991; Heart, 1992; Laurence & Weinhouse, 1994; Nechas & Foley, 1994). Dr. Robert Bonow of the National Heart, Lung and Blood Institute blamed women's anatomy: "breast tissue can interfere with tests that produce images of the heart, limiting their usefulness" [Altman, 1991, p. C8]. Many women having heart attacks present with "atypical" symptoms (Laurence & Weinhouse, 1994, p. 97): "Of course the term *atypical* is used because "typical" heart attack pain is that experienced by the majority of people who take part in medical studies: middle-aged white men." Women have also been known to discount the pain they feel during heart attacks, because it doesn't rival the pain they remember having experienced during childbirth.

Medical Research. Why are women under-treated or inappropriately treated? Because most medical research has not been done on women (Dresser, 1992). Astonishingly, even a recent Rockefeller University study (reported in Nechas & Foley, 1994, p. 22) of the relationship of obesity to breast and cervical cancer was conducted entirely on men! Why has this exclusion of women from medical research continued for so long? For one thing, our "complicated" cycling hormones, instead of being viewed simply as a variation of the norm, are seen as "confounding variables" in research on drug effects. We are, however, routinely given treatments and pharmaceuticals by doctors who can have no idea how, or whether, they work in women.

Another concern is the potential risk of testing experimental treatments on women who *might* be pregnant, especially because the worst teratogenic (birth-defect-causing) effects on fetuses occur early in pregnancy, before many women know they're pregnant. Researchers can surely figure out how to confirm or eliminate the possibility of pregnancy before including women of childbearing age in their studies. At issue is their mistrust of women subjects' agreement to remain nonpregnant for the duration of the study, and their fear of lawsuits for damaged fetuses. One problem relating to pregnancy is, of course, what women can do who become ill, and require medical treatment, during pregnancy. Since most drugs have not been tested on *any* women, much less on pregnant women, doctors are loath to offer them to pregnant women. Some women discover life-threatening conditions during pregnancy, and are confronted with life-or-death decisions: Undergo treatment and continue with the pregnancy, risking serious harm or death to the fetus; refrain from treatment until after the birth, risking serious harm or death to themselves; or terminate the pregnancy in order to undergo treatment.

Another major reason that women have been excluded from most medical research, and that women's health issues have not been studied, is that women, by and large, were not doing the research. Science research agendas are set by science researchers, and if they're all straight white men, issues of importance to women, people of color, gays, and lesbians will not likely be accorded the research attention they need. As former U.S. Congresswoman Pat Schroeder said, "You fund what you fear. They do not fear breast cancer, and they do not fear you" [Nechas & Foley, p. 71]. Research questions don't drop from the sky; they come from our life experiences. As women are increasingly able to conduct research, through increased opportunities for higher education, and appropriate levels of research funding, more women's health research will be carried out. Certainly, numerous women's health issues demanding more research attention have already been identified (e.g., Roberts, 1990, 1992; Nechas & Foley, 1994), but the research infrastructure is hardly in place. The National Institutes of Health, responding to demands from women's health researchers and activists, established the Office of Women's Health in 1990 and funded the Women's Health Initiative (Herman, 1994), and now screens all research proposals for inclusion of women subjects. But funding parity remains a distant goal.

In recent years, responding to the ongoing neglect of women's health issues by the medical establishment, women's health activists and experts have discussed the possibility of designating women's health a new medical specialty. Those in favor see a specialty designation as bringing new resources and energy to a sadly neglected field. Those opposed feel that the health concerns of half the species should not be "ghettoized" into one specialty, that *all* doctors and medical researchers must be knowledgeable about women's health matters (e.g., Harrison, 1994).

The women's health field started as a grassroots movement, and to this day, as much as in any area in health, the women's health research agenda has been shaped and informed by grassroots activists. Brown (1993) has examined the role of grassroots activism in identifying environmental hazards, and his model applies very well to women's health research. Brown describes how grassroots people identify a problem, their interaction and confrontation with public and private officials, and the difficulty, for laypeople, of producing sufficiently "scientific" data to prove their case. From breast cancer to AIDS, from abortion and reproductive rights to the conduct of hospital birth, women angry at our mistreatment at the hands of medical professionals or exclusion from the research agenda have petitioned, campaigned, demonstrated, and lobbied our needs and demands onto the health care bargaining table. Since we don't yet control the funding decisions, getting funding for research, and attention to our concerns in clinical medicine, is an ongoing struggle.

CONCLUSION

Our experience in the women's health movement has taught us that we can't ever let up. Merely exposing a problem isn't enough; the "manufacturers of illness," those forces who benefit from the status quo, have a disproportionate amount of power in getting the system to work for them. And just when we think we've beaten one problem, another crops up. Diethylstilbestrol (DES), an antinausea and antimiscarriage drug given to women in the 1950s and 60s, resulted in reproductive anomalies and cancers in their children, and getting it recognized, and victims compensated, has been a lengthy battle. Some would say, about a dangerous drug from twenty or thirty years ago, "that was then, this is now." But we are daily confronted with new drugs and treatments enthusiastically offered, with the same minimizing of risks, by the medical profession. One current example is the routine use of ultrasound in pregnancy. Useful in diagnosing fetal anomalies and multiple births, and in locating the fetus during amniocentesis, it is now being used routinely in pregnancy. Many women even have several routine ultrasound screenings during pregnancy. While there is no evidence of long-term effects in humans, early data indicated DNA effects in mice exposed to ultrasound in utero (Liebeskind et al., 1979). Will ultrasound be this generation's DES? And what about the routine use of electronic fetal monitoring during hospital birth? Originally developed for use in labors with fragile, preterm babies, it quickly became part of the routine standard of care in labor, though no data ever supported any advantage to either mother or baby. Even fragile babies have never been shown, after twenty years of routine use, to benefit from monitoring (Grant, 1989). Yet fetal monitoring, associated with the astronomical rise in cesarean section from 1970 to the present, continues to be used routinely. Menopause-related drugs are marketed enthusiastically regardless of evidence of, or lack of data on, long-term risks. For example, a brand-new drug, Fosamax, which restores bone mass in patients with osteoporosis, has been promoted as a *preventive* measure, without the slightest evidence that it has any such effect (Zones, 1996).

We need in each instance to employ a *risk-benefit analysis* to any proposed medical treatment: Do the benefits outweigh the risks? If there *is* no benefit, as in the case of electronic fetal monitoring, any risk at all is unacceptable. Sometimes the choice is simple, especially when we are educated about treatment options, but not always; one case in point is the recent nationwide uproar over whether, and at what age, women should get mammograms. Most data show that for the population as a whole, mammography screening becomes useful at around age 50, in that it starts to make a real difference in the number of lives saved by early detection. But many feel that age 40 should be the starting point. And some feel (e.g., Wright & Mueller, 1995) that mammography screening is *never* useful for the population as

a whole. What should women over 40 do? The federal government, aware of the controversy, called a 35-member expert panel together in 1996 to review the scientific evidence. The panel was so divided that their recommendation to the women of the United States was: Here are the risks and benefits. Make up your own minds on a case-by-case basis. Meanwhile, the federal government is moving to ensure that insurance companies don't deny mammography coverage to women in their 40s (Kolata, 1997).

I hope that this brief introduction will arm readers with an understanding of the issues involved in thinking about *any* women's health issue. Our place in society, the prevailing view of our bodies as complicated and pathological, the medicalization of normal physiological and life events and marketing of procedures and products to "fix" our "problematic" bodies, the over- and undertreatment of our health problems, the dearth of good medical research and education about women's health, and the need for every woman to understand her treatment options and the risks and benefits inherent in them: These are the tools we need to think about women's health.

REFERENCES

ACT UP/New York Women and AIDS Book Group. (1990). *Women, AIDS and Activism.* Boston: South End Press.

Altman, L. K. (1991, 6 Aug.). "Men, women and heart disease: More than a question of sexism." *The New York Times,* pp. C1, C8.

Angier, N. (1997, 17 Feb.). "In a culture of hysterectomies, many question their necessity." *The New York Times,* pp. 1, 14.

Bell, R. (1981, 1987). *Changing Bodies, Changing Lives.* New York: Random House/Vintage.

Boston Women's Health Course Collective. (1970). *Our Bodies, Our Selves: A Course by and for Women.* Boston: New England Free Press.

Boston Women's Health Book Collective. (1992). *The New Our Bodies, Our Selves.* New York: Simon & Schuster/Touchstone.

Brown, P. (1993). "When the public knows better: Popular epidemiology." *Environment,* 35, pp. 16–20, 32–41.

Centers for Disease Control and Prevention. (1993). "Rates of cesarean delivery: United States, 1991." *Morbidity and Mortality Weekly Report,* 42, pp. 285–289.

Coney, S. (1994). *The Menopause Industry: How the Medical Establishment Exploits Women.* Alameda, CA: Hunter House.

Doress-Waters, P. B., and Siegal, D. L. (1987) *Ourselves, Growing Older.* New York: Simon & Schuster/Touchstone.

Doress-Waters, P. B., and Siegal, D. L. (1994). *The New Ourselves, Growing Older.* New York: Simon & Schuster/Touchstone.

Doyal, L. (1995). *What Makes Women Sick.* New Brunswick, NJ: Rutgers University Press.

Dresser, R. (1992). Wanted: Single, White Male for Medical Research. *Hastings Center Report,* 22, pp. 24–29.

Edwards, M., and Waldorf, M. (1984). *Reclaiming Birth: History and Heroines of American Childbirth Reform.* Trumansburg, NY: The Crossing Press.

Ehrenreich, B., and English, D. (1978). *For Her Own Good: 150 Years of the Experts' Advice to Women.* Garden City, NY: Doubleday/Anchor.

Federation of Feminist Women's Health Centers. (1981). *How to Stay Out of the Gynecologist's Office.* Culver City, CA: Women to Women Publications.

Feldman, G. B., and Freiman, J. A. (1985). "Prophylactic cesarean at term." *New England Journal of Medicine,* 312, pp. 1264–1267.

"$5 Million awarded to woman who said doctor maimed her." (1991, 22 June). *The New York Times,* p. 9.

Fugh-Berman, A. (1992, 20 Jan.) "Tales out of medical school." *The Nation,* pp. 1, 54–56.

Grant, A. (1989). "Monitoring the fetus during labour." In I. Chalmers, M. Enkin, and M. Keirse (Eds.), *Effective Care in Pregnancy and Childbirth,* Vol. 2. Oxford: Clarendon Press.

Greenwood, S. (1989). *Menopause, Naturally.* Volcano, CA: Volcano Press.

Haire, D. B. (1972). "The cultural warping of childbirth." *ICEA News,* Spring; reprinted in *Environmental Child Health,* 19 (1973), pp. 171–191.

Harrison, B. G. (1994). "Why I don't feel so good about women's medicine." In K. M. Hicks (Ed.), *Misdiagnosis: Woman as a Disease.* Allentown, PA: People's Medical Society, pp. 209–214.

Harrison, M. (1982). *A Woman in Residence.* New York: Random House.

"Heart Drug Response in Women." (1992, 1 July). *The New York Times,* p. C12.

Herman, R. (1994). "What doctors don't know about women." In K. M. Hicks (Ed.), *Misdiagnosis: Woman as a Disease.* Allentown, PA: People's Medical Society, pp. 33–42.

Hubbard, R. (1990). *The Politics of Women's Biology.* New Brunswick, NJ: Rutgers University Press.

Hufnagel, V., and Golant, S. K. (1989). *No More Hysterectomies.* New York: Penguin/Plume.

Iezzoni, L. I., Ash, A. S., Shwartz, M., and Mackieman, Y. D. (1997). "Differences in procedure use, in-hospital mortality, and illness severity by gender for acute myocardial infarction patients." *Medical Care,* 35(2), pp. 158–171.

Kolata, G. (1997, 28 Jan.). "Stand on mammograms greeted by outrage." *The New York Times,* pp. C1, C8.

Kushner, R. (1984). *Alternatives: New Developments in the War on Breast Cancer.* New York: Warner.

Laurence, L., and Weinhouse, B. (1994). *Outrageous Practices: How Gender Bias Threatens Women's Health.* New Brunswick, NJ: Rutgers University Press.

Liebeskind, D., et al. (1981). "Morphological changes in the surface characteristics of cultured cells after exposure to diagnostic ultrasound." *Radiology,* 138, pp. 419–423.

Livingston, M. (1987). "Choice in childbirth: Power and the impact of the modern childbirth reform movement." *Women and Therapy,* 6, pp. 239–261.

Mitford, J. (1992). *The American Way of Birth.* New York: Dutton.

National Women's Health Network. (1995). *Taking Hormones and Women's Health: Choices, Risks and Benefits.* Washington, DC: National Women's Health Network.

Navarro, V. (1990). "Race or class or race and class: Mortality differentials in the United States." *The Lancet,* 336, pp. 1238–1240.

Nechas, F., and Foley, D. (1994). *Unequal Treatment: What You Don't Know and How Women Are Mis-*

treated by the Medical Community. New York: Simon & Schuster.

Reed, W. L., Darity, W., and Roberson, L. (1993). *Health and Medical Care of African-Americans.* Westport, CT: Auburn House.

Roberts, H. (Ed.). (1990). *Women's Health Counts.* London and New York: Routledge.

Roberts, H. (Ed.). (1992). *Women's Health Matters.* London and New York: Routledge.

Rothman, B. K. (1982). *In Labor: Women and Power in the Birthplace.* New York/London: W. W. Norton & Co.

Saslow, L. (1992, 10 May). "Women cautioned on heart disease." *The New York Times,* p. 7, L.I.

Seaman, B. (1969). *The Doctors' Case against the Pill.* New York: Avon.

Strausz, I. K. (1993). *You Don't Need a Hysterectomy.* Reading, MA: Addison-Wesley.

Wagner, M. (1994). *Pursuing the Birth Machine.* Camperdown, Australia: Ace Graphics.

Waldron, I. (1997). "What do we know about causes of sex differences in mortality?" In Conrad, P. (Ed.), *The Sociology of Health and Illness,* 5th ed. New York: St. Martin's Press, pp. 42–55.

Wertz, R. W., and Wertz, D. C. (1989). *Lying-In: A History of Childbirth in America.* New Haven: Yale University Press.

West, S., and Dranov, P. (1994). *The Hysterectomy Hoax.* New York: Doubleday.

White, E. (1995). *The Black Women's Health Book.* Seattle, WA: Seal Press.

Wright, C. J., and Mueller, C. B. (1995). "Screening mammography and public health policy: The need for perspective." *The Lancet,* 346, pp. 29–32.

Zones, J. S. (1996, 18 Nov.). "The new fountain of youth? Estrogen, synapses and secretions." Paper presented at the annual meeting of the American Public Health Association, New York.

Reading 2   Midwives and Women-Centered Care

LISA ROSS AND LINDA COLE

Questions to Consider:

1. According to Ross and Cole, how is a midwife's approach to childbirth different from that of an obstetrician? In what ways is it the same?

2. How is birth a powerful experience for women?

3. If you or your partner were to give birth, would you choose to use a midwife? Why or why not?

INTRODUCTION

Midwife is a Middle English word: *mid*-with and *wife*-woman, meaning one who brings forth by assisting women in childbirth. The World Health Organization (WHO) defines midwife as: "a person who, having been regularly admitted to a midwifery educational program fully recognized in the country in which it is located, has successfully completed the prescribed course of studies in midwifery and has acquired the requisite qualifications to be registered and/or legally licensed to practice midwifery. She must be able to give the necessary supervision, care, and advice to women during pregnancy, labor, and the postpartum period, to conduct deliveries on her own responsibility, and to care for the newborn and infant. This care includes preventive measures, the detection of abnormal conditions in mother and child, the procurement of medical assistance, and the execution of emergency measures in the absence of medical help. She has an important task in counseling and education, not only for patients, but

also within the family and community. The work should involve antenatal education and preparation for parenthood and extends to certain areas of gynecology, family planning, and childcare. She may practice in hospitals, clinics, health units, domiciliary conditions or any other service." The American College of Nurse-Midwives (ACNM), the professional organization representing Certified Nurse-Midwives (CNMS), defines CNM as: "an individual educated in the two disciplines of nursing and midwifery, who possesses evidence of certification according to the requirements of the ACNM." Another major midwifery organization in North America, the Midwives Alliance of North America (MANA), uses a slightly altered version of the WHO definition.

The work of midwives always includes care during the maternity cycle. Many midwives also provide well-woman gynecology services including annual physical examinations, pap smears, contraceptive management, perimenopausal care, and treatment of minor problems such as vaginal or urinary tract infections. The scope of midwives' practice depends largely on the norms of the country where they practice, the birth site in

Courtesy of Lisa Ross and Linda Cole

254

which they attend deliveries, and their access to, and relationship with, consulting physicians. In the United States, the majority of midwives confine their practice to the maternity and gynecologic care of essentially healthy women and newborns. Those with clinical hospital privileges often continue to care for women at higher risk during labor and delivery in collaboration with physician consultants. Worldwide, midwives attend births both in hospital and in out-of-hospital settings such as birth centers or clients' homes.

Traditional midwives were mature women who apprenticed with an experienced midwife. Their practice usually included comprehensive healing using herbs and other treatments and "laying out" the dead in addition to attending women in childbirth. There are few of these "Granny Midwives" remaining in the United States. Unlike most industrialized nations, which have clear definitions of what constitutes a midwife, what her independent scope of practice encompasses, and what her role is within the overall system of health care, the United States' recognition of midwives is fragmented and confusing. Legal authority to practice varies widely among states, some of which retain antiquated laws allowing the practice of midwifery with no standards of education or licensure. Others have regulated midwifery practice in minute detail, describing precisely what midwives may and may not do.

There are currently two organizations representing midwives in this country. Both the ACNM and MANA define educational requirements and certification procedures. All states now legally recognize the CNM, who must first be a registered nurse, complete an accredited program of education, and pass a national certification examination. Several states have begun to recognize the legal right to practice of midwives certified by the North American Registry of Midwives (NARM), the certification arm of MANA. Qualifications do not include a nursing degree, allow a variety of educational pathways including apprenticeship

and self-study as well as formal institutional programs, and assess competency by way of documented clinical experience, mastery of a set of clinical skills, and passing a certification examination. Those meeting the criteria are entitled to be called Certified Professional Midwife (CPM). This certification was developed to lend credibility and standardization for those midwives who choose a route to professional practice without a nursing prerequisite. There are also many midwives who practice without any formal certification, alternately known as "lay," "empirical," or "traditional" midwives. Many of these resist any form of certification as elitist, and fear that it might compromise their freedom to practice as they see fit.

Legal sanction or prohibition of these different types of practitioner varies by state, as does their access to the mainstream physician-dominated health care system. While lay midwives have almost complete autonomy, they are often shunned by the medical community, limiting their access to needed diagnostic procedures and pharmacological treatments as well as hospital and physician backup for complications. States recognizing the CPM title usually limit the scope of practice to the maternity cycle, and deny eligibility for hospital privileges and prescriptive authority. CNMs have the advantage of being universally recognized, but the requirement for formal physician "supervision" of practice confines CNMs to a dependent role. Consumers face the issues of flexibility of the individual midwife's criteria for acceptance into care, which birth sites she utilizes and the options possible in each, comparable fees and eligibility for third-party reimbursement, documentation of a standard level of competency, and the practitioner's carriage of professional liability insurance. The midwives themselves face serious choices about their level of independence and access to medical assistance when needed. The Carnegie Foundation funded an Interorganizational Work Group between ACNM and MANA to collaborate on standards of education and practice, to increase the supply of professional midwives, and to help balance the ratio of midwives to obstetricians in the United States to more accurately reflect the ratio of normal to complicated births. Despite consensus on many issues such as necessary skills, standards of care, and the need for practice guidelines, the two organizations could not agree on acceptable educational pathways. Although formal meetings have ceased, the ACNM has made a commitment to developing and accrediting non–nurse certified midwife educational programs, and MANA continues to pursue legal recognition of their certification process. There is hope in both groups for continued communication and cooperation with the goal of increasing the viability of midwifery as a profession.

Several major challenges face American professional midwives. Those certified by MANA/NARM continue to struggle for legal status in most states; in some they remain vulnerable to arrest for practicing medicine without a license. While some have been fortunate to find supportive obstetrical backup for complications, others may be forced out of the loop of care if referral to a physician or hospital is necessary. Nurse-midwives are legally perceived as nurses, and as such, are always dependent upon formal, written arrangements with physicians for consultation and referral. They must confine their scope of practice to what the obstetric community defines as low-risk and appropriate for midwifery care. To further challenge CNMs, hospitals in most states "may" grant hospital practice privileges, but rarely "must" admit midwives to their list of credentialed providers. This can be highly political, and communities with limited markets and an abundance of providers are often averse to the idea of increasing competition for clients. Most hospitals granting midwives privileges do so under the medical assistant or associate category, which requires that they admit patients under the physician's name and are strictly limited to performing procedures

approved by the OB/GYN Committee and Medical Board. They rarely have voting rights or the assurance offered to the medical staff for equitable treatment on issues such as granting, denial, or revocation of clinical privileges. In some states, CNMs have little or no prescriptive authority, limiting pharmacologial treatment of many commonly occurring problems. Third-party payment may be withheld altogether, particularly in managed care plans with defined provider panels. Even when payment is available, it is often at a lower rate than for obstetricians for identical services. CNMs in most states are supervised either by the Board of Nursing or the Board of Medical Examiners, neither of whom are peers. All of these factors combine to make it extremely difficult for CNMs to form private practices, usually relegating them to being employees of health facilities or physicians.

In stark contrast, England passed the Midwives Act of 1951, making clear that those becoming midwives post–nursing education and those attending direct-entry programs were comparable in preparation, competence, and professional stature. State Certified Midwives (SCMs) are defined as independent practitioners within the scope of normal maternity care, and as such are accepted members of the health care system with access to practice at home and in hospital with the guarantee of medical support as necessary. SCMs attend over 75 percent of deliveries in Great Britain. The United States, alone among the world's nations, has no national definition of a midwife, no clear role for them within the health care system, and no expectation that they will function as the primary maternity care giver for the majority of pregnant women. This problem not only causes confusion in the minds of consumers and a lack of confidence in midwives as highly skilled professionals, but also creates territorial conflict among midwives themselves. Insight into the historical development of childbirth and midwifery in America should help to clarify the basis for this anomalous situation.

HISTORY OF MIDWIFERY IN AMERICA

The first American midwives were undoubtedly Native American women. Unfortunately, little written history remains to detail their work. There is, however, bountiful documented evidence of colonial-period midwifery in town records of the mid-seventeenth century. The English practice of considering midwives under the control of religious leaders was continued in the colonies. An obsession with the practice of witchcraft at that time dominated the requirements for the practice of midwifery. Civil licensing in the colonies required midwives to take an oath promising to attend all women regardless of ability to pay, not to cause abortion through medication or other acts, and not to practice magic or witchcraft. They were also required to administer baptismal rights in emergency situations. Midwives were accorded considerable social and civic stature, and many communities supplied stipends and other support to ensure their ability to attend any woman in need. No formal training was required, and midwives apprenticed to learn their art. Only anecdotal evidence is available to document the outcomes of their practice. Poor outcomes, especially the birth of deformed or stillborn infants, were often attributed to witchcraft. The "guilty" midwives were sometimes enjoined from practice, sometimes actually prosecuted for dealing in magic.

By the middle 1700s, American medicine, including midwifery, began to be strongly influenced by European advances in knowledge of anatomy and physiology and new medical techniques. The trend of the wealthy being attended in birth by formally educated physicians slowly crossed the Atlantic, and traditional midwifery began to die. Midwives, as women, had little social status or power, were not given access to formal education in the burgeoning sciences, and failed to organize themselves into guilds to protect their vocation and standards. The middle and upper classes largely ceased to utilize midwives by the nineteenth century; those able to afford the services of educated physicians preferring what they believed to be the safer, more prestigious care of doctors. Concomitantly, large numbers of distinct ethnic groups began to immigrate to America. These groups, as well as isolated rural women and the urban poor, continued to seek the services of midwives.

Around 1800, physicians began to lobby for licensure laws restricting the practice of medicine to those who had received professional training. Several groups of alternative practitioners existed at the time, including botanists, homeopaths, eclectics, and hydrotherapists in addition to "regular" allopathic doctors. There was little control over standards of medical education until 1910, when the Flexner Report was issued. This report exposed the lack of standardization and the poor quality of medical education in most proprietary schools, and encouraged accreditation and regulation of medical education and licensure. Attending births became an area of intense competition as it was perceived to be the route of entry into sustained family practice.

As women were excluded from admission to regular schools of medicine, not only were midwives being forced out of practice, but women were effectively barred from any respectable, licensed practice of medical arts and sciences. The developing profession of nursing was assumed to be the proper place of women in the health sciences. Unlike Europe, where midwifery continued to have a respected place in the provision of maternity care, American development of medical education largely disenfranchised women as providers of health care. The profound effect of the exclusion of women from obstetric practice resulted in a sexist bias that remains today. Although more than half the doctors entering obstetric residency programs today are women, the Victorian assumptions prevail that women are weak and incapable and the process of childbirth is in need of medical intervention.

Investigation into the outcomes of maternity care, specifically maternal and infant mortality, began in the early twentieth century in the United States. Although there was little objective evidence that licensed physicians had superior outcomes, blaming "ignorant, incompetent" midwives for poor statistics became popular. Scientifically, it is far more likely that poor overall health status, lack of public health measures, inability to prevent or manage infection and hemorrhage, and the practice of limiting maternity care to the intrapartum and postpartum phases contributed much more to the alarmingly high maternal and infant death rates. Still, many states outlawed midwifery, and few of those in power saw the need for education programs for midwives. After educating midwives since 1911, the Bellevue School of Midwifery in New York City was closed because the Commissioner of Hospitals, a physician, felt midwives were no longer necessary. America lacked any widespread educational programs for midwives for many years. The Sheppard-Towner Act, passed in 1921, allocated federal funds to the improvement of maternal-child health, including the provision that public health nurses should educate and oversee the practice of lay midwives. In 1925, Mary Breckenridge, an American nurse trained in England, brought the first practice of nurse-midwifery to America. She established the Frontier Nursing Service in a remote Kentucky mining community. British-trained midwives brought professional care to mothers and babies who previously had no access, and the result was dramatically improved outcomes among some of the country's most socioeconomically disadvantaged people. The advent of the Second World War made English training impossible, and the Frontier Graduate School of Midwifery was opened in 1939. The Lobenstein Midwifery School, a creation of the Maternity Center Association (MCA) in New York, opened in 1932. The Maternity Center Association, founded in 1918, is a nonprofit health agency dedicated to the improvement of maternity and infant care. The MCA's ongoing mission is to promote safe,

affordable, family-centered maternity care through demonstration projects, educational programs, and advocacy, according to Kassabain (1995). This school educated public health nurses in midwifery and remains open today under the aegis of the State University of New York. These two schools educated all of American nurse-midwives until the mid-forties, and fewer than 10 programs existed at any one time until the late sixties. Accredited programs, largely housed in university colleges of nursing, currently number forty-seven. Until the 1970s, nurse-midwives were largely unable to clinically practice their profession and were mostly employed as nursing supervisors, administrators, educators, and public health consultants.

Many social developments in the seventies influenced the growth of nurse-midwifery education and clinical practice. Large-scale involvement in the women's movement gave women the impetus to assume control over their own lives, including their health care. Public outcry about male dominance of women's reproductive functions became common. This manifested in concern about reproductive freedom, the mystification and medicalization of childbirth, and women's lack of power in decisions relating to their own bodies. The advantages of natural or prepared childbirth and breastfeeding started to gain widespread interest. Counterculture living arrangements and mores, coupled with a belief that the medicalization of childbirth was not only unnecessary, but potentially physically and psychologically harmful, led to a resurgence of homebirth. Books such as *Our Bodies, Our Selves* shared both factual knowledge and an ethic of empowerment for women to control their own health care. Lay midwives, a few physicians, and CNMs began to attend homebirths in significant numbers for the first time since the mid 1930s, when childbirth had become an almost exclusively hospital domain.

Simultaneously, official recognition of nurse-midwives as an accepted part of the health care team was issued in a joint statement by the American College of Obstetricians and Gynecologists (ACOG), the Nurse Association of ACOG (NAACOG) and the ACNM in 1971. A perceived shortage of medical personnel practicing obstetrics further enhanced the growth of nurse-midwifery educational programs. Federally funded programs to improve maternal-child health status, such as the Indian Health Service and Maternal Infant Care Projects, began to rely heavily on CNMs to provide care for underserved populations. CNMs also began to be associates in private medical practices.

By the late seventies, a strong consumer movement toward humanization of the birth process was underway. Well-educated women began to demand alternatives to standard obstetric care, and increasing numbers sought the services of midwives. Nurse-midwives became leaders in the promotion of family-centered maternity care in hospitals, and, with the MCA, opened the first freestanding birth center in New York in 1975. While some CNMs had home-birth practices, this remained largely the province of midwives outside the medical system. Official opposition to birth outside the hospital was voiced by ACOG, and some physicians cited home birth as child abuse despite any objective evidence that it resulted in poor outcomes.

Although few in number and relatively powerless within organized medicine, midwives of all educational backgrounds have continued their commitment to work toward improved maternity care. Freestanding birth centers have proliferated, have documented excellent outcomes with well-controlled prospective studies, and are gaining recognition as a safe, cost-effective and consumer-satisfying alternative to routine hospital obstetric care. Home birth continues to have a small, but stable group of both providers and consumers. The numbers of midwives have increased, as has their voice in public policy and planning. Documentation of their excellent perinatal outcomes by the Public Citizen's Health Research Group has been widely disseminated, and policy makers have been urged to increase their utilization.

MIDWIFERY AND OBSTETRICS

Midwifery and obstetrics are very separate professions, sharing some knowledge, but differing in their basic philosophical beliefs and styles of practice. Obstetrics views women's health care and birthing from the perspective of the medical, or illness model, whereas midwifery promotes the social, or wellness model of caring for the whole woman and her family. Doctors tend to see labor and birth as something that happens to women, when, as women, midwives know that giving birth is something a woman does.

Within the medical model of birth, one views birth from a problem or risk perspective, ever vigilant for that subtle sign that would validate the need for technology, medicine, and surgery. Conversely, midwives believe that, in most cases, labor and birth progress normally without interference. Women who choose to give birth in hospitals with obstetric providers are more often than not subjected to the use of routine intervention in the normal birth process. These interventions include continuous electronic fetal monitoring (EFM); mandatory bedrest; intravenous fluid administration and withholding of food and liquids by mouth; epidural anesthesia; use of oxytocin, a potent medication which strengthens uterine contractions; artificial rupture of the amniotic fluid sack; and the cutting of an episiotomy—the surgical enlargement of the vaginal opening. Conversely, midwives find in their black bags not the means to intervene in birth, rather the tools to support women through this powerful journey. They do not adhere to any routine treatment of women during pregnancy and birth, but believe strongly that care must be administered individually for each woman, taking into account her values and life factors.

A midwife's most important and effective tool is the relationship she forms with her client, one of open communication and trust. A midwife views herself not as the harborer of all knowledge and decision-making power, but enters into a partnership with the woman and her family throughout the pregnancy and birth. Shared knowledge and informed choice making are of primary importance to both midwife and client.

Constant attendance during active labor and birth enables the midwife to offer encouragement when needed, use position changes creatively, promote walking and drinking, and touch the woman in ways that are relaxing and give the assurance of support. Other tools in her repertoire include hydrotherapy, or the use of water for labor and birth, facilitation of alternative positions for labor and birth, perineal support and massage to avoid lacerations or episiotomy, assisting women or their partners to "deliver" the baby themselves, and early promotion of family bonding and breastfeeding.

Midwives and obstetricians share concern for the health and safety of the woman and her child during pregnancy and birth, but approach their goal from widely divergent philosophies. Midwives are woman-centered providers, whereas obstetricians tend to be problem-, or disease-centered providers. For many women, finding a female provider leads them into their search for a midwife, although male midwives also exist, and comprise 4 percent of the membership of the ACNM. One might wonder, with 50 percent of students entering medical school being women, why a woman would not choose a female obstetrician as her provider. It is often only after a woman has experienced her first obstetrical hospital delivery that she questions the nature of the care she received, and realizes that her care was influenced not so much by gender as by philosophy. In the changing medical environment in our country, which is becoming ever more complex and disorganized, midwives offer the best option for providing excellent woman-centered care for most women.

MIDWIFERY IN THE CURRENT HEALTH CARE ARENA

That the American system of health care is in a state of crisis has been proclaimed since the mid-1980s. Staunch opposition to a single-payer system, that is, nationalized health care, has been mounted by the insurance industry, organized medicine, and the major political parties. Fear of any organization of the health system that smacks of socialized medicine runs deep in the United States. The public fears both the lack of choice of providers and the rationing of services. The health insurance companies are unwilling to compromise their profit margin, much less their existence. The government fears an uncontrollable increase in expenditures similar to what it encountered with the Medicare and Medicaid entitlement programs, as well as blame if highly technical and exorbitantly priced procedures must be rationed. Physicians are reluctant to support any measures that might limit either their autonomy or income maintenance.

The temporary compromise is "managed care" in which the government largely abdicates responsibility, and delegates management of the system to the third-party insurance carriers. Thus far, private practice physicians retain a large degree of control over accepting clients with various sources of payment. They generally are able to limit their caseload to a clientele whose carriers will reimburse them for any procedures they think warranted. While a growing number of physicians and other health providers are employees of health maintenance organizations (HMOs) and other managed care plans, physicians still figure prominently in deciding which procedures should be reimbursed at what level, and which type of providers should be admitted to their preferred provider panels. The system is so physician-centric that other professional groups are given little say in the development of policies within the insurance industry.

Containing costs while preserving quality of care is the stated goal of managed care organizations. What were once individual hospitals have evolved into health systems. These health systems attempt to capture a large and secure market of insured recipients of care by limiting their access to care to providers and facilities within system entities. To this purpose, everything from family practice physicians to subspecialists, as well as varied health facilities, have affiliated with these health systems. In order to retain expected profits and economies of scale, both health systems and physicians have had to devise methods of increasing utilization without similarly increasing operating expenses. In a rational system that would guarantee all residents of a country access to basic health services, practitioners such as midwives, advanced practice nurses, and physicians assistants could be an elemental part of assuring access and quality while containing costs. Much of the primary and some secondary-level care can be provided by these nonphysician providers. In particular, midwives, by virtue of their training and philosophy of practice, could dramatically reduce costs by limiting high-tech intervention for the rare times it is necessary while still achieving comparable or superior outcomes.

Many American midwives hoped that the managed care arena would finally open long-closed doors to their practice and put them into the mainstream of American health care. They envisioned increased access to hospital practice privileges, mandated equitable third-party reimbursement, and other widespread progress on issues that midwives have fought for over decades. Just as family practitioners consult with or refer patients to specialists when the complexity of the problem exceeds their areas of expertise, midwives hoped to establish a similar role in the system. Countries with midwives as the primary provider of maternity care have long demonstrated superior maternal and neonatal outcomes to those in the United States. Furthermore, American midwives have lower cesarean section rates, and less medical intervention with comparable outcomes and less expenditure than found in the usual style of obstetric care, as reported by Gambay and Wolfe (1995). Childbirth is the number-one indication for hospital admission in the United States. If the goal is reduced cost and assured quality of care, what could be more sensible than system changes including midwives as the predominant providers of maternity care?

American midwives have a long history of providing care to underserved populations, and few are unwilling to provide services to all socioeconomic strata. In a recent study of CNM practices, over 70 percent of the women cared for are members of "vulnerable" populations. Paine, DeJoseph, Scupholme, and Strobino (1994) defined vulnerable populations as "women or infants who are likely to experience poorer than average perinatal outcomes or who have problems with access to care by virtue of their age, race/ethnicity, education level, source of payment for care, and/or geographic location of residence." Most midwives are unwilling to compromise the relationships with women and their families so treasured by both the providers and consumers of midwifery care. Practicing in a climate in which high volume is paramount is antithetical to the midwifery model of care. To be "with-women," they must have time to individualize care to maintain both the physical and psychosocial benefits of midwifery services. Since midwives do not incur as high educational costs as physicians, since they rely more on support and education of their clients rather than technology, and expect lower incomes, they are capable of containing costs while preserving close provider/client relationships. Since most maternity and gynecology care is normal, the ratio of midwives to obstetrician/gynecologists could be reversed. As in many countries, every American woman could receive the benefits of midwifery care and simultaneously benefit from OB/GYN care as necessary. As a fully integrated part of the health care system, midwives can help teach medical students and residents a less expensive and less technological approach to maternity care, particularly the value of patience and the recognition that "normal" is not always "average." Creative approaches to this model of care are beginning to develop around the United States. There is great potential for physician/midwife collaboration within teaching institutions, public and private practices, and managed care systems. While this would not solve all the problems or right all the inequities of the current system, it would go a long way toward humanizing childbirth, offering equal access to high-quality care, and containing the spiraling costs of women's health care.

BENEFITS OF MIDWIFERY CARE FOR MOTHERS AND BABIES

The benefits of midwifery care for mothers and babies are both physical and psychological. Physical benefits can best be illustrated by comparing perinatal outcome statistics of midwives and obstetricians. Midwives have improved their data collection in recent years, realizing how important it is to document their excellent outcomes. In contrast to the hard data that illustrate physical benefits, psychological benefits are more easily described by soft data, or the experiences of women.

The use of analgesia and anesthesia for pain relief varies from region to region in this country. Nevertheless, it is the expectation of most women that they will need assistance from drugs to deal with the pain of labor. Midwives know that most women do well without it, and are highly satisfied with their ability to have a drug-free birth when all is done.

Analgesia used for labor is usually from the class of drugs known as narcotics. Narcotic analgesia carries with it the potential for respiratory depression in the neonate. It can also have a negative impact on early breastfeeding if a new mother is in an altered state of consciousness following the birth, and a baby is too sleepy to suckle. As a physiological response to poor feeding, a baby's blood sugar may drop to a dangerous level. Bottle-feeding may be introduced by medical personnel, which begins the cascade of nipple confusion and breastfeeding problems.

Anesthesia used for labor and birth fall into one of two categories, general or regional. General anesthesia is reserved for emergencies that arise when the baby must be "rescued" in a matter of a few minutes by cesarean section, or by surgical delivery through an abdominal incision. Under general anesthesia a woman is unconscious, therefore not aware of pain. Epidural anesthesia is the hallmark of modern obstetrics in hospitals across our nation. Epidural anesthesia involves the injection of an anesthetic agent into the epidural space surrounding the membrane that covers the spine and nervous system. It is a procedure that has the potential risks of infection, severe blood pressure changes, and even permanent back injury, though these are rare. These risks should be, and usually are, discussed with women prior to administration of the epidural. The risks that are almost never discussed are the common sequelae of being numb from the upper abdominal or chest area down to the tips of the toes during a physiological event that works best with the active body-mind participation of the woman giving birth. A woman cannot be an active participant in her own bodily functioning during birth when she is sensorially unaware. When a woman has an epidural, she cannot get out of bed to move around, and she must be strapped to the continuous electronic fetal monitor since fetal distress is more common with an epidural. She must have an intravenous drip, which further limits her mobility. She is likely to have diminished expulsive efforts when it is time to push her baby out into the world. This inability to push may lead to an episiotomy, the use of forceps or an instrument called a vacuum extractor to facilitate the birth, thus further removing power from the woman and placing it in the hands of the obstetrician.

Oakley et al. (1995) reported significantly different analgesia and epidural rates for women who were cared for by nurse-midwives than those cared for by obstetricians. Labor analgesia rates were 31.0 percent and 41.5 percent for the midwife group and the obstetrician group, respectively. The epidural rates were 14.6 percent and 39.6 percent, respectively for the two groups. A study of outcomes for 108 home-birth clients by Anderson and Greener (1991) reported only one laboring woman who received labor analgesia and one who received epidural anesthesia, both of these women having been transferred in labor to a hospital.

Childbirth used to occur primarily in the home, and children were able to see their mothers in labor and observe the unfolding of birth. Few women trust their body to function well in birth anymore, or have ever had birthing modeled for them by other women. As a result of the medicalization of birth, and childbirth moving into the hospital at the beginning of this century, women have lost the opportunity to learn birth from their mothers, and have given up birth to nurses, doctors, and epidurals. Midwives are helping women to once again trust their own inner strength and the power of birth. Women attended by certified nurse-midwives in hospitals may still employ the numbing effect of the epidural, but at a lower rate than women cared for by physicians. Most midwives, even in hospitals, choose to attend their clients during their entire labor and try to utilize nonmedical alternatives for pain relief. Women choosing an out-of-hospital birth in their home or a birth center rarely transfer to the hospital for the purpose of anesthesia. A supportive attendant in comfortable surroundings usually keeps the need for such intervention to a minimum.

Perineal integrity is another beneficial outcome of midwifery care. The perineum is the area between a woman's vagina and rectum, which is most likely to tear during delivery. Midwives take pride in using the "art" of their profession when they use techniques such as warm compresses, water immersion, perineal massage, gentle verbal guidance through "crowning" (when the widest diameter of the baby's head is coming over the perineum), to minimize the chance of tearing or needing an episiotomy. Episiotomy is only truly needed when the baby's heartrate drops dangerously and shows no sign of returning to normal as the baby is nearing birth. In this instance, a small episiotomy can improve the well-being of the neonate, and prevent the need for any resuscitative actions. The overall episiotomy rate in hospitals in the United States is 62.5 percent, according to Thacker and Banta (1983). Midwives perform episiotomies approximately 5 percent to 20 percent of the time, taking pride in the avoidance of this procedure. Obstetricians, on the other hand, trained as surgeons, believe that a clean, straight incision is preferable to a jagged tear. Certainly it is easier for the physician to repair, and requires less time in the delivery room preceding and following the birth. Many of these women, if given the chance, would have delivered with an intact perineum, avoiding physical and psychological scars. One problem with disturbing the integrity of the perineum is that once a cut is made, the tissue is much more likely to sustain even further tearing into the rectal tissue, placing the new mother at risk for postpartum complications and extreme discomfort. Many women suffer prolonged pain with intercourse following episiotomy. Though midwives are trained to perform an episiotomy, they reserve its use for times when it is truly necessary,

One of the disturbing trends of modern obstetrics in America is the soaring cesarean section rate. In 1970, the cesarean section rate was 5 percent, in 1978 it was 15 percent, and by 1990 was 23 percent. There are two primary explanations for this. First, with the burgeoning of technology, and specifically the electronic fetal monitor, came the overdiagnosis of fetal compromise, or fetal distress. The EFM was never intended to be used on all women in labor. Instead, it was intended for use with those women who had pregnancies requiring closer observation than usual. The medical profession has embraced science and technology with open arms, often unquestioningly and without regard for consequence. The fetal monitor is a perfect example of this. Rosen and Dickinson (1993) reported that continuous EFM has not been shown to improve perinatal outcomes for women and babies, and, according to Loveno (1986), it has only served to increase the cesarean section rate as a response to the false identification of fetal distress. It has also sent the message to women that their experience giving birth is of minimal significance in comparison to the importance of any presumed, but not documented, needs of the fetus.

The second explanation for the skyrocketing cesarean section rate is fear of medical malpractice by obstetricians. With the obstetrician at the pinnacle of power, controlling the use of all available technology, and choosing to perpetuate the myth that technology is the savior, it is no wonder that one would feel betrayed when this myth fails. Midwives, on the other hand, having entered into a relationship of mutual trust and respect with their clients, are rarely subject to litigation by their clients. Occasionally there will be a bad outcome surrounding pregnancy and birth. This is a fact of life, and is devastating to all involved when it occurs, but it is not necessarily attributable to poor care. Midwives practice their profession through the use of sound scientific rationale, as well as listening to what their intuition tells them. They trust their instincts as well as hard science, share information with the woman and her family, and do not base their clinical decisions on fear of litigation.

Rooks et al. (1989) reported the cesarean section rate to be 4.4 percent in a study of 11,814 birth center clients cared for by midwives. In a study comparing midwife-attended home birth with a sample of physician-attended hospital births, Duran (1992) found the cesarean section rates differed dramatically. The cesarean section rate for the women planning home birth was 1.5 percent, and for those having their babies in the hospital it was 16.5 percent.

The psychological benefits for women receiving midwifery care are equally as important as the physical benefits already discussed. Midwifery clients, many of whom are already very self-directed individuals, naturally assume an equal partner role with the midwife. They learn to view birth as normal and feel confident in their ability to actively give birth. They are supported by the midwife in labor and are able to give birth with dignity in an environment that promotes this. There is no greater joy for a midwife than to hear a woman who has just given birth say "I did it." The midwife knows she has done her work well if the client feels thus empowered. It is more common in a hospital, physician-attended birth, to hear a woman say "Thank you, doctor, I couldn't have done it without you."

Babies also benefit from care by midwives. Births attended by midwives are gentle births, especially those that occur at home or in a birth center. In an out-of-hospital birth setting, the woman and her family have more control in designing the birth environment that they feel is warm, gentle, and welcoming to their newborn. Dimmed lights, quiet music, warm water, continual close maternal-newborn contact, and freedom to follow one's natural instincts all lead to an optimal experience for the infant. In a hospital, this type of experience is more unusual, but not impossible, with a cooperative and respectful nursing staff and a midwife who will act as her client's advocate.

Nurse-midwives have excellent documented outcomes related to neonatal mortality. Rooks et al. (1989) reported in their study of 84 birth centers, in which midwives were the primary caregivers, a neonatal mortality rate of 0.8 per 1000 births. This compares nationally to a rate of 8.5 per

1,000 births reported by Wegman (1994). Low birth weight and prematurity are factors that place infants at risk of morbidity and mortality during the first year of life. Midwives have worked hard to improve the health of pregnant women in underserved areas. Through careful screening, nutritional counseling, education regarding good health habits, and spending an adequate amount of time during prenatal visits to address client concerns, midwives have improved perinatal outcomes for this vulnerable population of infants.

FEMINISM AND MIDWIFERY

Feminism and midwifery are closely allied. Feminism is predicated on the premise that women have a right to equal access to information, people, and resources. Feminist philosophy can be seen in the work midwives have accomplished and in their basic belief system. Liberal feminist views have had an impact on midwives seeking equal opportunity for their profession, struggling to obtain hospital-admitting privileges, third-party reimbursement, and prescriptive privileges. The word "privileges" itself implies exclusiveness, and midwives have historically been excluded from the male-controlled medical infrastructure of this country.

Radical feminist views have been put into practice by midwives who place the woman at the center of all management decisions. The client's input, values, needs, and priorities determine the services given in this woman-centered approach to care. Informed choice is the core of this type of care, and midwives place great importance on equipping women to make informed choices for themselves and their families. To truly engage in the practice of informed decision making, women must have access to unbiased information regarding benefits, risks, and alternatives relating to the issue in question. By helping in this process, midwives are truly giving birthing back to women. Women are empowered by making their own choices, acting on them, and finding their families

and themselves benefiting from those choices. They are finding that their birth choices are changing their lives in ways they never would have imagined. Many of these women have gone on to join in the consumer-driven movement that has already altered the delivery of birth services in many hospitals. Most hospitals have moved birth out of the delivery room, off of the cold metal table and into the birthing room with its birthing bed, birthing chair, or birthing tub. Labor-delivery-recovery-postpartum (LDRP) rooms, where women spend their entire hospital stay, instead of moving from room to room, were developed in response to consumer demand for a more comfortable and family-centered experience. Rooming-in and mother-baby postpartum units are also examples of changes brought about by consumers demanding a more humanistic approach to hospital care surrounding childbirth. Unfortunately, attitudes steeped in patriarchy for over a century surrounding birth have changed much more slowly than the physical nature of the birth environment. It will take continued effort by women to challenge the present system of medicalized childbirth.

Historically, male control over women's health and women's bodies has extended beyond childbirth to include areas such as infertility and menopause. It is the accepted belief within the medical, or illness model, that women's bodies are inherently flawed. With reproductive technology, women are the primary objects of medical manipulation and control. Treatment of infertility is often focused on the woman, at least initially, even though male and female factors contribute equally to the diagnosis. Midwives, who usually view infertility from a feminist perspective, promote information gathering for the couple, assisting them to become educated about self-monitoring of the menstrual cycle, self-testing of urine, and alternative treatment modalities.

Menopause, a natural event in a woman's life when reproductive capabilities cease, has also been defined by the medical community as a disease-like state requiring intervention and control. Recent research has shown a beneficial effect on the prevention of osteoporosis, cardiovascular disease, and even Alzheimer's disease in those women who take hormones during and after menopause. Linking these disease states with menopause directly, rather than considering menopause as a factor among many that can contribute to these disease states, contributes to the woman as flawed theory. This encourages women to rely on the medical model for health maintenance throughout their lifespan, rather than taking control and responsibility for their own health and well-being. Midwives believe in equipping women with the ability to accept the changing and aging of self, and to make healthy lifestyle choices throughout their years. These choices may or may not include use of allopathic medicines, as well as herbs and alternative therapies.

SUMMARY

Midwifery in America is changing to meet the needs of women, as health care continues to evolve. Historically, midwives have struggled to maintain their legal right to care for women, through continual involvement in public education, politics, and empowerment of women, even in the face of adversity from the medical profession. Midwifery has not only survived over time, but has flourished and become a well-respected profession of its own. Women are reaping the benefits of the midwifery model-of-care in larger numbers than ever before, and midwives have become the provider of choice for women of all walks of life.

REFERENCES

Anderson, R., & Greener, D. (1991). "A descriptive analysis of home births attended by CNMs in two nurse-midwifery services." *Journal of Nurse-Midwifery,* 36 (2), 623–631.

Duran, A. M. (1992). "The safety of home birth: The Farm study." *American Journal of Public Health,* 82 (3), 450–453.

Gabay, M., & Wolfe, S. (1995). "Encouraging the use of nurse-midwives: A report for policymakers." Public Citizen's Health Research Group.

Kassabain, L. (Ed.). (1995). *Prelude to Action II: Reforming Maternity Care.* New York: Maternity Center Association.

Loveno, K. J., (1986). "A prospective comparison of selective and universal electronic fetal monitoring in 34,995 pregnancies." *New England Journal of Medicine,* 315 (10), 615–619.

Oakley, D., Murtland, T., Mayes, F., Hayashi, R., Petersen, B. A., Rorie, C., & Andersen, F. (1995). "Processes of care: comparisons of certified nurse-midwives and obstetricians." *Journal of Nurse-Midwifery,* 40 (5), 399–409.

Paine, L. L., DeJoseph, J. F., Scupholme, A., Strobino, D. M. (1994). *Nurse-Midwifery Care for Vulnerable Populations in the United States.* Executive Summary Report Grant #18747. Washington, DC: American College of Nurse-Midwives.

Rooks, J. P., Weatherby, N. L., Ernst, E. K. M., Stapleton, S., Rosen, D., & Rosenfeld, A. (1989). "Outcomes of care in birth centers: The national birth center study." *New England Journal of Medicine,* 321 (26), 1804–1811.

Rosen, M. G., & Dickinson, J. C. (1993). "The paradox of electronic fetal monitoring: more data may not enable us to predict or prevent infant neurological morbidity." *American Journal of Obstetrics and Gynecology,* 168 (3), 745–751.

Thacker, S. B., & Banta, H. D. (1983). "Benefits and risks of episiotomy: an interpretive review of the English language literature, 1860–1980." *Obstetrics and Gynecology Survey,* 38 (6), 322–338.

Wertz, R., & Wertz D. (1977). *Lying In: A History of Childbirth in America.* New York: Shocken Books.

Weyman, M. E. (1994). "Annual summary of vital statistics." *Pediatrics,* 94 (6), 792–803.

Reading 3   Found Voices: Women, Disability and Cultural Transformation

DEBORAH LISI

Questions to Consider:

1. According to Lisi, how can people with disabilities transform culture?

2. How might your experience of your body be different if there were greater acceptance of physical diversity in our culture?

3. What changes would there be in the women's movement if the needs of women with disabilities were taken into account?

SUMMARY. This article explores the cultural consequences of disability on women. The author interviewed four women with disabilities and two mothers and shares some of her own experiences with disability. The relationship between disability rights and feminism and ethnic identity and the impact of disability on the sense of self and personal goals are considered, as is the transformative power of speaking to the larger culture about how disability experiences inform human perceptions and social practices.

Women's entrance into the disciplines brings a recovery of voice and with it the realization that if we do not end a tradition of storm and shipwreck, there may well be an end to nature and to civilization. But women's questions also stir up conflict and disagreement and thus are more likely to be spoken

© 1993, The Haworth Press Inc., Binghamton, NY.
Women and Therapy, 14, 3/4, pp. 195–209.

where no one will leave and someone will listen. (Gilligan, 1990, p. 27)

When individuals from a minority experience or culture enter the academic arena, they bring with them the voices of others of their kind, people whose life styles and personal connections have not led to the disciplines. It is not enough for these women and men to sit at the font of knowledge; they must enrich the substance of academia by adding to it the essence of the minority culture that has been left out of the thinking and debates of the universities and colleges. I believe in the value of those hidden and dishonored voices to strengthen, renew, and bring verity to our places of scholarship. So, I chose to interview women I know who deal with disability, not to write in the voice of the disciplines and scholarship but to honor what their experiences tell us about both the recovery of voice and the emergence of new voices among us.

Like the robin I saw outside my window this morning, red breasted in April snow, the voices of trailblazers carry spring seeds into a culture requiring change and renewal. The renewal of culture requires risk takers: individuals willing to challenge assumptions of accepted norms and values, new role models that help us see that it is possible to transcend old physical, intellectual, and emotional stereotypes, people willing to bring into action the necessary cultural transformation and give voice to the experience through their life stories.

The work of Carol Gilligan (1990) and Emily Hancock (1989) both identify a time in childhood when the girl challenges the voices of authority. In Hancock's book, *The Girl Within,* the state of being of young girls is more assured than challenged. It is as if the girl is so busy listening to the self and the universe she is engaged in exploring that she does not hear the voices of society that threaten her own voice. This early exploration of self is often interrupted and self awareness remains underdeveloped or not always fully regained. Feminists are now exploring what environments and opportunities need to exist for the self to be regained.

The voices of those experiencing disability as a part of their own whole and dynamic reality represent not so much the recovery of lost words as the emergence of words and voices that were silenced in past generations. For those of us whose experience of womanhood in America is shaped in contexts that somehow mark us as different or alien to those who surround us, the initial finding of voice may be a more solitary task. At least so it seems when I reflect back to what my own experience has been as a woman with a disability growing up in America of the fifties and sixties. So much of our presence was responded to with questions, doubts, and outright negation that affirmation was hard to come by.

We live at a time when the culture we are a part of is being challenged to embrace a broader range of diversity, to leave behind the melting pot to make room for the retention of ethnic identities, in an America of economic uncertainties and aging baby boomers. During this transition per-

haps the journeys of women with disabilities can remind the larger culture of the diverse ways available for individuals to develop and understand our own humanity; to retain diversity through that understanding; to allow each person to plumb the depths and find our own voices, our own selfhood in a community of diversity.

Twenty five, even ten years ago, many who lived with severe disabilities would have died. Others with a broad range of physical, intellectual, or mental conditions were locked up as misfits or patients. Treated not as individuals but as aberrations from human norms; many were placed in institutions for medical or custodial care and received either rehabilitation or neglect or an odd mix of the two as professionals tried to fix what they often did not begin to understand. Many of us have grown up now and have a story to tell about what it feels like to grow up disabled in a world seeking certainties. Sadly it's still happening; we live in a society that has begun to see the limitations of institutionalizing those among us who grow old or have physical or mental disabilities: after all, one day many of us will have lived into old age and will be expected to go quietly into those bleak wards of institutional night to count our breaths till morning, because we are not quite ready to shed the skin we've outgrown. Instead of alternatives we have a vacuum and it is filled by homeless, institutionalized, and marginalized people, by bored and angry people in settings where they do not belong or that have not yet accepted and made room for their difference, their experience. The elderly and those of us with disabilities join other minorities who are being marginalized by a society moving into obsolescence, living out outmoded and outdated stereotypes. Our culture needs an explosion of creativity (economic, technological, social and interpersonal) if it is to stay kinetic and responsive enough to give expression to the diversity and the gifts its members contain.

These are new voices calling, cajoling, and singing to be heard. I am not at all sure that it is a different story, but perhaps it needs to be brought home differently as new cultures and technologies evolve, bringing forth new conflicts and new opportunities. People who were considered unreachable now speak with the aid of interpreters, facilitated communication, and technological aids. Teens dance and do ropes courses in wheelchairs, instead of buying into a label of dysfunctional. Men and women I know speak of their experiences with psychiatric disabilities as a journey to connectedness, a healing process mislabeled as illness.

But it is a struggle to be heard. It is a struggle to hear your own voice when the experience you bring to the world is not one that others share. These are journeys of connectedness and separation, of conflict and reconciliation, of isolation, affirmation, and despair. They are not isolated from the experience of difference as felt through gender, race, cultural difference or class; but they have new elements, new turnings on an old wheel. Over time those of us with similar experiences have learned to search for kindred voices so that we too gain the hearing that Carol Gilligan (1990) has so clearly identified as essential to trust, community, and intimacy.

I met with six women to discuss the impact of disability on their lives, their sense of self, their womanhood. Four of these women had disabilities; two were parents of daughters with disabilities; each had professional as well as personal experience with disability issues. Disability experiences varied; the women quoted in this article had dealt with mobility related disabilities or psychiatric disabilities, though I also talked with a woman who has a severe and progressive hearing loss. Her perspective influenced this article even though she is not quoted. The shape and content of the writing is influenced by my own experience with disability and by the many women with physical, sensory, cognitive, and mobility related disabilities I have known over the years. In the interviews, I wanted to explore how the human experience with disability had transformed their lives and affected their perspectives. I chose women I sensed had a

story to tell; people born to struggle, make connections, women who seemed to be survivors. This was not random statistical research. I wanted to talk to people who were creating their own road maps.

Most of the women I spoke to saw themselves as rebels, either as a part of their character or because their individual gifts inadvertently challenged the status quo: young women whose athletic prowess and intellectual curiosity outstripped their brothers; women who opposed the Vietnam war during their college years; the girl who refused to lose herself in the role of patient in a family of medical professionals; and mothers who refused to accept the failure labels either for themselves as a parent or for their child who was born disabled. These woman by intent or accident were well suited to deal with the dichotomies presented by disability. They defined themselves as rebels, liked challenges, and liked to raise questions. The conflicts raised around disability were not always comfortable but they always raised necessary questions, inherent conflicts, issues that without the disability experiences might never have emerged.

Even a rebel may not be comfortable challenging the status quo without role models and peers, and may do so out of necessity, not choice. That is when an instinctive inclination for rebellion comes in handy. Lee and Peggy raised their children in the sixties and were part of a first generation of parents of children with severe disabilities who chose to raise them at home rather than sending them to institutions. For both of them and for their children the role models and support groups existed somewhere in the future, waiting somewhere to be created along with Head Start programs and local theater groups. Sometimes they were criticized by professionals who felt that their decision to raise severely disabled children at home went against the best interest of the disabled child and the family as a whole.

It was rare then for a mother to align herself with adults with disabilities, to imagine her severely disabled child as a person who would one day grow to adulthood and want to live independently. As Peggy said:

> *I know that what I wanted for Lisa, was for her as an adult to have her own life and for her to be around people, adults with disabilities, who could speak for themselves... there are some things I just realize need to happen because the most important thing is for a person to feel they have some self worth... Maybe [because of] my struggle internally...the fact that I grew up not knowing any self worth...perhaps my pain was also my gift to my children...*
>
> *And when I look back and think of what we did and what beautiful people my daughter was able to connect with...you see, because I believe that we can't be everything to everybody; if you surround yourself with people that you expect the best of, maybe I have that belief inside, that they can see different models. It is the most important part of education...to surround yourself with different people...the kids get the best of what a community has to offer.... somewhere inside I just trust that education isn't really in the schools. It just basically, bottom line, is really that we meet a lot of people and see how they live their lives.*

For women with disabilities the role models out there to meet in order to see how they live their lives are just beginning to emerge. I grew up needing to be my own role model in the same way that each morning when I sat up and put my feet on the floor of the bedroom I had to slowly rise and find my balance, moving across the floor with my arms out until I found my center and got oriented again to being in the body and moving through the world on my awkward legs. Ann, whom I interviewed, said that her first role model was an older disability rights activist she finally met when she was in her twenties. She had a friend with disabilities before then, but not a role model, the opportunity to see someone integrating disability into a strong self image. She had gone through her childhood and into college wanting to deny the part of her that was disabled, ('hating the lower half of my body,' as she put it); had been drawn to black studies and had thought the first disability rights activists she met were pretty bizarre for even considering disability a rights issue or a cultural concern.

Living one's life with a disability means kicking aside what Ann terms "ablisms." It means taking risks not just for the sake of challenging assumptions but in order to live an individual life. I'm glad that I've raised a kid and learned the value of massage, relaxation and fun so that I can say to other women with disabilities, "Yes; it's possible to raise a kid (and have a wonderful time doing it). Yes, it makes sense your legs (or arms, or brain) are tired; and no, walking more is not what you need: maybe you should get a good leg rub and back massage."

I'm glad—more than glad—that I've been able to have my own life, raise a kid, write poems and songs, find a sweetheart after years of living alone, speak in public, be alone, garden, ache, listen to other people's stories and take risks, because without risks there is no opportunity to experience a life that takes you beyond your original expectations. Ann and I talk about this: the importance of risk and the importance of day to day opportunities for happiness. Take away risk and how much opportunity for self determination is left? Diana's cerebral palsy makes her hands so jittery she can't hold ski poles, so she skies down Mount Ascutney (in Vermont) without poles. It's called creative problem solving, and it's not without risk. But Diana (who's braver than I am) would be the first to tell you it's fun.

She and I and all the women with disabilities I spoke to either had gone through or are still trying to deal with questions of body image and cultural expectations (but then, so are probably all the women we know). We live in a culture hung up on physical attributes and physical acceptance. One reason both aging and disability is hard for us to deal with is because they both require acceptance of realities and images our culture tries to overlook; but wrinkles and size and limps are just a few of the attributes our society questions. One young woman spoke of how hard it felt believing that the first man she loved didn't accept her because of her disability; and how liberating it was to find out later that her disability had nothing to do with it: he is gay and they are still good friends.

Our society is rather parochial and seems to cope with difference poorly: we want to integrate it, manage it, do something about it; anything but accept it. So we end up with special education instead of an education that integrates all learners. We end up with racial ghettos, minority movements, a covert class structure all because we have yet to learn how to create communities that allow for and embrace diversity.

Because so much of the women's movement in this country is based on pretty stereotypical assumptions, some of the issues other women fight about, and for, represent cultural norms (however limiting or faulty) that we are not viewed through or included in.

For example, not all of us take being a sex object for granted. For someone who does not expect to be viewed as attractive, a wolf whistle from a passing truck can be a great experience. On the other hand many men, with disabilities and without, may compound sexist attitudes when thinking about or relating to women with disability. We are sometimes treated not as individuals, but as many of the stereotypes of women's sexuality come to life; and when our disabilities cause mobility or communication problems, we may also be subjected to being objectified and subjected to unwanted attentions due to the effects of our disabilities. I still remember the French teacher who lived in the town in which I grew up who seemed to think that my cooking ability and my disability went hand in hand with my being a potentially good wife for some man who

wouldn't have to worry about me being too fast for him...(to use a loaded phrase).

Not all of us take jobs for granted either. Equality of opportunity has to come before equality of pay. Like Black women, women with disabilities are ranked far below White able-bodied men and women when it comes to career options and salary levels. Poverty or the fear of it is something we know about (Asch & Fine, 1984).

The feminization of poverty and the gender bias in our culture compound the unique issues relating to disability so that you have a double whammy of discrimination and stereotypes to deal with. The advantage being that women have been raised to expect discrimination; men with disabilities and without the experience of color bias or other minority identification are poorly prepared to challenge stereotypes. Yet men with disabilities must be willing to challenge stereotypes if they hope to find self esteem.

Growing up and dealing with hidden as well as the more visible aspects of disability, I often felt alien in the homes of my parents and our neighbors, as though I faced people from different cultures across the dinner table and the living room floor. My brothers and sisters didn't give me that feeling but almost everyone else did. I felt that if I was going to find myself and survive, I had to find ways to transcribe my life into a language that had no words for part of what my daily experience was. The women's movement only now is dealing with our issues and not always doing it well.

Such little actions challenge the status quo. A woman in Boston wears sneakers to work and gains the admiration of her nondisabled peers. She says:

> *A couple of months ago I realized that my body was responsible for giving me my politics...how if I didn't have cerebral palsy I wouldn't have the politics I've developed. Also, I don't dress to project myself as a good looking person...I dress how I want to*

dress, and that means being an individual and not wanting to buy into 'the way women should dress,' or it doesn't matter how people are going to look at me anyhow so I might just as well be comfortable.

I think all women struggle; we're told so often...I mean, just the phrase, the words, 'make up' itself says: You're not good enough. Every morning you need to make up ...'make up'...look different in order to be socially acceptable. That's wrong...and I find it...really silly.

We talked, laughing about the dangers of shaving your legs if you have involuntary movements. She said,

I think having a disability and not being about to shave my legs; because if I did... I'd never have made it...I would be a mess. If I tried to put on mascara, I'd put my eye out, you know; I could never physically do it. When I was a teenager it used to bother me; but now you know it doesn't.

It's interesting; I never thought of it this way, but it's true that I've had the experience that because I'm disabled I can't do certain things that other people do because that's what you're 'supposed to do'; like sports, or dressing up, walking a certain way, or wearing heels and other things relating to careers ...and I can't do certain things. The experience of disability allows us to think...like I have to think of my body. I can't keep working overtime, all the time; even though I can work for a long time. I have to give myself breaks...but having come to terms with that part of myself, it's meant that I'm dealing with having a better balance in life as a person, not just as a person with a disability. So I think that we're able to be who we are as women 'cause we don't fit into the stereotype maybe.

This is perhaps one of the more central messages that disability experience has to give the larger culture. We need to find ways to help people recognize and follow their own pole star. Kay speaks of this in her own experiences with mental illness: The doctor who helped her the most was the one who expected her to help herself. The ways she speaks of it, the kinetic quality of the relationship makes the human connection happen. As Kay put it:

I was laying in bed, I was fat, wouldn't brush my teeth, wouldn't comb my hair, also having major headaches at the time. Finally my psychologist comes in, a Ph.D.... he was the one bright spot in my life, he was very good looking...he had lots of positive energy. I wouldn't say I had a crush on him... although most of his female patients probably did...I had a crush on his energy.

He was very helpful to me in my process of getting well, if you will...but he came in one day, and he plopped himself down (with all this energy) and he had his hands on his legs; he would be right where I was: he didn't mind telling me a joke now and then. He said, 'I'll tell you what. I've been coming here for days and I don't see you doing anything, and I'm not going to waste my time. There are lots of other people who want to see me and want to get better. I'm going to come back in three days and see what your decision is; if you're not willing to help yourself, I'm bailing out of this mess.'

I just went...my mouth went down to the floor; and that's what my turning point was...for my recovery if you will...though I'm not sure it was an illness...but whatever... For me turning my life around for myself. Because before that I didn't have any sense of [who I was]. That little five year old had a clear sense and then it got lost in the shuffle...and everything became external...all those doctors, this medication and the hospital…and none of it doing any good and I realized that I had to do good for myself; whether it's mental illness, whether it's caused by whatever I've been through, whatever I've done, doesn't matter. I have to somehow take control of that. I have to be responsible and let the medications…I was on them for nine years, they're only tools, that I can use, and I have to make them work, or not, or nothing's going to work. In just that short session, I got up and I took a shower and I panted and puffed and almost fainted; I was heavy. I was in the hospital seventeen days and lost seventeen pounds. I lost the weight myself and I kept it off. I have a very strong core, that goes back to my younger girl, the stronger Kay, I really have depended on her to keep me going in life. Others say people have to have a support group to make it but the hardest things I've struggled with I've done by reaching down into my core.

Telling this story Kay talked about the time in her life just prior to the incident when she was having a harder and harder time coping. She spent a long time each morning having to put her mask on every day before she went to work. The make up again; to hide the nonacceptable self.

Living with disabilities—whether they be physical, mental or cognitive—demands such an array of responses that it is impossible to face your self without dealing with the disability that is part of one's unique human experience. It begins to transform your sense of each segment of the lifespan; it subtlety influences your experience of your body, your sense of self, your place in the world around you. It both points out and challenges limitations. For many of us our struggle for common ground and kindred understanding is not found in the women's movement but in the struggles of racial minorities and the poor. It is hard for girls and young women to see disability pride as something worth having; too many

attitudes and stereotypes pervade the way we are treated, the way we perceive our own bodies when we accept our body through the eyes and assumptions of the ablebodied. To take up our own vision and acknowledge our own experience is often a lonely task, difficult to come to.

As my friend Ann put it:

I think we are the only group of people who are trying to push that broadening of acceptance beyond culture and race, toward a broadening acceptance for everybody… that would free men and women from the stereotypes of how men and women need to be emotionally or physically…You know what I mean: I think we have the potential for questioning the culture and moving it into another direction…I think we're a very positive force in that sense. If we don't push the culture into having the physical and emotional diversity, medical technology is going to be used to rehabilitate us all onto a very rigid ground where everyone is going to get fixed, redone, whatever; you know, a white, blond, blue-eyed, perfect body image. As medical technology progresses, there is the tendency to use it for a pure fix and get us to conform to those stereotypes that men and women are struggling with in the culture. So just as technology is allowing people with disabilities to live longer and be more independent, the technology may also work against us if we're not careful. In trying to use technology to eliminate disability that also prevents human diversity and what we have as a race to learn from our own diversity. I think we need to resist that tendency in order to push the culture to having that physical and emotional diversity.

Ann went on to say that she wanted the culture to move to an acceptance of human life that was not so constrained by images and expectations of people limited by or locked into their physical bodies. One reason I feel so certain that the disability rights movement requires a transformation of culture is because the lessons I and others have learned through our individual and shared experience with disability stir up such fundamental conflicts (with the status quo and the myths and stereotypes about being human that our culture embraces), that our experiences cannot be voiced without changing the personal and social perspectives of those people able to hear what these experiences say about what it is to be human.

When I speak to audiences about disability rights and the awareness it requires, I tell them that we are remaking the cultures we live in and redefining what it is to be human. Individuals who would have died or been forced to live in institutions are now living to remake the meanings of disability, aging, and human potential. We are joined by others of different races and cultures whose perceptions, histories, and cultural identities are transforming America. Let's get on with it.

I believe the perspective Ann and others embrace speaks to a way of living that Bettina Aptheker (1989) referred to when she noted, "that the dailiness of women's lives structures a different way of knowing and a different way of thinking" (pp. 253–254).

This way of being may be feminist, but it goes beyond feminism. It speaks to what it is to be human. As she put it:

The process that comes from this way of knowing has to be at the center of a women's scholarship. This is why I have been drawn to the poetry and to the stories: because they are layered, because more than one truth is represented, because there is ambiguity and paradox. When we work together in coalitions, or on the job, or in academic settings, or in the community, we have to allow for this ambiguity and paradox, respect each other, our cultures, our integrity, our dignity. (pp. 253–254)

Bettina Aptheker's (1989) thoughts about the structure of women's lives representing a new structure, a more prism-like paradigm reminds me of one of the more striking allusions two women independently chose to use about their experiences with disability: life as a puzzle. Lee, the mother of a disability rights activist and one herself, used the image when I asked her what her love of art and theater had in common with the work she does in disability politics. She chose the image of puzzles to express their commonality. She spoke of both activities requiring the creation of expressions that spoke to cultural needs. And when Ann spoke of her involvement in adaptive recreation she spoke of the joy she experiences in puzzling out ways of interacting with a rocky cliff, a ropes course, or wheelchair races as solving a puzzle; finding, creating new ways to interact with the environment in a body that does not behave in the predictable and understandable ways of a human with no spinal cord injury. She also spoke eloquently of the art of climbing out of her wheelchair and feeling her way down a rocky slope to water as a way of communicating with the stones through touch. It makes perfect sense that problem solving and art occur together as we seek honest ways to live out our women's sense of being; makes perfect sense that coming to terms with age and disability takes on the tonal quality of jazz, a kind of free fall into composition, a note by note inquiry into life.

This kind of inquiry and openness requires a great deal of us, and also challenges our academic, political, social, and therapeutic institutions. We speak of nothing less than a different way of living into the future; moving beyond the constructs and constraints of old cultural and gender "isms." For those of us dealing personally with ageing or with disability or other minority experiences that the culture is not always able to understand and honor, the approach to life which I speak of is paramount to survival, expression, recognition, and joy. But as Bettina Aptheker (1989) recognized, the institutions, even those "isms" and systems that pride themselves for their radical spirit, often close the door on the new voice that seeks to speak to them:

> *As we have pressured against racial and sex discrimination, institutional doors have opened, however tenuously and with whatever reluctance. Some of us have been allowed in, but nothing about the values of those institutions or their rules of success have changed, whether they be academic, corporate, ecclesiastic, political, medical or juridical. The point is to change the values and the rules and to change the process by which they are established and enforced. The point is to integrate ideas about love and healing, about balance and connection, about beauty and growing into our everyday*

way of being. We have to believe in the value of our ways of knowing, our ways of doing things. (p. 254)

REFERENCES

Aptheker, B. (1989). *Tapestries of life.* Amherst, MA: The University of Massachusetts Press, (pp. 253–254).

Asch, A., & Fine, M. (1984). *Women with disabilities.* Philadelphia, PA: Temple University Press.

Gilligan, C. (1990). Teaching Shakespeare's sister: Notes from the underground of female adolescence. In Gilligan C., Lyons N. & Hanmer T. J., (Eds.), *Making Connections: The relational worlds of adolescent girls at Emma Willard School,* (p. 27). Cambridge, MA: Harvard Univ. Press.

Hancock, L. (1989). *The girl within.* New York, NY: Dutton.

Topic 8

Violence against Women

My Father's Bed

Legs to chest
forehead on knees,
I huddle in the corner
of my father's bed.

White sandals, favorite lemon
sundress with the rainbow seams
and panties drown in the orange puddle
cast by pulled polyester drapes.

Three windowless walls surround me:
one as headboard, one as footboard,
one solid along my left side
when I'm pinned on my back.

My seven-year-old eyes
travel the king-size distance
to him gazing at me from the edge,
and I think,

we both could lie on this bed and never
touch.

Anonymous

The year-long trial of O. J. Simpson brought the issue of violence against women into the living rooms of all Americans. More recently the media have portrayed the extensive sexual violence and sexual harassment within the armed forces. Beyond the headlines, however, are the millions of women who are sexually and physically abused every year. According to the U.S. Department of Justice (1995), among the 5 million women known to be raped, robbed, assaulted, and beaten, most are attacked by men who are known to them. Physical abuse of women by their husbands, former husbands, and boyfriends directly affects 2 to 4 million women each year (Novello, Rosenberg, Saltzman, & Shosky, 1992).

In addition to the various forms of interpersonal violence, there exists another pervasive form of violence against women that is rarely acknowledged as violence—poverty. Social scientists and social policy makers now speak of the growing "femininization of poverty," because women and children have a much greater risk of being poor than men do, and this greater risk is compounded if they are black or Hispanic. Poverty is both physically and psychologically damaging to women. Compared with economically privileged women, poor women are at greater risk for violence and for poor health; they are also more vulnerable to low self-esteem, chronic hopelessness, and depression.

Violence against women can be understood only in the context of the hierarchical social organization of our culture, which restricts the political, social, and economic power of certain social groups, in this case, females (Hall & Barongan, 1997). Violence and the threat of violence are forms of control used by powerful people (in this case, males) to maintain their power (Pharr, 1988). Our major social institutions (e.g., the family, legal systems, health care, education, churches, workplace, media) support male violence by continually reinforcing the message that women are inferior. This consistent message of unequal value causes many females and males to accept female subordination as deserved. Such cultural conditioning also contributes to male violence against women because it teaches that males are entitled to control. When this message is coupled with our socialization patterns of rewarding males for aggressive behavior, and our widespread acceptance of violence as an acceptable means of resolving conflict, a high-risk situation is created.

In 1994, the federal government assumed some responsibility for ending interpersonal violence against women by passing legislation in the form of the "Violence Against Women Act." This act represented government recognition that violence is the most serious health risk facing women. It provides for the following actions: battered women shelters that guarantee safety for women who leave their homes; tougher prison sentences for male perpetrators of violence against women; the removal of guns from men with criminal charges; and money for community education that challenges the sexist attitudes that support violence against women. Unfortunately, the government does not include poverty as a form of violence against women so the Act does not address this major health risk for women.

As devastating as the various forms of violence are, the strength, resilience, and courage shown by women who fight back on a personal and political level support a basic tenet of this book: Women are not passive victims of oppression. There have always been individual women, community actions, and social movements directed toward ending violence in all of its forms, and toward establishing equal rights for women. The following readings address the societal causes of interpersonal and economic violence against women, their health consequences for women, and strategies for reducing them.

In the first reading, "Battered Wives: Causes, Effects, and Social Change," Beverly Birns argues that wife battering is the most serious health risk confronting U.S. women today. According to her, the physical battering of women by men is rooted in a culture that encourages men to believe that they are superior to women, and that they are entitled to control women's lives. Within this culture of masculine entitlement, women are often blamed for their own victimization. Consequently, they are often revictimized by the legal and health care systems from which they seek help. Poor women, and women who were abused as children, are at the greatest risk of being the victims of male violence and of sexist legal and health care systems. According to Birns, women will continue to be victimized in great numbers until we design social policies and childhood socialization practices that challenge male supremacy and masculine entitlement.

The second and third readings in this chapter address the issue of rape—particularly of girls and of young women. Experts estimate that between 13 percent and 25 percent of women experience rape or attempted rape in their lifetime. The two readings present different contexts for and approaches to rape prevention.

The reading by Carole Baroody Corcoran and Deborah Mahlstedt, entitled "Preventing Sexual Assault on Campus: A Feminist Perspective," addresses rape on college campuses because of its prevalence in those settings, and because colleges are environments that often support social change. The authors criticize college rape prevention programs that target the behavior of women, the victims. Since it is not women's behavior that causes rape, teaching them safety strategies may give them a false sense of safety, instead of decreasing their risk. The authors claim that rape prevention should be directed to changing male attitudes and behavior toward women instead. A model program is described that provides intensive educational training to groups of men in a seminar. The trained men, now advocates for changing male attitudes and behavior, function as peer leaders with groups of fraternity men.

The reading by Charlene DiCalogero, entitled "A Women's Martial Arts School: Connecting Feminism, Community, and Activism," describes a feminist martial arts program for empowering women. DiCalogero agrees with Corcoran and Mahlstedt that teaching martial arts is insufficient to end rape. The program she describes emphasizes that women must become active agents of social change. In addition to self-defense, women also learn to organize programs, to work with diverse groups, and to become involved with community activities aimed at social change. The program also provides knowledge about the history and social context of violence against women, and the many personal and political actions necessary to end it.

In the final reading, entitled "Economic Violence Against Women," Ruth Brandwein states that the definition of violence should include all acts and situations that harm the health and well-being of women. Poverty directly harms the physical and mental health of women because it prevents them from securing adequate food, clothing, shelter, safety, and health care for themselves and their children. Economic violence also causes poor women to experience many life stresses that lead to high rates of depression and illness. Brandwein also explains why poverty and interpersonal violence are highly correlated. For example, some women remain in abusive relationships because they do not have the money to leave.

Because male violence against women is part of a larger system of inequality, to end this violence we must change that system. It is not enough to imprison individual men or provide shelter for individual women. Until we make changes in our institutions, in our cultural values, and in our socialization practices, violence will continue to be a way that people with power stay in power.

REFERENCES

Hall, G. C. N., & Barongan, C. (1997). "Prevention of sexual aggression: Sociocultural Risk and Protective Factors." *American Psychologist, 52* (1), 5–14.

Novello, A. C., Rosenberg, M., Saltzman, L., & Shosky, J. (1992). "From the surgeon general, U.S. Public Health Service." *The Journal of the American Medical Association, 267,* 3132.

Pharr, S. (1988). *Homophobia: A Weapon of Sexism.* Little Rock, AK: Chardon Press.

U.S. Department of Justice, Office of Justice Programs. (1995). *Violence Against Women: Estimates from the Redesigned Survey, August 1995.* Washington, DC: Author.

Reading 1   Battered Wives: Causes, Effects, and Social Change

BEVERLY BIRNS

Questions to Consider:

1. According to Birns, why do some men physically and sexually abuse their wives and girlfriends?

2. Birns argues that battered women show a variety of resistance strategies. Have you seen these strategies used by a battered woman you know? Explain. Were these strategies effective? Why or why not?

3. Imagine that you have been given a grant to initiate a domestic violence prevention program in high schools or colleges. Use what you have learned from Birns to discuss what your program would include.

In June 1983, Tracey Thurman, a married mother of a two-year-old son, was repeatedly beaten by her husband Charles and almost murdered. Earlier, Tracey—fearing for her life—left their house in Virginia, and returned to her hometown, Torrington, Connecticut. Charles followed, repeatedly threatened, beat, and abused her. Tracey often called the police. At her final call, her husband was screaming and pounding on her door. When the police arrived, having stopped to buy coffee, Charles was stabbing, beating, and stomping on his wife. They removed his knife, secured it in their car, but did not constrain Charles from stomping on his wife, or from throwing their son on top of his bleeding and screaming mother.

In July 1992, Kathy Germaine, a successful businesswoman and mother of two sons was shot to death by her estranged husband, Thomas. Thomas Germaine had a stable work history and appeared to be a loving husband early in their mar-

riage. However he beat his stepson, and became increasingly abusive to Kathy. Kathy filed for divorce and an Order of Protection, a document that orders abusers to stay away from their victims. Kathy's last days were filled with terror.

These two extreme cases illustrate the issues involved in understanding male violence towards wives. Although each has its own history, these cases share certain commonalities. Both of these women were protective of their children, recognized the lethality of their husbands' behavior, and tried to end the abuse. When the abuse escalated in frequency and severity, both attempted to enlist the help of law enforcement agencies, but help was either too little, too late, or ineffective. Both *did* leave, when they were terrified. Kathy was murdered after she served Thomas with divorce papers, and Tracey was almost murdered when she physically left.

Tracey Thurman sued the city of Torrington and the police department and was awarded over 2 million dollars because the police failed to protect her.

How can we understand the violence that many women experience at the hands of their boyfriends, husbands, and former husbands? What must be done to end this epidemic? This article addresses these questions by focusing on the following: definition and extent of the problem; description of the abusers and the abused; the change in relationships from "to love, honor and cherish" to physical harm and terror; physical and psychological effects of abuse; coping strategies of abused women; and societal roots of this violence and efforts to end it.

DEFINITION AND EXTENT OF THE PROBLEM OF WIFE ABUSE

Definition

A government panel of experts recently concluded that at present there is no agreed upon definition of violence against women. Sociologists, psychologists, criminologists, legal experts, and physicians ask different questions, use different definitions, and come up with different numbers.

Psychologists on the American Psychological Association Task Force on Male Violence Against Women define violence as "physical, visual, verbal, or sexual acts that are experienced by a woman or a girl as a threat, invasion, or assault and that have the effect of hurting her or degrading her and/or taking away her ability to control contact with another individual" (National Research Council, 1996). Most experts agree that a major attribute of violence against women by their partners is the abuse of power and control. Feminist scholars (Walker, 1979; Pagelow, 1984; Dobash, Dobash, Wilson & Daly, 1992) insist that men use physical force against their wives to coerce, demean, humiliate, or punish them. They exert their power to achieve what they consider to

be their rights: sex on demand, social isolation, food prepared to their liking, and perfectly behaved children. Violence against wives is the most extreme, most physically and psychologically damaging experience for millions of women.

Extent

In 1985, C. E. Koop, Surgeon General of the United States, stated "violence against women is the number one health problem of American women" (Koop, 1992). Five years later, Surgeon General Novello, reporting in the *Journal of the American Medical Association* (Novello, Rosenberg, Saltzman, & Shosky, 1992), claimed that between two and four million women are abused each year. Furthermore, violence is the leading cause of injury to women between the ages of fifteen and forty-four. According to Senator Joseph Biden (1993), spouse abuse is more common than automobile accidents, mugging, and cancer combined. Finally, according to the American Medical Association Guidelines (1992), 25 percent of women who attempt suicide are abused, and among pregnant women the rate of abuse is 25 percent.

Advocates who provide services to battered women insist that reported assaults underestimate the actual numbers, and furthermore do not explain the nature of the injuries or the physical and psychological trauma experienced by victims. Psychologists are well aware that counting single acts of abuse is insufficient for understanding the repetitive and dangerous behavior, and its consequences.

The definition of abuse depends on whom and what you ask. Sociologists (Straus, Gelles, & Steinmetz, 1980) ask large samples of married individuals how they resolve conflicts. Medical practitioners discover and may report abuse when they see physical evidence of injuries in pregnant or ill women. Police count the number of domestic incidents reported, and the number of arrests that they make. Shelters for abused women see only those who seek safety. The number of victims known to different agencies therefore varies considerably.

THE ABUSED AND THEIR ABUSERS

"Why do they stay?" is still asked today and implies that "they" are a homogenous group of women whose faulty personalities elicit the abuse. This myth impedes ending the violence, since it transfers the responsibility from the violent men to their victims. Therefore we will first discuss the perpetrators and ask, "why do men abuse women and how do they justify using physical force to control and dominate women?" Two major social factors are sexism and American tolerance for all forms of violence.

Sexism.   The introductory articles in this volume describe the nature of sexism and its impact on the lives of women. In all of our social institutions—law, business, government, education, and health care—men have the decision-making power. What is less obvious, but equally true, is that this control extends to family life, and to other intimate male-female relationships, particularly marriage. Dobash et al. (1992) state that "violence against women occurs in the context of continuous intimidation and coercion and is inextricably linked to attempts to dominate and control women." Men become physically, sexually, verbally, and emotionally abusive to women because they believe that it is their "right" to have their needs and desires fulfilled on demand.

America's Love of Violence.   The second root cause of men's violence toward intimate partners is the extent, severity, and tolerance for violence in contemporary America. Factors that prematurely killed adults and children at the beginning of the century (contagious diseases, and deaths during childbirth) have been reduced. However, the rates of death by violence have steadily

increased. The serious nature of the epidemic of violence in this country has been acknowledged by surgeon generals (Koop, 1992; Novello, 1992) and the public health service, and has finally been addressed in federal legislation (The Violence Against Women Act of 1994). The difficulty in passing gun control legislation is one example of our willingness in the United States to accept violence. We exceed all other industrialized nations in homicides, suicides, and assaults. Injuries by firearms cost the taxpayers millions of dollars every year. We also rank number one among industrialized nations on rates of rape and family homicides. Our support and tolerance for using lethal weapons as a means of resolving conflicts is well established.

Male Entitlement.   Feminist sociologists, psychologists, and advocates consider entitlement to be an essential element to explain male behavior. In a patriarchal culture, boys are raised in homes and schools that support the ideology of male privilege. When abusive men are confronted with the acts that they have committed, their first response is almost always denial: "I didn't do it."

However, the second line of defense is usually "It was her fault." Rape of acquaintances, the abuse of wives, or incest is most often justified by the perpetrators, who say "It is my right." Men who rape their wives claim it isn't rape, "She is my wife." Incestuous fathers often say, "She is my daughter, and I have a right to be affectionate with her." Physical wife abuse is justified by the statement, "Sure I hit her, she wouldn't stop nagging," or "I got tired of cold food." In each of these situations, men justify their acts by verbalizing their belief that, "It is my right."

Feminist scholars invoke sex-role socialization as one root cause of male dominance and entitlement. However, few have documented its evolution. In an elegant series of experiments, Maccoby (cited in Birns et al., 1994) described findings that indicated that, during the preschool years, boys and girls use different strategies to resolve conflicts. When preschoolers compete for a toy, the boys are likely to resort to pushing, shoving, and grabbing to get what they want when they are playing with other boys or with girls. Girls, in the same situation, when playing with other girls, are more likely to use conciliatory strategies, take turns, or share. However, when the girls and boys are together and competing, the girls try their negotiating strategies, and when their strategies don't work, they retreat or seek adult help.

Maccoby demonstrates the early appearance of these behaviors but insists that they are not learned because she falsely claims the American family is democratic. Maccoby believes that parents share decision making and power, and therefore children's behavior is not based on observed sexism. However, contrary to her belief, inequality pervades all of our social institutions, including the family. Very young boys use bullying strategies and force to solve conflicts, and girls are more likely to negotiate and try to use persuasion. In addition to the family, films, music, and television provide models of inequality.

Individual Factors. The ideology of male superiority and male entitlement is necessary—but not sufficient—to understand abuse. Individual factors also play a role. All American boys are raised in a "macho" culture, but most men do *not* grow up to rape and brutalize women. Individual life experiences and personality do play a role. Men who abuse their wives are not a homogeneous group, although many share certain attributes and background factors.

Gondolf (1993) claims that although there are different types of batterers, they all share one belief system. They are egocentric and believe that their own needs and desires are primary, and that their needs justify their behavior. Some men who beat their wives do behave aggressively to their peers, acquaintances, drinking buddies, and fellow athletes. Also, many men are arrested for other crimes before the wife abuse was reported

to the police. Many batterers, but not all, come from homes where they have witnessed their fathers beating their mothers. Alcohol abuse, frequently invoked as a cause, has been documented to be positively correlated with violence, but does not cause it. Abusive men who stop drinking do not stop the abuse. Abusive behavior toward animals or friends is often found in the history of abusive men. Abusive men share a cultural belief in male authority. However, each man has an individual history that contributes to the abuse.

Abused Women

Early advocates for battered women documented the fact that victims of domestic violence might be poor or rich, white or black, working or not working, and of any age. Among groups of battered and formerly battered women are physicians, lawyers, business executives, a former Miss America, the wives of senators, judges, and police officers, as well as beauticians, cleaning women, and welfare mothers. It is true that battered women are found in all groups. It is also true that in spite of many attempts to "profile" or characterize battered women, no such profile has been found. Women who are abused are not victims because of their personality traits.

However, if we consider risk factors, not psychological characteristics, current data from the Congressional Research Service (CRS, 1995) indicate that certain demographic factors have been identified. Although any woman may be abused, some women are more likely than others to experience violence at the hands of their partners. CRS quotes studies that indicate that women between the ages of 20 and 34 are most at risk. Women college graduates have lower rates of victimization than those with less education, and women with family incomes under $10,000 a year are more likely to be abused than women with higher incomes and more education. A major finding of many studies is that separated and divorced women are at higher risk of injury from their former mates than are married or never married women (Barnett & LaViolet (eds, 1993, cited in Ferraro, 1997).

From Happily Ever After to Unrelenting Harm. Some believe that women married to abusive men had knowledge of the abuse prior to the marriage and that they "chose" to marry abusive men. However, Dobash and Dobash (1979) found that for many women, the period of courtship was the happiest period of their lives because they were courted by men who appeared to be loving, concerned, caring, and totally attentive to them. In fact, many of the behaviors that are indicative of abuse such as possessiveness and jealousy are initially perceived as measures of love.

Specifically, many abusive men initially appear to be unusually concerned about their girlfriends' whereabouts, very determined to spend all of their time with the woman being courted, and very resentful of her other emotional commitments—whether parents, friends, or children by a previous marriage. Pathological jealousy after marriage initially appears as loving concern. "I love you so much I have to be sure you got to work alright; I love you so much I want to be only with you, not your family or friends." For many women, the intense degree of involvement is equated with love. In a culture that equates love with possessiveness and teaches women that their happiness depends on marriage, such attitudes are understandable, although they may be ultimately disastrous.

What then of the transition from love, honor, and cherish (and some even still say obey) to the black eyes, pulled hair, insults, threats, pushes, shoves, gashed face, kicks, blows to the head, and abject terror?

All human relationships involve some conflict. Marital conflicts concern whether a woman should work or return to school, where to live, how often to have sex, the number of children to have, or how to spend leisure time. When couples first date and become romantically involved, the

conflicts may seem unimportant compared to the strong positive emotional and sexual feelings. When couples commit to a long-term relationship, it is usually with the belief that differences can be resolved and that the relationship will provide warmth, friendship, sex, companionship, intimacy, and stability.

In abusive marriages, the early controlling behavior may be perceived as "strong, masculine, and decisive." What emerges as frequent violence may early on be perceived as something rare and therefore forgiven. When husbands initially become aggressive, some men apologize and promise that it will never happen again. In future episodes the men more often blame their wives. Initially, when men blame their wives for their own anger, many women accept the blame. When he says that "dinner was cold and inedible," some think he may be right. Many abusive men batter when they drink, and convince themselves, and sometimes their wives, that alcohol causes the aggression. However, both drinking and using fists are activities that are freely chosen. As stated earlier, men who "only" hit when they are drunk do not stop the aggression even if they stop drinking.

The Question That Won't Go Away—Why Don't They Leave? Returning to the case of Tracey Thurman, when Tracey tried to leave her assaultive husband and get a divorce, his behavior became more violent. The murderous violence did not end until the police arrested him— only after the ambulance arrived. Many women do not leave because they fear the violence will escalate—a rational fear.

These cases cited are among the most extreme. However, there are millions of American women who are seriously injured each year. Bones are broken, women are raped, some are knocked down stairs, and some pregnancies are terminated due to extreme physical harm. The most recent available data suggest that as many as 50 percent, and perhaps more, of the injured women have separated or divorced their husbands and therefore are not among the "counted" cases of domestic violence.

Physical and Psychological Effects.   The O. J. Simpson case occupied the front pages of newspapers, television, and the minds and passions of most Americans. The photos of Nicole Brown Simpson's face, from a previous episode, as well as tapes of her frantic call to 911 indicate that she incurred serious injury at the hands of her husband prior to her death. This case received the attention that it did because Simpson was a very famous black athlete, the trial was televised, and Nicole was a rich and beautiful woman. Nicole may have been one of 1500 known murders of wives by their husbands that occur each year. We know little about the hundreds of others, except what we read in the press.

Most wife abuse is never known to the police, hospitals, courts, shelters, or agencies that provide services to battered women. We, therefore, know little of the short- and long-term physical and psychological effects of abuse. According to the American Medical Association guidelines (1992), some common injuries are cuts, fractures, and sprains; and injuries to the head, neck, chest, breast, and stomach. Bruises and severe injures are not uncommon during pregnancy. McFarlane et al. (1992) determined that 17 percent of pregnant women are abused during pregnancy, which affects not only the woman but the pregnancy.

Medical problems that result from the stress of abuse include chronic pain, headaches, and sleep and food disorders. Articles on the physical and psychological damage caused by abuse are increasingly appearing in medical journals (Journal of the American Medical Association, 1992).

Stark and Flitcraft (1981) provided important data on the psychological impact of continuous and increasing levels of violence on women. At the time of their study (1981), records of patients who came to emergency rooms of hospitals had not been analyzed regarding abuse. For women who showed up repeatedly at an emergency room, each visit was recorded as if it were an independent event. This study explored explanations given for injuries and also the effects of repeated episodes. Women who came in with unexplained injuries were not asked the cause.

By searching files on women who made repeated trips to the emergency room, the authors documented the increasing severity of the injuries, and the psychological as well as physical harm. As the injuries became more frequent and severe, the women began to show marked deterioration in their physical and psychological status. As the violence became more severe, the women reported headaches, sleep problems, eating, drinking, and drug problems. The number of attempted suicides increased. This was the first scientific evidence of the fact that battered women develop psychiatric symptoms in response to the violence, rather than that these behaviors and problems were preexisting.

In 1992, Cascardi, Langhinrichsen, and Vivian studied 93 couples who came for counseling at a marital clinic. Although these investigators (using flawed measures) believed that men and women are equally violent, their concern in this study was the impact of the violence on husbands and wives. Although only 6 percent of women and 1 percent of men report acts of aggression on the first intake, when asked specific questions about acts of aggression, more than half answer yes. The data indicate that, although among distressed couples both the men and the women show depression, it is the wives who are the most seriously depressed. The major finding was that more than 25 percent of the women sustained injuries, whereas only 2 percent of the men were injured, and none of them seriously.

SURVIVAL STRATEGIES

A major theme of this book is that, in a society where male power is a defining feature, women's position has been one of subservience. However, an equally prominent theme is that some women at all times have struggled against this oppression. Whereas many people still mistakenly blame women for their victimization, most victims struggle to protect themselves and their children. Rather than being passive subjects, abused women try many different strategies to stop the violence, and many show incredible strengths in the attempts.

Personal Solutions

What do women do when they are faced with violence at the hands of their intimate partners? Initially, most women are surprised, upset, sad, frightened, and shocked. Sometimes even the man seems shocked, remorseful, and apologetic, leading some women to believe that it won't continue. Women may think that it is only under certain circumstances that the man becomes violent and that the fault may be partially theirs.

A woman may believe that if she is careful she can prevent the violence from recurring: "If dinner is on time; if I spend less time on the phone; if the kids are quiet in the evening; if my sister doesn't visit so often." A woman may try to change her behavior and give in to the man's demands.

When the violence escalates in frequency and severity, women try many strategies to avoid being hurt. Rather than being passive victims, many try to walk away, some try to hide, some cry and call for help, and others psychologically freeze, waiting for it to end. Some women also do fight back. Most hate the violence—but not necessarily their mates, particularly if the men try to make up afterwards and act contrite. When the women recognize the increasing frequency and the fear that is generated, many reach out to family and friends.

Interpersonal Supports

When personal strategies fail to stop the abuse, the next resource is usually family and friends. When women first enlist the help and support of relatives and friends they may receive sympathy

and support. Even parents who are critical and say, "It's your problem, deal with it," often soften when they see the physical and psychological scars. However, after repeated calls, or frequent requests to remain in others' homes, friends and family may exhaust their own resources. They may find the crowding impossible or become appropriately fearful themselves. As the violence escalates, men often lash out at the people who provide support for their wives, at times breaking down doors, harassing them, and threatening to harm them as well as their wives.

Institutional Support

Finally, to stop the violence, some women report to institutions established to protect victims of violence: the police, hospitals, physicians, psychotherapists, shelters, and other advocates for battered women.

During the past 20 years, as a result of advocacy and education by feminists and other support groups for battered women, many agencies have developed policies and guidelines to serve the needs of victimized women better. Changes have occurred at the local, state, and federal level.

Historically, it was shelters for battered women that first provided a safe place for a woman to go when she knew that she had to leave a threatening situation. Battered women who use shelters claim that they are the most helpful services available. Women who are afraid that their lives and the lives of their children are most in danger turn to shelters. Besides a safe place to stay, with staff who provide understanding, shelters also provide safety planning and legal assistance. The ideology of most shelters is to help women make their own decisions, recognizing that many women leave and return many times prior to making the final move. Staff provide job training, assistance in finding permanent housing, and help with the understanding and care of children—many of whom are traumatized by the violence they've witnessed, and also by having to move out of their homes, away from friends and school.

Besides shelters, some health care professionals, physicians, nurses, and psychologists have provided research and advocacy that have served to educate their colleagues about the importance of recognition and treatment of battered women.

Changes in local and state laws and practices are in the process of reform. Policies to have men who batter their wives treated as other criminals are increasingly put in place. Pro-arrest policies attempt to get the police to respond by arresting violent men rather then telling them to walk around the block or take a cold shower.

For the first time, federal legislation has been passed and signed into law by the president. The Violence Against Women Act (1994) promotes the arrest of batterers and the coordination of the various agencies. The law provides funding for the expansion of services to battered women, a national hotline, and funding for further research directed toward ending the violence against women (National Research Council, 1996).

CONCLUSIONS

Violence against women at the hands of their male partners is physically and psychologically the most extreme form of male control and dominance. As a consequence, local, state, and federal governments have passed laws requiring additional funding for shelters, severe punishment for convicted offenders, the removal of guns from men charged with domestic violence, and extensive community education.

To achieve primary prevention—ending the violence against women—we must educate our children to value women as well as men, cooperation as much as competition, and nurturance as well as competence. To diminish violence, we must establish sexual equality at the workplace, in government, and in all educational facilities, as well as in the home, where children first learn what it means to be a human being.

REFERENCES

Barnett, O. W. and A. D. LaViolette. (1993). *It Could Happen to Anyone: Why Battered Women Stay.* Newbury Park, CA: Sage Publications.

Biden, J. R. (1993). "Violence against women: The congressional response." *American Psychologist,* 48, 1059–1061.

Birns, B., & Birns, S. (1997). "Ending domestic violence." In S. Dreman (Ed.), *The Family on the Threshold of the 21st Century.* Hillsdale, NJ: Erlbaum.

Birns, B., Cascardi, M., & Meyer, S. (1994). "Sex-role socialization: Developmental influences on wife abuse." *American Journal of Orthopsychiatry,* 64, 50–59.

Bograd, M. (1988). "Feminist perspectives on wife abuse: An introduction." In K. Yllo & M. Bograd (Eds.), *Feminist Perspectives on Wife Abuse* (pp. 11–26). Newberry Park, CA: Sage.

Browne, A. (1992). "Violence against women: Relevance for medical practitioners." (Report of the Council on Scientific Affairs, American Medical Association.) *Journal of the American Medical Association,* 267, 3184–3189.

Browne, A. (1993). "Violence against women by male partners: Prevalence, outcomes, and policy implications." *American Psychologist,* 48, 1077–1087.

Cascardi, M. A., Langhinrichsen, J., & Vivian, D. (1992). "Marital aggression: Impact, injury, and health correlates for husbands and wives." *Archives of Internal Medicine,* 152, 1178–1184.

Crowell, N. A. and A. W. Burgess, eds. (1996). *Understanding Violence Against Women.* National Academy Press, Washington, D.C. (p. 10).

Council on Ethical and Judicial Affairs, American Medical Association. (1992). "Physicians and domestic violence: Ethical considerations." *Journal of the American Medical Association,* 267, 3190–3193.

Council on Scientific Affairs, American Medical Association (1992). *Journal of the American Medical Association.* 262:3132.

Dobash, R. P., Dobash, R. E., Wilson, M., & Daly, M. (1992). "The myth of sexual symmetry in marital violence." *Social Problems,* 39, 71–91.

Dobash, R. E. and Dobash, R. P. (1979). *Violence Against Wives.* NY: Free Press.

Flitcraft, A. H., Hadley, S. M., Hendricks-Matthews, M. K., McLeer, S. V., Warshaw, C. (1992). *Diagnostic and Treatment Guidelines on Domestic Violence.* Chicago, IL: American Medical Association.

Gondolf, E. W. (1993). Male Batterers. In R. Hampton and T. Gullotta (eds.), *Family Violence: Prevention and Treatment.* Newbury Park, CA: Sage.

Goodman, L. A., Koss, M. P., Fitzgerald, L. F., Russo, N. F., & Keita, G. P. (1993). "Male violence against women: Current research and future directions." *American Psychologist,* 48, 1054–1058.

Helton, A. S., McFarlane, J., & Anderson, E. (1987). "Battered and pregnant: A prevalence study." *American Journal of Public Health,* 77, 1337–1339.

Helton, A. S., & Snodgrass, F. G. (1987). "Battering during pregnancy: Intervention strategies." *Birth,* 14:3, 142–147.

Jones, R. F. (1993). "Domestic violence: Let our voices be heard." *Obstetrics and Gynecology,* 81, 1–4.

Koop, C. E. (1992). "Violence in America, A public health emergency: Time to bite the bullet back." *Journal of the American Medical Association,* 267, 3075–3076.

Koss, M. P., L. Goodman, A. Browne, L. Fitzgerald, G. P. Keita, and N. F. Russon. (1994). *No Safe Haven.* American Psychological Association, Washington, D.C.

McCleer, S. V. (1989). "Education is not enough: A systems failure to protect battered women." *Annals of Emergency Medicine,* 651–653.

McCleer, S. V., & Anivar, R. (1989). "A study of battered women presenting in an emergency department." *American Journal of Public Health,* 79, 65–66.

McFarlane, J., Parker, B., Soeken, K., & Bullock, L. (1992). "Assessing for abuse during pregnancy: Severity and frequency of injuries and associated entry into prenatal care." *Journal of the American Medical Association,* 267, 3176–3183.

Novello, A. C., Rosenberg, M., Saltzman L., & Shosky, J. (1992). "From the surgeon general, U.S. Public Health Service." *The Journal of the American Medical Association,* 267, 3132.

Pagelow, M. D. (1984). *Family Violence.* New York: Praeger Publishers.

Robinson, D. (1995). *Congressional Research Service Report for Congress.* Domestic Violence: Data, Federal Programs, and Selected Issues. Congressional Research Service, the Library of Congress, July 31, 1995.

Schecter, S. (1982). *Women and Male Violence: The Visions and Struggles of the Battered Women's Movement.* Boston: South End Press.

Stark, E., & Flitcraft, A. H. (1983). "Social knowledge, social policy and the abuse of women." In D. Finkelhor, R. Gelles, G. Hotaling, & M. Straus (Eds.), *The Dark Side of Families: Current Family Violence Research* (pp. 330–348). Beverly Hills, CA: Sage.

Stark, E., Flitcraft, A. H., & Frazier, W. (1979). "Medicine and patriarchal violence: The social construction of a private event." *International Journal of Health Services,* 9, 461–493.

Straus, M. A., Gelles, R. J., & Steinmetz, S. (1980). *Behind Closed Doors: Violence in American Families.* Garden City, NY: Doubleday.

Tayler, L., & Salcedo, M. (1992, July 14). "Germaine case cited as example: Proof of flawed system, advocates say." *Newsday,* pp. 3, 19.

Violence Against Women Act of 1994, National Resource Center on Domestic Violence and the Battered Women's Justice Project.

Walker, L. E. (1984). *The Battered Woman Syndrome.* New York: Springer.

Walker, L. E. (1979). *The Battered Woman.* NY: Harper & Row.

Walker, L. E. (1993). "The battered woman syndrome is a psychological consequence of abuse." In R. J. Gelles & D. Loseke (Eds.), *Current Controversies on Family Violence* (pp. 133–153). Newbury Park, CA: Sage.

Readings 2   Preventing Sexual Assault on Campus: A Feminist Perspective

CAROLE BAROODY CORCORAN AND DEBORAH MAHLSTEDT

Questions to Consider:

1. According to the authors, why is rape particularly prevalent on college campuses? Which of these factors exist on your campus? Explain.

2. How does feminist ideology influence the rape prevention program described by the authors?

3. What do the authors mean when they state that all men gain from rape? Do you agree? Explain your answer.

4. Based on this reading, what would you advise women to do if faced with date rape?

It was like any Friday night, my boyfriend and I were just relaxing in my room watching TV. I had a hard day and fell asleep during the evening news. Needless to say, I was not prepared for the experience that would shape my attitudes about safety for the rest of my life. During my sleep, I was awoken [sic] to a strange feeling. I awoke to the fact that I was being raped by my boyfriend whom I placed all my trust in. I didn't know what to do. I tried to defend myself though at that point I was defenseless to his strength. I just kept screaming NO! NO! NO! I did not know if I actually made any sound but the word NO just kept running through my head. I was a mess. I was never so scared, devas-tated, or humiliated in my life. I felt that all my self dignity was erased.

–Female student

A feminist perspective on sexual violence examines rape within the larger context of gender power relations that advantage men and disadvantage women. Indeed, many feminists view sexual assault as a consequence of the unequal power in "normal" heterosexual relationships, where the man assumes a dominant role and the female is in a passive role. By taking a feminist approach to the issues of sexual assault, this chapter will demonstrate how most campus sexual assault prevention programs are at best ineffective, and at worst, victim blaming. After briefly examining the extent of sexual assault among college students, we will consider how violence against women harms all women and benefits all men. Next, the two traditional approaches to campus sexual assault prevention

Courtesy of Carole Baroody Corcoran and Deborah Mahlstedt

will be presented and critiqued. Finally, a prevention seminar developed for fraternity men is offered as an example of a program with goals that are consistent with a feminist approach to ending sexual violence.

THE SCOPE OF THE PROBLEM

Globally, male violence constitutes the number-one threat to the physical and mental health of women (Russo, Koss, & Goodman, 1994). Although we like to think of college and university campuses as sanctuaries of higher learning, they are not exempt from harboring this threat.

Groundbreaking research conducted by Mary Koss and her colleagues (Koss, Gidycz, & Wisniewski, 1987) documents the frequency and extent of sexual abuse and assault on campus. Their survey of a representative national sample of 6,159 students at 32 institutions of higher education reveals that 53.7 percent of the 3,187 female respondents have experienced some form of sexual victimization, 12.1 percent of the women report experiences that meet the legal definition of attempted rape, and 15.4 percent describe experiences that legally constitute rape. However, only 27 percent of the women who report sexual assaults that fit the legal definition of rape *label* their experiences as rape. Further, only 5 percent of the women report their rapes to the police, only 5 percent seek rape crisis assistance, and 42 percent tell no one about the experience.

Data from the 2,972 males in the study indicate that 25.1 percent of the men admit to engaging in some form of sexual aggression, and 7.7 percent report perpetrating an act that meets the legal definition of rape or attempted rape. However, only 1 percent of these men acknowledge that the described incident is, in fact, rape.

The Koss et al. (1978) findings are important for several reasons. First, beyond demonstrating the pervasiveness of sexual assault, they illustrate that many college women and men do not perceive and *label* these occurrences as rape. This

study and subsequent research (e.g., Rappaport and Posey, 1991) also support the perspective of the "normality of rapists" (Malamuth, Haber, & Feshbach, 1980), since college men are responsible for widespread acts of sexual coercion. In addition, the vast majority of sexual assaults are committed by men known by their victims. Koss et al. (1987) found that 84 percent of the women knew the men who raped them, and Koss (1990) reported that romantic partners commit 57 percent of all assaults. Finally, although one would not expect the frequencies reported by female and male students to match, the discrepancies between victimization experiences reported by women and sexually aggressive acts reported by men imply that there is a gender gap in perceptions of what constitutes "real rape." Such a gap is consistent with a feminist analysis of sexual violence that places rape within the larger context of patriarchy. Accordingly, we would expect the dominant group, men, to be less aware of their advantaged position, while the disadvantaged group, women, would be more keenly aware of the power differential inherent in gender relations (see McIntosh, 1988). Ignoring sexual oppression (consciously or not) serves to benefit the advantaged group by upholding male supremacy.

HARM AND BENEFIT: SEXUAL TERRORISM AND CONSPIRACY OF SILENCE

At first the harassment was verbal, like name calling. They called her a fat ugly slut. Then all of a sudden violence entered the picture. One of the boys had a leather football in his hand. He told the girl that if she moved he would have all the guys hold her down and he would beat the shit out of her. So she just stood there as he repeatedly whipped the football at her head. I'll never forget the noise as the football hit her head, it made a loud thud. I'll never forget the expression of pain that crossed her face with each blow. No one did anything—many were laughing.

–Incident observed by a sorority woman

In a patriarchal culture, men maintain social, political, and economic power over women, and it is imperative to the status quo that women's bodies and sexuality remain under their control (Brownmiller, 1975). The threat of male violence reminds women of their vulnerability, and the fear of sexual assault subjugates all women and functions to keep them in their (subordinate) place. Warr (1985) reports that for women under the age of 35, rape is feared even more than murder, assault, or robbery. Women report living on a restrictive "rape schedule," and engaging in a number of daily rape avoidance behaviors (Riger and Gordon, 1981). Carole Sheffield (1995) calls the common characteristic of all forms of sexual violence "sexual terrorism because it is a system by which males frighten and by frightening, control and dominate females" (p. 1). The term *terrorism* captures the unpredictable and arbitrary nature of sexual violence against women. In addition to cutting across socioeconomic class, Sheffield notes that sexual crimes such as rape share the following characteristics: They are least likely to be reported, have the lowest conviction rates, are blamed on the victim, and fuse violence, power, and sex.

Just as all women are harmed by sexual assault, all men can be said to benefit from rape. That is, all men are privileged in status by violence against women, whether they want to be or not. In an essay called "The Lie of Entitlement," Terrance Crowley (1993) says "as a man, I accrue privilege simply by remaining silent, accepting this legacy, and saying nothing about its cost in terms of women's lives" (p. 347). Mandoki and Burkhart (1991) believe that the extent and frequency of sexual violence against women make it an inseparable part of women's ordinary life, and therefore, victimization cannot be viewed as a "disease" explained by the psychopathology of individual men. They conclude that, "To be consistent with the traditional male role—that is, to be 'normal'—men must accept some forms of violence against women" (p. 178). Given the pervasiveness of male domination, according to Bart and O'Brien (1985), "The question we should ask then, is not why men rape, but why don't **all** men rape?" (p. 102). Although we know that all men are not rapists, until men assume an active role in ending violence against women, there is no way for women to distinguish between men who accept and perpetuate violence against women and men who don't. Thus, women are left with little choice but to view all men as potential rapists.

Acquaintance rape is typically viewed as a woman's problem, and discussion of sexual assault can trigger defensive reactions in both male and female college students. Perhaps what is threatening is that male privilege will become visible and both men and women will have to identify men as central to the problem, thus disturbing the status quo. This is one reason for the "conspiracy of silence" among men on the subject of sexual assault. Instead of getting upset about not being distinguishable from men who do rape and breaking the silence, many men tend to distance themselves from the topic and retain their patriarchal privilege. Clearly, male sexuality needs to be reconstructed in a way that disentangles power and aggression from sexual pleasure (Jeffreys, 1991).

Before turning to a discussion of feminist programming aimed at preventing sexual assault, we will first describe and critique the two most common approaches to sexual assault prevention.

TRADITIONAL APPROACHES TO SEXUAL ASSAULT PREVENTION: VICTIM CONTROL AND RISK FACTORS

I feel that even though it may not be right or fair, that many of these violent acts are due to the way women dress, act, carry them-

selves and the things they say. Men should realize that this is not fair, but women should realize that rape does happen in these situations and that the safest way to "stop" or prevent them is to never get in them or lead a man on.

–Male student

Many sexual assault education and prevention programs place responsibility for rape avoidance on women and therefore indirectly (and perhaps unintentionally) support a victim-control perspective. In the past, rape was viewed as precipitated by the victim:

If the victim is not solely responsible for what becomes the unfortunate event, at least she is often the complementary partner.... Theoretically, victim precipitation of forcible rape means that in a particular situation the behavior of the victim is interpreted by the offender as a direct invitation for sexual relations or as a sign that she will be available for sexual contact if he will persist in demanding it. (Amir, 1967, p. 493)

Historically, the traditional approach to rape education and prevention has been to advise potential victims to control their behavior. The idea is that if a woman refrains from engaging in certain "risky" behaviors (e.g., going out alone at night, hitchhiking, leaving a door unlocked), she will be able to avoid sexual assault. This follows from the victim-precipitation view, and because, until recently, rape has been understood to mean stranger rape, education programs have primarily included prevention tactics that are consistent with a victim-control model. However, the victim-control perspective is also evident in education about date and acquaintance rape. For example, to avoid acquaintance rape, a woman is advised not to drink alcohol, dance "provocatively," or wear miniskirts. Thus, the cause of sexual assault is simply attributed to a different set of "risky behaviors." Many college students

feel that women can prevent rape by controlling and restricting their own behavior. Part of the appeal of the victim-control point of view is that it can serve a self-protective function for women. It may preserve one's belief in a just world (Lerner, 1970) and reinforce the idea that "rape won't happen to me."

Compared to research on risk factors that might identify male perpetrators, a disproportionate amount of research is conducted in an attempt to locate risk factors in either characteristics of the dating situation or in a woman's behavior. The research often depicts a no-win situation for women. For example, some studies indicate that a man's initiating, paying for expenses, and driving on a date are associated with sexual assault occurring (Muehlenhard and Linton, 1987). On the other hand, research findings have shown that if a woman initiates a date and shares expenses she is judged by others as being more willing to engage in sex and that it is more justifiable for a man to have sex with her against her will (Muehlenhard, 1988). Further, research indicates that men in general—and particularly sexually aggressive men—incorrectly attribute women's friendliness, nonsexual touch, clothing, and alcohol use to the woman's sexual intentions (Abbey, 1991). Consequently, the problem seems to be males' sexual objectification of women and feelings of sexual entitlement, and *not* female behaviors that are in need of being controlled.

It is problematic, then, to search for the causes of acquaintance rape in individual acts and situational factors that are under a woman's control. Current research shows that the best predictors of experiencing sexual assault are factors that are *not* under one's control, such as gender (e.g., the vast majority of sexual assaults are perpetrated against girls or women) and age. Russell (1984) reports that the highest risk of rape for women is between the ages of 16 and 24, and Koss et al. (1987) indicate that victimization rates for college-age women are about three times higher than that of the general population. Further, unequivocal evidence demonstrates that the most reliable predictor of sexual victimization is previous victimization (Koss & Dinero, 1989; Gidycz, Coble, Latham, & Layman, 1992). For example, in a probability sample, Russell (1986) finds that 65 percent of incest victims experience rape or attempted rape in adulthood, compared with 35 percent of women who were not sexually abused as children. Finally, research conducted by Mary Koss (1985) demonstrates that sexual assault is primarily the result of being exposed to sexually aggressive men and that it is not predictable on the basis of victim characteristics.

Obviously, there are a number of serious flaws associated with the victim-control model of sexual assault prevention. This view places responsibility for rape avoidance on the intended victim and does not challenge the existing sociocultural conditions that allow and cause sexual assaults to occur. It suggests that, to prevent rape, women should restrict their freedom and limit their actions. Closely associated with victim control is victim blame. Thus, if a woman is sexually assaulted, she (and others) may feel that she is to blame because she failed to engage in the necessary victim-control strategies (e.g., "this wouldn't have happened if I hadn't been drinking, invited him in, kissed him," etc.). In addition, this perspective allows the rapist to justify his behavior ("she asked for it") and divert the responsibility for sexual assault from the rapist to the victim. Further, unless all women lock themselves away or perhaps wear rape-proof armor, this approach will not affect the overall incidence of rape. The restriction and control of women are a heavy price to pay, particularly because victim control strategies do not have the desired impact of reducing the occurrence of sexual assault.

SELF-EMPOWERMENT AND MISCOMMUNICATION

Empowerment strategies do not seek to limit a woman's freedom; rather they try to provide women with more options and to strengthen their ability to resist and avoid rape. For example,

instead of a woman's staying at home, she would be advised to park in a well-lit parking lot and pay attention to surroundings at night. Other practices consistent with a self-empowerment model would include providing accurate information about the definition of sexual assault and its prevalence, assertiveness training, and self-defense skills.

Instead of restricting their behavior to prevent sexual assault, college women are admonished to be more forceful or assertive in their communication with male acquaintances. The majority of campus date rape programs promote this message (Lonsway, 1996) and indeed, self-empowerment (both physically and verbally) may help women avoid rape (Bart & O'Brien, 1985). Quinsey and Upfold (1985) report that any type of resistance is associated with decreased injury and an incompleted attack. Although the researchers observe that physical resistance is employed less frequently in the case of acquaintance rape, they find it to be effective in thwarting both acquaintance and stranger rape (see also Levine-MacCombie & Koss, 1986).

It is interesting that although research evidence supports the efficacy of *physical* resistance, most acquaintance rape programs stress miscommunication and misperception as the cause of date rape, and therefore suggest that the remedy lies in assertive *verbal* communication on the part of the female. In some programs, there is also the underlying message that women are sending out subtle nonverbal "signals" of which they may not be aware. In a chapter explaining how misperceptions lead to acquaintance rape, Abbey (1991) states that:

> Men need to know that when a woman says "no" she means it and that her desires must be respected, regardless of what she has said or done previously. For this to occur, women must say "no" only when they genuinely mean it and must be more aware of the way in which their behaviors are perceived by men. Certainly women have the right to

dress as they choose or drink alcohol on a date, but they need to realize how some men are likely to interpret these cues and counteract those assumptions by verbally making their intentions clear. (p. 107)

Such an emphasis on miscommunication places the onus for rape avoidance squarely on women. Further, it may be misleading and even dangerous to overemphasize assertive communication as a rape avoidance strategy when there is no evidence that a man whose goal is to have sexual intercourse (with or without consent) will be dissuaded by such a tactic. Hanson and Gidycz (1993) maintain that victimized women communicate just as clearly about sexuality as nonvictimized women and that it is the perpetrators who choose to ignore these communications and selfishly pursue their own sexual goals.

Many women who forcefully protest, scream, and physically fight are still victims of sexual assault by acquaintances. In one study (Koss, 1988), 70 percent of the women, most of whom were raped by acquaintances, report physically fighting with their attackers. Research conducted on date rapists and sexually coercive men suggests that many women are assertive and firmly establish their limits; however, their wishes are simply ignored. Using a scale that assesses sexually coercive methods, Rappaport and Posey (1991) indicate that males most frequently reported either ignoring a woman's protests or engaging in the behavior when they knew the woman did not want sexual contact. Thus, sexual assault is far from being a miscommunication problem, and the current emphasis on women's responsibility for assertive verbal behavior (while certainly it is healthy advice) also serves as a mechanism for deflecting blame from the perpetrator to the victim.

Self-empowerment strategies are certainly a preferable alternative to fear or restriction, but the burden for sexual assault prevention is still placed on the woman. Whenever the responsibility for rape avoidance remains with women, the potential for victim blaming is not far away. If a woman does not employ empowerment strategies (or if they are not effective), there is the danger she will blame herself ("I must have led him on or not communicated assertively enough") or be blamed by others for her sexual assault ("Why didn't you fight or resist?"). It is ironic that the major focus of most college and university acquaintance rape education programs can easily be twisted into yet another version of blaming the victim.

Finally, empowerment strategies and, specifically, physical resistance can be effective and prevent a particular individual woman from being sexually assaulted. However, this approach does not directly affect the overall incidence of rape. If a sexually aggressive man is deterred, he will most likely seek out another "more vulnerable" target. As Swift (1985) points out, "The net effect of successful rape avoidance, then, may be to displace victimization from informed women, prepared women, and women proficient in self-defense to the very young, the physically or mentally disabled, or the elderly" (p. 418).

In summary, the victim-control and self-empowerment models that underlie most acquaintance rape prevention programs are inadequate. Eliminating sexual assault will require a more comprehensive structural approach that is sensitive to the gender relationships central in feminist analyses of violence against women. Context-stripping (Wallston & Grady, 1985) or removing behavior from the larger social structure in which it occurs fail to acknowledge male power. Therefore, interpretations of cause and responsibility ignore or distort connections between actions and the patriarchal society in which they occur. Cause is attributed to the factor itself (e.g., alcohol), rather than its function within the system of patriarchy. Sexual assault is the product of a patriarchal culture that promotes and allows rape through gender socialization, power differences, the acceptance of sexual violence, and institutionalized misogyny.

FEMINIST APPROACHES TO SEXUAL ASSAULT PREVENTION

From a feminist perspective, the crucial issue that needs to be addressed in sexual assault prevention is not just male aggression, but male dominance. Men are socialized to assume a position of power within heterosexual relations in order to ultimately maintain male institutional and social dominance. Violence and the threat of violence toward women are merely one avenue through which male dominance is maintained. Therefore, the elimination of violence against women necessitates dismantling male-dominated institutions, as well as redefining how men use power in their daily lives. This final section will explore the challenges of prevention work with men and present a model program developed for fraternity men.

THE CHALLENGE OF PREVENTION WORK WITH MEN

For the most part, campus sexual assault prevention educators face doing their work in restricted time segments and with little money. This makes addressing the complexities of violence against women difficult. On the one hand, educators face an urgent need to reach women, who, as the victims of sexual assault, are also more accessible and motivated to attend programming. On the other hand, working with men to prevent dating violence addresses the root of the problem by reaching those who perpetuate violence.

Only recently, educators and researchers have begun to address a number of critical questions concerning male violence against women: What can happen in a one-hour workshop to reach a man who might commit date rape within the next two weeks? Whom are we trying to reach? How do we do it? Who would offer the most effective leadership? And what kind of resources are needed? To answer such questions, educators must begin with a clearly defined the-

oretical framework. Feminist approaches to prevention place responsibility on men to acknowledge that it is men who violate women and men who need to take action to dismantle the dynamics of male-institutionalized power. Only then can violence against women be eliminated. Feminist prevention efforts must inform men, as well as women, about the language, dynamics, behavior, and images of male power in everyday life. A feminist prevention framework must examine the complex processes through which contributing factors such as alcohol and alleged miscommunication play a role in patriarchy. Thus, when students examine alcohol and miscommunication within the context of male dominance and institutionalized power, they may come to understand how these factors function within a patriarchal culture to maintain power and control over women, rather than serving as primary causes of sexual assault.

A feminist perspective on prevention that holds all men accountable for violence implies that prevention should not only reach men with negative attitudes toward women, but should also promote the recognition that all men need to take an active role to end sexual violence. Most prevention workshops have the intent of changing the attitudes of as many men as they can fit in a room, with the hope that change will extend beyond the individuals. Unfortunately, group change requires more than changing individuals. In order to take action, men must have in-depth knowledge about sexual violence, support from other men, strategies for implementing group change, and the appropriate interpersonal skills.

To the prevention educator, such a model for change may seem ideal, but not feasible or even desirable because the need to reach women or next weekend's potential rapist seems so pressing. While educating individual women and men is necessary, prevention educators must think more broadly and in long-range terms about creating structures and processes aimed at cultural change. To illustrate these ideas, the next section will briefly describe a feminist dating violence prevention program developed for fraternity men at West Chester University that uses a minority influence model to effect change. (Footnote: For specific program materials, resources and evaluation of the program, contact the second author.)

A FEMINIST DATING VIOLENCE PROGRAM FOR MEN: A MINORITY INFLUENCE MODEL

Women are encouraged to take self-defense classes, to not walk alone at night, to not wear provocative clothing, and to not drink in excess. Men, oftentimes, are not asked to do anything to stop violence against women. The Fraternity Violence Education Project *asks that men realize this imbalance of responsibility and take action. It is not always that easy for men to challenge other men's behavior toward women even though they may not like it. We must* begin *to speak out more and support each other to do so.*

—FVEP male peer leader

The *Fraternity Violence Education Project (FVEP),* initially a one-year action-research study begun in 1989, evolved through a process of ongoing feedback and modifications in design into a multifaceted model for change. The project targets fraternity organizations for change using a minority influence approach. A central component of the process involves in-depth development of leaders drawn from the group targeted for change. Fraternity peer leaders influence their individual fraternities as well as the fraternity system at large by serving as constant reminders of prevention messages, as alternative role models for men, and as sources for ongoing dialogue. In addition, as active members of their respective fraternities, peer leaders are likely to be present as moderating influences when the potential arises for sexually violent incidents. In a typical college workshop for men, an educator, external

to the group, tries to reach as many individual men as possible before leaving the system. In a minority influence model, by contrast, an educator assumes the initial interventionist role, which is then taken on by an accepted member of the existing group of men. It is now this leader who continues to promote reflection and, from within the group, actively challenges the goals and behavior of his peers within system (Moscovici, Mucchi-Faina, & Maass, 1994; Wood, Lundgren, Ouelette, Busceme, & Blackstone, 1994). Thus, the presence of the peer leaders creates an outspoken minority perspective that presses upon the norms of the majority culture of the fraternity, such as male complicity to maintain silence, devaluation of women as sex objects, and peer pressure to prove masculinity.

Throughout one year's training program, fraternity men develop the skills necessary to assume a role of peer leadership and take action against dating violence. During the fall semester, the men take a semester-long, consciousness-raising seminar on violence against women for academic credit. Through readings, group discussions, and assignments, seminar participants gain extensive knowledge about sexual violence and have opportunities to reflect on their own behavior and learn group facilitation skills. In the spring semester, seminar participants apply their learning by coleading discussion groups and workshops within their fraternities with experienced peer leaders. Young men who have successfully completed the seminar will then facilitate upcoming seminars. The faculty coordinator of the project mentors the facilitators to help in developing their leadership skills.

The content of the seminar and its educational message are designed to be clear without oversimplifying the complexity of the causes of dating violence. The context for power relations becomes the backdrop for discussion of all other elements—sexual objectification, peer pressure, alcohol as a means to coerce women to engage in unwanted sexual behavior, and male responsibility for sexual assault. By stressing the misuse of institutional power as the root cause of violence against women, parallels can be drawn among sexism, racism, ageism, and other forms of oppression. When explained in this manner, the concepts of male power and control appear to make sense to men, become hard to deny, and reduce their defensiveness. The seminar must also include ways for men to take action, since its basic message is for men to take responsibility for ending all forms of violence against women.

The process for developing pro-feminist male leadership through an intensive seminar experience is as important as the content of what participants learn. The small group becomes a microcosm for how men can relate to one another in meaningful ways about issues they often do not discuss with other men, such as relationships, gender role expectations, power, and feelings. Through the process of working together to create skits tailored to address current campus situations, participants consciously explore the everyday behavior of power relations. Such an experience provides them with ample opportunity to practice new ways for men to work and live together and offer each other support.

After completing the seminar, peer leaders implement programming with fraternities and coordinate campuswide efforts aimed at men. Peer leaders coordinate activities ranging from educating pledges to presenting at their regional conferences. *FVEP* peer leaders also may help to resolve specific concerns and/or incidents that arise related to sexual harassment, battering, and acquaintance rape on campus.

I believe that the underlying cause of violence against women in our society is caused by the male-dominated power structure that continues to exist... I had a very hard time understanding this concept at first, and often tried to defend my case against its existence with examples of recent feminist movement/ equal rights successes. However, after read-

ing (and more importantly listening fully to many of the arguments) I began to realize that I was doing exactly what was predicted by some of the readings. It seems silly to me now that I could try to defend my point that in our society men don't hold all the power.
                                    –Male seminar participant

CONCLUSION

The majority of campus sexual assault prevention programs place responsibility for rape avoidance on women, provide support for victim-blaming ideology, and promote strategies that are ineffective in reducing and eliminating sexual assault. In contrast, a feminist analysis insists that men must recognize and take responsibility for ending male violence against women. The campus sexual assault prevention project described in this chapter is aimed at providing men with an understanding of institutional male power and the consequences of male dominance and the oppression of women. Recognizing and understanding the role of sexual violence within the context of patriarchal power is essential in order to achieve the feminist goal of transforming a rape supportive culture and putting an end to sexual assault.

REFERENCES

Abbey, A. (1991). "Misperception as an antecedent of acquaintance rape: A consequence of ambiguity in communication between women and men." In A. Parrot & L. Bechhofer (Eds.), *Acquaintance Rape: The Hidden Crime* (pp. 96–111). New York: John Wiley.

Amir, M. (1967). "Victim precipitated forcible rape." *Journal of Criminal Law, Criminology, and Political Science,* 58, 493–502.

Bart, P. B., & O'Brien, P. H. (1985). *Stopping Rape: Successful Survival Strategies.* New York: Pergamon.

Brownmiller, S. (1975). *Against Our Will.* New York: Simon and Schuster.

Crowley, T. (1993). "The lie of entitlement." In E. Buchwald, P. Fletcher, & M. Roth (Eds.), *Transforming a Rape Culture* (pp. 341–350). Minneapolis: Milkweed Editions.

Gidycz, C. A., Coble, C. N., Latham, L., & Layman, M. J. (1992). "Relation of a sexual assault experience on adulthood to prior victimization experiences: A prospective analysis." *Psychology of Women Quarterly, 7,* 151–168.

Hanson, K. A., & Gidycz, C. A. (1993). "An evaluation of a sexual assault prevention program." *Journal of Consulting and Clinical Psychology,* 61, 1046–1052.

Jeffreys, S. (1991). *Anticlimax.* London: The Women's Press.

Koss, M. P. (1985). "The hidden rape victim: Personality, attitudinal, and situational characteristics." *Psychology of Women Quarterly, 9,* 193–212.

Koss, M. P. (1988). "Hidden rape: Sexual aggression and victimization in a national sample of students in higher education." In A. W. Burgess (Ed.), *Rape and Sexual Assault* (Vol. 2, pp. 3–25). New York: Garland.

Koss, M. P. (1990). "The women's mental health research agenda: Violence against women." *American Psychologist,* 45, 372–380.

Koss, M. P., & Dinero, T. E. (1989). "Discriminant analysis of risk factors for sexual victimization among a national sample of college women." *Journal of Consulting and Clinical Psychology,* 57, 242–250.

Koss, M. P., Gidycz, C. A., & Wisniewski, N. (1987). "The scope of rape: Incidence and prevalence of sexual aggression and victimization in a national sample of higher education students." *Journal of Consulting and Clinical Psychology,* 55, 162–170.

Lerner, M. J. (1970). "The desire for justice and reactions to victims." In J. Macauley & Berkowitz (Eds.), *Altruism and Helping Behavior: Social Psychological Studies of Some Antecedents and Consequences* (pp. 205–229). New York: Academic Press.

Levine-MacCombie, J., & Koss, M. P. (1986). "Acquaintance rape: Effective avoidance strategies." *Psychology of Women Quarterly,* 10, 311–320.

Lonsway, K. A. (1996). "Preventing acquaintance rape through education: What do we know?" *Psychology of Women Quarterly,* 20, 229–265.

Malamuth, N., Haber, S., & Feshbach, S. (1980). "Testing hypotheses regarding rape: Exposure to sexual violence, sex differences, and the "normality" of rapists." *Journal of Research in Personality,* 14, 121–137.

Mandoki, C. A., & Burkhart, B. R. (1991). "Women as victims: Antecedents and consequences of acquaintance rape." In A. Parrot & L. Bechhofer (Eds.), *Acquaintance Rape: The Hidden Crime* (pp. 176–191). New York: John Wiley.

McIntosh, P. (1988). "White privilege and male privilege: A personal account of coming to see correspondences through work in Women's Studies." In M. Anderson & P. Hill Collins (Eds.), *Race, Class, and Gender: An Anthology* (pp. 76–87). Belmont, CA: Wadsworth.

Moscovici, S., Mucchi-Faina, A., & Maass, A. (1994). *Minority Influence.* Chicago: Nelson-Hall.

Muehlenhard, C. L. (1988). "Misinterpreted dating behaviors and the risk of date rape." *Journal of Social and Clinical Psychology,* 6, 20–37.

Muehlenhard, C. L., & Linton, M. A. (1987). "Date rape and sexual aggression in dating situations: Incidence and risk factors." *Journal of Counseling Psychology,* 34, 186–196.

Quinsey, V. L., & Upfold, D. (1985). "Rape completion and victim injury as a function of female resistance strategy." *Canadian Journal of Behavioral Science,* 17, 40–50.

Rapaport, K. R., & Posey, C. D. (1991). "Sexually coercive college males." In A. Parrot & L. Bechhofer (Eds.), *Acquaintance Rape: The Hidden Crime* (pp. 217–228). New York: John Wiley.

Riger, S., & Gordon, M. (1981). "The fear of rape: A study in social control." *Journal of Social Issues,* 37, 71–94.

Russell, D. E. H. (1984). *Sexual Exploitation: Rape, Child Sexual Abuse, and Work.* Beverly Hills, CA: Sage.

Russell, D. E. H. (1986). *The Secret Trauma: Incest in the Lives of Girls and Women.* New York: Basic.

Russo, N. P., Koss, M. P., & Goodman, L. A. (1994). "Male violence against women: A global health and development issue." In L. Adler & F. Denmark (Eds.), *Violence Prevention and Violence* (pp. 121–127). Westport, CT: Praeger.

Sheffield, C. J. (1995). "Sexual terrorism." In J. Freeman (Ed.), *Women: A Feminist Perspective.* (pp. 1–21). Mountain View, CA: Mayfield.

Swift, C. F. (1985). "The prevention of rape." In A. W. Burgess (Ed.), *Sexual Assault: A Research Handbook* (pp. 413–426). New York: Garland.

Wallston, B., & Grady, K. (1985). "Integrating the feminist critique and the crisis in social psychology: Another look at research methods." In V. O'Leary, R. Unger, & B. Wallston (Eds.), *Women, Gender and Social Psychology* (pp. 7–33). Hillsdale, NJ: Lawrence Erlbaum.

Warr, M. (1985). "Fear of rape among urban women." *Social Problems,* 32, 239–250.

Wood, W., Lundgren, S., Ouelette, J., Busceme, S., & Blackstone, T. (1994). "Minority influence: A meta-analytic review of social influence processes." *Psychological Bulletin,* 115, 323–345.

Reading 3   A Women's Martial Arts School: Connecting Feminism, Community, and Activism

CHARLENE R. DiCALOGERO

Questions to Consider:

1. According to DiCalogero, what are the benefits of teaching martial arts to women? How do women benefit from the approach to martial arts taken by the Center for Anti-Violence Education?

2. Why does DiCalogero see a feminist approach to martial arts as essential?

3. If you have studied the martial arts, what did you learn from that experience? If you haven't studied the martial arts, would you like to? Why or why not?

4. Would you recommend that martial arts training be made available and affordable to all women? Why or why not?

In order to ensure feminism's vitality, we as feminist scholars and activists continue to pose this question: How do we keep feminist thinking and the diverse realities of women's lives under sexism connected to each other to spark social change? How do we widen the circle of women who (a) incorporate the feminist critique of gender-linked social attitudes and behaviors into their worldviews and (b) organize to overcome these limitations and distortions of women's (and men's) lives? Or we can ask the question this way: How do we empower women by making feminism relevant and responsive to their concerns?

Through a historical and biographical case study of The Center for Anti-Violence Education (CAE), also known as Brooklyn Women's Martial Arts, of Brooklyn, NY, this research will illustrate some approaches a grassroots feminist organization used to connect women with diverse life experiences and backgrounds to each other and to the joint development of ideas and strategies for liberation.

ORGANIZATION HISTORY AND PRINCIPAL CHARACTERISTICS, 1981–91

CAE, which celebrated its twentieth anniversary in 1994, is one of the oldest and largest all-women's martial arts schools in the United States (Atkinson, 1983, p. 14). It was founded in 1974 by two women martial artists, and has a consistent student membership of 60 to 80 women in Okinawan goju karate, plus tai ji and children's classes, which equals a total in a typical month of over 100 students. Add to this program the five-week self-defense class cycles, which run several times a year, as well as off-site workshops, demonstrations, and classes conducted at street fairs, public schools, colleges, conferences, businesses, marches, and community organizations, and it becomes clear that hundreds of women and children come in contact with the school's students and staff each year. According to the Twentieth Anniversary invitation, CAE "has trained over 10,000 women and children in violence-prevention and self-defense." It is located on a busy commercial street in a mixed working-class and middle-class neighborhood that experienced gentrification in the 1970s and 1980s. Long-term students (those training a year or more) tend to reside within about a mile of the school, but some travel more than an hour each way by subway, bus, or car to attend classes.

These are some of the activities CAE does in the way of martial arts and self defense. This is the core of the school, and yet does not capture what may be most important about it as a feminist institution. This is its philosophy, and its philosophy-in-action. The moving force of this institution is the *empowering of each individual woman as the first step toward understanding why violence against women exists in our society and how to stop it* (Atkinson, 1983).

Empowerment in this sense has been called "psychological empowerment," which is defined as the process and result of people achieving "mastery over issues of concern to them.... The construct integrates perceptions of personal control, a proactive approach to life, and a critical understanding of the sociopolitical environment" (Zimmerman, 1995, p. 581). Women who believe they can act effectively to defend themselves, who pursue desirable activities regardless of the threat of sexist violence, and who understand the mechanisms of individual and institutional sexism, may be said to experience psychological empowerment with respect to issues of violence against women.

Empowerment in this school often takes the form of dramatic external changes, sometimes resulting from internal, soul-growing, idea trans-

formations. For women like myself, who had never been taught to believe in the possibility of self-protection, much less actual techniques, learning how a palm-heel strike could be effective against an attacker of any size was one of the first of many eye-opening lessons. Another woman spoke of the confidence she found from learning self defense that enabled her to tell her abusive partner, "You are never going to touch me again" (Pilcher, 1983). These are examples of the individual realizing and regaining her own power.

In the first week of a typical karate class at CAE, each woman learned to execute a middle punch and a front kick, to stand and move in a formal, solid posture, and to use the kiai. This last, the kiai, a Japanese word meaning "a gathering of...spiritual or internal energy" (Atkinson, 1983, p. 46), is a fierce shout that can be used by itself as a powerful self-defense technique. It was often introduced, after a demonstration by the teacher, with the class closing their eyes or facing away from each other and making noise all together. This teaching method allows women new to the technique to minimize feelings of self-consciousness and embarrassment, caused by fears of making the "wrong" sound, looking awkward, and worrying about others' judgments of us. The kiai was one of the first ways we became aware of our power as individuals and as a group, hearing how much noise we could make by ourselves and together, hearing our voices become a shield and a counterattack. In evaluations of a self defense course taught in 1996, students wrote that the kiai or verbal defense were among the most helpful techniques they learned (Center for Anti-Violence Education, 1996). Some classes explored diversionary tactics to interrupt an attack on others, ways to attract attention from potential allies if being harassed or attacked, and talking to other women about harassers at school or work. These strategies for *individual empowerment and group empowerment* are explicitly related to each other by teachers in the self-defense and karate classes.

Does this empowerment happen for women in all martial arts schools? It is probable that, as in universities and other organizations, not all education empowers (Belenky, Clinchy, Goldberger, & Tarule, 1986; Koegel, 1995). Subtle and overt forms of victim blaming, unrealistic and harmful limits on women's lives (e.g., don't go out at night, don't walk alone, get a man to protect you), and other types of disempowerment can be found in self-defense and martial arts teaching (Atkinson, 1983). A great deal depends on the school's *structure, philosophy, and leadership,* which encourages growth within a framework of discipline (Maton and Salem, 1995).

Structure

The structure of CAE/BWMA has evolved over time. During the 80s, it had a board of directors, which was composed of "regular teaching staff, the board officers, and elected student representatives" (Principles of Unity, n.d.; Valerie, 1986). All students were welcome to most board meetings. Many decisions were made informally, with few being put to a vote, in favor of a consensus model. However, this type of decision making was subject to confusion, due to such factors as fuzzy definition of the solution; or lack of implementation procedures, expected time frame or follow-up, all of which are hazards commonly encountered by informally run organizations. At least one attempt to formalize policies and shift some decision power from staff to volunteer student committees—in pursuit of feminist ideals—resulted in severe conflict, an organizational life-cycle phenomenon noted by other researchers (Riger, 1994). Much work required to run the school was accomplished through student committees and at yearly weekend retreats, in which all students were encouraged to participate in institutional assessment, policy decisions, and long-range planning (Maria Victoria, 1986). Becoming involved in these activities seemed to increase students' sense of ownership of and

responsibility for the continuance of the school as an institution. With this went at least some *willingness to endure conflict* (although making the process more conscious, less painful, and more productive is an ongoing challenge for the school).

These structures went through cycles of running well and less well, but to an as-yet-unmeasured extent did function as intended, to help women "gain experience in the running of the school" and to learn "new skills, such as decision making, bookkeeping, proposal writing, community outreach, planning, advertising, teaching and grassroots fundraising, [which] builds women's self-confidence and strength" (BWMA, Grant Proposal to Northstar Foundation, for year 1982–83). This feminist goal, to increase women's access to knowledge and experience, helped a number of women advance in their work or change careers. It also enlarged the pool of women with "organizational know-how" within what direct-action strategists Oppenheimer and Lakey call a type of "constructive program" (1964, p. 26). Such programs are useful for making a movement a part of—at home in a community—involving people who might not engage in more overt political action upon first joining, but seek some benefit the organization has to offer, such as classes or a hand with community betterment projects.

Philosophy

The school's philosophy has been overtly political from the beginning. From its Principles of Unity, first drafted in the early eighties: "We believe all women have the right to defend ourselves, and that training must be accessible to all women, especially to those of us who have the least power in this society: poor women, women of color, lesbians, older women.... We are committed to ending all forms of violence against women" (BWMA, Principles of Unity, n.d.). This philosophy grew out of the personal commitment and activities of the founders and many of the first students. They were involved in the feminist movement, civil rights, Black and Latina Power movements, Vietnam War resistance, peace and labor movements (Atkinson, 1983). It is important to note that, while the Asian martial arts became known in this country after World War II and the Korean War—imported mainly by returning white American soldiers (Kim, 1972)—the founders of CAE count two African American senseis (teachers) among their primary martial arts influences. Gerald Orange and Choka Zulu were unusual teachers who welcomed women in their classes, encouraged them to teach, and held a vision of martial arts as a path to liberation for oppressed people (Atkinson, 1983; Karate School for Women, 1983). The strength of this philosophy is the way it pervades the teaching of classes, and serves as a guide and measure for decisions and policies.

Leadership

Leadership from the Head Instructor/Executive Director of the school for all twenty years, and from other teachers and students who emerged over the years, has been vital to the internal growth of CAE and its impact on the community. CAE makes *training students to be teachers* one of its top priorities. Students do not wait many years to learn to teach, as they often do at more hierarchical, authoritarian karate dojos. Students start teaching in the first weeks of training by giving feedback to each other as partners and, a little later, in groups. After a year of karate training, students can take a formal self-defense teacher training course, followed by apprenticeship with more experienced teachers. The head instructor is a talented teacher who models the philosophy of cooperation and supportiveness in teaching and the running of the school. Her position is one of high visibility within the school, which attracts both admiration and criticism. Although the school is a nonprofit with heavy student involve-

ment, at many points the survival of CAE rested on her shoulders.

The limits of a school founded by white middle-class women were addressed by a group of women who formed a support group for women of color in 1984. Based on their leadership efforts, three workshops to combat racism were held for the school. Goals for the nurturance of leadership of women of color included identifying and training more such women to teach, holding special training events for women of color, and creation of an Anti-Racism Committee to formulate policy recommendations for CAE (Anti-Racism Committee, 1988; Anti-Racism Related Work at Brooklyn Women's Martial Arts, n.d.).

PHILOSOPHY IN ACTION

In an attempt to think systematically about what contributed to CAE's capacity to draw together diverse groups of women, enabling the communication of different types of knowledge, energizing and politicizing them as a group, I analyzed two primary activity areas: learning environment and methods, and social activism and community engagement.

Learning Environment and Methods

The learning environment had a number of features that appeared critical. Most obviously it was an *all female[1] and feminist context*, a rare experience for many women. This environment tends to avoid much of the overt sexism of mixed schools (Guthrie, 1995). It does *not*, however, protect against racism, classism and other oppressions (Riger, 1994). Since most women experience physical violence and sexual harassment at the hands of men, an appreciable amount of physical

---

[1] True for the adult karate, tai ji, and self-defense classes at the school, and for many workshops; children's classes and some workshops were mixed-gender.

and psychological safety was achieved through the all-female space. The school's relative *diversity* and openness to discussion of women's differences in race, sexuality, disabilities, class, and the like, promoted personal connections to form among women of different backgrounds through *extracurricular social opportunities* such as pot-luck meetings, cultural events, fund-raisers, dances, marches, trips to martial arts camps, and friendship networks.

Learning methods figure prominently in CAE's ability to integrate diverse women into the institution. *Action and multi-modal learning* included observing others, imitating, listening, experimenting, imagining, role playing, peer teaching, and observing ourselves in the mirror. We took part in discussions about personal experiences, and shared historical and theoretical information brought in from books, articles, and other sources. This is where part of the *academic connection* comes in: *making nonacademic learning accessible to women in academia, and making formal theory and research available to women outside academia*. Research on violence, the history of the martial arts, racism, and other topics were brought in and presented in classes or meetings. A school library was established in 1992, including many feminist and multicultural works. Some students were educators, college and graduate students, writers, artists, lawyers, filmmakers, and others who made their work and ideas available. In turn, the knowledge that academically employed women gained from members of the school who never went to college but had gotten their education from life (B. Richie, personal communication, 1989), was brought back with them to academia.

Because so few women seem to have much athletic or fighting skill, learning martial arts was *risky learning*, physically and socially. Challenging learning in areas previously closed to women and other socially subordinated groups helped break stereotypes *and* static self-concepts as we saw ourselves transcend artificial limits (Atkin-son, 1983; Guthrie, 1995). One Caribbean self-defense student said she discovered "you could be as small as a flea or as big as a ton" and be able to effectively use self defense (Pilcher, 1983). This belief in *all women's* ability to learn self-defense and martial arts was reinforced by news items posted on bulletin boards (e.g., a newspaper photo of a 90-year-old woman executing a flying front kick) and the telling of self-defense success stories in class. Research at a similar feminist martial arts school concurs that women find a combined physical and mental experience to be empowering and healing in a more comprehensive way than traditional therapeutic practices or feminist academicism (Guthrie, 1995).

Some of the riskiest learning for white women was going to the homes of women who lived in largely black or Latina neighborhoods, or collaborating with groups run by people of color. White women saw that these neighborhoods were not necessarily more dangerous than where they lived, but they did have to face the discomfort of being outside the norm—an experience more familiar to people of color within the dominant white society.

Important for many women was the *teaching style*, which emphasized *cooperation and mutual encouragement* rather than competition. Students were encouraged to progress at their own pace, to avoid comparison with other students, and to adapt or ask for help in adapting exercises to accommodate variations in physical mobility. Teachers were trained to concentrate more on each woman's strengths rather than her weaknesses. Role plays, attack simulations, and other aspects of the curriculum were reviewed and some redesigned when concerns about racial, age, and other stereotypes were raised. Women with past experiences of violence were encouraged to ask for emotional support and to modify participation in some exercises and role plays according to their own physical and emotional needs. Such approaches fall within the model of "feminist 'care of the self' ethic" (Guthrie, 1995, p. 108).

Open-ended learning is a part of practicing the martial arts, which entails the acquisition and use of information and skills that can be extended and refined on a lifelong basis. Although this is actually true of any area of human learning, traditional martial arts schools are among the few educational institutions in this country in which it is acknowledged that one never "graduates." At CAE there were *no ranks or tests;* as with most of human life, this martial arts school had no tests in which students pass or fail, or attain different color belts. CAE stood out in this respect, I believe, even among feminist martial arts schools. Occasional evaluations for kata, sparring, and self-defense were held to encourage each student to push to a new level of proficiency and to envision the ones beyond that.

School learning methods retained their vitality through *renewal of the pool of energy and knowledge* gained from new students, students who leave and return, and guests, including martial artists from other countries and other martial arts styles. Instructors learned from students who were different from them, revised their ideas of what feminism can mean thereby, and passed the information on to later participants (Rodriguez, 1987).

Social Activism and Community Engagement

CAE stated its ultimate goal is to end violence. Its contribution to this massive effort was to conduct activities of "education, community organizing, and political action" (Mission Statement, n.d.). There were *varied opportunities for political participation and different levels of involvement:* One could participate in discussions on the financial structure of the school (the reasons for the sliding-fee scale and the necessity of fund-raising and volunteer work to support its continuation), plan in-school presentations on sexual orientation, speak at street fairs and demonstrations about the mission of the school and its connection to liberation struggles, or do court watch for a battered woman on trial for killing her husband in self-defense, to name a few activities. This range of activity and commitment enabled women to choose a degree of involvement that was in accord with her own political thinking at that time. While some women could and did choose to concentrate on only the physical or sport aspect of classes, others found the political involvement an enriching, unexpected, and vital part of their training (B. D. Jones, personal communication, November 13, 1996). This aspect of the school's program, which focuses beyond personal learning to organizational and community betterment, is a feature that has been identified in other types of empowering groups (Maton and Salem, 1995).

In turn, opportunities occur in which participants see the *impact on people outside the organization:* as at martial arts demonstrations, where they were welcomed by cheering crowds at Lesbian and Gay Pride Marches; and at a public speaking engagement in 1987 with Yanira Corea, a survivor of contra terrorism in the U.S. and El Salvador, where CAE provided security (Anti-Racism Related Work, n.d.).

CAE's level of community engagement has increased over the years, as evidenced by its *presence in many different arenas:* from the street at fairs and marches, to elementary and high schools, colleges, neighborhood centers, civil disobedience and protests, corporations, homeless shelters, and local, national, and international conferences. Students and teachers were both presenters and attendees at the National Women and the Law Conference in 1985, attended by academics, lawyers, and activists from all over the United States (16th National Conference on Women and the Law, 1985). At the New York State Conference on Domestic Violence in 1984, in which legal justifications for and barriers to self defense for women were discussed, members of the school met attorneys and law professors working in the same struggle from a different perspective. For the past five years, at the Center for Women's Global Leadership annual two-week conference, CAE presented three-hour self-defense workshops.

During these workshops, teachers give women an opportunity to share information about what they are doing in their own countries on issues of violence against women. Among the exercises they typically led was the self defense voice circle: Women provide their own phrases (e.g., "Leave me alone, I don't know you!") to ward off an attacker and step forward to present them individually in front of the group. It has been such an empowering experience that women from as far away as Argentina have come to the conference on the strength of word of mouth about the self-defense class (B. D. Jones, personal communication, November 13, 1996).

The various media in which CAE appeared is reflective of its efforts to reach women in all walks of life: *New York Times, Newsday, New York* magazine, small neighborhood newspapers, television news, film, and even a music video, "A Priority," by Sweet Honey in the Rock. This is in addition to grassroots publicity: flyers, word of mouth, and referrals from other feminist and antiviolence groups. These occasional appearances in the media have been another form of validation for the participants: Representations of the school's philosophy and practice momentarily receive the stamp of mainstream social reality, in contrast to largely antifeminist discourses so often found in popular culture and mass communication (Faludi, 1991).

CONCLUSION

The Center for Anti-Violence Education was and remains a learning institution in the most complete sense of the word. It has enabled women to acquire knowledge and new ways of thinking and acting, incorporated new perspectives brought into the school by successive generations of non-academic, academic, and community activist contributors, and as an institution has reshaped itself numerous times to meet philosophical and practical challenges. Multiple features of its philosophy, structure, and practice seem in accord with

theoretical, empirical, and historical research on organizations that foster individual empowerment, organizational empowerment, and community empowerment (Zimmerman, 1995).

It is an institution feminist to its core, an example of what researchers of similar organizations have called women's "public homeplaces" (Belenky, Bond, & Weinstock, 1997, p. 156), with strengths from which other groups organizing for socially progressive ends can learn. Perhaps the most important lesson it offers is the way involvement in CAE can combine the fulfillment of needs for individual growth and self-expression with the desire to effect greater social change. Brenda Jones, assistant director, reflected that this came up in conversation with a number of students in the school: "People are able to go back and forth between the activism and the training. The training can feed you personally so you can continue on and do the work." The internal and external pressure that activists feel to "give and give and give is eased by the martial arts' ability to rejuvenate us." About her personal experience, as a student for 16 years, as well as karate and self-defense teacher, staff member, and/or governing board member for most of that time, she said it reassured her to have the long-term goal of ending violence (Mission Statement, n.d.), which the women realize is beyond the reach of their lifetimes. But "the self defense work, individual stories keep me going. It's drops of water. That's what it feels like: we're creating drops of water, and hopefully there will be many many more drops" (B. D. Jones, personal communication, November 13, 1996).

REFERENCES

Anti-Racism Committee. (1988, April). Anti-Racism Committee policy recomomendations [sic] for BWMA.

Anti-Racism Related Work at Brooklyn Women's Martial Arts. (n.d.).

Atkinson, L. (1983). *Women in the Martial Arts: A New Spirit Rising.* New York: Dodd Mead and Co.

Belenky, M. F., Bond, L. A., & Weinstock, J. S. (1997). *A Tradition That Has No Name: Nurturing the Development of People, Families, and Communities.* New York: Basic Books.

Belenky, M. F., Clinchy, B. M., Goldberger, N. R., & Tarule, J. M. (1986). *Women's Ways of Knowing: The Development of Self, Voice, and Mind.* New York: Basic Books.

BWMA (n.d.). Grant proposal to Northstar Foundation, for year 1982–83.

Center for Anti-Violence Education. (1996). [Evaluation of 5-Week Self-Defense Course]. Unpublished raw data.

Faludi, S. (1991). *Backlash: The Undeclared War Against American Women.* New York: Crown Publishers, Inc.

Guthrie, S. (1995). "Liberating the Amazon: Feminism and the martial arts." *Women & Therapy,* 16, (2–3) 107–119.

Karate School for Women. (1983). Special Training '83 [conference program].

Kim, J. H. (1972). *The History of Empty Hand Combat in the Orient and Development of the Oriental Martial Arts in America* [microform]. Thesis, M.A., Kent State University, UO-76 380-UO76 381.

Koegel, R. (1995). "Responding to the challenges of diversity: Domination, resistance, and education." *Holistic Education Review,* 5–17.

Maria Victoria. (1986, February). "The BWMA Retreat." *Dojo News.*

Maton, K. I., and Salem, D. A. (1995). "Organizational characteristics of empowering community settings: A multiple case study approach." *American Journal of Community Psychology,* 23, 631–656.

Mission Statement (n.d.). (Available from The Center for Anti-Violence Education, 412 Fifth Avenue, Brooklyn NY 11215.)

Oppenheimer, M., and Lakey, G. (1964). *A Manual for Direct Action.* Chicago: Quadrangle Books.

Pilcher, L. D. (1983). *Kiai! Women in Self-Defense* [film]. New York: Women Make Movies.

Principles of Unity. (n.d.). Brooklyn Women's Martial Arts.

Riger, S. (1994). "Challenges of success: Stages of growth in feminist organizations." *Feminist Studies,* 20, 2: 275–300.

Rodriguez, Y. (1987, June–July). "Children & martial arts." *Brooklyn Schools,* 8.

16th National Conference on Women and the Law. (1985). *Building Bridges, Not Walls.* New York City, March 21–24, 1985: Sourcebook.

Valerie. (1986, February). "The BWMA Board: What does it really do?" *Dojo News.* (Available from The Center for Anti-Violence Education, 412 Fifth Avenue, Brooklyn, NY 11215.)

Zimmerman, M. A. (1995). "Psychological empowerment: Issues and illustrations." *American Journal of Community Psychology,* 23, 5: 581–599.

Reading 4   Economic Violence against Women

RUTH BRANDWEIN

Questions to Consider:

1. When most speak about violence against women, they are speaking about physical violence. How does Brandwein justify including poverty as a form of violence against women? Do you agree with her? Explain.

2. According to Brandwein, how does poverty influence women's decisions to leave violent relationships?

3. Brandwein identifies poverty as a form of violence and describes measures to diminish poverty among women. Do you agree that we have a responsibility as a society to take steps to reduce the rate of poverty among women? Why or why not?

4. If you were a policy maker, which of Brandwein's suggestions would you enact first? Explain. Are there any suggestions you would not enact? Explain.

"Poverty is violence—violence against people. Physical, mental, psychological, intellectual, emotional, social, legal, political, you-name-it violence. It is ugly and angry and everywhere." Thirty years ago this statement was made by Norman Lourie, a distinguished social work educator, in a speech made before the Women's International League for Peace and Freedom (Lourie, 1968).

DEFINITIONS OF VIOLENCE

When we talk about violence, most people think about rape, murder, mugging, domestic violence, and other forms of personal assault. This is the interpersonal level of violence. There are, however, other types and levels of violence that are more indirect and therefore more insidious and more difficult to recognize.

The National Center for Injury Prevention and Control has defined violence as the "threatened or actual use of physical force against oneself or an individual or group that either results, or is likely to result, in injury or death" (National Crime Prevention Council, 1994). However, there is a broader definition of violence that encompasses more than direct physical force. Violence can be defined as any action or situation that harms the health and/or well-being of oneself or others. It can include both direct attacks on one's physical or psychological well-being as well as destructive acts that do not involve a direct relationship between the victim and those responsible for harm (Bulhan, 1985; NYC NASW Center, 1995; Salmi, 1993; Van Soest and Bryant, 1995).

According to Van Soest and Bryant, there are three levels of violence: (1) *the interpersonal*

Courtesy of Ruth Brandwein

level, which includes interpersonal acts of violence against persons or property, suicide and substance abuse, and acts by organized groups or mobs; (2) *the institutional level,* which includes harmful acts by organizations and institutions and official forms of violence such as state repression, war, torture, forced migration, unequal treatment under the law, and police brutality; and (3) *the structural level,* which includes oppression and deprivations built into the structure of society such as poverty, hunger, racism, and sexism (Van Soest and Bryant, 1995; Young, 1990).

We usually visualize violence only when it is immediate, active, and interpersonal but "poverty and inequity are passive forms of violence which impede human development" (NYC NASW Center, 1994).

Economic violence against women can be described as a gender-based, structural level of violence in which the society deprives women of economic well-being because of their gender. Such inequality affects women and their children in a number of harmful ways, including poverty, poor educational opportunities, poor or dangerous housing conditions, depression, loss of self-esteem, and other psychologically damaging conditions—as well as putting them at greater risk for physical violence. Poor women are more likely to be battered by their partners or live in high-crime neighborhoods, putting them at greater risk for muggings or rape.

Rosa was an unhappy teenager. Her father abused her and she escaped by moving in with her boyfriend. She got pregnant and dropped out of high school. By the time she was twenty her boyfriend had left her without any support for their three children. She has no high school degree or job skills and is on public assistance. Because she is Hispanic and has three children, most landlords will not rent to her. She was forced to move into the only place she could find—a dilapidated converted garage with two bedrooms in a part of town where she is afraid to let the kids go outside to play. This costs her $800

a month. Her welfare housing allowance is $422. The only way she could afford the rent was by having her mother move in with them. But Rosa does not like the way her mother is treating the children. She hits them and is verbally abusive. They live in close quarters and are always getting on each others nerves. Rosa and her children are victims of interpersonal, institutional, and structural violence.

DEFINITIONS OF POVERTY

Poverty may be seen as a form of structural violence but what is the definition of poverty? There are, in fact, two ways of defining poverty. One is the concept of "absolute poverty"; the other is "relative poverty."

Absolute poverty means that there is an absolute standard for determining if people are poor, based on objectively defined minimum needs. In the United States, the federal government developed a definition of poverty in 1964, based on a determination of a family's minimum needs for food, shelter, and other necessities. This standard varies with family size and has been adjusted annually since its inception in accordance with changes in the national cost-of-living index. Currently, for a family of four, this is slightly over $14,000. Any family of four whose income falls below this amount would officially be considered poor.

There are some major flaws in this definition of poverty.

(1) This standard ignores the different living costs in different parts of the country. While a family of four in rural Mississippi might be able to manage on $14,000, a similar family in Los Angeles or New York City, with higher housing, utility, and food costs, would probably be poor even if their family income were several thousand dollars more.

(2) When the standard was developed, the average family spent about one-third of its income on food. Therefore, in developing the

standard, the other two-thirds was considered adequate for housing, utilities, medical care, and other expenses. However, housing costs sky-rocketed in the 1970s and 1980s. By not taking this change into account, the poverty level is set inordinately low.

(3) Another problem built into the develop-ment of the poverty level was the amount esti-mated for food needs. Initially, it was to be based on the Department of Agriculture's "minimum but adequate" diet, but this definition would have classified too many people as poor, so, instead, the Department's "emergency" diet was used. Although this diet was considered nutritionally inadequate to sustain health over the long term, it was more politically acceptable. Cost-of-living increases in the poverty level since then have built on these original gaps in food and housing costs.

A major criticism of the concept of the abso-lute poverty level is that poverty is relative, depending on where you live and what others have. Critics of poverty programs often maintain that our poor people are better off than even the nonpoor in parts of Africa or India. That may be true. If everyone lives in a home with a dirt floor, that is the norm. But to expect someone in Chi-cago or another American city to live with a dirt floor when all around them have tile, carpet, or wood floors would make that person impover-ished despite how people live elsewhere in the world.

Television has had a profound impact in exposing poor people daily to consumer goods and wealthy lifestyles, in both programs and com-mercials. No longer are the poor isolated. They are acutely aware of the differences between the deprivations they suffer and the opulence all around them.

This comparative approach is the concept of *relative* poverty; that is, what one's income is in comparison to the general population. In coun-tries using this concept, poverty is measured in relation to the society's median income. Under this measure, poverty is often defined as an income that is below one-half of the median. In one suburban community in the East, the median family income is $65,000. Half of that would be $32,500. Yet the poverty level for a family of four in that community is the same as the national level—only slightly over $14,000, less than one-quarter of that median income. Rather than trying to determine the absolute minimum needed for survival, relative poverty focuses on the concepts of equality and equity.

In the United States, the gap between the richest and poorest people in the nation has grown dramatically in the last twenty-five years, since these figures began to be collected. In 1994, the top fifth of households in the United States received almost half (49.1 percent) of all the national income—meaning that this group received almost as much income as all the other households combined. The top 5 percent of households received 20 percent of all income. In contrast, the bottom fifth of households received less than 4 percent (3.6) of all income earned (U.S. Bureau of the Census, 1995).

WOMEN AND POVERTY

In 1978, Pearce coined the phrase "the feminiza-tion of poverty." By this, she did not mean to imply that women had not been poor in the past, but that women and women-headed families were making up an ever larger proportion of all the poor than previously. While the number of poor families remained fairly constant, or even decreased, the proportion of all those families headed by women began to increase in the 1970s and has continued to the present (Pearce, 1978).

In 1994, over one-third of all female-headed families fell below the poverty level as compared to only 6.5 percent of married-couple families. This phenomenon is exacerbated by race. For black female-headed families, 46 percent have incomes below the poverty level, and the rate is even higher for Hispanic female headed families (52 percent), (U.S. Bureau of the Census, 1995).

Looking at it another way, of all families in the United States that are poor, almost 53 percent are headed by women. This can be contrasted with Western European nations. In Sweden, only 6 percent of all poor families were headed by women; in France, 21 percent, and in the United Kingdom, just under 16 percent (Rainwater, 1992; Nichols-Casebolt, Krysik, & Hermann-Currie, 1994) Again, race exacerbated the situation. Of all poor black families, more than three quarters (77.5 percent) were headed by women.

The difference cannot be explained by the presence of two earners in many two-parent families. While female-headed families in 1993 had a median income of $17,443 and married-couple families had a median income of $43,005, families headed by men with no wife present had a median income of $26,467, almost $10,000 more than in women-only families (U.S. Women's Bureau, 1995).

Working women still earn less and have poorer pension and social security benefits than men. According to the 1994 U.S. Bureau of the Census data, women working full time, full year earn only 72 cents for every dollar men earn, and almost half of the women who work part-time do so because full-time work is unavailable (Bassuk, 1996).

Education alone is not the answer. When comparing earnings of men and women who have completed high school, there is a $10,000 discrepancy—men earn $22,966 to women's earnings of only $13,000. Moreover, men with a high school education earn the same as women who have completed college (Gottlieb, 1995; U.S. Bureau of the Census, 1994).

These discrepancies are more apparent as women age. In 1993, one-third of elderly women were poor or near poor, and for those living alone, one-third had incomes under the federal poverty level (Office of Senator Moseley-Braun, 1996). Elderly women over 65 are twice as likely to be poor as are elderly men. (Barusch, 1994; U.S. Bureau of the Census, 1995). If women earn less than men when they are younger, their Social Security benefits will be less when they grow older. Since more women work in low-paid, service sector jobs, and these jobs usually do not provide benefits, fewer women will have pensions to supplement their meager Social Security benefits. Many women working as domestics, waitresses, or other service jobs work "off the books"; their employers do not pay into the Social Security system, so they are not eligible for any benefits when they are too old to work.

THE IMPACT OF ECONOMIC VIOLENCE ON WOMEN

To consider poverty as economic violence, it is necessary to demonstrate how it causes injury to women. It causes both tangible material injury as well as injury to the spirit.

Poverty and inequality cause psychological damage. The effects of poverty in an affluent society destroy the spirit and violate one's self-worth. Women tend to have lower self-esteem than men, they are two to three times as likely to suffer from depression, and young poor women with children suffer the highest rates of depression (Gottlieb, 1995). Depression, low self-esteem, and little hope for the future are all risk factors in the abuse of alcohol and drugs, which are often used as "self-medication" to dull the anxiety and stress experienced in daily life.

According to Belle (1990, pp. 385–386), "Decades of research find poverty to be a correlate of psychological distress and diagnosable mental disorder…poor women experience more frequent, more threatening and more uncontrollable life events than does the general population." Single mothers and women of color are more likely to experience persistent, long-term poverty. Such chronic stress associated with poverty—financial uncertainty, poor housing, dangerous living conditions, illness of oneself and one's children—take a toll on one's mental health. A recent study by Bassuk and associates found that over 40 percent of poor women studied had a major depressive disorder—more than twice the rate of the general female population, over a fourth had attempted suicide at least once, and over one-third reported alcohol or drug dependence at some time in their lives, and the same number have experienced post traumatic stress (Worcester Family Research Project, 1996).

These conditions also put physical health at risk. Poor women are less likely to receive adequate health care. Fully one-fifth of people in female-headed families have no health insurance (U.S. Bureau of the Census, 1995). Poor women are less likely to have access to prenatal care, especially in the first and second trimesters. The lack of prenatal care increases the risk of infant and maternal mortality.

The rate of infant mortality in the United States is higher than in other industrialized nations, largely because of the higher rate for African Americans, who are more likely to be poor. In 1991, the infant mortality rate in the United States was 9.8 per thousand live births, while for African Americans it was 18.6 per thousand. In contrast, it was only 4.8 per thousand in Japan and 7.4 per thousand in Germany. Similarly, the maternal mortality rate was higher for African American women: 18.6 as compared to 5.4 white women who died in childbirth for every 1,000 births (U.S. Public Health Service, 1992).

The same study of both housed and homeless poor women in Worcester, Massachusetts, found that the physical health of both groups was significantly poorer than that of the general population for both acute and chronic health problems. For example, over 20 percent reported chronic asthma in contrast to only 5 percent in the general population. Similarly higher proportions of poor women suffered from chronic bronchitis, anemia, and ulcers (Bassuk et al., 1996).

The structural violence of poverty also puts women at higher risk for interpersonal violence. The poor, particularly in urban areas, are more likely to live in high-crime areas. Lack of access to safe housing in safe neighborhoods makes poor women and their children more likely to be victims of muggings, rape, and drug abuse. A divorced or single mother, who is more likely to be poor, is even more vulnerable in these circumstances.

Women who head families, who are at higher risk of being poor, are also increasingly at risk of being homeless. More than one-third of all homeless in the United States are now families with dependent children, and almost all of these families are headed by women (U.S. Conference of Mayors, 1995).

Because schools in the United States are primarily funded through local property taxes, living in a poor community is also likely to mean that a poor woman's children will attend poor schools. Not only are the children at greater risk of interpersonal violence in or on the way to school, but an inadequate education means that they will have fewer opportunities and be less able to compete economically, creating a cycle of poverty in the next generation.

THE LINKS BETWEEN ECONOMIC VIOLENCE AND FAMILY VIOLENCE

Between two and four million women are assaulted by their intimate male partners each year, according to current estimates. Twenty-five percent of all women have been abused by their male partners (Stark and Flitcraft, 1988; Strauss and Gelles, 1990). Poverty is a factor in causing and exacerbating such interpersonal violence. One study of poor women found that over 60 percent had been seriously abused by intimate male partners and over 80 percent had suffered from physical or sexual abuse over their life span (Worcester Family Research Project, 1996).

While domestic violence occurs in all socio-economic groups, poverty, male unemployment, and underemployment are related to higher rates of abuse (Davis, 1995; Gelles and Cornell, 1990). These conditions can create levels of stress, frustration, and anger in men that are often released in beating their wives or girlfriends. This should not be interpreted as an excuse or justification for this kind of scapegoating; it just means that men who are predisposed to violence may be more likely to engage in it under these conditions.

How does poverty or economic violence affect the female victim of domestic violence? Not only is a woman in a lower socioeconomic status more likely to be abused, but she has fewer options in extricating herself from an abusive situation. When the question is asked, "Why does she stay?" the answer often is that she cannot afford to leave. Particularly if she has children, a woman may fear that if she leaves her abuser she will be unable to support her family. Earlier we documented the lower incomes that women earn, even when they have more education.

Flo Kennedy, an African American lawyer-activist, once said that "every woman is one man away from welfare." A woman in a middle-class home may face poverty if she is divorced or separated. Her socioeconomic status is linked to her husband's career and salary. A woman who has only a high school education or less, and who has little or no job experience, is often faced with the tragic choice of staying with her abuser or having to go on welfare. Even a woman with a college degree who has stayed at home and raised her children, or worked at part-time jobs to supplement the family income, may have trouble earning enough to support herself and her children.

The recently passed welfare "reform" law imposes a five-year lifetime limit on receipt of financial aid. If a woman in an abusive situation has had previous episodes on welfare that total 60 months, she will be ineligible for any public assistance ever. Unless she had a family who could take her in, she would then be forced to stay with her abuser. Often such family arrangements are temporary. In many situations, the family may be unable to support her, or the woman has been so isolated from her family by her abuser that she cannot turn to them. Her only alternatives then would be homelessness, begging, prostitution, or crime.

The new welfare law (The Family Protection and Work Opportunity Reconciliation Act of 1996) also requires a mother on welfare to work after receiving aid for two years. But it has virtually eliminated education and job training programs, so even if she finds a job, unless she had education or training previously, she is doomed to a future of low-paid, low-skilled, often temporary jobs with few benefits.

And if a woman finds a job, she will have difficulty finding safe, accessible, and affordable child care. Full-time child care can cost $100 a week or more. For a woman earning $5 an hour, that would be half her wages, before any deductions. The United States is the only industrialized nation that does not provide child care as a matter of public policy.

Another problem in leaving an abuser is finding safe, affordable housing. Unless the abuser can be convinced to leave the family home, and even if he does, unless she can afford to stay there, a domestic violence victim will have difficulty finding safe, affordable housing. Over 80 percent of renters who are poor families spend more than a third of their income on rent (Bassuk et. al, 1996), and many spend 50 percent or more of their total income for housing, leaving little for other needs. If a woman is poor, and she is likely to become so after leaving her partner, she must face the choice of staying with her abuser or subjecting herself and her children to dilapidated, unsafe, and possibly dangerous housing conditions or even becoming homeless.

Although the father is supposed to continue to support his children, even if they are not living with him, current child support enforcement is inadequate. Currently, only half of all divorced women have child support orders, and of these only about half are receiving the full amount ordered by the court. Particularly in domestic violence situations, the abuser is often determined not to provide for his former partner and will go to considerable lengths to make it more difficult for her financially, as well as in other ways. He may even threaten to fight for custody, not because he wants to care for the children, but to intimidate her. If he leaves the state, works for himself, or works in the underground economy, it is unlikely that she will receive any support. Yet child support payments combined with a low-paying job can make the difference in enabling a woman to support her children. Women seeking public assistance are required to provide information about the father so the state can seek child support. Failure to cooperate may disqualify them or lead to sanctions. Yet for abused women, providing such information could seriously endanger them or their children. This is another example of how the institutional violence of the system can contribute to interpersonal violence.

WHAT CAN BE DONE: POLICY IMPLICATIONS

At the programmatic level, adequate, affordable, quality child care, health care, and housing should be available to all. This would help women to free themselves from domestic violence situations. It would also help to free all women from economic violence.

Pay equity and comparable worth laws would help to equalize women's salaries. Since women continue to be clustered in certain job areas known as the "pink collar ghetto" (such as secretarial work, nursing, teaching), equal pay for equal work is not sufficient to raise women's pay scales.

The concept of comparable worth means that different jobs performed by men and women are compared by variables including level of educational attainment required, preparation, difficulty, risk, responsibility, and number of people supervised. Then, even if the work is different, the pay would be equal for jobs that are comparable along those variables. For example, janitors, who are primarily male, often receive higher wages than women who are day care teachers. Because day care teaching requires a higher edu-

cational level, is more difficult, and requires greater responsibility, salaries for day care teachers should be increased. Using principles of comparable worth, some states have already instituted studies of pay scales to determine more equitable wages.

Existing federal programs such as the Earned Income Tax Credit (EITC), which is a negative income tax for low-paid workers, and Title IX, which ensures educational equity for women and girls, must be protected and expanded. With the recent increase in the minimum wage and the EITC, a woman working full time at minimum wage will be able to bring her family above the poverty line.

The recently passed welfare bill must be rescinded or revised. It is estimated that 1.5 to 2 million more children will be impoverished. Not only does it throw women and their children off welfare after a lifetime total of five years, but it prohibits any welfare payments or food stamps to most legal immigrants. Moreover, it eliminates Supplemental Security Income (SSI, which provides payments for the disabled) to many disabled children, which will make it harder for their mothers to stay home and care for them.

Real welfare reform can occur only if more jobs are available at wages that enable people to support a family above the poverty level. More, not less, education and training must be made available so that women will be prepared for these jobs, and individualized plans must be developed with each woman to assure that the training, education, or job is appropriate, that adequate time is allowed for each individual to prepare herself, and case management is provided during a transitional period. Emotional abuse may be so severe for domestic violence victims that it will take them longer to achieve self-confidence and learn how to deal appropriately with authority. Unrealistic time limits in the welfare legislation ignores their needs. Women who have been substance abusers (and many victims of violence use these drugs and alcohol to self-medicate) must be provided with treatment programs that allow them to keep their children.

Beyond these specific policy changes are the larger structural changes that will be needed to bring women out of poverty and eliminate the economic violence they suffer. Societal values that perpetuate patriarchy, traditional gender roles for women and men, and the traditional family must be challenged and eliminated. Until little girls are raised to believe they are of equal value, are imbued with self-esteem and self-confidence, and are given the same opportunities as little boys, economic violence against women will continue.

Currently, lawmakers at the federal and state levels are attempting to enshrine the traditional two-parent family as the only family of any value. In a recently passed federal law, same-sex marriages will not be recognized. Attempts are being made by some states to limit adoption of children to heterosexual married couples. Some states have adopted "wedfare," a policy that pressures women on welfare to marry in order to obtain higher welfare benefits.

Finally, economic injustice will continue as long as our economic system is founded on the principle of winners and losers. A few people are becoming extremely wealthy, many others are becoming poorer, and for the first time in the United States the middle class is shrinking. When wages are adjusted for inflation, even white male workers are earning less today than they were twenty years ago. That means more mothers, even of infants, are being forced into the workplace, and both men and women are working longer hours in order to maintain a livable family income. The stress and frustration of the middle class is reflected in the scapegoating of the poor—especially welfare mothers, African Americans, and immigrants. Economic violence against women is the natural outcome of an economy that can be healthy only if a certain percentage of people who are seeking work remain unemployed. It

will not end until a more equitable and just economic system replaces the current one.

REFERENCES

Barusch, A. (1994). *Older Women in Poverty: Private Lives and Public Policies.* New York: Springer.

Bassuk, E., et al. (1996). "Single mothers and welfare." *Scientific American,* October, pp. 60–67.

Belle, D. (1990). "Poverty and women's mental health." *American Psychologist,* 45:1, pp. 385–389.

Bulhan, H. (1985). *Frantz Fanon and the Psychology of Oppression.* New York: Plenum Press.

Davis, L. (1995). "Domestic violence." In R. Edwards (Ed.), *Encyclopedia of Social Work,* 19th ed., pp. 780–788. Washington, DC: NASW Press.

Gelles, R., and Cornell, C. (1990). *Intimate Violence in Families,* 2nd ed. Newbury Park, CA: Sage Publications.

Gottlieb, N. (1995). "Women overview." In R. Edwards (ed.), *Encyclopedia of Social Work,* 19th ed., pp. 2518–2529. Washington, DC: NASW Press.

Lourie, N. (1968). "Poverty Is Violence." Speech presented to conference of Women's International League of Peace and Freedom, Philadelphia, Pa. Sept. 28, 1968.

National Association of Social Workers. (1995). "Poverty: Ensuring Enough for Everyone" One in a series of six briefing papers produced by the Violence and Development Project. Washington, DC: NASW Office of Peace and International Affairs.

National Crime Prevention Council. (August 1994). *"Community Partnerships Bulletin: Partnerships to Prevent Youth Violence* (NCJ148459). Washington, DC: U.S. Department of Justice.

New York City NASW Center on Poverty, Violence and Development. (1994). Report submitted to the Violence and Development Project.

Nichols-Casebolt, A., Krysik, J., & Hermann-Currie, R. (1994). "The povertization of women: A global phenomenon." *Affilia: Journal of Women and Social Work,* 9:1, pp. 9–29.

Office of Senator Carol Moseley-Braun, "Statistics on Women, Pensions and Poverty—1996" Washington, DC: U.S. Senate.

Pearce, D. (1978). "Feminization of poverty: Women, work and welfare." *Urban and Social Change Review,* February.

Rainwater, L. (1992). *Poverty in American Eyes* (Luxembourg Income Study, Working Paper No. 80). Walfendange, Luxembourg: Center for the Study of Population, Poverty and Public Policy.

Salmi, J. (1993). *Violence and Democratic Society.* London: Zed Books.

Stark, E., and Flitcraft, A. (1988). "Violence among intimates: An epidemiological review." In V. Hassalt et al. (Eds), *Handbook of Family Violence,* pp. 293–327, New York: Plenum Press.

Strauss, M., and Gelles, R. (1990). "How violent are American families? Estimates from the National Family Violence Resurvey and other studies." In M. Straus and R. Gelles (Eds.), *Physical Violence in American Families,* pp. 341–367. New Brunswick, NJ: Transaction Books.

U.S. Bureau of the Census. (1995, March) *Current Population Reports.* Washington, DC: U.S. Government Printing Office.

U.S. Conference of Mayors (1995). A Status Report on Hunger and Homelessness in America's Cities. Washington D.C.: Author.

U.S. Public Health Service. (1992). *Health United States, 1991.* Washington, DC: U.S.: Government Printing Office.

U.S. Women's Bureau. (1995, May). "Twenty facts on women workers." *Facts on Working Women* 95:1. Washington, DC: U.S. Government Printing Office.

Van Soest, D., and Bryant, S. (1995). "Violence reconceptualized for social work: The urban dilemma." *Social Work,* 40:4, pp. 549–557.

Worcester Family Research Project. (1996). *Study Highlights: Major Findings Concerning Homeless Families,* August. Newton Centre, MA: Better Homes Fund.

Young, I. (1990). "Five faces of oppression." In *Justice and Politics of Difference.* Princeton, NJ: Princeton University Press.

Topic 9

Mental Health

Ghosts of Horses

straight steel posts
once boxed in this pasture
fresh
paint green soldiers
perfectly lined the perimeter
protecting against escape
or intrusion

trussed light
with high tinsel wire
and the surrounding shock
of invisible energy

those humming currents
and the thunder
of pounding hooves
have dissipated
swallowed by the land
pinned down
by the sporadic posts
left encircling
this overgrown pasture

I forced the last steel stake
crusted brown with rust
free from the earth
and blood welled up
from that empty space
and washed the tears
from my eyes
as the ghosts of horses
galloped away

Courtesy of Rhonda Barnett

The issue of gender differences in mental health is a very complex and controversial one. Considerable research has examined the link between gender and the frequency of disorders, and between gender and the type of disorder experienced. Although gender differences in the frequency of psychological disorders have not been established consistently, there is considerable evidence for differences in the types of disorders typically experienced by females and males. That is, females are much more likely to be diagnosed with depression, eating disorders, and anxiety disorders; while males are much more likely to be diagnosed with drug and alcohol addictions and with personality disorders.

One explanation for these gender differences is that conceptions of mental health and mental disorder are affected by gender stereotypes. For example, in a classic study (Broverman, Broverman, Clarkson, Rosenkrantz, & Vogel, 1970), psychologists and social workers were asked to describe a mentally healthy woman, a mentally healthy man, and a mentally healthy adult (no sex specified). Compared to the mentally healthy male, the mentally healthy female was described as being more submissive, more easily excitable, more emotional, and more vain. She was also described as less independent, less adventurous, less competitive, and less objective. Furthermore, the therapists' descriptions of a mentally healthy male were very similar to their descriptions of a mentally healthy adult. As Lips (1996) points out, this double standard of mental health created a double bind for women. If they met the cultural standard for a healthy female, they failed to achieve that of a healthy adult. In fact, their attitudes and behaviors more closely resembled those of people with low self-worth and feelings of powerlessness. On the other hand, if they met the cultural standard for a healthy adult by behaving in ways that are characteristic of empowered people, then they were considered unfeminine. Either way, they were vulnerable to depression.

More recent research with mental health professionals has revealed considerably less *overt* sexism concerning conceptions of mentally healthy women and men. However, the double standard of mental health still exists in more *subtle* forms, as documented in naturalistic studies that observe interactions between therapists and their clients (Hare-Mustin, 1983). This finding suggests that gender biases are so deeply embedded in our cultural thinking that they continue to surface in unintentional ways in the therapeutic relationship and may be harmful to the mental health of females. Gender stereotypes (as well as racial, ethnic, and social class stereotypes) also influence the diagnosis and treatment of psychological disorders. For example, the widespread assumption that women are easily excitable relative to men may help explain why women are much more likely to be diagnosed with anxiety disorders, and to be receiving drug treatment for them.

Gender oppression offers a second explanation for differences in the type of psychological disorders experienced by females and males. For example, the gender difference in depression may be linked to several disempowering life experiences that are more common to women than to men. Among these are the limits placed on many women's lives in the family, community, and workplace; the caretaking burden that women shoulder in the family, community and workplace; single parenting; and the heightened vulnerability of women to several forms of violence—battering, sexual assault, sexual harassment, and poverty. Similarly, gender oppression may account for some of the gender difference in eating disorders. For example, childhood sexual abuse and the cultural standard of attractiveness for women have each been linked to anorexia and bulimia.

This section introduces the work of several social scientists who have addressed these issues by challenging the sexism inherent in diagnostic categories (such as PMS), by targeting specific life conditions of women that contribute to psychological disorders, and by showing how life conditions are linked to race and ethnicity.

In the opening reading, entitled "Gender Issues in the Diagnosis of Mental Disorder," Paula Caplan highlights several examples of the ways that gender biases in the labeling and diagnosis of disorders are a reflection of widespread sexism among mental health professionals. For example, in the Diagnostic and Statistical Manual of Mental Disorders (DSM-III-R), premenstrual syndrome (PMS) is classified as a psychological disorder—"late luteal phase dysphoric disorder."[1] This has occurred despite the absence of scientific support for any underlying psychological causes of premenstrual syndrome. Caplan calls attention to the fact that there is no equivalent diagnostic category involving male hormone cycles, such as "testosterone-based aggressive disorder," and alerts us to the problems and dangers involved in this and other misogynist diagnostic categories.

In the second reading, entitled "Depressed Mood and Self-Esteem in Young Asian, Black, and White Women in America," Nancy Fugate Woods and her colleagues test a model of depression and self-esteem that connects women's psychological state to the conditions of their daily lives. Because their model connects life conditions to ethnicity as well as gender, depression and self-esteem were examined for Asian, black and white women living in the United States. For each group of women, the researchers examined the effects of personal resources (income and education), social demands, social resources, level of feminine socialization, and social roles (employment, marital status and parenting). Although several of these life conditions were predictors of depression and self-esteem for all three groups (especially personal resources and social networks), a different model of depression and self-esteem emerged for each group. This was due to the variability of daily experiences among the three groups.

In the third reading, entitled, "'A Way Outa No Way': Eating Problems among African-American, Latina, and White Women," Becky Wangsgaard Thompson uses life history interviews with culturally diverse women to challenge several assumptions about eating disorders that have emerged from research focused on white, middle- and upper-class heterosexual women. For example, while acknowledging the importance of the "culture-of-thinness" model to understanding eating disorders, she challenges its theoretical emphasis. She argues that it is limited in its ability to account for eating problems, and that it may unintentionally reinforce the sexist assumption that women are obsessed with their appearance. By extending her research to groups of women who have been excluded, Thompson shows that eating problems are often survival strategies for coping with a variety of social injustices such as sexual abuse, emotional abuse, physical abuse, racism, heterosexism and poverty. For example, bingeing was reported as the most common method of coping among survivors of sexual abuse in Thompson's study. Bingeing helped the women block painful feelings by numbing them against the pain. According to Thompson, treatment of eating disorders should go beyond individual healing to focus on changing the social conditions that underlie their cause.

NOTE

1. In the latest edition of the Diagnostic and Statistical Manual of Mental Disorders (DSM-IV), the diagnostic category "late luteal phase dysphoric disorder" (LLPDD) has been replaced with the category "premenstrual dysphoric disorder" (PMDD).

REFERENCES

Broverman, I. K., Broverman, D. M., Clarkson, F. E., Rosenkrantz, P. S., & Vogel, S. R. (1970). "Sex-Role Stereotypes and Clinical Judgments of Mental Health." *Journal of Consulting and Clinical Psychology,* 34 (1), 1–7.

Hare-Mustin, R. (1983). "An Appraisal of the Relationship Between Women and Psychotherapy: 80 Years after the Case of Dora." *American Psychologist,* 38, 593–601.

Lips, H. (1996). *Sex and Gender: An Introduction.* Mountain View, CA.: Mayfield Publishing Company.

Reading 1   Gender Issues in the Diagnosis of Mental Disorder

PAULA J. CAPLAN

Questions to Consider:

1. According to Caplan, why are the learning disabilities of girls more likely to be overlooked and underdiagnosed than are those of boys? What is your reaction to her claims?

2. According to Caplan, "self-defeating personality disorder" and "late luteal phase dysphoric disorder" (premenstrual syndrome) are misogynist diagnostic categories. Do you agree with her reasoning? Explain your answer.

3. According to Caplan, what are some of the ways that females have been harmed by sexism among mental health professionals? Have you, or someone you know, been harmed by this sexism? If so, explain.

Historically, it has been considered acceptable—indeed, womanly—for two or more women or girls to band together to help the poor, the sick, the helpless, the oppressed, children, or men. The only time it has not been considered acceptable for women to do this has been when the help was for themselves or for other women. Women who have done the latter have been branded as selfish, unwomanly, belligerent, strident, and so on; they have been accused of complaining too much or of ignoring the needs of other people. They have been threatened with ostracism by the host culture.

In spite of such threats, some women have continued to insist that women's concerns be given high priority. It was high time for a feminist conference on gender, science, and medicine—like this one—which Dr. Elaine Borins so beautifully put together.

I shall present a very brief sampling of some of the ways in which sexism among mental health professionals has resulted in serious oversights, inadequate treatment, and even mistreatment and harm—primarily to females but also sometimes to males. It is important to keep in mind that sexism is not the only bias that profoundly skews and twists the process of diagnosis. Racism, ageism, classism, and homophobia are some of the other deep-seated prejudices that are reflected in the creation and assignment of diagnostic labels by mental health professionals.

Although there is space here to mention only a few examples, I have chosen these carefully to provide a sense of the enormous range of diagnostic problems and harm that result from sexism.

© 1992, The Haworth Press, Inc., Binghamton, New York, *Women and Therapy,* "Gender Issues in the Diagnosis of Mental Disorder," *12,* (4), pp. 71–79.

LEARNING DISABILITIES

In my earliest years as a clinical psychologist, I specialized in children's learning problems (Kinsbourne & Caplan, 1979). One of the most widely accepted bits of "wisdom" in that field was, and still is, that far more boys than girls have learning disabilities. Recent research (Shaywitz, Shaywitz, Fletcher, & Escobar, 1990) suggests that, in fact, learning disabilities are equally common in both sexes. Nevertheless, in virtually all clinical settings, more boys than girls are brought in with complaints about learning problems; and I wondered whether that pattern of *noticing* and referral for learning disabilities reflected the pattern of *real* learning disabilities. My own research (Caplan, 1973, 1977; Caplan & Kinsbourne, 1974) a number of years ago suggested that girls' learning disabilities and other academic problems are more likely than boys' to be overlooked and underdiagnosed, and there seemed to be several reasons for this:

First, since it is considered less important for girls than for boys to be academically successful, low academic performance by girls appears less likely to be labeled a problem than low academic performance in boys; therefore, girls' learning difficulties are unnoticed or, when noticed, not considered to warrant referral, remediation, or any other kind of treatment (this is the "As long as she's pretty and nice, she'll get a husband. She doesn't need to be smart" attitude).

Second, girls are socialized to deal with frustration and failure in less disruptive, antisocial ways than are boys. As a consequence, a learning disabled girl is less likely than an equally learning disabled boy to deal with that frustration in ways that lead her teachers or parents to take her to professionals in the hope that they can "do something" to keep her under control.

This pattern is harmful to girls and to boys in different ways. Many girls' learning problems are simply never noticed, and boys who already have one problem (e.g., learning disability) develop a second problem (disruptive behavior) as part of their attempt to cope in a sex-appropriate, traditionally masculine way. Canadian psychologist Meredith Kimball (1981) has identified the deep-seated sexism in North American educational systems' allocation of funds for remediation of learning disabled children. Kimball points out that it is commonly believed (although by no means based on solid evidence) that boys have more reading disabilities than girls and that girls have more trouble (although, interestingly, these are not usually dignified with the term "learning disability") with so-called "visual-spatial tasks," which are assumed to be important for doing math and sciences.

Where do public monies for remediation go? Overwhelmingly, they are poured into remedial *reading* programs, and little or no remediation is provided for children with visual-spatial problems. A similar disproportion characterizes the research that is done on learning disabilities: Overwhelmingly, it is focused on reading problems, the problems thought to plague boys far more than girls. Although some might argue that reading is the most important school-related skill and therefore deserves more attention and funding, even North America's post-Sputnik stress on the importance of education in mathematics and sciences did not result in any substantial increase in a focus on visual-spatial problems.

PSYCHIATRIC DIAGNOSES

When the American Psychiatric Association last revised its massive handbook, *Diagnostic and Statistical Manual of Mental Disorders* (DSM)—which is probably the most widely used listing of psychiatric labels—they included two new, dangerously misogynist diagnostic categories. A great deal has been written elsewhere (see Caplan, 1987, for details and additional references) about the numerous problems and dangers involved in these categories, which are "self-defeating personality disorder" (SDPD) and "late luteal phase dysphoric disorder" (LLPDD), but I shall briefly mention some of the major ones here.

Self-defeating personality disorder was initially to be called "masochistic personality disorder," and even though the title was changed, the criteria and the implications are the same. The criteria applied to these people include putting other people's needs ahead of their own, not feeling appreciated even though they really are, and settling for less when they could have more.

This diagnostic label is dangerous because:

1. It applies to what I call the "good wife syndrome": Women in North America are traditionally raised to put other people's needs ahead of their own and to settle for less when they could have more (it's called being unselfish, not being a demanding shrew, and/or having poor self-esteem so that one doesn't *realize* that one could do better), and it has been well-documented that women's traditional work (housework and childcare) in fact *is not* appreciated. Thus, after a woman has conscientiously learned the role her culture prescribes for her, the psychiatric establishment calls her mentally disordered. It does *not* do anything similar for men. It does not classify as a psychiatric disorder the inability to identify and express a wide range of emotions, a "disorder" which has been proven to characterize enormous numbers of North American males.

2. It is a description of the typical battered or severely emotionally abused woman. Such women characteristically experience a dangerous plummeting in their self-esteem because of the abuse, and, trying to be good women and good wives, they may become even more self-denying, giving, and undemanding than other women in an attempt to persuade the abuser to stop the abuse. Applying the label of "self-defeating personality disorder" to these women is a pernicious form of victim-blaming. Although users of

the DSM are cautioned not to apply this label when abuse was the major cause of the woman's apparently "self-defeating" behavior, it has been well-documented (see Firsten, 1991, for a review) that therapists almost never ask their clients about abuse, and when they do, the clients are reluctant (ashamed, scared) to talk about it. As Poston and Lison (1989) report, "Many would sooner ask a client if she is hearing voices than ask her if she has sexual abuse in her background, even though figures would indicate that the chances of an abusive background far outweigh the occurrence of hearing voices" (p. 21).

3. The label is dangerous because it leads both therapists and the women so diagnosed to believe that the problems come from within, that the women have a sick need to be hurt, humiliated, unappreciated, etc. Since my book, *The Myth of Women's Masochism,* was published (1987), hundreds of women·have told me that in years of traditional psychotherapy, their therapists told them regularly that they brought all their problems on themselves. When the women say, for instance, "But Fred was wonderful to me when we were dating. It wasn't until our wedding night that he started to beat me," the therapist all too often replies, "Ah, yes! So *consciously* you didn't choose an abusive man. But your self-defeating motives are *unconscious*!" Such "treatment" is, I believe, a major cause of depression in women: They are unjustifiably given the message that there is no point in their trying to get out of an abusive or otherwise distressing relationship or situation, because their sick, unconscious motives will inevitably lead them straight into more trouble.

4. Prime movers of the DSM revisions have themselves pointed out that people diagnosed in this way typically have what is called a "negative therapeutic reaction," that psychotherapy makes them worse (Kass,

MacKinnon, & Spitzer, 1986). No surprise, I say, because if I have a broken leg, and the doctor puts a cast on my arm instead, my leg will certainly get worse. If a woman is being abused or severely emotionally neglected and unappreciated by her intimate partner, then a therapist who takes the approach that she enjoys her misery and has an unconscious need to suffer not only does not help but actively makes her worse.

The other misogynist diagnosis, LLPDD, is a fancy term for premenstrual syndrome as a psychiatric disorder. What's wrong with that? Several things.

1. While we all know women who have genuine physical or mood problems that seem to be regularly associated with their menstrual cycle, the danger is in calling these troubles psychiatric problems. Robert Spitzer, chief author of the most recent DSM revisions, told a press conference that psychiatrists don't know any psychiatric treatment that will help women with PMS but that PMS as a psychiatric diagnosis is essential to enable psychiatrists to figure out what they can do for these women. Although Spitzer may have good intentions, since psychiatric labelling tends to have negative and even dangerous consequences, until there is reason to believe that PMS is a psychologically caused problem *and/or* is helped by psychiatric treatment, there is no justification for using this label. Women who have PMS have enough trouble without having to worry that they are crazy. Furthermore, our society typically seizes on any suggestion of women's emotional weakness to justify keeping women out of well-paying responsible jobs. (By contrast, although it is known that men's job performance varies according to predictable cycles, since there is no easy-to-pinpoint marker like monthly bleeding with which to associate those changes, men are regularly

allowed to work at such dangerous jobs as piloting airplanes without being checked for where they are in their cycles.)

2. Nutritional, vitamin, and exercise treatments of various kinds have been shown to be helpful to many women who have PMS. These forms of treatment are not widely recommended (perhaps not even known) by the psychiatric and medical community, and calling PMS a psychiatric problem makes it even less likely that women will be told about such useful courses of action.

Perhaps the most striking feature of SDPD and LLPDD is that the DSM includes no equivalent diagnostic categories for males, that is, there is no male SDPD parallel in the sense of having a category that describes an extreme form of males' socialization, such as "Macho Personality Disorder," and there is no male equivalent of LLPDD such as "Testosterone-Based Aggressive Disorder."[1]

WHY ISN'T THE HEALTH INSURANCE INDUSTRY SCARED?

The health insurance industry ought to be up in arms about both of these diagnoses. Why?

---

1. After this paper was presented at the 1988 Gender, Science, and Medicine Conference, Margrit Eichler and I proposed, for educational and consciousness-raising purposes, the diagnostic category described in the Appendix as a way to redress the sexist imbalance in the DSM. Curious to see what would happen, we submitted the category to the DSM-IV Revisions Task Force, and excerpts from the disturbing, sometimes hilarious, but always revealing correspondence from some of the Task Force members about this category have now been published in a paper called "How *Do* They Decide Who Is Normal? The Bizarre, But True, Tale of the *DSM* Process" (Caplan, 1991). A comprehensive review of the research relevant to the category has also been published (Pantony & Caplan, 1991). We note that, in our hurry to get the proposal circulated, we inadvertently omitted a great many possible criteria that we feel ought to have been included, such as some related to homophobia, racism, classism, materialism, ableism, weightism, and so on.

Because most nice women and virtually all battered women could be erroneously given the label of "self-defeating personality disorder," and once they are in psychiatric treatment, since they are not psychiatrically disordered they will be unlikely to "get well"; thus, the therapy is likely to be interminable. Women who enter psychiatric treatment for their PMS will, of course, experience little or no improvement for this physiologically based disorder, and since they don't "get well," they may regularly lie on a psychiatrist's couch—until they reach menopause, at which time they will no doubt be considered in need of psychotherapy for their menopausal disorder. I have repeatedly contacted the health insurance lobby in the United States and the Canadian department of Health and Welfare, but they have chosen not to express any opposition to these categories, even though one would think that they would be worried that their coffers will be rapidly drained.

THE ABUSE OF MOTHERS OF SEXUALLY ABUSED CHILDREN

After a few, brief years during which many brave adults revealed that they had been sexually abused as children and were believed, there has been a dangerous, unbelieving backlash. The media are filled with allegations that children claim they are sexually abused by their fathers only because the children's nasty, scheming mothers force them to say it, in an effort to hurt their ex-husbands. Some mental health professionals, egged on by an enthusiastic legal profession, have legitimized this backlash through the use of the psychiatric label, "Munchausen's syndrome by proxy." The label "Munchausen's syndrome" is a psychiatric diagnosis applied to people (usually women) who are described as going from one physician to another in the mistaken belief that they have something physically wrong with them, that they have a pathological need to believe they are physically ill. Typically, I have heard psychiatrists describe such a person as "never being satisfied until she gets someone to operate on her." Now, "Munchausen's by proxy" is being applied to a woman whose child reports being sexually abused. The diagnosis is supposed to indicate that the woman has a need to believe that something terrible is happening not to her but rather to her child.

This is a particularly terrifying, nauseating development. For so long, mothers have been damned by therapists for *not* reporting sexual abuse in their children—mothers' explanations that they *did not know* it was happening are ignored, and therapists say they *must have known unconsciously*—and now, they are being damned and pathologized if they *do* make the report. When their children are being seriously harmed, the harm to the children is too often ignored and disbelieved, while the spotlight is turned on the allegedly sick mother. This is one of the more vicious and irresponsible forms of mother-blaming, a phenomenon whose pervasiveness among mental health professionals has been well-documented.

CONCLUSION

The sheer variety of gender biases in diagnoses represented in this brief paper reflects the power and the pervasiveness of sexism in the realm of diagnosis. This means that both conclusions drawn from research mired in these biases and the clinical and human applications of biased categories need rapid and radical transformation.

REFERENCES

Caplan, Paula J. (1973) The role of classroom conduct in the promotion and retention of elementary school children. *Journal of Experimental Education, Spring. 41(3).*

Caplan, Paula J. (1977) Sex, age, behavior, and subject as determinants of report of learning problems. *Journal of Learning Disabilities, 10,* 314–316.

Caplan, Paula J. (1987). *The myth of women's masochism.* NY: Signet.

Caplan, Paula J. (1991) How *do* they decide who is normal? The bizarre, but true, tale of the *DSM* process. *Canadian Psychology 32(2),* 162–170.

Caplan, Paula J., & Kinsbourne, Marcel. (1974) Sex differences in response to school failure. *Journal of Learning Disabilities, 7,* 232–235.

Firsten, Temi (1991). Violence in the lives of women on psych wards. *Canadian Woman's Studies, 11(4),* 45–48.

Kass, Frederic, Mackinnon, Roger A., & Spitzer, Robert L. (1986). Masochistic personality: An empirical study. *American Journal of Psychiatry, 143,* 216–218.

Kinsbourne, Marcel, & Caplan, Paula J. (1979). *Children's learning and attention problems.* Boston: Little, Brown.

Kimball, Meredith (1981). Women and science: A critique of biological theories. *International Journal of Women's Studies, 4,* 318–335.

Pantony, Kaye Lee, & Caplan, Paula J. (1991) Delusional dominating personality disorder: A modest proposal for identifying some consequences of rigid masculine socialization. *Canadian Psychology, 32(2),* 120–133.

Poston, Carol, & Lison, Karen. (1989) *Reclaiming our lives: Hope for adult survivors of incest.* Boston: Little, Brown

Shaywitz, Sally E., Shaywitz, Bennett A., Fletcher, Jack M., & Escobar, Michael. (1990) Prevalence of reading disability in boys and girls: Results of the Connecticut longitudinal study. *Journal of American Medical Association, 264(8),* 998–1002.

Appendix

DELUSIONAL DOMINATING PERSONALITY DISORDER (DDPD)*

Individuals having this disorder are characterized by at least 6 (?) of the following 14 criteria (note that such individuals nearly always suffer from at least one of the delusions listed):

1. Inability to establish and maintain meaningful interpersonal relationships

---

*The Criteria for Delusional Dominating Personality Disorder was first printed by *Canadian Psychology* 32(2), pp. 120–333.

2. Inability to identify and express a range of feelings in oneself (typically accompanied by an inability to identify accurately the feelings of other people)

3. Inability to respond appropriately and empathically to the feelings and needs of close associates and intimates (often leading to the misinterpretation of signals from others)

4. Tendency to use power, silence, withdrawal, and/or avoidance rather than negotiation in the face of interpersonal conflict or difficulty

5. Gender-specific locus of control (belief that women are responsible for the bad things that happen to oneself, and the good things are due to one's own abilities, achievements, or efforts)

6. An excessive need to inflate the importance and achievements of oneself, males in general, or both. This is often associated with a need to deflate the importance of one's intimate female partner, females in general, or both

7. The presence of any one of the following delusions:

   A. the delusion of personal entitlement to the services of

      1. Any woman with whom one is personally associated
      2. Females in general for males in general
      3. Both of the above

   B. the delusion that women like to suffer and to be ordered around

   C. the delusion that physical force is the best method of solving interpersonal problems

   D. the delusion that sexual and aggressive impulses are uncontrollable in

      1. Oneself
      2. Males in general
      3. Both of the above

   E. the delusion that pornography and erotica are identical

F. the delusion that women control most of the world's wealth and/or power but do little of the world's work

G. the delusion that existing inequalities in the distribution of power and wealth are a product of the survival of the fittest and that, therefore, allocation of greater social and economic rewards to the already privileged are merited

(Note: the simultaneous presence of several of these delusions in one individual is very common and frequently constitutes a profoundly distorted belief system)

8. A pronounced tendency to categorize spheres of functioning and sets of behavior rigidly according to sex, e.g., belief that housework is women's work

9. A pronounced tendency to use a gender-based double standard in interpreting or evaluating situations or behavior (e.g., a man who makes breakfast sometimes is considered to be extraordinarily good, but a woman who sometimes neglects to make breakfast is considered deficient)

10. A pathological need to affirm one's social importance by displaying oneself in the company of females who meet any three of the following criteria:

A. are conventionally physically attractive

B. are younger than oneself

C. are shorter in stature than oneself

D. weigh less than oneself

E. appear to be lower on socioeconomic criteria than oneself

F. are more submissive than oneself

11. A distorted approach to sexuality, displaying itself in one or both of these ways:

A. A pathological need for flattery about one's sexual performance and/or the size of one's genitals

B. An infantile tendency to equate large breasts on women with their sexual attractiveness

12. A tendency to feel inordinately threatened by women who fail to disguise their intelligence.

13. Inability to derive pleasure from doing things for others

14. Emotionally uncontrolled resistance to reform efforts that are oriented toward gender equity

Note: In keeping with the stated aims of the DMS, the proposed category is atheoretical, but there is little or no evidence that it is biologically based. In fact, there is a great deal of evidence that it is an extremely common disorder that involves a great deal of psychological upset both to the patient and to those with whom the patient deals. There is also evidence that the disorder is socially-induced and…that the younger patient when…treatment is begun, the better the prognosis.

Reading 2   Depressed Mood and Self-Esteem in Young Asian, Black, and White Women in America

NANCY FUGATE WOODS, MARTHA LENTZ,
ELLEN MITCHELL, AND L. D. OAKLEY

Questions to Consider:

1. In their introduction, the authors review theory and research that connects the life conditions of women to their mental health. What are some of these life conditions, and what is their connection to mental health in your own life?

2. According to the authors, why is it important to explore the connection between life conditions and mental health for different groups of women? What similarities and differences do you perceive in the daily lives of Asian-American, African-American and white women?

3. What insights into the connections between specific life conditions and mental health (depression and self-esteem) for different groups of women did you gain from this study? How is this information useful to you?

During the last two decades, investigators have explored the relationship between women's life conditions and their mental health. Some have related women's socially disadvantaged status, or their socialization to a traditional feminine role, to depression and low self-esteem. Others have emphasized the consequences of women's roles, or the balance of social demands and resources, on their well-being. More recently, feminist scholars have proposed a developmental account of depression. We tested a model comparing the

effects of personal resources, social demands and resources, socialization, and women's roles, on self-esteem and depressed mood in young adult Asian, Black, and White women in America. Women who resided in middle-income and racially mixed neighborhoods were interviewed in their homes. Personal resources were indicated by education and income and social resources by unconflicted network size as measured by Barrera's (1981) Arizona Social Support Interview Schedule. Social demands were assessed by conflicted network size as measured by the Barrera scale and by the Positive Life Events and Negative Life Events scales from Norbeck's (1984) revision of the Sarason Life Events Scale. Women's roles included employment, parenting, and partnership with an adult (e.g., marriage). Self-esteem was assessed with the Rosenberg

Reprinted with permission from *Health Care for Women International*, 15, 1994, pp. 243–262.

This research was supported by Grant NU01054 (Prevalence of Perimenstrual Symptoms) from the National Center for Nursing Research.

Self Esteem Scale (Rosenberg, 1965) and depressed mood with the Center for Epidemiologic Studies Depression scale (Radloff, 1977). Although models for Asian, Black, and White women differed, social network and social demands as well as personal resources were common to each group as predictors of self-esteem and depression.

The prevalence of depression, in various forms, is higher among women than among men, and birth cohort studies indicate that the incidence for women is increasing (Nolen-Hoeksma, 1990; Weissman & Klerman, 1987). Recently, much effort has been placed on discerning the roles played by genetic history and endocrine physiology in variations and subtypes of depression. Despite the potential explanatory power of neurotransmitter models, locating the explanation of depression solely within human biology cannot negate the need to comprehend the human experience of depression as it occurs within the social context of ordinary life.

The experience of depression ranges from feeling blue to feelings of despair, helplessness, hopelessness, guilt, and self-hate (Formanek & Gurian, 1987). The multiple dimensions of depression include negative thinking, sadness, loss of energy, loss of appetite, difficulty concentrating, changes in sleep patterns, negative comparison of the self with others, and the perception that people are unfriendly (Ross & Mirowsky, 1984). The experience of depressed mood ranges from low mood to severe dysphoria that includes hopelessness, loss of self-esteem, helplessness, and the perception that one is powerless to effect change in one's life. Self-concept becomes constricted; the ability to function independently is decreased; and, when the dysphoria is acute, the risk of suicide is increased.

Whereas sadness is a normal feeling, depressed mood can be experienced as a nonfeeling state in which some emotions are constricted and overlaid with dysphoria. Because of the subjective pain associated with depressed mood, the depressive experience itself is socially isolating and threatens the individual's self-esteem. In contrast to depressed mood, sadness does not decrease one's ability to function interpersonally and does not lower self-esteem.

Stiver and Miller (1988) pointed out that women are more vulnerable to depressed mood when their daily life experiences are disconnected from the relationships that are important to them. They suggest that depression develops when a woman perceives her social environment as a context in which her sadness cannot be experienced, expressed, and validated. From Stiver and Miller's perspective, treatment for depression should include the goal of helping women to move from the nonfeeling of depression to the less destructive feelings of sadness by validating their perceptions of distress.

Self-esteem, the positive valuation of oneself, has been linked to women's social experiences. Indeed, Jack (1991) has argued that a woman's self-esteem is influenced by her sense of herself in intimate interaction. Women's place in society, including the value accorded women's usual roles, also influences self-esteem. Powerful external judgments about women's value are transmitted through their restricted access to social resources (Jack, 1991). Although depression is not merely the absence of self-esteem, self-hatred and negative comparisons of oneself to others are frequent accompaniments of depressed mood. In addition, the experience of being depressed may produce low self-esteem (Formanek & Gurian, 1987; Ross & Mirowsky, 1984).

Our purpose in the present study was to explore a model of depressed mood and self-esteem that connects women's affective experience and the conditions of their lives. Because the conditions of women's lives are linked to their ethnicity, self-esteem and depressed mood were examined for Asian, Black, and White women. Five models accounting for women's experiences of depressed mood and self-esteem permeate contemporary works: the social disadvantage model, the social roles model, the feminine socialization model, the balance of demands and resources model, and a developmental model.

CONTEMPORARY MODELS OF WOMEN'S DEPRESSED MOOD AND SELF-ESTEEM

Social Disadvantage Model

Proponents of the social disadvantage model argue that women are vulnerable to depressed mood and low self-esteem because discrimination makes it difficult for them to achieve personal mastery of their lives. Reduced legal, economic, political, and social power is viewed as a product of women's social disadvantage, a disadvantage that lowers individual self-esteem and aspirations (Weissman & Klerman, 1987).

According to the social status disadvantage model, women become depressed when their restricted access to personal resources such as income and education subsequently restricts their opportunity to develop social resources. Education and income directly influence women's access to and use of social resources such as support. Low levels of personal and social resources have been linked to women's psychological distress (Belle, 1982, 1987, 1990; Woods, 1985). Alternatively, high levels of education and income can expand individual attitudes concerning health. Well-educated women are more likely to report eudaimonistic visions of health than are women who have less education (Woods et al., 1988). Moreover, supportive, interpersonal relationships seem more evident among women with high levels of income and education (Riley & Eckenrode, 1986).

Social Roles Model

Others have argued that the nature of women's social roles explains their experiences of depressed mood and low self-esteem (McBride, 1990; McLaughlin & Melber, 1986). Nathanson (1980) proposed that women experience symptoms of psychological distress because the social roles assigned to them are inherently stressful. There is no evidence of a direct relationship between the number of roles (e.g., employee, parent, and spouse or partner) women perform and their mental health (Woods, 1985). Indeed the evidence suggests just the opposite. Women who perform multiple roles may have a health advantage over women who perform one or two roles (Verbrugge, 1986).

Verbrugge (1986) proposed that the psychological and social burdens associated with women's roles, rather than the types or numbers of roles performed, negatively affect women's health. Van Fossen (1981) found that support inequity or lack of reciprocity in partner relationships produced depressed mood in employed women who felt overloaded by the demands of the relationship. Just the opposite has been observed for women who have reciprocal partner relationships. Positive affirmation from the spouse was associated with positive health outcomes for women who worked at home. Woods (1985) observed that women whose husbands shared homemaking tasks and were emotionally supportive reported fewer symptoms of poor mental health.

Socialization Model

Socially transmitted negative images of women have been argued to contribute to the development of individual attitudes that are not supportive of women's assertive and independent behaviors (Weissman & Kierman, 1987). According to the socialization model, traditional feminine sex role socialization is a source of stress for women.

Contemporary women perform new combinations of social roles that require new expectations for behavior. Norms influence the meaning individuals attribute to events in their lives. In western culture, new roles and expectations have led to dramatic changes in how women view themselves and their roles. Women with contemporary versus traditional sex role norms report more positive mental health (Gump, 1972; Levy, 1976; Powell & Reznikoff, 1976; Woods, 1985).

Women who have contemporary social expectations for themselves but live within a relatively unchanged social milieu may not attribute their subsequent psychological distress to their nonsupportive social environment. These women may respond with feelings of depression and discouragement rather than with increased use of support. Women who can attribute their distress to social expectations for women that constrain their performance of valued social roles may respond with actions that lead to increased social support for their contemporary social roles.

Social Resources and Social Demands Model

Some researchers propose that depressed mood is a psychological response to stressful life events and chronic life stress in the absence of social support. Role-specific support from a significant other, partner, or peer can reduce the level of psychological distress experienced by women (Muhlenkamp & Sayles, 1986; Norbeck, 1988; Woods, 1985). However, for some women the high personal cost of using the social support available within their relationships exceeds the benefit of the support (Killien & Brown, 1987; Tilden & Galyen, 1987). Of particular importance is the dilemma of secondary demand. In Western culture, women are the traditional providers of emotional support. When a woman uses support for her personal benefit, a second level of relational consent and obligation can be activated. Some women expect to return the resource by being willing to provide support, on demand, for those who assisted them (Belle, 1982; Stack, 1974). Support itself, then, can be a stressor for women when they are culturally obligated to provide support because they are women and have previously accepted support. Norbeck (1984) has identified specific stressors that emerge from women's social relationship obligations associated with work, school, love, marriage, family, close friends, finances, and parenting.

Developmental Model

Current revisionist theories of women's social development offer a more specific framework for understanding the connection between women's social development, the social demands placed on women, and women's experience of depressed mood. Self-in-relation theory, a product of thinkers such as Gilligan (1977, 1982), Miller (1986), Chodorow (1978), and Jack (1991), views women's involvement with social relationships as fundamental to their development from childhood through adulthood. Self-in-relation theorists argue that the behavioral norm for women's relationships is interdependence. Intimacy is an essential feature of female interpersonal interactions. According to self-in-relation theory, a woman's self-concept is relational. Creativity, autonomy, competence, and self-esteem develop for women within rather than separate from their relationships. Interpersonal conflict and social development failure for some women may result not from a failure to obtain and maintain autonomy but from a failure to maintain intimacy with others while asserting a distinct sense of self.

The dilemma contemporary women face is defined by gender-typed socialization that values women's participation in relationships as providers of emotional support but does not value adult interdependence. Ambivalence toward women's development presents a no-win situation for the contemporary woman. From early childhood, women expect to define themselves, psychologically and socially, through their relationships with others. Yet in an achievement-oriented environment such as Western culture, interpersonal attachment is valued less than individual accomplishments (Jack, 1987). Women who subscribe to attachment behavior norms risk being perceived as adults who are unable to compete or perform autonomously.

Evidence of an association between relational stressors and women's depression was provided by the classic work of Brown and Harris (1978). The context for each of four predictors of depression was relational: the presence of three or more children in the home who were less than 14 years of age, the loss of one's mother before age 11, the lack of employment, and the lack of a confiding relationship with a husband or male partner.

Ethnicity

To date, there has been limited exploration of which model best accounts for self-esteem and depressed mood in women from different ethnic groups. Indeed, results of most studies reflect White women's experiences. What is missing from most work on women's mental health is consideration of the effects of the interactive effects of gender, race, and social class. More surprisingly, the effects of racism are rarely considered. Although many social risk factors for depression are likely to affect women from underrepresented American ethnic groups, they are explored without reference to the context of women's lives (Barbee, 1992). Often, researchers attribute Black American women's experience of depression to social class (Steele, 1978). More recently, investigators have considered the influence of women's support networks on their mental health (Dressler & Badger, 1985). Asian American women also must contend with racial and ethnic discrimination and the gender stereotyping of them as docile and subservient (Lott, 1990). Low self-esteem in some Asian women has been linked to the expectation that they accommodate men rather than assert themselves (Loo & Ong, 1982).

In sum, several models link women's experiences of depressed mood to their social environment. Our purpose in the present study was to test a model of personal resources, social resources,

socialization, social demands, and social roles in association with the experience of depressed mood and their self-esteem in Black, Asian, and White women.

METHOD

Sampling

We used a multistage sampling framework in which census block groups (fractions of census tracts) in which 40% or more of the population reported an income between $12,900 and $39,900 were identified from the 1980 census data from King County, Washington. Of the 901 block groups that met the initial income criterion, in only 119 was 10% or more of the population Black or Asian. Profiles of the number of women between the ages of 15 and 59 (the age bands used in reporting census data) and of these women's educational status (completion of more than elementary school) were generated for each ethnic group in each of the 119 block groups. We selected the most suitable block groups from the standpoint of age, ethnicity, and education. We randomly ordered street segments of the selected block groups with a computer program. The numbers of the street segments within block groups provided the link between this initial set of criteria and a city directory from which potential participants' telephone numbers were obtained.

Design

The data presented herein were obtained on a single-occasion, in-home interview. The interview was a cross-sectional component of a larger study of the prevalence of perimenstrual symptoms (Woods et al., 1987).

Measures

The concepts included in the model of women's experience of depressed mood and low self-esteem were personal resources, social resources, socialization, social demands, and roles. The instruments used to measure these concepts were as follows.

Personal Resources. Personal resources ensure women's access to social resources associated with positive mental health. Income was included in the analyses as an ordinal variable coded according to more than 20 categories. In addition, education was included in the model and measured by years of formal education.

Social Resources. Social resources included support available to women from their network members as measured by their responses to Barrera's (1981) Arizona Social Support Interview Schedule (ASSIS). Barrera conceived of social support as individuals' subjective and objective appraisal of their interaction with their environment. The ASSIS includes six areas: material aid, physical assistance, intimate interactions, guidance, feedback, and social participation. Individuals are asked to enumerate important relationships and whether they have interacted with each person within the past month. Psychometric assessment by Barrera indicated test-retest reliabilities of .88 for unconflicted network size and .54 for conflicted network size.

Socialization. Socialization was indicated by women's gender role norms and religiosity. Scores on the Attitudes Toward Women scale (ATW; Spence & Helmreich, 1978) indicated women's gender role norms. The 15-item ATW contains statements that describe the roles, rights, and privileges women should have. A 4-point scale is used, ranging from *agree strongly* to *disagree strongly*. Items are scored 0–3, with high scores indicating a profeminist, egalitarian attitude. Possible total scores range from 0 to 45. Internal consistency was high (Cronbach's alpha = .86) in the present sample.

Women's self-rating of religiosity was also used as an indicator of socialization. Women

rated themselves as very religious, somewhat religious, or not at all religious, so that religiosity was indicated by a lower score.

Social Demands. The centrality of women's relationships to their lives has negative as well as positive consequences. Social demands were indicated by Norbeck's (1984) adaptation of the Sarason Life Events Survey (LES). This 91-item scale describes events related to health, work, school, residence, love and marriage, family and close friends, personal and social matters, financial matters, crime and legal matters, and parenting. Participants indicate whether each event occurred during the past year, whether they perceived it as good or bad, and the magnitude of the effect of the event (from 0 for no effect to 3 for great effect). Total positive events, total negative events, and total events are scored. The Negative Life Events score was found to correlate positively with state (but not trait) anxiety and with depression (Norbeck, 1984). It also discriminated between counseling center clients and undergraduate students. Scores on the Positive Life Events scale did not correlate with the anxiety measures. Norbeck (1984) modified the LES to increase its relevancy to women's lives by adding items related to fertility control, finding a job, and being assaulted. Single mothers, female graduate students, single women, and partnered women participated in studies to develop the instrument. Test-retest reliability for 1 week was found to be .78 for the Negative Life Events scale, .83 for the Positive Life Events scale, and .81 for the total score. Cronbach's alpha levels were .80 for Negative Life Events, .37 for Positive Life Events, and .71 for the total score (Norbeck, 1984). Both the Negative Life Events and Positive Life Events scales were used in the present study. An additional indicator of social demands was the conflicted network size as measured with the ASSIS.

Roles. Women's roles included employment, marital status, and parenting. Employment was coded as a dummy variable (1 = employed, 0 = not employed). Parenting was reflected in the number of children living at home. Marital status was coded as partnered or not partnered.

Mood. Depressed mood was assessed by the Center for Epidemiologic Studies Depression scale (CES-D; Radloff, 1977). The CES-D was designed for use with community population. On the 20-item scale, respondents rate how often the symptoms occurred during the past week, and responses are scored on a scale of 0–3. A single summarized score is generated, with those below 16 indicating the absence of depression. The scale correctly identified 71% of minor and 57% of depressive personalities. Clinical diagnosis was based on the Schedule for Affective and Schizophrenic Research Diagnostic Criteria (Roberts & Vernon, 1983). The CES-D has a false-positive rate of 16.6% and a false-negative rate of 40% for major depression. Selected sample means include 3.6 for working women and 4.5 for homemakers (Newberry et al., 1979). Dimensions of the CES-D evident on factor analysis included depressed affect, enervation, positive affect, and interpersonal relations (Ross & Mirowsky, 1984). The reliability of the CES-D in the present sample was high (alpha =.89).

Self-Esteem. Self-esteem refers to positive valuations of the self and was measured by the 10-item Rosenberg Self Esteem Scale (Rosenberg, 1965). This scale incorporates a 7-point Likert-type scale from *strongly agree* (1) to *strongly disagree* (7). Participants are asked to respond to items such as "I feel that I have a number of good qualities." Total scores can range from 10 to 70, with higher scores indicating higher self-esteem. Although this scale was initially developed for adolescents, it has been used in numerous studies with adults and has high internal consistency in samples of adult women (19–45 years of age) we have studied. Cronbach's alpha values exceeded .70 in this sample.

Analysis

Data analysis included assessment of relationships using Pearson's product-moment correlation (r) and multiple regression analysis. Multiple regression analyses were used to develop a model relating indicators of personal resources, social resources, socialization, social demands, and roles to self-esteem and mood.

RESULTS

Respondents

A total of 656 women participated in the larger study. Complete data were available for the present analyses from 75 Asian, 91 Black, and 295 White women. The women ranged in age from 18 to 45 years, with a mean of 32. As Table 1 indicates, significant differences were found between the groups of women for most measures. In general, Asian-American women were most likely to be employed, had the highest education levels and incomes, had the fewest children, had experienced the fewest negative life events, had the smallest conflicted network size, and had the lowest depression scores. Black women had the greatest number of children, the lowest education and income, the greatest number of negative and positive life events, and the smallest unconflicted network size. White women had the largest unconflicted network size, the largest conflicted network size, the most contemporary sex role norms, and were the most likely to be married....

Depressed Mood

Models for depressed mood for the three groups of women are given in Table 2. For Asian women, income and unconflicted network size both were associated with lower depression scores, accounting for 22% of the variance. For Black women, number of negative life events, conflicted network size, and low religiosity were associated with higher depression scores, and

TABLE 1   Personal and Social Resources, Socialization, Social Demands, Roles, Self Esteem, and Depression for Asian, Black, and White Women

Variable	Asian ($n = 75$)	Black ($n = 91$)	White ($n = 295$)
Personal resources			
Mean years of education	14.77 (1.85)[a]	13.77 (2.02)	14.37 (2.08)
Median income category	16	14	15
Social resources			
Mean unconflicted network size	9.54 (6.02)	7.50 (3.45)	10.24 (5.91)
Socialization			
Mean score on ATW[b]	75.00 (11.25)	75.64 (12.75)	81.86 (11.50)
Median religiosity category	2	2	2
Social demands			
Negative events	6.75 (5.88)	13.55 (10.61)	9.89 (8.49)
Positive events	15.88 (9.25)	24.83 (13.61)	21.95 (13.25)
Mean conflicted network size	1.55 (2.44)	1.62 (1.53)	1.91 (1.80)
Mean age in years	30.9 (8.4)	31.55 (10.61)	32.8 (6.3)
% employed	93	79	80
Mean no. of children	0.9 (1.2)	1.5 (1.5)	1.1 (1.2)
% married	45	39	71
Mean self-esteem score	56.1 (7.8)	55.2 (10.0)	54.7 (8.9)
Mean depression score	10.0 (7.4)	14.0 (9.9)	11.4 (10.2)

[a]Standard deviation.

[b]Attitudes Toward Women scale.

education was associated with lower depression scores, accounting for 31% of the variance. For White women, number of negative life events and conflicted network size were associated with higher depression scores, and education and number of children with lower depression scores, accounting for 26% of the variance.

Self-Esteem

Regression models for self-esteem in the three groups of women are presented in Table 6. For Asian women, number of children, unconflicted network size, and number of positive life events were positively associated with self-esteem and accounted for 28% of the variance. For Black women, conflicted network size had negative effects and education positive effects on self-esteem; together, they accounted for 19% of the variance. For White women, number of negative life events and conflicted network size had negative effects on self-esteem, but nontraditional attitudes toward women's roles and higher income had positive effects on self-esteem. Together, these variables accounted for 22% of the variance in self-esteem.

TABLE 2 Regression Models Predicting Depressed Mood in Asian, Black, and White Women

Variable	beta	p	R^2 (cumulative)
Asian			
Income	−.304	.008	.157
Unconflicted network size	−.263	.022	.217
Black			
Negative Life Events	.304	.002	.148
Education	−.283	.003	.201
Conflicted network size	.277	.004	.270
Religiosity	.195	.033	.308
White			
Negative Life Events	.423	.000	.217
Conflicted network size	.141	.007	.236
Education	−.129	.012	.249
Number of children	−.117	.022	.263

TABLE 6 Regression Models Predicting Self-Esteem in Asian, Black, and White Women

Variable	beta	p	R^2 (cumulative)
Asian			
Number of children	.463	.000	.158
Unconflicted network size	.255	.016	.213
Positive Life Events	.251	.018	.274
Black			
Conflicted network size	−.339	.001	.084
Education	.332	.001	.193
White			
Negative Life Events	−.283	.000	.127
Attitudes Toward Women	.229	.000	.188
Conflicted network size	−.121	.023	.202
Income	.118	.028	.216

DISCUSSION

As anticipated, the models of self-esteem for Asian, Black, and White women differed. For Asian women, having children, network members with whom there was no conflict, and positive life events were all important predictors of self-esteem. Alternatively, for Black women, the positive effect of education and the negative effect of conflicted network members were important. For White women, number of negative life events, conflicted network, income, and attitudes toward women's roles were important.

Common to all three groups, however, was the influence of a woman's network. Both conflicted network size and unconflicted network size were important, with number of unconflicted members of Asian women's networks most important, probably because of this group's social status advantage and the cultural emphasis on achieving consensus (Belle, 1987). Conflicted network size was more influential for Black and White women, reflecting the erosion of self-esteem that can occur as a consequence of involvement in a network of relationships in which conflict exists.

Life events were also significant. Of interest was that positive events fostered self-esteem for Asian women and negative events eroded self-esteem for White women. The influence of positive events on the Asian women's self-esteem may be explained by their social status advantage (Belle, 1987), whereas the influence of negative events on the White women's self-esteem is consistent with research linking social demands to distress (Norbeck, 1984).

As anticipated, personal resources, including education and income, predicted these women's self-esteem. For White women, income was influential, whereas for the Black women, education was influential. This difference may reflect White women's earning capacity in contrast to the constrained income range for Black women. Socialization also was important for White women. Having a contemporary attitude toward women positively influenced their self-esteem. The belief that women's roles in society need not be restricted by gender predicted positive self-image, similar to findings of earlier studies of predominantly White women (Gump, 1972; Levy, 1976; Powell & Reznikoff, 1976; Woods, 1985). Of interest is this variable's lack of influence on Asian and Black women's self-esteem. This may be a function of the social environments of these two groups, which restrict women's achievements, as well as overshadowing by other factors, in particular, the nature of their relationships with network members.

Women's roles were noticeably absent from the models of self-esteem, with one exception: The number of children positively influenced Asian women's self-esteem. Women's relationships and the social demands associated with their relationships, not simply their roles, influenced self-esteem.

Depressed mood, like self-esteem, was explained by a different model for each group of women. For Asian women, unconflicted network size and income reduced the likelihood of depressed mood. For Black women, number of negative life events, conflicted network size, and low religiosity fostered depression, but education reduced its likelihood. For White women, like Black women, number of negative life events, conflicted network size, and education were important. For White women, however, the number of children was negatively associated with depressed mood. This may reflect the positive

effects of parenting for White women with higher incomes.

Of particular interest is the level of interpersonal conflict the three groups of women faced and the balancing effect of personal resources. Black and White women were significantly influenced by the level of interpersonal conflict in their relationship network. Asian women also experienced interpersonal conflict, but they were influenced more by unconflicted relationships. All of the women benefited from the personal resources they held. For Asian and White women, income had a protective influence, but Black women were highly benefited by education.

Taken together, these models of depression and self-esteem underscore the importance of women's social networks in protecting them from depression and enhancing their self-esteem when these networks are characterized by little conflict. When conflict characterizes the relationships, however, the network erodes self-esteem and contributes to depression. Likewise, number of negative life events, usually an indicator of social demands, figures prominently in the models. Personal resources of education and income also influence depressed mood and self-esteem. Socialization and women's roles have little effect on either self-esteem or depressed mood.

These results support elements of both the social disadvantage model and the social resources and demands model as accounting for women's depression and low self-esteem. In addition, some support for the socialization model and its influence on self-esteem is evident. Taken together, the results indicate the utility of an integrative model such as the newer developmental model that encompasses the dimensions of socialization, social disadvantage, and social resources and demands.

What is clear from the present analyses is the importance of considering the uniqueness of these models for women from different ethnic groups as they reflect the context for women's lives. The centrality of women's social networks and the different ways in which networks function to promote self-esteem and reduce the incidence of depressed mood warrant further consideration. The health-limiting as well as health-enhancing effects of women's networks warrant careful attention in health programs for women, as does the variability of experience among women from different ethnic groups.

REFERENCES

Barbee, E. L. (1992). African American women and depression: A review and critique of the literature. *Archives of Psychiatric Nursing, 6,* 257–265.

Barrera, M. (1981). Social support in the adjustment of pregnant adolescents: Assessment issues. In B. Gottlieb (Ed.), *Social networks and social support* (pp. 69–96). Beverly Hills, CA: Sage.

Belle, D. (1982). *Lives in stress: Women and depression.* Beverly Hills, CA: Sage.

Belle, D. (1987). Gender differences in the social moderators of stress. In R. Barnett, L. Biener, & G. Baruch (Eds.), *Gender and stress,* (pp. 257–277). New York: Free Press.

Belle, D. (1990). Poverty and women's mental health. *American Psychologist, 45,* 385–389.

Brown, G., & Harris, T. (1978). *Social origins of depression: A study of psychiatric disorders in women.* New York: Free Press.

Chodorow, N. (1978). *The reproduction of mothering: Psychoanalysis and the sociology of gender.* Berkeley: University of California Press.

Dressler, W., & Badger, L. (1985). Epidemiology of depressive symptoms in black communities. *Journal of Nervous and Mental Disease, 173,* 212–220.

Formanek, R., & Gurian, A. (Eds.). (1987). *Women and depression: A lifespan perspective.* New York: Springer Publishing Company.

Gilligan, C. (1977). In a different voice: Women's conception of the self and of morality. *Harvard Educational Review, 47,* 481–517.

Gilligan, C. (1982). *In a different voice: Psychological theory and women's development.* Cambridge, MA: Harvard University Press.

Gump, J. P. (1972). Sex role attitudes and psychological well-being. *Journal of Social Issues, 28,* 79–92.

Jack, D. (1987). Self-in-relation theory. In R. Formanek & A. Gurian (Eds.), *Women and depression: A lifespan perspective* (pp. 41–45). New York: Springer Publishing Company.

Jack, D. (1991). *Silencing the self.* Cambridge, MA: Harvard University Press.

Killien, M., & Brown, M. (1987). Work and family roles of women: Sources of stress and coping strategies. *Health Care for Women International, 8,* 169–184.

Levy, R. (1976). Psychosomatic symptoms and women's protest: Two types of reaction to structural strain in the family. *Journal of Health and Social Behavior, 17,* 122–134.

Loo, C., & Ong, P. (1982). Slaying demons with a sewing needle. Feminist issues for Chinatown's women. *Berkeley Journal of Sociology, 17,* 77–88.

Lott, J. (1990). Portrait of Asian and Pacific American women. In S. Rix (Ed.), *The American women, 1990–1991: A status report* (pp. 258–264). New York: Norton.

McBride, A. (1990). Mental health effects of women's multiple roles. *American Psychologist, 45,* 381–384.

McLaughlin, S., & Melber, B. (1986). *The changing life course of American women: Life-style and attitude changes.* Seattle, WA: Batelle Human Affairs Research Center.

Miller, J. (1986). *Toward a new psychology of women.* Boston: Beacon Press.

Miller, J. (1991). The development of women's sense of self. In J. Jordan et al. (Eds.), *Women's growth in connection: Writings for the Stone Center* (pp. 11–26). New York: Guilford Press.

Muhlenkamp, A., & Sayles, J. (1986). Self esteem, social support, and positive health practices. *Nursing Research, 35,* 334–338.

Nathanson, C. (1980). Social roles and health status among women: The significance of employment. *Social Science and Medicine, 14A,* 463–471.

Newberry, P., Weissman, M., & Myers, J. (1979). Working wives and house wives: Do they differ in mental states and social adjustment? *American Journal of Orthopsychiatry, 49,* 282–291.

Nolan-Hoeksma, S. (1990). *Sex differences in depression.* Palo Alto, CA: Stanford University Press.

Norbeck, J. (1984). Modification of life event questionnaires for use with female respondents. *Research in Nursing and Health, 7,* 61–71.

Norbeck, J. (1988). Social support. In J. Fitzpatrick, R. Taunton, & J. Benoliel (Eds.), *Annual review of nursing research* (Vol. 6, pp. 209–236). New York: Springer Publishing Company.

Powell, B., & Reznikoff, M. (1976). Role conflict and symptoms of psychological stress in college-educated women. *Journal of Consulting and Clinical Psychology, 44,* 473–479.

Radloff, L. (1977). The CES-D scale: A self-report depression scale for research in the general population. *Applied Psychological Measurement, 1,* 385–401.

Riley, D., & Eckenrode, J. (1986). Social ties: Subgroup differences in costs and benefits. *Journal of Personality and Social Psychology, 51,* 770–778.

Roberts, R., & Vernon, S. (1983). The Center for Epidemiological Studies Depression Scale: Its use in a community sample. *American Journal of Psychiatry, 140,* 41–107.

Rosenberg, M. (1965). *Society and adolescent self-image.* Princeton, NJ: Princeton University Press.

Ross, C., & Mirowsky, J. (1984). Components of depressed mood in married men and women. *American Journal of Epidemiology, 119,* 997–1004.

Spence, J., & Helmreich, R. (1978). *Masculinity and femininity: Their psychological dimensions, correlates, and antecedents.* Austin: University of Texas Press.

Stack, C. (1974). *All our kin.* New York: Harper & Row.

Steele, R. (1978). Relationship of race, sex, social class and social mobility to depression in normal adults. *Journal of Social Psychology, 104,* 34–47.

Stiver, I., & Miller, J. (1988). From depression to sadness in women's psychotherapy (Work in Progress 36). Wellesley, MA: Stone Center.

Tilden, V., & Galyen, R. (1987). Cost and conflict: The darker side of social support. *Western Journal of Nursing Research, 9,* 9–18.

Van Fossen, B. (1981). Sex differences in the mental health effects of spouse support and equity. *Journal of Health and Social Behavior, 22,* 130–143.

Verbrugge, L. (1986). Role burdens and physical health of women and men. *Women and Health, 11*(1), 47–77.

Weissman, M., & Klerman, G. (1987). Gender and depression. In R. Formanek & A. Gurian (Eds.), *Women and depression: A lifespan perspective* (pp. 3–15). New York: Springer Publishing Company.

Weissman, M., & Paykel, E. *The depressed woman: A study of social relations.* Chicago: University of Chicago Press.

Woods, N. (1985). Employment, family roles, and mental ill health in young adult married women. *Nursing Research, 34*(1), 4–9.

Woods, N., & Hulka, B. (1979). Symptom reports and illness behavior among employee women and homemakers. *Journal of Community Health, 5,* 36–45.

Woods, N., Laffrey, S., Duffy, M., Lentz, M., Mitchell, E., Taylor, D., & Cowan, C. (1988). Being healthy: Women's images. *Advances in Nursing Science, 11*(1), 36–46.

Woods, N., Lentz, M., Mitchell, E., Lee, K., & Allen-Barash, N. (1987). Perimenstrual symptoms: Another look. *Public Health Reports,* Supplement (July–August), 106–112.

Reading 3 "A Way Outa No Way": Eating Problems among African-American, Latina, and White Women

BECKY WANGSGAARD THOMPSON

Questions to Consider:

1. According to Thompson, how have African American and lesbian women been hurt by the stereotype among mental health professionals that mainly white, heterosexual women suffer from eating problems?

2. How does Thompson reframe the "culture of thinness" model of eating disorders? Does her new model fit with your own experience with eating problems, or with the experiences of someone close to you? Why or why not?

3. According to Thompson, how has the theoretical overemphasis on the "culture of thinness" contributed to sexist portrayals of women? Do you agree? Why or why not?

4. Imagine that you are a therapist specializing in women with eating problems, and that you have adopted Thompson's model for treatment and prevention. What steps would you take to help your clients heal and to prevent eating problems from developing in young females?

This article offers a feminist theory of eating problems (anorexia, bulimia, extensive dieting,

Becky Wangsgaard Thompson, "'A Way Outa No Way'": Eating Problems among African-American, Latina and White Women," *Gender and Society, 6,* (4), pp. 546–561, copyright © 1992 by Sage Publications, Inc. Reprinted by permission of Sage Publications, Inc.

Author's Note: The research for this study was partially supported by an American Association of University Women Fellowship in Women's Studies. An earlier version of this article was presented at the New England Women's Studies Association Meeting in 1990 in Kingston, Rhode Island. I am grateful to Margaret Andersen, Liz Bennett, Lynn Davidman, Mary Gilfus, Evelynn Hammonds, and two anonymous reviewers for their comprehensive and perceptive comments on earlier versions of this article.

and binging) based on life history interviews with African-American, Latina, and white women. Until recently, research on eating problems has focused on white middle- and upper-class heterosexual women. While feminist research has established why eating problems are gendered, an analysis of how race, class, and sexual oppression are related to the etiology of eating problems has been missing. The article shows that eating problems begin as strategies for coping with various traumas including sexual abuse, racism, classism, sexism, heterosexism, and poverty. Identifying eating problems as survival strategies shifts the focus from portraying them as issues of appearance to ways women take care of themselves as they cope with trauma.

Bulimia, anorexia, binging, and extensive dieting are among the many health issues women have been confronting in the last 20 years. Until recently, however, there has been almost no research about eating problems among African-American, Latina, Asian-American, or Native American women, working-class women, or lesbians.[1] In fact, according to the normative epidemiological portrait, eating problems are largely a white, middle-, and upper-class heterosexual phenomenon. Further, while feminist research has documented how eating problems are fueled by sexism, there has been almost no attention to how other systems of oppression may also be implicated in the development of eating problems.

In this article, I reevaluate the portrayal of eating problems as issues of appearance based in the "culture of thinness." I propose that eating problems begin as ways women cope with various traumas including sexual abuse, racism, classism, sexism, heterosexism, and poverty. Showing the interface between these traumas and the onset of eating problems explains why women may use eating to numb pain and cope with violations to their bodies. This theoretical shift also permits an understanding of the economic, political, social, educational, and cultural resources that women need to change their relationship to food and their bodies.

EXISTING RESEARCH ON EATING PROBLEMS

There are three theoretical models used to explain the epidemiology, etiology, and treatment of eating problems. The biomedical model offers important scientific research about possible physiological causes of eating problems and the physiological dangers of purging and starvation (Copeland 1985; Spack 1985). However, this model adopts medical treatment strategies that may disempower and traumatize women (Garner 1985; Orbach 1985). In addition, this model ignores many social, historical, and cultural fac-

tors that influence women's eating patterns. The psychological model identifies eating problems as "multidimensional disorders" that are influenced by biological, psychological, and cultural factors (Garfinkel and Garner 1982). While useful in its exploration of effective therapeutic treatments, this model, like the biomedical one, tends to neglect women of color, lesbians, and working-class women.

The third model, offered by feminists, asserts that eating problems are gendered. This model explains why the vast majority of people with eating problems are women, how gender socialization and sexism may relate to eating problems, and how masculine models of psychological development have shaped theoretical interpretations. Feminists offer the culture of thinness model as a key reason why eating problems predominate among women. According to this model, thinness is a culturally, socially, and economically enforced requirement for female beauty. This imperative makes women vulnerable to cycles of dieting, weight loss, and subsequent weight gain, which may lead to anorexia and bulimia (Chernin 1981; Orbach 1978, 1985; Smead 1984).

Feminists have rescued eating problems from the realm of individual psychopathology by showing how the difficulties are rooted in systematic and pervasive attempts to control women's body sizes and appetites. However, researchers have yet to give significant attention to how race, class, and sexuality influence women's understanding of their bodies and appetites. The handful of epidemiological studies that include African-American women and Latinas casts doubt on the accuracy of the normative epidemiological portrait. The studies suggest that this portrait reflects which particular populations of women have been studied rather than actual prevalence (Andersen and Hay 1985; Gray, Ford, and Kelly 1987; Hsu 1987; Nevo 1985; Silber 1986).

More important, this research shows that bias in research has consequences for women of color. Tomas Silber (1986) asserts that many well-trained professionals have either misdiagnosed or delayed their diagnoses of eating problems among African-American and Latina women due to stereotypical thinking that these problems are restricted to white women. As a consequence, when African-American women or Latinas are diagnosed, their eating problems tend to be more severe due to extended processes of starvation prior to intervention. In her autobiographical account of her eating problems, Retha Powers (1989), an African-American woman, describes being told not to worry about her eating problems since "fat is more acceptable in the Black community" (p. 78). Stereotypical perceptions held by her peers and teachers of the "maternal Black woman" and the "persistent mammy-brickhouse Black woman image" (p. 134) made it difficult for Powers to find people who took her problems with food seriously.

Recent work by African-American women reveals that eating problems often relate to women's struggles against a "simultaneity of oppression" (Clarke 1982; Naylor 1985; White 1991). Byllye Avery (1990), the founder of the National Black Women's Health Project, links the origins of eating problems among African-American women to the daily stress of being undervalued and overburdened at home and at work. In Evelyn C. White's (1990) anthology, *The Black Woman's Health Book: Speaking for Ourselves,* Georgiana Arnold (1990) links her eating problems partly to racism and racial isolation during childhood.

Recent feminist research also identifies factors that are related to eating problems among lesbians (Brown 1987; Dworkin 1989; Iazzetto 1989; Schoenfielder and Wieser 1983). In her clinical work, Brown (1987) found that lesbians who have internalized a high degree of homophobia are more likely to accept negative attitudes about fat than are lesbians who have examined their internalized homophobia. Autobiographical accounts by lesbians have also indicated that secrecy about eating problems among lesbians partly reflects their fear of being associated with a stigmatized illness ("What's Important" 1988).

Attention to African-American women, Latinas, and lesbians paves the way for further research that explores the possible interface between facing multiple oppressions and the development of eating problems. In this way, this study is part of a larger feminist and sociological research agenda that seeks to understand how race, class, gender, nationality, and sexuality inform women's experiences and influence theory production.

METHODOLOGY

I conducted 18 life history interviews and administered lengthy questionnaires to explore eating problems among African-American, Latina, and white women. I employed a snowball sample, a method in which potential respondents often first learn about the study from people who have already participated. This method was well suited for the study since it enabled women to get information about me and the interview process from people they already knew. Typically, I had much contact with the respondents prior to the interview. This was particularly important given the secrecy associated with this topic (Russell 1986; Silberstein, Striegel-Moore, and Rodin 1987), the necessity of women of color and lesbians to be discriminating about how their lives are studied, and the fact that I was conducting across-race research.

To create analytical notes and conceptual categories from the data, I adopted Glaser and Strauss's (1967) technique of theoretical sampling, which directs the researcher to collect, analyze, and test hypotheses during the sampling process (rather than imposing theoretical categories onto the data). After completing each interview transcription, I gave a copy to each woman who wanted one. After reading their interviews, some of the women clarified or made additions to the interview text.

Demographics of the Women in the Study

The 18 women I interviewed included 5 African-American women, 5 Latinas, and 8 white women.

Of these women, 12 are lesbian and 6 are hetero-sexual. Five women are Jewish, 8 are Catholic, and 5 are Protestant. Three women grew up outside of the United States. The women represented a range of class backgrounds (both in terms of origin and current class status) and ranged in age from 19 to 46 years old (with a median age of 33.5 years).

The majority of the women reported having had a combination of eating problems (at least two of the following: bulimia, compulsive eating, anorexia, and/or extensive dieting). In addition, the particular types of eating problems often changed during a woman's life span. (For example, a woman might have been bulimic during adolescence and anorexic as an adult.) Among the women, 28 percent had been bulimic, 17 percent had been bulimic and anorexic, and 5 percent had been anorexic. All of the women who had been anorexic or bulimic also had a history of compulsive eating and extensive dieting. Of the women, 50 percent were compulsive eaters and dieters (39 percent) or compulsive eaters (11 percent) but had not been bulimic or anorexic.

Two-thirds of the women have had eating problems for more than half of their lives, a finding that contradicts the stereotype of eating problems as transitory. The weight fluctuation among the women varied from 16 to 160 pounds, with an average fluctuation of 74 pounds. This drastic weight change illustrates the degree to which the women adjusted to major changes in body size at least once during their lives as they lost, gained, and lost weight again. The average age of onset was 11 years old, meaning that most of the women developed eating problems prior to puberty. Almost all of the women (88 percent) consider themselves as still having a problem with eating, although the majority believe they are well on the way to recovery.

THE INTERFACE OF TRAUMA AND EATING PROBLEMS

One of the most striking findings in this study was the range of traumas the women associated with the origins of their eating problems, including racism, sexual abuse, poverty, sexism, emotional or physical abuse, heterosexism, class injuries, and acculturation.[2] The particular constellation of eating problems among the women did not vary with race, class, sexuality, or nationality. Women from various race and class backgrounds attributed the origins of their eating problems to sexual abuse, sexism, and emotional and/or physical abuse. Among some of the African-American and Latina women, eating problems were also associated with poverty, racism, and class injuries. Heterosexism was a key factor in the onset of bulimia, compulsive eating, and extensive dieting among some of the lesbians. These oppressions are not the same nor are the injuries caused by them. And certainly, there are a variety of potentially harmful ways that women respond to oppression (such as using drugs, becoming a workaholic, or committing suicide). However, for all these women, eating was a way of coping with trauma.

Sexual Abuse

Sexual abuse was the most common trauma that the women related to the origins of their eating problems. Until recently, there has been virtually no research exploring the possible relationship between these two phenomena. Since the mid-1980s, however, researchers have begun identifying connections between the two, a task that is part of a larger feminist critique of traditional psychoanalytic symptomatology (DeSalvo 1989; Herman 1981; Masson 1984). Results of a number of incidence studies indicate that between one-third and two-thirds of women who have eating problems have been abused (Oppenheimer et al. 1985; Root and Fallon 1988). In addition, a growing number of therapists and researchers have offered interpretations of the meaning and impact of eating problems for survivors of sexual abuse (Bass and Davis 1988; Goldfarb 1987; Iazzetto 1989; Swink and Leveille 1986). Kearney-Cooke (1988) identifies dieting and binging as common ways in which women cope with frequent psychological consequences of sexual abuse (such as body image disturbances, distrust of people and one's own experiences, and confusion about one's feelings). Root and Fallon (1989) specify ways that victimized women cope with assaults by binging and purging: bulimia serves many functions, including anesthetizing the negative feelings associated with victimization. Iazzetto's innovative study (1989), based on in-depth interviews and art therapy sessions, examines how a woman's relationship to her body changes as a consequence of sexual abuse. Iazzetto discovered that the process of leaving the body (through progressive phases of numbing, dissociating and denying) that often occurs during sexual abuse parallels the process of leaving the body made possible through binging.

Among the women I interviewed, 61 percent were survivors of sexual abuse (11 of the 18 women), most of whom made connections between sexual abuse and the beginning of their eating problems. Binging was the most common method of coping identified by the survivors. Binging helped women "numb out" or anesthetize their feelings. Eating sedated, alleviated anxiety, and combated loneliness. Food was something that they could trust and was accessible whenever they needed it. Antonia (a pseudonym) is an Italian-American woman who was first sexually abused by a male relative when she was four years old. Retrospectively, she knows that binging was a way she coped with the abuse. When the abuse began, and for many years subsequently, Antonia often woke up during the middle of the night with anxiety attacks or nightmares and would go straight to the kitchen cupboards to get food. Binging helped her block painful feelings because it put her back to sleep.

Like other women in the study who began binging when they were very young, Antonia was not always fully conscious as she binged. She described eating during the night as "sleep walking. It was mostly desperate—like I had to have it." Describing why she ate after waking up with nightmares, Antonia said, "What else do you do? If you don't have any coping mecha-

nisms, you eat." She said that binging made her "disappear," which made her feel protected. Like Antonia, most of the women were sexually abused before puberty; four of them before they were five years old. Given their youth, food was the most accessible and socially acceptable drug available to them. Because all of the women endured the psychological consequences alone, it is logical that they coped with tactics they could do alone as well.

One reason Antonia binged (rather than dieted) to cope with sexual abuse is that she saw little reason to try to be the small size girls were supposed to be. Growing up as one of the only Italian Americans in what she described as a "very WASP town," Antonia felt that everything from her weight and size to having dark hair on her upper lip were physical characteristics she was supposed to hide. From a young age she knew she "never embodied the essence of the good girl. I don't like her. I have never acted like her. I can't be her. I sort of gave up." For Antonia, her body was the physical entity that signified her outsider status. When the sexual abuse occurred, Antonia felt she had lost her body. In her mind, the body she lived in after the abuse was not really hers. By the time Antonia was 11, her mother put her on diet pills. Antonia began to eat behind closed doors as she continued to cope with the psychological consequences of sexual abuse and feeling like a cultural outsider.

Extensive dieting and bulimia were also ways in which women responded to sexual abuse. Some women thought that the men had abused them because of their weight. They believed that if they were smaller, they might not have been abused. For example when Elsa, an Argentine woman, was sexually abused at the age of 11, she thought her chubby size was the reason the man was abusing her. Elsa said, "I had this notion that these old perverts liked these plump girls. You heard adults say this too. Sex and flesh being associated." Looking back on her childhood, Elsa believes she made fat the enemy partly due to the shame and guilt she felt about the incest. Her belief that fat was the source of her problems was also supported by her socialization. Raised by strict German governesses in an upper-class family, Elsa was taught that a woman's weight was a primary criterion for judging her worth. Her mother "was socially conscious of walking into places with a fat daughter and maybe people staring at her." Her father often referred to Elsa's body as "shot to hell." When asked to describe how she felt about her body when growing up, Elsa described being completely alienated from her body. She explained,

> *Remember in school when they talk about the difference between body and soul? I always felt like my soul was skinny. My soul was free. My soul sort of flew. I was tied down by this big bag of rocks that was my body. I had to drag it around. It did pretty much what it wanted and I had a lot of trouble controlling it. It kept me from doing all the things that I dreamed of.*

As is true for many women who have been abused, the split that Elsa described between her body and soul was an attempt to protect herself from the pain she believed her body caused her. In her mind, her fat body was what had "bashed in her dreams." Dieting became her solution, but, as is true for many women in the study, this strategy soon led to cycles of binging and weight fluctuation.

Ruthie, a Puerto Rican woman who was sexually abused from 12 until 16 years of age, described bulimia as a way she responded to sexual abuse. As a child, Ruthie liked her body. Like many Puerto Rican women of her mother's generation, Ruthie's mother did not want skinny children, interpreting that as a sign that they were sick or being fed improperly. Despite her mother's attempts to make her gain weight, Ruthie remained thin through puberty. When a male relative began sexually abusing her, Ruthie's sense of her body changed dramatically. Although she weighed only 100 pounds, she began to feel fat

and thought her size was causing the abuse. She had seen a movie on television about Romans who made themselves throw up and so she began doing it, in hopes that she could look like the "little kid" she was before the abuse began. Her symbolic attempt to protect herself by purging stands in stark contrast to the psychoanalytic explanation of eating problems as an "abnormal" repudiation of sexuality. In fact, her actions and those of many other survivors indicate a girl's logical attempt to protect herself (including her sexuality) by being a size and shape that does not seem as vulnerable to sexual assault.

These women's experiences suggest many reasons why women develop eating problems as a consequence of sexual abuse. Most of the survivors "forgot" the sexual abuse after its onset and were unable to retrieve the abuse memories until many years later. With these gaps in memory, frequently they did not know why they felt ashamed, fearful, or depressed. When sexual abuse memories resurfaced in dreams, they often woke feeling upset but could not remember what they had dreamed. These free floating, unexplained feelings left the women feeling out of control and confused. Binging or focusing on maintaining a new diet were ways women distracted or appeased themselves, in turn, helping them regain a sense of control. As they grew older, they became more conscious of the consequences of these actions. Becoming angry at themselves for binging or promising themselves they would not purge again was a way to direct feelings of shame and self-hate that often accompanied the trauma.

Integral to this occurrence was a transference process in which the women displaced onto their bodies painful feelings and memories that actually derived from or were directed toward the persons who caused the abuse. Dieting became a method of trying to change the parts of their bodies they hated, a strategy that at least initially brought success as they lost weight. Purging was a way women tried to reject the body size they thought was responsible for the abuse. Throwing up in order to lose the weight they thought was making them vulnerable to the abuse was a way to try to find the body they had lost when the abuse began.

Poverty

Like sexual abuse, poverty is another injury that may make women vulnerable to eating problems. One woman I interviewed attributed her eating problems directly to the stress caused by poverty. Yolanda is a Black Cape Verdean mother who began eating compulsively when she was 27 years old. After leaving an abusive husband in her early 20s, Yolanda was forced to go on welfare. As a single mother with small children and few financial resources, she tried to support herself and her children on $539 a month. Yolanda began binging in the evenings after putting her children to bed. Eating was something she could do alone. It would calm her, help her deal with loneliness, and make her feel safe. Food was an accessible commodity that was cheap. She ate three boxes of macaroni and cheese when nothing else was available. As a single mother with little money, Yolanda felt as if her body was the only thing she had left. As she described it,

> I am here, [in my body] 'cause there is no where else for me to go. Where am I going to go? This is all I got…that probably contributes to putting on so much weight cause staying in your body, in your home, in yourself, you don't go out. You aren't around other people…You hide and as long as you hide you don't have to face…nobody can see you eat. You are safe.

When she was eating, Yolanda felt a momentary reprieve from her worries. Binging not only became a logical solution because it was cheap and easy but also because she had grown up amid positive messages about eating. In her family, eating was a celebrated and joyful act. However, in adulthood, eating became a double-edged sword. While comforting her, binging also led to weight gain. During the three years Yolanda was on welfare, she gained seventy pounds.

Yolanda's story captures how poverty can be a precipitating factor in eating problems and highlights the value of understanding how class inequalities may shape women's eating problems. As a single mother, her financial constraints mirrored those of most female heads of households. The dual hazards of a race- and sex-stratified labor market further limited her options (Higginbotham 1986). In an article about Black women's health, Byllye Avery (1990) quotes a Black woman's explanation about why she eats compulsively. The woman told Avery,

> I work for General Electric making batteries, and, I know it's killing me. My old man is an alcoholic. My kid's got babies. Things are not well with me. And one thing I know I can do when I come home is cook me a pot of food and sit down in front of the TV and eat it. And you can't take that away from me until you're ready to give me something in its place. (p. 7)

Like Yolanda, this woman identifies eating compulsively as a quick, accessible, and immediately satisfying way of coping with the daily stress caused by conditions she could not control. Connections between poverty and eating problems also show the limits of portraying eating problems as maladies of upper-class adolescent women.

The fact that many women use food to anesthetize themselves, rather than other drugs (even when they gained access to alcohol, marijuana, and other illegal drugs), is partly a function of gender socialization and the competing demands that women face. One of the physiological consequences of binge eating is a numbed state similar to that experienced by drinking. Troubles and tensions are covered over as a consequence of the body's defensive response to massive food intake. When food is eaten in that way, it effectively works like a drug with immediate and predictable effects. Yolanda said she binged late at night rather than getting drunk because she could still get up in the morning, get her children ready for school, and be clearheaded for the college classes she attended. By binging, she avoided the hangover or sickness that results from alcohol or illegal drugs. In this way, food was her drug of choice since it was possible for her to eat while she continued to care for her children, drive, cook, and study. Binging is also less expensive than drinking, a factor that is especially significant for poor women. Another woman I interviewed said that when her compulsive eating was at its height, she ate breakfast after rising in the morning, stopped for a snack on her way to work, ate lunch at three different cafeterias, and snacked at her desk throughout the afternoon. Yet even when her eating had become constant, she was still able to remain employed. While her patterns of eating no doubt slowed her productivity, being drunk may have slowed her to a dead stop.

Heterosexism

The life history interviews also uncovered new connections between heterosexism and eating problems. One of the most important recent feminist contributions has been identifying compulsory heterosexuality as an institution which truncates opportunities for heterosexual and lesbian women (Rich 1986). All of the women interviewed for this study, both lesbian and heterosexual, were taught that heterosexuality was compulsory, although the versions of this enforcement were shaped by race and class. Expectations about heterosexuality were partly taught through messages that girls learned about eating and their bodies. In some homes, boys were given more food than girls, especially as teenagers, based on the rationale that girls need to be thin to attract boys. As the girls approached puberty, many were told to stop being athletic, begin wearing dresses, and watch their weight. For the women who weighed more than was considered acceptable, threats about their need to diet were laced with admonitions that being fat would ensure becoming an "old maid."

While compulsory heterosexuality influenced all of the women's emerging sense of their bodies and eating patterns, the women who linked heterosexism directly to the beginning of their eating problems were those who knew they were lesbians when very young and actively resisted heterosexual norms. One working-class Jewish woman, Martha, began compulsively eating when she was 11 years old, the same year she started getting clues of her lesbian identity. In junior high school, as many of her female peers began dating boys, Martha began fantasizing about girls, which made her feel utterly alone. Confused and ashamed about her fantasies, Martha came home every day from school and binged. Binging was a way she drugged herself so that being alone was tolerable. Describing binging, she said, "It was the only thing I knew. I was looking for a comfort." Like many women, Martha binged because it softened painful feelings. Binging sedated her, lessened her anxiety, and induced sleep.

Martha's story also reveals ways that trauma can influence women's experience of their bodies. Like many other women, Martha had no sense of herself as connected to her body. When I asked Martha whether she saw herself as fat when she was growing up she said, "I didn't see myself as fat. I didn't see myself. I wasn't there. I get so sad about that because I missed so much." In the literature on eating problems, *body image* is the term that is typically used to describe a woman's experience of her body. This term connotes the act of imagining one's physical appearance. Typically, women with eating problems are assumed to have difficulties with their body image. However, the term body image does not adequately capture the complexity and range of bodily responses to trauma experienced by the women. Exposure to trauma did much more than distort the women's visual image of themselves. These traumas often jeopardized their capacity to consider themselves as having bodies at all.

Given the limited connotations of the term body image, I use the term *body consciousness* as a more useful way to understand the range of bodily responses to trauma.[3] By body consciousness I mean the ability to reside comfortably in one's body (to see oneself as embodied) and to consider one's body as connected to oneself. The disruptions to their body consciousness that the women described included leaving their bodies, making a split between their body and mind, experiencing being "in" their bodies as painful, feeling unable to control what went in and out of their bodies, hiding in one part of their bodies, or simply not seeing themselves as having bodies. Binging, dieting, or purging were common ways women responded to disruptions to their body consciousness.

Racism and Class Injuries

For some of the Latinas and African-American women, racism coupled with the stress resulting from class mobility related to the onset of their eating problems. Joselyn, an African-American woman, remembered her white grandmother telling her she would never be as pretty as her cousins because they were lighter skinned. Her grandmother often humiliated Joselyn in front of others, as she made fun of Joselyn's body while she was naked and told her she was fat. As a young child, Joselyn began to think that although she could not change her skin color, she could at least try to be thin. When Joselyn was young, her grandmother was the only family member who objected to Joselyn's weight. However, her father also began encouraging his wife and daughter to be thin as the family's class standing began to change. When the family was working class, serving big meals, having chubby children, and keeping plenty of food in the house was a sign the family was doing well. But, as the family became mobile, Joselyn's father began insisting that Joselyn be thin. She remembered, "When my father's business began to bloom and my father was interacting more with white businessmen and seeing how they did business, suddenly thin became impor-

tant. If you were a truly well-to-do family, then your family was slim and elegant."

As Joselyn's grandmother used Joselyn's body as territory for enforcing her own racism and prejudice about size, Joselyn's father used her body as the territory through which he channeled the demands he faced in the white-dominated business world. However, as Joselyn was pressured to diet, her father still served her large portions and bought treats for her and the neighborhood children. These contradictory messages made her feel confused about her body. As was true for many women in this study, Joselyn was told she was fat beginning when she was very young even though she was not overweight. And, like most of the women, Joselyn was put on diet pills and diets before even reaching puberty, beginning the cycles of dieting, compulsive eating, and bulimia.

The confusion about body size expectations that Joselyn associated with changes in class paralleled one Puerto Rican woman's association between her eating problems and the stress of assimilation as her family's class standing moved from poverty to working class. When Vera was very young, she was so thin that her mother took her to a doctor who prescribed appetite stimulants. However, by the time Vera was eight years old, her mother began trying to shame Vera into dieting. Looking back on it, Vera attributed her mother's change of heart to competition among extended family members that centered on "being white, being successful, being middle class,... and it was always, 'Ay Bendito. She is so fat. What happened?'"

The fact that some of the African-American and Latina women associated the ambivalent messages about food and eating to their family's class mobility and/or the demands of assimilation while none of the eight white women expressed this (including those whose class was stable and changing) suggests that the added dimension of racism was connected to the imperative to be thin. In fact, the class expectations that their parents experienced exacerbated standards about weight that they inflicted on their daughters.

EATING PROBLEMS
AS SURVIVAL STRATEGIES

Feminist Theoretical Shifts

My research permits a reevaluation of many assumptions about eating problems. First, this work challenges the theoretical reliance on the culture-of-thinness model. Although all of the women I interviewed were manipulated and hurt by this imperative at some point in their lives, it is not the primary source of their problems. Even in the instances in which a culture of thinness was a precipitating factor in anorexia, bulimia, or binging, this influence occurred in concert with other oppressions.

Attributing the etiology of eating problems primarily to a woman's striving to attain a certain beauty ideal is also problematic because it labels a common way that women cope with pain as essentially appearance-based disorders. One blatant example of sexism is the notion that women's foremost worry is about their appearance. By focusing on the emphasis on slenderness, the eating problems literature falls into the same trap of assuming that the problems reflect women's "obsession" with appearance. Some women were raised in families and communities in which thinness was not considered a criterion for beauty. Yet, they still developed eating problems. Other women were taught that women should be thin, but their eating problems were not primarily in reaction to this imperative. Their eating strategies began as logical solutions to problems rather than problems themselves as they tried to cope with a variety of traumas.

Establishing links between eating problems and a range of oppressions invites a rethinking of both the groups of women who have been excluded from research and those whose lives have been the basis of theory formation. The construction of bulimia and anorexia as appearance-based disorders is rooted in a notion of femininity in which white middle- and upper-class women are portrayed as frivolous, obsessed with their bodies, and overly accepting of narrow gender roles. This portrayal fuels women's tremendous shame and guilt about eating problems—as signs of self-centered vanity. This construction of white middle- and upper-class women is intimately linked to the portrayal of working-class white women and women of color as their opposite: as somehow exempt from accepting the dominant standards of beauty or as one step away from being hungry and therefore not susceptible to eating problems. Identifying that women may binge to cope with poverty contrasts the notion that eating problems are class bound. Attending to the intricacies of race, class, sexuality, and gender pushes us to rethink the demeaning construction of middle-class femininity and establishes bulimia and anorexia as serious responses to injustices.

Understanding the link between eating problems and trauma also suggests much about treatment and prevention. Ultimately, their prevention depends not simply on individual healing but also on changing the social conditions that underlie their etiology. As Bernice Johnson Reagon sings in Sweet Honey in the Rock's song "Oughta Be a Woman," "A way outa no way is too much to ask/ too much of a task for any one woman" (Reagon 1980).[4] Making it possible for women to have healthy relationships with their bodies and eating is a comprehensive task. Beginning steps in this direction insuring that (1) girls can grow up without being sexually abused, (2) parents have adequate resources to raise their children, (3) children of color grow up free of racism, and (4) young lesbians have the chance to see their reflection in their teachers and community leaders. Ultimately, the prevention of eating problems depends on women's access to economic, cultural, racial, political, social, and sexual justice.

NOTES

1. I use the term *eating problems* as an umbrella term for one or more of the following: anorexia, bulimia, extensive dieting, or binging. I avoid using the term eating disorder because it categorizes the problems as individual pathologies, which deflects attention away

from the social inequalities underlying them (Brown 1985). However, by using the term *problem* I do not wish to imply blame. In fact, throughout, I argue that the eating strategies that women develop begin as logical solutions to problems, not problems themselves.

2. By trauma I mean a violating experience that has long-term emotional, physical, and/or spiritual consequences that may have immediate or delayed effects. One reason the term trauma is useful conceptually is its association with the diagnostic label Post Traumatic Stress Disorder (PTSD) (American Psychological Association 1987). PTSD is one of the few clinical diagnostic categories that recognizes social problems (such as war or the Holocaust) as responsible for the symptoms identified (Trimble 1985). This concept adapts well to the feminist assertion that woman's symptoms cannot be understood as solely individual, considered outside of her social context, or prevented without significant changes in social conditions.

3. One reason the term *consciousness* is applicable is its intellectual history as an entity that is shaped by social context and social structures (Delphy 1984; Marx 1964). This link aptly applies to how the women described their bodies because their perceptions of themselves embodied (or not embodied) directly relate to their material conditions (living situations, financial resources, and access to social and political power).

4. Copyright © 1980. Used by permission of Song-talk Publishing.

REFERENCES

American Psychological Association. 1987. *Diagnostic and statistical manual of mental disorders*. 3rd ed. rev. Washington, DC: American Psychological Association.

Anderson, Arnold, and Andy Hay. 1985. Racial and socioeconomic influences in anorexia nervosa and bulimia. *International Journal of Eating Disorders* 4:479–87.

Arnold, Georgiana. 1990. Coming home: One Black woman's journey to health and fitness. In *The Black women's health book: Speaking for ourselves,* edited by Evelyn C. White. Seattle WA: Seal Press.

Avery, Byllye Y. 1990. Breathing life into ourselves: The evolution of the National Black Women's Health Project. In *The Black women's health book: Speaking for ourselves,* edited by Evelyn C. White. Seattle, WA: Seal Press.

Bass, Ellen, and Laura Davis. 1988. *The courage to heal: A guide for women survivors of child sexual abuse*. New York: Harper & Raw.

Brown, Laura S. 1995. Women, weight and power: Feminist theoretical and therapeutic issues. *Women and Therapy* 4:61–71.

———. 1987. Lesbians, weight and eating: New analyses and perspectives. In *Lesbian psychologies,* edited by the Boston Lesbian Psychologies Collective. Champaign: University of Illinois Press.

Chernin, Vim. 1981. *The obsession: Reflections on the tyranny of slenderness.* New York: Harper & Row.

Clarke, Cheryl. 1982. *Narratives.* New Brunswick, NJ: Sister Books.

Copeland, Paul M. 1985. Neuroendocrine aspects of eating disorders. In *Theory and treatment of anorexia nervosa and bulimia: Biomedical sociocultural and psychological perspectives,* edited by Steven Wiley Emmett. New York: Brunner/Mazel.

Delphy, Christine. 1994. *Close to home: A materialist analysis of women's oppression.* Amherst: University of Massachusetts Press.

DeSalvo, Louise. 1989. *Virginia Woolf: The impact of childhood sexual abuse on her life and work.* Boston, MA: Beacon.

Dworkin, Sari H. 1989. Not in man's image: Lesbians and the cultural oppression of body image. In *Loving boldly: Issues facing lesbians,* edited by Ester D. Rothblum and Ellen Cole. New York: Harrington Park Press.

Garfinkel, Paul E., and David M. Garner. 1982. *Anorexia nervosa: A multidimensional perspective.* New York: Brunner/Mazel.

Garner, David. 1985. Iatrogenesis in anorexia nervosa and bulimia nervosa. *International Journal of Eating Disorders* 4:701–26.

Glaser, Barney G., and Anselm L. Strauss. 1967. *The discovery of grounded theory: Strategies for qualitative research.* New York: Aldine DeGruyter.

Goldfarb, Lori. 1987. Sexual abuse antecedent to anorexia nervosa, bulimia and compulsive overeating: Three case reports. *International Journal of Eating Disorders* 6:675–80.

Gray, James, Kathryn Ford, and Lily M. Kelly. 1987. The prevalence of bulimia in a Black college population. *International Journal of Eating Disorders* 6:733–40.

Herman, Judith. 1981. *Father-daughter incest.* Cambridge, MA: Harvard University Press.

Higginbotham, Elizabeth. 1986. We were never on a pedestal: Women of color continue to struggle with poverty, racism and sexism. In *For crying out loud,* edited by Rochelle Lefkawitz and Ann Witborn. Boston: MA: Pilgrim Press.

Hsu, George. 1987. Are eating disorders becoming more common in Blacks? *International Journal of Eating Disorders* 6:113–24.

Iazzetto, Demetria. 1989. When the body is not an easy place to be: Women's sexual abuse and eating problems. Ph.D. diss., Union for Experimenting Colleges and Universities, Cincinnati, Ohio.

Kearney-Cooke, Ann. 1988. Group treatment of sexual abuse among women with eating disorders. *Women and Therapy* 7:5–21.

Marx, Karl. 1964. *The economic and philosophic manuscripts of 1844.* New York: International.

Masson, Jeffrey. 1984. *The assault on the truth: Freud's suppression of the seduction theory.* New York: Farrar, Strauss & Giroux.

Naylor, Gloria. 1985. *Linden Hills.* New York: Ticknor & Fields.

Nevo, Shoshana. 1985. Bulimic symptoms: Prevalence and ethnic differences among college women. *International Journal of Eating Disorders* 4:151–68.

Oppenheimer, R., K. Howells, R. L. Palmer, and D. A. Chaloner. 1985. Adverse sexual experience in childhood and clinical eating disorders: A preliminary description. *Journal of Psychiatric Research* 19:357–61.

Orbach, Susie. 1978. *Fat is a feminist issue.* New York: Paddington.

———. 1985. Accepting the symptom: A feminist psychoanalytic treatment of anorexia nervosa. In *Handbook of psychotherapy for anorexia nervosa and bulimia,* edited by David M. Garnet and Paul E. Garfinkel. New York: Guilford.

Powers, Retha. 1989. Fat is a Black women's issue. *Essence,* Oct., 75, 78, 134, 136.

Reagon, Bernice Johnson. 1980. Oughta be a woman. On Sweet Honey in the Rock's album, *Good News.* Music by Bernice Johnson Reagon; lyrics by June Jordan. Washington, DC: Songtalk.

Rich, Adrienne. 1986. Compulsory heterosexuality and lesbian existence. In *Blood bread and poetry.* New York: Norton.

Root, Maria P. P., and Patricia Fallon. 1988. The incidence of victimization experiences in a bulimic sample. *Journal of Interpersonal Violence* 3:161–73.

———. 1989. Treating the victimized bulimic: The functions of binge-purge behavior. *Journal of Interpersonal Violence* 4:90–100.

Russell, Diana E. 1986. *The secret trauma: Incest in the lives of girls and women.* New York: Basic Books.

Schoenfielder, Lisa, and Barbara Wieser, eds. 1983. *Shadow on a tightrope: Writings by women about fat liberation.* Iowa City, IA: Aunt Lute Book Co.

Silber, Tomas. 1986. Anorexia nervosa in Blacks and Hispanics. *International Journal of Eating Disorders* 5:121–28.

Silberstein, Lisa, Ruth Striegel-Moore, and Judith Rodin. 1987. Feeling fat: A woman's shame. In *The role of shame in symptom formation,* edited by Helen Block Lewis. Hillsdale, NJ: Lawrence Erlbaum.

Smead, Valerie. 1984. Eating behaviors which may lead to and perpetuate anorexia nervosa, bulimarexia, and bulimia. *Women and Therapy* 3:37–49.

Spack, Norman. 1985. Medical complications of anorexia nervosa and bulimia. In *Theory and treatment of anorexia nervosa and bulimia: Biomedical sociocultural and psychological perspectives,* edited by Steven Wiley Emmett. New York: Brunner/Mazel.

Swink, Kathy, and Antoinette E. Leveille. 1986. From victim to survivor: A new look at the issues and recovery process for adult incest survivors. *Women and Therapy* 5:119–43.

Trimble, Michael. 1985. Post-traumatic stress disorder: History of a concept. In *Trauma and its wake: The study and treatment of post-traumatic stress disorder,* edited by C. R. Figley. New York: Brunner/Mazel.

What's important is what you look like. 1988. *Gay Community News,* July, 24–30.

White, Evelyn C., ed. 1990. *The Black women's health book: Speaking for ourselves.* Seattle, WA: Seal Press.

———. 1991. Unhealthy appetites. *Essence,* Sept, 28, 30.

Topic 10

Aging

Living by Holding Back

I am landlocked.
A backyard creek is no
ocean. Low-slung
hills surround me.
Clouds hang
in the air and
the branches, bare,
grip the claws
of crows that crouch,
scrutinize. The rain
sputters and spits.
Guttered leaves
crumble, and I
have been on hold
for forty years.

Courtesy of Nancy Edmondson

While older women constitute the largest growing segment of the population in the United States, the double oppression of ageism and sexism has meant that the truth of older women's lives has not been told. Aging women are often portrayed as unattractive, sexually inactive, no longer useful, and unhappy, but in reality, women's experiences in old age often contradict these stereotypes. For example, it has been assumed that when children leave home, women will experience an empty-nest syndrome, feeling depressed and useless. Research indicates that while this is true for some women, most welcome the new opportunities for personal fulfillment that the end of child rearing provides. Menopause too, although it may bring some uncomfortable symptoms, is rarely experienced as the stereotyped traumatic event. Instead, many women report that it brings new sexual freedom.

Women live longer than men, so they are more likely to experience widowhood or divorce, and to live alone in old age. Because women are believed to be the dependent sex, it is expected that they will fare more poorly than widowed men, but the opposite is true. Men whose wives die either remarry within a year, or are more likely to die within a year than are women. Women are less likely to remarry, but they survive physically and psychologically better than men, perhaps because women have stronger support networks.

Women experience a "double standard" when they age. While aging often brings to men an increased status as they become more powerful economically, aging women tend to become less powerful because they are seen as less physically attractive. As women age, they are more likely to live in poverty than men, and this is particularly true for women of color.

While aging is the result of biological changes in the body, cultural factors play an important role in how these changes are experienced. For example, as we learned in the section on adolescence, African Americans are less likely than European Americans to see youth as a criterion for being judged beautiful (Parker et al., this volume). As a result, African American women may not experience the same feelings of undesirability and unattractiveness that are frequently felt by aging European American women. The three readings in this section look at how culture shapes women's experiences of aging, and how women meet the challenges that aging presents.

The first reading, "Women of a Certain Age," gives us an overview of the issues faced by older women. Laura Cartensen and Monish Pasupathi argue that aging is not the same experience for women and men. Women outlive men, are more often widowed, are more likely to live alone in old age, are the majority of nursing home residents, and have higher rates of poverty. A lifetime of disadvantage due to sexism shows cumulative effects in old age. For example, women's responsibility for caregiving often leads to career compromises which mean that women do not have the retirement benefits men do. It also means that elderly women are much more likely to be responsible for caring for an aged parent or an elderly spouse. While Carstensen and Pasupathi paint a pessimistic picture of aging for women, they also remind us of the psychological resilience older women have shown, and they offer suggestions for changing the inequities. These suggestions focus on change at the individual and societal level, encouraging women to plan for their old age, and demanding modification of public policy on aging.

Carstensen and Pasupathi point out that because of racism, minority women face even greater challenges in aging than white women. In the second reading, "Puerto Rican Elderly Women: Shared Meanings and Informal Supportive Networks," Melba Sánchez-Ayéndez looks at how a group of Puerto Rican elderly women living in Boston deal with the challenges of aging. Her description demonstrates ways that cultural values can affect the experience of aging. Sánchez-Ayéndez describes how the women's support networks are shaped by their view that men and women should play different roles (the woman's role is in the home), and their belief in family unity and interdependence. These cultural values lead Puerto Rican women to rely on their families for support in old age. These values also mean that elderly women continue to play an important role in supporting their children and their children's families. As this reading demonstrates, it is especially important to understand cultural value orientations if we wish to understand how minority women face the challenges of growing old.

In the final reading of this section, "Confronting Ageism: A Must for Mental Health," 70-year-old Shevy Healey describes her struggles with ageism and the ways she has internalized her culture's view of old women. She describes her shock at being treated as "old" by other people, and her attempts to deny to herself that she was aging. Eventually, however, she had to confront the fact that she was an old woman, and in doing so she found an opportunity to reevaluate most of her values and beliefs. As an example, she describes how she learned to let go of her preconceived notions of beauty, and to broaden her definition of what was beautiful. She also learned to listen to her body in ways she hadn't when she was younger. For Healey, confronting ageism has been an opportunity to grow, to learn, and to create a richer life.

As the readings in this section demonstrate, women face discrimination and prejudice in old age, but they also have resisted oppression by developing supportive networks and challenging the limitations they face as old women.

Reading 1   Women of a Certain Age

LAURA L. CARSTENSEN AND MONISHA PASUPATHI

Questions to Consider

1.   What challenges do you see yourself facing in old age? Are these challenges related to your gender? What plans do you have for dealing with these challenges?

2.   Carstensen and Pasupathi argue that structural inequalities especially exploit married women. Why do single women fare better than widows in old age?

3.   What changes should take place in public policy and in individual retirement planning to prevent the scenario experienced by Helen?

The whole meaning of our lives is in question. If we do not know what we are going to be, we cannot know what we are. Let us recognize ourselves in this old man or in that old woman. It must be done if we are to take upon ourselves the entirety of our human state.[1]

Medicare, social security, national health insurance, nursing-home placement, and other pressing issues are receiving increasing attention in the media. Rarely do we hear them framed as "women's issues." On the contrary, age is treated as the great equalizer—men and women, rich and poor, regardless of background, escape old age only through premature death. It is true that both women and men suffer the biological deterioration that advanced age brings, and both men and women face ageist stereotypes and misconceptions. Both men and women experience loss with age.

From *American Women in the Nineties: Today's Critical Issues* edited by Sherri Matteo. Copyright 1993 by Northeastern University Press. Reprinted with permission.

Aging, however, is not a process that occurs evenly for women and men in the United States. In this [article] we will review briefly some basic facts that distinguish older women from older men, illustrate the impact of these differences in everyday life, and suggest ways people might modify the inevitability of deleterious outcomes and the course of their own aging process.

THE FACTS

The fact that our elderly population is rapidly growing has become common knowledge. During the twentieth century, the proportion of elderly people in the population grew from 3 percent to 12 percent.[2] By the year 2040, 23 percent of the population will be over 65.[3] However, the fact that *most* of these people are women is largely ignored. At 65, women outnumber men by 100 to 83; by 85, women outnumber men by 100 to 39.[4] The over–85 age segment is the fastest growing segment of the population. Indeed, "the world of the very old is a world of women."[5]

These population statistics reflect the fact that women outlive men by about seven years.

For reasons as yet unknown, the survivability of females is greater than males from conception on. The average life expectancy for white women in the United States is 79; for men it is 72. For most ethnic minorities in the United States, life expectancy is lower. For black women, the average life expectancy is 73 years; for black men it is 64 years. The difference of roughly seven years between men and women in longevity holds across ethnic groups.

In part because of the difference in longevity and in part because women traditionally marry older men, women are far more likely than men to be widowed in old age. In fact, even though 95 percent of Americans marry at some point during their lives, only 35 percent of women over 65 are married. After 85, only 21 percent of women are married. Moreover, when men *are* widowed, they are four times more likely to remarry than women who are widowed. For women, the average length of widowhood is 15 years; once widowed, women are at high risk for a number of age-related problems.

It is important to note that the jeopardy widowed women face is not the result of being without a man, but from widowhood itself. Women who have always been single fare much better than widows in late life; they are better off financially[6] and less likely to be depressed or lonely. Very little is known about older lesbians, but they are included in statistics about single women. Also included among single women are women who live in religious communities. Nuns enjoy a life expectancy six years longer than the average woman in the United States. Thus, it is not being *single* that puts women at risk; it is, as we will illustrate, the result of a complex system of structural inequities that exploit all women and especially married women.

Living alone is a risk factor for a number of negative outcomes in old age and widowed women are far more likely to live alone than other older people. Most men live out their lives living with a spouse in the community. Among elderly men, 76 percent of whites, 66 percent of Hispanics, and 63 percent of blacks live with a spouse. Among elderly women, these percentages are substantially lower—41 percent of whites, 35 percent of Hispanics, and 27 percent of blacks live with a spouse.[7]

Twenty-five percent to 30 percent of older people will reside in nursing homes at some point in their lives.[8] These facilities are virtual worlds of women. Seventy-five percent of nursing-home residents are female.

Not surprisingly, older women are more likely than older men to be poor. Twenty-five percent of elderly white women are poor. Much higher poverty rates are found among minority women.

One more statistic—we hear a fair amount these days about caregivers of the elderly, what we don't hear is that the caregivers of the elderly are, for the most part, elderly women.

A CASE STUDY

What do these numbers really mean for the lives of elderly women? Consider the following scenario, a story that is more common than most of the us would like to admit.

Married since 1947, Helen and Paul—a white American, middle-class couple—are expecting to spend a relaxed and satisfying old age together. Paul retired from his engineering job a year ago with a good pension. Helen had worked on and off over the years in a day-care center. Because she worked only part time at a relatively low-paying job, she has not accrued any retirement benefits, but she does qualify for social security. Between Paul's pension and the couple's social-security benefits, they feel relatively secure and optimistic about their future. Their two sons, Michael and Robert, are both married and live out of state with children of their own. Both sons have jobs they like. Neither makes a lot of money, but they manage to make ends meet. Helen and Paul see their grandchildren once or twice a year and enjoy frequent telephone contact with them.

About one year after Paul retires, he begins to behave peculiarly. Always an active person, he now seems anxious in conversations with old friends and spends more and more time alone. One day Helen finds a note in Paul's pocket that gives directions from their house to the market only six blocks away. When she asks him what the instructions are for, he gets angry and accuses her of invading his privacy. During the next two months she finds him to be increasingly forgetful. Occasionally, he acknowledges problems in performing familiar tasks, but usually he claims that it is "just old age."

One day, the doorbell rings. The local police bring Paul home. They tell Helen that they found Paul wandering in a park and that, while he could tell them his name, he could not remember his address. After looking up the address at the police station, the officers brought Paul home. They suggest to Helen that she take him to a physician for a thorough medical evaluation.

Helen calls Dr. Frierson, their longtime physician, and makes an appointment. After a lengthy workup, he informs Helen that Paul appears to be in the early stages of Alzheimer's disease, a chronic debilitating disease that ultimately ends in death. Helen is devastated, but is determined to do the best she can to make sure that Paul lives out his life as comfortably as possible.

Paul gets worse and worse. He has difficulty with basic grooming and bathing. She can dress him, but cannot bathe him without assistance. Paul is a large man and Helen cannot physically lift him. She hires help to come in three times a week to help Paul shower, but the aides quit regularly and Helen is forced to hire new people and sometimes go without assistance. Besides, she is quickly spending their savings to pay aides. As time passes, Paul loses the ability to tell night from day. He gets up many times throughout the night and wakes Helen. During the day, he naps frequently, but Helen cannot do the same. It is unusual for Helen to sleep more than three hours a night. She feels that she cannot afford to hire someone to stay in the evenings. She becomes increasingly depressed and physically exhausted.

Helen rarely sees her friends. She cannot bring Paul out with her because he becomes agitated in unfamiliar places. Her friends feel for her, but are uncomfortable coming to the house. It's hard for them to see Paul and, in some ways, Helen prefers that they stay away. Michael and Robert call regularly. They are obviously concerned for her so she tries to minimize the gravity of the situation. Susan, her daughter-in-law, tries especially hard to help. She even stops working full-time so that she can visit once a month and alleviate some of the burden, but she has young children so she cannot stay more than a day or two.

When Paul becomes incontinent, Helen realizes that she can no longer manage him at home. She looks at several nursing homes. Some are horrible—understaffed and overcrowded. Eventually, she finds a nice place where the staff are kind, the food is good, and Paul can have a room with a view of the park. They had saved about $200,000 toward their retirement so Helen feels that she can afford a decent place for him. The cost of the nursing home is $40,000 a year. Helen assumes that her insurance will pay some of the nursing-home costs, but is told that less than 5 percent is covered. She decides that she has no choice, however, and admits Paul to the facility.

Helen visits every day even though Paul no longer recognizes her. She cannot stay away. She loves Paul very much and this is the only way left for her to show her love. Medicare pays for 80 percent of Paul's medical treatment, but virtually nothing toward the nursing home expenses. She inquires about Medicaid, but is told that she has too much money to qualify for assistance. Rather, she must spend down their savings to $60,000 before Paul can qualify. Just a few years later, they qualify for Medicaid assistance. Seven years later, Paul dies.

Shortly after Paul's death Helen learns that Paul's pension pays only minimal survivor benefits. Helen, now 77 years old and alone, is living on far less income than she had anticipated. Her car engine fails one day. She decides to sell the car rather than pay the cost of repair. Then, one morning she slips on the sidewalk, breaks a hip, and is hospitalized. Her physician is pleased with her recovery progress and releases her after three weeks, but her cost of medical care, even with Medicare insurance, totals $40,000. Without savings to supplement her income, she can no longer make ends meet.

She considers asking her sons for financial assistance, but decides that the house is too big for her, anyway, and, after all, they have expenses of their own. She decides that if she sells the house, she can live more cheaply and perhaps leave some money for her grandchildren, as Paul had so hoped to do. She is surprised to see how high the rent is in her neighborhood. Eventually someone tells her about a housing unit, called the Rainbow House, in the center of the city and takes an apartment there.

In some ways, life is better now. Her financial concerns are somewhat alleviated and she is proud that she is not a burden on her children. She does not let them visit because she doesn't want them to see her apartment. It might concern them to see the neighborhood and she doesn't want to worry them. With her old furniture, her apartment is fairly comfortable, but the neighborhood is quite dangerous. Her friends from the old neighborhood telephone occasionally, but they do not visit. She leaves the building only when necessary. Unfortunately, Helen feels that she has nothing in common with the other tenants.

Helen's long-standing cardiac arrhythmia worsens. Normally, she would see her physician, but she can't get to Dr. Frierson without an expensive taxicab ride and she puts off finding a new physician in the neighborhood. Her diet is poor and, without exercise, her arthritis worsens.

One day, a worker from Adult Protective Services is called. A neighbor had reported that several newspapers had piled up outside Helen's door. The worker finds Helen weak and disoriented. She urges her to move into a state-funded nursing home nearby. When Michael and Robert find out how sick Helen is they want to help, but neither can afford to do very much. Michael visits once, but it breaks his heart to see his mother in the condition she is in and he never returns. Five years later, at the age of 85, Helen dies.

THE ISSUES

Sound extreme? Probably the worst thing you can do is to think that this cannot happen to you. A major part of the problem is that, in our society, older women and their problems are invisible. We are just beginning to fully realize the problems older people face. Only rarely do we hear that these issues are especially relevant to women. Instead, we hear in the media that older people wield more power than any other age group, are draining the social-security system, and hold positions of power. True, the U.S. government is a gerontocracy, but it is extremely important to realize that the power age affords is not evenly distributed across gender, class, or ethnicity.

Even aspects of aging that on the surface affect men and women equally, do not. For example, the incidence of Alzheimer's disease is equal for men and women, but since the chances increase with age, and women live longer, more women develop it. Moreover, because husbands are typically older than wives, elderly women are far more likely to care for a spouse who has dementia.

As our case study illustrates, caregiving takes its toll in many ways, affecting both physical and mental health. A large amount of literature documents the considerable physical and mental strain of caregiving.[9] Luck and fate may have some impact on who gets ill in old age, but they do not determine who becomes a caregiver. The vast majority of unpaid caregivers are women.[10] Wives care for their husbands; elderly daughters care for elderly mothers. The path of responsibility does not just flow directly down through bloodlines and generations. In families where there are only sons, daughters-in-law provide care. When daughters-in-law are not available, the burden is likely to fall on a granddaughter or a niece. Only rarely are caregiving responsibilities assumed by sons.[11]

Interestingly, when husbands do become caregivers, their experience is different from that of wives. For one, when husbands provide caregiving, they often receive help from other relatives and friends or hire professional help.[12] When women provide caregiving, they are reluctant to seek *any* help. Instead, they often try to protect other loved ones from the burden that they bear.[13] Subsequently, caregiving is typically more stressful for women than men.[14] The extent of the stress is evidenced in the fact that 50 percent of caregivers become clinically depressed.[15]

The cornerstone of the U.S. Department of Health and Human Services social policy is that caregiving falls in the private domain and is supported by the government *only as a last resort.*[16] Despite the fact that home-based care is relatively cheap, Congress imposes major restrictions on this funding, which forces families—in most cases, women—to provide an abundance of unpaid labor in order to provide home care. It is their only alternative to institutionalization of loved ones.[17]

In our story, Helen's daughter-in-law, Susan, helped her the most, compromising her career to do so. As noted above, this is common and occurs for a variety of reasons at different points in the life cycle. Young women often make career concessions by working part time or taking years off to care for children. Later in life, women often retire early to care for ailing spouses, parents, or siblings. Social security penalizes women for these work patterns. Because social-security benefits are based on income, working part time or taking years off reduces social-security entitlements.

The insidiousness of the disadvantages for women is apparent in two ways. First, since wives usually make less than husbands, they are the logical candidates for career compromises. Second, those compromises reduce the likeli-

hood that they will accrue private pension benefits to supplement their already lower social security. Subsequently, elderly women are far more likely than elderly men to rely exclusively on minimal social security benefits. Elderly women receive approximately 24 percent less than elderly men in social-security benefits *and* have less private supplemental income.[18]

You can see the beginning of this process in our story when Susan begins working part time to help Helen. In the unwritten epilogue, Susan reaches old age having only worked part time. Subsequently, under current regulations, she will be entitled to lower social-security benefits. Moreover, as a widow, she will not have a private pension and will very likely live at poverty level. Sadly, even young women today, who work for most of their lives, will receive comparable retirement benefits to their mothers who were never employed.[19]

With Paul's illness, Helen's financial difficulties worsened considerably. A couple's entire life savings can be quickly exhausted providing medical intervention for a spouse, leaving a widow destitute. When Medicaid is required to pay for health care, as is the case in the vast majority of nursing-home placements, assets must be spent down before eligibility requirements are met.[20] Again, because of the shorter life span and accompanying morbidity of men, women are more likely to be left destitute after the death of their husbands. Interestingly, widowed women are worse off financially than single and divorced women.[21]

Many women come to old age poor, but others, like Helen, become poor for the first time in their lives in old age. A cogent argument can be made that public policy surrounding old age is inherently discriminatory because it fails to take into account the cumulative economic disadvantages women bring to old age. The poverty of old age is especially intractable due to very limited opportunities to generate more income.[22]

Among minorities, poverty is far more widespread than among whites. Over *half* of black and

Hispanic elderly females not living with their families are living at or below poverty level.[23] These alarming statistics are not simply an artifact of past eras. It is estimated that 25 percent of young women today will live at or near the poverty level in old age.

Living alone increases the likelihood of institutionalization because no one is available to assist in daily care. Poverty drastically limits the available options for nursing homes or board-and-care facilities. Again, women are more likely than men to experience the consequences. In people 85 and over, one in four women lives in a nursing home, whereas only one in seven men lives in a nursing home.[24] The quality of nursing homes ranges from excellent to very poor and, not surprisingly, high quality care inevitably requires money. Here again we are confronted with the cumulative discrepancies between men and women in financial security garnered across the life span.

Less obvious are the combined ramifications of poverty and widowhood. For example, the health of low-income patients with heart disease is more likely to worsen[25] and, if they live alone, they are almost twice as likely to suffer another heart attack.[26] Once again, women are more likely to experience both risk factors.

Double jeopardy refers to being old and female; *triple jeopardy* refers to being a member of a minority group, as well. The terms are problematic because they imply that the problems are additive when, in fact, the problems older black women face are qualitatively different from those older white women face.[27] But they are fitting in suggesting that problems are greater for minority elderly. Reading the case study in this chapter, you may have felt that we were presenting the worst case scenario. Not so. We provided you with a case study about people who had come to old age privileged in many ways. Helen and Paul were white and middle-class. They planned for their retirement, saved thousands of dollars, and enjoyed excellent health care. To many Americans, these are luxuries.

Virtually every risk factor we have discussed is greater for minority elderly. For example, non-Hispanic blacks and Puerto Ricans are the least likely groups to have private health insurance.[28] Sixty-four percent of black women living alone live below the poverty level.[29] Elderly blacks are twice as likely as elderly whites to report fair or less than fair health.[30]

In addition to problems that result from a lifetime of disadvantage, elderly minorities are more likely to face the disadvantages of more current social crises. In the midst of a drug epidemic, which is hitting the inner-city particularly hard, black grandmothers have become the most likely caregivers for grandchildren whose parents have become addicted to drugs.[31] Native American grandparents are also increasingly likely to assume primary caretaking roles for grandchildren, for reasons ranging from the desire to preserve native culture to the drug dependency of parents.[32]

The picture we have painted is, indeed, pessimistic. If there is a positive element to this at all it is that, despite the problems, older women are doing quite well psychologically. For some reason, they are less likely to be depressed[33] or lonely[34] than their younger counterparts. Instead, reading the literature on aging invokes the adage "what doesn't kill you makes you stronger." Older women appear to have impressive resilience despite the uneven odds.

The labeling of older women as a *special* or *needy* population is ironic. Older women, by and large, face the cumulative disadvantages of lifelong discrimination and, *in spite of that,* cope reasonably well. The problem is not a needy population; rather, the problem stems from massive structural inequities. Government policy does not adequately address the concerns of minorities, women, or elderly people. Those inadequacies in policy translate into cumulative disadvantages that are dramatically evident in old age.

In theory, the inequities can be changed. The first step is to recognize the problem. Subsequent steps fall in two domains: personal planning and political restructuring. We offer the following suggestions: At the individual level, women must plan for their futures. Find out about health-insurance policies, survivor benefits, and retirement income. Plan for an old age without a spouse. Most women do not think about widowhood until they are nearing old age even though only a small minority of married women live out their lives with their spouses. Carefully think through alternative living arrangements. The second domain involves public policy. Write letters to state and local representatives. Insist on a national health-insurance plan. Affordable health care is possible if it is made a national priority. Medicaid laws can be changed to reduce the inherent discrimination toward women. We can reduce the likelihood of problems if we become informed about the future.

We need to act. Older women, who have a lifetime of experience on which to draw, may be our best spokespersons. We'll leave you with a last word from Maggie Kuhn, founder of the Gray Panthers:

> *What can we do? Those of us who have survived to this advanced age? We can think and speak, we can remember. We can give advice, and make judgments. We can dial the phone, write letters and read. We may not be able to butter our bread, but we can still change the world.*[35]

Acknowledgments

Preparation of this chapter was facilitated by grants AG07476 and AG08816 from the National Institute on Aging. Many thanks go to Edwin L. Carstensen, Marty Lynch, Julio Garcia, Diana Pierce, Chantal Piot-Ziegler, Lillian Rabinowitz, and Susan Turk for their critical and constructive comments on an earlier draft of this chapter. Correspondence concerning this chapter should be directed to Laura L. Carstensen, Ph.D., Department of Psychology, Bldg. 420, Jordan Hall, Stanford University, Stanford, CA 94305.

ENDNOTES

1. S. de Beauvoir, *The Coming of Aging* (New York: Putnam, 1972), 12.

2. National Center for Health Statistics, *Vital and Health Statistics: Current Estimates from the National Health Interview Survey, 1990* (DHHS Publication No. PHS 92–1509) (Washington, D.C.: U.S. Government Printing Office, 1991).

3. Special Committee on Aging, United States Senate, *Aging America: Trends and Projections* (Serial No. 101-E) (Washington, D.C.: U.S. Government Printing Office, 1989).

4. Ibid.

5. G. Hagestad, "The Family: Women and Grandparents as Kinkeepers," in *Our Aging Society: Paradox and Promise,* ed. A. Pifer and L. Bronte (New York: W. W. Norton, 1986),147.

6. Special Committee on Aging, 1989.

7. Ibid.

8. C. Lesnoff-Caravaglia, "The Five Percent Fallacy," *International Journal of Aging and Human Development* 2 (1978–79): 187–192.

9. D. E. Biegel, E. Sales, and R. Schulz, *Family Caregiving in Chronic Illness* (Newbury Park, Calif.: Sage Publications, 1991); L. George and L. P. Gwyther, "Caregiver Well-being: A Multidimensional Examination of Family Caregivers of Demented Adults," *The Gerontologist* 26 (1986): 253–259; and D. Gallagher, J. Rose, P. Rivera, S. Lovett, and L. Thompson, "Prevalence of Depression in Family Caregivers," *The Gerontologist* 29 (1989): 449–456.

10. S. E. England, S. M. Keigher, B. Miller, and N. Linsk, "Community Care Policies and Gender Justice," in *Critical Perspectives on Aging: The Political and Moral Economy of Growing Old,* ed. M. Minkler and C. Estes (Amityville, N.Y.: Baywood Publishing, 1991), 227–244.

11. A. Horowitz, "Sons and Daughters as Caregivers to Older Parents: Differences in Role Performance and Consequences," *The Gerontologist* 25 (1985): 612–617.

12. S. H. Zarit, N. K. Orr, and J. M. Zarit, *The Hidden Victims of Alzheimer's Disease: Families Under Stress* (New York: New York University Press, 1982).

13. Ibid.

14. A. S. Barusch and W. M. Spaid, "Gender Differences in Caregiving: Why Do Wives Support Greater Burden?" *The Gerontologist* 29 (1989): 667–675.

15. Gallagher et al., 1989.

16. England et al., 1991.

17. Ibid.

18. T. Arendel and C. Estes, "Older Women in the Post-Reagan Era," in *Critical Perspectives on Aging: The Political and Moral Economy of Growing Old,* ed. Minkler and Estes, 209–226.

19. Older Women's League, "Heading for Hardship: Retirement Income for American Women in the Next Century," *Mothers' Day Report,* 1991.

20. Spend-down rules have changed a great deal over the last few years. As of 1992, states vary considerably in the level of assets individuals are allowed to keep before they are eligible for Medicaid assistance.

21. Special Committee on Aging, 1989.

22. G. J. Duncan, *Years of Poverty, Years of Plenty: The Changing Economic Fortunes of American Workers and Families* (Ann Arbor: Institute for Social Research, University of Michigan, 1984).

23. Special Committee on Aging, 1989.

24. American Association of Homes for the Aging, "Fact Sheet: Nursing Homes" (Washington, D.C.: 1991).

25. R. B. Williams, J. C. Barefoot, R. M. Califf, T. L. Haney, W. B. Saunders, D. B. Pryor, M. A. Hlatky, I. C. Siegler, and D.B. Mark, "Prognostic Importance of Social and Economic Resources Among Medically Treated Patients with Angiographically Documented Coronary Artery Disease," *New England Journal of Medicine* 267(4) (1992): 520–524.

26. R. B. Case, A. J. Moss, N. Case, M. McDermott, and S. Eberly, "Living Alone After Myocardial Infarction: Impact on Prognosis," *New England Journal of Medicine* 267(4) (January 22/29, 1992): 515–519.

27. P. L. Dressel, "Gender, Race and Class: Beyond the Feminization of Poverty in Later Life," in *Critical Perspectives on Aging: The Political and Moral Economy of Growing Old,* ed. M. Minkler and C. Estes (Amityville, N.Y.: Baywood Publishing, 1991).

28. National Center for Health Statistics, *Health United States 1990* (DHHS Publication No. PHS 91–1232) (Washington, D.C.: U.S. Government Printing Office, 1991).

29. Special Committee on Aging, 1989.

30. U.S. Department of Health and Human Services, 1990.

31. M. Minkler, "Forgotten Caregivers: Grandparents Raising Infants and Young Children in the Crack Cocaine Epidemic," *Symposium Presented at the 44th Annual Scientific Meeting of the GSA,* San Francisco (1991).

32. J. Weibel-Orlando, "Grandparenting Styles: Native American Perspectives," in *The Cultural Context of Aging: Worldwide Perspectives,* ed. J. Sokolovsky (New York: Bergin & Garvey, Publishers, 1991), 109–125.

33. D. Blazer, "Depression in Late Life: An Update," in *Annual Review of Geriatrics and Gerontology,* ed. M. P. Lawton (New York: Springer, 1989), 197–215.

34. T. A. Revenson, "Social and Demographic Correlates of Loneliness in Late Life," *American Journal of Community Psychology* 12 (1984): 338–342.

35. M. Kuhn, *No Stone Unturned: The Life and Times of Maggie Kuhn* (New York: Ballantine, 1991), 212–213.

Reading 2   Puerto Rican Elderly Women: Shared Meanings and Informal Supportive Networks

MELBA SÁNCHEZ-AYÉNDEZ

Questions to Consider:

1. How do gender roles influence these Puerto Rican women's experiences of being elderly?

2. What cultural values have influenced the experience of aging in your family and community? Are elderly women's lives similar to the lives of the Puerto Rican women described in the reading? Explain.

3. What advantages do you see to aging in a culture (as described in the reading) that values family interdependence and different roles for women and men? What disadvantages do you see?

INTRODUCTION

Studies of older adults' support systems have seldom taken into account how values within a specific cultural context affect expectations of support and patterns of assistance in social networks. Such networks and supportive relations have a cultural dimension reflecting a system of shared meanings. These meanings affect social interaction and the expectations people have of their relationships with others.

Ethnicity and gender affect a person's adjustment to old age. Although sharing a "minority" position produces similar consequences among members of different ethnic minority groups, the groups' diversity lies in their distinctive systems

of shared meanings. Studies of older adults in ethnic minority groups have rarely focused on the cultural contents of ethnicity affecting the aging process, particularly of women (Barth 1969). Cultural value orientations are central to understanding how minority elders approach growing old and how they meet the physical and emotional changes associated with aging.

This article describes the interplay between values and behavior in family and community of a group of older Puerto Rican women living on low incomes in Boston.[1] It explores how values emphasizing family interdependence and different roles of women and men shape the women's expectations, behavior, and supportive familial and community networks.

BEING A WOMAN IS DIFFERENT FROM BEING A MAN

The women interviewed believe in a dual standard of conduct for men and women. This dual standard is apparent in different attributes assigned to women and men, roles expected of them, and authority exercised by them.

The principal role of men in the family is viewed as that of provider; their main responsibility is economic in nature. Although fathers are expected to be affectionate with their children, child care is not seen to be a man's responsibility. Men are not envisioned within the domestic sphere.

The "ideal" man must be the protector of the family, able to control his emotions and be self-sufficient. Men enjoy more freedom in the public world than do women. From the women's perspective, the ideal of maleness is linked to the concept of *machismo*. This concept assumes men have a stronger sexual drive than women, a need to prove virility by the conquest of women, a dominant position in relation to females, and a belligerent attitude when confronted by male peers.

The women see themselves as subordinate to men and recognize the preeminence of male authority. They believe women ought to be patient and largely forbearing in their relations with men, particularly male family members. Patience and forbearance, however, are not confused with passivity or total submissiveness. The elderly Puerto Rican women do not conceive of themselves or other women as "resigned females" but as dynamic beings, continually devising strategies to improve everyday situations within and outside the household.

Rosa Mendoza,[2] now sixty-five, feels no regrets for having decided at thirty years of age and after nine years of marriage not to put up with her husband's heavy drinking any longer. She moved out of her house and went to live with her mother.

I was patient for many years. I put up with his drunkenness and worked hard to earn money. One day I decided I'd be better off without

him. One thing is to be patient, and another to be a complete fool. So I moved out.

Although conscious of their subordinate status to their husbands, wives are also aware of their power and the demands they can make. Ana Fuentes recalls when her husband had a mistress. Ana was thirty-eight.

I knew he had a mistress in a nearby town. I was patient for a long time, hoping it would end. Most men, sooner or later, have a mistress somewhere. But when it didn't end after quite a time and everyone in the neighborhood knew about it, I said "I am fed up!" He came home one evening and the things I told him! I even said I'd go to that woman's house and beat her if I had to.... He knew I was not bluffing; that this was not just another argument. He tried to answer back and I didn't let him. He remained silent.... And you know what? He stopped seeing her! A woman can endure many things for a long time, but the time comes when she has to defend her rights.

These older Puerto Rican women perceive the home as the center around which the female world revolves. Home is the woman's domain; women generally make decisions about household maintenance and men seldom intervene.

Family relations are considered part of the domestic sphere and therefore a female responsibility. The women believe that success in marriage depends on the woman's ability to "make the marriage work."

A marriage lasts as long as the woman decides it will last. It is us who make a marriage work, who put up with things, who try to make ends meet, who yield.

The norm of female subordination is evident in the view that marriage will last as long as the woman "puts up with things" and deals with marriage from her subordinate status. Good relations with affinal kin are also a woman's responsibility. They are perceived as relations between the wife's domestic unit and other women's domestic units.

Motherhood

Motherhood is seen by these older Puerto Rican women as the central role of women. Their concept of motherhood is based on the female capacity to bear children and on the notion of *marianismo*, which presents the Virgin Mary as a role model (Stevens 1973). *Marianismo* presupposes that it is through motherhood that a woman realizes herself and derives her life's greatest satisfactions.

A woman's reproductive role is viewed as leading her toward more commitment to and a better understanding of her children than is shown by the father. One of the women emphasized this view:

> It is easier for a man to leave his children and form a new home with another woman, or not to be as forgiving of children as a mother is. They will never know what it is like to carry a child inside, feel it growing, and then bring that child into the world. This is why a mother is always willing to forgive and make sacrifices. That creature is a part of you; it nourished from you and came from within you. But it is not so for men. To them, a child is a being they receive once it is born. The attachment can never be the same.

The view that childrearing is their main responsibility in life comes from this conceptualization of the mother-child bond. For the older women, raising children means more than looking after the needs of offspring. It involves being able to offer them every possible opportunity for a better life, during childhood or adulthood, even if this requires personal sacrifices.

As mother and head of the domestic domain, a woman is also responsible for establishing the bases for close and good relations among her children. From childhood through adulthood, the creation and maintenance of family unity among offspring is considered another female responsibility.

FAMILY UNITY AND INTERDEPENDENCE

Family Unity

Ideal family relations are seen as based on two interrelated themes, family unity and family interdependence. Family unity refers to the desirability of close and intimate kin ties, with members getting along well and keeping in frequent contact despite dispersal.

Celebration of holidays and special occasions are seen as opportunities for kin to be together and strengthen family ties. Family members, particularly grandparents, adult children, and grandchildren, are often reunited at Christmas, New Year's, Mother's and Father's days, Easter, and Thanksgiving. Special celebrations like weddings, baptisms, first communions, birthdays, graduations, and funerals occasion reunions with other family members. Whether to celebrate happy or sad events, the older women encourage family gatherings as a way of strengthening kinship ties and fostering family continuity.

The value the women place on family unity is also evident in their desire for frequent interaction with kin members. Visits and telephone calls demonstrate a caring attitude by family members which cements family unity.

Family unity is viewed as contributing to the strengthening of family interdependence. Many of the older women repeat a proverb when referring to family unity: *En la unión está la fuerza.*

("In union there is strength.") They believe that the greater the degree of unity in the family, the greater the emphasis family members will place on interdependence and familial obligation.

Family Interdependence

Despite adaptation to life in a culturally different society, Puerto Rican families in the United States are still defined by strong norms of reciprocity among family members, especially those in the immediate kinship group (Cantor 1979; Carrasquillo 1982; Delgado 1981; Donaldson and Martínez 1980; Sánchez-Ayéndez 1984). Interdependence within the Puerto Rican symbolic framework "fits an orientation to life that stresses that the individual is not capable of doing everything and doing it well. Therefore, he should rely on others for assistance" (Bastida 1979: 70). Individualism and self-reliance assume a different meaning from the one prevailing in the dominant U.S. cultural tradition. Individuals in Puerto Rican families will expect and ask for assistance from certain people in their social networks without any derogatory implications for self-esteem.

Family interdependence is a value to which these older Puerto Rican women strongly adhere. It influences patterns of mutual assistance with their children as well as expectations of support. The older women expect to be taken care of during old age by their adult children. The notion of filial duty ensues from the value orientation of interdependence. Adult children are understood to have a responsibility toward their aged parents in exchange for the functions that parents performed for them throughout their upbringing. Expected reciprocity from offspring is intertwined with the concept of filial love and the nature of the parent-child relationship.

Parental duties of childrearing are perceived as inherent in the "parent" role and also lay the basis for long-term reciprocity with children, particularly during old age. The centrality that motherhood has in the lives of the older women

contributes to creating great expectations among them of reciprocity from children. More elderly women than men verbalize disappointment when one of their children does not participate in the expected interdependence ties. Disappointment is unlikely to arise when an adult child cannot help due to financial or personal reasons. However, it is bound to arise when a child chooses not to assist the older parent for other reasons.

These older Puerto Rican women stress that good offspring ought to help their parents, contingent upon available resources. Statements such as the following are common:

Of course I go to my children when I have a problem! To whom would I turn? I raised them and worked very hard to give them the little I could. Now that I am old, they try to help me in whatever they can.... Good offspring should help their aged parents as much as they are able to.

Interdependence for Puerto Rican older parents also means helping their children and grandchildren. Many times they provide help when it is not explicitly requested. They are happy when they can perform supportive tasks for their children's families. The child who needs help, no matter how old, is not judged as dependent or a failure.

Reciprocity is not based on strictly equal exchanges. Due to the rapid pace of life, lack of financial resources, or personal problems, adult children are not always able to provide the care the elder parent needs. Many times, the older adults provide their families with more financial and instrumental assistance than their children are able to provide them. Of utmost importance to the older women is not that their children be able to help all the time, but that they visit or call frequently. They place more emphasis on emotional support from their offspring than on any other form of support.

Gloria Santos, for example, has a son and a daughter. While they do not live in the same state as their mother, they each send her fifty to seventy dollars every month. Yet, she is disappointed with her children and explains why:

> They both have good salaries but call me only once or twice a month. I hardly know my grandchildren. All I ask from them is that they be closer to me, that they visit and call me more often. They only visit me once a year and only for one or two days. I've told my daughter that instead of sending me money she could call me more often. I was a good mother and worked hard in order for them to get a good education and have everything. All I expected from them was to show me they care, that they love me.

The importance that the older women attach to family interdependence does not imply that they constantly require assistance from children or that they do not value their independence. They prefer to live in their own households rather than with their adult children. They also try to solve as many problems as possible by themselves. But when support is needed, the adult children are expected to assist the aged parent to the degree they are able. This does not engender conflict or lowered self-esteem for the aged adult. Conflict and dissatisfaction are caused when adult children do not offer any support at all.

SEX ROLES AND FAMILIAL SUPPORTIVE NETWORKS

The family is the predominant source of support for most of these older women, providing instrumental and emotional support in daily life as well as assistance during health crises or times of need. Adult children play a central role in providing familial support to old parents. For married women, husbands are also an important component of their support system. At the same time, most of the older women still perform functional roles for their families.

Support from Adult Children

The support and helpfulness expected from offspring is related to perceptions of the difference between men and women. Older women seek different types of assistance from daughters than from sons. Daughters are perceived as being inherently better able to understand their mothers due to their shared status and qualities as women; they are also considered more reliable. Sons are not expected to help as much as daughters or in the same way. When a daughter does not fulfill the obligations expected of her, complaints are more bitter than if the same were true of a son: "Men are different; they do not feel as we feel. But she is a woman; she should know better." Daughters are also expected to visit and/or call more frequently than are sons. As women are linked closely to the domestic domain, they are held responsible for the care of family relations.

Motherhood is perceived as creating an emotional bond among women. When daughters become mothers, the older women anticipate stronger ties and more support from them.

> Once a daughter experiences motherhood, she understands the suffering and hardships you underwent for her. Sons will never be able to understand this.
>
> My daughter always helped me. But when she became a mother for the first time, she grew much closer to me. It was then when she was able to understand how much a mother can love.

Most of the older women go to a daughter first when confronted by an emotional problem. Daughters are felt to be more patient and better able to understand them as women. It is not that older women never discuss their emotional problems with their sons, but they prefer to discuss them with their daughters. For example, Juana Rivera has two sons who live in the same city as she and a daughter who resides in Puerto Rico.

She and her sons get along well and see each other often. The sons stop by their mother's house every day after work, talk about daily happenings, and assist her with some tasks. However, when a physical exam revealed a breast tumor thought to be malignant, it was to her daughter in Puerto Rico that the old woman expressed her worries. She recalls that time of crisis:

Eddie was with me when the doctor told me of the possibility of a tumor. I was brave. I didn't want him to see me upset. They [sons] get nervous when I get upset or cry.... That evening I called my daughter and talked to her.... She was very understanding and comforted me. I can always depend on her to understand me. She is the person who better understands me. My sons are also understanding, but she is a woman and understands more.

Although adult children are sources of assistance during the illnesses of their mothers, it is generally daughters from whom more is expected. Quite often daughters take their sick parents into their homes or stay overnight in the parental household in order to provide better care. Sons, as well as daughters, take the aged parent to the hospital or doctors' offices and buy medicines if necessary. However, it is more often daughters who check on their parents, provide care, and perform household chores when the parent is sick.

When the old women have been hospitalized, adult children living nearby tend to visit the hospital daily. Daughters and daughters-in-law sometimes cook special meals for the sick parent and bring the meals to the hospital. Quite often, adult children living in other states or in Puerto Rico come to help care for the aged parent or be present at the time of an operation. When Juana Rivera had exploratory surgery on her breast, her daughter came from Puerto Rico and stayed with her mother throughout the convalescence. Similarly, when Ana Toledo suffered a stroke and remained unconscious for four days, three of her six children residing in other states came to be with her and their siblings. After her release from the hospital, a daughter from New Jersey stayed at her mother's house for a week. When she left, the children who live near the old woman took turns looking after her.

Most adult children are also helpful in assisting with chores of daily living. At times, offspring take their widowed mothers grocery shopping. Other times, the older women give their children money to do the shopping for them. Daughters are more often asked to do these favors and to also buy personal care items and clothes for their mothers. Some adult offspring also assist by depositing Social Security checks, checking post office boxes, and buying money orders.

Support from Elderly Mothers

The Puerto Rican older women play an active role in providing assistance to their adult children. Gender affects the frequency of emotional support offered as well as the dynamics of the support. The older women offer advice more often to daughters than to sons on matters related to childrearing. And the approach used differs according to the children's gender. For example, one older woman stated,

I never ask my son openly what is wrong with him. I do not want him to think that I believe he needs help to solve his problems; he is a man.... Yet, as a mother I worry. It is my duty to listen and offer him advice. With my daughter it is different; I can be more direct. She doesn't have to prove to me that she is self-sufficient.

Another woman expressed similar views:

Of course I give advice to my sons! When they have had problems with their wives, their children, even among themselves, I lis-

ten to them, and tell them what I think. But with my daughters I am more open. You see, if I ask one of my sons what is wrong and he doesn't want to tell me, I don't insist too much; I'll ask later, maybe in a different way; and they will tell me sooner or later. With my daughters, if they don't want to tell me, I insist. They know I am a mother and a woman like them and that I can understand.

Older mothers perceive sons and daughters as in equal need of support. Daughters, however, are understood to face additional problems in areas such as conjugal relations, childrearing, and sexual harassment, due to their status as women.

Emotional support to daughters-in-law is also offered, particularly when they are encountering marriage or childrearing problems. Josefina Montes explains the active role she played in comforting her daughter-in-law, whose husband was having an extramarital affair.

I told her not to give up, that she had to defend what was hers. I always listened to her and tried to offer some comfort. . . . When my son would come to my home to visit I would ask him "What is wrong with you? Don't you realize what a good mother and wife that woman is?" . . . I made it my business that he did not forget the exceptional woman she is. . . . I told him I didn't want to ever see him with the other one and not to mention her name in front of me. . . . I was on his case for almost two years. . . . All the time I told her to be patient. It took time but he finally broke up with the other one.

When relations between mother and daughters-in-law are not friendly, support is not usually present. Eulilia Valle says that when her son left his wife and children to move in with another woman, there was not much she could do for her daughter-in-law.

There was not much I could do. What could I tell him? I couldn't say she was nice to me. . . . Once I tried to make him see how much she was hurting and he replied: "Don't defend her. She has never been fond of you and you know it." What could I reply to that? All I said was, "That's true but, still, she must be very hurt." But there was nothing positive to say about her!

Monetary assistance generally flows from the older parent to the adult children, although few old people are able to offer substantial financial help. Direct monetary assistance, rarely exceeding fifty dollars, is less frequent than gift-giving. Gift-giving usually takes the form of monetary contributions for specific articles needed by their children or children's families. In this way the older people contribute indirectly to the maintenance of their children's families.

The older women also play an active role in the observance of special family occasions and holidays. On the days preceding the celebration, they are busy cooking traditional Puerto Rican foods. It is expected that those in good health will participate in the preparation of foods. This is especially true on Christmas and Easter when traditional foods are an essential component of the celebrations.

Cooking for offspring is also a part of everyday life. In many of the households, meals prepared in the Puerto Rican tradition are cooked daily "in case children or grandchildren come by." Josefina Montes, for example, cooks a large quantity of food everyday for herself, her husband, and their adult children and grandchildren. Her daughters come by after work to visit and pick up their youngest children, who stay with grandparents after school. The youngest daughter eats dinner at her parents' home. The oldest takes enough food home to serve her family. Doña[3] Josefina's sons frequently drop by after work or during lunch and she always insists that they eat something.

The older women also provide assistance to their children during health crises. When Juana Rivera's son was hospitalized for a hernia operation, she visited the hospital every day, occasionally bringing food she had prepared for him. When her son was released, Doña Juana stayed in his household throughout his convalescence, caring for him while her daughter-in-law went off to work.

The aged women also assist their children by taking care of grandchildren. Grandchildren go to their grandmother's house after school and stay until their parents stop by after work. If the children are not old enough to walk home by themselves, the grandparent waits for them at school and brings them home. The women also take care of their grandchildren when they are not old enough to attend school or are sick. They see their role as grandmothers as a continuation or reenactment of their role as mothers and childrearers.

The women, despite old age, have a place in the functional structure of their families. The older women's assistance is an important contribution to their children's households and also helps validate the women's sense of their importance and helpfulness.

Mutual Assistance in Elderly Couples

Different conceptions of women and men influence interdependence between husband and wife as well as their daily tasks. Older married women are responsible for domestic tasks and perform household chores. They also take care of grandchildren, grocery shopping, and maintaining family relations. Older married men have among their chores depositing Social Security checks, going to the post office, and buying money orders. Although they stay in the house for long periods, the men go out into the community more often than do their wives. They usually stop at the *bodegas*,[4] which serve as a place for socializing and exchange of information, to buy items needed at home and newspapers from Puerto Rico.

Most married couples have a distinctive newspaper reading pattern. The husband comments on the news to his wife as he reads or after he has finished. Sometimes, after her husband finishes reading and commenting on the news, the older woman reads about it herself. Husbands also inform their wives of ongoing neighborhood events learned on their daily stops at the *bodegas*. Wives, on the other hand, inform husbands of familial events learned through their daily telephone conversations and visits from children and other kin members.

The older couple escort each other to service-providing agencies, even though they are usually accompanied by an adult child, adolescent grandchild, or social worker serving as translator. An older man still perceives himself in the role of "family protector" by escorting the women in his family, particularly his wife.

Older husbands and wives provide each other with emotional assistance. They are daily companions and serve as primary sources of confidence for each other, most often sharing children's and grandchildren's problems, health concerns, or financial worries. The couple do not always agree on solutions or approaches for assisting children when sharing their worries about offspring. Many times the woman serves as a mediator in communicating her husband's problems to adult children. The men tend to keep their problems, particularly financial and emotional ones, to themselves or tell their wives but not their children. This behavior rests upon the notion of men as financially responsible for the family, more self-sufficient, and less emotional than women.

Among the older couples, the husband or wife is generally the principal caregiver during the health crises of their spouse. Carmen Ruiz, for example, suffers from chronic anemia and tires easily. Her husband used to be a cook and has taken responsibility for cooking meals and looking after the household. When Providencia Cruz's husband was hospitalized she spent many hours each day at the hospital, wanting to be certain he was comfortable. She brought meals she had cooked for him, arranged his pillows, rubbed him with bay leaf rubbing alcohol, or watched him as he slept. When he was convalescing at home, she was his principal caregiver. Doña Providencia suffers from osteoarthritis and gastric acidity. When she is in pain and spends the day in bed, her husband provides most of the assistance she needs. He goes to the drugstore to buy medicine or ingredients used in folk remedies. He knows how to prepare the mint and chamomile teas she drinks when not feeling well. He also rubs her legs and hands with ointments when the arthritic pain is more intense than usual. Furthermore, during the days that Doña Providencia's ailments last, he performs most of the household chores.

While both spouses live, the couple manages many of their problems on their own. Assistance from other family members with daily chores or help during an illness is less frequent when the woman still lives with her husband than when she lives alone. However, if one or both spouses is ill, help from adult children is more common.

FRIENDS AND NEIGHBORS AS COMMUNITY SOURCES OF SUPPORT

Friends and neighbors form part of the older women's support network. However, the women differentiate between "neighbors" and "friends." Neighbors, unlike kin and friends, are not an essential component of the network which provides emotional support. They may or may not become friends. Supportive relations with friends involve being instrumental helpers, companions, and confidants. Neighbors are involved only in instrumental help.

Neighbors as Sources of Support

Contact with neighbors takes the form of greetings, occasional visits, and exchanges of food, all of which help to build the basis for reciprocity when and if the need arises. The establishment and maintenance of good relations with neighbors is considered to be important since neighbors are potentially helpful during emergencies or unexpected events. Views such as the following are common: "It is good to get acquainted with your neighbors; you never know when you might need them."

Josefina Rosario, a widow, has lived next door to an older Puerto Rican couple for three years. Exchange of food and occasional visits are part of her interaction with them. Her neighbor's husband, in his mid-sixties, occasionally runs errands for Doña Josefina, who suffers from rheumatoid arthritis and needs a walker to move around. If she runs out of a specific food item, he goes to the grocery store for her. Other times, he buys stamps, mails letters, or goes to the drugstore to pick up some medicines for her. Although Doña Josefina cannot reciprocate in the same way, she repays her neighbors by visiting every other week and exchanging food. Her neighbors tell her she is to call them day or night if she ever feels sick. Although glad to have such "good neighbors," as she calls them, she stresses she does not consider them friends and therefore does not confide her personal problems to them.

Supportive Relationships Among Friends

Although friends perform instrumental tasks, the older women believe that a good friend's most important quality is being able to provide emotional support. A friend is someone willing to help during the "good" and "bad" times, and is trustworthy and reserved. Problems may be shared with a friend with the certainty that confidences will not be betrayed. A friend provides emotional support not only during a crisis or problem, but in everyday life. Friends are companions, visiting and/or calling on a regular basis.

Friendship for this group of women is determined along gender lines. They tend to be careful about men. Relationships with males outside the immediate familial group are usually kept at a formal level. Mistrust of men is based upon the women's notion of *machismo*. Since men are conceived of as having a stronger sexual drive, the women are wary of the possibility of sexual advances, either physical or verbal. None of the women regards a male as a confidant friend. Many even emphasize the word *amiga* ("female friend") instead of a *amigo* ("male friend"). Remarks such as the following are common:

> *I've never had an* amigo. *Men cannot be trusted too much. They might misunderstand your motives and some even try to make a pass at you.*

The few times the women refer to a male as a friend they use the term *amigo de la familia* ("friend of the family"). This expression conveys that the friendly relations are not solely between the woman and the man. The expression is generally used to refer to a close friend of the husband. *Amigos de la familia* may perform instrumental tasks, be present at family gatherings and unhappy events, or drop by to chat with the respondent's husband during the day. However, relations are not based on male-female relationships.

Age similarity is another factor that seems to affect selection of friends. The friendship networks of the older women are mainly composed of people sixty years of age and older. Friends who fill the role of confidant are generally women of a similar age. The women believe that younger generations, generally, have little interest in the elders. They also state that people their own age are better able to understand their problems because they share many of the same difficulties and worries.

Friends often serve as escorts, particularly in the case of women who live alone. Those who know some English serve as translators on some occasions. Close friends also help illiterate friends by reading and writing letters.

Most of the support friends provide one another is of an emotional nature, which involves sharing personal problems. Close friends entrust one another with family and health problems. This exchange occurs when friends either visit or call each other on the telephone. A pattern commonly observed between dyads of friends is daily calls. Many women who live alone usually call the friend during the morning hours, to make sure she is all right and to find out how she is feeling.

Another aspect of the emotional support the older women provide one another is daily companionship, occurring more often among those who live alone. For example, Hilda Montes and Rosa Mendoza sit together from 1:00 to 3:00 in the afternoon to watch soap operas and talk about family events, neighborhood happenings, and household management. At 3:00 P.M., whoever is at the other's apartment leaves because their grandchildren usually arrive from school around 4:00 P.M.

Friends are also supportive during health crises. If they cannot come to visit, they inquire daily about their friend's health by telephone. When their health permits, some friends perform menial household chores and always bring food for the sick person. If the occasion requires it, they prepare and/or administer home remedies. Friends, in this sense, alleviate the stress adult children often feel in assisting their aged mothers, particularly those who live by themselves. Friends take turns among themselves or with kin in taking care of the ill during the daytime. Children generally stay throughout the night.

Exchange ties with female friends include instrumental support, companionship, and problem sharing. Friends, particularly age cohorts, play an important role in the emotional well-being of the elders.

The relevance of culture to experience of old age is seen in the influence of value orientations on the expectations these Puerto Rican women have of themselves and those in their informal supportive networks. The way a group's cultural tradition defines and interprets relationships influences how elders use their networks to secure the support needed in old age. At the same time, the extent to which reality fits culturally-based expectations will contribute, to a large extent, to elders' sense of well-being.

NOTES

1. The article is based on a nineteen-month ethnographic study. The research was supported by the Danforth Foundation; Sigma Xi; the Scientific Research Society; and the Delta Kappa Gamma Society International.

2. All names are fictitious.

3. The deference term *Doña* followed by the woman's first name is a common way by which to address elderly Puerto Rican women and the one preferred by those who participated in the study.

4. Neighborhood grocery stores, generally owned by Puerto Ricans or other Hispanics, where ethnic foods can be purchased.

REFERENCES CITED

Barth, F.
1969 *Introduction to Ethnic Groups and Boundaries,* F. Barth, ed. Boston: Little, Brown.

Bastida, E.
1979 "Family Integration and Adjustment to Aging Among Hispanic American Elderly." Ph.D. dissertation, University of Kansas.

Cantor, M. H.
1979 "The Informal Support System of New York's Inner City Elderly: Is Ethnicity a Factor?" In *Ethnicity and Aging,* D. L. Gelfand and A. J. Kutzik, eds. New York: Springer.

Carrasquillo, H.
1982 "Perceived Social Reciprocity and Self-Esteem Among Elderly Barrio Antillean Hispanics and Their Familial Informal Networks." Ph.D. dissertation, Syracuse University.

Delgado, M.
1981 Hispanic Elderly and Natural Support Systems: A Special Focus on Puerto Ricans. Paper presented at the Scientific Meeting of the Boston Society for Gerontological Psychiatry, November, Boston, Mass.

Donaldson, E. and E. Martinez.
1980 "The Hispanic Elderly of East Harlem" *Aging* 305–306: 6–11.

Sánchez-Ayéndez, M.
1984 "Puerto Rican Elderly Women: Aging in an Ethnic Minority Group in the United States." Ph.D. dissertation, University of Massachusetts at Amherst.

Stevens, E. P.
1973 "Marianismo: The Other Face of Machismo in Latin America." In *Female and Male in Latin America,* A. Pescatello, ed. Pittsburgh: University of Pittsburgh Press.

Reading 3   Confronting Ageism: A Must for Mental Health

SHEVY HEALEY

Questions to Consider:

1. In what ways is Healey's experience of being old unlike her other experiences of being different?

2. What are the characteristics of internalized ageism?

3. How do you feel about your own aging?

4. What steps can you take to combat the ageism in our culture? What steps can you take to combat your own internalized ageism?

SUMMARY. This is a personal account by a 70 year old lesbian of how she came to the conclusion that without confronting ageism it is impossible to have a good old age.

The equation of old women with undesirability is so pervasive that no one is immune from its destructiveness. The fear about age, reaching phobic proportions among white skinned women of European background, has grave repercussions for us as we experience our own aging. We can attempt to deny our aging for a while at least, through the almost universal practice of trying to pass for younger; we can accept the ugly stereotypes about ourselves and become increasingly depressed and alienated; or we can embark on the struggle to confront the ageism of our culture as well as our own internalized ageism.

As an old woman who has chosen the latter course, the impact upon my life has been tremendous. In this article I speak of my struggles against my own internalized ageism and how this path led me to a renewed social activism, sense of purpose, and inner exploration. I have been forced to explore the actuality of my aging vs. my ageist expectations, which I have found repeatedly to cloud my ability to experience my life. This process has brought excitement and fullness to my life, making my old age a time rich in learning and insight.

Old age crept upon me and caught me unawares.

Shevy Healey is a retired 70 year old psychotherapist with a PhD in Clinical Psychology from The Ohio State University. Formerly in private practice, she is feminist actively involved as a writer, presenter, and facilitator, as well as one of the founders of the Old Lesbians Organizing for Change (OLOC), a national organization by and for old lesbians 60 and over dedicated to confronting ageism.

Like most women, I had never thought about my own growing old. When I was young I felt invincible. In my 30's I was too busy struggling through my life to think about any future. I do remember thinking longingly of "retirement" but that was because I didn't like my life very much and felt powerless to change it.

In my 40's and 50's, with my life exploding in many new directions, I felt, in my heart of hearts, that I was beating the clock. I first began my college education at age 43 and not too long thereafter got divorced after some 22 years of marriage. I continued and finished my undergraduate work while my only child was herself away at college. Deciding to go for broke, at 47 I left Southern California where I had lived most of my adult life to go to graduate school in Ohio, and at 54 I finally got a Ph.D. in clinical psychology. At 50 I made another drastic life change when I fell in love with a woman and came out as a lesbian.

With so much going on for me, I did not feel in sync with my peers and fooled myself into thinking, when I thought of age at all, that it was "a state of mind," nothing else. The experience of being out of sync was, in fact, what felt most familiar.

My mother, father, and I arrived in this country from Poland in 1923. Within six months my father died, and at age 24 my mother was left alone without any close family to raise a two year old child. I started kindergarten not knowing a word of English, and my sense of shame and alienation was more profound when my first name was arbitrarily changed by the school registrar. My own name was too "foreign" sounding; thus Sheva became Evelyn.

Although almost all immigrants were poor, we were in an especially impoverished category. At the height of the Great Depression when my mother got sick and could no longer bring home even the four dollars a week she was earning we were forced to go on county welfare to survive.

I was out of sync even as a Jewish child raised in a Jewish ghetto, for my mother was a revolutionary and an atheist. I was the only child I knew who ate bread on Pessach (Passover), and who "on principle" did not say aloud the Pledge of Allegiance to a government which hypocritically claimed to be for liberty and justice for all, while favoring the rich at the expense of the poor. At five I proudly marched with my mother, a garment worker, on my first picket line. I clearly remember running with her down an alley to escape the Philadelphia mounted police, who, with horses rearing and stomping, charged into the picket line of mostly women and children in an attempt to break the strike. By age eleven I was a seasoned Junior Pioneer leader wearing my red bandanna and marching in picket lines and May Day Parades. From the rebellious tom boy to the high school rebel, I was an "expert" in knowing what it felt like to be other than the mainstream, while at the same time having a strong sense of place and solidarity with my own political comrades.

The closest I came to being mainstream was when I finally got my Ph.D., but by then I was an "out" lesbian and feminist—both of which did not exactly clothe me in respectability.

Surely then, with all of my previous experience of otherness, I could be expected to make a relatively easy transition to the otherness experienced so acutely by old women. Absolutely not so. I continued through my 50's steadfast in my delusion that age, *my* age, was irrelevant. More and more in social circles I experienced myself as the "older" woman in the group, but coming out as a lesbian at 50 and having a wonderfully exciting decade only promoted my sense of myself as an exception. It is true that I began to fret about my outward appearance more than I ever had. The wrinkles, loose flesh, the changes in my body left me worried and split. How could my body feel so charged and sexual, my self be so full of plans and dreams and energy, while at the same time it was registering the signs of growing old? Although I never dyed my hair, by now a lovely steel gray, I did seriously consider a face lift. Only at the last minute did I acknowledge to myself that it would take more than surgery to help me resolve my internal split about my own aging.

My growing external change of status forced my growing internal discomfort to reach more conscious levels. My first intimations of what age stereotyping was all about occurred when I moved into a new community and was shocked to find myself addressed by younger people, with the ritual respect reserved for—not Mother—but Grandmother, at a time when my own grandchild had not yet been born. I began to work only part time and this meant increasing isolation from colleagues and work-related sources of respect. I found also that younger professionals who were meeting me for the first time and knew that I too was a professional assumed a respectful rather than collegial stance, while those who knew nothing about me most often ignored me completely.

My own mother and step-father, now in their early 80's, seemed to be having increasing health difficulties, but I must admit, strange as that seems to me now, I simply did not pay much attention and blithely assumed that they would go on as always, at least until some far-off future. My world changed radically and shockingly when my step-father died unexpectedly after surgery, leaving my mother alone, in failing health and total panic. Suddenly I found myself solely and increasingly responsible for my mother's care, a task which took enormous energy and struggle.

When she died some two years later at age 85, no amount of preparation helped me to experience my new position in the world, feeling orphaned at 63! I became the oldest living member of my very small family. In a way I could not foresee I was catapulted into an active awareness of my own mortality, my own vulnerability, myself as an old woman.

There ensued a series of struggles and learnings which I think are relatively typical, though at the time I thought were unique. The invisibility I experienced as an old woman felt much different from all the experiences of otherness I had ever known. Being subject to special oppression was certainly familiar enough. What was different this time, however, was how I felt inside as I experienced this oppression. Whatever fear I had experienced in being "other" throughout my life, I had always felt a core of strength and pride in who I was and what I stood for—in my poor and working class background, my Jewishness, my atheism, my foreignness, my political radicalism, my being a girl, a woman, a lesbian. Now, I was attempting to deny my otherness by denying my own aging, a denial that masked the tremendous fear I felt about being an old woman, about being "over the hill," for I had internalized the ageist stereotype that my life was all but over and I did not want it to be! Neither did I want to be part of a group stigmatized as ineffectual, useless, ugly, asexual, whining, passive, lifeless, sick, dependent, powerless—the antithesis of everything I had tried to be and make of my life.

What a dilemma: hating and dreading what being old represented, while each year becoming more clearly identifiably old. All I really wanted was to hold back the clock by some magical act of will. Truth is, I think I tried that—for a while convincing myself that if only I exercised the right way, ate the right food, lived the right kind of pure and glowing life, I would "beat" old age. I never, as yet, questioned the validity of my ageist assumptions. My fears were reinforced by watching my mother grow old and die, an old age that was full of denial and fear of the changes occurring in her body and her life, and rage at what she considered the whittling away of her self and the ending of a life that felt unfulfilled.

Looking back on that time, only now can I see how hard I was working to deny my feelings and my confusion. It was, of course, not possible to deal with a problem that I refused to identify, for I was doing what all oppressed groups try to do; I was trying to pass—to myself at least.

Knowing that I felt inside a continuity with the person I always was, instead of idealizing that growing old does not mean dropping off a precipice, I decided I felt "young" inside. But no matter how automatic and unconscious this universal practice of passing for younger is, it remains a deeply alienating experience. Begging the question, refusing to acknowledge my age did nothing but rob me of the core of strength I needed to sustain and guide me through this great life change, crossing the bridge between mid-life and old.

Finally, the reality of my life forced me to go beyond denial and into acknowledging and coping somehow with my unaccustomed and unwanted status of being an old woman. In the beginning of this struggle I found myself wavering between rage—at the patronizing dismissals meted out to me in many different forms, and anxiety and foreboding about my future.

Having just turned 70, I can look at my last decade and chart my progress to a rich and rewarding old age. I am able to view my own process within the context of the political, not simply the personal. This pushes me to share my experience in the hope that it can be useful to other women learning to grow up to be old. But although I think the issue has universal significance, denial about the process is so ingrained that it seems somewhat daring, even brave, to speak in detail about my own struggles to explore the dimensions of being an old woman. For the most part, neither books nor songs are written about the every day, heroic and ordinary lives of old women. Talk about being old by the old is a conversational taboo. Interestingly, only young and mid-life women feel free to speak easily and insultingly of their dread of coming into my time of life.

I owe a huge debt to Barbara Macdonald and the book she wrote with Cynthia Rich, *Look Me In The Eye—Old Women Aging and Ageism* (1991). When I read and reread this book I felt a profound and exhilarating relief. For in writing about her own life Macdonald had also named my experience and made me feel sane, less alone and less fearful. It reminds me of the excitement of discovery we women experienced in the early days of the women's movement when we learned through our consciousness raising groups as nothing else could teach us, that what was happening in our lives was not a matter of individual flaw or problem but a common experience of oppression.

So, too, has this time of my life been a sorting, testing, learning, both as I become more mindful and attentive to my own experience and as I share with other old women and learn from our common experience. Yet this ongoing process is complex and I often feel muddled and overwhelmed. When that happens, I long to find some systematic simple way, because I am that kind of a person, to categorize and define the various components of my experience.

Am I dealing, in any given instance, with the ageism, sexism, heterosexism, or anti-Semitism of our society? Am I being "too" sensitive? Certainly as an old Jewish lesbian I can expect to and mostly do get treated in certain predictable ways in our oppressive mainstream culture, but my dismay is more acute when I experience the same slights, the same invisibility in my own special lesbian and feminist community. Since old women, lesbian or heterosexual, are invisible in our society, it is easy to grow used to that condition and sometimes the only clue I have that I am in the world but not part of it is an uneasy delayed reaction I have to my own invisibility. It is not always clear at first.

Or am I dealing not just with external ageism but a response that arises from my own internalized ageism, buttressed by the sexist and heterosexist models of aging I have from my mother and her generation?

Or, finally, can I trust that my response is actually coming from inside me, from my own body of life experience?

Sometimes there seems almost no area of behavior and emotion in which I can totally trust my first reaction. In almost every part of my life

I am forced again and again to examine my ageist expectations, not because I necessarily want to do so from some intellectual curiosity, but because if I do not do this, false expectations and assumptions cloud and diminish my ability to actually experience my life.

I think often of the most important model I've had—my own mother and her unfulfilled old age. I have to remind myself that her life and my life have been vastly different, that the times in which we both lived, the options we had and choices we made were vastly different. I remind myself also of the research that points out that in old age there is greater heterogeneity than at any other developmental stage, which provides even less basis for the existing stereotypes about old women. Yet these cultural assumptions harden into oppressive dogmas. Ageism, primarily a woman's issue, is the extension of the sexism, heterosexism, racism, and rampant consumerism of our multi-corporate society. Old women, outliving men in greater numbers, have lost their special capacity for service to the patriarchy. They no longer function as ornaments, lovers, domestics, bearers and rearers of children, or as economic drudges in the work place. To quote Copper (1988), "The ageism which old women experience is firmly embedded in sexism, an extension of the male power to define, control values, erase, disempower and divide."

The expressions of ageism are many. A core area of my ongoing examination of my own aging is my self and my relationship to my body. This is a most complex relationship, encompassing issues of illness and wellness, fear of incapacity and actual disability, loss of independence and acceptance of interdependence, the intricate relationship of my body and appearance to my sense of self and self-esteem, my own standards and politics of beauty, and more. The interrelationship and the complexity of all of these issues make them difficult to untangle. I find comfort in reminding myself that I am not dealing with trivialities but with the core issues that we all face throughout our entire lives. The fear of aging, reaching phobic proportions among white skinned women of European background, has grave repercussions for women as they experience their own aging. My greater urgency to confront these issues is my conviction that my health, well being and life itself rest on finding my way through the swamp of the ageist myths and assumptions.

My appearance was the first indicator I could see of my own aging. The face lift that I didn't get compelled me instead to examine my assumptions about beauty and appearance. It forced me to begin specifically to confront the basic assumption underlying ageism, that youth is good, desirable, and beautiful; old age is bad, repulsive and ugly. Otherwise every time I look in the mirror I must feel contempt and aversion for how I look, or avoid looking altogether because, by patriarchal standards of beauty, I will find no beauty there. The most frequent "compliment" given to old women is "you don't look your age." Consider for a moment that what is really being said is that if you did look your age you would look ugly. There is an erosion of the self which occurs when who you are is everywhere made synonymous with unattractiveness and undesirability.

I was thrilled to read Cynthia Rich's article on Ageism and the Politics of Beauty (1988), which challenges us to look at how we arrive at our ideas about beauty and to reconsider the "mysteries of attraction." For unless we examine these "mysteries" we may well exclude, to our impoverishment, whole categories of women as attractive, particularly those who are disabled or old. Rich says, "Our task is to learn, not to look insultingly beyond these features to a soul we can celebrate, but instead to take at these bodies as parts of these souls—exciting, individual, beautiful."

My first big stretch then was to examine my own conditioned notions and reconsider more open ways to experience beauty. Most helpful to me in this process is the greater reliance I have been developing on my own senses, rather on preconceived ideas. Skin that is old and wrinkled is soft and lovely, and as I touch my own skin and that of my lover I feel deep pleasure. Letting go more and more of my conditioning makes it possible for me to look with a clearer more loving vision at myself and the other old women around me. A shift, not yet complete, is taking place.

My relationship to my body has always been somewhat problematic. I have lived much of my life in my head and was trained, even more so than most women, to ignore my body's demands either for rest or attention. With growing psychological sophistication I talked about and regularly included in my practice as a therapist the notion of making friends with one's body. However, outside of sporadic frenzied efforts, I myself continued largely to ignore my body, and seemed to be able to do so with impunity since for the most part I was blessed with good health.

But starting in my 60's, my body no longer permits me to ignore her; she has begun to speak most loudly on her own behalf. Although I've always eaten too quickly and too much, for the first time I began to develop digestive problems. My vision, even with glasses, has become strained, and I've had laser surgery for glaucoma in both eyes. I have found that it takes me longer to recuperate, either after hard work or a transient illness, and I get downright cranky with insufficient rest. In other words, my body is showing some wear and tear after a long and arduous life. Certainly an acceptable proposition in a sane society and one that can be lived with, particularly since so many of us have paid such lip service to the need for women to attend to ourselves and our bodies with kindness and care, not only to others.

But in our culture, one of the first ageist assumptions is that to be old automatically means to be in some state of failing health and decrepitude, physical, mental, or both, and, further, to be in this state means to be valueless and a nonperson. It is no wonder, then, that women from their thirties on begin to lament their failing physical abilities, as if the standard set in the teens and 20's are the normative standards for life. My experiences with health limitations were so tied in with ageist expectations that at the first signs of what turned out to be a relatively mild condition I had a life crisis. I will not ever forget the absolutely unreasoning fear I felt the night I finally called the paramedics for what I thought was probably gas, but "given my age" could perhaps be chest pains, and signal the "beginning of the end." I'm not sorry I called the paramedics that time, or the time after. What I see in retrospect is that my fears, fed by the ageism of the medical establishment, were in large part due to my ageist expectations that my body was supposed to give out.

That incident provided me with some firsthand education about the rampant ageism of the medical establishment. I was referred from one doctor to another, experiencing a range of attitudes from the paternalistic "what do you expect at your age" to the downright incompetent in which, despite all medical information that *less* rather than *more* medication is indicated with age, I was, without diagnosis, prescribed heart medication to take for the rest of my life "just in case." Only after I became very much sicker (from the side effects of the medication) and after many expensive intrusive tests was it determined that nothing much was wrong with me that could not be controlled simply by proper diet and exercise. Of course a part of me felt foolish. But the havoc created by this series of events impressed upon me as probably nothing else would have how crucially my own welfare depends upon my confronting and challenging ageism, the ageism of the medical establishment as well as my own internalization of it. I was forced as well to learn in a new way how I must indeed listen to and attend to my body.

Medical research shows that there is no reason that most of us cannot remain in relatively good health until all but the very last stages of life, particularly if we take proper care of our bodies. With age our bodies do demand more time and attention, and for the most part we learn to live with that greater demand. Like any other stage of life, there is a downside to old age, and I believe this is it. For all of us, young and old, our worst fear is what will happen to us in the event of chronic or severe illness in a society without adequate universal health care coverage, with a medical establishment that is racist, ageist, and sexist to the core, and with disability a social stigma. We are all haunted by the specter of being warehoused into nursing homes should we become disabled through accident or illness and unable to care for ourselves. We are taught to hate and fear disability and the disabled, and our society has tried to isolate and segregate the disabled, both young and old.

In addition, given that old age in white western European culture is thought of as a disease rather than a stage of life, it is not surprising to find that problems of living arising from greater fragility are reduced to medical problems requiring medical solutions. The medicalization of old age means that government funding gets funnelled through the medical establishment into nursing homes, vastly more expensive for the consumer and vastly more profitable for the provider than home health care.

The whole issue of possible disability raises another new area for reevaluating long held beliefs and attitudes. I have worked hard to become self-reliant and independent, and my ability to be "my own" person and do it "on my own" has been a source of pride for me. Lesbians, who do not look to men to be taken care of, place a high premium on that quality and have much difficulty in asking for help. Now, as an old woman, I am forced to reexamine the value I have placed upon personal independence at the expense of interdependence. There is much stretching to do in knowing that I am not diminished by asking for help. Should I become chronically disabled, I know I will face more critically the ongoing struggle to maintain an intact sense of myself while relying more upon others.

One thing is certain, our society makes interdependence difficult, for we live in a society segregated by race, ethnicity and age. Before I became conscious of my own ageism, I assiduously avoided anything that had to do with "old," including activities at our local Senior Center. As I began to acknowledge and accept my aging, I also began eagerly to seek out the companionship of old women, in my local neighborhood and in the lesbian community. It didn't take me long to know that the best of my learning and growth could take place here with these old women, as together we confronted the gripping issues of our lives.

Without any apparent loss of the energy and excitement of my youth, I once again became an activist, as one of the founders and organizers of the First West Coast Conference and Celebration of Old Lesbians (1987), as well as of the national Old Lesbians Organizing for Change (OLOC), which grew out of the Second West Coast Conference in San Francisco (1989). Lesbians, this time old lesbians, are once again in the forefront, on the cutting edge of the struggle for women's liberation.

We did an enormous amount of hard work to clarify our purpose and our goals as we hammered out a policy to confront the ageism within our lesbian community as well as the larger community. The uncompromising nature of our struggle was set from the start when we limited our group to old lesbians sixty and over, and when we insisted on calling ourselves OLD. The age limit exists so that old women have the opportunity to speak for ourselves, for, as an OLOC brochure (1992) says, "we are especially sensitive to those who see themselves as committed to the old, doing 'good' for the old, speaking for us. That is ageism!"

The insistence, for the first time, on 60 as an exclusive limit for belonging made 60 plus an important and empowering time in women's lives. I pointed out in my welcoming talk at the First West Coast Conference that important and painful as the problems of mid-life women may be, "to lump aging from 40 to 90+ is once again to trivialize the problems of old women—and once again to defer to younger women. We are expected to be available to nurture young and mid-life lesbians. Instead we boldly say 'No, this is our space.' We take this strong stand to affirm ourselves."

The "O" word is probably more dreaded than the "L" word. I have never yet attended a group, as either leader or participant in which the issue has not come up. Why use that word. I will never forget one group in which an old lesbian talked about how disgusting, revolting, and actually nauseating that word was. Yet we old lesbians again stood firm, accepting none of the euphemistic substitutes that came pouring in.

The OLOC brochure says that although "Old has become a term of insult and shame...we refuse the lie that it is shameful to be an old woman." We are neither "older" (than whom?), nor "elder," nor "senior." We name and proclaim ourselves as OLD for we no longer wish to collude in our own oppression by accommodating to language that implies in any way that old means inferior, ugly or awful. For to the degree that old women deny our own aging we cripple our ability to live. By naming ourselves old, we give up the attempt to pass. And as we break our silence, we empower ourselves and each other.

The excitement of this struggle is enormous. There were approximately 200 old lesbians attending each of the West Coast Conferences, and within a year when OLOC began to issue a Newsletter the mailing list grew to over 700 names. Now there are clusters of old lesbians meeting in at least 14 states, with plans for some of us to caravan around the country to meet and organize additional old lesbians. There is no question that old lesbians want to network with each other and share their experiences so that they can become a force in changing the ageism of our society.

Such an exciting endeavor! I often feel astonished at how rich in exploration and discovery my

life is. This is not what I expected. This self of mine, that I always characterized at its best as a seeker after truth, is still in there doing her thing! And I am surprised, for I believed the same things we were all taught about what it means to be old.

I am learning better than ever before just how political the personal is. Never has my political life been so intertwined with my personal thrust toward clarity and resolution. I believe that our work has impact, that I have impact as we old lesbians continue to organize and make ourselves visible.

As part of our active engagement with life I and my partner are constantly building our friendship circle, a community of old and new friends and comrades, based first on our own special group of old lesbians but extending intergenerationally to many women. For our community of women strengthens and sustains us.

I have always wanted to live a mindful life, and I believe that my ongoing process of checking the dimensions of my own reality keep me mindful, alert and aware.

I am bemused when I think of my many fears about growing old. I was even afraid to retire and waited an extra year because I wasn't sure that I would have either enough to do or enough money to do it with. Although money is not abundant, I am fortunate that it is an occasional rather than a chronic worry. Since we hear only the down side of growing old, I was unprepared for my life as it is now. It is different from what I expected. Not until I stopped working could I even begin to imagine the exhilarating sense of freedom which unstructured open-ended time makes possible, a delicious experience I am having for the first time in my life.

How could I expect that my old age would be so full of life and love and excitement? All the ageist cliches depict old age as a static time, and the major gerontological theories reinforce those cliches, categorizing old age as a time of disengagement, when the biological clock winds down and the spirit and psyche withdraw. I do not dispute that such characterizations may be true for some. That is not the way, however, I am experiencing my life. I am not unaware that my body is moving closer to dying, and that at the time of my actual dying, if the process is natural and not precipitated by trauma, I may indeed have a different agenda.

For now, however, my life is very much in process, full of opening new doors while looking back at old and treasured experiences. My past gives my present a richness and a backdrop for the exploration which is happening in the present. Almost every value and belief I have held is up for reexamination and reevaluation.

In speaking of my old age, I once declared with some disappointment that I have not miraculously arrived at a state of grace or of wisdom, that I am still in process. This, then, is perhaps the greatest miracle of all. That so long as there is life, there is the possibility of growth and change. Old age provides no guarantees but death. However, it does provide us with a special gift, the final challenge and the final opportunity to grow up.

REFERENCES

Copper, B. (1988). *Over the hill, Reflections on ageism between women.* Freedom, CA: The Crossing Press.

Macdonald, B. & Rich, C. (1991). *Look me in the eye—old women aging and ageism.* San Francisco, CA: Spinsters Book Company.

OLOC Brochure (1992). OLOC, P.O. Box 980422, Houston, TX 77098.

Rich, C. (1988). Ageism and the politics of beauty. In Macdonald, B. & Rich, C. (1991) *Look me in the eye—old women aging and ageism* (pp. 139–146), San Francisco, CA: Spinsters Book Company.

Perennial

We make fists in silence
Our anger shallow on this endless wall of rhetoric
Debasing the integrity of spirit
That flows, then ebbs in the heat of desert; mine
Yours—Like rivers who once sang songs
Endless at night when stars were low
And touched us.

Girl, woman, wife, worker
At the skills taught by mentors, mothers.
Quiet, sure hands, open and calm
Suffer mute despair.
Minds desire release from manmade oppression
But quiver with dark fear
Of the freedom escape could bring
To tired souls.

Tomorrow the fruit will be ripe
But unpicked. Colder nights
Steal the succulence of soft-skinned perfection
Paling, useless, dying
Unnoticed, untouched, unsavored
Then Autumn comes
To shrink and rob beauty
From the branches of our eyes.

We are perennial. Rise up.
Rise up, tender innocence
And not be swayed by insolence
That fills the stream with silt
And kills the spring that waters
Our predecessors. Rise up
From muddy waters
Restore the banks in fullness
Now abraded by subservience.
Follow the course of our river
Marked by the smooth stones of yesterday
On the way to destiny with the stars.

Courtesy of Barbara Koehler